Adolescents

Readings in Behavior

and Development

Edited by

ELLIS D. EVANS

University of Washington

THE DRYDEN PRESS INC.
Hinsdale, Illinois

Copyright © 1970 by The Dryden Press Inc.
All Rights Reserved
Library of Congress Catalog Card Number: 79–113204

ISBN: 0-03-089015-2

Printed in the United States of America

1234   090   98765432

A Word of Thanks

Whatever success a volume such as this may enjoy depends directly upon the cooperation of many people. The editor wishes to express his deep gratitude to the authors for their contributions of high quality and the publishers whose generous permissions have enabled previously published material to be reproduced. With due respect to all contributors the royalties from the sale of this book have been earmarked for charitable purposes.

This volume is dedicated to my parents and Boyd R. McCandless whose respective influences have contributed significantly to this project.

Preface

Introduction

Any scientific discipline depends for its viability upon continued research and theory development. And the achievement of growth by a viable discipline is marked explicitly by its professional literature. The literature on developmental psychology, including adolescent behavior and development, is no exception. It becomes increasingly difficult, however, for one to maintain a perspective upon all trends and changing viewpoints in a rapidly proliferating field such as the psychology of adolescence. This difficulty is magnified by the dispersion of published material throughout a large number of professional journals and monographs. A periodic compilation of scholarly contributions to the adolescence literature, however, can do much to reduce this difficulty, especially for beginning students. This volume, therefore, has a basic objective: to provide for students a convenient source of representative material from current developments in adolescence research and theory. To suggest that this volume covers all points of significance in the adolescence literature would be fallacious. Inevitably, a compiler's biases will influence the content selection for any book of readings. Nevertheless, in the writer's opinion, a study of this volume can represent a large step toward the achievement of a fruitful perspective on contemporary adolescent psychology.

Criteria for Selection of the Papers

At lease three objective criteria have been employed to shape the content of this book. These include timeliness, variety, and readability. One of this volume's strongest assets is its twelve original essays prepared especially in relation to these three criteria. This seemed the best way to cope with the wide variance in the quality of research on adolescents. This feature also helps to establish the relevance of this text for use in conjunction with current adolescent psychology textbooks. Recommended in this connection is *Adolescents: Behavior and Development* by Boyd R. McCandless and published by The Dryden Press Inc. (1970).

Timeliness   The topical coverage represented by the selections contained herein reflects areas of research and theoretical interest clearly illuminated in the current literature. Topics range, for example, from school-related phenomena such as student dissent, sex education, and underachievement, to broader problems such as drug use and delinquency. The timeliness of these topics is reinforced by this writer's observation that adolescents, parents, and teachers alike express interest and concern about them. Moreover, issues associated with these and other topics covered in this reader have continually been preferred for discussion among students in his own classes. This timeliness is even further accentuated by the fact that, with few exceptions, all papers presently included either come from literature published since 1967 or appear here in published form for the first time.

Variety   Adolescent behavior and development is studied in many different ways and with varying degrees of specificity. In this volume the student will encounter various types of studies, examples of critical research reviews, and running accounts of ongoing research, the results of which remain to be finalized. Particular care has been exercised by the editor to incorporate examples of major research strategies for psychological study. These strategies, all of which are explained at the appropriate time, include the longitudinal and cross-sectional approaches and the causal-comparative and experimental methods. Major activities of psychologists concerned with adolescence are also exemplified. At one level this involves primarily the description of behavior. At another level the interest centers around the identification of cause–effect relationships. At still another level, efforts are directed toward the modification of behavior. All three levels are represented by research presented in Part III. In contrast, Parts I and II are dominated by reviews, analyses, syntheses, and critical evaluations of research and theory pertinent to adolescence. As such a variety of theoretical interpretations and positions are presented for the reader's contemplation.

Further elements of variety are twofold. First, the content of the volume variously deals with the full range of adolescence (the teen years) and extends into young adulthood. For example, Sullivan's essay on political development (Part I) is concerned mainly with early and middle adolescence; the selections concerned with student dissent (Keniston, Part II; Haan *et al.*, Part III) deal with late adolescence and young adulthood. Secondly, the content of this volume is not limited to contributions by psychologists *per se*. The reader is treated to perspectives from allied fields, notably sociology (Akers, Part II) and cultural anthropology (Spindler, Part II).

Readability With perhaps two or three exceptions, skill in the interpretation of statistical data and a technical vocabulary are not prerequisites for an understanding of these selections. Papers which rely heavily upon complex statistical analyses have largely been avoided, primarily out of regard for readers whose experience with statistical data may be limited.[1] Contributors to this volume have been remarkably successful in applying their graphic communication skills for the benefit of reader comprehension.

Organization of the Book

The content of many papers appearing in this book is such that any number of codes could be utilized for organizational purposes. Rarely is a piece of literature on adolescence conceived so that its focus is exclusive. In other words, the psychology of adolescence deals ultimately with the whole person; although a given paper may deal with one facet of behavior or development it is never really independent of a holistic context. For example, the study of adolescent sexuality may deal with specific

---

[1] For those readers desirous of refining their concepts of psychological study and statistical analysis a good starting point is Chapter 2, "Methods and Problems in the Study of Adolescence," of the aforementioned McCandless text.

forms of sexual behavior. Yet implicitly there exists the relationship of
sexuality to other dimensions of behavior, such as social and emotional
development. These interrelationships frequently complicate the formulation of an abstract conceptual framework within which to organize data.
Hence the organization portrayed in this volume is only one of many
alternatives which could be rationalized. It was the editor's intent to
provide an alternative sufficiently flexible for individual classroom adaptation.

For present purposes a tripartite structure has been established within
which to sequence content. To begin with, Part I provides the reader
with a foundation upon which to build successive conceptual overlays
relevant to the general study of adolescence. Included in this first section
are discussions of theoretical viewpoints and summarizations of empirical
data appropriate to puberty, identity, cognition, sexuality, and the adolescent "society," to name a few. In one way or another this frame of
reference taps the major dimensions of adolescent development—physical,
cognitive, emotional, and social.

Part II consists essentially of special interest topics, that is, specific
areas of particular interest to psychologists at this point in time which
encompass a number of issues in regard to the socialization process during
adolescence. It would be accurate to state, however, that these areas actually represent a combination of long-standing and emergent issues. An
example of the more traditional problem areas is the psychology of vocational choice; the student protest movement personifies an emergent
complex of research problems and issues. All topics presented in Part II
are unquestionably contemporary in their orientation, however.[2]

Equipped with the conceptual tools made available in Parts I and II
the reader hopefully will succeed in building for himself an interpretative
framework appropriate for Part III. This last segment of the volume
provides a foray into the territory of empirical research on adolescence.
The research comprising this territory touches many of the bases covered
in the earlier two sections. It also illustrates many and varied skills that
researchers bring to bear upon psychological phenomena. Most of the
studies or research reports are outgrowths of areas explored in the earlier
sections of the volume. The creativity research of Parloff *et al.* (Part III),

---

[2] The resultant separation of Parts I and II should not be taken to imply
that material in the former part is without contemporary support by psychologists. The separation is both a matter of specificity and organizational convenience. For example, one could rationalize the placement of Sullivan's essay
on political development and Wagner's discussion of adolescent sexuality in
Part II as well as Part I.

for example, continues along an avenue formulated by Golann's (Part II) insightful overview of creativity research and issues. Still other studies serve to merge developmental coordinates such as moral and political behavior. An example of this function is the Haan *et al.* (Part III) research which nests comfortably in the anatomy created by Sullivan (Political Development) and Keniston (Student Dissent) in Part II. It is hoped that the sampling of research in Part III whets sufficiently the reader's appetite for continued study and perhaps even some original research activity of his own.

Additional Features of this Book

Each selection is prefaced by an orientation statement whose general purpose is fourfold: First, to provide some background to the basic theme(s) inherent in each selection; second, to identify unique attributes of each article; third, to suggest some relationships among various selections where applicable, and fourth, to introduce or clarify overriding issues which may be associated with a selection. In this way, the editor hopes to provide interpretative assistance to the student as well as provoke thought for discussion purposes.

In addition to each respective orientation a brief list of recommended readings is provided for further study. Space permitting, the editor would have liked to include the full text of many of these references in this volume. Use of these references should add significantly to the student's sophistication in the formal study of adolescent behavior and development.

Seattle, Washington   E.D.E.
January 1970

Contents

Some Theoretical and Conceptual Foundations of Adolescent Behavior and Development

1.1 Orientation

One appropriate way to inaugurate a formal study of adolescence is to examine various theoretical viewpoints on adolescent development in their historical contexts. An excellent vehicle for this purpose is the following paper by Rolf E. Muuss. Professor Muuss has devoted a substantial portion of his professional career to the analysis of theories of adolescence and their educational implications. The current selection introduces the reader to the contribution of major philosophical figures to contemporary thinking about adolescence. Noteworthy issues with which Muuss confronts his readers include the nature of human nature, the long-standing nature—nurture controversy, mind-body dualism, and theological influences, which, in many instances, have been dissonant with the scientific approach to developmental study.

A major point in the Muuss discussion is that "pre-scientific" approaches to human behavior and development provide in varying degrees the philosophical underpinnings for modern psychology. For example, John Locke's *tabula rasa* proposition anticipated the heavy environmentalist leanings of modern day behavioristic psychologies. Rousseau's belief in the innate goodness of the child perhaps bears less directly upon modern psychology than does Locke. However, vestiges of Rousseauian thought are reflected in Montessori education, John Dewey's progressive education, and today's humanistic psychologies. Despite technical advances in the study of human behavior by psychologists, the human nature issue is one with which psychologists continually grapple. And, at the base of any cohesive theory of behavior and development inevitably rest unproven assumptions about human nature.

The Muuss essay concludes with a reference to G. Stanley Hall (1844–1924) whose work is frequently credited with having provided a transition from a pre-scientific to a scientific approach to human development. Hall's heavily genetic theory of development generally has been discounted over the years. Nevertheless, Hall's contributions to psychology can hardly be overestimated. The reader is encouraged to consult the recommended reading for elaborations on Hall's work.

RECOMMENDED READINGS

Burgess, Charles, and Borrowman, Merle L.   *What Doctrines to Embrace.* Glenview, Illinois: Scott, Foresman, 1969, 73–100.

Grinder, Robert E., and Strickland, Charles E.   G. Stanley Hall and the social significance of adolescence. *Teachers College Record*, 1963, **64**, 390–399.

Grinder, Robert E.   The concept of adolescence in the genetic psychology of Stanley Hall. *Child Development*, 1969, **40**, 355–369.

Muuss, Rolf E.   *Theories of Adolescence* (2d Ed.) New York: Random House, 1968.

1.1 Theories of Adolescent Development—
Their Philosophical and Historical Roots

Rolf E. Muuss, GOUCHER COLLEGE

Long before psychology became a science we find philosophical, theological, educational and psychological theories that contribute to an understanding of human nature and human development. It is G. Stanley Hall with his famous two-volume *Adolescence*[12] who is credited as the father of a scientific "Psychology of Adolescence." He seems to stand on the threshold between the philosophical and the scientific approaches to adolescence. Prior to Hall we find that it is frequently the philosopher-educator who is especially concerned with a theory of human development, as well as its implications for teaching, as is the case with Plato, Aristotle, Comenius, Rousseau, Herbart, Froebel, and Pestalozzi.

The difficulty in identifying pre-scientific theories of adolescent development is due to the fact that prior to Hall adolescence was considered a part or a stage of human development and received no special emphasis. The word "adolescence" first appears in the fifteenth century, indicating that historically adolescence is subordinated to theoretical considerations about the general nature of human development. Contemporary theories of adolescence have their historical roots frequently in general theories of development. Some important ideas about human development come from philosophers who are primarily concerned with the question: What is the nature of man? For example, Locke and Darwin do not develop a theory of adolescence, but what each has to say about the nature of man is so profound that it is utilized and reflected in the writings of Rousseau and Hall respectively and thus constitutes a philosophical basis for a theory of development. This article will reflect these difficulties and deal with questions of the nature of man, as well as with theories of human development and, if appropriate, emphasis will be placed on adolescent development. Many of our present controversial issues related to development have ideational roots that go far

---

A modified version of this paper is found in Chapter 2 of Professor Muuss' book, *Theories of Adolescence* (2d Ed.), Random House, 1968. This version is reprinted by permission of Random House and the author.

It is also based partially upon Chapter 2 of the author's dissertation "Theories of Adolescence: An Analysis of Selected American and European Positions," submitted in partial fulfillment of requirements for the Ph.D. degree at the University of Illinois.

back into the philosophical thought of the past. We also observe that some ideas that we consider new discoveries have been expressed before.

In classifying theories of development, Ausubel[6] makes an interesting distinction between preformationistic and predeterministic approaches to human development on the one side, and *tabula rasa* approaches on the other side. The preformationistic theory is reflected in the theological proposition of man's instantaneous creation, in the homunculus theory, and the doctrine of man's basic sinfulness as well as in the more recent theories emphasizing instincts and innate drives. Predeterministic theories postulate universally fixed stages of development but allow for environmental influences as is obvious in the case of Rousseau, Hall's theory of recapitulation, Freud's stages of psycho-sexual development and Gesell's emphasis on maturation. In contrast to this are the *tabula rasa* approaches which minimize the biological and genetic factors and place the emphasis on environmental determinants of human development. As the name implies, this includes Locke's *tabula rasa* theory, the humanistic approaches, and the related modern theories of behaviorism and cultural determinism. It is with some of these basic contemporary issues in mind that the theories presented here have been selected. The presentation follows a chronological sequence since developments of ideas follow at times in opposition to each other, e.g., the theological concept of man's instantaneous creation vs. Darwin's theory of evolution; at times in an expansion, elaboration, but continuation of thought, as one might consider the influence of Plato on Aristotle or of Locke on Rousseau; at times compatible ideas are expressed without any interaction as seems to have been the case with the writings of Comenius and Locke.

Early Greek Concern with Human Nature

An historical approach to a theory of adolescence requires some concern with the early Greek ideas about human development since their influence remained prevalent through the Middle Ages and is still noticeable today. Plato made a clear distinction between two aspects of human nature: soul and body. This position is known as dualism. He expounded that both were different substances, and that although there was some interaction between them the soul was an entity in itself, capable of leaving the body without losing its identity. The soul was the essential quality. It could perceive more clearly and reach higher realities when freed from the body; *soma sema* (the body is the grave of the soul) he declared. The body and sensuality are the fetters which hinder the soul in reaching those higher realities, since body is matter and has all the defects of matter. "And thought is best when the mind is gathered into herself and none of these things trouble her—neither sounds, nor sights, nor pain, nor any pleasure—when she takes leave of the body, and has as little as possible to do with it, when she has no bodily sense or desire, but is aspiring after true being."[20] The idea of dualism between mind and body reappeared later in Christian theology and becomes of primary importance in the philosophical thinking of the seventeenth century, especially under Descartes, Leibnitz and Spinoza.

Of greater interest from a developmental point of view is the idea of the layer structure of the soul which Plato developed in the dialogue, *Phaedo*.[20] According to Plato the soul has three distinguishable parts, or layers, or levels. Thus, probably for the first time in the history of psychology a three-fold division of soul, mind or psyche is advanced. The lowest layer of the soul is described as man's desires and appetites. Today we might describe this level in terms of drives, instincts, and needs, and its resemblance to Freud's concept "id" can hardly be denied. According to Plato, this part of the soul is located in the lower part of the body and is primarily concerned with the satisfaction of the physical needs. ". . . it fills us full of love, and lusts, and fears, and fancies of all kinds, and endless foolery, and . . . takes away the power of thinking at all."[21] The second layer of the soul, the spirit, includes courage, conviction, temperance, endurance and hardihood; aggressiveness and fierceness also originate here. Man has both the first and the second layer in common with the animal world. These two layers belong to the body and die with it. The third layer is divine, supernatural and immortal, it constitutes the essence of the universe. This is the real soul, which Plato describes as reason and which has its temporary seat in the body. "This separation and release of the soul from the body is termed death."[20] Plato's theory concerning the layer structure of the soul closely resembles several contemporary central European personality theories, which are developed on the assumption of a layer-like stratification of personality, by Rothacker, Lersch and Remplein. They perceive development as a process by which the lower layers mature earlier and are superseded by higher layers as the child grows older. Plato already postulated such a developmental theory. Reason is latent during the first stage when perception is most important. The second stage of development is characterized by conviction and understanding and brings the second layer of the soul, spirit, into the foreground of psychological development. The third stage, which we might identify with adolescence and maturity, but which, according to Plato, is not reached by all people, relates to the development of the third part of the soul, reason and intelligence.[17]

Interspersed in most of Plato's dialogues—but particularly in *Laws* and in *The Republic*—are descriptive accounts of children and youth as well as advice concerning the control of their behavior. While this material does not constitute a theory of development as we understand it today, it does give some rather basic insight into Plato's conception of the nature of development.

During the first three years of his life the infant shall be free from fear and pain and sorrow. This point of view would be endorsed by many psychologists today. Interestingly enough, in the dialogue Cleinias suggests that in addition we ought to provide the infant with pleasure. However, the Athenian Stranger objects, since this would spoil the child; during the early years "more than at any other time the character is engrained by habit."[19] Character is formed at such an early age since the experience and impressions leave a lasting influence.

From three to six the child needs sports and social contact with age-mates in order to get rid of his self-will. Plato would punish but not disgrace the child. Social development is taken into consideration at this age, children ought to come together in a kind of kindergarten arrangement under the supervision of a nurse but they themselves should find for themselves the "natural modes of amusement" which children have at this age.

Already at six, Plato suggests to divide the sexes. "Let boys live with boys and girls . . . with girls." The boy now has to learn horsemanship, the use of bow and arrows, the spear and the sling. Plato makes an interesting comment on the artistic taste of children as a function of their age. Children are believed to prefer the puppet-show, youth comedy, young men tragedy, and older men prefer Homer and Hessiod.

Boys will not be allowed to drink wine until they are eighteen because of their easy excitability, "fire must not be poured upon fire." Related are adolescents' desire to argue for amusement's sake. In their enthusiasm they will leave no stone unturned and in their delight about the first taste of wisdom they will puzzle and annoy anybody with their arguments. Even though Plato—as discussed above—believed that the character is formed through habit at a very early age, he at other times feels that "the characters of young men are subject to many changes in the course of their lives." The argument about the consistency of personality versus its modifiability has continued and proponents for both of Plato's statements can be found today. The contemporary concern with this issue is illustrated by a 1964 monograph by B. Bloom, *The Stability and Change in Human Characteristics*.

Plato develops his educational philosophy especially in *The Republic*.[21] He perceives education as the development of the soul under the influence of the environment "and this has two divisions, gymnastic for the body, and music for the soul." Reasoning in the young child is undeveloped but since the young child is impressionable Plato suggests "to establish a censorship of the writers of fiction" since "anything that he receives into his mind is likely to become indelible and unalterable: and therefore it is most important that the talks which the young first hear should be models of virtuous thoughts." Rational and critical thought are not yet predominant during childhood but develop mainly during adolescence. The training begins with music and gymnastics during childhood, is continued through adolescence with mathematical and scientific studies. The latter bring out critical thought and dissatisfaction with direct sense-knowledge; during this training students would develop methods to find the truth and to become able to distinguish truth from opinion. Plato speaks of education as "that training which is given by suitable habits to the first instincts of virtue in children—when pleasure, and friendship, and pain, and hatred are rightly implanted in souls not yet capable of understanding the nature of them, and who find them, after they have attained reason, to be in harmony with her."[19] In other words education means to provide experiences to children prior to the development of reason that are nevertheless in agreement with reason when it does develop.

Plato postulated that one of the means of explaining the attainment of knowledge is through his doctrine of innate ideas. Innate ideas are undeveloped, vague and nebulous, nevertheless they are present at birth. Learning is a process of remembering these ideas, which once, probably before the soul entered the body, were clear. Sensation helps in reawakening these partially lost ideas. The mind-body dualism is of relevancy here since the body contributes sensation, while the mind contains the ideas. In a way, Plato opens the discussion about the influence of heredity and environment by his theory of innate ideas.

Aristotle, in contrast to Plato, denied the separation of body and soul and returned to the older Greek idea of the unity of the physical and mental worlds. Body and soul for him were related in structure and function. The relationship between body and soul was the same as that between matter and form, body was matter and soul was form. Psychic life, for which Aristotle used the word *entelechy*, was the principle by which the body lives. Aristotle accepted Plato's idea concerning the levels of the soul life; however, he viewed soul structure from a biological, almost evolutionary, point of view. The lowest soul-life form is that of the plant, the life-functions of which are supply of nourishment and reproduction. The next higher form of soul-life is also found in animals, its additional functions are sensation, perception and locomotion. The third soul-life function is distinctly human—and sets men apart from the animal world. It includes the ability to think and to reason. Consequently there are three layers of soul-life, the food supplying or plant soul, the perceiving or animal soul, and the thinking or human soul. Aristotle further divided the thinking or human part of the soul into two different parts, the practical soul by which we "deliberate about those things which depend upon us and our purpose to do or not to do"[3] and the theoretical soul which deals with higher and abstract knowledge such as distinguishing between what is true and what is false.

Aristotle advanced a theory of development concerning the layer structure of the soul which appears to have some resemblance to Darwin's more scientific biological theory of evolution, even though it does not include the idea of evolution of one species to another. Furthermore, Aristotle made an impassable division between the different levels of soul-life. Plato, in describing the stages of development, held that the plant soul level developed before the animal soul level and this again was a prerequisite for the rational soul level. Aristotle followed this idea of the level structure of the soul and applied it to the development of the child, as becomes obvious from the following quotation:

As the body is prior in order of generation to the soul, so the irrational is prior to the rational. The proof is that anger and wishing and desire are implanted in children from their very birth, but reason and understanding are developed as they grow older. Wherefore, the care of the body ought to precede that of the soul, and the training of the appetitive part should follow; none the less our care of it must be for the sake of the reason, and our care of the body for the sake of the soul.[4]

He then proceeded by dividing the developmental period of the human being into three distinguishable stages of seven years each. The first seven years he named infancy; the period from seven to the beginning of puberty, boyhood; and from puberty to twenty-one, young manhood. This division of the period of development into three stages was generally accepted during the Middle Ages and recurs in some modern psychological theories of development, such as Kroh, Remplein and Zeller in Germany. Infants and animals are alike in that both are under the control of their appetites and emotions. "Children and brutes pursue pleasures."[1] Aristotle emphasized that moral character is the result of choice "for by choosing what is good or bad we are men of a certain character. . . ." Even though young children are able to act voluntarily they do not have choice; "for both children and the lower animals share in voluntary action, but not in choice, and acts done on the spur of the moment we describe as voluntary, but not as chosen."[1] This seems to imply that children first go through an animal-like stage of development; what distinguishes them from animals is that children have the potential for higher development which animals do not have "though psychologically speaking a child hardly differs for the time being from an animal."[2] It is the characteristic of adolescence to develop the ability to choose. Only if the youth voluntarily and deliberately chooses will he develop the right kind of habits and this in the long run will build the right kind of character. Thus by choosing, the adolescent actively participates in his own character formation. Voluntary and deliberate choice thus becomes an important aspect in Aristotle's theory of development, since it is necessary for the attainment of maturity. This idea is expressed today by modern writers. For example, both Margaret Mead and Edgar Friedenberg have stated that today with prolonged education and prolonged dependency we have reduced choices for adolescents to the extent that we interfere with their attainment of maturity.

Aristotle, even though he does not give us a systematically stated theory of adolescence, provides us with a rather detailed description of the "Youthful type of character" part of which is not unlike descriptive statements that could have been written by G. Stanley Hall or Arnold Gesell. "Young men have strong passions, and tend to gratify them indiscriminately. Of the bodily desires, it is the sexual by which they are most swayed and in which they show absence of self-control."[5] Sexuality in adolescence is of concern in any contemporary text whether theoretically, empirically or clinically oriented. Among the more recent theoretical positions, Otto Rank in particular describes promiscuity as an adolescent defense mechanism against sexual urges, "since sexual gratification takes place without genuine love and ego involvement."[16] Aristotle in his description of the adolescent comments on their instability: "They are changeable and fickle in their desires, which are violent while they last, but quickly over: their impulses are keen but not deep-rooted."[5] Lewin and Barker among the contemporary writers deal with the instability of the psychological field of the adolescent since he stands in a psychological no-man's-land "moving into an unstructured social and psychological field."[16] This makes many socio-psychological situations unclear, indefinite and ambiguous and the resulting behavior is "changeable and fickle." "For owing to their love and honour they cannot bear being slighted, and are indignant if they imagine themselves unfairly treated."[5] Adolescent complaints about being "unfairly treated" in home, school, and society in general are so common today that they need no further elaboration. The list of quotes from *Rhetoric* contemporary theory, observation and empirical data would not be too difficult to find. Aristotle discusses, among other issues, adolescent desire for success, their optimism, trust, concern with the future rather than the past, their courage, conformity, idealism, friendship, aggressiveness and gullibility.

In education, the adolescent was to study mainly mathematics including astronomy and theory of music and geometry, since these subjects teach abstraction but do not require the life experiences and wisdom necessary to be a philosopher or a physicist.

MEDIEVAL CHRISTIAN VIEW OF HUMAN DEVELOPMENT

The theological view of human nature and development cannot as readily be identified in terms of one man, a specific period of time in history or even a particular church. We find the idea of original sin expressed by Tertullian in the second century when he speaks of the depravity of human nature. It is emphasized by John Calvin in the sixteenth century, and is prevalent in Catholic scholasticism, Protestant Calvinism and American Puritanism.

The theological view of human nature and development as we find it in the medieval–early reformation period encompassed several ideas relevant to our topic:

  (a) man's unique position in the universe, being created in the image of God,
  (b) man's evil due to Adam's original sin,
  (c) man's dualistic nature, a spiritual immortal soul and a material, mortal body. Salvation and the life after death places the immortal soul on a higher level of importance,
  (d) knowledge is revealed to man from without; it comes from God and is revealed to us through the Bible,
  (e) the homunculus idea of instantaneous creation. The last point is not so much biblical as it is medieval.

The origin of most of these ideas can be found in biblical sources; they are also influenced by Greek philosophy; Plato especially spoke about man's dualistic nature. We will see later that theories that follow in the seventeenth, eighteenth and nineteenth century, especially those advanced by Locke, Rousseau and Darwin, can partly be understood as antitheses to these earlier theological ideas.

The idea that God created man in his own image and thus gave him a unique position in the universe is expressed in Genesis I. 27:28: "And God created man to his own image: to the image of God he created him: male and female he created them." Furthermore, he gives them the power to rule over all living creatures. This point of view of the divine creation of the human being was held in early centuries. Prior to Darwin man was seen as being basically different from the animal world.

The second important idea concerning the nature of man is the theological doctrine of human depravity. The human being was seen as having innate tendencies toward ungodliness and sinfulness, man is fundamentally bad and his badness will become stronger during the developmental years if it is not counteracted by stern discipline. The idea of original sin as based on Genesis III. 6:7 relates the sinfulness of each individual to Adam's first sin. And "as sin came into the world through one man and death through sin, and so death spread to all men because all men sinned. . . . Yet death reigned from Adam to Moses, even over those whose sins were not like the transgression of Adam . . ."[7] (Romans V. 12:14). This pessimistic view of human nature even so prevalent in Catholic theology before the Reformation receives a new impetus with Calvin's theology and thus sets the intellectual climate for Puritanism. The educational objective in this theory is to bring forth the innate ideas which are God given, knowledge of his laws and commands. This was accomplished by stern mental and moral discipline. There is little room for individual differences since the quality of the mind is the same for all individuals and the child who fails to learn is seen as willfully resisting the efforts of the teacher. The role of the teacher is defined by his authority and a belief that learning can be facilitated by physical punishment, and the role of the child by obedience. Nevertheless, Calvin in particular expressed a strong faith in the value of education.

The theological point of view that man was the result of instantaneous creation results in preformationist thinking.[6] It was believed that the child came into the world as a miniature adult. The difference between a child and an adult was only a quantitative one, not a qualitative one. Therefore children wore dresses of adult style, only smaller in size, as is obvious from many medieval paintings. "Little girls wore long dresses and corsets,"[11] just as mature women did. The qualitative difference in body build, body function and mental abilities was disregarded. Growth was understood to be only a quantitative increase of all physical and mental aspects of human nature, not a qualitative one. This theory of preformationism held that children had the same interests as adults and therefore should be treated correspondingly which meant that adult requirements were put upon them and were enforced by stern discipline. According to this view the child did not "develop" since it was preformed. This idea of "homunculism" was even utilized in pre-scientific theory of embryology.

It was seriously believed that a minature but fully-formed little man (i.e., an homunculus) was embodied in the sperm, and when implanted in the uterus simply grew in bulk, without any differentiation of tissues or organs, until full-term fetal size was attained at the end of nine months.[6]

This idea of homunculism was soon to be challenged by the beginning of modern science and advancements in the field of medicine. Pediatricians learned that the young child has qualitative and quantitative characteristics of his own and is not a miniature adult. One might speculate that the reason for the limited concern of Pre-Hallian writers with the basic physiological changes that take place during pubescence—many of these changes are obvious to the keen observer and their detection does not require medical knowledge or technology—are due to the theoretical position that the child is a miniature adult. If one were to accept this point of view then it follows that there should be no difference in the physiological functions of the child and the adult. In the philosophical realm it was Rousseau who stated that "nature would have children be children before being man. If we wish to prevent this order, we shall produce precocious fruits which will have neither maturity nor flavor, and will speedily deteriorate; we shall have young doctors and old children."[18] Thus a new conception of human nature contributed to a more scientific concept of growth and development.

John Amos Comenius' Development-Centered Theory of Education

The Renaissance may be seen as a revolt against authoritarianism in church, school and society. The Aristotelian logic, the presupposition of universal ideas and scholasticism in general is challenged by Erasmus and Vives. Vives felt that one had "to begin with individual facts of experience and out of them to come to ideas by the natural logic of the mind."[7] Learning is no longer seen as a deductive process but as an inductive process beginning with experiences, and he suggests that an understanding of the learning process comes from psychology. Learning is determined by the mind of the learner, and therefore, education becomes concerned with individuality in pupils.

Comenius accepts these new ideas of the Renaissance, combines them with Aristotle's classification of development and advances a theory of education which is based on psychological assumptions. In his *Great Didactic*[9] Comenius suggests a school organization based on a theory of development. Rather than dividing the developmental period into three stages of seven years, as Aristotle did, Comenius proposes four developmental stages of six years each and a different kind of school for each of these four stages. However he maintains the three divisions of the soul. "For here we live a threefold life, the vegetative, the animal, and the intellectual or spiritual."[9]

The suggested school organization is based on assumptions concerning the nature of human development and a specific theory of learning, that of faculty psychology. Interestingly enough, present day school organization in parts of the United States closely resembles this pattern. The temporal sequence of the curriculum content—Comenius argued—should be borrowed from nature, in other words it should be suitable to the psychological development of the child. "Let our maxim be to follow the lead of nature in all things, to observe how the faculties develop one after the other, and to base our methods on this principle of succession."

The child in the first six years of his life learns at home in the Mother-School at his mother's knee. He should exercise the external senses and learn to discriminate between the various objects around him. The nature of the development of the faculty of sense perception is such that it precedes all other faculties and consequently sensory experiences and sensory knowledge should be provided first. The child through sensory experiences becomes familiar with his world.

The child from six to twelve attends the vernacular-school and receives a general well rounded elementary education, which is provided for all children, rich or poor, boy or girl. Included in the curriculum is the correct use of the vernacular language, social habits and religious training. The program at this level would emphasize training of the "internal senses, the imagination and memory in combination with their cognate organs." Comenius accepts the faculty psychology point of view in respect to memory. "The memory should be exercised in early youth since practice develops it, and we should therefore take care to practice it as much as possible. Now, in youth, labour is not felt, and thus the memory develops without any trouble and becomes very retentive."

For the next six years, from 12 to 18, which includes the adolescent period as we understand it today, education is provided in the Latin school. The psychological purpose of the school at this age is to train the faculty of reasoning. The student learns to "understand and pass judgment on the information collected by the senses." Included are judgments about relationships of the things perceived, imagined and remembered. Understanding here implies utilization of the principle of causality. The curriculum of the school is divided into six years, which results in the following six classes: Grammar, Natural Philosophy, Mathematics, Ethics, Dialectics and Rhetoric.

The following six years from 18 to 24 consist of university education and travel and it is at this point that the faculty of the will is to be trained. Considering our present conception of will this appears to be a strange notion and becomes more meaningful only if we consider that the concept of will, as used by Comenius, includes the self-direction of one's own life.

Comenius rather strongly advocates that the instructional procedure fits the level of comprehension of the child in contrast to the scholastic education which he attacks. For Comenius, development is not uniform, continuous and gradual—as the homunculus theory of development implies—but each stage of development has its own characteristics, "teachable moments" as Havighurst would say today. Development is a process of increased "domination of the intellect over the other souls."[17]

To attempt to cultivate the will before the intellect (or the intellect before the imagination, or the imagination before the faculty of sense perception) is mere waste of time. But this is what those do who teach boys logic, poetry, rhetoric, and ethics before they are thoroughly acquainted with the objects that surround them. It would be equally sensible to teach boys of two years old to dance, though they can scarcely walk.[9]

The right time for the education of each of the faculties must be chosen correctly and the sequence must be "borrowed from nature." In his continuous focus on what children can do, know and are interested in at each stage of development, we seem to find the historical roots of a child centered theory of education.

JOHN LOCKE'S EMPIRICISM

The idea of homunculism with its emphasis on preformationism and Plato's theory about innate ideas—which was accepted as a basic scholastic principle at Locke's time—was most seriously challenged and opposed by John Locke. Locke was influenced by Thomas Hobbes' idea that the human being, including his body as well as his mind, is part of the natural order; he further expanded Hobbes' theoretical position, known today as empiricism, which states that all of our knowledge is derived from sensation. Hobbes had stated that "there is no conception in man's mind, which has not at first, totally, or by parts, been begotten upon the organs of sense."[13] Locke further develops the theory that there are no innate ideas; ideas that we hold in our consciousness are either obtained through our senses directly or are derived from those ideas that have been obtained through sensations previously. The child's mind at the time of birth is, according to an anology used by Locke, a *tabula rasa*, a blank tablet. He made the following famous statement concerning the nature of the human mind:

Let us then suppose the mind to be, as we say, white paper, void of all characters, without any ideas:—How comes it to be furnished? . . . To this I answer, in one word, from EXPERIENCE. In that all our knowledge is founded; and from that it ultimately derives itself. Our observation employed either, about external sensible objects, or about the internal operations of our minds perceived and reflected on by ourselves, is that which supplies our understandings with all the materials of thinking. These two are the fountains of knowledge, from whence all the ideas we have, or can naturally have, do spring.[14]

From this assumption followed other important ideas that have had far reaching influence in social theory and have become the cornerstone of democracy; i.e., that since the minds of all men at birth are a *tabula rasa*, all ideas and all knowledge that men have come from experience; therefore, present differences and inequalities that can be found in people are due to environment and experiences; and therefore men are completely equal at birth. Thus the principle of democracy is in part derived from a philosophical-psychological theory concerning the child's mind at birth. Locke discussed his views concerning democracy in "Treatise of Civil Government."[15] He blamed environmental conditions, such as poor education and poor social environment, for the human misery in the world and gave hope to those who lived under unfavorable conditions.

Locke found rather enthusiastic followers in Helvetius and Condillac in France who carried his empiricism to its extreme since for them even the powers of faculties of the mind are the result of sensation. Furthermore, since poor living conditions existed for the French lower and middle classes prior to the revolution, many people in France were especially susceptible to such ideas. Thus the words *liberté, égalité, fraternité* became the powerful symbols of a new concept of human nature. A new hope emerged: that by changing the environment, human nature could be changed; and from it then followed that mankind could determine its own destiny. Thus a theory emerged which is an expression of faith in the perfectibility of the human race.

Locke's proposition that there are no innate ideas and that the human mind is a *tabula rasa* contrasted sharply with several of the theories of human development already discussed. The more outstanding examples are:

(1) The doctrine of human depravity and original sin appeared to be in open contradiction to Locke's new concept of the human mind. If our mind is formed by experience only, then it follows that whether a child becomes "good" or "bad" is due to environmental experiences. It is important to point out that Locke did not have a clear concept or understanding of the nature of heredity; nevertheless his psychology stresses nurture rather than nature.

(2) The medieval class system of Europe was based on what we would consider today as hereditary assumptions. The nobility was noble by birth, regardless of personal merits and qualities. This notion was challenged by the empiricist assumption that "all men are born equal." If all men are alike and begin life at the same point, everyone should have the same rights and opportunity to obtain a better social position. King and subject, rich and poor begin life at the same zero point. Therefore support for social mobility is found in this theory. Locke's early form of environmentalism,

even though it is not directly related to behaviorism and cultural relativism may be viewed as a historical forerunner to these schools of thought.

(3) The doctrine of innate ideas was interpreted by the medieval period to imply that the child is a miniature adult and only grows quantitatively. Locke's *tabula rasa* concept implied that the child at birth is fundamentally different from the adult both qualitatively and quantitatively. If ideas are not innate then the newborn child is radically different from the adult in respect to intellectual properties. Locke pointed out that the child's personality is basically different from that of the adult and thus laid the foundation for a new theory of child development; he also urged the scientific study of human nature. Development, he believed, occurred in a gradual process from mental passivity in the early years of childhood to increased mental activity in adolescence through a series of developmental progressions. The rational faculty emerges toward the end of this developmental process and therefore is characteristic of the period of adolescence.

Locke himself, even though he has much to say about human nature, does not develop a specific theory of human development, but gives many important ideas to it and foresees it; it is Rousseau who, influenced by Locke, advances a new theory of child development.

JEAN JACQUES ROUSSEAU'S ROMANTIC NATURALISM

Rousseau was greatly influenced by Locke's ideas; however, he not only opposed some of Locke's propositions, he developed his own theoretical positions concerning human nature. While for Locke reason was the most important aspect of human nature, Rousseau considered human nature as primarily feeling. While Locke was concerned with constitutional government, Rousseau made a great plea for individualism and individual freedom, and directed his criticism and attack against society and social institutions. Although he, too, was concerned with the social well being of all, he distinguishes between the "will of all" (majority will, determined by vote) and the "general will" (that which is really best for every member of the society). Rousseau was not truly democratic for he was afraid that a majority vote could be as bad as any monarchy. Ideally the majority will and the general will would coincide. This, however, was only possible if men were educated and wise.

Rousseau brought about a revolutionary change in the thinking concerning the nature of human development and the corresponding educational implications, the main ideas of which he expressed in his famous book *Emile*.[18] The traditional approach toward childhood education had been to see the child from the adult point of view, adult interests and adult social life. Rousseau claimed that such an approach is not only false, but may even be harmful. He started with the needs and interests of the child and saw development as a natural preplanned process. If one were to free the child from the restrictions, unnatural limitations and the rigid discipline of the adult world, nature would assure a harmonious and healthy development. The child was innately good, but the restrictions of adult society and poor education had corrupted the child. To correct this, he advocated a natural development in a sound and healthy environment, which for him was one that posed little restrictions on the child, especially in the first twelve years. Rousseau was one of the strongest proponents of individualism in education, and he expressed a deep faith in the natural good of man.

Rousseau's naturalism considered the nature of the child of greatest importance; if development were left to the laws of nature the outcome would be most desirable. Environment and education in the past had had a predominantly negative influence. Rousseau in his belief that the child is by nature good gives further impetus to the doctrine of the modifiability and perfectibility of human nature. A child-centered approach in education and a non-directive approach in therapy do seem to have historical roots that go back to Rousseau's naturalism.

Rousseau advocated a revision of the treatment children should receive at home and in the school as well as changes in the methods of instruction. Each of the four stages of development has specific psychological characteristics. Consideration of these characteristics results in definite educational objectives, the attainment of which helps children grow toward maturity. The educational methods, the content to be taught and the educational objectives at each age level are to be determined by the characteristics of the child at that developmental level. Learning is most effective if the child has freedom and can learn and grow according to his own impulses. Erich Fromm in his introductory comments to Neill's *Summerhill* sees a historical relationship between Rousseau's emphasis on freedom and this contemporary educational experiment.

Rousseau most strongly opposed the homunculus idea and asserted that it was the plan of nature that children play, live and behave like children before they become adults. "Childhood has its own way of seeing, thinking, and feeling, and nothing is more foolish than to try to substitute ours for them."[18] Even though Rousseau himself had only limited and not always successful educational experiences—his five children lived in a foundling asylum—his theory had a tremendous impact on educational practice in the latter part of the eighteenth and most of the nineteenth century. Rousseau's ideas are obvious in the works of Pestalozzi, Froebel, Basedow, Spencer, Horace Mann and John Dewey.

Rousseau advised teachers and parents, "You ought to be wholly absorbed in the child—observing him, watching him without respite, and without seeming to do so, having a presentiment of his feelings in advance."

He, like Aristotle, saw the development of the child occurring in certain stages—however, he identified four stages rather than three— and believed that teaching and training should be in harmony with the developmental nature of each of these stages. According to Rousseau these various stages are breaks in the developmental process and each can be distinguished because each has special characteristics and functions. He spoke of a metamorphosis that takes place when the child changes from one stage to another. Thus Rousseau introduced a saltatory theory of human development according to which the nature of development is seen as change which is more sudden at certain age levels than at others. He like G. Stanley Hall speaks of puberty as a new birth. New functions may emerge rather suddenly and become dominant in the psychological organization. We might better understand this saltatory aspect of development in Rousseau's theory if we recall his own temperamental saltatory experiences.

The first stage, that of infancy, includes the first four to five years of life. The child is dominated by the feeling of pleasure and pain. This period is called the animal stage because the child is like an animal in regard to its physical needs and undifferentiated feelings. This notion we encountered earlier in the writings of Aristotle. Education, such as training motor coordination, sense perception and feeling, is primarily physical. He advocates to mothers that the method of nature be followed in everything and proposed the following rule: "Observe nature, and follow the route which she traces for you. She is ever exciting children to activity; she hardens the constitution by trials of every sort; she teaches them at an early hour what suffering and pain are."

The second stage, which Rousseau characterized as the savage stage, includes the years from five to twelve. Dominant during this stage is the faculty of sense. Sensory experiences are provided by play, sport and games, and the curriculum is centered around the training of the senses. During this stage self-consciousness and memory develop and human life in the proper sense begins here. The child still lacks reasoning ability and is not yet sufficiently aware of moral considerations. Education during this stage should be free from external, social and moral control. Formal training in reading and writing are seen as harmful and therefore postponed until the beginning of the third developmental stage. In the first twelve years education

. . . ought to be purely negative. It consists not at all in teaching virtues or truth, but in shielding the heart from vice, and the mind from error. If you could do nothing and allow nothing to be done, if you could bring your pupil sound and robust to the age of twelve years without his being able to distinguish his right hand from his left, from your very first lesson the eyes of his understanding would be open to reason.

Rousseau's method of "negative education," based on the assumption that there was an innate developmental plan in the organization which cannot be improved upon by environmental factors, finds its corresponding modern psychological concept in "maturation." The defenders of the maturational concept of development advocate, as did Rousseau, a permissive and unrestricted atmosphere for child rearing.

The third stage, from the age of twelve to fifteen, is characterized by an awakening of the rational functions, including reason and self-consciousness. Youth at this age possess an enormous amount of physical energy and strength. The excess of energy leads to curiosity. Since curiosity is a characteristic of this developmental stage, the school curriculum should be built around the child's natural interest, his exploratory behavior and the desire to discover what is true about the world. The only book that should be read during this stage was *Robinson Crusoe*. Rousseau saw in Crusoe the great model and idea for the pre-adolescent since his style of life characterized by exploration of the world and a primitive curiosity, corresponds to the needs and interests of this developmental stage. The curriculum should be geared to the study of nature, astronomy, science, art and crafts. Rousseau in agreement with contemporary educational theory emphasizes the learning process rather than the product. "He is not to learn science, he is to find out for himself." This is the age of reason; curiosity and personal utility are the main motives for behavior; social conscience and emotionality are still undeveloped. It is interesting to observe that, in opposition to other developmental theories, the rational aspect of personality develops prior to the emotional. Rousseau's theory was a reaction to the historically earlier philosophy of rationalism. Modern theory of personality stratification sees in emotionality the deeper and therefore the historically and developmentally earlier layer of personality.

The fourth period, adolescence proper, from the age of fifteen to twenty, finally culminates in the maturation of the emotional functions and brings about a change from selfishness to self-esteem and social consideration. The adolescent is no longer self-sufficient but develops a strong interest in other people and a need for genuine affection. This stage is characterized—late by comparison to knowledge about youth today—by the emergence of the sex drive, which Rousseau considered a second birth. "We have two births, so to speak—one for existing and the other for living; one for the species and the other for the sex." Now conscience is acquired and morals and virtues become possible. This is the period of preparation for marriage, which ideally coincides with the attainment of maturity.

Maturity could be considered as a fifth stage in the process, but it appears to be less clearly defined. The faculty which becomes dominant during this period is will. The will is the faculty of the soul by which we choose between two alternatives.

These stages of development, according to Rousseau, correspond to certain stages in the development of the human race. Thus it was assumed by this recapitulation theory that the human race had gone through the stages of animal like living, the stage of savagery, the stage of reason and finally, through a stage of social and emotional maturity. He used the historical development of the race in order to explain the development of the individual child. This hypothesis was taken up again and further developed by educators such as Froebel and Ziller as well as by G. Stanley Hall and the Child Study Movement of America.

Critics have pointed out that Rousseau overemphasized the individual nature of human growth and development and underemphasized the importance that education and culture have in the developmental process and especially in the formation of the human personality. "He neglected the importance of the culture in the human development and turned the eye of the teachers away from the necessity of realizing that society has great influence upon the development of individual personality."[18] Maybe it would be more appropriate to say that he saw the influence of education and culture as negative forces in personality development which he wanted to remove to make possible the free natural development of what is good in the child.

CHARLES DARWIN'S THEORY OF BIOLOGICAL EVOLUTION

A new trend of thought concerning the nature of development, although not primarily concerned with child and adolescent development, results from the publication of Darwin's *Origin of Species*.[19] The impact that this book, published in 1859, had on advancement of knowledge in many fields was considerable. Darwin's idea of evolution, growth and development from the simpler to the more complex forms of organic life has been one of the most revolutionary and influential ideas in man's thinking about himself and the nature of his development. Every living organism from the simplest organic structure to the complexity of human biology is brought together under the lawfulness of natural explanation. The psychological implications resulting from the biological concept of development were accepted, elaborated and applied to adolescent development by G. Stanley Hall, thus leading to a science of adolescent development.

Since Darwin's theory is well known, only its basic principles will be stated. Darwin collected substantial, though not complete, evidence for a theory which claimed that the evolution of biological life was continuous, from a single cell organism, through numerous higher developmental stages, to the complexity of human mind and body. This evolutionary theory assumed variability and adjustability in all organisms as well as the overproduction in the number of offspring of each species. Darwin showed that the overproduction of offspring outnumbered their capacity to survive. The result is a "struggle for existence." In this struggle selection of some and elimination of others, a "natural selection process" takes place by which the increase in population is checked. The stronger, the healthier, faster, more immune, more intelligent and physically better developed and adjusted organisms survive and reproduce, while the weak, sick and less adaptable species perish. In time this leads to the "survival of the fittest." The qualities which account for the survival of the fittest are inherited by the offspring. Since the conditions for survival frequently differ in various kinds of environments basic changes in the organism occur. Thus in the selection process, variations, new kinds, new races and eventually new organisms come into existence. This process began with the simple one cell organism, and from the lower forms of organic life more and more complex forms have developed. The last link in this biological evolution is the human being. Since the climate, geological and general life conditions change, the evolutionary process is a perpetual one.

This theory of evolution is in complete contrast to the theological doctrine of the Divine Creation of each individual. Through Darwin's theory man was placed in the order of nature. Most theological and many philosophical positions previous to Darwin,—e.g., Aristotle—had postulated an essential dualism between man and nature. This absolute distinction between human nature and the nature of the organic world was seriously challenged by Darwin. Man was now seen not only as a more advanced and more intelligent species in the organic world, but also as a part of it.

The acceptance of these principles by the natural and the social sciences resulted in an increased concern with the nature of the human mind and its development. G. Stanley Hall, deeply impressed by this theory of biological evolution, began to study the nature of child and adolescent development from the standpoint of an evolutionary oriented psychology.

Many of these theoretical trends, especially those of Rousseau and

Darwin, but also those of Aristotle and Locke, culminate in the psychology of human development promulgated by G. Stanley Hall. Since he uses the philosophical thought of the past as well as the beginning scientific approach of the present, his theory of adolescence is in general well known and in many texts on adolescence constitutes the beginning of the discussion. Because of lack of space his theory cannot be discussed in detail, however, the reader is referred to the literature[16] for a discussion of the theme begun in this article.

REFERENCES

1. Aristotle. "Ethica Nicomachea." Trans. W. D. Ross, in *The Basic Works of Aristotle*, R. McKeon (Ed.) New York: Random House, 1941.
2. Aristotle. "Historia Animalium." Trans. D. W. Thompson, in *The Basic Works of Aristotle*. R. McKeon (Ed.) New York: Random House, 1941.
3. Aristotle. "Magna Moralia." Trans. G. Stock, in *The Works of Aristotle*. W. D. Ross (Ed.) Vol. IX, Oxford: The Clarendon Press, 1925.
4. Aristotle. "Politica." Trans. B. Jowett, in *The Basic Works of Aristotle*. R. McKeon (Ed.) New York: Random House, 1941.
5. Aristotle. "Rhetorica." Trans. W. R. Roberts, in *The Basic Works of Aristotle*. R. McKeon (Ed.) New York: Random House, 1941.
6. Ausubel, D. *Theory and Problems of Child Development*. New York: Grune & Stratton, 1958.
7. Boyd, W. *The History of Western Education*. New York: Barnes & Noble, 1965.
8. Butts, R. F. *A Cultural History of Western Education*. 2d ed. New York: McGraw-Hill, 1955.
9. Comenius, J. A. *The Great Didactic*. M. W. Keating (Ed. and trans.) London: A. & C. Black, Ltd., 1923.
10. Darwin, C. R. *The Origin of Species by Means of Natural Selection*. London: J. Murray, 1859.
11. Eby, F. *The Development of Modern Education*. New York: Prentice-Hall, 1952.
12. Hall, G. S. *Adolescence*. 2 Vols. New York: Appleton & Co., 1916.
13. Hobbes, T. *Leviathan*. Reprint of the Edition of 1651. Oxford: The Clarendon Press, 1929.
14. Locke, J. *An Essay Concerning Human Understanding*. A. C. Fraser (Ed.) Oxford: The Clarendon Press, 1894.
15. Locke, J. *Treatise of Civil Government*. New York: Appleton-Century Co., 1937.
16. Muuss, R. E. *Theories of Adolescence*. New York: Random House, 1962.
17. Price, K. *Education and Philosophical Thought*. Boston: Allyn and Bacon, Inc., 1962.

18. Rousseau, J. J. *Emile*. W. H. Payne (Trans.) New York: Appleton & Co., 1911.
19. Plato. "Laws." B. Jowett (Trans.) *The Dialogues of Plato*. Vol. IV, 4th ed. Oxford: The Clarendon Press, 1953.
20. Plato. "Phaedo." B. Jowett (Trans.) *The Dialogues of Plato*. Vol. I, 3d ed. New York: Random House, 1937.
21. Plato. *The Republic*. B. Jowett (Trans.) Oxford: The Clarendon Press, 1921.

1.2 *Orientation*

A major influence in the birth of psychology as a scientific discipline was the study of the individual differences among people. This influence, rooted in Darwinian biology, was intensified by selected British psychologists who during the latter nineteenth century explored ways to measure individual differences and analyze such measurements statistically. One precipitous outgrowth of this exploration was the mental test movement which gathered momentum in this country shortly after the turn of the century. Among the early interests of psychologists identified with the testing movement was sex differences in intelligence and other psychological characteristics. Not only has this interest been sustained, but it has been magnified by many provocative sex differences disclosed through psychological study since that time. Rare are studies involving both sexes which do not reveal sex differences even though a researcher may not have initially sought to discover them.

The paper that follows represents a crisp overview of physiological, psychological, social, and cognitive differences between the sexes apparent immediately prior and subsequent to puberty. As such, this overview is a valuable precursor to papers that appear later in this volume, particularly those on adolescent sexuality, the identity crisis, identification, and sex education. It is important to note that this survey is composed largely of generalizations derived from *nomothetic* study, that is, methods and procedures designed to formulate general principles of development, and *normative* study, or the attempt to describe group characteristics in terms of statistical averages. Data reported by the author of the proceeding paper are, with few exceptions, based upon comparisons of groups of males and females. Thus, while a generalization holds true for a comparison group, it obviously may not be reflected in the behavior of a given individual from that group. Although this limitation may be considered serious, reliable group-derived generalizations are extremely helpful to psychologists in many ways, including theory formulation and behavioral diagnosis. In addition, they occasionally offer significant implications for social and educational planning.

RECOMMENDED READINGS

Brown, Daniel G.   Sex-role development in a changing culture. *Psychological Bulletin*, 1958, **55**, 232–242.

Maccoby, Eleanor (Ed.)   *The Development of Sex Differences*. Stanford, Calif.: Stanford University Press, 1966.

Tanner, J. M.   *Growth at Adolescence*. Oxford, England: Blackwell Scientific Publications, 1962.

1.2   Differences between the Sexes at Puberty

Barbara B. Hauck, UNIVERSITY OF WASHINGTON

Much of the psychological data on puberty has not been devised for, directed toward, nor evaluated in a way consistent with maximizing all possible information on sex differences. Nonetheless, important information on dissimilarities between the sexes can be found in the literature —and there are indications that such differences may be far more numerous than has been assumed to date. All too frequently, data on boys and girls have been pooled *prior to* statistical evaluation, and the resultant findings reported for *children* or *youths* instead of for *boys* or for *girls*. Valuable information on inter-sex diversity and significantly different patterns of intercorrelations of variables for one sex or the other may thereby be submerged (Kagan & Moss, 1962). In considering sex differences at puberty it is important to note that some of these dissimilarities are *innate* and biological in origin; even more probably they are *learned* within the context of interpersonal experiences or as an outgrowth of group membership.

The psychologist concerned with adolescence must, like Janus, look both backward and forward in order to assess and explain the sex differ-

---

An original paper prepared especially for this volume.

ences that exist at puberty. Transescence, the period which begins prior to pubescence and extends into early adolescence, encompasses many physical and psychological changes which transform boys and girls into adolescent youth. During this period boys and girls differ significantly from one another in the *hormonal constitution* and *sequence* which actuates physiological and sexual maturation; in the *age* at which sexual maturity is reached; in the *rate* at which various levels of maturity are attained; in the *stability* of personality traits over time; in the *socio-cultural expectations* held for each sex; in the *patterns of child rearing* which mold them; and in the *psychological responses* each sex makes to the internal and external changes which impinge upon them.

PHYSIOLOGICAL DIFFERENCES

Puberty is the climax of the pubescent period, distinguished by specific, physiological clues to maturity in each sex. The most precise of multiple clues for girls is the arrival of menarche. For boys, the most precise single clue is the presence of live spermatozoa in the urine; however, since this fact can be noted only by clinical means, a combination of observable factors (ejaculation, pigmented pubic hair, deepening voice, and so on) more commonly serve to indicate sexual maturity in the male. These maturational events occur in response to hormonal stimulation. The endocrine glands, including the thyroid, adrenals, and the pituitary, secrete hormones or chemical substances which then are carried to another organ where they stimulate some specific activity.

Tanner's review (1962) of the findings on gonadotropic excretion in children indicates that such hormones are clinically detectable several years before puberty. They increase quite rapidly during the adolescent years, then level off in adulthood. In females, the hormone level fluctuates not only longitudinally, but also within the menstrual cycle.

Low levels of estrogen are found in both boys and girls until pubescence, but at that time the rate of estrogen production increases markedly in girls, and finally is established as a cyclic excretion about eighteen months before menarche. The female growth spurt begins at about age 10 and crests at about age 12 (Meredith, 1967). Breast enlargement begins at a mean age of 10.5 and reaches fullest development in about three years. Pigmented pubic hair appears at about age 11. Menarche, which occurs at a mean age of 13 in white girls of the present generation, reportedly occurred at age 14.5 or later only 100 years ago. This increasingly rapid physical maturation appears to be related to the better state of nutrition, general improvement in standard of living, and higher quality of medical care which has come about in past decades.

There are no significant differences in the amounts of ketosteroids (adrenal androgens) excreted by boys and girls up to the time of puberty. At this point, however, there is a sharp increase for both sexes, with boys eventually reaching levels twice as high as those of girls (Group for the Advancement of Psychiatry, 1968). The slight rise in estrogen production in boys during puberty is minor in comparison with the prominent increase in the ketosteroids (Hamburg & Lunde, 1966). The mean age for the beginning of testicle enlargement in males is age 12, and growth to maturity takes up to seven years. Penis enlargement begins at about age 12.5, and mature size is attained in about five years. The male growth spurt begins at about 12.5 and peaks at 14. Pigmented pubic hair appears at a mean age of 13 in boys (Meredith, 1967).

Mussen, Conger, and Kagen (1963) report the average boy to be taller than the average girl until about the age of 10, and heavier until about 11. By age 13, girls are both taller and heavier, but this trend is again, and permanently, reversed by ages 16 or 17. By this time, boys are taller, heavier, and have greater muscular strength than girls. At most ages the basic sex differences in size override the relationship of size to maturation rate. Among boys, physiological variation is greatest at about 14 years of age. Girls show maximum physical variation at about age 12 (Eichorn, 1968). In skeletal age girls are two years ahead of boys at age 13, but by the age of 18 the sex group norms are similar. In addition to being two years ahead of boys in skeletal maturation, girls also are advanced in dentition, onset of procreative ability, and in completion of physical growth (Flory, 1935).

The activity of sex hormones in conjunction with growth hormones brings about the adolescent growth spurt. On the average, both sexes grow two or three inches during the tenth to eleventh year for girls, and during the fourteenth to fifteenth year for boys. In addition to height increases, the shoulder and chest areas broaden and musculature increases dramatically in males. In females, the pelvic area broadens and the waist narrows. These physiological changes are due to the influence of specific sex hormones which affect differential growth of the body parts in each sex. For instance, there is a more rapid growth of the lower extremities just prior to puberty. This period is more protracted in boys, thus permitting the development of longer legs in relation to trunk length in males than is possible in the more rapidly maturing females (Group for the Advancement of Psychiatry, 1968).

It is difficult to determine the age at which fertility is attained. Although the Kinsey study (1948) indicated that the majority of early adolescents of both sexes are capable of sexual response, it appears that sexual responsivity is not synonymous with fertility. Evidence from cultures which permit adolescent pre-marital intercourse indicates that both sexes are sterile for some indefinite period after the beginning of menstruation or ejaculation. Tanner (1961) concludes that conception is very unlikely during the first year to eighteen months after these processes begin. Maximum fertility probably is not reached until the twenties.

PSYCHOLOGICAL AND EMOTIONAL DIFFERENCES:
THE PERSONALITY VARIABLES

The occurrence of body changes associated with sexual development and functioning, as well as those changes related to physical size and strength, demand modification of the pubescent's previous body image and feelings about himself. To a larger extent, one's feelings of adequacy or inadequacy about oneself occur as a result of, and in reaction to, the real or imagined assessments of others. Therefore, a boy or girl at puberty judges his or her adequacy as a male or as a female against a cultural standard or a composite, idealized image.

Although the acquisition of a sex role standard—a learned association between typical male and female physical attributes, overt behaviors, and covert attitudes—apparently occurs during the years 3–6 in both sexes (Kagan, 1964), there is a continual refinement and redefinition of these qualities as children grow toward puberty. Some sex dissimilarities appear to be inborn, appearing significantly more often in one sex or the other across cultures regardless of differing socialization practices (Whiting, 1963; Spiro, 1956). However, these innate tendencies, as well as the much larger group of potential behaviors that do not have biological roots, may both be emphasized or deemphasized by particular child rearing practices. While there appears to be some evidence that aggression in boys, and seriousness and responsibility in girls have genetic underpinnings, it is also clear that specific pressures tend to propel boys toward more aggressive behaviors (Bandura, 1965), toward becoming independent problem-solvers, and toward being the sexual pursuers while encouraging girls to be dependent, confirming, affiliative, nurturant, passive, poised, and friendly (Bennett & Cohen, 1959).

In most cultures different behaviors are elicited from boys than from girls, and there is a surprisingly high consistency across cultures in the nature of these sex-connected expectations. Nurturance, obedience, and responsibility training are significantly more often aimed toward girls in all cultures; achievement striving and training in self-reliance are more frequently a part of a boy's rearing practices. These behaviors are consistent with the adult sex roles which involve women in child care and family responsibility and men in self-reliant, productive family support and protection activities (Barry, Bacon, & Child, 1957).

Sex differences in the longitudinal stability of personality traits in this culture are apparent (Kagan & Moss, 1962). As would be expected, girls show greater stability in the degree of passivity they evince over time. Boys who have been passive prior to school entrance tend to shift toward greater activity when they enter school. Since school entrance marks a point of discontinuity with previous cultural expectations for children, it is not surprising that formerly passive boys now are nudged toward the masculine typed behavior of heightened activity.

A similar trend is noted in the stability patterns of independence behavior. Girls show stability in independence behavior from ages 3–14, but boys do not. Again, this probably relates to differential age-sex cultural expectations. Although girls are encouraged from infancy to be dependent, society does not necessarily impose punishment upon those girls who show independence. This is tolerated. Therefore, a given girl may be either dependent or independent over time, but whichever trend she follows tends to have high temporal stability. Although boys are expected to be independent at all ages, dependent behavior is tolerated during their pre-school years. However, upon school entrance, boys are pushed to become independent. Thus those boys who were dependent pre-schoolers now will be forced to modify their previous behavior in the direction of greater independence.

More aggression is expected, and therefore tolerated in boys than in girls, so there tends to be high stability of aggressive behavior in males of all ages. The only trend toward increased aggression noted in girls was reported by Livson and Bronson (1961), and indicated that the daughters of well-educated parents were verbally aggressive. Since educated families may be more likely to treat girls and boys alike, rearing them democratically, permitting and encouraging their involvement in decision-making, such girls may feel freer to speak their minds, and less needful to act the passive, compliant female role. Probably because society at all levels considers aggressive behavior normal for males, the level of aggression in boys seems to be unrelated to the educational level of the family.

The fluctuation of achievement motives appears to be highly sex related. Girls appear to strive for intellectual mastery at an earlier age than boys, but boys are more likely than girls to continue recognition-seeking behavior between childhood and puberty. This may be due to a discontinuity of cultural expectation for females which arises at puberty—such as the demand that now she become sought-after by boys. Or it may relate to the biological and psychological intricacies of the puberty period itself—as when the girl becomes so intrigued with the opposite sex that she lets her studies slide. Conversely, societal expectations for boys at puberty include some explicit demands from parent and from school that it is time to settle down, study, and prepare for college entrance or a job. For both sexes, high intellectual mastery during transescence tends to be a good index of adult achievement.

Girls who are described as "bold, fearless, and daring" during the pubescent period appear to be those who will become the intellectually oriented women (Kagan & Moss, 1962). Since the adjectives "bold, fearless, and daring" tend to have masculine connotations, and since intense intellectual drive in adulthood tends to be viewed as more masculine than feminine, it may be that only those girls who have personality traits tending toward the masculine end of the continuum either desire to undertake, or manage to survive intellectual orientation. Girls with a more passive, non-competitive, and dependent nature may well find it easier to accept the traditionally feminine roles of wife and mother; and upon accepting these roles, eschew intellectual mastery.

Girls must assess their attractiveness, poise, and passivity in continual interaction with others in order to get the feedback which indicates how well they are meeting the cultural expectations for their sex. Thus, a girl is initiated early into a system of dependency upon others; into courting their acceptance as the price which must be paid for their help in molding her into an acceptable woman. This need for acceptance and feedback from others may underlie the consistent finding that by junior high age, the anxiety level of girls is significantly higher than that of boys. At the elementary school level the differences between boys and girls are insignificant (Keller & Rowley, 1962).

Boys are able to develop many male sex-typed behaviors in situations where other persons are not necessarily present. For example, they can perfect gross motor and mechanical skills without feedback from others. A boy's skill at mastering the bicycle is perfectly obvious to him, with or without the help of others, and is largely dependent upon his innate aptitude plus a large amount of practice. This he can accomplish on his own, or incidental to other pursuits. Since independence of the attitudes and opinions of others is deemed a favorable masculine trait, doing things on his own is both "favorably perceived and encouraged by peers and adults" (Kagan, 1964).

Bronfenbrenner (1961) believes that boys develop the optimal qualities of independence, initiative, and self-sufficiency in response to parental affection coupled with strong parental discipline. He suggests that there is a much greater risk of "oversocializing" girls—that is, in developing such traits as timidity, overdependency, sensitivity to rejection—because parents more often use love-oriented or psychological disciplinary techniques with girls. This leads to greater internalization of parental standards and a higher degree of superego development in girls than in boys.

However, Douvan (1960) states that the internalization of standards is *more* important to mature male ego development, while the development of interpersonal skills is more important for girls.

Pubescent girls report more love and nurturance from their parents than boys do (Droppleman & Schaefer, 1963), while boys state that they receive more physical punishment, control, hostility, and neglect from both parents. Under such circumstances, Bronfenbrenner predicts that boys develop fewer internalized behavioral controls than girls—and this appears to be the case. Livson and Bronson (1961), investigating patterns of impulse control in adolescents, found extreme impulsivity and under-control make for moderate personal adjustment in males, but for poor adjustment in females.

If it is assumed that personal adjustment is related to the individual's perception of how closely he achieves the social expectations for his own sex, this is understandable. If boys are expected to be less controlled and more impulsive, and girls are expected to be the opposite, then fulfilling that expectation would make for better adjustment than not doing so.

Throughout middle childhood, boys consistently display more frequent and severe conduct (acting-out) disturbances than girls (Peterson, Becker, Hellmer, Shoemaker, & Quay, 1959). This undoubtedly relates to the different set of social expectations and a higher tolerance level for misbehavior in boys. By the time girls are in the fifth or sixth grades, they show a higher percentage of personality problems than boys. This may be connected with the onset of puberty in girls at these grade levels where the boys have not yet reached this degree of maturation. However, it could relate also to the fact that while conduct problems are more characteristic of, expected from, and perhaps even elicited in boys, so personality problems are more likely to be socially acceptable, even encouraged deviations in girls.

Since realistic acceptance of one's own physique and functioning is basic to the achievement of identity (Erikson, 1959), each sex must come to terms with and integrate the reality aspects of puberty. Girls must accept the menstrual cycle and its implications for normal womanhood —the female body changes, and the disquieting stirrings of sexual feeling. They must modify former aggressive or competitive tactics in dealing with boys and begin to display the more acceptably feminine attributes of compliance, passivity, and receptivity.

Boys must learn to deal constructively with their greater physical size and strength. This means facing and managing aggressive urges which have a different implication once body size and strength are increased. Since fantasy now could become reality in regard to physical assault or aggression against peer or parent, this can constitute an area of anxiety. There may be concern over penis and testes development, often some difficulty in comprehending the physiology and implications of ejaculation, and concern over masturbatory activity.

Heterosexual intercourse prior to marriage is considered a violation of the restrictive middle-class moral code. Constant pressure is exerted on the teenager to eschew any form of sexual behavior until marriage. Despite recent evidence that youth are adhering less and less to what many of them consider an outworn and hypocritical moral code, nonetheless it is unlikely that many of the younger adolescents have either opportunity or adequate sophistication to find and establish stable heterosexual outlets. Thus, masturbation necessarily continues to be the primary sexual outlet for a good many years. Because of parental admonitions, old wives' tales, and individual adolescent's fantasy, involvement in masturbation exacts penalties in feelings of unworthiness, shame, guilt, and fear.

A larger percentage of boys (82 percent) than girls admit to masturbation (Kinsey, 1948; Willoughby, 1937), but both sexes do engage in it, and both suffer conflict over participation in an act which they have been led to believe is morally wrong and/or physically harmful (Landis, 1940). Some boys attempt to deny or cover up their feelings of guilt or anxiety by boasting about their sexual virility. The existence of the double standard of expected sexual behavior deters most girls from admitting to or discussing freely their own sexual activities. Boasting about sexual matters is acceptable in the male but not in the female.

Despite the toll in worry and concern engendered by masturbation, it tends to serve a useful function for youth by providing a learning situation during which the sexual urges are gradually brought under individual control and management. It permits, through sexual fantasy situations, role practice for new relationships. Thus, masturbation not only serves to relieve sexual tensions and to provide the pubescent with some assurance that he is functioning normally, but it also may indicate to him that one comes gradually to achieve a degree of control in the execution of the sexual act. This is a necessary prerequisite for successful heterosexual relationships at a later date (Group for the Advancement of Psychiatry, 1968).

Since the male self-image and developing ego are so intimately bound to the appropriate and timely maturation of the external genitalia, boys who are late to develop or those who consider their physical endowment less than optimal suffer keenly. Because early maturing boys tend to be perceived more favorably by peers and others (Jones & Bayley, 1950; Weatherley, 1964), their evaluations of themselves tend to be more positive. If a boy matures early, whatever his eventual size or body build will be, the fact persists that at a crucial point he has been reassured about his maleness. Since in this way he also is spared from months of needless concern about whether he is developing normally, positive self-feelings are established early. He receives salubrious feedback from peers and parents. Therefore, if several years hence some of his later-blooming friends eventually surpass him, his acceptance of himself is not likely to be shaken. Late maturing boys, however, tend to maintain their relatively poor self-concepts and related personality tendencies which originated at the time they were deeply concerned about their maturation (Mussen & Jones, 1957).

Early development in girls is not perceived as especially favorable either by the girl herself or by others. Parents are concerned about the dangers inherent in their young daughter's sexuality. Peers of either sex do not accord favorable recognition to the girl who suddenly towers above them by three inches. The girl herself may feel miserably out of step with her age-mates. At a time when her interests are focused on the changes in her body and in her evolving feelings toward boys, she finds little to discuss with her still-childish girl friends. Boys her own chronological age are perceived as hopelessly small in size and infantile in outlook. Boys of the appropriate—and interesting—maturational level are older, and are not always to be found at her school level. Thus, the early maturing girl remains an outsider for at least as long as her physical setting keeps her from easy contact with other youths of the same developmental stage.

The late maturing girl is in a somewhat better position than the late maturing boy, because she fits better with age-mates, and poses no threat to those who have not yet begun their developmental spurt. Besides, her parents are much more accepting of their "little girl" being slow to mature than they would be of her brother under the same circumstances. Small girls can still be feminine. Parents may be quite relieved at not yet having to face the problem of a dating daughter. Thus, they do not communicate to her any feelings of concern or dissatisfaction over her physical status. The rate of physical maturation is a much less influential variable mediating future personality development in girls than in boys. Nonetheless, late maturation in both sexes appears to have less desirable long-term consequences than does early maturation (Weatherley, 1964). Early maturers of both sexes earn higher reading achievement and IQ test scores, remain in school longer, and are higher in school performance than late maturers (Douglas & Ross, 1964).

Long (1968) found several developmental changes in the self-concept during adolescence which seem to be sex-related rather than to stem from the individual timing of puberty. Boys appear to decline in identification with their fathers at about the fourth grade level. This drop evens out after the sixth grade, but then declines markedly after the twelfth grade. Girls, however, tend to make their dramatic shift away from others right at the time of puberty. This corresponds to Tryon's observation (1939) of emotional upheavals in junior high girls but not boys, and to the fact that the peak of a girl's bad relations with parents occurs at puberty (Buhler, 1931). The difficulties appear to resolve themselves early in adolescence, because by ninth or tenth grades, a new high point in girls' self-esteem is reached (Long, 1968).

At the beginning of puberty and in early adolescence, boys are relatively more stable than girls in terms of perception of distance from others. This may be because boys have been testing themselves in independent activities all along, and have had considerably more practice in learning just how much need they have of others. Where the girl seems to withdraw and then reapproach, the boy begins his independence striving early, levels off before puberty, but then pulls farther from parents as he reaches late adolescence (Long, 1968).

SOCIAL DIFFERENCES BETWEEN BOYS AND GIRLS

Just as there are identifiable differences between the sexes in personality and trait stability factors, so there are distinctive differences in social factors, interests, and outlets. Despite the superficial impression that a boy's social life is less rule-bound than a girl's, less supervised, and with greater adult tolerance toward boisterousness, aggression, and impulsivity, the picture may be misleading. In fact, adult expectations for feminine behavior, being clearly defined and consistent, provide more secure guidelines and support for girls at all ages (Peltier, 1968). Thus, a girl more safely can predict the consequences of her behavior. In contrast, a boy who has been permitted to be active, aggressive, and rebellious in some situations is forced to make accurate and perceptive assessments of specific occasions and modify his behavior appropriately. A fellow can be rough-and-tumble on the playground, but he must settle down in the classroom.

Mature adolescent behaviors for each sex differ from those of childhood, so discontinuities abound. The well-adjusted child who fails to alter his behavior appropriately may become the poorly adjusted adolescent.

From a very early age girls consistently are encouraged to respond sensitively to social feedback. However, boys are encouraged to make their own decisions and to act autonomously. This emphasis can adversely affect social interaction where cooperation and sensitivity toward others is imperative.

These boy and girl behavioral differences are apparent in the like-sex clubs and cliques to which both sexes adhere in pubescence. Girls form such groups earlier than boys, and behave in quite opposite ways. While 12-year-old boys are being aggressive, competitive, and active, girls of corresponding age are acting neat, prim, and docile. It is not until several years later that both groups actively strive for social conformity, with the boys gradually becoming less boisterous and more poised, and the girls becoming increasingly sophisticated (Tryon, 1944).

Pubescents and early adolescents appear to be making earlier and more frequent cross-sex friendship choices than they did a generation ago (Kuhlen & Houlihan, 1965). Although girls supposedly show earlier social and heterosexual interests than do boys, this study found a higher frequency of cross-sex choices by the boys. This may indicate either less reticence on the part of boys in displaying overt interest in the opposite sex, or it may signify earlier or stronger interest than had been suspected.

By 14 when most girls start dating, generally they are anxious and defensive. They still cling tenaciously to their girl friends for advice, comfort, and support (Douvan & Adelson, 1966). Boys begin dating between 14 and 15, while they are involved in learning a new and expanded masculine role. In social-sexual affairs they are uncertain about how far they should go, how far the girl expects them to go, and how to behave in any eventuality. Ordinarily, it is the girl who feels keenly that it is her social and moral responsibility to keep the sexual part of the dating relationship within proscribed limits (Schwartz & Marten, 1967) thus putting a greater burden of anxiety on her shoulders from the start. Boys are perceived as morally immature and incapable, therefore, of assuming the leadership role in keeping sexual impulses under control. The cultural assessment of young males as a dangerous, hot-blooded minority (Friedenberg, 1965) tends, apparently, to be internalized to a degree by boys, and they then act upon this cultural assignation.

That girls assume more responsibility to keep the dating relationship under control is hardly surprising. Girls are constantly bombarded with warnings about the social consequences of a pre-marital pregnancy; they are impressed with the idea that the boy will "go as far as you let him" and the fact that "he is only concerned with his own satisfaction." In addition to these emotional appeals to a girl's self-preservation instincts, personal esteem, and pride, is the fact that specific child rearing practices apparently have inculcated a greater sense of responsibility in girls. By the sixth grade level, girls show a higher degree of internal locus of control (feeling of personal responsibility for one's actions) than do boys of any age all through high school (Crandall, Katkovsky, & Crandall, 1965). Douvan (1957) states that boys are more likely to consider parental rules as external controls, a means of keeping out of trouble rather than as internalized guidelines. Girls, on the other hand, tend to internalize parental rules and to consider them in terms of personal guidance and safety.

Anti-social, amoral, and deviant behavioral tendencies in males are higher in all cultures, in all historical periods, and throughout the age range from pre-school to adulthood. Lerman (1967) notes that the verbal use and understanding of slang, swearing, and argot is significantly higher for boys than for girls through transescence, puberty, and adolescence. Probably this is due to the less restrictive rearing of boys in which they are free to roam around and be exposed to seamy language and situations far more frequently than their sisters. There is also greater permissiveness extended to males in relation to using certain words and expressions—the verbal double standard.

School dropout rates are higher for boys than for girls at all educational levels (Voss, Wendling, & Elliott, 1966) with boys representing approximately 55 percent of the total. In all, about 35 percent of a potential high school graduating class drops out between fifth and twelfth grades. Age 16 is the median age for leaving school, although boys leave at a somewhat later age than girls. The reasons for dropping out differ somewhat between males and females, with boys more often succumbing to the pressures of educational retardation and general factors of alienation, and girls leaving school more frequently because of disinterest, to get married, or because they are pregnant.

Several factors appear to bear upon the differential dropout rates for males and females. Boys, lagging developmentally at the beginning of their school life, may get off to a poor learning start which plagues them all through the grades. For some, this results in educational retardation of such severity that school is synonymous with frustration and failure. Dropping out relieves the immediate problem (Voss *et al.*, 1966). Boys also are permitted greater autonomy in decision-making than are girls. Parents tend to feel that boys can take care of themselves better than girls can sexually, as well as economically. Insisting that a daughter remain in school has sexual-safety implications in that it is a means of keeping her off the streets during the critical period during which she is only marginally mature enough for marriage. If she drops out in order to *get* married, parents may be satisfied; if she drops out because of pregnancy, the family must bow to the inevitable and make the best of it.

Delinquency figures also show higher incidences for boys of all ages (Schreiber, 1964). About 3/4 of all delinquents are boys, and 3/4 of these are in the 14–16-year age range. The most common offenses resulting in institutional commitment for boys are burglary and theft (including car theft), being ungovernable, and for running away. Girls are most often committed for running away, being ungovernable, and for sex offenses. Obviously running away and being ungovernable may well be an integral part of committing sex offenses. The aggression theme that recurs in every area of a boy's life expression, is implicit in the "theft" category, while the focus on interpersonal relationships, so important to a girl, clearly plays a part in her anti-social activities.

Weinstein (1960) found pubescent girls higher than boys on a variety of personal adjustment scores. He concludes that girls have an easier time because societal expectations for girls are more clearly defined and consistently stated and imposed than for boys. Further, the expectations of behavior for girls are more consistent with the avenue of behavior actually open than is the case for boys.

Vocational choices ordinarily are not made at puberty, but, for both sexes, this is the time when fantasy career choices are made. In boys these appear to relate to the firm establishment of masculine identity rather than being based upon actual abilities. Girls' career interests in early puberty appear to be psychological techniques for channeling unconscious desires for marriage and a family which must, in fact, be delayed for some years. The temporary choices may serve to deny these unfulfillable wishes and also may provide a last fling at aggression before a girl permanently settles into the passive, feminine role (Matthews, 1963).

Girls' career choices at all ages from puberty on are less likely to be free, autonomous selections to the same degree that boys' choices are. Many career areas are not open equally to girls. Some families still consider money invested in girls' education to be a waste—especially if she later marries. Thus, parents do not support her career aspirations as wholeheartedly as her brother's. Many girls elect marriage as their prime choice, and therefore are diffident about selecting an interim job. For girls who elect marriage, social identity is much more closely tied to choice of mate and his vocation rather than to her own occupation. Social identity for a girl married to a doctor, but who is a secretary by training is distinct from that of a girl married to a fireman, but who is a secretary by training. There is also evidence that while bright boys make significantly more realistic vocational choices than duller boys at the junior high level, girls, whatever their ability levels, tend not to make realistic vocational choices (Krippner, 1962).

COGNITIVE DIFFERENCES BETWEEN THE SEXES

Because tests of general intelligence were devised specifically to minimize sex differences, any substantial dissimilarities between mean IQ scores of boys and girls imply differential inclusion of items favoring one sex or the other (Eichorn, 1968). In Rusk's (1940) report on the intelligence of Scottish children, the mean score for all boys was 103 and for all girls, 101. However, he found the boys' intellectual spread was more variable than that of the girls. This variability is highlighted in the fact that longitudinal studies of gifted children tend to identify more boys as gifted than girls, and, conversely, there are substantially larger numbers of boys who are mentally subnormal than there are girls. Girls' scores tend to cluster more closely around the mean.

Girls consistently tend to earn higher IQ scores and better school grades during the early school years up to adolescence. Boys earn higher scores on IQ tests during the high school period (Sontag, Baker, & Nelson, 1958). Much of this probably is due to girls' developmental advantage, as well as to the gradual change in children's perceptions of the sex-typed characteristics of school and academic work. The first few years of school are seen as more appropriate to girls than to boys. This also corresponds to the period most dominated by female teachers. Later, girls' motivation perhaps decreases somewhat as a result of their anxiety over feeling more intellectually competent than boys, and their conflict over excessive competitiveness. Maccoby (1966) suggests that family and community pressures to suppress intellectuality converge on girls at puberty. Preparation for higher education or a vocation may seem inimical to finding a husband, and therefore be derogated. Matthews (1963) believes that girls' achievement superiority in the grades is confusing to both sexes and may have long-range effects on each. In boys, feelings of inferiority engendered during the time girls were surpassing them academically may underlie future resentment toward vocational competition with women. In girls, it may herald the beginning of a competitive striving which is damaging to the necessary cooperative functions of marriage. However, once boys reach puberty, they have closed the intellectual gap which has separated them from girls, and now are in an equitable position. High school boys begin to connect academic proficiency with future vocational success. Further, they find high school more appropriate to their needs, as well as better stocked with male teacher-models (Maccoby, 1966).

Underachievement is patterned differently for boys than for girls. Boys are more consistent in both achievement and underachievement from the second grade on. Thus high achievement between the ages of 6 and 10 is more predictive of adult intellectual mastery in males than in females (Sontag & Kagan, 1967). Girls more often achieve until puberty and then become underachievers in junior and senior high school (Shaw & McCuen, 1960).

Social demand for specific sex-typed behaviors such as conformity-passivity in girls and aggression in boys appears to be important in producing identifiable sex differences in cognitive performance. Aggression in boys appears to underlie their better analytic thinking abilities. Girls' strong affiliative needs help them to function well in group problem-solving situations, but not in analytic thinking. Witkin (1962) related girls' conformity and dependency to their field dependence. That is, dependent and conforming individuals are oriented toward stimuli outside themselves rather than toward internal analytic thinking processes. A study by Sigel (1963) confirms this. Sigel found that transescent girls make more test errors because of difficulties in perceptual discrimination than do boys. He believes this reflects girls' more global approach in contrast to boys' more analytic one.

Skills and problems requiring analysis and reasoning are culturally viewed as more male-appropriate behaviors. Analytic thinking, as well as creativity and high general intelligence, appear to be cross-sex-typed in that boys and girls who score high possess a spread of abilities encompassing some of those traits considered more appropriate or more common to the opposite sex (Sontag & Kagan, 1967).

Although overall intelligence scores are comparable for boys and girls, differences between the sexes, in *particular* cognitive abilities, tend to be larger and tend to increase with increasing age. Clear differences favoring girls are noted in word fluency, rote memory, and reasoning (Carlsmith, 1964). Boys excel in spatial and quantitative abilities. Ausubel (1968) states that the only sex difference in cognitive ability which is evident at the pre-school level is in verbal fluency, therefore the other differences are possibly culturally determined rather than sex-linked factors.

To date, researchers have found a few identifiable differences between boys and girls in cognitive style—the consistent pattern of cognitive organization and functioning that a person uses. Boys are more likely to be analytic-descriptive rather than inferential-descriptive or relational in a picture grouping task (Kagan, Moss, & Sigel, 1962). Boys and girls not only differ in some aspects of cognitive style but also a particular cognitive style is different psychologically to each sex. Certain styles of mental operation have different personality correlates in boys than in girls. For instance, use of the descriptive part-whole approach correlates positively with cautiousness in boys but negatively in girls.

In their recent comprehensive assessment of developmental factors at pre-adolescence, Gardner and Moriarty (1968) found very few sex differences in the areas of cognitive functioning and control. They conclude that this lack may be attributable to the fact that this culture does not make significantly different cognitive demands on one sex or the other during the period when patterns of cognitive functioning are being established. The more-or-less equivalent intellectual-scholastic experiences for boys and girls in the public schools probably tend to even out potential differences rather than to emphasize them.

SUMMARY

Differences between boys and girls at puberty can be found in the physical, psychological, social, and intellectual areas. Some of these are inborn, sex-related factors, but more frequently they are traits that have been culturally influenced. Clear-cut knowledge of the differences between the sexes is important to future educational and social planning. Such information is more likely to become available as researchers make a concerted effort to plan their studies and assess their data in ways designed to maximize rather than minimize single-sex information and the interacting variables pertinent to it.

REFERENCES

Ausubel, D. P. *Educational Psychology. A Cognitive View.* New York: Holt, Rinehart and Winston, 1968.

Bandura, A. Influence of models' reinforcement contingencies on the acquisition of imitative responses. *Journal of Personality and Social Psychology,* 1965, 1, 589–595.

Barry, H., Bacon, Margaret K., and Child, I. L. A cross-cultural survey of some sex differences in socialization. *Journal of Abnormal and Social Psychology,* 1957, 55, 327–332.

Bennett, E. M., and Cohen, L. R. Men and women: personality patterns and contrasts. *Genetics Psychology Monograph,* 1959, 60, 101–153.

Bronfenbrenner, U. The changing American child—a speculative analysis. *Journal of Social Issues,* 1961, 17, 6–18.

Buhler, Charlotte. The social behavior of the child. In C. Murchison (Ed.) *Handbook of Child Psychology.* Worcester, Mass.: Clark University Press, 1931, 392–431.

Carlsmith, L. Effect of early father absence on scholastic aptitude. *Harvard Educational Review,* 1964, 34, 3–21.

Clark, W. W. Boys and girls—are there significant ability and achievement differences? *Phi Delta Kappan,* 1959, 41, 73–77.

Crandall, Virginia C., Katkovsky, W., and Crandall, V. J. Childrens' beliefs in their own control of reinforcements in intellectual achievement situations. *Child Development,* 1965, 36, 91–109.

Douglas, J. W. B., and Ross, J. M.   Age of puberty related to educational ability, attainment and school leaving age. *Journal of Child Psychology and Psychiatry*, 1964, 5, 185–196.

Douvan, Elizabeth.   Independency and identity in adolescence. *Children*, 1957, 4, 186–90.

Douvan, Elizabeth.   Sex differences in adolescent character process. *Merrill-Palmer Quarterly*, 1960, 6, 203–211.

Douvan, Elizabeth, and Adelson, J.   *The Adolescent Experience*. New York: John Wiley, 1966.

Droppleman, L. F., and Schaefer, E. S.   Boys' and girls' reports of maternal and paternal behavior. *Journal of Abnormal and Social Psychology*, 1963, 67, 648–654.

Eichorn, Dorothy H.   Variations in growth rate. *Childhood Education*, 1968, 44, 286–291.

Erikson, E. H.   *Identity and the Life Cycle*. New York: International Universities Press, 1959.

Flory, C. D.   Sex differences in skeletal development. *Child Development*, 1935, 6, 205–212.

Friedenberg, E. Z.   *Dignity of Youth and Other Atavisms*. Boston: Beacon Press, 1965.

Gardner, R. W., and Moriarty, Alive.   *Personality Development at Preadolescence*. Seattle: University of Washington Press, 1968.

Ginzberg, E., Ginsberg, S. W., Axelrae, S., and Herma, J. L.   *Occupational Choice*. New York: Columbia University Press, 1951.

Group for the Advancement of Psychiatry, Committee on Adolescence.   *Normal Adolescence: Its Dynamics and Impact*. New York: Charles Scribners, 1968.

Hamburg, D. A., and Lunde, D. T.   Sex hormones in the development of sex differences in human behavior. In Eleanor E. Maccoby (Ed.) *The Development of Sex Differences*. Calif.: Stanford University Press, 1966, 1–24.

Jones, H. E.   *Development in Adolescence*. New York: Appleton-Century-Crofts, 1943.

Jones, H. E., and Bagley, Nancy.   Physical maturing among boys as related to behavior. *Journal of Educational Psychology*, 1950, 41, 129–148.

Kaczkowski, H.   Sex and age differences in the life problems of adolescents. *Journal of Psychological Studies*, 1962, 13, 165–169.

Kagan, J.   Acquisition and significance of sex typing and sex role identity. In M. L. Hoffman and Lois W. Hoffman (Eds.) *Review of Child Development Research, Part I*. New York: Russell Sage Foundation, 1964, 137–167.

Kagan, J., and Moss, H. A.   *Birth to Maturity*. New York: John Wiley, 1962.

Kagan, J., Moss, H. A., and Sigel, I. E.   The psychological significance of styles of conceptualization. In *Proceedings of Conference on Cognitive Processes*. J. F. Wright and J. Kagan (Eds.) *Monograph of Social Research in Child Development*, 1962.

Keller, E. D., and Rowley, V. N.   Junior high school and additional elementary school normative data for the children's manifest anxiety scale. *Child Development*, 1962, 33, 675–681.

Kinsey, A., Pomeroy, W., and Martin, C. *Sexual Behavior in the Human Male.* Philadelphia: Saunders, 1948.

Kohlberg, L. Moral education in the schools: a developmental view. *School Review,* 1966, **64,** 1–29.

Krippner, S. Sex, ability, and interest: a test of Tyler's hypothesis. *The Gifted Child Quarterly,* 1962, **6,** 105–110.

Kuhlen, R. G., and Houlihan, Nancy B. Adolescent heterosexual interest in 1952 and 1963. *Child Development,* 1965, **36,** 1049–1052.

Landis, C. *et al. Sex in Development.* New York: Hoeber, 1940.

Lerman, P. Argot, social deviance, and subcultural delinquency. *American Sociological Review,* 1967, **32,** 209–224.

Livson, N., and Bronson, Wanda C. An exploration of patterns of impulse control in early adolescence. *Child Development,* 1961, **32,** 75–88.

Long, B. H. *et al.* Developmental changes in the self-concept during adolescence. *School Review,* 1968, **76,** 210–230.

Maccoby, Eleanor. *The Development of Sex Differences.* Stanford, Calif.: Stanford University Press, 1966.

Matthews, Esther. Career development for girls. *Vocational Guidance Quarterly,* 1963, **2,** 273–277.

Meredith, H. V. Synopsis of puberal changes in youth. *Journal of School Health,* 1967, **37,** 171–176.

Mills, C. A., and Ogle, C. Physiologic sterility of adolescence. *Human Biology,* 1936, **8,** 607–615.

Mussen, P. H., and Jones, Mary C. Self-conceptions, motivations and interpersonal attitudes of late and early maturing boys. *Child Development,* 1957, **28,** 243–256.

Mussen, P. H., Conger, J. J., and Kagan, J. *Child Development and Personality.* New York: Harper, 1963.

Peltier, G. L. Sex differences in the school: problem and proposed solution. *Phi Delta Kappan,* 1968, **50,** 182–185.

Peterson, D. R., Becker, W. C., Hellmer, L. A., Shoemaker, D. J., and Quay, H. C. Parental attitudes and child adjustment. *Child Development,* 1959, **30,** 119–130.

Rusk, R. R. The intelligence of Scottish children. In G. M. Whipple (Ed.) *Intelligence: Its Nature and Nurture.* Thirty-ninth Yearbook of the National Society for the Study of Education. Bloomington, Ill.: Public School, 1940.

Schreiber, D. (Ed.) *Guidance and the School Dropout.* Washington, D.C.: National Education Association, 1964.

Schwartz, G., and Merten, D. The language of adolescence: an anthropological approach to the youth culture. *American Journal of Sociology,* 1967, **62,** 453–468.

Sears, Pauline S. *The Effect of Classroom Conditions on the Strength of Achievement Motive and Work Output on Elementary School Children.* Final Report, Cooperative Research Project, No. 873, Stanford University, 1963.

Shaw, M. C., and McCuen, J. T.   The onset of academic achievement in bright children. *Journal of Educational Psychology*, 1960, **51**, 103–108.

Sigel, I. E.   How intelligence tests limit the understanding of intelligence. *Merrill-Palmer Quarterly*, 1963, **9**, 39–56.

Sontag, L. W., Baker, C. T., and Nelson, Virginia A.   Mental growth and personality development: a longitudinal study. *Monograph of Social Research in Child Development*, **23**, 1958.

Sontag, L. W., and Kagan, J.   The emergence of intellectual-achievement motives. *American Journal of Orthopsychiatry*, 1967, **37**, 8–21.

Spiro, M. E.   *Kibbutz: Venture in Utopia*. Cambridge: Harvard University Press, 1956.

Tanner, J. M.   *Education and Physical Growth*. London: University of London Press, 1961.

Tanner, J. M.   *Growth at Adolescence* (2d ed.) Oxford: Blackwell Scientific Publications, 1962.

Tryon, Carolyn M.   Evaluations of adolescent personality by adolescents. *Monographs of Social Research in Child Development*, 4, No. 4, 1939.

Tryon, Carolyn M.   The adolescent peer culture. *Yearbook of the National Social Studies Education*, 1944, **3**, 217–239.

Voss, H. L., Wendling, A., and Elliott, D. S.   Some types of high school dropouts. *Journal of Educational Research*, 1966, **59**, 363–368.

Weatherley, D.   Self-perceived rate of physical maturation and personality in late adolescence. *Child Development*, 1964, **35**, 1197–1210.

Weinstein, E. A.   An analysis of the sex differences in adjustment. *Child Development*, 1960, **31**, 721–728.

Whiting, Beatrice B. (Ed.)   *Six Cultures: Studies of Child Rearing*. New York: John Wiley, 1963.

Willoughby, R. R.   Sexuality in the second decade. *Monograph of Social Research in Child Development*, **2**, 1937.

Witkin, H. A., Dyk, R. B., Faterson, H. F., Goodenough, D. R., and Karp, S. A. *Psychological Differentiation*. New York: John Wiley, 1962.

1.3   *Orientation*

If for no other reason, the psychological concomitants of sexual motivation could provide psychologists with justification to study adolescence as a distinct stage of development. The onset of puberty requires the socialization of new features of the sex drive, a requirement that presents myriad problems to any organized society. Cross-cultural studies indicate that societies vary widely in the extent to which they place sanctions on the sexual behavior of adolescents (Ford & Beach, 1951). Our own society seems to fall near the restrictive end of a restrictive-permissive continuum with its social, moral, and legal sanctions against various forms of sexual behavior. The extremes to which adults frequently go to control adolescent sexual behavior is perhaps a testimony to the strength of sexual motivation among adolescents. As Ford and Beach (1951) indicate, the most nearly effective preventative method is complete segregation and constant supervision of the sexes. The effects of these and other practices, including permissive ones, upon attitudes toward sex, preferred forms of sexual behavior, and the like are not clear. It is abundantly clear, however, that sexual problems often accompany personal maladjustment in adulthood. Whether in any given case a sexual problem is the result or cause of personal maladjustment is not easily determined. Reasoned speculation, however, points to a relationship between childhood socialization practices and adult sexual beliefs and attitudes.

From a mental health point of view the socialization of the sexual drive creates something of a dilemma. On the one hand, the internalization of impulse control is imperative for ordered social existence. On the other hand, the promotion of guilt and shame over sexual feelings and genital functions is generally viewed negatively (McCandless, 1970). And there exists the still further issue of a moral code from which adolescents can take cues for appropriate sexual behavior. Into the muddy waters created by such issues has plunged the author of the following concise essay. Dr. Wagner's expressed objective is to stimulate a rational, honest inquiry into the psychodynamics of adolescent sexual behavior and the responsibilities of society to assist in the process of psychosexual development.

Several noteworthy aspects are to be found in Wagner's essay. One is the skill with which the author dissects crucial psychosocial issues related to adolescent sexual behavior—the issue of sexual responsibility, for example. Another is Wagner's description of the complex array of motives thought to give rise to sexual responses. Still another is his comment on differences in the meaning of sex between males and females.

Wagner concludes with a discourse on sundry issues such as out of wedlock births, dualisms associated with cultural views on sexual behavior, contraception, and the need for a meaningful, consistent morality of sexual behavior. A plea for more effective sex socialization practices glistens brightly in the final stages of this essay. Wagner's plea anticipates an elaboration of this topic by David Payne in Part II of this reader.

RECOMMENDED READINGS

Atkinson, Ronald. *Sexual Morality*. New York: Harcourt, Brace & World, 1966.

Beach, F. A. (Ed.) *Sex and Behavior*. New York: John Wiley, 1965.

Ford, C. S., and Beach, F. A. *Patterns of Sexual Behavior*. New York: Harper & Brothers, 1951.

Simon, William, and Gagnon, John H. On psychosexual development. In David A. Goslin (Ed.) *Handbook of Socialization Theory and Research*. Chicago: Rand McNally, 1969, 733–752.

1.3   Adolescent Sexual Behavior

Nathaniel N. Wagner, UNIVERSITY OF WASHINGTON

Although the adult society appears very interested, if not preoccupied, with the sexual behavior of adolescents, there has been relatively little scientific study of this important area. The taboos concerning the study of sex have affected the social sciences as well as the medical sciences. Two examples will illustrate this reticence. In an excellent volume on pre-marital sexual standards in America, Ira Riess (1960), an eminent sociologist, goes to considerable length in his introduction to "apologize" for the nature of his topic. He states, in essence, he has chosen to study sex because it is a good field to test sociological theory. It is sociological theory that is important and sexual behavior is only a convenient example of a complex set of behaviors. It is my considered judgment that Ira Riess need not be ashamed of his considerable contribution to our knowledge of *sexual behavior* whether or not he has contributed to "sociological theory."

The second example concerns medical science where, until the very recent past, sexual behavior, as separate from reproductive behavior, was not an accepted topic for scientific investigation. A specific and pointed illustration (which for added emphasis does not concern itself with the controversial area of teenage sexual behavior), a male in his early forties has a myocardial infarction (heart attack). During his convalescence his physician is very explicit about the amount and type of physical exercise the patient should follow. If the patient asks about when he should resume sexual relations with his wife, he would receive

---

An original paper prepared especially for this volume.

the following answer if his physician was being totally honest: "There is not a single research study (as of 1969) directed to this question. If I assume sexual intercourse is similar to playing handball or running upstairs, then there is a great deal of data available and I can advise you." In point of fact, that is what most physicians do—make clinical assumptions and inferences—as they sometimes are faced with such questions from anxious and frank patients.

Clearly, sexual behavior is an emotional area which produces intense feelings and strong resistances to honest and rational inquiry. This is particularly so for teenage sexual behavior where questions of pre-marital sexual behavior, sex education, illegitimacy, and promiscuity are just some of the topics guaranteed to make adults uncomfortable and for which teenagers are confused and receive little genuine assistance.

The following short essay drawn from the writer's professional experience and originally written for a television series entitled "Teenagers and Sex: A Dialogue with Parents" highlights some of the problems facing teenagers, particularly females, today.

"I AM NOT THAT KIND OF A GIRL"

A group of eight pregnant girls all under the age of 18 sat in a circle around a table. This group session was a regular part of the education program offered them by the city schools special education program in conjunction with a local voluntary social agency. There were two group leaders, a psychologist and a social worker.

During the many sessions of the group (they met once a week for an hour and a half) a variety of topics were discussed. Whether to relinquish the baby for adoption, to keep it, to get married, were the alternatives available. Many had considered abortion, but for this group this was not a viable alternative. Half the girls were white, half were black; the whites from the outer fringes of the city, the blacks from the central core.

The discussion turned to the question of the unplanned quality of their pregnancies. Every girl present indicated that if she could have controlled it she would not be pregnant. The obvious question was raised, since they did not abstain from intercourse, why were adequate contraceptive measures not used? "I am not that kind of girl" was the almost uniform response phrased in a variety of ways but still with the same message.

I have heard variations of this statement "I am not that kind of girl" from so many pregnant teenage females that I no longer smile even inwardly at its absurdity. I believe that although it represents many honest emotional feelings, in the final reality it is a cop-out, an extraordinarily effective dodge of responsibility.

The concept of premeditation making an act more serious is well understood. A murder that was carefully planned and executed has a very different response from a judge and a jury than a murder that occurs in a tavern where there was a disagreement, strong words were exchanged, and then a bottle is shattered with the intent to kill. In this latter instance we talk of murder in the second degree or manslaughter, whereas premeditation means murder in the first degree. The differences in prison terms, the differences in moral judgment about these crimes are considerable. It is important to remember, however, that in each instance the victim is dead.

For many, if not all teenagers in America today, sexual behavior has the sense of wrong-doing about it. It may be one of the reasons it is so exciting. Sexual intercourse outside marriage for teenagers is almost uniformly judged as an evil. For young girls or young boys to take contraceptive steps to prevent a pregnancy it is an indication of premeditated sex. Thus, a double evil is perpetrated—sex outside marriage and in cold blood.

To avoid the "in cold blood" charge, many young people, both boys and girls, evade the issue of premeditation. While doing so they also evade the issue of responsibility. The young person may tell themselves at the beginning of the evening "I'm going to be good, I'm not going to do anything wrong," or they may consciously suppress any thoughts of sexual activity. Then with the titillation of the society at full work, with the perfumes with names suggesting sin, indiscretion, and a variety of exciting wrong-doing; with the hair creams guaranteed to make one sexually irresistible, with the tight sweater and the miniskirt, with the mood music in that sexual symbol the automobile, "love" takes over. There is the major cop-out—"we didn't do it because we planned it, we did it because we love each other." Everyone knows that evil committed in the passion of emotion is really not an evil. That is true whether a wife's lover is killed or if sexual intercourse occurs in the back seat of an automobile.

The society aids and abets in this moral cop-out. Where can young people receive assistance in dealing with their feelings honestly? How helpful has the church, the school, parents been? Everywhere one sees the advertisement of things to make one sexually attractive. There is no need to catalog the list, it would be much too long. The things to make one sexually responsible, however, are hidden under the druggist's counter or need a prescription from that pillar of moral respectability, the family doctor.

In the vernacular of the teenage world—doesn't it blow your mind to imagine for a moment contraceptive devices being advertised in the media as we do with cigarettes? Young people on a sailing craft having a great time, young people on horses in the great open spaces, young people running across a hillside—and on, and on, and on.

I am not suggesting that we advertise contraceptives in the media. I am suggesting that we devote as much attention to the question of sexual responsibility as we do appeals to sexual attractiveness. I am suggesting it is a strange morality that sees millions of dollars spent on the advertisement of products we know are harmful to health and life, and yet provides little help in assisting young people to become sexually responsible human beings. To help those young people who feel the proper place for sex is within marriage deal with their sexual feelings and drives; to help those who will have sex outside marriage be more responsible for their behavior—this is what I am suggesting—for without such assistance, children will be born every day into this world to parents who did not plan for them and do not want them . . . but then they are not "that kind of people."

TEENAGE SEXUALITY

At this point it may be helpful to look at the context and meaning of teenage sexual behavior. The importance of the adolescent years does not need to be highlighted for the reader. The fact of this volume speaks for the interest of the contributing authors. In terms of sheer numbers there were over 24 million young people in the 13–19 age range in 1969. This is the largest 7-year age grouping in the American population due to the high birth rate in those years following World War II.

The central task of adolescence is that of finding one's identity. By identity I mean the developing of beliefs and values, deciding on what one wants to do and get out of life—in essence, coming to know who one is. In terms of sexuality, the teenager must adjust to changes in the size and shape of the body with possibilities for different and more mature behavior. The concept of self undergoes rapid change as people begin to respond differently to the individual because of his or her changing physical appearance. The desire for independence becomes an important vehicle in the search for identity. If one conforms to parental values and behavior then one's identity is fused with the parental identity. Developmentally in children, the concept of difference appears before the concept of sameness, and the negativism of a 2-year-old can be viewed as the first real statement of independence and of a developing independent identity.

Adolescence is usually demarcated by a physiological, sexual event. For girls the menarche (the first menstrual flow) and for boys a number of indications—the most scientifically reliable one being the presence of spermatozoa (detectable by microscopic examination) in the urine—mark the beginning of sexual maturity. Changes in body shape, the deepening of the voice, facial and pubic hair are the most noticeable indications of puberty. This demarcation, however, is rarely clear-cut. For girls the menstrual flow may be quite skimpy and irregular and there may be months between periods. A few never menstruate. For boys, although they may frequently have erections (often but not invariably associated with the presence of females), they may still be unable to ejaculate. A nocturnal emission usually proceeds a consciously produced ejaculation. Generally puberty comes about two years earlier for females than for males.

The sexual behavior of young people cannot be understood as a manifestation of any single motive, either psychological or physiological. Like other human behavior, it is complex and over-determined; that is, a variety of motives combine to produce any single behavior. For teenagers the physical changes and, more importantly, the awareness of those changes through the pleasure accompanying sexual stimulation or thoughts, together with the striving for independence and maturity are some of the most powerful motives seeking expression. The need to belong, manifesting itself in the herd-like conformity of this age, is another powerful determinant. Without benefit of meaningful data, the mass media and adults who speak and write about adolescent sexuality combine to present an unrealistic picture of rampant teenage sexuality. The adolescent who is relatively sexually inexperienced (by far the great majority according to all evidence) feels that he or she is different, not partaking in the activities of the others.

Other motivations relating to sexual behavior are the need for the comfort and security of a "steady" so that the adolescent can be ready for any social eventuality. Related to this and of real importance is the need to be liked and the complementary need to express affection. For girls, affectionate feelings for boys can often be related to sexual feelings. Sexual desire seems to develop much later for females and be much less specific than for males in this society. More important for most females are such concepts as "romance," "love," and security of romantic attachment.

Sexual feelings initially felt by boys are not usually accompanied by feelings of love or affection and for some boys these emotional components remain separate from the physical for many years. In some, they are capable of separation indefinitely. For most boys, however, sexual and affectual feelings fuse with the first experience of an extended boy-girl relationship.

For girls, affection or love usually precedes sexual feelings. The female adolescent places a very high value on falling in love. This may result from the feeling that female identity cannot be complete without the presence of a strong and powerful male. This may be the reason that athletes are so attractive to young girls. Whatever the basis for this feeling, it does present real conflict to many young people, for to some females it implies sexual surrender. While all adolescents need to develop a healthy identity of self, there is real question and controversy as to the merit of experiencing sexual intercourse for its evolvement.

These differences between males and females derive, in part, from the society's double standard of sexual behavior. Females are supposed to have less sexual interest than boys, and the societal judgment is uniformly negative concerning extensive sexual activity of young females. Although young boys may receive the same admonitions about petting and intercourse, they also receive indirect encouragement especially from peers and from overly anxious fathers. The cliche "to sow some wild oats" beautifully describes the underlying expectation for the behavior of young males.

This double standard of sexual behavior appears to be under direct attack presently by young females. Although there has been considerable speculation about changing American sexual behavior in the 1960s, the most recent investigation of college-age youths (Luckey & Nass, 1969) indicates that it is among the females where the largest change has occurred. That is, for American samples, the behavior of males has been relatively similar for the last 20 years, while females have changed in the direction of more frequent sexual intercourse before marriage. This change in female attitude appears to be part of a general "revolt" on the part of minority groups who are seeking equal status with the dominant minority. Females, in contrast to such ethnic groups as Blacks, Chicanos, and Indians, are the only minority group which in fact is a majority. Despite this, their status, self-concept, and societal practices clearly define females as a minority group.

Interestingly, the change in female teenage sexual behavior so that it more closely approximates male behavior has had the effect of decreasing the importance of prostitution in early sexual experiences of American males.

There are no reliable data, however, on American teenagers other than college data, as we have not had a comprehensive survey such as the English have with Schofield's (1965) excellent study. Hopefully this lack of knowledge will be corrected in the near future.

POPULATION, UNWANTED PREGNANCIES, AND CONTRACEPTION

Any discussion of adolescent sexual behavior would be inadequate without a discussion of the problems of population, unwanted pregnancies and unwanted children, and the factor of contraception.

The population explosion is the world's biggest problem. There are at present 3.5 billion people in the world. By the year 2000 the population will double. Simply to keep up with the increase in the United States we should build a new city of 250,000 (the size of Tulsa, Oklahoma) each month. By the end of this century we will have an additional 100 million people. All this assumes no drastic change in the rate of population increase.

Not only is there the problem of population growth but the related problem of unwanted pregnancies. Unfortunately, there are no hard data on the frequency of unwanted pregnancies and the closest approximation we have is the number of "illegitimate" births. Obviously not all "illegitimate" births represent unwanted pregnancies and conversely not all pregnancies within marriage are wanted. It is a reasonable assumption, however, that a large majority of "illegitimate" births are unwanted. The concept of an illegitimate birth is a most unfortunate one for a variety of reasons and we prefer the term "out of wedlock." Are there really illegitimate births or illegitimate children?

In the last 25 years the rate of out of wedlock births in America has tripled. This is the rate per 1,000 unmarried women between 15 and 44 and not the actual number of children born out of wedlock, which has been increasing at an even higher rate because of population increases. Figures from the National Center for Health Statistics for 1967 indicate that 1 out of every 12 children born in America is born out of wedlock. This rate of 1 out of 12 compares to the 1940 figures of 1 out of 33. This startling rise has occurred at the same time as major advances in contraceptive techniques. What this figure of 1 out 12 represents in human misery is staggering.

The condition for young people is particularly striking, because 42 percent of the out of wedlock births occur to females under 20. For females under 15, 3 out of 4 children are born out of wedlock, and for females in the 15–19 age range, 1 out of 5 children are born out of wedlock. This does not consider the startling fact that out of all American first marriages, 1 out of 6 women have a child in less than 8 months from the time of their marriage. Estimates for teenage marriages are that 50–75 percent of the brides are pregnant at the time of marriage. These statistics suggest an unbelievable problem in terms of human suffering. We know that unwanted children—and the large majority of children conceived and born out of wedlock are unwanted—suffer major psychological damage. The evidence is extensive and powerful and has no rebuttal.

These related problems of population and unplanned and unwanted children stem in part from the inability and/or refusal of society to accept the fact that the sexual act and the reproductive act are not one and the same. This becomes vital in understanding the adolescent years as the young person is capable of both the sexual and reproductive functions in a physiological sense but in the vast majority of instances, adolescents are not ready or capable for the responsibilities of parenthood. It is within the context of a seductive society with its confused messages concerning sex—it is fun, it is wrong, it is grown up, it is cheap, it is sophisticated, it is dirty, it is beautiful—that teenagers search for standards that are consistent and meaningful.

One of the central facts of our time that we have real difficulty in facing is that the sexual act is a fundamentally different act with contraception than without it. The admonition to teenagers to avoid sexual intercourse because of the possibility of unwanted pregnancy is a strange hypocrisy in view of the increasing sophistication and reliability of contraceptives. Society can no longer expect ignorance through isolation; it can no longer expect scare and fear tactics to control behavior. If we wish young people to abstain from sexual intercourse before marriage we shall have to develop more rational and meaningful reasons for this behavior. We shall need to do more than to say pre-marital intercourse is wrong because it is wrong—but supply reasons that define its wrongness.

More importantly, we shall need to develop a morality of sexual behavior distinct from reproductive behavior. In the evolution of man from lower forms the instinctual quality of his sexual behavior has diminished to where only his sexual responsiveness is instinctual and he needs to learn about sexual behavior in order to perform. Concomitant with this loss of instinctual quality comes the reality that it is only humans, as compared to other mammals, who engage in sexual behavior essentially unrelated to times of fertility and conception.

We need to acknowledge this cerebral control of sexual behavior, its possibility of total separation from reproductive behavior, and develop standards of sexual conduct that define sexual behavior as it really is— an important human interpersonal communication. We owe it to our young people to develop such standards or we can expect continued human suffering and misery as they search for their own way, their own identity, as they will continue to be sexual human beings as they have no other choice.

REFERENCES

Luckey, Eleanore B., and Nass, Gilbert D. A comparison of sexual attitudes and behavior in an international sample. *Journal of Marriage and the Family*, 1969, 21, 364–379.

Riess, Ira L. *Premarital Sexual Standards in America.* New York: Free Press, 1960.
Schofield, Michael. *The Sexual Behavior of Young People.* Boston: Little, Brown, 1965.

1.4 *Orientation*

Over the past half-century, several major theoretical concepts for use in interpreting adolescent behavior and development have been shaped. Many of these concepts appear in various guises throughout this volume. Some have been spawned directly from learning theory; for example, the concepts of *modeling* (imitation learning) and *reinforcement.** Others are more clearly the product of sociological and anthropological study; for example, such notions as *opportunity failure* and *alienation.*† Still another is based upon the *sexual impulses* activated by puberty and the accompanying conflicts which the adolescent encounters in his movements toward sexual gratification. An emphasis upon sexuality has been principally supported by psychoanalytic thought, notably Sigmund Freud and his disciples.

Possibly the most popular of explanatory hypotheses treated in the literature on adolescence, however, is one which represents a broad fusion of various theoretical viewpoints, namely, the *identity crisis.* According to this conceptualization, adolescence is most fundamentally a period for the crystallization of one's sense of self— a satisfactory integration of sexual identity, goals and aspirations, personal ethics, and emotional independence. Identity formulation, of course, does not await the period of adolescence; one's concept of self has its underpinnings in infancy and early childhood (Ausubel, 1958). Nevertheless, several factors are thought to operate during adolescence, at least in Western cultures, to provoke a reorganization of one's identity. For one thing, pubertal changes require a refocus of one's body image. For another, there are mounting cultural pressures upon adolescents to make decisive commitments—personal and vocational—especially during late adolescence. The assumption of personal liability, the cornerstone of this so-

---

* Most broadly, the notion of reinforcement is based upon the principle that behavior is shaped by its consequences. See the Staats and Butterfield study in Part III for an application of this concept. Modeling is examined by Sarason in Part III.

† See the Burlingame paper in Part I.

ciety's legal system, also requires the development of responsible action by adolescents and young adults within the larger society.

The purposes of the following essay are threefold: to examine some evolutionary aspects of the identity crisis hypothesis, discuss some major ideas associated with contemporary protagonists of this hypothesis, and reflect briefly upon the validity of the identity theme by a reference to empirical study. A fundamental issue for the reader's consideration is whether a crisis in identity (as defined below) is inevitable during adolescence.

RECOMMENDED READINGS

Erikson, Erik H. *Identity: Youth and Crises.* New York: W. W. Norton, 1968.

Masterson, James F., Jr. *The Psychiatric Dilemma of Adolescence.* Boston: Little, Brown, 1967.

Rosenberg, Morris. *Society and the Adolescent Self-Image.* Princeton, N.J.: Princeton University Press, 1965.

Schacter, Burt. Identity crisis and occupational processes: an intensive exploratory study of emotionally disturbed male adolescents. *Child Welfare*, 1968, **47**, 26–37.

1.4 Identity Crisis: A Brief Perspective

Ellis D. Evans, UNIVERSITY OF WASHINGTON
Thomas H. Potter, UNIVERSITY OF WASHINGTON

The concept of identity crisis may be defined contemporaneously as "a necessary turning point, a critical movement, when development must move one way or another, marshaling resources of growth, recovery, and further differentiation." (Erikson, 1968, p. 16.) It seems fair to say, however, that the modern psychological roots of the identity concept extend to Sigmund Freud's (1856–1939) psychoanalytic theory of personality development. Roughly 75 years have passed since the inception of psychoanalysis, yet this theory, despite modifications, has continued to exert a strong influence upon many students of child and adolescent development. Classical psychoanalytic theory (Freud, 1917) did not attend ex-

An original paper prepared especially for this volume.

tensively to the adolescent period[1]; however, adolescence as perceived by Freud represents a final stage in psychosexual development during which the identification process is culminated (or at least continued). (In psychoanalytic terms, identification is a mechanism by which psychic energy is diverted for the purpose of ego development.) This stage, termed by Freud the *genital period*, normally involves a number of developmental features including (1) a shift away from narcissism (self-love) to altruism, (2) a final coming to terms with reality, and (3) reciprocal heterosexuality. It also is seen by Freud to be a time of anxiety, particularly in relation to heightened sexual motivation which is blocked by cultural sanctions. Such blocking, however, is considered to have its positive attributes, particularly by way of the *sublimation* mechanism. For example, through the sublimation process, an individual may channel his sexual energy in socially acceptable, although frequently disguised forms. The expansion of interests during adolescence is thought to be one positive outcome of such redirected energy.

Freud's work on personality development has been continued by his daughter, Anna, who has enlarged upon many psychoanalytic details with respect to the adolescent period. In a fashion similar to that of her father's, Anna Freud has dealt primarily with deviant behavior; little attention has been paid by her to "normal" psychosexual development. She does, however, acknowledge the need for psychoanalysts to attend more specifically to normal development. For Anna Freud, "teenage emotional upset" is not only inevitable but imperative if an adolescent is to become an adequately functioning adult. For example, she observes that many youngsters may be admired because they progress smoothly through the genital period when in fact they remain adolescents all their lives. Thus a major issue is introduced, namely, the extent to which conflict and emotional upheaval is actually a necessary precondition for personality maturation. Clearly Anna Freud observes that conflict is necessary; adolescent development neither is nor should be smooth and predictable. In this connection she sympathizes with the practitioner or parent who attempts to sort out "normal difficulties" (phasic) from those genuinely pathological. However, according to Anna Freud, even severe pathological upsets (to the point of psychosis) may be "normal" *if* they are transitory in the developmental cycle.

Anna Freud perhaps makes her greatest contribution by identifying typical patterns of ego defenses utilized by adolescents and the characteristics of adolescents who have satisfactorily repressed their sexual

---

[1] Freud's core ideas are concerned with early childhood development and psychopathologies which assumedly have their source in developmental problems.

impulses. For example, her description of the ascetic adolescent who foregoes all pleasure as evil presents a classical model of personality dynamics. A second broadly defensive syndrome is represented by the uncompromisingly idealistic adolescent who effectively intellectualizes all of his problems to the point of detached abstraction. Such tendencies may be present to some extent in all adolescents; in psychoanalysis abnormal behavior is perceived as basically an exaggeration, albeit often bizarre, of normal behavior.

SOME CONTEMPORARY CHAMPIONS OF THE IDENTITY CONCEPT

Modification and extensions of psychoanalytic thought are apparent in the work of many others, including Erich Fromm. Fromm's significant works have come in the years following 1940 and thus reflect life in the world somewhat different from that of Sigmund Freud's (Fromm, 1941; Fromm, 1956; Fromm, 1961). His works are also oriented more explicitly toward the warping and frustrating nature of society than were Freud's. The critical problem for humans, Fromm maintains, is *isolation*, an isolation borne of the incompatibility between human nature and organized society. The only acceptable solution to this incompatible situation, Fromm believes, is for men and woman to unite with each other in a spirit of love and cooperative interaction. Society prevents this, however, by its demands for conformity. Such demands, coupled with the authoritarianism found in any society, are thought to impair both man's ability to love and his creative propensities. This impairment leads to a sickness which is further fed by a pervasive system of pathological, frequently violence-oriented ethics characteristic of organized society. Hence, Fromm's "patient" is not so much the individual as it is the society of which the individual is a part.

Fromm has no single, articulated theory of adolescence. Yet his views clearly convey a primary concern for emotional growth and love during this developmental period. And among the basic needs of man postulated by Fromm is the need for identity. Moreover, the supreme human service is that which fosters mature love (Fromm, 1956). Mature love (the emotional union of one person with another without a loss of one's individuality or personal integrity) has, Fromm states, four essential elements:

(1) *care* (assisting the loved one to realize his/her own potential, that is, to serve as a catalyst for further growth);
(2) *responsibility* toward the loved one (tantamount to complete honesty);
(3) *respect* for and acceptance of the loved one as he/she is; and
(4) *full knowledge* of the person loved.

According to Fromm, the problem for adolescents in the matter of love is at least twofold. First, adolescent love frequently tends to be a matter of idolatry, thus perverted, although adolescents are rarely sufficiently insightful to discriminate this from mature love. Secondly, the capacity for mature love is dependent upon a clear, firm personal identity, an attribute neither easily nor quickly achieved during the adolescent years. The reader again is reminded of Fromm's conviction that societal values impede this achievement. For example, Fromm believes that money and power are valued more highly than love in our society. Further complicating factors are described by Fromm as "dichotomies of existence." An example of such a dichotomy is provided by Fromm's observation that while man "loves" peace, he wages war.

In summary, Fromm maintains that while individual behavior is shaped by society, this same society poses nearly insurmountable obstacles to personal development. Such obstacles may be particularly apparent during adolescence when the individual finds it necessary to make significant decisions about his own existence. Although Fromm expresses hope for man's condition and expresses faith in man's capacity to solve social problems, a certain pessimism inheres in Fromm's writings. For Fromm, there exists no strong probability that the child will develop into an adequately functioning, non-despairing adult as long as the child is immersed in a sick society.

From a theoretical foundation based upon the psychoanalytic-sociological views of Fromm and the interpersonal developmental views of Harry Stack Sullivan (1953), Edgar Friedenberg (1959; 1965) has brandished an incisive literary sword. Together with personalities such as Paul Goodman (1956), Friedenberg is frequently credited with furnishing an intellectual rationale, if not an impetus to the student activist movement. A principal target for Friedenberg has been the "melting-pot" tendencies in our society, that is, those forces that tend to minimize or reduce individuality and heterogeneity, thus destroying creativity and uniqueness. For Friedenberg the central developmental task of adolescence is *self-definition*:

Adolescence is the period during which a young person learns who he is, and what he really feels. It is the time during which he differentiates himself from his culture, though on the culture's terms. It is the age at which, by becoming a person in his own right, he becomes capable of deeply felt relationships to other individuals perceived clearly as such. (Friedenberg, 1959, p. 29).

Basic hazards to self-definition in Friedenberg's terms include societal obsessions with "group adjustment" and "mutual cooperation." These emphases frequently translate, Friedenberg feels, to conformity pressures which consequently overwhelm the adolescent and prevent his full development as an individual. What is needed, rather, is what Friedenberg calls *dialectical conflict*.[2] For self-definition, much conflict must take place with reference to clearly defined values communicated by adults who themselves are secure with such values. Friedenberg believes that our problems in this regard are that (1) adults neither embrace nor communicate clearly defined values which they are willing to examine dialectically with adolescents and (2) adults seemingly do everything possible to eliminate conflict with adolescents. The latter includes the "buddy-daddy" or "good guy" tendency among parents and teachers, psychological counseling in the schools, and the non-contingent over-provision of material possessions to adolescents. Facing these combined problems, it becomes increasingly difficult for Friedenberg's adolescent to achieve mature personality growth. As conflict is eliminated, the essential nutrient for personality growth is also eliminated. Therefore, adolescence as a period of growth is believed by Friedenberg to be vanishing from our society.

Paradoxically, Friedenberg's recent works have seriously questioned whether it is a "good idea" to be a creative or self-defined individual. If society, particularly the educational establishment, actively punishes such behavior (especially in bright students), perhaps adolescents should succumb or adjust to the system in their own best self-interests. Friedenberg, through the use of case study and interview techniques has painted a bleak picture of the purportedly damaging effects of rigid and demeaning secondary schools. He points out the absence of civil liberties and civil rights within the schools and espouses the thesis that adolescents are seldom treated with respect by teachers. In the final analysis, Friedenberg's theory is less a theory of adolescence than a defense of this age group and a condemnation of society and public education. Nevertheless, his collective works dramatize the identity crisis hypothesis in many provocative ways.

Similar to Friedenberg's thinking is that of Paul Goodman (1956; 1964). The latter's approach, however, involves perhaps an even greater emphasis on sociological and anthropological methods with a good many philosophical condiments sprinkled throughout. Goodman has focused upon the general uselessness of the adolescent in our society. He feels that the American people have lost sight of the important goals in life such as self-worth and the values of excellence. Rather, we are now excessively devoted to the means of material productivity and collective aggrandizement. Our society no longer is really interested in people, says

---

[2] *Dialectical* in this sense generally refers to discussion by reasoning and dialogue as a means of intellectual investigation. Thus, conflicting, alternative positions and contradictory ideas would be argued on logical grounds.

Goodman, and therefore the adolescent has few, if any, adequate role models for identification purposes. Without this necessary identification, the child has developmental difficulties or may never become an adult. (This line of thought is not far afield from the identification research and theory reported by Heilbrun in Article 1.5 of this volume.) Goodman feels that one of the necessary components of self-worth is meaningful accomplishment. Without a basic feeling of self-accomplishment, adult roles are not effectively fulfilled. Thus, not only do we deprive youth of adequate role models, but we also prevent them from fulfilling any meaningful tasks themselves. With few if any models and no feeling of accomplishment, our youth would rather "drop out" than take part in self-alienation. In contrast to Friedenberg, however, Goodman seems to have remained hopefully optimistic. Goodman also has addressed himself to changes that must be made in order to "save" our society and adolescents (Goodman, 1956; 1964).

Another author whose investigative approach is similar to that of Friedenberg and Goodman is Jules Henry (1963). Henry considers that the major problem for human development in our culture is posed by a compulsive achievement drive. Our society, feels Henry, is more interested in technology than people. In order to worship and value *things*, we must weaken our impulse controls and permit our collective id to take over and point our lives toward pleasure, however meaningless this pleasure may be. While Henry is particularly interested in how this affects youth, he also takes time to study the destruction and despair of our aged. In a life tuned to technology, production, and fun, those who cannot produce are discarded—such is the lot of the elderly. Henry attacks industry and advertising for creating this "pleasure-drive." But the schools, organized religion, and other social institutions are also criticized scathingly by Henry for pandering to this end.

Henry points out that education should free us, not shackle us to the constant custom of pleasure seeking and release at the expense of value. Because adolescents have created not a sub-society, but their own culture, they do not wish to resolve their developmental tasks, but instead, to remain forever adolescent. The problem is that, as Freud has pointed out, such perennial self-indulgence by an adolescent can never be fully met nor allowed by his ego. Therefore, the system of dynamics as pictured by Henry is heavily tension-producing. Such constant tension causes ever more searching for the myth of pleasure, thus perpetuating a vicious circle. Under such circumstances the identity crisis may be infinitely prolonged or perhaps resolved negatively.

Although the visibility of social critics and defenders of youth such as Friedenberg, Goodman, and Henry has been high, perhaps the most widely quoted authority on identity formulation is the influential psycho-analyst, Erik Erikson (1968). From a wealth of clinical experiences with children and adults, Erikson has built a theoretical framework based upon a series of psychosocial crises thought to confront the individual in successive fashion throughout the course of development. Erikson maintains that such crises (eight in all) present themselves at predictable periods during the developmental sequence, the first of which is asso-ciated with infancy and the last with senectitude. For continued per-sonal growth each crisis must be coped with successfully. The adequate resolution of each major crisis or conflict is believed by Erikson to result in the establishment of a basic personality characteristic. Specifically for the adolescent, this crisis involves the "final establishment of a domi-nant positive ego identity" (Erikson, 1963, p. 306).

For Erikson, the "danger" of the developmental stage of adolescence is "role confusion." To illustrate, Erikson refers to the dilemma of Biff in Arthur Miller's *Death of a Salesman*: "I just can't take hold, Mom, I just can't take hold of some kind of life." In other words, doubt, bewilderment, sexual insecurity, a lack of autonomy, and a failure to arrive at an occupational commitment all contribute to identity con-fusion. Phenomena such as an "over identification" with heroes and the general clannishness and conformity behavior of adolescents are Erik-sonian indications of a *defense* against identity confusion. This implies that adolescents in effect may help each other through much develop-mental discomfort by forming cliques and stereotyping themselves, their ideals, and their enemies. In addition, Erikson interprets the testing by adolescents of each other's capacity to pledge fidelity and the tendency to commit themselves totally to idealistic causes as part and parcel of the identity-striving process.

Erikson suggests that virtually all adolescents experience temporarily some degree of identity confusion. While most adolescents overcome this confusion, failure to do so may result in a variety of unfortunate out-comes, for example, a persistent inability to "take hold" as in Biff's case or the jelling of a negative identity. Such outcomes may be manifested, according to Erikson, in "devoted attempts" by adolescents to become precisely what culture, school, or parents do not wish them to be. For Erikson, tolerance, acceptance, and understanding are essential ingre-dients for facilitative adult-adolescent relationships during this time, but not to the point where complete and total freedom prevails. Rea-soned guidance, ample experiences to learn about human behavior, and a variety of vocational opportunities and avenues for personal achieve-ment are advised.

A person who emerges from the adolescent period with a firm sense of identity is prepared, states Erikson, to fuse that identity with others. In short, one is "ready" for *intimacy*. This means one has the "capacity to commit oneself to concrete affiliation and partnerships and to develop the ethical strength to abide by such commitments, even though they may call for significant sacrifices and compromises" (Erikson, 1963, p. 263). The hazardous counterpart of adolescent identity confusion during this superordinate stage is *isolation*, that is, one's consistent avoidance of relationships which involve intimate commitment.

The above discussion, beginning with the views of Freud and extending through the contemporary insights of Erikson has attempted to illustrate how the concept of identity crisis has been woven into the fabric of contemporary thinking about adolescence. Over the years this concept has relied increasingly upon cultural or sociological contexts for its meaning. As such the concept has grown in complexity. It has also been assigned the properties of a *process*, that is, one's identity is thought to be ever changing and developing, continually to be undergoing differentiation in terms of one's growing awareness of others and the problems of society of which one is a part. And, as Erikson (1968) suggests, it thus seems impossible to separate personal growth from communal change. The conceptual complexities implied by this are well illustrated by Erikson's own words:

In psychological terms, identity formation employs a process of simultaneous reflection and observation, a process taking place on all levels of mental functioning, by which the individual judges himself in the light of what he perceives to be the way in which others judge him in comparison to themselves and to a typology significant to them; while he judges their way of judging him the light of how he perceives himself in comparison to them and to types that have become relevant to him. This process is, luckily, and necessarily, for the most part unconscious except where inner conditions and outer circumstances combine to aggravate a painful, or elated, identity-consciousness. (Erikson, 1968, pp. 22–23).

The above suggests that the study of identity simultaneously requires insight into a person's subjective experience (including self-perceptions) and a full understanding of cultural forces (including interpersonal relationships) which currently may be impinging upon that person. Such a requirement, at the very least, complicates the empirical study by psychologists of identity formulation and the components of crisis. How, for example, does one measure, objectively and reliably, an adolescent's identity or the degree to which an adolescent is bathed in role confusion? At issue ultimately is the nature of the evidence which serves to validate the identity crisis concept.

VALIDATING EVIDENCE: SOME EXAMPLES

Data utilized to support the identity crisis hypothesis have come from diverse sources, although these data tend to be indirectly, rather than directly relevant. In addition, much of the evidence is the result of subjective interpretation by psychologists predisposed to accept this hypothesis. Notable among those with psychoanalytic leanings has been the use of clinical data, especially the results of counseling and psychotherapeutic sessions with adolescents. This is patently true of Erikson (1963; 1968), although he has synthesized data from other fields, particularly cultural anthropology, to develop his theory. A good example of clinical case study material utilized in the context of identity formulation is the recent work of Galinsky and Fast (1966). These psychologists have taken the position that vocational indecision is frequently an indication of identity difficulties. One characteristic of indecisive college students observed by Galinsky and Fast is a feeling of incompetence or unworthiness. A second is a lack of conviction to do work, a characteristic localized in Eriksonian terms as a problem of initiative and industry. Clinical data such as these unfortunately have at least two shortcomings. For one thing, they do not allow one confidently to determine the extent to which vocational indecision pervades the adolescent population as a whole. For another, these data do not necessarily indicate the magnitude of confusion that may prevail. Galinsky and Fast have presumedly based their comments upon college students who voluntarily seek counseling. This does not represent a random sample of college students and one cannot generalize the problems reported by self-referred late adolescents to the adolescent population as a whole. Such clinical data most clearly reveal the fact that vocational choice conflicts frequently motivate students to seek guidance.

The cross-cultural insights of Ruth Benedict (1938), although formulated several decades ago, are perhaps illustrative of the contribution of allied fields to the understanding of adolescent conflict and role confusion. Benedict's principal thesis is based upon the notion of *cultural discontinuity*. Discontinuity in socialization occurs when children or adolescents are required to "unlearn" a form of behavior previously reinforced or to learn something directly opposite of that for which they were earlier rewarded or punished. According to Benedict, certain role status conflicts provide the breeding ground for discontinuity problems in our culture. For example, the child who fulfills (and is rewarded for) a non-responsible, submissive, asexual role is expected adequately to fulfill a responsible, dominant, and sexual role as an adult. The inconsistencies in cultural conditioning created by such role contrasts, with concomitant anxieties or insecurities, have been postulated to be in large part responsible for the "storm and stress" of adolescence.

More recently, McNassor (1967) has developed a comparative portrait of identity development specific to adolescents in America and Western Europe. McNassor maintains that one's personal destiny (including one's occupational identity) forms at an earlier age in Europe than in America. In fact, the entire transition from childhood to adulthood is seen by McNassor to take less time and involve less personal estrangement or insecurity in European cultures. For evidence, McNassor points to differences in goals, educational systems, and socialization practices (less permissiveness in Europe) between American and European culture. He also believes that European adolescents are treated to more "tightly woven" norms of social and geographical bands and clearer role and authority hierarchies. Thus, these features of European life are thought by McNassor to facilitate identity formulation. In contrast, for American youth, maturity is thought to carry a higher price tag in terms of anxiety, tentativeness, and "personality dispersion." (This observation is buttressed by McNassor's interviews with American and European adolescents although we are not told from how many subjects he gathered data.)

One of McNassor's (1967) more intriguing speculations is that the comparatively safer passage to adulthood for European youth also is infested with social censorships which may limit youth's exploration of its creative potentialities. Such exploration is more likely in America, McNassor states, if and when adolescents learn to live adequately with uncertainty and tentativeness.

The McNassor (1967) report is a good example of intuitive reasoning about identity formation based upon cultural phenomena and clinical data. To these data frequently are added the results of *projective testing*. This approach to testing attempts to catalog the responses of adolescents to relatively ambiguous stimulus materials where it is assumed that each respondent will subconsciously project into the testing situation his own attitudes, values, conflicts, and aspirations. Projective techniques include the Rorschach Inkblot Test, the Thematic Apperception Test, and the Incomplete Sentence technique used by Friedenberg (1959) and others (for example, Marcia, 1966).

The research of Tooley (1967) exemplifies the projective testing approach to adolescent personality development. Investigated were the writing styles of three age groups (adolescent, late adolescent, and adult) for insight into the characteristics of personal expression and adaptation modes of these subjects. All participants (normal) wrote stories in response to pictures from the Thematic Apperception Test (Murray, 1943). Resultant stories then were analyzed by judges according to specific criteria. Focal was the hypothesis that expressive style becomes more emotionally moderate and rational through the adolescent period. This hypothesized trend further assumes the achievement, with age, of higher levels of personal identity and independence.

As compared to their younger and older counterparts, late adolescents were judged by Tooley (1967) and company to be less "flamboyant" (melodramatic) and more "impersonal" (detached and controlled intellectualizations). Tooley concluded that the expressive style of late adolescence reflects a moderation in emotional tone and a dependence upon intellectualizing defenses (recall Anna Freud's contentions in this context). This style is thought by Tooley to be appropriate for coping with the developmental tasks of late adolescence. Although tantalizing, the Tooley data are not unambiguous with respect to identity formulation. They may, however, be interpreted to suggest an objectivity peculiar to late adolescence which is relevant to one's preparation for intimacy (Erikson, 1963) and diminished dependence upon one's parents.

Closely related to projective assessments is the use of questionnaires and checklists. Among the best examples of this relevant to identity formulation is the research on adolescents by Douvan and Adelson (1966). One conclusion drawn by these researchers is that the process of identity formulation tends to be more difficult for girls in our society than for boys. Whereas a male's occupation serves a critical identity-defining function, a female must, according to Douvan and Adelson, rely largely upon her marriage for self-definition. In other words, an adolescent male may begin to solidify his identity by voluntarily choosing and preparing for an occupation. Douvan and Adelson feel that this activity can "focus and stabilize" for the male adolescent many transitional conflicts and problems. In contrast, the female's task is thought to be more ambiguous. Marriage is not only a matter for the undefined future, but it requires the initiative and decision of someone else. This situation does not lend itself to "rational planning" beyond a female making herself attractive and personable. These sex differences are reinforced by Douvan and Adelson's finding that boys receive their greatest feelings of esteem through personal achievement. In contrast, girls generally reported acceptance by others and gratifying interpersonal relations as their greatest source of self-esteem.

Still other theoretical vantage points, specifically self-theory (see, for example, Moustakas, 1956; Combs & Snygg, 1959; Wiley, 1961; Jersild, 1963; Hamachek, 1965) have provided relevant data on the development and psychological functions of self-esteem, self-evaluation, and personal expectancies, all of which relate to the identity concept. The study of the self-concept has itself, however, been characterized by thorny problems, including measurement. (See the Williams and Byars paper in this volume for an example of self-concept research.) Furthermore, there exists the question of whether the self-concept is an objective entity suitable for scientific research or whether it is a metaphysical creation of psychologists to provide an explanatory construct without which certain behavior could not be understood (Lowe, 1961). In short, clinical and self-concept data, both of which frequently require elaborate inference and unproven assumptions for their interpretation, are not fully acceptable to many psychologists.[3]

A suitable example of self-concept research is that of Carlson (1967) who believes that one manifestation of a sense of identity is in terms of self-image changes which occur during the adolescent years. Included in her theory is the proposition that identity formulation requires an adaptation by adolescents to culturally defined sex roles. Thus, somewhat different identity channels would be prescribed for the two sexes. Carlson administered at one point in time a two-dimensional self-concept measure to 49 sixth graders. The same measure was again administered when these same subjects were high school seniors. One dimension was self-esteem. The second was personal-social orientation. (Personal orientation refers to self-conceptions not contingent upon the nature of one's social experience; social orientation is the degree to which one's interpersonal experiences figure prominently in one's view of himself. Social orientation further implies a vulnerability to social appraisals by others.)

Carlson found, as expected, that self-esteem was both relatively stable over the 6-year period and independent of sex role identification. Changes on personal-social orientation were observed, however, with girls becoming progressively more socially oriented and boys more personally oriented during the teen years. These data comment most specifically upon the salient influences of sex role norm qualities upon self-image development during adolescence. As such they fit nicely with the Douvan and Adelson (1966) data mentioned earlier. Unfortunately they do not permit authoritative comment on the difficulties which adolescents may encounter as self-images are changed or the degree to which genuine conflict is involved in this process.

Constantinople (1969) has recently devised an instrument specifically to test Eriksonian personality theory. This study of nearly 1,000 college students of both sexes (ranging from freshman to seniors) disclosed a consistent increase in the "successful resolution" of identity through the college years. This pattern of increasing maturity was more clearly marked among males than females (a finding also relevant to the Douvan and Adelson thesis discussed earlier), although females are reported

[3] See Crowne and Stephens (1961) for a critical review of self-concept methodology.

initially to enter college with a more advanced degree of maturity. Constantinople, aside from having encountered problems with her measuring instrument, has raised some questions about Eriksonian theory. Particularly at issue for her (and Erikson) is the potency of the college social environment to affect personality development. Further research may clarify this relationship. Meanwhile, Constantinople's work represents one of the few attempts to operationalize Eriksonian concepts by way of test construction.

Aside from a relative paucity of impressive *empirical* research attendant to the validity of the identity crisis hypothesis, there are authorities who flatly prefer alternative concepts of adolescent development. For example, Coleman (1965), whose research on the adolescent society is discussed by William Burlingame in this volume, does not envision the adolescent to be preoccupied with self-discovery. Coleman's concern is that adolescents experience sufficient freedom to act autonomously, yet feel clearly the *consequences* of their actions in order to learn better for the future. As Coleman states:

The best learning has always proceeded in this way: one feels directly the consequences of his action and, if necessary, modifies his actions to make these consequences beneficial. The critical problem for the adolescent in modern society is that the consequences of his actions are indirect and far in the future; thus they can have little impact on his current actions. (Coleman, 1965, Preface).

Coleman's contention most clearly relates to the nature of reinforcement and the extent to which reinforcements are either absent or delayed as adolescents test their skills in a social context. Relevant to this contention is a paper in this volume by Herbert Lefcourt (Part I) which introduces the construct, *locus of control*. Also pertinent to Coleman's position is the concept of opportunity failure basic to Rivera and Short's discussion of adolescent gang behavior found in Part III of this reader. These phenomena are not *necessarily* incompatible with the identity crisis hypothesis, however, and may in fact reflect the influence of environmental conditions which contribute to role confusion.

The Coleman hypothesis above may serve to highlight a general issue in psychology, namely, the degree of parsimony inherent in theoretical constructs. In other words, are there more economical means of explaining (and predicting) adolescent behavior than is represented by the identity crisis approach? Generally speaking, the more assumptions and inferences with which one must deal in regard to a given theoretical construct or hypothesis the greater are the chances for error. An empirical concept of reinforcement, for example, represents a conceptual tool with a substantially lower error risk for psychologists than does an existential concept of the self-concept. Generally psychologists whose affinity is for social learning and reinforcement interpretations of behavior are not impressed by popularized versions of adolescent crises, identity or otherwise (Bandura, 1964). Clinical psychiatrists also number among those who question the crisis point of view. Masterson (1967), for example, has concluded from his clinical studies that the significance of adolescent turmoil tends to be overplayed in our society.

Finally, a more extreme (and perhaps cynical) argument against the identity crisis hypothesis might incorporate Merton's (1948) notion of the *self-fulfilling prophecy*. Adolescents possibly would not experience an identity crisis if only they were not told by society that it was expected of them.

CONCLUSION

This essay has had only the modest objectives of introducing some of the thinking of scholars who variously incorporate the identity concept in their analyses of the adolescent period and some of the evidence pertinent to this concept. By no means have all of the relevant data been presented. Yet what data are available indicate most clearly that (1) sex differences and (2) occasional prolonged vocational indecision characterize the identity formation process as this process is currently studied. This alone may be sufficient to provide a valid toehold for the identity crisis hypothesis. Protagonists of the hypothesis may justifiably claim that the major validation problem is that behavioral scientists have not yet perfected the means to investigate appropriately the identity crisis phenomenon. On the other hand, one might argue that the hypothesis is largely academic or that adolescents may have identity problems primarily because they have not learned to behave otherwise. Elsewhere the universality of the identity crisis and its mechanisms has been called into question (Hersheson, 1967). In final analysis, it is the student of adolescent behavior who should weigh the evidence and determine for himself the viability of the identity crisis hypothesis.

REFERENCES

Ausubel, D. P. *Theory and Problems of Child Development.* New York: Grune & Stratton, 1958.

Bandura, Albert. The stormy decade: fact or fiction? *Psychology in the Schools,* 1964, **1,** 224–231.

Benedict, Ruth. Continuities in cultural conditioning. *Psychiatry*, 1938, 1, 161–167.

Blos, Peter. *On Adolescence: A Psychoanalytic Interpretation*. New York: Free Press, 1962.

Carlson, Rae. Stability and change in the adolescent's self-image. *Child Development*, 1965, **36**, 659–666.

Coleman, James S. *Adolescents and the Schools*. New York: Basic Books, 1965.

Combs, Arthur W., and Snygg, Donald. *Individual Behavior* (Rev. Ed.) New York: Harper and Row, 1959.

Constantinople, Anne. An Eriksonian measure of personality development in college students. *Developmental Psychology*, 1969, 1, 357–372.

Crowne, D. P., and Stephens, M. W. Self-acceptance and self-evaluative behavior: a critique of methodology. *Psychological Bulletin*, 1961, **58**, 104–121.

Douvan, Elizabeth, and Adelson, Joseph. *The Adolescent Experience*. New York: John Wiley, 1966.

Erikson, Erik H. Identity and the life cycle: selected papers. *Psychological Issues Monograph Series*, I: No. I. New York: International Universities Press, 1959.

Erikson, Erik H. *Childhood and Society* (2d Ed.) New York: W. W. Norton, 1963.

Erikson, Erik H. *Identity: Youth and Crisis*. New York: W. W. Norton, 1968.

Freud, Sigmund. *A General Introduction to Psychoanalysis* (1917). Garden City, N.Y.: Doubleday, 1953.

Freud, Sigmund. *An Outline of Psychoanalysis* (1938). New York: Norton, 1949.

Freud, Anna. *The Ego and the Mechanism of Defense*. New York: International Universities Press, 1948.

Friedenberg, Edgar Z. *The Vanishing Adolescent*. Boston: Beacon Press, 1959.

Friedenberg, Edgar Z. *Coming of Age in America: Growth and Acquiescence*. New York: Random House, 1963.

Friedenberg, Edgar Z. *The Dignity of Youth and Other Atavisms*. Boston: Beacon Press, 1965.

Fromm, Erich. *Escape from Freedom*. New York: Rinehart, 1941.

Fromm, Erich. *The Sane Society*. New York: Holt, Rinehart and Winston, 1955.

Fromm, Erich. *The Art of Loving*. New York: Harper and Row, 1956.

Fromm, Erich. *May Man Prevail?* Garden City, N.Y.: Doubleday, 1961.

Galinsky, M. David, and Fast, Irene. Vocational choice as a focus of the identity search. *Journal of Counseling Psychology*, 1966, **13**, 89–92.

Goodman, Paul. *Growing Up Absurd*. New York: Random House, 1956.

Goodman, Paul. *Compulsory Mis-Education*. New York: Horigon Press, 1964.

Hamachek, Don E. (Ed.) *The Self in Growth, Teaching, and Learning*. Englewood Cliffs, N.J.: Prentice-Hall, 1965.

Henry, Jules. *Culture against Man*. New York: Random House, 1963.

Hersheson, D. B. Sense of identity, occupational fit, and enculturation in adolescence. *Journal of Counseling Psychology*, 1967, **14**, 319–324.

Jersild, Arthur T.   *The Psychology of Adolescence* (2d Ed.) New York: Macmillan, 1963.

Lowe, C. Marshall.   The self-concept: fact or artifact? *Psychological Bulletin*, 1961, **58**, 325–336.

McNassor, Donald.   Social structure for identity in adolescence: Western Europe and America. *Adolescence*, 1967, **2**, 311–334.

Marcia, James E.   Development and validation of ego-identity status. *Journal of Personal and Social Psychology*, 1966, **3**, 551–558.

Merton, R. K.   The self-fulfilling prophecy. *Antioch Review*, 1948, **8**, 193–210.

Moustakas, Clark E. (Ed.)   *The Self*. New York: Harper and Row, 1956.

Murray, Henry A.   *Manual of Thematic Apperception Test*. Cambridge, Mass.: Harvard University Press, 1943.

Tooley, Kay.   Expressive style as a developmental index in late adolescence. *Journal of Projective Techniques and Personality Assessment*, 1967, **31**, 51–59.

Wiley, Ruth.   *The Self-Concept*. Lincoln, Nebraska: University of Nebraska Press, 1961.

1.5 *Orientation*

The concept of identification in psychology has been variously influential in the study of moral and cognitive development, sex role development, and psychopathology among children and adults. Many psychologists, including the author of the following paper, believe that identification is a superordinate mechanism for general psychological development. Out of this belief have been carved many research hypotheses involving same- and cross-sex parent-child relationships. It is within the context of parent-child relationships that Professor Heilbrun summarizes his recent work on identification. Critical to an understanding of this work is Heilbrun's interpretation of identification learning as incidental learning, that is, learning that does not reflect the direct attempts of parents to mold the behavior of their children.

Heilbrun begins by highlighting several major developmental tasks faced by college students, although these tasks are not necessarily exclusive to the college population. His primary concern is the degree to which effectiveness in coping with these tasks during late adolescence is associated with patterns of parent identification. The investigation of this relationship has required the construction of an extensive chain of researches into the identification phenomenon. A major link in this chain was an instrument invented by Heilbrun to measure parent-child similarity. From this measure the extent of parent identification is inferred which may characterize a given parent-child (adolescent) relationship. Heilbrun's Identification Scale is clearly an example of the psychometric approach to such measurement. Other approaches exist, however, including projective techniques (recall the discussion of these techniques in the earlier paper concerning identity crisis), and the measurement of autonomic reactivity (Kagan & Phillips, 1964). None are problem-free yet all have been fruitful in achieving a greater understanding of identification.

The reader will note that Heilbrun does not deal directly with the motives that may underlie identification learning. To do so would traverse another avenue of identification theory beset with its own obstacles and space requirements. A study of alternative explanations and interpretations of identification is essential, however, for a student who wishes to become thoroughly conversant with this concept and its contributions to developmental psychology. The references immediately below are excellent beginning points for this purpose. Finally, consistent with the tone established by Professor Hauck's earlier discussion of sex differences at puberty, significant sex differences in parent identification patterns are documented by Heilbrun's research.

RECOMMENDED READINGS

Bandura, Albert. Social learning theory of identificatory processes. In David A. Goslin (Ed.) *Handbook of Socialization Theory and Research.* Chicago: Rand McNally, 1969, 213–262.

Bronfenbrenner, Urie. Freudian theories of identification and their derivatives. *Child Development,* 1960, **31,** 15–40.

Hill, Winfred F. Learning theory and the acquisition of values. *Psychological Review,* 1960, **67,** 317–331.

Kagan, Jerome. Acquisition and significance of sex typing and sex role identity. In M. L. Hoffman and Lois W. Hoffman (Eds.) *Review of Child Development Research.* New York: Russell Sage Foundation, 1964, 137–167.

Kagan, Jerome, and Phillips, William. Measurement of identification: a methodological note. *Journal of Abnormal and Social Psychology,* 1964, **69,** 442–444.

Lynn, David B. *Parental and Sex Role Identification: A Theoretical Formulation.* Berkeley: McCutchan Publishing Corporation, 1969.

Sears, Robert R. Dependency motivation. In M. R. Jones (Ed.) *Nebraska Symposium on Motivation.* Lincoln: University of Nebraska Press, 25–64.

1.5 Identification and Behavioral Effectiveness during Late Adolescence

Alfred B. Heilbrun, Jr., EMORY UNIVERSITY

The fact that late adolescents vary considerably in their ability to cope with the multifarious demands of college life is obvious. Crowded mental health facilities, high dropout rates, student unrest in search of a cause, and occasionally more tragic incidents serve as testimony to this fact and to the importance of a continuing search for the reasons why this is so.

Put in simple perspective, the student's development in college can be considered to fall into three areas: (1) His academic progress which includes the various motivational and intellectual concomitants which go into becoming an educated person, (2) his social maturation as he works toward adult interpersonal roles involving more responsibility and mutuality, and (3) an evolving plan which should combine academic goals and social aspirations into a realistic formulation of where he is going after college and how he is going to get there. The extent to which these categories exhaust the possible classes of behavior relevant to personal growth in college is not important. They do at least exemplify some of the major dimensions along which college students could be ordered in degree of effectiveness.

The term "behavioral ineffectiveness" has been chosen to describe the failure of late adolescents to meet these pre-adult challenges and to avoid the use of standard psychiatric labels. The behaviorally ineffective student does not necessarily fall into a nosological class used to understand more disturbed behaviors. For purposes of this chapter, degrees of behavioral effectiveness will be inferred from whether the student has found it necessary to seek professional assistance with problems in his life and from the type of problem which he identifies as requiring resolution.

PARENT IDENTIFICATION—ITS MEANING AND MEASUREMENT

Since the concept of identification will receive ample attention elsewhere in this book, it will not be necessary to present a discussion in depth in this chapter. Accordingly, the reader will be given only the most basic assumptions relating to identification. First and foremost, parental identification is considered to be *a* learning process through

An original paper prepared especially for this volume.

which the child becomes more similar to a parent. Complicating attempts to understand identification is the fact that it is not the only learning process through which the child's similarity to a parent may be enhanced. Parents, intentionally or unintentionally, set up systems of reward and punishment that may be directed toward modifying child behavior in ways that make him more like the parent. For example, if the parent has extremely strong values about honesty, he is likely to strongly reinforce honesty in the child. If honesty is learned as a guiding value by the child because of parental reward and punishment, parent-child similarity in this regard cannot be considered as evidence of identification.

Since identification learning is to exclude the explicit attempts of the parents to modify the child's behavior by use of reinforcement, another form of learning is required. Imitation learning or modeling is considered to be the process through which the child comes to incorporate aspects of parent behavior into his own behavior repertory. It is not necessary to assume that imitative behaviors occur beyond the awareness of the child (that is, imitative behavior is unconscious).

There are other sources of similarity between parent and child which further complicate the study of identification. Genetic transmission and outside social forces that act upon both parent and child are but two. It is probably safe to assume though that these will in most cases be less influential determinants of parent-child similarity than imitative learning or learning through parent reward-punishment systems.

The fact that parent-child similarity may have multiple determinants creates a very real problem for identification research. Since identification is typically studied by assessing the likeness between parent and child, it is impossible to extricate the amount of similarity that can be attributed to the various sources. Knowledge about parent identification has continued to grow despite the limitation, but at a snail's pace dictated by imprecision.

Given a process through which a child comes to display behavioral similarities to one or both parents, the measurement of the process has logically involved some means of estimating how similar the parent and the child are. Numerous approaches to measuring similarity have been attempted, including the one (to be described below) from which the empirical evidence to be presented later in this chapter was derived.

The degree of parent-child similarity (and, indirectly, the degree of identification) in prior research by the writer has been derived from the Identification Scale. A more complete description, rationale, and summary of validity evidence is available elsewhere (Heilbrun, 1965a). The technique elicits two sets of ratings from the child. One set is comprised of self-descriptive responses from which 15 personality scores are obtained. The personality variables, originally cataloged within Murray's need system (1938), include:

(1) Achievement: to strive to be outstanding in pursuits of socially recognized significance.
(2) Dominance: to seek and sustain leadership roles in groups or to be influential and controlling in individual relationships.
(3) Endurance: to persist in any task undertaken.
(4) Order: to place special emphasis on neatness, organization, and planning in one's activities.
(5) Intraception: to engage in attempts to understand one's own behavior or the behavior of others.
(6) Nurturance: to engage in behaviors that extend material or emotional benefits to others.
(7) Affiliation: to seek and sustain numerous personal friendships.
(8) Heterosexuality: to seek the company of and derive emotional satisfactions from interactions with opposite-sex peers.
(9) Exhibition: to behave in such a way as to elicit the immediate attention of others.
(10) Autonomy: to act independently of others or of social values and expectations.
(11) Aggression: to engage in behaviors that attack or hurt others.
(12) Change: to seek novelty of experience and avoid routine.
(13) Succorance: to solicit sympathy, affection, or emotional support from others.
(14) Abasement: to express feelings of inferiority through self-criticism, guilt, or social impotence.
(15) Deference: to seek and sustain subordinate roles in relationships with others.

The second set of ratings involve the child's perception of both parents on the same 15 variables and his judgment about which parent is best described by each. The measurement procedure is a subtle one so that the rater is not likely to be aware that parent-child similarity is being measured. The final score indicates whether the child perceives himself behaviorally more similar to the father or to the mother.

PARENT SEX ROLE

Research inquiring into the relations between parent identification and maladjustment in late adolescents has provided some modest returns. It has been rather well established that males are more likely to be better off if they have chosen their fathers as a primary model for identification (Gray & Klaus, 1956; Heilbrun, 1962; Helper, 1955; Osgood, Suci, & Tannenbaum, 1957). However, the expected relationship between a maternal identification in daughters and more effective behavior has rarely been reported. Rather, equivocal results have been the order of the day (Emmerich, 1959; Gray, 1959; Heilbrun, 1962; Helper, 1955; Johnson, 1955; Mussen & Distler, 1959; Osgood, Suci, & Tannenbaum, 1957).

The obvious reason for the expectation that identification with the same-sex parent will facilitate development has to do with the budding sex role identity of the child. It is reasoned that if a boy identifies with his father, he will be masculine and will be rewarded by society for conforming to the appropriate sex role. Similarly, the girl should model after the mother, learn to be feminine, and reap her rewards. The fact that this simple rationale has held for males testifies to the more rigid expectancies maintained for men in our culture. Yet the equivocal results for females, which have failed to follow simplistic laws, make it clear that other factors need be considered before progress toward understanding of the relationship between sex role adoption and adjustment of the female can be achieved.

One such factor not considered in the earlier investigations of parent identification and filial adjustment is the sex role identity of the parents. Although there would be little argument with the statement that all fathers are not equally masculine nor are all mothers equally feminine, the variability of the parents in masculine-feminine sex role adoption was not considered until fairly recently. Heilbrun and Fromme (1965) discovered that when the masculinity or femininity of the parent models were considered, some illumination of the effects of identification for daughters was possible. Given parents who provide sex-typical models (that is, a masculine father and a feminine mother), the choice of model for identification was important for the female, but the surprising feature was that identification with the masculine father was more closely tied to psychological health than was identification with the feminine mother. When the sex roles were reversed between the parents (that is, a feminine father and masculine mother) the nature of the daughter's identification was not clearly tied to her effectiveness as a person. As was expected, the males again demonstrated father identification to be a correlate of health, but this was even clearer when parent sex roles were considered. A masculine-father identification was closely linked with good adjustment, whereas a feminine-mother identification portended personal problems.

This finding for the female instigated two further studies. One (Heilbrun, 1965b) found that the daughter's identification with a masculine father was conducive to greater feminization of behavior than would be expected, but it is a femininity lacking the dependency which is one of the hallmarks of the feminine sex role. Subsequently, Heilbrun (1968a) elaborated upon this finding by noting that college girls, considered masculine by usual testing standards, actually combined masculine goal-orientation and feminine interpersonal sensitivity, but feminine girls evidence only the interpersonal sensitivity. The predominant pattern of identification for the masculine girls was with the masculine father; the modal pattern of identification for the feminine girl involved the feminine mother as the primary model.

Synthesis of the evidence regarding parent identification for the female (Heilbrun, 1968b) led to a proposed principle of contrast relating identification to sex-role identity for the female in our society:

The most effective mediation of a feminine sex role identity in the daughter occurs under conditions of maximum within-parent model or between-parent model contrast in sex role behavior.

In line with this principle, a feminine identity will be facilitated when the primary identification model is a feminine mother whose behavior contrasts with that of a masculine father. Similarly, identification with a masculine father will facilitate the learning of feminine behaviors as his daughter-directed feminine behavior stands in contrast to his own masculinity. Outcome differences were proposed between these two alternatives. Both would include the potential for feminine behaviors but identification with the father would add a more assertive goal orientation.

Since these studies focused upon the college female, they seem to offer a way of explaining the prior evidence which pointed toward feminine-mother identified girls as behaviorally ineffective. It was reasoned that their lack of goal orientation in a college environment would disrupt their academic and vocational progress.

Closer scrutiny of the relationship between the female's sex role and the presence of behaviorally disruptive problems made it clear, however, that being masculine served as no protection. Essentially equal numbers of masculine and feminine girls availed themselves of a mental health agency on the campus because of personal problems in the course of the Heilbrun (1968a) study. This left many questions unanswered. Does either sex role for the female college student carry with it the potential for different but equally disruptive problems? Will these problems vary in intensity and kind depending upon whether the father or mother provided the model for the sex role? How important is having both parents present sex-typical models no matter which is chosen as the primary model for identification? These and other questions must await further research for definitive answers, although it is hoped that a new look at some old data at this point will generate some hypotheses to guide these efforts.

PARENT SEX ROLE, IDENTIFICATION, AND BEHAVIORAL EFFECTIVENESS

Over the past 6 years our research efforts on two college campuses have accumulated a sizeable number of measurements of parent identification and parent sex role.

The parent sex roles, as judged by the child, have been inferred from the Identification Scale comparisons of the two parents. College students rated 9 of the 15 personality variables as sex-typed for parents (achievement, endurance, dominance, and autonomy as masculine and nurturance, affiliation, succorance, abasement, and deference as feminine) (Heilbrun, 1964). Comparisons between parents on these nine variables apprise us of whether the parents present a typical sex role pattern (father masculine and mother feminine) or an atypical one (father feminine and mother masculine).

The 599 late-adolescent college students from whom the measures were collected were sampled from a large midwestern state university and a smaller southeastern private university, thus providing some degree of geographic and socio-economic spread. Most important for our purpose, the samples have been collected from sources which insure clear differences between those individuals we will assign to different levels of effectiveness.

Low effective students are those who have initiated contact with a mental health agency on campus and requested psychotherapeutic help for personal problems. Such persons are commonly estranged from rewarding peer relationships, still actively involved in dependency-independency conflicts within their family, plagued by emotional distress over which they lack control, impoverished in their self-concept, and generally unable to take advantage of the educational and social opportunities of the university.

Intermediate effective students have initiated contact with the same mental health agencies but have presented problems involving academic studies or vocational choice. Although they are understandably concerned about the problems they present, signs of emotional distress are uncommon. They usually present the picture of being effective persons beyond the boundaries of the dilemmas for which they seek professional guidance.

High effective students were obtained as volunteers for research and were screened for anyone who had availed himself of the professional help described above. It would be accurate enough to assume that these students would compare somewhat favorably to a representative cross section of college students as far as their effectiveness as persons is concerned.

Let us now turn to the data, keeping in mind that the goal is to generate some hypotheses about how patterns of parent identification may contribute in a positive or negative way to subsequent competence of the student in college. Since statistics will not be used, the reader should not lose sight of the tentative nature of any conclusion. Figure 1 summarizes the incidence of parent identification patterns for college students of differing levels of behavioral effectiveness.[1]

If we examine first the incidence of parent identification patterns among students judged to be most highly effective in their behavior, the masculine father as the identification model emerges as the most facilitative pattern. The fact that the masculine father occurs as the most facilitative model for identification for both sons and daughters is intriguing. It would seem to require that the masculine father provides a somewhat different array of behaviors as he relates to the boy or to the girl, after which the child will model, and, indeed, this has been proposed previously (Heilbrun, 1965b). Such fathers are more prone to relate with warmth and softness to their daughters than to their sons, which would have the effect of allowing the daughter to learn both masculine and feminine attributes through modeling but the son a more exclusively masculine set of behaviors.

Intermediate effectiveness again is tied most closely to the same pattern of identification for males and females—in this case identification with a masculine mother. Since having problems of an academic or vocational planning nature represents the common theme among these students, it would be logical to look there first for understanding of this communality. There is some evidence (Heilbrun, in press) that identi-

---

[1] The reader should be aware of what assumptions are required before data can be objectively presented as in this figure. To speak of being identified with one parent more than the other or of the parents being either typical or atypical in their sex roles requires some standards or points of reference for comparison, and behavioral standards are usually arbitrary in nature. When "identified with" is used we are actually saying that the boy or girl demonstrates more similarity to that parent than the average among his peers. "Sex-typical parents" refers to the fact that in most ways, actually on at least seven of the nine personality variables, the father is judged to be masculine and the mother is judged as feminine. "Sex-atypical parents" means that on at least three of these personality traits there is a reversal of the expected masculine or feminine role behaviors.

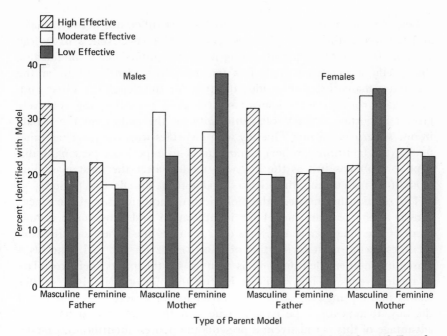

FIGURE 1. Incidence of Parent Identification Patterns for Male and Female College Students Varying in Degree of Behavioral Effectiveness

fication with the mother has the common effect of interfering with the crystallization of vocational interest patterns in male and female college students, but this was true only when the feminine mother was the selected model. Perhaps the most promising direction that future inquiry might take would have to do with the sex role reversal feature of this pattern. It is unlikely that a woman can present as adequate a masculine model as the biologically male father. It seems possible that masculinity in a woman is more blended with feminine qualities, whereas masculine men are likely to behave discretely in masculine or, under special conditions, in feminine ways. If so, the sex role reversed masculine mother will present a somewhat blurred model of masculine and feminine behaviors for either the son or the daughter to emulate.

It is also tempting to attribute some importance to the "masculine protest" implied by masculinity in a woman. Since such protest conveys not only an endorsement of the masculine role but an often subtle rejection of femininity, certain attitudinal or motivational conflicts may be inherited through identification with this model which interfere with educational or vocational commitments, especially for the daughter.

Low effective behavior brings us to the first difference between males and females. Although the greatest behavioral ineffectiveness in college students is most likely found among mother-identified males or females, the specific associated pattern is a female-mother identification for the son and a masculine-mother identification for the daughter. These findings again confirm what many have observed regarding the relatively greater importance of sex-role conformity for the male than the female in our American society. The boy who identifies with the most feminine model (the feminine mother) is most likely to experience personally disruptive problems just as the boy who models after the most masculine model (the masculine father) is most likely to be an effective person.

The relationship between the biological-psychological sex of the parent chosen as the primary model for identification and subsequent competence of the daughter is a strange one. A masculine-father identification qualifies as the most facilitative of effectiveness for the girl, whereas a masculine-mother identification is seen to be the most likely correlate of ineffectiveness. Thus, while it is true that the girl is given greater leeway in adopting cross-sex role behavior in our society than is accorded the boy, it appears to be equally true that the mother who has taken advantage of this permissiveness presents the poorest identification model for her daughter.

Although other observations might be made from the graph data, perhaps enough has been said to stress the importance of the *pattern* of parental identification, meaning here the combination of both the biological and psychological sex of the identification model, for behavior development into the college years.

Two potentially important directions for future inquiry can be identified. One would be a far closer scrutiny of how sex-role reversal between the parents influences the development of problems in the daughter. Paramount here is the question of whether the father tends to value or devalue the masculine behaviors which the daughter comes to emulate in the mother. The second direction that should be promising is how the pattern of identification relates to sexual orientation (for example, heterosexuality versus homosexuality).

REFERENCES

Emmerich, W. Parental identification in young children. *Genetic Psychology Monographs*, 1959, **60**, 257–308.

Gray, S. W. Perceived similarity to parents and adjustment. *Child Development*, 1959, **30**, 91–107.

Gray, S. W., and Klanc, R. The measurement of parental identification, *Genetic Psychology Monographs*, 1956, **54**, 87–114.

Heilbrun, A. B. Parental identification and college adjustment. *Psychological Reports*, 1962, **10**, 853–854.

Heilbrun, A. B. Social value-social behavior consistency, parental identification and aggression in late adolesence. *Journal of Genetic Psychology*, 1964, **104**, 135–146.

Heilbrun, A. B. The measurement of identification. *Child Development*, 1965, **36**, 111–127. (a)

Heilbrun, A. B. An empirical test of the modeling theory of sex-role learning. *Child Development*, 1965, **36**, 789–799. (b)

Heilbrun, A. B. Sex role, instrumental-expressive behavior, and psychopathology. *Journal of Abnormal Psychology*, 1968, **73**, 131–136. (a)

Heilbrun, A. B. Sex-role identity in adolescent females: a theoretical paradox. *Adolescence*, 1968, **3**, 79–88. (b)

Heilbrun, A. B. Parental identification and the patterning of vocational interests in college males and females. *Journal of Counseling Psychology*, in press.

Heilbrun, A. B., and Fromme, D. K. Parental identification of late adolescents and level of adjustment: the importance of parent-model attributes, ordinal position and sex of the child. *Journal of Genetic Psychology*, 1965, **107**, 49–59.

Helper, M. M. Learning theory and self-concept. *Journal of Abnormal and Social Psychology*, 1955, **51**, 184–194.

Johnson, M. M. Instrumental and expressive components in the personalities of women. Unpublished doctoral dissertation, Radcliffe, 1955.

Murray, H. A. *Explorations in Personality: A Clinical and Experimental Study of Fifty Men of College Age.* New York: Oxford University Press, 1938.

Mussen, P., and Distler, L. Masculinity, identification and father-son relationships. *Journal of Abnormal and Social Psychology*, 1959, **59**, 350–356.

Osgood, C., Suci, G., and Tannenbaum, P. H. *The Measurement of Meaning.* Urbana: University of Illinois Press, 1957.

1.6 *Orientation*

Among the most influential theoreticians on the contemporary psychological scene is the Swiss epistemologist, Jean Piaget. Piaget's study of developmental processes in cognition and morality has spanned well over four decades. From his prolific pen a wealth of insights has been recorded. These insights have done much to stimulate the thinking of psychologists the world over. (An example of empirical research relevant to Piaget's view of adolescent mental development is provided in Part III of this volume.)

Piaget's genetic approach to thought development maintains that the human organism strives toward successively higher levels of cognitive integration as the organism confronts and adapts to physical reality. Such adaptation is viewed to be sequential and invariant. It also involves the evolution of four successive developmental stages all of which are briefly reviewed in the following paper by David Elkind. Although many "master concepts" pervade Piagetian theory, it is *egocentrism* that receives Elkind's primary attention. Egocentrism, as Elkind indicates, appears in different forms as Piaget's child proceeds toward cognitive maturity. Within a Piagetian framework, egocentrism serves as a conceptual tool helpful for the understanding of adolescent behavior. It is also revelant to a clarification of the relationship between intellectual development and personality dynamics.

Elkind deals principally with adolescent egocentrism in terms of the adolescent's belief that his appearance and actions are items of absorbing interest and concern to other people. Other manifestations of adolescent egocentrism have been discussed, however. For example, Flavell's (1963) interpretation has centered upon the adolescent's proclivity for criticizing and theorizing. In Piagetian terms, this proclivity is thought to generate from a newly discovered cognitive power during adolescence. In other words, adolescents (now in the cognitive stage of "formal operations") are able for the first time to envision alternatives to the way things are done by adults (for example, child-rearing, education, and political organization). In turn, the idealism of adolescents is fed by this increased cognitive sophistication. When idealism is combined with an adolescent's proposals for change a last "high water mark" in egocentrism is likely. This is because such proposals are typically accompanied by a "cavalier disregard" for their practical limitations (Flavell, 1963).

RECOMMENDED READINGS

Flavell, John H. *The Developmental Psychology of Jean Piaget.* Princeton, N.J.: Van Nostrand, 1963.

Furth, Hans G. *Piaget and Knowledge.* Englewood Cliffs, N.J.: Prentice-Hall, 1969.

Inhelder, Barbel, and Piaget, Jean. *The Growth of Logical Thinking from Childhood to Adolescence.* New York: Basic Books, 1958.

1.6 Egocentrism in Adolescence

David Elkind, UNIVERSITY OF ROCHESTER

Within the Piagetian theory of intellectual growth, the concept of egocentrism generally refers to a lack of differentiation in some area of subject-object interaction (Piaget, 1962). At each stage of mental development, this lack of differentiation takes a unique form and is manifested in a unique set of behaviors. The transition from one form of egocentrism to another takes place in a dialectic fashion such that the mental structures which free the child from a lower form of egocentrism are the same structures which ensnare him in a higher form of egocentrism. From the developmental point of view, therefore, egocentrism can be regarded as a negative by-product of any emergent mental system in the sense that it corresponds to the fresh cognitive problems engendered by that system.

Although in recent years Piaget has focused his attention more on the positive than on the negative products of mental structures, egocentrism continues to be of interest because of its relation to the affective aspects of child thought and behavior. Indeed, it is possible that the study of egocentrism may provide a bridge between the study of cognitive structure, on the one hand, and the exploration of personality dynamics, on the other (Cowan, 1966; Gourevitch & Feffer, 1962). The purpose of the present paper is to describe, in greater detail than Inhelder and Piaget (1958), what seems to me to be the nature of egocentrism in adolescence and some of its behavioral and experiential correlates. Before doing that, however, it might be well to set the stage for the discussion with a brief review of the forms of egocentrism which precede this mode of thought in adolescence.

FORMS OF EGOCENTRISM IN INFANCY AND CHILDHOOD

In presenting the childhood forms of egocentrism, it is useful to treat each of Piaget's major stages as if it were primarily concerned with resolving one major cognitive task. The egocentrism of a particular stage can then be described with reference to this special problem of cognition. It must be stressed, however, that while the cognitive task characteristic of a particular stage seems to attract the major share of the child's mental energies, it is not the only cognitive problem with which

Reprinted from *Child Development*, 1967, **38**, 1025–1034, by permission of the author and the Society for Research in Child Development.

the child is attempting to cope. In mental development there are major battles and minor skirmishes, and if I here ignore the lesser engagements it is for purposes of economy of presentation rather than because I assume that such engagements are insignificant.

Sensori-motor Egocentrism (0–2 Years)

The major cognitive task of infancy might be regarded as *the conquest of the object*. In the early months of life, the infant deals with objects as if their existence were dependent upon their being present in immediate perception (Charlesworth, 1966; Piaget, 1954). The egocentrism of this stage corresponds, therefore, to a lack of differentiation between the object and the sense impressions occasioned by it. Toward the end of the first year, however, the infant begins to seek the object even when it is hidden, and thus shows that he can now differentiate between the object and the "experience of the object." This breakdown of egocentrism with respect to objects is brought about by mental representation of the absent object.[1] An internal representation of the absent object is the earliest manifestation of the symbolic function which develops gradually during the second year of life and whose activities dominate the next stage of mental growth.

Pre-operational Egocentrism (2–6 Years)

During the preschool period, the child's major cognitive task can be regarded as *the conquest of the symbol*. It is during the preschool period that the symbolic function becomes fully active, as evidenced by the rapid growth in the acquisition and utilization of language, by the appearance of symbolic play, and by the first reports of dreams. Yet this new capacity for representation, which loosed the infant from his egocentrism with respect to objects, now ensnares the preschool children in a new egocentrism with regard to symbols. At the beginning of this period, the child fails to differentiate between words and their referents (Piaget, 1952b) and between his self-created play and dream symbols and reality (Kohlberg, 1966; Piaget, 1951). Children at this stage believe that the name inheres in the thing and that an object cannot have more than one name (Elkind, 1961a; 1962; 1963).

The egocentrism of this period is particularly evident in children's linguistic behavior. When explaining a piece of apparatus to another child, for example, the youngster at this stage uses many indefinite terms

---

[1] It is characteristic of the dialectic of mental growth that the capacity to represent internally the absent object also enables the infant to cognize the object as externally existent.

and leaves out important information (Piaget, 1952b). Although this observation is sometimes explained by saying that the child fails to take the other person's point of view, it can also be explained by saying that the child assumes words carry much more information than they actually do. This results from his belief that even the indefinite "thing" somehow conveys the properties of the object which it is used to represent. In short, the egocentrism of this period consists in a lack of clear differentiation between symbols and their referents.

Toward the end of the pre-operational period, the differentiation between symbols and their referents is gradually brought about by the emergence of concrete operations (internalized actions which are roughly comparable in their activity to the elementary operations of arithmetic). One consequence of concrete operational thought is that it enables the child to deal with two elements, properties, or relations at the same time. A child with concrete operations can, for example, take account of both the height and width of a glass of colored liquid and recognize that, when the liquid is poured into a differently shaped container, the changes in height and width of the liquid compensate one another so that the total quantity of liquid is conserved (Elkind, 1961b; Piaget, 1952a). This ability, to hold two dimensions in mind at the same time, also enables the child to hold both symbol and referent in mind simultaneously, and thus distinguish between them. Concrete operations are, therefore, instrumental in overcoming the egocentrism of the preoperational stage.

Concrete Operational Egocentrism (7–11 Years)

With the emergence of concrete operations, the major cognitive task of the school-age child becomes that of *mastering classes, relations, and quantities.* While the preschool child forms global notions of classes, relations, and quantities, such notions are imprecise and cannot be combined one with the other. The child with concrete operations, on the other hand, can nest classes, seriate relations, and conserve quantities. In addition, concrete operations enable the school-age child to perform elementary syllogistic reasoning and to formulate hypotheses and explanations about concrete matters. This system of concrete operations, however, which lifts the school-age child to new heights of thought, nonetheless lowers him to new depths of egocentrism.

Operations are essentially mental tools whose products, series, class hierarchies, conservations, etc., are not directly derived from experience. At this stage, however, the child nonetheless regards these mental products as being on a par with perceptual phenomena. It is the inability to differentiate clearly between mental constructions and perceptual givens which constitutes the egocentrism of the school-age child. An example may help to clarify the form which egocentrism takes during the concrete operational stage.

In a study reported by Peel (1960), children and adolescents were read a passage about Stonehenge and then asked questions about it. One of the questions had to do with whether Stonehenge was a place for religious worship or a fort. The children (ages 7–10) answered the question with flat statements, as if they were stating a fact. When they were given evidence that contradicted their statements, they rationalized the evidence to make it conform with their initial position. Adolescents, on the other hand, phrased their replies in probabilistic terms and supported their judgments with material gleaned from the passage. Similar differences between children and adolescents have been found by Elkind (1966) and Weir (1964).

What these studies show is that, when a child constructs a hypothesis or formulates a strategy, he assumes that this product is imposed by the data rather than derived from his own mental activity. When his position is challenged, he does not change his stance but, on the contrary, reinterprets the data to fit with his assumption. This observation, however, raises a puzzling question. Why, if the child regards both his thought products and the givens of perception as coming from the environment, does he nonetheless give preference to his own mental constructions? The answer probably lies in the fact that the child's mental constructions are the product of reasoning, and hence are experienced as imbued with a (logical) necessity. This "felt" necessity is absent when the child experiences the products of perception. It is not surprising, then, that the child should give priority to what seems permanent and necessary in perception (the products of his own thought, such as conservation) rather than to what seems transitory and arbitrary in perception (products of environmental stimulation). Only in adolescence do young people differentiate between their own mental constructions and the givens of perception. For the child, there are no problems of epistemology.

Toward the end of childhood, the emergence of formal operational thought (which is analogous to propositional logic) gradually frees the child from his egocentrism with respect to his own mental constructions. As Inhelder and Piaget (1958) have shown, formal operational thought enables the young person to deal with all of the possible combinations and permutations of elements within a given set. Provided with four differently colored pieces of plastic, for example, the adolescent can work out all the possible combinations of colors by taking the pieces one, two, three and four, and none, at a time. Children, on the other hand, cannot formulate these combinations in any systematic way. The ability to conceptualize all of the possible combinations in a system allows the adolescent to construct contrary-to-fact hypotheses and to reason about such propositions "as if" they were true. The adolescent, for example, can accept the statement, "Let's suppose coal is white," whereas the child would reply, "But coal is black." This ability to formulate contrary-to-fact hypotheses is crucial to the overcoming of the egocentrism of the concrete operational period. Through the formulation of such contrary-to-fact hypotheses, the young person discovers the arbitrariness of his own mental constructions and learns to differentiate them from perceptual reality.

ADOLESCENT EGOCENTRISM

From the strictly cognitive point of view (as opposed to the psychoanalytic point of view as represented by Blos (1962) and A. Freud (1946) or the ego psychological point of view as represented by Erikson (1959), the major task of early adolescence can be regarded as having to do with *the conquest of thought*. Formal operations not only permit the young person to construct all the possibilities in a system and construct contrary-to-fact propositions (Inhelder & Piaget, 1958); they also enable him to conceptualize his own thought, to take his mental constructions as objects and reason about them. Only at about the ages of 11–12, for example, do children spontaneously introduce concepts of belief, intelligence, and faith into their definitions of their religious denomination (Elkind, 1961a; 1962; 1963). Once more, however, this new mental system which frees the young person from the egocentrism of childhood entangles him in a new form of egocentrism characteristic of adolescence.

Formal operational thought not only enables the adolescent to conceptualize his thought, it also permits him to conceptualize the thought of other people. It is this capacity to take account of other people's thought, however, which is the crux of adolescent egocentrism. This egocentrism emerges because, while the adolescent can now cognize the thoughts of others, he fails to differentiate between the objects toward which the thoughts of others are directed and those which are the focus of his own concern. Now, it is well known that the young adolescent, because of the physiological metamorphosis he is undergoing, is primarily concerned with himself. Accordingly, since he fails to differentiate between what others are thinking about and his own mental preoccupations, he assumes that other people are as obsessed with his behavior and appearance as he is himself. *It is this belief that others are preoccupied with his appearance and behavior that constitutes the egocentrism of the adolescent.*

One consequence of adolescent egocentrism is that, in actual or impending social situations, the young person anticipates the reactions of other people to himself. These anticipations, however, are based on the premise that others are as admiring or as critical of him as he is of himself. In a sense, then, the adolescent is continually constructing, or reacting to, *an imaginary audience*. It is an audience because the adolescent believes that he will be the focus of attention; and it is imaginary because, in actual social situations, this is not usually the case (unless he contrives to make it so). The construction of imaginary audiences would seem to account, in part at least, for a wide variety of typical adolescent behaviors and experiences.

The imaginary audience, for example, probably plays a role in the self-consciousness which is so characteristic of early adolescence. When the young person is feeling critical of himself, he anticipates that the audience—of which he is necessarily a part—will be critical too. And, since the audience is his own construction and privy to his own knowledge of himself, it knows just what to look for in the way of cosmetic and behavioral sensitivities. The adolescent's wish for privacy and his reluctance to reveal himself may, to some extent, be a reaction to the feeling of being under the constant critical scrutiny of other people. The notion of an imaginary audience also helps to explain the observation that the affect which most concerns adolescents is not guilt but, rather, shame, that is, the reaction to an audience (Lynd, 1961).

While the adolescent is often self-critical, he is frequently self-admiring too. At such times, the audience takes on the same affective coloration. A good deal of adolescent boorishness, loudness, and faddish dress is probably provoked, partially in any case, by a failure to differentiate between what the young person believes to be attractive and what others admire. It is for this reason that the young person frequently fails to understand why adults disapprove of the way he dresses and behaves. The same sort of egocentrism is often seen in behavior directed toward the opposite sex. The boy who stands in front of the mirror for 2 hours combing his hair is probably imagining the swooning reactions he will produce in the girls. Likewise, the girl applying her makeup is more likely than not imagining the admiring glances that will come her way. When these young people actually meet, each is more concerned with being the observed than with being the observer. Gatherings of young adolescents are unique in the sense that each young person is simultaneously an actor to himself and an audience to others.

One of the most common admiring audience constructions, in the adolescent, is the anticipation of how others will react to his own demise. A certain bittersweet pleasure is derived from anticipating the belated recognition by others of his positive qualities. As often happens with such universal fantasies, the imaginary anticipation of one's own demise has been realized in fiction. Below, for example, is the passage in *Tom Sawyer* where Tom sneaks back to his home, after having run away with Joe and Huck, to discover that he and his friends are thought to have been drowned:

But this memory was too much for the old lady, and she broke entirely down. Tom was snuffling, now, himself—and more in pity of himself than anybody else. He could hear Mary crying and putting in a kindly word for him from time to time. He began to have a nobler opinion of himself than ever before. Still, he was sufficiently touched by his aunt's grief to long to rush out from under the bed and overwhelm her with joy—and the theatrical gorgeousness of the thing appealed strongly to his nature too—but he resisted and lay still.

Corresponding to the imaginary audience is another mental construction which is its complement. While the adolescent fails to differentiate the concerns of his own thought from those of others, he at the same time over-differentiates his feelings. Perhaps because he believes he is of importance to so many people, the imaginary audience, he comes to regard himself, and particularly his feelings, as something special and unique. Only he can suffer with such agonized intensity, or experience such exquisite rapture. How many parents have been confronted with the typically adolescent phrase, "But you don't know how it feels. . . ." The emotional torments undergone by Goethe's young Werther and by Salinger's Holden Caulfield exemplify the adolescent's belief in the uniqueness of his own emotional experience. At a somewhat different level, this belief in personal uniqueness becomes a conviction that he will not die, that death will happen to others but not to him. This complex of beliefs in the uniqueness of his feelings and of his immortality might be called *a personal fable*, a story which he tells himself and which is not true.

Evidences of the personal fable are particularly prominent in adolescent diaries. Such diaries are often written for posterity in the conviction that the young person's experiences, crushes, and frustrations are of universal significance and importance. Another kind of evidence for the personal fable during this period is the tendency to confide in a personal God. The search for privacy and the belief in personal uniqueness leads to the establishment of an I-Thou relationship with God as a personal confidant to whom one no longer looks for gifts but rather for guidance and support (Long, Elkind, & Spilka, 1967).

The concepts of an imaginary audience and a personal fable have proved useful, at least to the writer, in the understanding and treatment of troubled adolescents. The imaginary audience, for example, seems often to play a role in middle-class delinquency (Elkind, 1967). As a case in point, one young man took $1,000 from a golf tournament purse, hid the money, and then promptly revealed himself. It turned out that much of the motivation for this act was derived from the anticipated response of "the audience" to the guttiness of his action. In a similar vein, many young girls become pregnant because, in part at least, their personal fable convinces them that pregnancy will happen to others but never to them and so they need not take precautions. Such examples could be multiplied but will perhaps suffice to illustrate how adolescent egocentrism, as manifested in the imaginary audience and in the personal fable, can help provide a rationale for some adolescent behavior. These concepts can, moreover, be utilized in the treatment of adolescent offenders. It is often helpful to these young people if they can learn to differentiate between the real and the imaginary audience, which often boils down to a discrimination between the real and the imaginary parents.

THE PASSING OF ADOLESCENT EGOCENTRISM

After the appearance of formal operational thought, no new mental systems develop and the mental structures of adolescence must serve for the rest of the life span. The egocentrism of early adolescence nonetheless tends to diminish by the age of 15 or 16, the age at which formal operations become firmly established. What appears to happen is that the imaginary audience, which is primarily an anticipatory audience, is progressively modified in the direction of the reactions of the real audience. In a way, the imaginary audience can be regarded as hypothesis—or better, as a series of hypotheses—which the young person tests against reality. As a consequence of this testing, he gradually comes to recognize the difference between his own preoccupations and the interests and concerns of others.

The personal fable, on the other hand, is probably overcome (although probably never in its entirety) by the gradual establishment of what Erikson (1959) has called "intimacy." Once the young person sees himself in a more realistic light as a function of having adjusted his imaginary audience to the real one, he can establish true rather than self-interested interpersonal relations. Once relations of mutuality are established and confidences are shared, the young person discovers that others have feelings similar to his own and have suffered and been enraptured in the same way.

Adolescent egocentrism is thus overcome by a twofold transformation. On the cognitive plane, it is overcome by the gradual differentiation between his own preoccupations and the thoughts of others; while on the plane of affectivity, it is overcome by a gradual integration of the feelings of others with his own emotions.

SUMMARY AND CONCLUSIONS

In this paper I have tried to describe the forms which egocentrism takes and the mechanisms by which it is overcome, in the course of mental development. In infancy, egocentrism corresponds to the impression that objects are identical with the perception of them, and this form of egocentrism is overcome with the appearance of representation. During the pre-school period, egocentrism appears in the guise of a belief that symbols contain the same information as is provided by the objects which they represent. With the emergence of concrete operations, the child is able to discriminate between symbol and referent, and so overcome this type of egocentrism. The egocentrism of the school-age period can be characterized as the belief that one's own mental constructions correspond to a superior form of perceptual reality. With the advent of formal operations and the ability to construct contrary-to-fact hypotheses, this kind of egocentrism is dissolved because the young person can now recognize the arbitrariness of his own mental constructions. Finally, during early adolescence, egocentrism appears as the belief that the thoughts of others are directed toward the self. This variety of egocentrism is overcome as a consequence of the conflict between the reactions which the young person anticipates and those which actually occur.

Although egocentrism corresponds to a negative product of mental growth, its usefulness would seem to lie in the light which it throws upon the affective reactions characteristic of any particular stage of mental development. In this paper I have dealt primarily with the affective reactions associated with the egocentrism of adolescence. Much of the material, particularly the discussion of the *imaginary audience* and the *personal fable* is speculative in the sense that it is based as much upon my clinical experience with young people as it is upon research data. These constructs are offered, not as the final word on adolescent egocentrism, but rather to illustrate how the cognitive structures peculiar to a particular level of development can be related to the affective experience and behavior characteristic of that stage. Although I have here only considered the correspondence between mental structure and affect in adolescence, it is possible that similar correspondences can be found at the earlier levels of development as well. A consideration of egocentrism, then, would seem to be a useful starting point for any attempt to reconcile cognitive structure and the dynamics of personality.

SUMMARY

This paper describes the different forms of egocentrism characteristic of each of the major stages of cognitive growth outlined by Piaget. Particular attention is paid to the egocentrism of adolescence which is here described as the failure to differentiate between the cognitive concerns of others and those of the self. This adolescent egocentrism is said to give rise to 2 mental constructions, the imaginary audience and the personal fable, which help to account for certain forms of adolescent behavior and experience. These considerations suggest, it is concluded, that the cognitive structures peculiar to a given age period can provide insights with respect to the personality characteristics of that age level.

REFERENCES

Blos, P. *On Adolescence*. New York: Free Press, 1962.

Charlesworth, W. R. Development of the object concept in infancy: methodological study. *American Psychologist*, 1966, 21, 623. (Abstract)

Cowan, P. A. Cognitive egocentrism and social interaction in children. *American Psychologist*, 1966, 21, 623. (Abstract)

Elkind, D. The child's conception of his religious denomination, I: The Jewish child. *Journal of Genetic Psychology*, 1961, 99, 209–225. (a)

Elkind, D. The development of quantitative thinking. *Journal of Genetic Psychology*, 1961, 98, 37–46. (b)

Elkind, D. The child's conception of his religious denomination, II: The Catholic child. *Journal of Genetic Psychology*, 1962, 101, 185–193.

Elkind, D. The child's conception of his religious denomination, III: The Protestant child. *Journal of Genetic Psychology*, 1963, 103, 291–304.

Elkind, D. Conceptual orientation shifts in children and adolescents. *Child Development*, 1966, 37, 493–498.

Elkind, D. Middle-class delinquency. *Mental Hygiene*, 1967, 51, 80–84.

Erikson, E. H. Identity and the life cycle. *Psychological Issues*. Vol. 1, No. 1, New York: International Universities Press, 1959.

Freud, Anna. *The Ego and the Mechanisms of Defense*. New York: International Universities Press, 1946.

Gourevitch, Vivian, and Feffer, M. H. A study of motivational development. *Journal of Genetic Psychology*, 1962, 100, 361–375.

Inhelder, Barbel, and Piaget, J. *The Growth of Logical Thinking from Childhood to Adolescence*. New York: Basic Books, 1958.

Kohlberg, L. Cognitive stages and preschool education. *Human Development*, 1966, 9, 5–17.

Long, Diane, Elkind, D., and Spilka, B. The child's conception of prayer. *Journal for the Scientific Study of Religion*, 1967, 6, 101–109.

Lynd, Helen M. *On Shame and the Search for Identity.* New York: Science Editions, 1961.

Peel, E. A. *The Pupil's Thinking.* London: Oldhoume, 1960.

Piaget, J. *The Child's Conception of the World.* London: Routledge & Kegan Paul, 1951.

Piaget, J. *The Child's Conception of Number.* New York: Humanities Press, 1952. (a)

Piaget, J. *The Language and Thought of the Child.* London: Routledge & Kegan Paul, 1952. (b)

Piaget, J. *The Construction of Reality in the Child.* New York: Basic Books, 1954.

Piaget, J. *Comments on Vygotsky's Critical Remarks Concerning "The Language and Thought of the Child" and "Judgment and Reasoning in the Child."* Cambridge, Mass.: M. I. T. Press, 1962.

Weir, M. W. Development changes in problem solving strategies. *Psychological Review,* 1964, **71,** 473–490.

1.7 Orientation

Rare are events that occur on a national (or international) level which do not carry political overtones. Political events of the last several years provide an especially rich context for Edmund Sullivan's scholarly discussion of political development. Sullivan devotes a majority of his attention to the period of early and middle adolescence. This feature is integrated with commentary based upon a political science-psychology relationship infrequently explored in psychology textbooks. Moreover, Sullivan's observation that systematic research into political socialization is a comparatively recent enterprise suggests the influence of changing sociopolitical conditions on psychologist's choices of problems to study.

After a bout with definitional issues in the beginning stages of his discussion, Sullivan examines data pertinent to the evolution of political concepts in childhood. Childhood experiences, of course, provide the background for any changes that may occur during adolescence. Sullivan's strategy is therefore reminiscent of Shakespeare's notion that "the child is father to the man." Available data strongly indicate the salient influence of parental beliefs upon children's political concepts.

What developmental changes in political concepts and attitudes transpire during adolescence are, in Sullivan's view, largely a function of increased cognitive sophistication. Some of the more explicit formulations in this regard are fostered by Piaget's cognitive-developmental theory discussed earlier by David Elkind. Piagetian thought also encourages a linkage between moral and political development, facets of which are touched by the Haan *et al.* research in Part III of this reader. Sullivan neatly draws our attention to the relevancy of moral orientation for political ideology. With this in mind, the reader is urged to analyze introspectively his own political development and the conditions which have accompanied this process.

Finally, the many features of Sullivan's article combine to provide a valuable precursor to Kenneth Keniston's forthcoming evaluation of the student dissent movement.

RECOMMENDED READINGS

Adelson, Joseph, Green, Bernard, and O'Neill, Robert. Growth of the idea of law in adolescence. *Developmental Psychology,* 1969, 1, 327–332.

Christie, Richard, and Geis, Florence. Some consequences of taking Machiavelli seriously. In Edgar F. Borgatta and William W. Lambert (Eds.) *Handbook of Personality Theory and Research.* Chicago: Rand McNally, 1968, 959–973.

Hess, Robert D. Political socialization in the schools. *Harvard Educational Review,* 1968, **38**, 528–536.

1.7   Political Development during the Adolescent Years

Edmund V. Sullivan, ONTARIO INSTITUTE FOR STUDIES IN EDUCATION

INTRODUCTION

Chapter headings in textbooks on adolescence have not, to my knowledge, included a separate coverage for political development. Until recently, there was no necessity for the inclusion of such a topic, since theoretical discussions of adolescent political development were rare, and research in this area even rarer. The future of this topic looks more promising in the 1970s, however, assuring it at least a place in chapters on adolescent values and moral development, if not a chapter all its own. This confident prediction is made for two reasons: (1) adolescents are political whether we study the topic or not, and (2) they are increas-

---

An original paper prepared especially for this volume.

ingly making known their political interests and persuasions. What started as political activism in some college students during the 1960s appears now to be filtering down into certain segments of adolescent high school populations and there is some degree of assurance that this phenomenon will increase in the 1970s.

The purpose of the present paper is to give an overview of certain salient aspects of political development that occur during the adolescent years. The analysis will be confined to adolescents of high school age and will only touch on political activity in late adolescence (or young adulthood). Political behavior in the latter age range has become a popular topic with the advent of "political activism" on American college campuses, and it is not possible to discuss it adequately here. Accordingly, this paper will be restricted to the years just previous to the onset of young adulthood. In order to set the topic in context, the discussion of political development will be preceded by a description of the field of inquiry and by a summary of relevant findings on political development in the period antedating adolescence and will be followed by a retrospective and prospective summary and analysis.

BASIC DEFINITIONS AND DELIMITATION OF THE FIELD OF POLITICAL DEVELOPMENT

The domain of political life is very difficult to define and there is by no means general agreement, even among political scientists, as to the most appropriate procedures for theorizing and researching in this area (Dahl, 1963). Although broad definitions frequently remain vague and abstruse, they nevertheless may have the virtue of preventing premature closure and narrowness in the initial definition of an area of research. In its broadest possible sense, the political system is any persistent pattern of human relationships that involves, to a significant extent, power, rule, or authority (Dahl, 1963). Politics can be considered as the activity of attending to the general arrangements of a set of people who were brought together by choice and whose political systems have given them a communal awareness of the past, a present, and a future (Oakeshott, 1966). These arrangements are encompassed by the categories of power, rule, and authority. Obviously, these political arrangements are generated from the basic value and moral commitments of the society involved. The political ideology of a particular society stems from the basic moral premises held by the society as to what types of political arrangements are to be maintained and what types are to be changed if the society is to develop its institutions. Political ideology does not place its emphasis on simple philosophical analysis and deduction nor on sociological generalization, but on moral reflection about elaborating and advocating conceptions of the good life and prescribing the forms of social actions and organization necessary for their achievement (Partridge, 1967). Societies frequently lag behind their basic moral-political commitments, as is evident in the United States. Nevertheless,

If political changes are to last, it appears that they must ring true and have some moral basis. In spite of the great shortcomings of Athenian democracy with all its restrictions concerning sex, race, and color and with its slavery, its great moral contribution was that it did introduce for the first time into the world the idea of individual freedom and individual responsibility within a civic organization. (Cantril, 1961, pp. 53–54).

It is not known just how political ideology affects political activity and one author has argued that a society's ideological commitments are abstracted from the daily habits of the society's institutional arrangements (Oakeshott, 1966). At present, it is difficult to give a definitive answer to this question or to the question of the relationship between attitudes and ideology. It is in the attempt to answer such questions that the relationship between political science and psychology becomes important. Certainly the early conceptualizations on how psychology and political science were to be related centered on some of the problems previously mentioned (Lane, 1963). Lane (1963), in his earlier theorizing, felt that the area of psychology which offered the greatest contributions to political science were social and clinical psychology and the interrelationship between them. The combination of the two disciplines provides no easy answers to political questions, however, as can be seen in the treatments by the two disciplines of the question of *ideology*. As Lane (1963) points out:

. . . ideology is relatively unsophisticated in both disciplines—indeed, each asks wholly different questions in this area. The political scientist wants to know the events of the arrangements of institutions proposed by each ideology. He argues the case for democracy, for socialism, for welfare states, and, elsewhere, for communism, for monarchy or facism. He argues in familiar terms employing logic, historical illustration, assumes facts about the nature of man, deductions from ethical premises, and so forth. The psychologist is interested in why the individual has adopted this particular ideology and penetrates the events of the case only in so far as its postulates about the human mind requires corrections. (p. 598).

It is interesting to note that the earlier efforts relating political science to psychology have peculiarly ignored the possible contribution of developmental psychology, and this is evident in Lane's theoretical article. More recent conceptualizations of this domain of inquiry have certainly reversed this earlier omission (Dennis, 1968). Dennis, in outlining problems of political socialization, poses questions that are clearly *developmental*, such as the following:

When does political learning begin?
How rapidly does it take place?
What are the most crucial developmental periods?
When, if ever, does it terminate?

Since political socialization, as an area of inquiry, is in its infancy, we can expect no definitive answers to these questions at this time. Our present overview will only attempt to summarize the developmental studies that have been accomplished thus far.

POLITICAL DEVELOPMENT IN CHILDHOOD

The accumulation of knowledge in the area of citizenship and political behavior in children is a phenomenon of recent origin. The earlier vacuum is probably somewhat related to the fact that American society has not, in the past, been characterized by any notable degree of political involvement and participation by most of its citizens (Brim, 1967). Recently the rapid social and political changes in the contemporary world and their corresponding precipitation of instability in ongoing political structures have made this topic important in the study of child development (Sigel, 1965). The vast majority of studies on political development in children completed thus far have centered around such topics as conceptions of nationality, partisanship and identification, attitudes toward and knowledge of political figures, and political trust and cynicism.

The child's comprehension of political institutions is limited by many factors, one of which is his lack of cognitive sophistication. The limited social experience of a 6-year-old makes it difficult for him to differentiate clearly such concepts as "town" and "country" (Jahoda, 1963a). Conceptions of "nationality" are slowly differentiated during the elementary school years (Jahoda, 1963b), although conflicts between certain nations are associated with earlier ideological differentiation (for example, American and Russian flags) (Lawson, 1963). Research on partisanship and identification indicates that children learn to identify with political parties during the elementary school years (Greenstein, 1965; Hess & Torney, 1967). In addition to expressing party preference rather early in life, it appears that children follow the preferences expressed by their parents (Lane & Sears, 1964). Political figures (for example, the President) enjoy a choice status with children, with a vast majority of American children viewing their nation, government, and its representatives as wise, powerful, and benevolent (Greenstein, 1965; Hess, 1968; Hess & Easton, 1960; Hess & Torney, 1967). Uncritical favorable attitudes toward representatives, however, decrease with age (Hess, 1968; Hess & Torney, 1967). The pattern of benevolence toward leaders is also evident in the child's unquestioning trust and lack of cynicism toward political institutions. Feelings of political efficacy and perceptions of control over political figures and institutions develop as early as grade three in children (Easton & Dennis, 1967) and increase with age (Easton & Dennis, 1967; White, 1968). It would appear that both the trust and lack of cynicism results from the child's lack of information and cognitive awareness (Easton & Dennis, 1967). Also, it is probably a result of cognitive confusion created by the schools when they present the nation as a picture of unity, equality, and freedom, thus distorting and oversimplifying the political institutions to a certain degree (Hess, 1968).

The developmental findings just quoted are also influenced by individual differences and sociocultural variables. For example, sex and IQ differences are apparent, boys acquiring political attitudes more rapidly than girls and having more interests in political matters (Hess & Torney, 1967). More intelligent children regard the political system in less absolutistic terms and have more reservations about the competence and intentions of governmental figures and institutions (Hess & Torney, 1967). The child's sense of political efficacy is greater in middle class than in lower class children (Easton & Dennis, 1967; Hess, 1968; Hess & Torney, 1967; White, 1968) but this result is usually confounded with intelligence (White, 1968). The relationship between political efficacy and IQ is fairly constant over the elementary school years; children with greater intellectual abilities have greater feelings of efficacy over political figures and institutions (Easton & Dennis, 1967; White, 1968). At present, the most salient lacuna in child political socialization literature is the topic of political orientations of Negro children (Jennings & Niemi, 1968a).

POLITICAL DEVELOPMENT IN ADOLESCENCE

Political Attitudes, Interests, and Activities

Concerning the scope and intensity of adolescent political involvement, there appear to be no major changes during the adolescent period with regard to political affairs, political activities, party identification, and a variety of opinions about public life and government in general (Greenstein, 1965; Hess & Torney, 1967). These types of conclusions are reached by noting, for example, that differences in political participation of adults of different social class backgrounds and of men and women are presaged by similar differences amongst preadolescent children (Greenstein, 1965). At a superficial level, one could draw from the above findings the conclusion that political development has been consolidated during the childhood years and that adolescent political development is a rather static phenomenon. Several criticisms must be leveled at this conclusion, however, since it focuses interest in political development away from the adolescent years and places greater stress on the childhood years as critical periods of development. First of all, political attitudes, interests and partisanship undergo substantial development during the adolescent years even though at a superficial level there is stability from childhood to adulthood (Jennings & Niemi, 1968a; Lane & Sears, 1964). Jennings & Niemi (1968a) stress the point further by noting that . . .

. . . although the evidence is imperfect, the pattern of development seems to include fluctuations in political inference over the entire life span. Expressions of absolute interest apparently decline somewhat during the elementary years, although the willingness and ability to convert this interest into reading, discussion, and so on, tend to climb. During high school, the interest probably increases, perhaps a great deal. Among young adults there is a further increase in political awareness which is maintained until retirement age. (p. 449).

Second, the focus of interest in childhood political socialization studies contributes to a rather conservative and static view of American political life (Easton, 1968; Greenstein, 1968; Litt, 1968). Thus, the numerous studies in adolescence and young adulthood extending the political socialization research from childhood give the impression of stability in acquisition of norms of stable allegiance to the governmental regime and in addition reveal that political attitudes are based on non-rational and apolitical factors (Litt, 1968). The focus of this type of research is conservative, since it directs its domain of inquiry to those aspects of political life which are designed to maintain the stability of the present political system (Easton, 1968; Litt, 1968). To study the processes of political change within the system is more difficult since it involves focusing on future events and change agents within the society. In general, the vast majority of studies of this type are done in the years of young adulthood rather than adolescence. With these reservations in mind, let us now review some of the studies on adolescent attitudes, interests, and activities before turning to adolescent political ideology.

The advance in cognitive sophistication from childhood to adolescence should be accompanied by an increase in depth and sophistication of political attitudes and interests. Although we shall see that this is frequently the case, one reservation should be noted. As already mentioned, the young child has an overidealized view of the political regime which declines with age during the elementary school years. Although we would expect the trend to continue into the adolescent years, it is worthwhile noting that there is a considerable amount of uncritical chauvinism in adolescents. For example, Litt (1963) found that a substantial number (1/5–1/3) of high school children in the Boston area could be classified as very chauvinistic. The extensiveness of this finding must be tempered by the fact that it may be just a regional phenomenon.

Nevertheless, there are subtle changes in political development that are indicative of the adolescent's expanding cognitive sophistication. Although it is evident that by the end of elementary school most children have had occasional use of the mass media concerning political topics, it is assumed that adolescents' use of the mass media for political information becomes more widespread during the high school years because of class assignments, if for no other reason (Jennings & Niemi, 1968a). In addition, high school students show a considerable increase in discussions of politics with friends (Hyman, 1959).

The studies on political partisanship in childhood indicated a substantial degree of consistency in party affiliation between child and parent. Similar findings on adolescent political partisanship have also been reported (Jennings & Niemi, 1968a, 1968b) but certain reservations must be made when adolescents are considered. First, although adolescents frequently follow their parents' political party affiliation there is a considerable increase in independent party affiliations away from parental party affiliations (Jennings & Niemi, 1968b). A developmental change that is more important than party preference involves knowledge about differences between the parties; this undergoes rapid learning during the high school years when compared to the elementary school years (Jennings & Niemi, 1968a). This increase in knowledge may make the phenomenon of similiarity of party preference between adolescent and parent a rather superficial finding when stated without elaboration. As Lane and Sears (1964) point out, it would be highly misleading, for example, to say that just because an adolescent adopts the party affiliation of one of his parents, this produces stability in the political system. There appears to be a generational difference that can be obscured; for example, despite their similarity in party preference, the father's reason for voting for the Democrat Al Smith in 1928 may be quite different from his son's reason for voting for John Kennedy in 1960 (Lane & Sears, 1964).

The question of "adolescent rebellion" is legitimate in the political domain since the rebellion hypothesis in adolescence occupies a considerable portion of the theoretical literature. Researchers have been hard pressed to uncover any significant adolescent rebellion in the realm of political affairs (Jennings & Niemi, 1968b; Lane & Sears, 1964). When political rebellion does occur, it is partially related to the closeness of the relationship between parent and child (Lane & Sears, 1964). Adolescent political rebellion is more likely to occur when the adolescent feels alienated from his parents, especially where parents are interested in politics than when they are not (Lane & Sears, 1964). Lower-class adolescents who feel that they have suffered from over-strict discipline from parents are likely to rebel politically. In such cases it appears that the adolescent uses parental political interest for his more general rebellion from his parents, but in general, rebellion in adolescence does not take on political overtones (Jennings & Niemi, 1968b). For example, when disagreements are reported with parents it was found that only a small proportion of these disagreements could be broadly defined as being in the area of politics (Jennings & Niemi, 1968b). Lack of political rebellion from parents is also accompanied by the trust in political institutions and low degree of cynicism which we have already seen in the childhood years (Jennings & Niemi, 1968a; 1968b). Part of this trust is probably related to the civic training which fosters rituals of system support that go unquestioned (Jennings & Niemi, 1968b). Jennings and Niemi (1968a) find a remarkably smaller amount of cynicism among students than among parents. While a fifth of the students were more cynical than their parents, three times this number of parents were more cynical than their children. Although there is some minor indication that adolescents are retreating from the trusting attitudes about the political system which they held earlier, it may be said that when compared to parents they still see little to be cynical about in national political activity (Jennings & Niemi, 1968b). It appears that changes in placement of trust and confidence in the political system occur almost entirely in the post-adolescent period (Jennings & Niemi, 1968a). A considerable amount of reservation must be maintained at present, however, concerning the conclusions made about political trust and cynicism in both childhood and the adolescent years because of the paucity of studies done on those subpopulations in the society where we might expect a considerable amount of cynicism and mistrust. For example, when trust and cynicism scales were administered to children and adolescents in the rural Appalachian region of the United States (that is, poor whites), it was found that these children were considerably more mistrustful and cynical about the political system and political figures (for example, the President) than other populations studied to date (Jaros, Hirsch, & Fleron, 1968). These authors point out that their findings have at least two implications for political socialization research:

. . . First, they point to the possibility that the often emphasized highly positive character of children's views of politics may be a culturally bound phenomenon. Secondly, the occurrence of such divergent findings underscores the desirability of explaining children's political orientations. (Jaros et al., 1968, p. 575).

Their findings question the thesis that the family is the prototypical structure that links the child to the political system. They find no evidence that disrupted family structure, measured by father-absence, contributes to negative political evaluation. Interestingly enough, the absence of the father is associated with more favorable political evaluations in the Appalachian children (Jaros *et al.*, 1968). To unravel the full implications of this interesting result is not our task here, but it indicates the necessity for more extensive exploration of subpopulations in the United States. As pointed out earlier, there has been little research on political socialization in Negro children and adolescents. No one can predict in advance the results but it would be interesting to investigate political postures of father-absent and father-present Negro families and its effects on the children, as well as the extent of Black Nationalism and separatism advocated in these family structures. Investigations of this kind may temper the conclusion that the political regime is generally perceived as benevolent by both children and adolescents.

Adolescent Political Ideology

Thus far we have centered our discussion on such topics as the political interests, attitudes, and party preference of the adolescent, but as yet we have not dealt with the political-ideological commitments that the adolescent perceives as the basis for a good and ideal social order. Without entering into elaborate discussions of the definition of ideology, let us here briefly use the term "ideology" to mean the system of ideas or cognitions that an adolescent has concerning the goodness or badness of social institutions within a social order. The adolescent's political ideological development should be closely related to his general moral development since, as pointed out earlier, political ideology stems from some basic moral convictions that the individual has about the social order and its political institutions. The moral component of political ideology is in a sense both a source of system maintenance and system change. In other words, political ideological statements are *moral prescriptions* about what portions of the political system's institutions are to be maintained and what portions are to be changed and revitalized.

The ideology in childhood years appears to be concerned with system maintenance and much less with ideas about change in political institutions. Inhelder and Piaget (1958) make some interesting observations about the correspondence between changes in intellectual and political development that take place in the adolescent years. It is their contention that significant changes in both these areas occur with the transition from the "concrete operational stage" (approximately 5 through

11 years) to the "formal operational stage" (approximately 11 years and upward) of thought. At the stage of formal operational thought the adolescent is able to manipulate intellectually the hypothetical, and to systematically evaluate a lengthy set of alternatives. In the scientific domain, this transition enables him to entertain "hypotheses" that are only possibilities and he is no longer restricted to the *concrete* realities of *what is*. In the moral-political domain, the child now begins to entertain possible social orders and is no longer restricted to the concrete institutions in which, at present, he is taking part. Inhelder and Piaget (1958) see this as one of the reasons for the "political idealism" seen in European adolescents. Just how closely American adolescents follow European adolescents in this trend is an open question, but there are some interesting parallels in studies conducted on adolescent moral development in the United States. We will now turn to these.

The relationship between moral and political development is closely intertwined in the area of ideology, moral development being more generic concerning both private and public morality. Political ideology is more specific and deals with that particular aspect of the moral domain which relates to public political institutions. Kohlberg (1964, 1969) has elaborated a stimulating theory of morality, centered on the development of moral judgments during the elementary and secondary school years, which is pertinent to the topic at hand. He has delineated a stage theory formulation of moral development which includes three levels and six stages of moral ideology that develop in a hierarchical and sequenced order in response to moral dilemma stories. An example of one of the stories is the following:

In Europe, a woman was near death from a special kind of cancer. There was one drug that the doctors thought might save her. It was a form of radium that a druggist in the same town had recently discovered. The drug was expensive to make, but the druggist was charging ten times what the drug cost him to make. He paid $200 for the radium and charged $2000 for a small dose of the drug. The sick woman's husband, Heinz, went to everyone he knew to borrow the money but he could only get together about $1000 which is half of what it cost. He told the druggist that his wife was dying, and asked him to sell it cheaper or let him pay later. But the druggist said "No. I discovered the drug and I'm going to make money from it." So Heinz got desperate and broke into the man's store to steal the drug for his wife. Should the husband have done that? Why? (Kohlberg, 1969).

On the basis of responses to these dilemma situations the moral judgments were classified developmentally as follows:
1. Pre-moral level
   Stage 1. Punishment and obedience orientation.

Stage 2. Naive instrumental hedonism. The child conforms in order to obtain rewards, and so on.
2. Morality of conventional rule conformity level
Stage 3. Good-boy morality of maintaining good relations. The child conforms to avoid disapproval.
Stage 4. Authority maintaining morality. The child conforms to avoid censure by authorities and resultant guilt.
3. Morality of self-accepted moral principles level
Stage 5. Morality of contract. A duty is defined in terms of contract, general avoidance of violation of the rights of others.
Stage 6. The morality of individual principles or conscience. The child conforms to avoid self-condemnation.

The last three stages which are closely related to the transition from childhood to adolescence and to development throughout the adolescent years are of particular relevance to adolescent political development; hence they are elaborated more fully here.

Stage 4: Authority and social order maintaining orientation. Orientation to "doing duty" and to showing respect for authority and maintaining the given social order for its own sake. Regard for earned expectations of others.

Stage 5: Contractual legalistic orientation. Recognition of an arbitrary element or starting point in rules or expectations for the sake of agreement. Duty defined in terms of contract, general avoidance of violation of the will or rights of others, and majority will and welfare.

Stage 6: Conscience or principle orientation. Orientation not only to actually ordained social rules but to principles of choice involving appeal to logical universality and consistency. Orientation to conscience as a directing agent and to mutual respect and trust. (Blatt & Kohlberg, 1968, p. 2).

Blatt and Kohlberg (1968) report a substantial change in moral orientation between the ages of 14 and 17 years away from a predominantly conventional authority maintaining stage to the more principled level of thought which constitutes stage 5 and stage 6 morality. This trend in moral stage development is of particular significance when it is compared with parallel age trends reported in studies specifically designed to tap adolescent political ideology (for example, Adelson & O'Neil, 1966; Adelson, Green, & O'Neil, 1968; Gallatin, 1967).

The recent more direct investigation of the development of political concepts in adolescence carried out by Adelson and collaborators (Adelson & O'Neil, 1966; Adelson *et al.*, 1968; Gallatin, 1968) has used an approach similar to Kohlberg's. These investigators have studied such political concepts as law, rights, and community by having the adolescent respond to hypothetical problem situations. For example, the adolescents were told that a thousand people are dissatisfied with their present government and decide to form a new one on a fictional island. The adolescent was then presented with an extensive series of questions on imaginary problems dealing with the specific concepts mentioned above. The situations are designed to be imaginary and remote so that the adolescent will not respond with cliches on these concepts that come from his own culture and therefore, his own idiosyncratic ways of dealing with political situations are assessed. Responses by adolescents to these problems reveal interesting developmental trends in the political orientation of adolescents. Adelson and O'Neil (1966) find that the sense of community is hardly developed in early adolescence and that before the age of 13, youngsters find it difficult to imagine the social consequences of political action. Before 15 years, adolescents have a difficult time in conceptualizing the community in its entirety and perceive government in terms of specific tangible services. During this early phase of adolescence the youngster is insensitive to individual civil liberties and opts for authoritarian solutions to political problems. The period between 13 and 15 years is a transitional period; most 15 year olds begin to look beyond the constraining functions of law and recognize that laws may aim to promote the general good and achieve moral and social benefits. Several examples will clarify this transition in the concept of law and its users.

Eleven years old: Well, so everybody won't fight and they have certain laws so they won't go around breaking windows and stuff and getting away with it.

Thirteen: To keep the people from doing things they're not supposed to like killing people and like . . . if you're in the city like speeding in the car and things like that.

Fifteen: To help keep us safe and free.

Eighteen: Well, the main purpose would be just to set up a standard of behavior for people, for society living together so that they can live peacefully and in harmony with each other. (Adelson, Green, & O'Neil, 1968, pp. 4–5).

As can be seen, with increasing age there is a greater awareness of the terms of the social contract between individual and state. Concurrent with this development is an expanding awareness of individual rights and recognition of the need to limit the government's control over its citizens (Gallatin, 1967). The latter developmental pattern transcends differences in sex, intelligence, and social class. The pattern also holds cross-nationally in adolescent populations interviewed in the United States, England, and Germany (Gallatin, 1967). Since rights depend on some awareness of social contract, the growth of a "sense of community" probably furthers this recognition of individual rights (Gallatin, 1967).

The parallels between the above findings and Kohlberg's stages of moral development are quite striking. If one reviews Kohlberg's stage 5, one can see it is a "social contract" definition of morality. The ages of transition in Kohlberg's and Adelson's work also parallel one another, supporting our contention of the close relationship between morality and political ideology. Adelson, Green, and O'Neil (1968) attempt to account for this transition as follows:

For one thing, the young adolescent is locked matter-of-factly into benignly authoritarian relationships to his milieu, both at home and at school. He takes it for granted that authority exercises its dominion over its subjects—teacher over student, parent over child—and almost casually, he generalizes this direction of ordinance to the domain of government. With the easing of control that accompanies adolescence, with the adolescent's sharp surge towards autonomy there is a gradual yielding of this way of looking at the politics of household and schoolroom, and ultimately of politics at large. (p. 6).

RETROSPECT AND PROSPECT: A SUMMARY

We have attempted to provide a focused summary of political development during the adolescent years, while providing a brief theoretical framework and relevant findings in child political socialization as a convenient backdrop for our analysis of the adolescent research. The fact that the topic of political development is a rather new area in developmental psychological research, with gaps in both data and theory, demands that the reader maintain a tentative attitude toward the findings quoted. Many of the studies discussed in both child and adolescent political development have been restricted to select populations and, as is suggested by the Appalachian study, the inclusion of a detailed analysis of certain subpopulations, such as Negroes and poor whites, may alter our conclusions substantially. Cultural change may also alter the pattern of findings even in Negro populations where there is some indication of political cynicism and alienation (Marvick, 1965). The political effects of Black Nationalism may enhance political involvement in black populations, as is indicated by the increasing propensity of younger Negro youths to involve themselves in political agitation (Marvick, 1965). There is also no guarantee that certain types of home environments that contribute to political stability at one portion of the life cycle will of necessity contribute to stability at another. The high school students coming from stable, liberal, middle-class homes are frequently amongst the political activists on college campuses (Flacks, 1967; Haan, Smith, & Block, 1968; Keniston, 1969). It would be most interesting to study the transition from late adolescence to early adulthood, especially of youth who go on to be politically active college students. Noteworthy is the fact that some "political activists" who "sit-in" on college campuses are frequently classified in the highest stage (that is, Stage 6) of moral reasoning (Haan *et al.*, 1968). As Keniston (1969) points out, "You have to grow up in Scarsdale to know how bad things really are"; that is, the difficulty encountered in trying to understand why students protest when they have everything results from the frequent confusion of equating economic affluence with political stability. The well-fed, well-heeled, affluent middle-class adolescent from the most excellent schools has apparently reached the point of realizing that in his own life:

Economic affluence does not guarantee a feeling of personal fulfillment; political freedom does not always yield an inner sense of liberation and cultural freedom; social justice and equality may leave one with a feeling that something else is missing in life. (Keniston, 1969).

It seems possible that the poor and the rich will be the significant change agents in the political structures of the future, but for different reasons.

REFERENCES

Adelson, J., and O'Neil, R. P. Growth of political ideas in adolescence: the sense of community. *Journal of Personality and Social Psychology*, 1966, **4**, 295–306.

Adelson, J., Green, B., and O'Neil, R. The growth of the idea of law in adolescence. Unpublished Paper, Michigan, 1968.

Blatt, M. M., and Kohlberg, L. The effects of classroom moral discussion upon children's level of moral judgment. University of Chicago and Harvard University, Unpublished Paper, 1968.

Brim, O. G. Adult socialization. In J. A. Clausen (Ed.) *Socialization and Society*. Boston: Little, Brown, 1967, Chap. 5.

Cantrill, H. *Human Nature and Political Systems*. New Brunswick, N.J.: Rutgers University Press, 1961.

Dahl, R. A. *Modern Political Analysis*. Englewood Cliffs, N.J.: Prentice-Hall, 1963.

Dennis, J. Major problems of political socialization research. *Midwest Journal of Political Science*, 1968, **12**, 85–114.

Easton, D. The theoretical relevance of political socialization. *Canadian Journal of Political Science*, 1968, **1**, 125–146.

Easton, D., and Dennis, J. The child's acquisition of regime norms: political efficacy. *American Political Science Review*, 1967, **61**, 25–38.

Flacks, R. The liberated generation: an exploration of the roots of student protest. *Journal of Social Issues*, 1967, **23**, 52–75.

Gallatin, Judith Estelle. The development of the concept of rights in adolescence. *University of Michigan Microfilm #68-7603*, 1967, **28**(12B), 1968b, 5204.

Greenstein, F. I. *Children and Politics*. New Haven: Yale University Press, 1965.

Greenstein, F. I. Political socialization. In *The Encyclopedia of Social Science*. New York: Collier-Macmillan, 1968, 551–555.

Haan, M., Smith, B., and Block, Jeanne. Moral reasoning of young adults: political-social behavior, family background, and personality correlates. *Journal of Personality and Social Psychology*, 1968, **10**, 183–201.

Hess, R. D. Political socialization in the schools. *Harvard Educational Review*, 1968, **38**, 528–536.

Hess, R. D., and Easton, D. The child's changing image of the President. *Public Opinion Quarterly*, 1960, **24**, 632–644.

Hess, R. D., and Torney, Judith V. *The Development of Political Attitudes in Children*. Chicago: Aldine Publishing Co., 1967.

Hyman, H. *Political Socialization*. Glencoe, Ill.: The Free Press, 1959.

Inhelder, B., and Piaget, J. *The Growth of Logical Thinking from Childhood to Adolescence*. New York: Basic Books, 1958.

Jahoda, G. The development of children's ideas about country and nationality, Part 1: The conceptual framework. *British Journal of Educational Psychology*, 1963, **33**, 47–60. (a)

Jahoda, G. The development of children's ideas about country and nationality, Part 2: National symbols and themes. *British Journal of Educational Psychology*, 1963, **33**, 143–153. (b)

Jaros, D., Hirsch, H., and Fleron, F. J., Jr. The malevolent leader: political socialization in an American sub-culture. *American Political Science Review*, 1968, **62**, 564–575.

Jennings, M. K., and Niemi, R. G. Patterns of political learning. *Harvard Educational Review*, Summer, 1968, **38**, 443–467. (a)

Jennings, M. K., and Niemi, R. G. The transmission of political values from parent to child. *American Political Science Review*, 1968, **62**, 169–184. (b)

Keniston, K. You have to grow up in Scarsdale to know how bad things really are. *The New York Times Magazine*, April 27, 1969.

Kohlberg, L. Development of moral character and moral ideology. In M. L. Hoffman and L. W. Hoffman (Eds.) *Review of Child Development Research*. New York: Russell Sage Foundation, 1964, 383–431.

Kohlberg, L. Stages in the development of moral thought and action. New York: Holt, Rinehart and Winston, 1969.

Lane, R. E. Political science and psychology. In S. Koch (Ed.) *Psychology: A Study of a Science*. New York: McGraw-Hill, 1963, **6**, 583–638.

Lane, R. E., and Sears, D. O. *Public Opinion*. Englewood Cliffs, N.J.: Prentice-Hall, 1964.

Langton, K. Peer group and school and the political socialization process. *American Political Science Review*, 1967, **61**, 751–758.

Lawson, E. D. Development of patriotism in children: a second look. *Journal of Psychology*, 1963, **55**, 279–286.

Litt, E. Civic education, community norms, and political indoctrination. *American Sociological Review*, 1963, **28**, 69–75.

Litt, E. Public knowledge and private men: Political impact in the post-Kerr era. *Harvard Educational Review*, December 1968, **38**, 495–505.

Marvick, D. The political socialization of the American Negro. *Annals of American Academy of Political and Social Science,* September 1965, **361**, 112–127.

Oakeshott, M. Political education. In I. Scheffler (Ed.) *Philosophy and Education: Modern Readings*, 2d ed. Boston: Allyn and Bacon, 1966, Chap. 16.

Partridge, P. H. Politics, philosophy, ideology. In A. Quinton (Ed.) *Political Philosophy*. London: Oxford University Press, 1967, 32–52.

Sigel, R. Assumptions about the learning of political values. *Annals of the American Academy of Political and Social Science*, 1965, **361**, 1–9.

White, E. S. Intelligence and sense of political efficacy in children. *Journal of Politics*, 1968, **30**, 710–731.

1.8 *Orientation*

Apathy, low aspiration level, and mistrust are problems long associated with undesirable social conditions, notably poverty and racism. Recent federal efforts to improve such conditions have thus provided a very practical dimension for a psychological construct, known as *locus of control*. Central to this construct is the notion of *instrumentality*. Instrumentality refers to the existence of a contingent relationship between one's behavior and the consequences of his behavior, that is, whether a consequence (reinforcement or reward) is dependent upon the quality of one's volitional behavior. The unique characteristic of locus of control is, however, one's *perception* of reinforcement and its source(s). Specifically at issue is the extent to which an individual perceives that a given reinforcement results from his own behavior (therefore being to a large degree under his personal control) versus the extent to which a person perceives reinforcement as being controlled by external forces independent of his instrumental behavior. Accordingly, the effect of a reward or reinforcement is a function of the degree to which an individual perceives a causal relationship between his behavior and the consequences which follow that behavior.

Theoretically, one's perception of causality generates expectancies concerning the source of reinforcements (Rotter, 1954). If, across various situations, a person expects that reinforcement is directly contingent upon his own behavior or attributes, he is thought to be operating from an *internal* locus of control. Moreover, this sort of expectancy is relevant to one's acceptance of personal responsibility. If, however, one expects that reinforcement is basically unrelated to his own behavior or attributes (therefore subject to the control of forces such as "luck," "chance," "fate," or "the whim of powerful others"), that person is operating from an *external* locus of control. According to the theory, it is not a simple matter of being either internal or external. Rather, it is the degree to which one is internal or external and the stability of one's control orientation across situations that are important.

Herbert Lefcourt provides a succinct review of research on the internal-external control phenomenon. This review is organized into two broad categories: (1) studies that concern the influences of task variables upon control orientation, and (2) studies that view control orientation as a relatively stable personality characteristic. Lefcourt astutely suggests implications of locus of control for the study of apathy, alienation, and psychopathology.

Lefcourt's observations are augmented by an independent synthesis of control orientation research (Rotter, 1966). Rotter suggests that an individual with a strong belief in his ability to control his own destiny is likely to (1) be alert to environmental events which provide useful information for future behavior, (2) take steps to improve upon his environmental circumstances, and (3) place a high value upon reinforcements that are contingent upon personal skill and achievement. The reader is urged to reflect upon the network of generalizations surrounding locus of control when studying other topics covered in this volume, including underachievement, student dissent, opportunity failure, and self-esteem.

RECOMMENDED READINGS

Julian, James W., Lichtman, Cary M., and Rychman, Richard M. Internal-external control and the need to control. *Journal of Social Psychology*, 1968, **76**, 43–48.

Katkovsky, Walter, Crandall, Virginia C., and Good, Suzanne. Parental antecedents in children's beliefs in internal-external control of reinforcements in intellectual achievement situations. *Child Development*, 1967, **38**, 765–776.

McGhee, Paul E., and Crandall, Virginia. Beliefs in internal-external control of reinforcements and academic performance. *Child Development*, 1968, **39**, 91–102.

Phares, E. Jerry, Ritchie, D. Elaine, and Davis, William L. Internal-external control and reaction to threat. *Journal of Personal and Social Psychology*, 1968, **10**, 402–405.

Rotter, Julian B. Generalized expectancies for internal vs. external control of reinforcement. *Psychological Monograph*, 1966, **80** (1), No. 609, 28 pp.

1.8 Internal versus External Control of Reinforcement: A Review

Herbert M. Lefcourt, UNIVERSITY OF WATERLOO[1]

Under various rubrics, and from diverse orientations, investigators have concerned themselves repeatedly with man's ability to control his personal environment. Concepts such as competence, helplessness, hopelessness, mastery, and alienation have all been utilized in one way or another to describe the degree to which an individual is able to control the important events occurring in his life space.

The theorist who has most extensively written about the overcoming of helplessness and the development of mastery is Alfred Adler (Ansbacher & Ansbacher, 1956). Adler's concept of "striving for superiority" is posited as a universal, basic motive deriving from man's inherent, initial inferiority. As opposed to popular distortions of Adler's superiority concept, Adler's concern was for man's becoming more effective in controlling his personal world. R. W. White's constructs, which he called competence and effectance (White, 1959), can be viewed as describing the same referents as Adler's superiority striving.

Research conducted by Richter (1959) and Mowrer and Viek (1948) has been concerned with this area of interest in studies of animal behavior. Richter reported that even vigorous animals, when placed in situations where no solutions (escape) were possible, ceased efforts and rapidly succumbed to death. Controlling for all alternative hypotheses, Richter concluded that the loss of hope (of being able to effect a change) was the crucial variable.

In an investigation of helplessness, Mowrer and Viek (1948) found that matched pairs of shock-controlling and shock noncontrolling rats differed in eating inhibition after the shock periods. They concluded that an

Reprinted from *Psychological Bulletin*, 1966, **65**, 206–220, by permission of the author and the American Psychological Association.

[1] The author would like to express appreciation to Irwin W. Silverman for his critical reading and encouragement throughout the preparation of this paper.

uncontrollable painful stimulus arouses an apprehension that this stimulus could last indefinitely or get worse, whereas the same stimulus, if subject to control, arouses little or no apprehension. Mowrer labels this apprehension of uncontrolled pain as "fear from a sense of helplessness."

Common to Richter's, Adler's, White's, and Mowrer's formulations is the emphasis on instrumentality, the strength of contingency between acts and their effects. All four theorists stress the importance of instrumentality for survival and adequate behavior.

It is the purpose of this paper to present the background and research on a construct labelled internal-external control of reinforcement which has facilitated the exploration of this problem of contingency between act and effect.

The internal-external control construct (subsequently referred to as "control") differs from the aforementioned concepts (hopelessness, helplessness, competence, and so on) in being an integral unit of an elaborated theory. It is an expectancy variable rather than a motivational one (as is White's competence, for instance). In Rotter's social learning theory (Rotter, 1954), the potential for any behavior to occur in a given situation is a function of the person's expectancy that the given behavior will secure the available reinforcement, and the value of the available reinforcements for that person. In a particular situation, the individual, though desirous of an available goal, may believe that there is no behavior in his repertoire that will allow him to be effective in securing the goal. Within this specific situation, the person may be described as anticipating no contingency between any effort on his part and the end results in the situation. This description of an external-control expectancy is not merely applicable to the extreme punishing situations described by Mowrer and Richter but can be seen as applicable in many events in most persons' lives, for example, after wagering on a horse at a race track, only very odd persons may entertain the belief that they can exert some control over the outcome (legally). In Rotter's theory, the control construct is considered a generalized expectancy, operating across a large number of situations, which relates to whether or not the individual possesses or lacks power over what happens to him. Throughout this article, individuals are labelled external controls when they are said to have a generalized expectancy that reinforcements are not under their control across varying situations. In layman's language, these persons may be described as lacking self-confidence, or in Adler's terminology, suffering from inferiority feelings.

In the first expository paper dealing with the control dimension (Rotter, Seeman, & Liverant, 1962), the construct was described as distributing individuals according to the degree to which they accept personal responsibility for what happens to them. As a general principle, *internal control refers to the perception of positive and/or negative events as being a consequence of one's own actions and thereby under personal control; external control refers to the perception of positive and/or negative events as being unrelated to one's own behaviors in certain situations and therefore beyond personal control.*

In describing the research completed with the control construct, this paper is divided into two sections. The first presents findings from experiments in which task structure was varied, inducing a specific expectancy of high or low control. The second section presents the results of experimentation with perceived control as a generalized expectancy (personality characteristic).

Internal-External Control as Determined by Task Structure

The earliest published report of task structuring of control from a social learning theory framework is that of Phares (1957). Phares gave one group of subjects instructions which emphasized that success on a task (color or length-of-line matching) was due to skill. A second group was given instructions which emphasized that success on the same task was due to chance. Despite the fact that all groups received the same number and sequence of reinforcements, subjects with skill directions changed expectancies more frequently and more in the direction of previous experience (fewer unusual shifts such as raises in expectancy following failure or decreases in expectancy following success). Phares concluded that his findings support the view that "categorizing a situation as skill leads the subject to use the results of his past performance in formulating expectancies for future performances."

A second study in this series was reported a year later (James & Rotter, 1958). In this investigation, the effects of partial versus 100 percent reinforcement schedules upon trials to extinction was explored with reference to a skill versus a chance-task categorization. As in Phares' experiment, a task (a simple card-guessing problem) was used in which success was completely controlled by the experimenter although it could appear noncontrolled to the subject. Subjects in chance- and skill-direction groups were instructed that success was controlled by chance or by their own skill, respectively. The findings revealed that under the skill condition the usual superiority of partial reinforcement for resistance to extinction did not obtain. In fact, under these conditions the 100 percent reinforcement schedule led to less (though not significantly so) rapid extinction than the 50 percent reinforcement schedule. The chance condition produced findings typical of prior partial reinforcement studies: the 100 percent reinforced chance group was significantly quicker to extinguish than the 50 percent reinforced chance group (and the 100 percent reinforced skill group). The 50 percent reinforced chance group was significantly slower to extinguish than the 50 percent reinforced skill group.

James and Rotter explain their findings on the basis of subjects' perceptions or categorization of the task: in chance (externally controlled) situations, the change from 100 percent to 0 percent reinforcement clearly signals a change in the situation (experimenter's manipulation). Consequently, extinction or a change in behavior is rapid. The partially reinforced chance condition, however, does not allow for the quick perception of a changed situation. Consequently, extinction is more gradual until the change becomes evident to the subject. Under skill conditions, subjects would be more likely to explain the nonreinforced extinction trials as reflecting their own lack of skill rather than reflecting changed operations in the task, and they might therefore persist in an attempt to improve their performance. Consequently, James and Rotter attribute the lack of difference between partial and 100 percent reinforcement on extinction trials with skill directions to the way subjects perceive the task, demonstrating the importance of the subjects' expectancies of internal or external control.

To make the James and Rotter (1958) findings more analogous to classical extinction studies in which responses rather than verbal statements are obtained, Holden and Rotter (1962) replicated the James and Rotter study with the 50 percent reinforcement groups using a direct-response technique (betting) rather than the stated expectancy method. Briefly, these investigators found the same effects of skill and chance instructions when money betting was used to index experimental extinction, skill subjects taking considerably less time to extinguish than chance subjects in the partial-reinforcement extinction experiment.

A second experiment by Rotter, Liverant, and Crowne (1961) sought to replicate the James and Rotter findings without using differential instructions as the experimental manipulation. In this investigation, subjects were presented with either of two tasks which would be regarded as skill- and chance-controlled tasks on the basis of the previous cultural experiences of the subjects. One task involved a motor-skill apparatus (vertical Level-of-Aspiration Board) while the other involved the card-guessing procedure used in the James and Rotter (1958) study. The results strongly supported the hypotheses that greater increments and decrements in verbalized expectancies would be found under skill conditions and that extinction of expectancies under continuous negative reinforcement reverses under chance and skill conditions (a 50 percent reinforcement group is more resistant to extinction than the 100 percent group only under chance conditions, while the reverse holds true under skill conditions). The interpretations drawn from these findings are similar to those in the James and Rotter (1958) article. The one exception to the findings is that unusual shifting was not more common to either group. However, the low number of training trials (nine) may have attenuated a possible distribution of unusual shifts.

Blackman (1962) undertook an investigation to determine whether the apparent patterning of events, as opposed to short, seemingly nonpatterned sequences, in the presentation of two flashing lights would lead to extinction results similar to those found under skill and chance conditions. He reasoned that long or patterned sequences would lead a subject to believe that predictions of the event could be made depending upon his skill to comprehend the pattern, whereas short sequences would lead the subject to perceive the patterns as unpredictable (external control). Blackman found that sequence length and number of sequences significantly affected the number of "wrong" guesses (selection of the light that was no longer being illuminated during extinction) throughout extinction trials. The more sequences and the shorter the sequences during training, the more wrong responses were given, and the greater was the expectancy associated with these wrong responses found during extinction. Subjects who were given the "skill" or internal-control facilitating sequences were found to make fewer errors, or, in other words, to adapt to the new sequencing in extinction more readily. This study, however, contained no description of reinforcement schedules so that the results were not directly comparable with the previous studies. Secondly, trials to extinction (the complete elimination of wrong responses) were not significantly predicted on the basis of sequencing. Nevertheless, the results provide an interesting finding in that when the subject perceives that he is able, through some modicum of personal activity, to predict the events occurring in a given situation, he becomes more accurate in his perception of changes in that situation. The lack of prediction of trials to extinction suggests that subjects under long sequencing probably interpreted the extinction series as just another long sequence, and still attempted to predict its termination, consequently making occasional "errors."

Phares (1962) reported a second experiment in which skill versus chance directions were used to differentially affect the perceptual thresholds for nonsense syllables, half of which were paired with shock. The experiment was designed to test the hypothesis that when escape from a painful stimulus is possible only on a chance basis, the difference between pre- and postexperiment recognition thresholds for shock-associated stimuli will be smaller than in a skill situation where escape depends on the subjects' ability to perceive the same stimuli. The experimental design, excepting the perceptual-response variable, was very similar to Mowrer's (1948) and Richter's (1959) experiments, described earlier. All involved avoidance of painful stimuli with interest focused on the effects of controllability of the escape. Phares based his predictions on the rationale that an expectancy of control in this shock situation would lead the subject to behave in a manner most likely to capitalize on his ability to control the situation, which in this experiment consisted of lowering thresholds of recognition. Phares' subjects in the internal-control conditions learned to press buttons associated with given shock-related syllables to terminate shock. Subjects under chance conditions, on the other hand, were told that the correct button for terminating shock changed continuously so that escape occurred only on a random basis. As in the Mowrer and Viek (1948) experiment, chance subjects were matched with skill subjects with respect to number of escapes and syllables on which escape occurred. The results indicated that threshold decrements were significantly greater for skill than chance subjects for both shock- and nonshock-related syllables. Phares included one control group in his design which received no shock so that their behavior as indicated by the pre-post measures was not instrumental for pain release. The nonshock control group performed remarkably like the skill-shock group. Both groups differed significantly from the chance or external-control group. This latter finding is very interesting in light of Mowrer's description of his shock-controlling rats. Those rats who could control the shock demonstrated no fear and acted almost "nonchalant" in face of the painful stimulus. No interference with activities such as eating was found. Likewise Richter's "hopeful" rats (Richter, 1959) resumed what appeared to be normal, vigorous responding as soon as anticipation of effective escape was restored. The similarity between humans and rats in their nondisturbance with pain when control of that pain is possible suggests that the control dimension may have relevance to a wide range of human and infrahuman responses.

At this point, it might be relevant to cite two research findings with animals which indicate the importance of locus of control for predicting differential responses to the same stimuli. The Walter Reed Army Institute of Research group (Brady, 1958; Brady, Porter, Conrad, & Mason, 1958) has reported studies concerning the development of ulcers in rhesus monkeys. Although these writers have become more involved in the effects of sequence and duration of trials as determinants of ulcer formation, one remarkable finding they reported was that only monkeys who exerted control over a painful stimulus developed ulcers, while their partners who were linked in series connections and passively received the same shock failed to develop ulcers. In these experiments, the production of ulcers seems to be related to having control over aversive stimulation. An animal experiment reported by Malmo (1963) described a differential response to extinction of septal stimulation by rats in classical versus instrumental conditioning situations. Malmo explained the phenomena as follows:

In the passive (classical conditioning) situation it were as though "hope" was not aroused by the tone (CS), or, if it was aroused, that "anger" failed to occur, when in extinction the tone was not followed by septal stimulation. Anthropomorphically considered, it were as if having exerted no effort to obtain the septal stimulation the animal had not earned the right to object to its omission! Seriously though, it would appear that the animal's bar pressing response in producing the brain stimulation (and the proprioceptive feedback) was essential for the appearance of the expectancy frustration phenomena. (p. 19).

Briefly, Malmo's rats acted "angry" and fitful when responses previously reinforced in instrumental conditioning ceased to evoke the reinforcement, while the same reinforcement (CS-UCS linkage) in classical conditioning with subsequent extinction led to no such reaction.

Although there is no ready explanation for these findings, they seem relevant enough to the human and animal work reported above to suggest that the locus-of-control variable may have implications for a wider spectrum of problems and species than previously believed.

The remainder of this paper presents a review of the literature dealing with predictions of individual differences from measures of internal-external control as a generalized expectancy.

INTERNAL-EXTERNAL CONTROL AS AN INTRAPERSONAL VARIABLE

The first attempt to measure the internal-external control dimension as a personality variable in social learning theory was reported in a doctoral dissertation by Phares (1955). Phares designed a 13-item scale to measure a general attitude or personality characteristic of attributing the occurrence of reinforcements to chance rather than oneself. Within groups receiving skill versus chance directions for color- and line-matching tasks, he found some low-level predictions of frequency of shifting and unusual shifts with his scale of chance orientation.

With a more lengthy revision of the Phares scale, James (1957) found a significant correlation between the James-Phares Likert-type scale and the Incomplete Sentences Blank personal adjustment score (Rotter, 1950). The relationship appeared to be curvilinear, extreme internals and extreme externals appearing less adjusted. In two subsequent master's theses (Holden, 1958; Simmons, 1959) additional correlates of the James-Phares scale were investigated. Briefly, the James-Phares scale was found to correlate ($r = .51$, $N = 101$, with intelligence partialed out) with the

California F Scale which was interpreted as reflecting the successful measurement in both scales of the degree to which individuals see the world as containing powerful forces that they cannot influence.[2] Secondly, behavior on the Level of Aspiration Board (Rotter, 1954) was related to the James-Phares scale. For clarity of presentation, the description of the subjects on the internal-external control dimension will be discussed in terms of degree of externality. Highly external subjects shifted estimates frequently, apparently unable to arrive at a stable evaluation of their own skill. Patterns derived from Level-of-Aspiration performance (Rotter, 1954) which indicate cautious-defensive or failure-avoidant strategies seemed more characteristic of highly external persons on the James-Phares scale, while the more aggressive, success-striving patterns seemed more common to those scoring low in externality on the James-Phares scale.

Since the presentation of the James-Phares scale, a series of new scales have been utilized, some designed for testing special age groups. The Internal-External Control Scale is a forced-choice-type measure offering alternatives between internal- and external-control interpretations of various events (Rotter, Seeman, & Liverant, 1962). A monograph which provides extensive data on the development, validity, and reliability of the Internal-External Control Scale has been published (Rotter, 1966). The Locus of Control Scale for children is an orally administered true-false scale (Bialer, 1961); The Childrens' Picture Test of Internal-External Control presents a series of cartoons about which a child states "what he would say" in the depicted lifelike situations which involve attribution of responsibility (Battle & Rotter, 1963); The Intellectual Achievement Responsibility Questionnaire contains forced-choice items for children pairing an internal and external interpretation of achievement outcomes. This scale provides for possible differences between responsibility attribution for failure and success outcomes (Crandall, Katkovsky, & Crandall, 1964); The Powerlessness and Normlessness Scales contains Likert-type scales derived from sociological studies of alienation (Dean, 1961).

One set of research findings with the control dimension involves the prediction of externality in known ethnic groups. With the assumption that Negroes in the United States can easily perceive impediments in

[2] It has been posited by critics of the F scale that acquiescence or agreeing response tendencies account for a considerable proportion of the results obtained with the F scale. However, a recent review by Rorer (1965) has demonstrated that response styles are inadequate as alternate interpretations of data derived from measures such as the F scale. There appears to be less consistency between measures of response styles than between attitude measures of authoritarianism.

the way of goal striving, several studies have successfully predicted greater externality among Negroes than among whites. Battle and Rotter (1963) found an interaction between race and social class on the control variable as measured by a projective device called The Children's Picture Test of Internal-External Control. Lower-class Negroes were significantly more external than lower-class whites or middle-class Negroes and whites. In addition, highly external children reported significantly lower mean expectancies for success on a line-matching test. For comparative purposes, the Bialer Locus of Control Scale was compared with the Picture Test for 40 subjects and correlated significantly with it ($r = -.42$, $p < .01$). A high score on the Bialer scale indicates low externality while a high score on the Picture Test indicates high externality. Since the two measurement devices differ so greatly in format and the sample-size used was small, the relationship between them may be more significant than the obtained magnitude suggests. The Bialer scale also related significantly to the number of unusual shifts made in expectancy statements in the line-matching task ($r = -.47$, $p < .01$, $N = 40$). Highly external subjects raised their expectancies after failure and lowered them after success more often than subjects low in externality.

Using a similar argument—that racial segregation and discrimination means to Negroes that their own efforts will lead to no reinforcements unless adventitious circumstances make it so—Lefcourt and Ladwig (1965a; 1966) successfully predicted higher external-control expectancies among Negro than among white prison inmates (most of whom were from low socioeconomic backgrounds) on six different measures: the Internal-External Control Scale, Dean's Powerlessness and Normlessness Scales, and three indices derived from performance on the Level of Aspiration Board—number of shifts, number of unusual shifts, and patterns. Negroes scored significantly higher in externality on the three scales and performed in ways interpreted as reflecting external control on the Level of Aspiration indices. In a comparison of the reformatory samples with a normative population on the Powerlessness and Normlessness Scales, Negro inmates scored significantly higher on the powerlessness variable. White inmates failed to differ from the normative population on the powerlessness measure though scoring higher in normlessness. (Powerlessness refers to the lack of power to cause ends and is more similar to the control construct. Normlessness refers to the belief that conventionally approved pathways cannot be used effectively to attain desired ends.)

In a third ethnic-group investigation, Graves (1961) and Jessor adapted the Internal-External Control Scale for high school students and studied ethnic differences in an isolated tri-ethnic community. They found whites to be least external, followed by Spanish-Americans. Indians were the most external in attitudes. These findings were consistent with predictions about the groups. Although economic factors undoubtedly contributed to differences, Graves felt that "ethnicity" was an important source of variance after other factors were controlled.

From a different orientation, Strodtbeck (1958) has discussed a construct called "mastery" and presents research relating religious, national, and social-class orientations within families to the development of mastery. Strodtbeck's scale of mastery seems very similar to the control dimension stressing effectance belief. Strodtbeck found Jewish middle- and upper-class subjects more mastery believing than lower-class Italians. Most of the variance was attributable to social class.

Using subjects enrolled in a southern Negro college, Gore and Rotter (1963) found that the Internal-External Control Scale predicted the type and degree of commitment behavior manifested to effect social change. Those subjects scoring lowest in externality signed statements expressing the greatest amount of interest in social action (the March on Washington and forming a freedom riders group) while the more external subjects either expressed no interest in participation or minimal involvement (willingness to attend a rally). This study has since been replicated with nearly identical results (Strickland, 1965).

In all of the reported ethnic studies, groups whose social position is one of minimal power either by class or race tend to score higher in the external-control direction. Within the racial groupings, class interacts so that the double handicap of lower-class and "lower-caste" seems to produce persons with the highest expectancy of external control. Perhaps the apathy and what is often described as lower-class lack of motivation to achieve may be explained as a result of the disbelief that effort pays off. In short, the "oppressed" groups can be described as analogous to Mowrer's rats whose "fear of fear" led to nonsurvival behavior. Bettelheim (1952) discussed an analogous accommodation to decreased opportunity in Nazi concentration camps. He found that prisoners ceased to be active and responsible "subjects" and became passive, irresponsible, and childlike "objects" under such oppressive conditions.

Two other studies have concerned group differences in perceived control with reference to pathological populations. Bialer (1961) administered a Locus of Control Scale orally to retarded and normal children (mean ages of 10 years 4 months and 10 years, respectively). Rather than compare the two groups, Bialer combined them into one large sample and sought intercorrelations among mental age using the Peabody Picture Vocabulary Test (Dunn, 1959), locus of control, preference for return to completed versus interrupted tasks, and gratification patterns (immediate versus delayed-reinforcement preference). Bialer predicted that all of these variables would be interrelated, reflecting "conceptual maturity." Contrasting the relationships of chronological and mental age, he found that mental age accounted for most of the variance involved among three criteria variables. With an N of 89, locus of control (the higher the score, the lower the externality) correlated positively with mental age ($r = .56$) and with deferred gratification preference ($r = .47$), both significant at the .01 level. An obtained relationship between locus of control and chronological age ($r = .37$, $p < .01$) was minimized when mental age was partialed out (partial $r = .02$). On the other hand, mental age and locus of control remained strongly related ($r = .47$) with chronological age partialed out.

In a study comparing schizophrenics and normals, Cromwell, Rosenthal, Shakow, and Kahn (1961) used the James-Phares scale, an early form of the Internal-External Control Scale, and the Bialer-Cromwell Locus of Control Scale. On all three measures, they found schizophrenics to be significantly higher in externality than normals. In addition, they were interested in investigating the differential effect of autonomous (internal) and control (external) conditions upon reaction time (RT). Conflicting findings about schizophrenics' RT deficiencies had prompted Shakow (1950) to note that some of the RT tasks differ in the degree to which they allow the subject autonomy for initiating his response. Cromwell et al. conducted an RT experiment with their subjects under four conditions, two of which were self-directing, and two of which differed in degrees of external control. They found that normals did better (lower RT) in and preferred situations allowing autonomy, while schizophrenics did better in and preferred externally controlled situations. This was interpreted as reflecting the external-control schizophrenics' distress at decision-making in autonomous conditions. Within the normal sample, the James-Phares scale correlated significantly with RT superiority in autonomous situations ($r = .74$, $p < .05$, $N = 13$). The greater the tendency of normal subjects to answer in the direction of external control on the James-Phares scale, the less they improved their performance in the autonomous conditions over and above that in the controlled conditions. While superiority of performance in autonomous conditions correlated with the other scales (highly external subjects performing less adequately with autonomous conditions) the relationships fell short of significance due to the small sample size though all were in the same direction. Within the schizophrenic group, however, correlations all approached zero. The lack of relationship in the latter group may be accounted for by the small variance in and extremity of external control in that group.

The remaining studies reported in this paper concern specific behavioral correlates of the control dimension rather than group differences on that dimension.

LEARNING AND ACHIEVEMENT

Since the control dimension is usually measured by scales stressing academic interests, it would seem likely that learning skills and achievement behaviors would be highly related to control. Early grade school children differed according to sex on the Intellectual Achievement Responsibility Questionnaire (Crandall, Katkovsky, & Crandall, 1965), girls being more prone to assign responsibility to themselves for results eventuating from intellectual achievement efforts (Crandall, Katkovsky, & Preston, 1962). In the same investigation, the Intellectual Achievement Responsibility Questionnaire and other measures were compared with four achievement-related activities (time spent in intellectual free-play activities, intensity of striving in intellectual free-play pursuits, intelligence test performance, and reading and arithmetic test performances). Briefly, responsibility attribution was significantly related to most criteria for males but not for females. Male subjects who attributed achievement responsibility to themselves spent more time in intellectual free-play activities ($r = .70$, $p < .05$, $N = 20$), demonstrated greater intensity of striving in intellectual free-play pursuits ($r = .66$, $p < .05$), scored higher on intelligence tests (Stanford-Binet, $r = .52$, $p < .05$), on reading achievement tests ($r = .51$, $p < .05$), and arithmetic achievement tests ($r = .38$, $p < .10$). In the same investigation, a TAT measure of need for achievement failed to relate to any of the criterion situations.

In two studies deriving from a sociological emhasis on alienation, Seeman (Seeman, 1963; Seeman & Evans, 1962) has reported differential learning between internals (low alienated) and externals (high alienated) in two field settings. With groups matched on socioeconomic and hospital-experience variables, Seeman and Evans found that hospitalized tuberculosis patients characterized as external controls had less objective knowledge about their own conditions. This differential knowledge about health matters was evidently revealed in their ward behavior, as indicated by the fact that multiple and independent staff describers of the patients were in agreement concerning the low information possessed by the more external-control patients. The scale used for differentiating low and high externals was a shortened version of the Internal-External Control Scale. In the second investigation (Seeman, 1963), an attempt was made to control for intelligence and the novelty of the stimulus materials to be learned. Seeman presented materials related to correctional matters to a sample of reformatory inmates. Three kinds of information, differing chiefly in immediate relevance to inmate attempts to control important goals, were presented to the prisoners. This information concerned (a) the present reformatory setting, (b) factors related to achieving successful parole, and (c) long-range prospects for a noncriminal career. The essential prediction was that inmates scoring low in externality would show superior retention of the parole material, since this material most clearly implies the possibility and value of personal control. The findings demonstrated no differences in learning the materials in the first and last categories above. However, inmates low in externality learned the parole-related material significantly better than inmates high in externality. When inmates were divided into "Square Johns" (inmates who had earned merits demonstrating conformity to institution demands) and "Real Cons" (those with no merits) the control measure showed significant prediction of parole-knowledge learning only in the "Square John" group. The "unconventional" inmates demonstrated no relationship between alienation and learning. Among those committed to habilitation values, expectation of personal control was significantly related to learning of relevant information. Again no differences were found in the learning of information that was not relevant to personal control of important goals. These findings indicate the importance of values as well as expectancies for making differential predictions of learning. For control purposes, Seeman also administered the Marlowe-Crowne Social Desirability Scale (Crowne & Marlowe, 1960). The social desirability measure was found to have no relationship with the criteria.

In summary, in investigations concerned with learning and achievement-related variables, the control construct allows some prediction when the materials are relevant to the subjects' goal strivings. However, successful predictions in this area were found only in male samples. The one study that included female subjects (Crandall et al. 1962) revealed no relationship between perceived control and achievement behaviors for girls (correlations averaged around zero). Perceived control, as need achievement, may be less useful for predicting females' achievement behaviors than it is for males'. More investigations including sex as a variable are necessary.

The remainder of the studies to be reported do not fall into any convenient cluster for reporting purposes and are presented as miscellaneous investigations.

CONFORMITY

In a study concerning personality characteristics of conformers (Odell, 1959), a significant relationship was found between the Internal-External Control Scale and Barron's (1953) Independence of Judgment Scale, with subjects high in externality showing greater tendencies to conform. As part of a larger investigation concerning conformity, Crowne and Liverant (1963) reported supporting evidence for Odell's findings. When subjects in Asch-type conformity situations had to make bets concerning their accuracy, subjects high in externality were found to conform significantly more than subjects low in externality (as measured by the Internal-External Control Scale). Additionally, with confidence in outcomes expressed in terms of amount wagered, highly external subjects tended to be less confident than low-external subjects. Differences in relative amounts bet on "conforming" and "independent" trials were also found between low- and high-exernal subjects. Low externals bet approximately the same on both conforming and independent trials, while high externals bet significantly less on independent trials than on trials in which they yielded ($t = 2.68$, $p < .02$). Also, the greatest differentiation between low- and high-external subjects in amounts bet occurred on independent trials, low externals betting more than high-external subjects.

Crowne and Liverant also used Level-of-Aspiration patterns (Rotter, 1954) for the prediction of conformity. As described in the Lefcourt and Ladwig (1965a) study, patterns "one" and "three" represent the low externality patterns. These patterns are characterized by average to moderately high mean difference scores with an average number of shifts, and no or rare unusual shifts. Crowne and Liverant describe patterns one and three as indicative of confidence and an achievement or success orientation, while patterns "four" and "seven" represent a more failure-avoidant, defensive, goal-setting behavior. These patterns are characterized by either continuous shifting with each outcome or by an excessively high negative difference score average with unusual shifting, primarily downward after success. The results comparing Level-of-Aspiration performance and conformity are included here because of their previously explored relationship with the control dimension (Lefcourt & Ladwig, 1965a; Simmons, 1959). Failure-avoidant groups conformed more than subjects with achievement patterns and tended to be less confident, as expressed in expectancies and betting, than the achievement-oriented groups, though the difference failed to reach statistical significance. Crowne and Liverant interpreted their results as portraying the conformer as one who has low expectancies of success in socially evaluative situations, as reflected in a high external-control or defensive Level-of-Aspiration pattern.

RISK-TAKING

Liverant and Scodel (1960) hypothesized that subjects low in externality would believe that they could exert a modicum of control in chance-determined situations while subjects high in externality would view outcomes in such situations as occurring randomly. Subjects were engaged in a risk-taking situation in which they were required to bet on the outcome of 30 trials of dice throwing. Subjects had to select amounts to bet, as well as to choose one of seven alternative bets with given objective probabilities. Liverant and Scodel predicted that low-external subjects would select more high-probability, low-payoff bets than high-external subjects. They found that low externals chose significantly more bets of intermediate probability and significantly fewer low-probability bets than did high-external subjects. Also, more low externals than high externals never selected an extreme high- or low-probability bet. Low externals wagered more money on cautious than risky bets. In short, perceived control was found to differentiate behavior in the risk-taking situation, low externals revealing a greater tendency toward self-regulation with regard to objective probabilities.

In a near replication of the Liverant and Scodel study, Lefcourt (1965) compared the risk-taking behavior of Negroes and whites whose behavior had reflected high-external and low-external-control orientations, respectively, in previous experimentation in skilled tasks (Lefcourt & Ladwig, 1965a). On the assumption that a chance task would elicit less defensiveness or failure avoidance than a skill task for Negroes, it was predicted that Negroes would prove less external than whites in a chance situation. Using the same task and the same indices as Liverant and Scodel, Negroes were found to choose less low-probability bets, and were generally less risk-taking than whites. This reversal of internal-control reflecting behavior in skill versus chance situations was interpreted as being due to Negroes' disbelief that achievement in self-evaluative, skill-demanding tasks is controllable. Success in externally controlled situations (luck- or fate-determined) seems more controllable for the Negro who believes that goals derived through achievement will be denied him regardless of his effort, while externally controlled goals are, at least, obtained fairly.

FURTHER CORRELATES OF THE CONTROL DIMENSION

In an investigation of strategy preference, Lichtman and Julian (1964) had subjects estimate their performance at each of a number of distances in throwing 12 darts at a target. After having established the distance from which the subject judged he could score with five and seven darts respectively, the subject was asked to choose the distance from which he would prefer to throw, given the conditions that at the closer distance he would be provided with only five darts while at the farther position he would receive seven. Consequently, the conditional probabilities of success were equated at the two distances though they differed in the degree of actual control that the subject could probably exert over the outcome. With the Internal-External Scale, Lichtman and Julian found a significant difference between low-external and high-external subjects in choice of position, subjects low in externality more often choosing the closer distance, while subjects high in externality preferred the farther distance at a 4:1 ratio. This finding parallels that of Liverant and Scodel (1960) in that low-external subjects prefer the high-probability choices through which to maximize their successes. An additional finding in the Lichtman and Julian study is a reported correlation with the Marlowe-Crowne Social Desirability Scale (1960) ($r = -.39$, $p < .05$, $N = 28$), and an insignificant relationship ($r = -.27$, $N = 28$) with a measure of need for achievement. The former finding indicates a weak but significant tendency for persons with high need for approval to be doubtful about their personal efficacy. This relationship has also been reported in a study by Strickland and Rodwan (1963). However, several other studies (Crowne & Liverant, 1963; Seeman, 1963) have reported no relationship between social desirability and control measures. The statistically insignificant but negative relationship between need achievement and external control supports a previously reported finding by Odell (1959) in which need achievement and externality were significantly related ($r = -.25$, $p < .05$). In the Odell study, a larger sample allowed for greater statistical significance. However, the magnitude of the relationship seems fairly consistent. The need achievement measure used by Odell derives from TAT-like stimuli whereas the Lichtman and Julian study utilized the French (1958) method. The similarity of results despite different techniques used argues for the stability of this modest relationship. Theoretically, one would expect internal-control persons to demonstrate the search for mastery that need achievement defines.

Two other correlates of interest have been reported by Butterfield (1964). In an extensive correlational study, Butterfield found strong correlations among the Internal-External Control Scale and the Child and Waterhouse (1953) Frustration-Reaction Inventory, and the Alpert-Haber Facilitating-Debilitating Test Anxiety Questionnaire (1960). Responses to the Child and Waterhouse measure are categorized into three groups: constructive response to frustration, intropunitive response, and extrapunitive response to frustration. Butterfield predicted and found a relationship between external control and constructive response to frustration scores ($r = -.37$, $p < .02$, $N = 47$). Partial correlations between each frustration-reaction score and external control when each of the other two reaction scores were held constant were $r = .57$, $p < .01$ be: tween externality and intropunitive, and $r = -.86$, $p < .01$ for constructive reactions. As perceived locus of control became more external, constructive responses decreased, and intropunitive responses increased when the other response scores were partialed out. No relationship with extrapunitive responses was found. This finding indicates that the less-external individual claims that he reacts in a more problem-solving direction despite frustration, wasting less time on guilty rumination and self-accusatory gestures that detract from problem-solving efforts.

In regard to the Alpert-Haber measure, two scores are derived—a debilitating-anxiety and a facilitating-anxiety measure. The former produced an insignificant $r = .23$ $(N = 47)$, while the latter measure produced an $r = -.68$, $p < .01$ with external-control scores. Facilitating anxiety correlated with constructive response to frustration (Child-Waterhouse measure), $r = .49$, $p < .01$. Other subscales of the two measures were unrelated. Partial correlations between each anxiety score and external control, with the other anxiety type held constant, were presented. The results were as marked as with the frustration-response measure. External control correlated ($r = .61$, $p < .01$) with debilitating-anxiety scores when facilitating-anxiety scores were partialed out; external control correlated with facilitating anxiety ($r = -.82$, $p < .01$) with debilitating-anxiety scores held contant. Facilitating anxiety decreased and debilitating anxiety increased as locus of control became more external.

Since both the frustration and anxiety indices are self-report measures, the findings suggest that subjects who are less external depict themselves as goal-directed workers who strive to overcome hardships, whereas high-external subjects portray themselves as suffering, anxious, and less concerned with achievement per se than with their affect responses to failure. The high multiple correlation ($r = .81$), which does not differ significantly from one approaching unity, between locus of control and the facilitating- and debilitating-anxiety scores raises a question about the independence of these scales. The items and format of the scales are sufficiently different that one would not anticipate such relationships as were obtained. However, the facilitating-debilitating anxiety scale does concern responses to achievement situations, as do several items in the locus-of-control scale. Consequently, the strong relationships obtained may indicate the greater success expectancies in achievement situations of the less-external-control individuals. It should be noted that the Alpert-Haber anxiety measure derives from work concerning test anxiety (Mandler & Sarason, 1952), the measure of which has been used as an index of fear or expectation of failure in achievement situations by Atkinson and Litwin (1960).

SUMMARY AND CONCLUSIONS

Research findings from experiments manipulating apparent controllability and investigations using measures of locus of control to make differential predictions of control-related behaviors have been reported.

It can be concluded that perceived control is a useful variable, and, in relation to the types of experiments noted in the introductory section, may be related to problems such as psychopathology, apathy, and withdrawal phenomena. It is no mean coincidence in time that writers such as Piaget (Flavell, 1963) and Michotte (1963) have also been doing extensive research into the causal relationships which Western man imposes upon his world; and that psychotherapists such as Adler (Ansbacher & Ansbacher, 1956) have concerned themselves with man's development of mastery. White's concern with effectance and competence mirrors this same focus of interest in personality psychology. As indicated in the range of studies described, this concern with control is amenable to research, though more investigation is needed.

At a time when problems of response sets and response styles beset any investigator making use of questionnaire materials, it is particularly encouraging to note the successful use of these scales in predicting complex behaviors. The research reviewed in this paper, while predominantly deriving from one theoretical orientation, has involved the use of several different measurement techniques. Forced-choice, Likert-type scales, true-false scales, projective devices, and performance measures drawn from Level-of-Aspiration tasks have all been utilized and have demonstrated some efficacy in predicting different criteria related to the locus-of-control dimension. The success of a variety of techniques in measuring the control dimension provides support for the construct validity of that dimension and argues against a response-style interpretation of scale performance.

Insofar as response set is concerned, several investigators have reported correlations between perceived control and social desirability. Overall results indicate that the relationship varies from one of bare significance to nonsignificance. With but a small proportion of the variance accounted for in the relationship between control and social desirability, the response-set interpretation of control-scale data appears nondefensible. In addition, social desirability has proven ineffective in the prediction of criteria related to the control dimension in several investigations.

Another question may be raised regarding the relationship between the control dimension and intelligence. As indicated in two studies (Bialer, 1961; Crandall, Katkovsky, & Preston, 1962) intelligence is positively related to perceived internal control. Cromwell (1963) has cogently discussed how retardation can eventuate in lower success expectancies with a concomitant decrease in efforts toward achievement. On these bases, it might be argued that locus of control merely represents the phenomenological response to one's own intelligence. If such were the case, then a measure of intelligence would perhaps be preferable to the attitude scales used in measuring the control variable. However, in studies where the range of intelligence is not as extensive as in the above-mentioned investigations (Bialer used retardates in his study), little relationship has been found between intelligence and control measures. In fact, one investigation (Battle & Rotter, 1963) reported a reversal—lower-class Negroes with high IQs being more external than middle-class whites with lower IQs.

Two questions of immediate interest that have not been investigated in any depth concern the origins and sources of control orientations and the operations for altering such orientations. Pertinent to the origins problem is the study by Strodtbeck (1958) in which attitudes similar to those of internal-control expectancies were investigated relative to family structure. Relevant to expectancy alteration, one study by Lefcourt and Ladwig (1965b) sought to vary expectancy by a "reference group manipulation." In this study, Negroes who had previously been characterized as highly external were led to believe that they were being studied as jazz musicians. In a game situation, the usually high external-control Negroes persisted in competition against a white opponent despite continuous losses when they believed that the experimenter was interested in them as jazz musicians. Two control groups (a second jazz musician group for whom jazz cues were irrelevant, and a nonmusician group) failed to show the same persistence. In this experiment where external-control orientations should predict failure-avoidance (quitting the experiment), Negroes continued to meet competitive challenges if they maintained expectancies other than those for themselves as Negroes.

Despite the leads from these research reports, little has been reported on how internal- or external-control expectancies become generalized across differing situations. Work needs to be done on specific antecedents of internal- and external-control orientations, and on the factors leading to the generalization of these orientations. In addition, the breakdown of external-control expectancies assumes more than a theoretical interest when programs are currently being devised by governmental agencies seeking to ameliorate problems of poverty and racial barriers, the very problems which seem to generate external-control orientations and their concomitants of apathy and lack of goal-striving behavior.

SUMMARY

A summary of research concerning the construct, internal vs. external control of reinforcement is presented. Investigations with this variable have utilized situational manipulations of locus of control or have involved differential predictions to given situations based on measures of the internal-external control dimensions. In both types of investigation, locus of control is found predictive to different social behaviors, learning performances, and to more and less achievement-related activities. Suggestions for further areas of study are presented.

REFERENCES

Alpert, R., and Haber, R. N.   Anxiety in academic achievement situations. *Journal of Abnormal and Social Psychology*, 1960, **61**, 207–215.

Ansbacher, H., and Ansbacher, R.   *The Individual Psychology of Alfred Adler.* New York: Basic Books, 1956.

Atkinson, J. W., and Litwin, G. H.   Achievement motive and test anxiety conceived as a motive to approach success and motive to avoid failure. *Journal of Abnormal and Social Psychology*, 1960, **60**, 52–63.

Barron, F.   Some personality correlates of independence of judgment. *Journal of Personality*, 1953, **21**, 287–297.

Battle, E., and Rotter, J. B.   Children's feelings of personal control as related to social class and ethnic group. *Journal of Personality*, 1963, **31**, 482–490.

Bettelheim, B.   Individual and mass behavior in extreme situations. In G. E. Swanson, T. M. Newcomb, and E. L. Hartley (Eds.) *Readings in Social Psychology.* New York: Holt, Rinehart and Winston, 1952.

Bialer, I.   Conceptualization of success and failure in mentally retarded and normal children. *Journal of Personality*, 1961, **29**, 303–320.

Blackman, S.   Some factors affecting the perception of events as chance determined. *Journal of Psychology*, 1962, **54**, 197–202.

Brady, J. V.   Ulcers in "executive" monkeys. *Scientific American*, 1958, **199**, 95.

Brady, J. V., Porter, R. W., Conrad, D. G., and Mason, J. W.   Avoidance behavior and the development of gastroduodenal ulcers. *Journal of the Experimental Analysis of Behavior*, 1958, **1**, 69–72.

Butterfield, E. C.   Locus of control, test anxiety, reactions to frustration, and achievement attitudes. *Journal of Personality*, 1964, **32**, 298–311.

Child, I. L., and Waterhouse, I. K.   Frustration and the quality of performance: III. An experimental study. *Journal of Personality*, 1953, **21**, 298–311.

Crandall, V. C., Katkovsky, W., and Crandall, V. J.   Children's beliefs in their own control of reinforcement in intellectual-academic achievement situations. *Child Development*, 1965, **36**, 91–109.

Crandall, V. J., Katkovsky, W., and Preston, A.   Motivational and ability determinants of young children's intellectual achievement behaviors. *Child Development*, 1962, **33**, 643–661.

Cromwell, R. L.   A social learning approach to mental retardation. In N. R. Ellis (Ed.) *Handbook of Mental Deficiency.* New York: McGraw-Hill, 1963, 41–91.

Cromwell, R., Rosenthal, D., Shakow, D., and Kahn, T.   Reaction time, locus of control, choice behavior and descriptions of parental behavior in schizophrenic and normal subjects. *Journal of Personality*, 1961, **29**, 363–380.

Crowne, D. P., and Liverant, S.   Conformity under varying conditions of personal commitment. *Journal of Abnormal and Social Psychology*, 1963, **66**, 547–555.

Crowne, D. P., and Marlowe, D.   A new scale of social desirability independent of psychopathology. *Journal of Consulting Psychology*, 1960, **24**, 349–354.

Dean, D. G.   Alienation: its meaning and measurement. *American Sociological Review*, 1961, **26**, 753–758.

Dunn, L. M.   *Peabody Picture Vocabulary Test Manual.* Nashville: Peabody College for Teachers, 1959.

Flavell, J. H.   *The Developmental Psychology of Jean Piaget.* Princeton, N.J.: Van Nostrand, 1963.

French, E.   Development of a measure of complex motivation. In J. W. Atkinson (Ed.) *Motives in Fantasy, Action, and Society.* New York: Van Nostrand, 1958, 242–248.

Gore, P. M., and Rotter, J. B.   A personality correlate of social action. *Journal of Personality*, 1963, **31**, 58–64.

Graves, T. D.   Time perspective and the deferred gratification pattern in a tri-ethnic community. Research Report No. 5, Tri-Ethnic Research Project. University of Colorado, Institute of Behavioral Science, 1961.

Holden, K. B.   Attitude toward external versus internal control of reinforcement and learning of reinforcement sequences. Unpublished master's thesis, Ohio State University, 1958.

Holden, K. B., and Rotter, J. B.   Supplementary report: a nonverbal measure of extinction in skill and chance situations. *Journal of Experimental Psychology*, 1962, **63**, 519–520.

James, W.   Internal versus external control of reinforcements as a basic variable in learning theory. Unpublished doctoral dissertation, Ohio State University, 1957.

James, W., and Rotter, J. B.   Partial and 100% reinforcement under chance and skill conditions. *Journal of Experimental Psychology*, 1958, **55**, 397–403.

Lefcourt, H. M.   Risk-taking in Negro and white adults. *Journal of Personality and Social Psychology*, 1965, **2**, 765–770.

Lefcourt, H. M., and Ladwig, G. W.   The American Negro: a problem in expectancies. *Journal of Personality and Social Psychology*, 1965, **1**, 377–380. (a)

Lefcourt, H. M., and Ladwig, G. W.   The effect of reference group upon Negroes' task persistence in a biracial competitive game. *Journal of Personality and Social Psychology*, 1965, **1**, 668–671. (b)

Lefcourt, H. M., and Ladwig, G. W.   Alienation in Negro and white reformatory inmates. *Journal of Social Psychology*, 1966, **68**, 153–157.

Lichtman, C. M., and Julian, J. W.   Internal vs. external control of reinforcement as a determinant of preferred strategy on a behavioral task. Paper read at Midwestern Psychological Association, St. Louis, 1964.

Liverant, S., and Scodel, A.   Internal and external control as determinants of decision-making under conditions of risk. *Psychological Reports*, 1960, **7**, 59–67.

Malmo, R. B.   On central and autonomic nervous system mechanisms in conditioning, learning, and performance. *Canadian Journal of Psychology*, 1963. **17**, 1–36.

Mandler, G., and Sarason, S. B.   A study of anxiety and learning. *Journal of Abnormal and Social Psychology*, 1952, **16**, 115–118.

Michotte, A.   *The Perception of Causality*. New York: Basic Books, 1963.

Mowrer, O. H., and Viek, P.   An experimental analogue of fear from a sense of helplessness. *Journal of Abnormal and Social Psychology*, 1948, **43**, 193–200.

Odell, M.   Personality correlates of independence and conformity. Unpublished master's thesis, Ohio State University, 1959.

Phares, E. J.   Changes in expectancy in skill and chance situations. Unpublished doctoral dissertation, Ohio State University, 1955.

Phares, E. J.   Expectancy changes in skill and chance situations. *Journal of Abnormal and Social Psychology*, 1957, **54**, 339–342.

Phares, E. J.   Perceptual threshold decrements as a function of skill and chance expectancies. *Journal of Psychology*, 1962, **53**, 399–407.

Richter, C. F.   Sudden death phenomenon in animals and humans. In H. Feifel (Ed.) *The Meaning of Death*. New York: McGraw-Hill, 1959.

Rorer, L. G.   The great response-style myth. *Psychological Bulletin*, 1965, **63**, 129–156.

Rotter, J. B.   *Social Learning and Clinical Psychology*. Englewood Cliffs, N.J.: Prentice-Hall, 1954.

Rotter, J. B.   Generalized expectancies for internal versus external control of reinforcement. *Psychological Monographs*, 1966, **80** (1, Whole No. 609).

Rotter, J. B., Liverant, S., and Crowne, D. P.   The growth and extinction of expectancies in chance controlled and skilled tasks. *Journal of Psychology*, 1961, **52**, 161–177.

Rotter, J. B., and Rafferty, J. E.   *The Rotter Incomplete Sentences Blank Manual*. New York: Psychological Corporation, 1950.

Rotter, J. B., Seeman, M., and Liverant, S.   Internal versus external control of reinforcements: a major variable in behavior theory. In N. F. Washburne (Ed.) *Decisions, Values, and Groups*, Vol. 2. London: Pergamon Press, 1962, 473–516.

Seeman, M.   Alienation and social learning in a reformatory. *American Journal of Sociology*, 1963, **69**, 270–284.

Seeman, M., and Evans, J.   Alienation and learning in a hospital setting. *American Sociological Review*, 1962, **27**, 772–782.

Shakow, D.   Some psychological aspects of schizophrenia. In M. L. Reymert (Ed.) *Feelings and Emotions: The Mooseheart Symposium*. New York: McGraw-Hill, 1950, 383–390.

Simmons, W.   Personality correlates of the James-Phares scale. Unpublished master's thesis, Ohio State University, 1959.

Strickland, B.   The prediction of social action from a dimension of internal-external control. *Journal of Social Psychology*, 1965, **66**, 353–358.

Strickland, B., and Rodwan, A. S.   The relationship of certain personality variables to decision making in perception. Paper read at Midwestern Psychological Association, Chicago, 1963.

Strodtbeck, F. L.   Family interaction, values and achievement. In D. McClelland (Ed.) *Talent and Society*. New York: Van Nostrand, 1958.

White, R. W.   Motivation reconsidered: the concept of competence. *Psychological Review*, 1959, **66**, 297–333.

1.9 Orientation

The existence of an adolescent society or subculture, as separate from the larger adult culture, has been debated at great length in the literature on adolescence (Smith & Kleine, 1966). Some authorities argue vociferously for this separatism while others discount it with equal vigor. Protagonists and antagonists alike seem able to find reasonable support for their views, a fact that has led some writers to declare the entire question a "pseudo issue" (Jahoda & Warren, 1965). Controversy nothwithstanding, the genesis, psychological functions, and social implications of youth culture currently number among the favorite topics of scholars concerned with adolescence. This favoritism is embodied in the ensuing paper by William V. Burlingame, a clinical professor of psychology.

Burlingame first draws the reader's attention to youth culture components, such as adornment styles and musical preferences. These components, suggests the author, signal a shift by adolescents toward increasingly idiosyncratic tastes—tastes which, collectively, create for youth a distinct image. From this colorful introduction, Burlingame proceeds to define the basic characteristics of youth culture in terms of a generalized belief system. This belief system, inferred largely from the customs and verbal behavior of adolescents, includes a quartet of related propositions. Once this quartet has been established, Burlingame briefly examines alternatives that attempt to account for the emergence of youth culture. These alternatives include the "changing social fabric," "market," "threshold," "alienation," and "ego process" theories. It is during this portion of Burlingame's essay that the reader will encounter some further ideas of personalities introduced previously by Evans and Potter (Part I), including the ideas of Friedenberg, Goodman, and Erikson. Consistent with the Evans and Potter review, Burlingame observes that diverse interpretations of youth culture and its functions may be more complementary than contradictory.

Additional particulars to be culled from Burlingame's analysis include (1) sex differences in the extent and timing of youth culture involvement, (2) academic and social characteristics of adolescents who vary in their adherence to youth culture norms, and (3) the differential meaning of the youth culture to its various "constituents." Embellishments of these three particulars are based upon Burlingame's own research with adolescent groups.

The present essay concludes with a refined statement on the implications of youth culture for psychological development. These conclusions thus provide a constructive linkage to the first selection in Part II (George D. Spindler). Burlingame's overriding conceptual preference becomes clear during this concluding portion, namely, his view of youth culture as an assist to identity formulation and a transitory mechanism for the achievement of autonomy and responsibility. After a study of this paper the reader may wish to consider further whether adolescence represents (in Western cultures) a relatively distinct cultural existence or more accurately reflects the adult value system (although perhaps in exaggerated form).

RECOMMENDED READINGS

Alexander, C. Norman, and Campbell, Ernest Q. Peer influences on adolescent educational aspirations and attainments. *American Sociological Review*, 1964, **29**, 568–575.

Jahoda, Marie, and Warren, Neil. The myths of youth. *Sociology of Education*, 1965, **38**, 138–149.

Smith, Louis M., and Kleine, Paul F. The adolescent and his society. *Review of Educational Research*, 1966, **36**, 424–436.

Smith, Thomas S. Conventionalization and control: an examination of adolescent crowds. *American Journal of Sociology*, 1968, **74**, 172–183.

1.9   The Youth Culture

William V. Burlingame, UNIVERSITY OF NORTH CAROLINA

INTRODUCTION

It is scarcely unique for one to observe the obvious discrepancy that exists between certain sentiments and predispositions of young people and those of their elders. Within recent years, it has become increasingly common

An original paper prepared especially for this volume.

to hear of these adolescent tastes as constituting a discrete culture which has been alternately referred to as "the adolescent society," "the teenage peer culture," or "the adolescent subculture." More disciplined social scientists would surely take affront. The term "culture" has a technical and restricted usage, and may seem inappropriate to describe the propensities of one peculiar age stratum which exists within a larger cultural matrix. In the same vein, if culture implies a shared base of values and attitudes, it has yet to be demonstrated that young people are not maturing to resemble previous generations. The foci of friction, the areas that approach schism, and the conspicuous dissent of a few may be quite visible, but they do not obscure that which is common and shared among generations. To some extent, then, it is as sensible to examine the given culture, to note the eccentricities of particular groups, and to account for divergence according to the principles of social and economic change or human growth and development. To do so is to pose the following questions: In the maturation of Western culture, what develpments have fostered this subset of beliefs and practices among the young? What is their psychological meaning and their utility in promoting growth toward autonomy and maturity? In the present discussion the term "youth culture" is used loosely and advisedly, with greater emphasis placed on the word "youth" with its connotations of growth and development than upon the word "culture."

Documenting the age level separation is not difficult; the following is the colorful if not inflammatory observation of social critic Paul Goodman (1966):

"Teenagers" are not adolescents in a total society of all ages; they are a race with a distinct plumage and music. Their high priests, unlike the movie heroes or athletes of other times who were grownup models, now tend to perform specifically for the teen audience and are hardly (or not yet) out of their teens themselves.

Such a subculture is not a subsociety, like the youth houses of primitive tribes, which were organized around the interests and secrets of adolescents but still took part in community life. Rather, it is a language and mores *against* the adults, or at best excluding them, as if they were a foreign tribe, probably hostile. In principle, every teenager is a delinquent. (pp. 18–19) .

Goodman cites plumage and music, although most authorities would view these as peripheral rather than fundamental aspects of culture. There is merit in briefly examining these expressive modes as examples of youth culture adherence.

In the years following World War II, the prototype for male adolescent appearance was the crew-cut collegian, who, in turn, had adopted his garb from the tastes of returning servicemen. The transmission of dress style was orderly, direct, and non-controversial, with the young borrowing in large part from their senior counterparts. By 1955, the process had been decisively interrupted. Such teen heroes as Elvis Presley and James Dean dictated taste; for secondary school boys, this included blue denim (not khaki) trousers which were close fitting, lightened by laundering or bleach, and hung at a precise and controversial point on the hips without benefit of a belt. Closely cropped hair was summarily abandoned in favor of elaborate and massive sideburns combed back to fall in the neck and maintained in place by substantial doses of hair oil. The atmospheric qualities conveyed were rebelliousness, thinly disguised sexuality, and arrogance. In the early 1960s, youthful models continued to prevail, although the form differed. At this time, it was the California surfer whose hair was equally long but fell instead over the forehead. Both hair and denim were now bleached either by sun, salt, or chemical, and pants were severed above the knee in order to enhance mobility in the surf. What had emerged as functional or accidental was rapidly integrated into a carefully specified style which was nearly as common in Michigan as in California. In the late 1960s, a plethora of tastes occurred which differed widely in form but had, in common, their origin in the youth culture. Loose and flowing bell-bottom trousers competed with brief "mini-skirts," while expensive "mod" attire was juxtaposed with the discarded fur coats, uniforms, and work clothing found in thrift shops and rummage sales. The Hippie, mod, and psychedelic influences combined to promote a taste that was as ornate, elaborate, flamboyant, and unconventional as anything yet produced in the twentieth century.

Developments in adolescent cult music paralleled. The subdued rhythms of the "big band" sound predominated throughout the 1940s and into the 1950s. The names of Benny Goodman, Glen Miller, and the Dorsey Brothers were accepted by both young and old; there was Guy Lombardo who produced the "sweetest music this side of heaven" and the crooners of the Crosby tradition, including Frank Sinatra who emerged as a hero of youth but was gradually assimilated as a stock item of middle-class musical taste. By 1955, a dramatic change had occurred as Elvis Presley, among others, drew upon the Negro rhythm and blues, and country and western musical traditions to produce hard-driving "rock and roll." The music of that period was predictable with its four-four beat and banal lyrics: "Who put the bomp in the bomp-ba bomp-a bomp? Who put the ram in the ram-a-lam a-ding-dong?" (*Time Magazine*, 1969). During the early 1960s youthful musicians, in apparent reaction, utilized the heritage of American folk music to produce a sound that had the peaceful, poetic, and soulful qualities previously absent. By 1965, the integration of folk, rock, and Indian raga music together with usage of psychedelic drugs, amplifiers, loud speakers, electrified instruments, and other sorts of electronic paraphernalia had produced music identified variously as "acid rock," "folk rock," or "revolution rock." The lyrics were sexually provocative, preoccupied with drug experiences, or in direct opposition to the usual political and economic institutions. An English group proposed that the time was propitious for "palace revolution" and its recordings was subsequently banned in that country, while American groups sung of "a magic carpet ride" and a "trip" that was "eight miles high."

The content inherent in this revolution in plumage and music is significant, but of greater import is the fact that the form as well as content had been generated from within the youthful constituency itself. Most observers have been inclined to view the decade of the 1950s as a decisive period in which the tastes of adolescents achieved cultural autonomy. This is not to deny the earlier manifestations of a youth culture, such as that noted in the "flaming youth" of the 1920s. Rather, it is to suggest that in the course of evolution a critical threshhold has been crossed with youth presently proposing its own tastes, testing these in the adolescent marketplace, accepting some items while rejecting others, and then passing on in fickle fashion to the latest innovation. Not only had custom been generated from within, but there was firm evidence that it was being emulated from above. Adolescents wryly commented to the effect that immediate demise is the fate of any fad adopted by adults. A teenager once informed this writer that a particular dance step had been ". . . killed by middle-aged women in hot pink stretch pants." The homogeneity of youthful taste has since assumed international proportions as well. Without doubt, the mass media have provided national and international coverage, and the message has fallen upon the receptive audience. Youth culture garb and musical taste are common throughout the industrial, urban centers of both Western and Communist nations.

YOUTH CULTURE DIMENSIONS

Music and dress have been noted as conspicuous examples of one of the parameters of youth culture practice. Because they are highly visible, it is a comparatively simple matter to illustrate their presence. There remain, however, a number of other features that are more central and pervasive but fall in the ambiguous realm of values and attitudes. The following four categories are intended to encompass the youth culture's core values; the attempt is to provide descriptive clarity, while recognizing that these propositions are at times overlapping or mere extensions of one another.

I. Construing the Youth Culture as Possessing Independent Cultural Existence

The presence of this attitude among adults and adolescents underscores a general cultural recognition of the distinct and separate existence of youth. The discontinuity with other generations is emphasized and an aura of uniqueness and desirability is attached. Childhood is disdained; there is abstentian from the responsibilities of adulthood; age is the primary criterion for providing distinction. It is no accident that romantic literature has idealized youth to the extent that "youth" and "beauty" have been seen as virtually synonymous. The companion fiction is that youth exists for its own ends and pleasures but will inevitably be corrupted by age and experience. Youth, then, is viewed as a suspension, a limbo-like state, which denies any organic continuity with childhood and is briefly spared the decay and doldrums inherent in adult status. Although empirical data are sparse, social scientists have not been loath to recognize a subculture of adolescents nor to account for adolescent behavior utilizing such a construct. As early as 1942, Parsons (1958) applied the term "youth culture" and attributed similar qualities to it. More recently, Keniston argued that the youth culture is not simply transitional:

For the essence of the youth culture is that it is not a rational transitional period—were it one, it would simply combine the values of both childhood and adulthood. Instead it has roles, values, and ways of behaving all its own. (Keniston, 1962).

II. Valuing Peer Group Sociability: A Range of Behaviors from Constituting Peers as a Reference Group to Seeking Group Esteem and Participating in Social Rating Practices

There are many data that describe the reliance of adolescents on the youth culture and peer group as a reference group for decision-making. When Coleman (1961, pp. 5, 6, 140) asked adolescents to decide whose disapproval would be most difficult to accept, he found a roughly even division between "parents" and "friends," with "teachers" accounting for a very small proportion. Considering that all subjects were secondary school students and resided in the parental home, the figures are somewhat startling. Of even greater significance was the discovery that members of the "leading crowds" (that is, the socially elite) were significantly inclined to regard peer disapproval as more difficult to receive. Thus, those who were considered leaders and pace-setters were oriented toward peers to even greater degree. An additional aspect is the preference for peer group association in contrast to solitary activity. This proliferation of group endeavor, whether formal or loose, whether purposeful or seemingly random, has long been a hallmark of adolescence. In the Coleman (1961, pp. 12–13) research, more than 80 percent of high school students listed choices of preferred ways of spending leisure time which were distinct peer group activities ("organized outdoor sports": 22 percent of boys; "being with the group": 32.5 percent of girls).

Beyond the participation in peer group association rests a higher order value, the search for status, which is somewhat more compelling if not actually coercive. This indulgence in social rating and rank ordering, including the pursuit of group esteem or what is commonly referred to as "popularity," is often one of the most offensive traits of adolescents in adult eyes. On occasion, it appears as if the sense of fair play and democracy so carefully inculcated by middle-class teachers and parents during grammar school years is openly discarded in favor of evaluation based on trivial or superficial criteria. In part, each adolescent's foray into group activity is to expose himself to group judgment regarding his personal adequacy and competence; self-esteem is based on group esteem and the judgment may be painful or inflated. In the Coleman (1961, p. 30) study, high school students were offered choices as to how they would prefer to be remembered at school. The "most popular" item was selected by 25 percent of boys and 35 percent of girls. Equally revealing was the "athletic star" choice of 44 percent of boys and "leader in activities" of 36 percent of girls. These latter activities are usually considered to be direct routes to group esteem. Further manifestations of the drive for social status include the "dating and rating" practice wherein esteem is accorded depending on the prestige of the dating partner, the arranging of social groups ("cliques") into status hierarchies within the social system of the high school, and, in the absence of other data, granting status to an individual according to the reputation of his group (Hollingshead, 1949).

III. Subscription to a Variety of Practices and Beliefs:
The Willingness to Adopt These Customs in the Pursuit
of Affiliation and Esteem

This proposition recognizes that with the advent of culture come artifacts or customs, and that membership requires conformity in various signal aspects of behavior. These constitute a badge of admission and offer a common base for shared activity. Whether these particular adolescent customs are but extensions of present middle-class culture, or operate in the ambiguous or irrelevant interstices, or are truly in conflict with prevailing society is of lesser consequence for present purposes.

The most obvious feature is the adoption of various subcultural trademarks, including approved music, dance, idiosyncratic language, modes of personal adornment, and means of transportation. Since these expressions are particularly conspicuous, they serve not only to differentiate teenagers from others, but offer a visible means of identifying adolescents of kindred sentiment. Of all the characteristics of the youth culture, these alone reveal the greatest flux; although the mode of expression remains, the specific esteemed style may change several times in the course of a year. In the milieu of the junior high school, mastering the current dance step, becoming familiar with this week's favored cult music recordings, adopting the preferred slang or jargon, and dressing to meet the "fad" may possess as much urgency for students as the lessons of their teachers. Due to the rapid exchange of item, these aspects have been less well investigated in formal research. Studying the then current styles of popular music, Coleman (1961, p. 23) discovered near universal agreement as to its acceptance. With popular music, two forms of six accounted for 70 percent of the favored choice; "rock and roll" music (the form most commonly attributed to the youth culture) received 50 percent of the total choice. Dance, idiosyncratic language, dress, and hair style are less well investigated, but equally pervasive. Automobile ownership, however, has been subject to greater study. With one exception, twelfth grade boys owned cars at levels between 40 and 80 percent in all of Coleman's settings. The finding that socially prominent boys were more likely to own cars led Coleman to interpret access to an automobile as contributory to social status (Coleman, 1961, p. 128).

Aside from the attention to symbols, there are other beliefs and practices that have potential for conveying social and self-esteem. Among these are the valuing of athletic prowess for boys, physical beauty and participation in activities for girls, seeking risk, stimulation, action, and excitement, and giving at least lip service to a non-scholarly orientation. Of the several routes to status none is so clearly evident as athletics for the young male. Over the past half century, studies have consistently revealed athletic success to be most strongly linked with social acceptance. Coleman (1961, pp. 30, 194), for example, found that each of the members of the leading freshman clique played either football or basketball. Similarly, almost 50 percent of high school boys would prefer to be remembered as "athletic star" in preference to "brilliant student" or "most popular," and the desire to be a nationally famous athlete led a field of four options. For girls, the analogous attribute appears to be a cluster of qualities best labeled as "glamor" and "personality," which includes physical beauty, a general gregarious quality, and participation in activities. It is not surprising, then, for Coleman (1961, p. 48) to note that the female role most equivalent to athletic star was that of cheerleader. The willingness to undertake activities where there is risk, limited danger, stimulation, and action has often been attributed to youth. Many years ago Kuhlen and Lee (1943) determined that the trait, "willing to take a chance," significantly discriminated between popular and unpopular groups at the sixth, ninth, and twelfth grade levels. Much later, Coleman (1961, p. 124) found that 30 percent of boys and 24 percent of girls checked the item "stirring up a little excitement," as a trait relevant to acceptance within their group. Of note is the finding that socially prominent boys, those most often selected as "friends," and those most often named as someone to emulate, checked this item more often than did other boys.

The reliance upon scholastic achievement appears to relate negatively to group acceptance and runs counter to youth culture values. It may not be that the culture is hostile to academics, as much as it is that this route rules out other avenues that are esteemed. Sole reliance on study and scholastic achievement suggests the "grind," "brain," or "teacher's pet," stereotypes that effectively eliminate the valued athletic orientation for boys, and the participation in recklessness, thrill-seeking, and risk-taking. This interpretation is less pessimistic but consistent with Coleman who viewed the youth culture as actively antischolastic. His evidence repetitively demonstrated the disadvantages of scholarly achievement as a single path to popularity, to acceptance by the opposite sex, and to being chosen for friendship (Coleman, 1961, pp. 31, 41, 148, 244, 245).

IV. Recognition of Alienation and Conflict between Generations

This general proposition contains a syndrome of attitudes that underscores the separation, mutual lack of understanding, antipathy between generations, and the consequent predisposition of adolescents to withdraw allegiance from adults and societal institutions. At its most benign level, it includes the tendency to view adults as dated, dull, bumbling, awkward, but generally well intentioned. For some 30 years the "Archie" comic strip has promoted the stereotype of adults as rather harmless, ineffectual, impotent creatures who must be indulged because society has delegated greater power to them. At a second level of intensity, there exists an overt and recognized hiatus between generations, emphasizing such qualities as alienation, separation, the inability to communicate, and the lack of bases for understanding. A further step is to acknowledge the previous, and to develop a mild, but critical attitude toward the practices of adults, with the occasional implication that these do not serve as models worthy of imitation. The projection mechanism may define yet another level in which adults are construed as possessing hostile and depreciating motives toward adolescents. With the acceptance of the foregoing, young people may take the final step of renunciation in which they deny allegiance, responsibility, and duty to parents and adults.

The separation between generations is likely a companion piece to the investment in peers. The same citations to research apply, and it would seem redundant to refer to any of the sizable fund of lay and scholarly opinion on this issue. It should be noted that neither the above proposition nor any of the previous intends to suggest that these motives are present in all adolescents. They are present to some degree among many, but their significance inheres in the fact that they are institutionalized within the belief system of the youth culture.

RATIONALES FOR THE EMERGENT YOUTH CULTURE

To date several distinct explanations have been proposed in attempting to account for the youth culture. As a group, the proposals tend to separate along disciplinary lines and to contain premises that are partially complete rather than mutually exclusive. Most commonly advanced is the "changing social fabric" theory which includes an amalgam of economic and sociological assumptions. In general, these social scientists have stressed industrialization and its manifold effects. As the nation has moved from a rural economy, the locus and unit of production have gradually transcended the home and farm. The wage earner and the means by which one is productive are no longer visible, and young people cannot learn to be productive at the knees of their parents. Nor can children themselves be productive, for there is little for them to produce; in effect, the United States has been the first nation to transform youth from "a family asset as labor to a family liability as student consumer (Denney, 1962). With long preparation being required in order to assume vocational responsibility, and with the adolescent being essentially useless and frequently unwanted on the labor market, an extended period of dependency occurs and learning has been institutionalized. Thus, secondary schools and colleges consist of many individuals of the same age, from whom society can demand little, and provide little in the way of concrete evidence regarding progress toward maturity. The conditions are set for an independent subculture with goals, tasks, and landmarks of its own.

He is "cut off" from the rest of society, forced inward upon his own age group, made to carry out his whole social life with others his own age. With his fellows he comes to constitute a small society, one that has most of its important interactions *within* itself, and maintains only a few threads of connection with the outside adult society. (Coleman, 1961, p. 3).

Although the above rationale is useful in accounting for age level separation, it does not contribute particularly to an understanding of youth culture content or its meaning and utility for adolescents.

A second set of interrelated theoretical postures is entitled the "threshold" and "market" explanations. They tend to cite such factors as population change, advances in technology, economic well being, and the mass media in accounting for the youth culture. These writers are apt to hold that the youth of today are little different from adolescents of distant generations, and that the youth culture construct is not particularly advantageous. The emergence of a so-called adolescent society is, in part, an artifact devolving from the rapid increase in sheer numbers of adolescents. A visibility threshold has been crossed to the extent that a homogenized subculture has emerged, with adolescents now being so conspicuous to one another that their conformity has produced a national and international uniformity. Census statistics are cited to the effect that the adolescent population is expanding at a rate four times as great as the national average with the median age of the total population having dropped to the late twenties. Advances in technology, particularly in the mass media, have enhanced the trend toward homogeneity. Radio, with the "disk jockey" who caters to adolescents, has produced a cult music and jargon. Television has permitted adolescent music and dance to take on national uniformity, while the microgroove record has allowed adolescents to carry their cult music beyond the television screen or radio set. The only necessary concomitant is the relative affluence that has occurred since World War II. Akin to the above reasoning is the "market" theory which holds that the youth culture is the product of the acumen and salesmanship of the advertising industry. There is no subculture other than that created by stimulated need, and the behavioristic assumption is made that any product can become a need if packaged and peddled to advantage.

Such contentions have limitations. The very need for conformity remains unexplained as does the apparent need for flux within the conformity pattern. Nor are the constant and repetitious youth culture themes accounted for, nor the failure of certain promotional schemes to succeed. The threshold and market theories suffer from severely simplified assumptions regarding the nature of human motivation.

Several volumes of social criticism have appeared in recent years which point up the plight of adolescents in an organized society. The notion of "alienation" is presented in which society appears to have conspired to deny the promise inherent in adolescence by rewarding mediocrity, conformity, and superficiality, thus preventing the decisive articulation of identity. The youth culture, then, is logically merely an age level manifestation of deteriorating adult values. To the extent that it is in conflict with adults, it may be commendable, but too often, even this reaction is inarticulate and misguided. In *The Vanishing Adolescent*, Friedenberg

(1959) held that adolescence is disappearing as a stage when identity can be achieved; the adolescent ". . . merely undergoes puberty and stimulates maturity." Goodman (1956) in *Growing Up Absurd* is also representative of the "alienation" point of view. He contended that society has ceased to make sense for the adolescent. Objective opportunity is lacking, and "security," that is, ". . . the sense of being needed for one's unique contribution . . ." (Goodman, 1956, p. 22) is not easily obtained.

It's hard to grow up when there isn't enough man's work. There is "nearly full employment," but there get to be fewer jobs that are necessary or unquestionably useful; that require energy and draw on some of one's best capabilities; and that can be done keeping one's honor and dignity. In explaining the widespread troubles of adolescents and young men, this simple objective factor is not much mentioned. (Goodman, 1956, p. 17).

The outcome has been a youth culture which provides a series of eccentric, substitute vehicles toward the achievement of independence and maturity. Goodman suggested by implication that in the proportion to which "objective opportunity" (meaningful activity, in terms of part-time jobs with utility, experiences relating to actual vocational preparation, and significant, engaging academic work) is lacking, adolescents are apt to demonstrate ". . . all the more fierce gang loyalty to their peers." (Goodman, 1956, p. 44).

Both Friedenberg and Goodman have made similar assumptions regarding human motivation. Youth, by being human, strives toward securing meaning, utility, integrity, competence, and the attainment of potential. Society, by virtue of bureaucracy, inefficiency, fear, and stupidity, has succeeded in thwarting youth. By dehumanization and violation of the conditions required for meaningful human existence, identity has been threatened. Goodman stated, "If there is nothing at all, when one does nothing, one is threatened by the question, *is* one nothing?" (Goodman, 1956, p. 41). The result is alienation both from one's own identity and from those individuals and institutions which create the debilitating conditions. The youth culture represents young people's turning in upon themselves in the futile search for meaning, escaping from that which is barren and offensive, and protesting against the absence of promise. Unfortunately, the youth culture seldom approximates much more than adolescent artifices mirroring similar adult practices.

A final position has come from individual psychology and is termed "psycho-social" or "ego process" theory. For these observers, the youth culture offers a sort of "way-station, . . . a temporary stop-over in which one can muster strength for the next harrowing stage on the trip." (Keniston, 1962, p. 161). It is a period of delay during which time a reorganization must be effected before adult responsibilities are assumed. The ego functions of the young person are assaulted from within and without: Full sexual drive is experienced, together with demands for controlled release, impulse management, object choice, and re-evaluation of moral commitments; physical and intellectual growth have occurred, thus requiring a re-assessment of body image and cognitive competency; with the maturation of capacity emerges the necessity to make value choices regarding what it is that is worthwhile; the environment, on viewing impending maturity of adolescents, exerts control on impulse and expects preparation for vocational achievement; by anticipating independence and judgment, the environment also serves as the principal agency which withholds the same, thus creating a task requiring delicate maneuvering on the part of the adolescent; subtly and gradually the capacity for interpersonal relationships of depth which are characterized by mutual and reciprocity has developed, and with it, the necessity to re-test and re-cast social relationships.

Such are the tasks of adolescence and it is the responsibility of the ego to secure synthesis and direction. Achieving "identity" is the term commonly applied to this process and, of several theorists, Erik Erikson has likely spoken most directly. The Eriksonian point of view has been summed as follows:

One of the main psychological functions of a sense of identity is to provide a sense of inner self-sameness and continuity, to bind together the past, the present, and the future into a coherent whole; and the first task of adolescence and early adulthood is the achievement of identity. The word "achieve" is crucial here, for identity is not simply given by the society in which the adolescent lives; in many cases and in varying degrees, he must make his own unique synthesis of the often incompatible models, identifications, and ideals offered by society. The more incompatible the components from which the sense of identity must be built and the more uncertain the future for which one attempts to achieve identity, the more difficult the task becomes. (Keniston, 1962, p. 162).

The peer group and the youth culture provide the medium for securing identity. Because the adolescent must separate himself from the identities of his parents, he must reject their dictates and, occasionally, their values; for "achieving" identity is an active process, rather than one of passive purchase of the achievements of others. Because society has been deficient in providing clear landmarks and in institutionalizing the steps to autonomy, the adolescent constitutes his own society. It is characteristically non-adult, but, at the same moment, encourages conformity and stereotypy. By demanding this concensus, it provides its own tasks and landmarks and offers a useful series of demarcations to identity. Although a different master, the authority of peers is constituted; this new master effects a break in the dependency on parents. The youth culture also has its lawful season and must be abandoned as autonomy and self-direction evolve.

Each of the dimensions of the youth culture can profitably be conceptualized within the psycho-social model. The tendency to idealize the teenage years is clearly the attempt to forestall adult responsibility during which time synthesis may be achieved. A modicum of irresponsibility of flirtation with risk is permitted in order to test possible alternatives. Age-mates are billed as authorities and reference groups, not necessarily in the interest of abandoning adult values, but as a means of breaking with adult authority. Conflict may be the possible consequence; however, it may also be initiated by adolescents who are seeking to document their progress to autonomy or to wrest control more abruptly (often in league with peers). The status-seeking and rank-ordering practices offer certainty as to position and self-definition during a time when these matters are ambiguous; in fact, the highly *social* nature of the youth culture permits it to serve as a constant mirror, feeding back data to the emergent and crystallizing identity. The subcultural symbols (language, music, dress) allow protective coloration and temporary comfort to prevent identity diffusion, but also constitute visible and definite tasks. Stereotyping is useful, for if an adolescent cannot remain the child of his parents and is as yet unable to proclaim independence, he can hide within the conventions of his peers. Finally, participation in risk, danger, and physical activity, while possibly serving as sublimations for genital drive, have the function of permitting young people to test the limits of their maturing physical bodies.

The four positions that have been set forth do not conflict as rival theories. In fact, they tend to be complementary. Sociological approaches have paid heed to industrialization, division of labor, the removal of the locus of production from the home and from the observation of the young, and the growth of institutionalized education with its body of age-equals. These foregoing events have created a need for new institutions or subcultures to assist in articulating the young to adult status. Psycho-social theory, using the concept of "identity," permits explanation of the psychological meanings of the youth culture, its manifestations, and its utility as a bridge from childhood to adulthood. For individual adolescents, it offers a viable account of growth or blockage. The market and threshold accounts are not first order, but contribute ancillary postulates. They do explain the homogeneity and uniformity but not the reason why it should occur. The alienation concept may offer a rationale to account for the present difficulties in attaining identity and may explain why so many recent encounters between adults and youth are laden with conflict and confrontation.

Since the Coleman study, a substantial research effort has been mounted in the attempt to add further clarity and definition. An attitude scale was derived from the several aspects of youth culture adherence previously described and was subsequently administered to thousands of young people in diverse settings (Burlingame, 1967). A number of propositions were tested to determine whether the existence of the youth culture and the nature of its content could be construed according to the identity construct. By way of example, if the youth culture were a "way-station," then adherence to it ought to vary according to age, and if it serves as a vehicle in the attainment of identity, then greater or lesser adherence should be related to the abundance or poverty of other forms of environmental provision. The findings were numerous and suggestive. Adherence to youth culture values occurred less among girls than boys of high school age. The peak of adherence for girls occurred in middle or late junior high school, while some boys were still increasing in their sensitivity to its demands through the tenth grade. However, once the apex was achieved, regardless of sex, the larger part of the high school experience was less subject to its waning effects. Secondary school teachers confirm these results; they routinely observe that conflict with authority and the corresponding idolatry of peers peaks at the thirteenth or fourteenth year for girls and a year or so later for boys. The environmental correlates of youth culture subscription pointed to a triad of associated conditions. Those who adhered to the culture to a greater extent had lesser academic success and more limited educational goals, participated less in adolescent social activities and received lesser social recognition, and came from families of lower socio-economic status. In specific terms, they had lower grade point averages, had lower intelligence quotients, were less likely to attend college, and studied less. Socially, they participated in fewer school and community activities both of task and social nature, spent less time in these activities, and were less likely to be designated for positions of task and social leadership by their peers. Economically, they were more likely to come from settings that contained large lower social class elements, and, in other settings, were likely to represent the more disadvantaged groups. The emergent picture of youth culture adherence very much implies deficit and compensation as causal factors.

It was no surprise to discover that adolescents of different ages and sex employed the youth culture's dimensions differently according to their own needs as well as to society's demands. Factor analytic study revealed that boys, regardless of age, emphasized the risk, action, and danger aspects. Mastery of the physical world and securing an estimate of masculine capacity appeared to be the need, with the youth culture as the means. Linked to this dimension was a preoccupttion with authority conflict. Interpretation remains open as to whether the authority issue is an artifact of indulgence in activities disapproved by adults or whether it represents a separate mastery struggle. Boys of all ages relegated group status and popularity concerns to a lesser role. For girls, the situation was reversed. Risk, danger, and physical mastery were insignificant, while social esteem presumed enormous importance. These findings are congruent with the Western cultural expectation that males secure mastery and dominance, particularly in the objective world as providers, while females become specialists in the interpersonal world which reaches culmination in the rearing of children. In an absolute sense, males seem to make greater use of the youth culture. It may not be that their needs are greater so much as that industrial society is impoverished in its opportunities for adolescent boys. If mastery of the physical world and securing an estimate of one's own competencies in relation to it are the vital concerns, it may be that there is no orderly transition to adult male productivity. It could be that boys remain captive in the American secondary school "preparing" for vocation instead of experiencing it, and that their needs are discharged in some counterfeit form into the argot of the youth culture.

Age-level trends support further generalizations regarding the meaning of the youth culture. Among younger adolescents of both sexes were indications of concern regarding impulse control. This finding is consistent with those personality theories which possess well-defined impulse systems and phase systems of growth and development. Early adolescence is often viewed as particularly difficult with the recrudescence of early impulse together with powerful new drives and cathexes. With the ego beset by drive and unable to balance control and drive, the youth culture provides an avenue of controlled expression and, at the same moment, raises new fears as to impulse mastery. Older adolescents arranged dimensions quite differently. Among both boys and girls, factors appeared which suggest personal independence, and, in one case, both adult and peer controls were rejected on the same dimension. The similarity with ego psychological principles is apparent: With maturity comes the installation of autonomy and self-direction in a personality free of compelling internal drive and environmental demand (in the form of dictates from either peers or elders) (Burlingame, 1967).

SUMMARY AND IMPLICATIONS

Youth culture features include the tendency to view the adolescent years as idyllic and developmentally distinct, the tendency to constitute age-mates as a reference group for decision making and for the generation of codes of behavior, and the tendency to come into conflict with the usual representatives of societal authority. Within these broad propensities exist a cluster of specific attributes, including the valuing of social status and participation in social ranking practices, the creation of idiosyncratic subcultural expressions for dance, music, dress, and language, the valuing of risk and stimulation, and the devaluing of academic achievement. Judgmentally, the above attitudes reflect a preference for the worldly and the material, the compromise with principle, immediate gratification, and conformity to the mass; these attitudes are taken in favor of deferred gratification, individual integrity and responsibility, social justice and equality, and worthwhile individual achievement. When studied empirically, youth culture adherence is found to be associated with a triad of conditions. Those who subscribed to greater extent had lesser academic success and more limited educational goals, participated less in adolescent social activities and received lesser social recognition, and came from families of lower socio-economic status.

How then may the youth culture be interpreted? Adolescence has been viewed as a time of identity crystallization and synthesis, with bodily growth and sexual drive occurring temporally with increased capacity for interpersonal relationships and increased demand from society for productivity and responsibility. To meet the demand from within and without, the young person must secure balance, direction, and purpose to the end that, at the close of adolescence, he views himself and is viewed by others as self-directing and autonomous. In part, these ego shifts and syntheses must transpire as the young adolescent wrests or takes responsibility for his activities from conspicuous adults and places it under the auspices of his developing ego. Such a process appears to require an additional step—that of constituting the society of his peers as a mediating agent, because he seems less able to acquire the ready-made identities of his parents and not yet able to constitute his own. The youth culture contains elements and fictions that meet the needs of transition. A group ego encourages conformity and provides protective coloration, thus preserving the adolescent ego from risk and extension. Social rating and social exposure offer an arena for role playing and a mirror for self-evaluation. Indulgence in risk-taking and the experimentation with dangerous or forbidden activity allows for needed experience in knowing the limits of newly developed capacity. Conflict with authority serves the whole by providing feedback as to progress toward autonomy and by securing the needed freedom to experiment. As synthesis is achieved, the youth culture and the society of peers is abandoned in favor of the responsibility for production and reproduction.

Such a process cannot be examined without reference to available avenues within the environment that have utility in promoting adolescent ego synthesis. A stable and respectable definition of self seems dependent upon provision within the life space: supportive family relationships, achievement, and social esteem from one's contemporaries. As these are available, the transition is facilitated and the use of the youth culture as an "ego bridge" is decreased. However, when these conditions are absent, the culture of age-mates may remain as the only alternative. The evidence is relatively conclusive. As adolescents have lesser aptitude, lesser achievement, lesser social esteem, lesser social contact, and lesser economic means, they over-value the youth culture. In short, it is those who are on the perimeter observing and not receiving who believe. Excessive adherence is related to deprivation. In psychodynamic terms, this interpretation is not without precedent. The exaggerated and distorted usage of the youth culture by some adolescents seems to reflect their own deflated and damaged ego capacities. A history of coercive or debilitating conditions coupled with a poverty of supportive feedback from the environment, which is met at adolescence by massive internal drive and external demand, produces disorganization. The behavior of this adolescent is identical to those who respond to the extremes of youth cultism; behavior is characterized by the need for immediate gratification and impulsive outbreak; proving and testing behavior are endless since self-perception is rooted in defeat; conflict with authority serves the twin needs to "get even" and to "get free."

Based on the assumption that the youth culture is a useful growth medium and, in those cases of extreme reliance, the result of deficit conditions, the following implications are suggested. Adolescence seems less a time for the inculcation of society's ways and more a time for the exploration of individual meaning and motivation. Children, in most strata of society, are well aware of what behaviors constitute the "right" and the "wrong" or the "good" and the "bad." By rejecting the earlier means of value transmission (parents and adults) in favor of peers, adolescents are not so much rejecting adult values as they are transferring authority into their own ego systems. This transference calls not for restriction, re-training, or scare and threat tactics, but for freedom and support for investigation. For most adolescents, some temporary adherence to the youth culture seems inevitable and useful for growth. Excessive or prolonged addiction to the society of teenage equals is a diagnostic sign of growth blockage, conflict, or fixation as surely as the signs that can occur at other stages in the life cycle. Further, provisions should be made for the existence of the youth culture, knowing that it will be abandoned with growth. This suggests a measure of privacy for adolescents and the separation of adult and adolescent recreation. A fair proportion of the conflict between generations is generated by "rubbing elbows" as each lives out his own needs. It suggests a policy of toleration for such recreational features as adolescent night clubs, dance halls, and coffee houses. In educational institutions and social agencies the tendency for adolescents to rank and rate should be recognized. Adults should not, in the name of democracy or bad publicity, drive social groups underground. The course of wisdom would be to offer sensitive adult leadership to high school fraternities and sororities, for example, which could curb excesses and remove the attractiveness of a forbidden activity. Conflict with authority appears to be a necessary ingredient for some adolescents and particularly for young males. Conflict in the guise of peer group activity may serve in the articulation of identity by breaking the dependency bond with parents and parent surrogates. All things considered, however, the provision for individual success and self-esteem remain the best guarantees, not against the development of a youth culture, but for the rapid attainment of identity and purpose.

REFERENCES

Burlingame, William V.   An investigation of the correlates of adherence to the adolescent peer culture. Unpublished Doctoral Dissertation, University of Washington, Seattle, 1967.
Coleman, James S.   *The Adolescent Society*. Glencoe, Ill.: The Free Press, 1961.
Denney, Reuel.   American youth today: a bigger cast, a wider screen. *Daedalus*, 1962, **91**, 124–144.
Friedenberg, Edgar Z.   *The Vanishing Adolescent*. New York: Dell, 1959.
Goodman, Paul.   *Growing Up Absurd*. New York: Alfred A. Knopf, 1956.
Goodman, Paul.   A social critic on "moral youth in an immoral society." *The Young Americans*. New York: *Time*, 1966, 18–19.
Hollingshead, August B.   *Elmtown's Youth*. New York: John Wiley, 1949.
Keniston, Kenneth.   Social change and youth in America. *Daedalus*, 1962, **91**, 161.
Kuhlen, Raymond G., and Lee, Beatrice J.   Personality characteristics and social acceptability in adolescence. *Journal of Educational Psychology*, 1943, **34**, 321–340.
Parsons, Talcott.   Age and sex in the social structure of the United States. In Herman D. Stein and Richard A. Cloward (Eds.) *Social Perspectives on Behavior*. Glencoe, Ill.: The Free Press, 1958, 193.
Time Magazine, August 15, 1969, p. 57.

part two

Some Contemporary Issues
in Socialization
and Development
during Adolescence

2.1 Orientation

A most significant and persisting set of issues imbedded in the affairs of any society concerns education. This set of issues demands attention to many facets of education, including goals, methods, and content. It is concern for educational issues that underlies the following paper by the distinguished anthropologist, George D. Spindler. Spindler begins his stimulating treatise with a discussion of puberty rites practiced in certain exotic cultures. This discussion emphasizes the apparent psychological functions of such initiatory rites. These various functions are subsumed by what Spindler terms *cultural compression*, that is, an intensified program of experiences which clarify for youth the transition from childhood to adulthood and formally ascribe adult status for the initiates. Spindler contends that no such clarification and formal recognition occurs in this society. He believes that due to this lack, adolescents establish unique "formal rites" in order to clarify for themselves their status and collective identity. Thus, Spindler supports the concept of a bonafide adolescent society in United States culture. The reader is alerted to the evidence utilized by Spindler to support his thesis. This evidence includes the existence of an adolescent speech community and ritualized behavioral patterns which distinguish the adolescent from the child he was and the adult with whom he is in conflict.

Spindler continues by suggesting that society should devise ways to incorporate teenagers into the mainstream of society. He further suggests that the closest thing to a fully institutionalized medium for this purpose currently in existence is the high school. The problem as Spindler sees it, however, is that the high school does not serve capably the functions for which it has been established. Thus, Spindler casts himself in the role of a critic of secondary education and calls for a vigorous re-examination of the character of education for adolescents. Concrete proposals for solving the problem as defined by Spindler are not included in this paper. Perhaps the reader will be motivated to offer some creative suggestions in this regard.

RECOMMENDED READINGS

Bower, Eli M., and Hollister, William G. *Behavioral Science Frontiers in Education.* New York: John Wiley, 1967.

Boyle, Richard P. The effect of the high school on students' aspirations. *American Journal of Sociology,* 1966, **71,** 628–639.

Brown, Judith K. A cross-cultural study of female initiation rites. *American Anthropologist,* 1963, **65,** 837–853.

Cohen, Yehudi A. *Transition from Childhood to Adolescence.* Chicago: Aldine, 1964.

Klausmeier, Herbert J. Balance in high school education. *Teachers College Record,* 1965, **67,** 18–25.

Schwartz, Gary, and Merten, Don. The language of adolescence: an anthropological approach to the youth culture. *The American Journal of Sociology,* 1967, **72,** 453–468.

Simonsen, Solomon. A new curriculum for teenagers. *Clearing House,* 1965, **40,** 13–19.

Young, Frank W. The function of male initiation ceremonies: a cross-cultural test of an alternative hypothesis. *American Journal of Sociology,* 1962, **67,** 379–391.

2.1   The Education of Adolescents: An Anthropological Perspective

George D. Spindler, STANFORD UNIVERSITY

The most intensive period of education occurs in many cultures at or about the time of puberty. I am going to talk about what happens at the time of puberty in other cultures and in ours. I will look at the crises and tasks of adolescence from the viewpoint of ego and from the viewpoint of society. I will examine the American high school as a four-year initiation, or puberty rite, and then look at college as a related experience.

Let me introduce the subject by reading a short section from a paper written by a colleague who studied with the Tiwi of north Australia (Hart, 1963):

Among the Tiwi of north Australia one can see the traumatic nature of the initiation period in very clear form and part of the trauma lies in the sudden switch of personnel with whom the youth has to associate. A boy reaches 13 or 14 or so and the physiological signs of puberty begin to appear. Nothing happens possibly for many months and then suddenly one day toward evening when the people are gathering around their campfires for the main meal of the day after coming in from their day's hunting and food gathering a group of 3 or 4 heavily armed and taciturn strangers appear in camp. In full war regalia they walk in silence to the camp of the boy and say curtly to the household, we have come for so and so. Immediately pandemonium breaks loose. The mother and the rest of the old women begin to howl and wail. The father rushes for his spears. The boy himself, panic stricken, tries to hide. The younger children begin to cry and the household dogs begin to bark. It is all terribly similar to the reaction which is provoked by the arrival of police at an American home to pick up a juvenile delinquent. This similarity extends to the behavior of the neighbors, these carefully restrained from identifying with either the strangers or with the stricken household. They watch curiously the goings on but make no move that can be identified as supporting either side. This is more particularly notable in view of the fact that the strangers are strangers to all of them. That is, they are men from outside the encampment, or outside the band, who under ordinary circumstances would be greeted with a shower of spears, but not under these circumstances. In fact, when we know our way around this culture we realize that the arrival of the strangers is not as unexpected as it appears. The father of the boy and other adult men of the camp not only knew they were coming, but had agreed on a suitable day for them

A lecture given at the meeting of the California Association of School Psychologists and Psychometrists, Disneyland Hotel, March 19, 1964 (edited from tape). Reproduced by permission of Professor Spindler.

to come. The father's rush for his spears to protect his son and preserve the sanctity of his household is make-believe, and if he puts on too good an act, the senior men will intervene and restrain him from interfering with the purpose of the strangers. With the father immobilized, the child clings to the mother, but the inexorable strangers soon tear him literally from his mother's arms and from the bosom of his bereaved family and still as grimly as they come, bear him off again into the night. No society could symbolize more dramatically that initiation necessitates the forceable taking away of the boy from the bosom of his family, his village, his neighbors, his intimates, and his friends.

What Hart has described makes clear one aspect of the period of education at adolescence that is, though not universal, widespread among the world's cultures. And that aspect is the forceable, and from our point of view, traumatic separation of the individual from everything that he has known and held dear up to that time. Another aspect—atmosphere— is important for the thesis as I will try to develop. I will quote further from his description of Tiwi initiation to show you what I mean (Hart, 1963, p. 410).

So far his life has been easy, now it is hard. Up to now he has never necessarily experienced any great pain. In the initiation period in many tribes, pain, sometimes horrible intense pain, is an obligatory feature. The boy of 12 or 13 used to noisy, boisterous, irresponsible play is expected and required to sit still for hours and days at a time saying nothing whatsoever, but concentrating upon and endeavoring to understand long intricate instructions and lectures given to him by his hostile and forbidding preceptors—who are of course the people who carried him away from camp in the first place, the strangers. Life has become suddenly real and earnest and the initiate is required literally to put away the things of a child and even the demeanor. The number of taboos and unnatural behaviors enjoined upon the initiate is endless. He mustn't speak unless he is spoken to, he must eat only certain foods, and often only in certain ways at certain fixed times and in certain fixed positions. All contact with females, even speech with them, is rigidly forbidden and this includes mothers and sisters. He cannot even scratch his head with his own hand, but must use a long stick, and so on through a long catalog of special unnatural but obligatory behaviors covering every daily activity and every hour of the day and night. And during this time he doesn't go home on a 48 hour pass, but remains secluded in the bush, literally a prisoner of his preceptors months or even for years at a time. If he is allowed home on rare intervals he carries his taboos with him. Nothing more astonished me in Australia than to see some youth whom I'd known the year before as a noisy, brash, boisterous 13-year-old sitting the following year after his initiation had begun in the midst of his family with downcast head and subdued air, not daring even to smile, still less to speak. He was home on leave, but he might just as well have stayed in camp for all that his freedom did for him.

I must make it clear that the description that I have just read of the initiation proceedings among the Tiwi is a relatively extreme case, but equally clear that most societies do pay special attention to the adolescent period. Here is another example. Among the Ojibwa and the Menomini that my wife and I have worked with, the culture, the character of which has been maintained to some extent into the present among a small minority of "conservatives." In this society, instead of strange and hostile strangers coming to get the youngster, he was asked each morning after he had reached about 10 years of age, "Will you have bread or charcoal?" If he chose bread, this meant that he was not ready to begin the puberty rite. If he chose charcoal his face was marked with it and the initiation period began. He would be taken out to the brush some distance from any human habitation and left alone in a rude shelter. He would have no food or water and would be expected to stay until such time as he had what we would call a vision. This might take 24 hours if he were really lucky, it might take a week, it might take 2 weeks.

The nature of vision and dream experience is so totally different in a culture of this kind that it is very difficult for us to conceive of the nature or meaning of that experience. Perhaps I can give you some suggestion as to the significance of dreaming and of vision experience in this culture by saying that during the 7 summer seasons we worked with Menomini we never recorded any significant decision made by an individual excepting on the basis of a dream.[1] Furthermore, we never once saw an innovation in song, music, dance, ritual, or decorative arts, excepting as it was given to an individual through a dream experience.

The relationship of the individual to his unconscious and the relationship of the unconscious to the culture is very different among the Menomini than among ourselves. We think of inspiration as something produced through one's thinking and study. To them inspiration can come only from being passive, by relaxing and letting the message come to one from the outside forces. This is how it is with the boy out in the bush, lonely, hungry, cold, and more than just a little scared. Sometime during his time out there a creature, sometimes in human form, sometimes in animal form, comes to him and then takes him on a long journey. This supernatural figure instructs him about the legends and origins of the tribe, the social organization and the nature of the major rituals. The initiate returns from his journey with a tremendous amount of material. Now this is very strange. The boy goes out ignorant, he comes back instructed. Who teaches him? The creature, the vision, the experience

[1] This statement applies only to the small, tradition-oriented enclave of Menomini. The majority of Menomini have become acculturated. (See Spindler, 1955.)

that he has had? Apparently latent learning is triggered. Most of what
he has learned and comes back knowing cannot be learned overtly by a
pre-adolescent individual, because all of these things carry sacred connotations and are too dangerous for a child. Nevertheless he does learn these
forbidden things by observation and indirect participation. He comes
back with a fairly incoherent version of this culture to be sure, but then
he goes to a medicine man to get this all straightened out. The old man
will talk to him about his experiences, what spirit came to him, where
did it take him, what did it tell him, what songs did he learn, and all the
rest of it. The boy explains all of this, and of course, there are many incoherent and jumbled parts of the learning because the latent learning,
so called, has not been perfect, but the medicine man does straighten it
out for him, and at the conclusion of this period of time the individual
has become a member of society. The vision experience that one has
determines what kind of an individual he can become. If one dreams of
the moon, he will either go insane some time in the middle years of life
or commit a murder. If one dreams of the bundle carrier, a mythological
figure that carries a bundle around on his back and searches aimlessly
and constantly throughout the world for something unknown, then one
is bound like this bundle carrier to be a wanderer, an unsatisfied person.

I think I've said enough to indicate that societies have different ways of
handling the adolescent period, but that most societies pay a considerable
amount of attention to it. In the more extreme cases an experience is
provided that constitutes a sharp break with formerly established routines
and roles, and an intensified period of education. I have used the term
"cultural compression" to describe this period (Spindler, 1963). The
individual is "compressed" into the cultural mold decisively and finally
at this period of time in most human cultures. It may be that the compression occurs as a climax to a more or less gradual series of educational
experiences in terms of intensity and difficulty, or it may be as in the case
of the Tiwi that there is an abrupt transformation at this time. In any
event, most initiatory rites are characterized by isolation and separation
from familiar things and people and emphasize the dramatic aspects of
information giving and getting. The atmosphere is sacred. Strangers are
used as instructors rather than familiar friendly people. Rigid rules for
the conduct of the individual and for the conduct of the educational
experience as a whole are maintained.

What I have described to you is the Menomini and the Tiwi equivalent
of high school in our culture. Most broadly we can simply say that virtually no culture in the world leaves the internalization and acceptance
of the basic values of the culture up to chance. Almost all of them are
particularly concerned with the incorporation of the young males into

the framework of adult male responsibility and less concerned about the incorporation of females into adult female responsibility. This is probably because in no culture do women assume the major public and institutionalized roles. Males take responsibility for these roles in most cultures, and it is this set of responsibilities that the initiatory rites center upon.

Furthermore, the initiation rites resolve tensions because they separate the child from the family at the period of time when the child is most likely to challenge adult authority. The child, and most particularly the male child, increases in power and ability so dramatically during adolescence that parents are no longer able to cope with them very effectively, not only in our society, but in others. The tension is reduced by removing the child from the family so there is no conflict between the adolescent and the parent, and no threat to adult authority. The adolescent is regarded in many societies as a potential threat to society. The initiation rites make it so tough for them that the initiate's attitude becomes, "Well, you can't lick them, so let's join them." He learns then what it means to become a man, responsible to the state, responsible to other men, within whatever framework of values is operating in his culture.

Now I would like to talk about the adolescent in our culture. I think the situation is a little different for our adolescents. There are many books on adolescence, and each book contradicts every other book, partly because each book is written either on the basis of personal experience or on the basis of examination of one particular group, and there are many different kinds of adolescents just as there are many different kinds of adults in American society. We cannot expect the adolescent subgroup to be any less heterogeneous than the adult mix from which adolescents come. Nevertheless, there are certain tendencies that appear. One of the tendencies that is quite marked is the devlopment of an adolescent speech community. There is no single speech community for all adolescents, of course, although there is a surprising degree of commonality in the basic vocabulary. But the argot of the American adolescent is extensive and constitutes a separate speech community—one which has very distinctive features in the use of words and which is very creative; and it changes rapidly. One of my fellow anthropologists, Henry Angelino (1956), compiled an argot containing some 3000 words. It is now completely outmoded. More recently a young woman named Dilys Jones (Jones, 1963) who looks young enough to get around in the high schools and pose as a high school student gave a very interesting analysis of the private language of Bay area teenagers. She made it clear that there was not only an extensive adolescent vocabulary but that this vocabulary tends to be different in different schools, so we have proliferation of speech communities.

The existence of a speech community is much more significant than the mere fact that a certain group of individuals use a different set of words than another group. Language is a set of symbols that stands for everything in experience. People in different speech communities express certain differences in their values, and even in their way of thinking. Enough of that for the moment. I simply want to establish that in one of the most obvious aspects of culture, teenagers are different than adults. Teenagers tend to establish a separate framework of communication in our society.

Teenage subcultural patterning in our society runs the gamut from harmless deviation in speech to serious offenses against the law and against basic morality. Teenage culture also includes patterning for behaviors that are not quite illegal, but are not quite legal either, and are threatening to adults and threatening to the stability and the peace of the community. One particular complex of behaviors that anthropologists would regard as culturally patterned, in fact, constituting a subculture in itself, is what I have come to call the car cult.[2]

The car cult is extremely important in California. I am not talking here about every adolescent that drives a car to and from high school. I am referring to a group that constitutes a systematic kind of deviation from the acceptable norms of behavior for teenagers as a whole. In some communities or social class sectors the car-cult group will constitute a majority, in others a minority. We have had some students doing studies on the use of cars and the complex behaviors centering upon them characteristic of teenagers in the high schools in the Bay area, and we find that the car-cult group has a definite culture of its own. For instance, one of the important communication devices is where the girl sits in relationship to the boy as the couple drives about from one drive-in to another or back and forth down a street where they can be seen. A girl who is sitting against the door away from the boy is either a girl whom the boy has known for a long time or who is mad at him. A girl who is sitting draped over the boy (and the boy does not usually put his arm around the girl) so that she is really a part of him, is not likely to be really going steady with the boy. This is a situation where the girl is trying to give the boy a build-up—not necessarily in relationship to her so much, but in relationship to the perception others have of him. The whole act is a part of the build-up that she is giving him for an outside audience. Other teenagers note who is in the car, what car, who is driving, what direction they are headed, and who is doing what in the car.

There are many other patterns of behavior associated with the car-cult

[2] I am indebted to Mrs. Jack Peltz for her interesting observations on car-cult behavior.

group. A suburban street that is not fully developed and has a little cul-de-sac at one end will be surrounded by cars, the lights will be turned on, the radios turned up and a street dance held. This in itself is harmless enough. But the car-cult culture goes further. Hatred of police, hatred of authority, being home as little as possible, are also part of the patterning, at least for the really "in" members. Special mannerisms of avoidance are developed—to avoid betrayal to adults of what is going on among teenagers.

The situation of the adolescent in our culture is dramatically different than the situation of the adolescent in the other cultures that I have described. The major difference is that our adolescent is providing his own rite of passage—his own initiation rite—and in other societies adults are providing it. This has implications that move us in many directions and I am really frustrated because I would like to take up all of them. For instance, one might ask, what kind of a society does this kind of self-created adolescent initiation period function most effectively in? I would be inclined to say that it is a culture that is in rapid and continuous change, because each generation manufactures its own culture. Although each generation comes back to a position roughly resembling the adjustment and values of the adult generation before it, still the fact that the transitional period has been marked by a self-invented culture moves the whole society along in unanticipated directions. There is no way in this kind of system for society in its traditional form to perpetuate itself. Each new generation recreates the culture.[3] It also means that in some ways no basic problems can be solved, because new problems are created as soon as the old ones are recognized. Our culture is maintained by change, by transformation, because continuous change is its most important and vital characteristic. Perhaps, then, the absence of compressive initiation rites, and the subcultural deviation of the adolescent group fits our situation. The large groups of disenchanted teenagers today suggest, however, that our culture is threatened with rejection and destruction, not reconstitution. I believe we have a serious problem on our hands. We must devise ways to incorporate teenagers into society, not alienate them. So I turn to the major institutions that are responsible for the education of adolescents in our society.

In the short time I have left I want to talk about the high school as an extended puberty rite. I think we can say that irrespective of the specific form of education during adolescence in different cultures there

[3] This statement is only relatively true. Of course no culture can be recreated with each generation and the degree of continuity outweighs the degree of change.

are certain basic kinds of functions, tasks, or crises that must be in some way passed through. From the viewpoint of ego, I would say that the important tasks are self-definition, securing independence, securing recognition, and seeking models for behavior. From the viewpoint of society, the most important tasks are co-opting the adolescent into the structure of adult responsibility and social control, transmitting the core values of the culture, and transmitting cultural content that is probably not learnable within the family. Education during adolescence must give recognition to the transition to adult status and must communicate to adolescents the nature of adult responsibility and authority. The rituals I have described for esoteric culture like the Menomini and Tiwi do perform these functions. Does our high school perform them?

Having given you the criteria, I think that you can examine the high school and see for yourself that generally speaking, it does not, and there are all sorts of reasons why it does not. From the viewpoint of those functions that are important from ego's viewpoint the high school is only partially successful. The school peer group itself creates such strong conformative pressure upon the individual within the framework of the adolescent subculture that it is impossible for the individual adolescent to develop a strong sense of self-definition. Or apply another criterion— does the adolescent achieve independence? Only very slightly so. Since the high school is a day school there is little real independence from home or family possible. Securing recognition? The high school can provide some social recognition, but most of the social recognition that occurs that is most meaningful within the framework of the peer group, is non-functional in terms of adult values and roles. Academic recognition helps because this is a prerequisite for advancement to middle-class status, but how about those who cannot achieve academically? Given a normal distribution of intelligence there is always a sizeable minority who cannot.

From the viewpoint of society, the American high school is probably even less effective than it is from ego's viewpoint. With respect to co-opting the adolescent into the structure of control and responsibility in our society, the high school can do very little because all of our laws mediate against giving any real responsibility to anyone under 21. With respect to transmitting values, the citizenship programs and the social studies programs are attempts at transmitting values, particularly those values that are concerned with the maintenance of our culture, but they are largely ineffective. They are so removed from social, political, economic reality and they are so limited in most communities by community pressure that they cannot possibly be effective.

With respect to providing models there is a very interesting problem.

What kinds of models does the high school provide for the youngsters? We have something very interesting in our educational system that no other culture has ever done. We have not assigned the education of children to those people that the children are going to become like as adults —in terms of their major adult roles. It is remarkable that we have institutionalized the role of teacher in such a way that the teacher by definition is one who does not participate in the mainstream of our society. In the most direct occupational model sense, only the boy or girl who is going to become a teacher finds a model, and these are a very small minority. Significant role models are pretty much unavailable to high school youngsters. The difficulty is compounded by the fact that role models are frequently not provided in the family either—particularly for boys. Consequently a child in our society can very well grow up, and in fact, I think the majority do grow up without ever really having close identifying relationships with any real model.

With respect to the fourth function—transmitting culture content— probably the high school does relatively well here, but the academic package selection is extremely selective and tends to be non-functional for many adolescents. Actually it is functional in most high schools only for those children who go on to college. Again the academic pressure is very intense and given the normal distribution of abilities many youngsters cannot achieve within the framework of the academic criteria.

Lastly, there is in the American high school no formal, no public recognition, of transition to adult status and adult responsibility. The high school is virtually a total failure at this point. The high school is either considered a step to college, or the end, for many children, of an unwanted and basically alienating experience.

It seems to me that the functions that I have described for the initiation period of other cultures are carried out in our society more effectively by colleges and universities than by high schools. In the first place, in the college there is separation from home and community. At least this is true with the exception of the junior colleges and I think perhaps for that reason the junior colleges will never fill their full function as culture-maintaining institutions in our society—adolescents should leave home to go to college. There is also in the college situation a wider range of channels to recognition and self-definition. There is some reduction of group conformity pressure. There are many alternatives provided in the form of groups and even in the form of models, although the models, like the culture transmitted in college by the faculty, suffer from lack of relevance in many critical ways. There is also a definite attempt made in the college to co-opt the individual into the control structure of society through preparation for an occupational role and particularly in the more responsible professional and semi-professional sectors. And there is a less constricted and a more critical attempt (than in the high school) to transmit the basic cultural values of our society in the liberal arts and general studies programs of the 4-year college. However ineffective they may be, they are not limited, so terribly limited, by local community pressure. Lastly the college can provide formal recognition for the transition to adulthood. The college diploma is the only really meaningful symbol of this transition that we have in our society, but even this symbol becomes less meaningful each June. It is really regrettable, in fact tragic, that college in our society is not a universal experience, and that non-college youth are effectively isolated from the central values of our culture. Frequently the young people who do not enter college are already alienated from society due to inadequacies in family culture or due to economic disadvantage. Their alienation from society is reinforced by not going to college. This is, of course, particularly true of ethnic minorities in American society.

I will conclude by saying that the discussion emphasizes the extreme need for a significant culture-transmitting and socializing institution at the high school level. The present high school is not adequate to the functional demands of adolescent education. Indeed, the same may be said of our colleges and universities, although they seem to serve better the purposes of an institution rite than do the high schools. The inadequacies of these institutions as cultural mechanisms certainly make them objects for scrutiny and call for a very vigorous reconsideration of the functions, purposes, and character of adolescent education in the United States.

REFERENCES

Angelino, Henry. *The Argot of the American Adolescent*, Preliminary Issue, Mimeograph. Norman, Oklahoma, 1956.

Hart, C. W. M. Contrasts between prepubertal and postpubertal education. In G. Spindler (Ed.) *Education and Culture: Anthropological Approaches.* New York: Holt, Rinehart and Winston, 1963.

Jones, Dilys. The astonishing private language of the Bay area teenagers, People. *The California Weekly, San Francisco Examiner*, October 27, 1963.

Spindler, George D. *Menomini Acculturation*, Vol. 5, Culture and Society Series, U. C. L. A., 1955.

Spindler, George D. The transmission of American culture. In G. Spindler (Ed.) *Education and Culture: Anthropological Approaches.* New York: Holt, Rinehart and Winston, 1963.

2.2 *Orientation*

Among the most complex and controversial issues faced by the public schools in our society is sex education. The most basic issue is, of course, whether schools should attempt to have sex education at all. Once an affirmative judgment is made one faces such issues as the content of a sex education program, when to introduce such content, whether a program should be coeducational, who should serve in what kind of instructional capacity, and what would constitute evidence of an "effective" sex education program. The following paper by David C. Payne represents an effort to provide the reader with background information useful to an examination of these and other issues provoked during discussions of sex education. In this regard it is important to note early Payne's accurate distinction between sex education and sexual education.

The substantive course of Payne's discussion begins with a consideration of the "indirect" socialization practices relative to sexuality which apparently pervade in most American homes. He also examines some misconceptions about sex which frequently result from such practices. Noteworthy is the indication that, in comparison to our knowledge of child-rearing practices in areas such as aggression training, independence training, and achievement training, psychologists know very little about sex and modesty training in this society. What data are available, however, indicate that many adults are unrealistic if they believe that sex information and sexual interest are the exclusive province of adolescents and adults. Clearly, much sex information is acquired by most children prior to pubescence although, unfortunately, it may be replete with inaccuracies and partial truths. Also significant is the nearly universal finding that the peer group (versus parents and teachers) is the major source of sex information for adolescents.

Features of the Payne paper specific to public school sex education include the rationale for such education, the problems and challenges faced by society in this area, the variety of programs currently underway, and the impact (or lack of impact) of such programs. The latter is a matter of particular interest to psychologists as is the sequential arrangement of educational experiences appropriate to the developmental characteristics of children and adolescents. The reader is encouraged to consider for himself purpose(s) or goal(s) of sex education. A fundamental issue in this connection is the degree of correspondence, if any, between increased knowledge about sex and changes in one's sexual behavior. For example, could we expect that "successful" sex education would be associated with lowered rates of illegitimate child birth, venereal disease, and sexual maladjustment? Such a concern would reflect pragmatic goals. Other goals, such as an increased capacity for feelings of spiritual union through heterosexual relations would be idealistic, although less tangible and easily determined. Finally, the reader may wish to integrate the insights of the Payne paper with those provided earlier by Wagner (Part I) enroute to a refinement of his own views on sexuality and sex education.

RECOMMENDED READINGS

Broderick, Carlfred B., and Bernard, Jessie (Eds.) *The Individual, Sex, and Society*. Baltimore: Johns Hopkins Press, 1969.

Handbook on Sex Instruction in Swedish Schools. Halsingbord, Sweden: Royal Board of Education in Sweden, 1964.

Kirkendall, Lester A., and Miles, Greg J. Sex education research. *Review of Educational Research*, 1968, **38**, 528–544.

Schur, Edwin M. (Ed.) *The Family and the Sexual Revolution*. Bloomington, Indiana: Indiana University Press, 1964.

2.2   Sex Education and the Sexual Education of Adolescents

David C. Payne, UNIVERSITY OF CONNECTICUT

INTRODUCTION

The purposes of this article are twofold. The first is to provide a descriptive account of how and what adolescents learn about sex. The second is to use the understanding that can be gained from such an account as a framework for developing guidelines for sex education programs at the secondary school level.

The reader should understand that the statement of these goals is much easier than their accomplishment since research in the area of human sexuality has focused primarily on adult and college student sexual behavior and little descriptive data are available on the topics of adolescent sexual behavior or adolescent sexual knowledge in the United States. At some time in the future the sexual education of adolescents may have

---

An original paper prepared especially for this volume.

been studied to the point where a straightforward descriptive account will be a simple matter. Until that time, however, our understanding of the overall process will necessarily be limited to whatever bits and pieces of information are available.

THE SOCIALIZATION OF SEX AND SEX EDUCATION

Human sexuality consists of a complex matrix of concepts, information, attitudes, emotions, and behaviors. Since sexuality has been found to assume widely different forms from culture to culture, it can be taken for granted that learning plays an extremely important role in its development. As a result, a variety of forms of sexual education are necessary for the development of culturally appropriate sexual behaviors. In every culture each individual must learn to identify what is and what is not sexual, how to be sexual, when to be sexual, and with whom to be sexual.

It is possible to distinguish between "sex education" in terms of learning about sex, and "sexual education" in terms of learning how to be sexual. It is also possible to make some educated guesses concerning some general relationships between these two areas. Since human sexuality has been found to occur at a very early age (Berelson & Steiner, 1964, p. 299) and is capable of persisting until a very late age (Masters & Johnson, 1966, p. 270), sexual knowledge in the individual probably progresses through several developmental stages in a manner similar to the development of sexual behavior. Thus, an understanding of sex education in adolescence can be enhanced by an understanding of the process in children. Furthermore, the existence of wide cultural and subcultural differences in the area of sexual behavior suggests the likelihood of considerable variability in the content and concepts that individuals use to view and understand sexuality.

THE SEXUAL EDUCATION OF CHILDREN

Sex education in childhood can be expected to have important implications for adolescents insofar as adolescents will naturally view educational efforts in this area in the context of their own past experiences. Although the literature is hardly replete with studies of sexuality during childhood, it is possible to sketch a tentative outline of the process of sexual learning during this period of life.

In their study of *Patterns of Child Rearing*, Sears, Maccoby, and Levin (1957) pointed out that mothers exert efforts to control and shape the sexuality of young children just as they do in other areas of behavior (feeding, toilet-training, and aggression). In contrast to the techniques used in these other areas, however, maternal controls in the area of sexuality emphasize inhibition rather than substitute gratification and also tend to be indirect rather than direct (p. 185). This emphasis on indirect socialization methods is most noticeable in the mothers' tendency to avoid the use of labels in connection with sex training (p. 189). Although mothers are not excessively punitive in the area of sexual controls, they do attempt to interfere with and inhibit masturbation (p. 199). Although there are considerable differences in the manner in which mothers deal with the existence of sex play with other children, most feel it should not be allowed (p. 206).

Gagnon (1965) has suggested that this combination of inhibitory parental handling techniques (in which sexual behaviors are discouraged) and indirect socialization procedures (in which sexual behaviors or topics are not given explicit or direct labels) has broad implications for sexual learning. In the first place, Gagnon suggests that many behaviors and topics that are negatively labeled in childhood never really get revised. Second, feelings that relate to one aspect of sexuality may "spill over" into other sexual areas because the child has no explicit cognitive structure in which to place sexual phenomena.

As an illustration of this indirect socialization process in the area of sexuality, this author frequently conducts the following poll in his college classes. Students are first asked whether they believe Santa Claus to be an actual person who visits every house on Christmas eve. (So far, 100 percent have stated they do not believe this.) Then students are asked whether they feel they would be able to have an enjoyable sexual relationship with their brothers or sisters. (So far, 100 percent have stated they would not.) These questions are followed with the question of whether students can remember *when* they learned that Santa Claus was not a real person (about 50 percent can remember) and *when* they learned that incest was not culturally acceptable (about 1 or 2 percent can remember). In essence, then, although college students have learned with equal effectiveness both that Santa Claus is not real and incest is not acceptable, 50 percent can remember learning the former but almost none can remember learning the latter.

Although it is frequently emphasized that much of the information made available to children in the area of sexuality is erroneous or fable-like (babies under rosebushes, babies ordered from doctors, or babies brought by storks), this is also true of information in non-sexual areas. The major point is that although fables such as Santa Claus are usually revised and handled directly later on, fables in the sexual area are much less likely to be directly dealt with or revised. Thus, although the word "incest" seems to be seldom used by parents, about 50 percent of the author's students remember being told that "Cousins don't marry" or that "brothers and sisters don't kiss"; both of which relate to the general concept of incest but in an indirect rather than a direct manner.

An overview of childhood sexuality reveals that it focuses very much on curiosity, exploration, and experimentation (Ausubel, 1954, p. 397). Furthermore, sexuality in childhood tends to occur in a pattern reflective of general childhood relationships among age-mates. Thus, Elias and Gebhard (1969) have found that 52 percent of males report sex play with the same sex prior to puberty and 34 percent report sex play with the opposite sex. The corresponding figures for girls were 35 percent reporting sex play with same sex partners and 37 percent with the opposite sex.

In summary, children probably acquire most of their information on sex from parents and peers, although there are no data that clarify the extent to which parents or peers are the primary source. Parents are no doubt very influential in providing children with technical information, behavioral guidance and controls, and attitudes toward sex. Peers are probably more influential sources of non-technical information and, except in rare cases, the sole source of information resulting from behavioral experience.

THE SEXUAL KNOWLEDGE OF ADOLESCENTS

Although the acquisition of sexual knowledge during adolescence is a continuation of a process that began long ago in the life of most individuals, it is imperative to realize that adolescents approach the topic of sexuality in a much more complicated manner than is true of children. Although curiosity is still a major component of sexuality during adolescence, it is far from the only component. As noted by Ausubel (1954, pp. 390–397), additional factors such as gonadal maturation, sexual expression and gratification, biological sex roles, and social expectations all result in an increasing degree of differentiation and complexity during adolescence.

Most of the research on the sexual knowledge of adolescents has focused on two major questions: First, what percentage of a given age-group of adolescents is acquainted with various sexual topics and second, what are the primary sources of this information?

What Do Adolescents Know about Sex?

Adolescents are very much involved in the process of learning to be sexual in addition to the process of learning about sex. Both male and female pre-adolescents experience hormone changes preparatory to pubescence, between the ages of 8 and 9. Estrogenic hormones increase rapidly in girls at age 11 and the average age of menarche (first menstruation) is 12.5 years (Maccoby, 1966, pp. 3–6).

Consistent with these pre-adolescent physiological events is a corresponding interest in heterosexual relationships. Broderick (1966) has conducted very interesting research in this area and has found that pre-adolescents, far from being uninterested in the opposite sex, are frequently involved in fantasied and actual heterosexual relationships. Thus, in Broderick's sample of 10- to 11-year-olds, 46 percent of the girls and 33 percent of the boys had played "kissing games" during the preceding year, 28 percent of both boys and girls claimed to have begun dating, and 78 percent of the girls and 58 percent of the boys reported having a "sweetheart" (although 40 percent of the latter relationships were so secret that the other party did not know about it).

In terms of the more technical aspects of sexual knowledge, a majority of the population probably knows the "basics" of intercourse by the age of 10. Gagnon (1965) cites data showing that 57 percent of boys and girls of age 10 know about intercourse and 69 percent know about fertilization or conception. He also states that by age 14, 92 percent of a sample of boys are acquainted with both of these topics. This finding is consistent with other studies of adolescents in general. Schofield (1965), in a study of adolescents in England, found that 95 percent of 14- to 15-year-old boys and 98 percent of girls the same age knew the "facts of life." Elias and Gebhard (1969) reported that 50 percent of 8- to 10-year-old lower socio-economic level girls knew about intercourse, the corresponding figure for upper socio-economic level girls of the same age being 75 percent. In general, the majority of the population acquires a fairly basic understanding of sexual intercourse and fertilization by or before pubescence.

There seem to be some important differences in sexual knowledge which are associated with socio-economic level and which are masked when the major focus of research is defined as adolescents in general. Elias and Gebhard (1969) report that although 96 percent of lower socio-economic level boys have a knowledge of intercourse, only 4 percent of this sample have a knowledge of fertilization. The same pattern existed in their sample of lower socio-economic girls, with 50 percent of 8- to 10-year-olds having a knowledge of intercourse but virtually none being acquainted with conception. These researchers reported the opposite pattern existing in the upper socio-economic levels, with larger percentages being acquainted with the facts of fertilization than with intercourse. Similar differences were found in how many girls were acquainted with facts relating to menstruation (approximately 75 percent of the upper socio-economic 8- to 10-year-old girls, but only approximately 25 percent of lower socio-economic girls the same age). Thus, these authors concluded that the lower socio-economic levels are probably less knowledgeable about sexuality in general when compared with their upper socio-economic age-mates.

Interestingly, there do not appear to be many major differences between boys and girls in terms of the ages at which sexual information is acquired, despite the fact that, physiologically, girls mature earlier than boys. Although longitudinal or cross-sectional data on this topic are scarce, Schofield's (1965) findings on English adolescents suggest that approximately the same percentage of boys as girls are acquainted with the facts of reproduction at all age levels between 10 and 17. The same is apparently true in Sweden, not only in terms of knowledge of reproduction but also in terms of knowledge of venereal disease and contraception (Linner, 1967). Thus, it seems safe to conclude that greater differences in sexual knowledge exist between different age groups and socio-economic levels than between males and females. Possibly the fact that it is still somewhat more acceptable for boys to be interested in sex offsets the differences that might be expected to exist because of earlier physiological maturation in girls.

Sources of Sexual Knowledge during Adolescence

In almost every study that has been conducted, peers have been found to be the major source of sexual knowledge during adolescence. Gagnon (1965) cites four studies conducted during the period of 1915 through 1965 which found peers to be the overwhelming source of sex information. However, more males are likely to cite peers as a primary source of sex information than females. The specific figures have been between 50 and 65 percent in the case of males (Ehrman, 1959; Schofield, 1965; Libby[1]; Linner, 1967). Among girls, the range has been between 34 and 49 percent citing peers as the primary source (Libby[1]; Linner, 1967).

In contrast to peers being a more frequent primary source for boys, mothers are a more frequent primary source for girls. Schofield (1965) cites 4 percent of adolescent males reporting mothers; Ehrman (1959) reports 15 percent, and Linner reports 21 percent (1967). For the same sources, the figures for girls can be obtained by adding approximately 20 percent to the figures given for boys.

It is interesting to note that fathers play almost no role at all as a primary source of sex information, unless in combination with mothers (Gagnon, 1965; Schofield, 1965). This is less true in Sweden than in the United States or England, although even in Sweden fathers play a relatively small role as a primary source: 16 percent for males and 13 percent for females (Linner, 1967).

Like fathers, schools also appear to play a minimal role as a primary source of sex information in that they are listed as such by only 6 percent

[1] Personal communication with the author. Unpublished data.

of English adolescents (Schofield, 1965), 10 percent of United States adolescents (Ehrman, 1959), and 16 percent of Swedish adolescents (Linner, 1967). This latter finding is especially interesting in that the research was conducted a decade after sex education became compulsory at every grade level in Swedish schools.

As was the case with sexual knowledge, a focus on adolescents in general masks some important socio-economic differences in terms of primary sources of sex information. Elias and Gebhard (1969) report that while peers are the primary source for lower socio-economic boys (75–88 percent), and a fairly large source for lower socio-economic girls (30 percent with 45 percent saying they had no primary source); they are the primary source for only 8 percent of upper socio-economic boys and 7 percent of upper socio-economic girls. On the other hand, mothers were the primary source of information for 48 percent of upper socio-economic level boys and 75 percent of upper socio-economic level girls.

In summary, peers provide the major source of sex information for the majority of adolescents. This is not surprising, since adolescence is a period when it is appropriate to learn how to be sexual (in various ways) and this learning process is very much a function of interaction with peers. Mothers are second as a primary source, with books, schools, and fathers playing only minimal roles.

SEX EDUCATION PROGRAMS DURING ADOLESCENCE

Given the fact that adolescents have already acquired a considerable amount of information, concepts, attitudes, and behavioral experience in the area of sexuality, it is not unwise to ask the question of whether programs in sex education are too late, in terms of developmental timing, to be of any practical benefit to the adolescent. The answer to such a question depends, of course, on the content and approaches used in sex education programs. The determination of appropriateness of content and approach can and should be aided considerably by keeping such questions within the context of what is known about adolescence as a developmental stage in individual maturation.

The Need for Sex Education during Adolescence

Since almost all sex education programs are organized and staffed by adults, formal statements of the need for such programs should be construed as reflecting adult, rather than adolescent, perceptions. It should also be recognized that there is probably as much variation in our culture in the way in which sex education programs are perceived as there is in the way sex, *per se*, is viewed.

In cases where sex education is part of a larger institutional program (such as church, school, youth organization), it is logical to expect program emphases to be in line with broader institutional goals. Thus, an educational agency such as SIECUS states the need in educational and secular terms (SIECUS Study Guide #1, 1965, pp. 10–11). Religious organizations, on the other hand, usually view their efforts in this area as based on the need for adolescents to receive spiritual education and guidance in the area of sex (Phillips, 1968).

Most statements by individual adults and adolescents concerning the need for sex education programs express a recognition of the fact that sexuality is a factor in everyone's life about which judgments have to be made. As such, the need for accurate information concerning sex is as important as it is in other areas. In general, both adults and adolescents feel that they could have received a more adequate education in the area of sexuality and both tend to support, in the abstract at least, the need for improved sex education.

Many writers in the area stress that the manner in which sex is socialized in our culture is in itself a factor which argues for the need for sex education programs. Gagnon (1965) suggests that there is nothing in the usual cultural treatment of sexual learning that necessarily fosters the development of an "integrated body of sexual knowledge" (p. 224). He goes further to state that children learn about sex in a "clandestine and subversive" manner with the possible result that ". . . the sexual learning process contributes another element to the child's future character structure—the capacity and need to keep sexuality secret, especially from those one loves" (p. 225). Although there are major differences of opinion about how openly and directly sexuality should be treated, it is clear that many children learn to be indirect and keep sexuality hidden from their parents. An interesting bit of data which relates to the need for sex education programs during adolescence is Schofield's (1965) finding that very few parents initiated sex education attempts after their children became 13 years of age, whether or not they had made attempts earlier in their child's life.

Sex Education in the Schools: Problems and Challenges

The general facts that (1) adolescents seem to be asking for sex education in the high school curriculum, and (2) that parents approve of such efforts do not imply, by any stretch of the imagination, that successful school programs in this area are easily accomplished. In fact, there are many factors that make the accomplishment of the goals behind sex education programs extremely difficult. This section attempts to place these factors within the context of what is known concerning the process of learning about sex, with particular emphasis on how these factors relate to school programs for the adolescent.

Adult-adolescent perceptual differences   Few parents of adolescents can be expected to approach the topic of sex education from a detached, objective point of view. Parents can reasonably be expected to emphasize not only the goal of increasing information in the area of sexuality but also the goal of control. This is especially true since parents have, prior to adolescence, invested a considerable amount of time and effort toward the well being of their children and may, out of concern, tend to emphasize the dangers that relate to sexuality more than their adolescent off-spring might wish. This emphasis on the part of parents concerning the dangers that relate to sexuality is also fostered by the fact that they are held responsible (partially at least) if their children get into difficulty. An additional complicating factor is that it is sometimes difficult for parents to perceive that their children are growing into adults, and this is as true of sexuality as it is of other areas.

Adolescents, on the other hand, are very much concerned with the issue of looking independent and being independent. Although they too are concerned with the issues of controls and dangers, they are also very concerned with being responsible for themselves and are, in fact, under considerable cultural pressure to assume more responsibility in almost every social area.

School personnel in charge of developing and implementing sex educa-tion programs for the adolescent are frequently faced with the problem that the same program will be evaluated from these two different points of view. Adolescents may want a program that is rather open-ended and that focuses on the behavioral aspects of sexuality, while parents may want a program that focuses on the non-behavioral aspects and empha-sizes, wherever possible, a rule-giving approach. To further complicate the matter, school personnel share, with adults in general, the problem of being viewed by adolescents as somewhat incapable of understanding their problems.

Adolescent heterogeneity   Despite the fact that both adults and adolescents may view each other in a rather simplistic, stereotyped manner at times, the actual characteristics of either group encompass an enormous range of differences. Thus, although lower socio-economic level adoles-cents are likely to have had more behavioral experience in the area of sexuality than their upper socio-economic level age-mates, they lag con-siderably behind in the area of technical knowledge. As stated earlier, the opposite pattern exists in the upper socio-economic levels.

Developmental timing is also a crucial factor that could be expected to play a major role in adolescent interest and knowledge of sexuality. Adolescents who are ahead of their peers in physical and social develop-ment are also more likely to be interested in the topic of sex in general and are also more likely to see it relating to them personally instead of as an abstract area.

Sex education and social change   In addition to the complicating factors of adolescent-adult perceptual differences and adolescent heterogeneity, it must also be emphasized that the impetus behind the development of sex education programs is a relatively recent phenomenon. Furthermore, it is a phenomenon that is part of a more general social change which focuses on the meaning of sexuality in our society and especially on the manner in which sexuality is and should be socialized. There seems to be considerable movement away from the point of view that sexuality should be discussed only with parents at all age levels and that peers are a relevant, but an undesirable, source of sex information. Many parents today are not only recognizing the possibility that there are other acceptable sources of sex information other than themselves, but are also coming to view other sources as a useful and desirable social force. Since this process is still taking place, however, it can be anticipated that some parents will continue to view school programs in sex education as more threatening than useful.

Another factor related to the recency of social change in the area of sexuality is that there are few qualified personnel available for the conduct of sex education programs in the high school. This statement should not be taken to imply that school personnel have not been able to keep up with relevant research, but rather that there has been no research with which to keep up until fairly recently. The fact that sex education is also a new curricular area also implies that interested school personnel have to move into it from other fields. This is further complicated by the fact that the behavioral sciences seem to have become much more popular at the college level than at the high school level. Thus, while research in human sexuality frequently relates closely to the behavioral sciences, the lack of these sciences in the secondary school curriculum serves to further delimit qualified personnel.

Parental attitudes concerning high school sex education programs
Since parents are such an influential force in the socialization of sexuality, it is important to consider how they feel about sex education programs in the high school. When asked the extent to which they approve of including sex education (specifically defined as discussion of sexual attitudes, standards, and behavior) in the high school curriculum, parents respond with 82.0 percent approval, 15.2 percent partial approval, and 2.8 percent disapproval (Libby, 1969). Despite this overwhelming approval on the *idea* of sex education, parental agreement seems to decline as one moves into the more specific aspects of programs. Thus, in the same

study, only 4 topics received over 90 percent parental approval for inclusion in secondary school programs (these were venereal disease, conception, menstruation, and illegitimacy). Interestingly, these are the four topics adolescents are most likely to know about by age 13. On the other hand, only 2 of a total of 22 topics received less than 50 percent approval by parents (these were oral-genital contacts and sexual techniques). This indicates that although a consensus does not exist on topics, there is certainly enough approval to support the existence of programs.

Even less agreement exists among parents in relation to the question of desirable personnel for the planning of high school programs. Although 92 percent saw doctors as highly desirable in planning such programs, only 74 percent saw family life and sex education consultants in the same light (Libby, 1969). This is rather incongruous in that family life consultants are doubtlessly much better trained in the area of sex education than are doctors.

Libby's (1969) data seem to substantiate a tendency, hypothesized earlier, on the part of parents, to indicate a differential attitude toward topics that relate to sexual behavior and topics that relate to sexuality without strong behavioral overtones. Parents seem to approve of the latter more readily than the former. Of 11 non-behavioral sexual topics, average parental approval for inclusion in high school sex education programs was 84.4 percent, whereas average parental approval for 11 behavioral topics dropped to 70.5 percent. Libby also found that parents with pre-pubertal children were significantly more liberal in their approval of sex education than parents with post-pubertal children, an item that would also support a non-behavioral parental preference. This same preference could perhaps explain the higher approval rate among doctors (who might focus more on medical and physiological topics) than among family life education consultants (who might include more of a behavioral emphasis).

Other pertinent findings in Libby's study were that liberality toward sex education in the high school increases proportionally with the socioeconomic level of the parents and that it is related to religious denomination. However, liberality was not related to sex of parent or to age of parent with the exception of the interval between 66 to 80 years of age).

The variety of sex education programs in the high school   Sex education programs can be expected to differ markedly from school to school, depending somewhat upon the demographic qualities of the areas that the schools serve and, more directly, on the orientations of those responsible for planning and conducting the programs. The author has observed a high school sex education program which emphasized that sex is something to avoid completely during adolescence because of its potential dangers (V.D., illegitimate babies, being used for someone else's gratification) in a format which included strong sanctions against question-asking among students. The author has also noted a program that took a fairly neutral stance on values relating to sexuality, although most of the adolescents present seemed to be unwilling to ask questions because of their own embarrassment. In a third program witnessed by the writer, sexuality was viewed as part of everyone's life; adolescent girls asked questions which revealed that their technical knowledge in this area was somewhat more detailed than their mothers', who were also participating in the program. All three of these programs have taken place within a 25-mile radius of where the author teaches.

The impact of high school sex education programs on the adolescent
It is important to realize that sex education programs can have a negative impact on the adolescent if they fail to take into account his or her needs or general situation. Few adolescents are so naive about sexuality that they will accept uncritically and without resentment a presentation which emphasizes only the potential dangers of sexuality. Neither do they approve of an approach in which they are cast as a derelict generation so devoid of acceptable values and behavior that they have to be told over and over that they cannot be trusted.

On the other hand, most adolescents can appreciate that the area of sexuality includes dangers in addition to gratification and fulfillment. Furthermore, most are more interested in and cognitively able to view sexuality as a part of life in general than they have been able to do in the past. Thus, few adolescents are interested in only the technical side of sexuality and almost all want to be able to include in their discussions its relationship to interpersonal relations and dynamics, love, family, and the future. As far as the author's experience is concerned, adolescents are also able to accept the fact that it is impossible for adults to solve their problems, present or future, but they are also cognizant of the fact that both facts and viewpoints can be helpful. In general, it is wise for both planners and personnel of high school sex education programs to keep in mind the general principle that while young children seem to want to be given all answers and no discussion when they ask a question, adolescents frequently want no answers and all discussion!

In considering the impact of sex education programs on adolescents, it seems realistic to recognize that such programs are unlikely to have a dramatic impact or to produce dramatic changes. It also seems reasonable to expect their impact to be distributed along the following lines: highest impact in the area of sexual information, next in the area of sexual attitudes, and least in the area of sexual behavior.

Although parents sometimes voice the concern that sex education programs might result in an earlier onset of sexual experience, such a result seems highly unlikely. This is due to the fact that the timing of sexual behavior is influenced primarily by maturational and social-developmental factors rather than informational ones. Thus, Linner (1967) reported data which reveal that the average age of onset of heterosexual petting in Sweden is 15.7 years in boys and 16.3 years in girls. These findings are very close to Schofield's (1965) data on heterosexual petting in English adolescents, despite the fact that there are marked differences in the availability and perceived appropriateness of sex education programs in the two countries.

Although high school sex education programs are unlikely to have any massive or immediate impact on the lives of adolescents, it would be erroneous to completely discount their import which, while probably limited to the area of information, can still be beneficial. The area of sexuality and sexual development is an extremely significant area of research. This is so not only because sex has been a "forbidden" social topic in the past, but also because sexual development is a complicated and many-faceted process which persists over the entire life span of the individual. As such, the study of sexuality and the information which accrues as a result may yield valuable insights into the areas of human development, human relationships, psychology, morality, and social values, in addition to a better understanding of sex itself.

Perhaps the most important contribution that secondary school sex education programs can make is to assist the individual adolescent with the development of an explicit cognitive frame of reference within which he may view himself. Those programs which are descriptive and allow the individual adolescent to make his own judgments concerning the personal relevance or import of various sexual topics and questions are likely to be more helpful in this process than those which attempt to take over this function. Finally, while it is necessary to keep in mind that any program or curriculum will achieve this result to different degrees (depending on the individual), those which include the most diversity of content and format are those most likely to succeed.

REFERENCES

Ausubel, David P. *Theory and Problems of Adolescent Development.* New York: Grune and Stratton, 1954.

Berelson, B., and Steiner, G. A. *Human Behavior: An Inventory of Scientific Findings.* New York: Harcourt, Brace and World, Inc., 1964.

Broderick, Carlfred B. Socio-sexual development in a suburban community. *The Journal of Sex Research*, 1966, **2**, 1–24.

Ehrmann, Winston. *Premarital Dating Behavior.* New York: Holt, Rinehart and Winston, 1959.

Elias, James, and Gebhard, Paul. Sexuality and sexual learning in childhood. *Phi Delta Kappan*, 1969, **7**, 401–405.

Gagnon, John H. Sexuality and sexual learning in the child. *Psychiatry*, 1965, **28**, 212–228.

Libby, Roger W. Liberalism-traditionalism and demographic correlates of parental attitudes toward high school sex education programs. Unpublished Master's thesis, University of Connecticut, Storrs, 1969.

Linner, Birgitta. *Sex and Society in Sweden.* New York: Random House, 1967.

Maccoby, Eleanore E. (Ed.) *The Development of Sex Differences.* Stanford, Calif.: Stanford University Press, 1966.

Masters, William H., and Johnson, Virginia E. *Human Sexual Response.* Boston: Little, Brown, 1966.

Phillips, John H. Sex education in major Protestant denominations. Pamphlet of the National Council of the Churches of Christ in the U.S.A., Council Press, New York, 1968.

Schofield, Michael. *The Sexual Behavior of Young People.* Boston: Little, Brown, 1965.

Sears, Robert R., Maccoby, Eleanore E., and Levin, Harry. *Patterns of Child Rearing.* New York: Row, Peterson and Company, 1957.

SIECUS Study Guide No. 1, Sex Education. Pamphlet published by the Sex Information and Education Council of the U.S., New York, 1965.

2.3 *Orientation*

Our examination of selected educational issues and implications of adolescent development continues with a specific look at the psychology of moral reasoning. Previously, the importance of a consistent, functional morality for purposes of intelligent self-direction was introduced by Nathaniel Wagner (Part I) within the context of sexuality. The reader will recall Wagner's explicit concern for the content of a moral code characterized by consistency and rationality. In the following paper, Lawrence Kohlberg extends this concern to issues of the sequence and processes of moral development. Kohlberg's train of thought begins with an evaluative review of past research into moral development, travels the main roads of his own research into this phenomenon, and arrives at some intriguing implications of these findings for moral education. This train of thought is spiced with a variety of Kohlberg's personal anecdotes and includes a detailed exposition of *stages* in moral development first cited in this volume by Sullivan (Part I). The Kohlberg approach to the assessment of these stages in judgment is further illustrated by Haan *et al.* in Part III.

Kohlberg has long maintained that an adequate concept of morality in psychology must extend beyond the level of behavioral conformity. This view helps to establish Kohlberg's research on moral judgment as one striking departure from the mainstream of traditional moral character research; his approach clearly distinguishes moral judgment from moral conduct. The influence of Jean Piaget (see Elkind, Part I) is especially apparent in Kohlberg's stage concept of moral reasoning, an influence neatly acknowledged by the phrase "cognitive-developmental theory." Still other recent variations in the study of moral development exist, however. For example, a mixture of psychoanalytic and social learning theory underlies the Sears, Rau, and Alpert (1965) investigations of conscience development in children. These researchers have arrived at a workable definition of conscience in terms of the (1) ability to resist temptation, (2) exercise of responsibility when dealing with younger children, and (3) willingness to admit transgressions. A second variation is Aronfreed's (1968) analysis of the origins of internalized behavior control and self-criticism; conscience development for Aronfreed involves several socialization mechanisms including behavior-contingent learning, observational learning and imitation, and vicarious experience. The reader will note that Kohlberg keys on the mechanism of "cognitive conflict" with regard to the achievement of higher levels of moral judgment.

Finally, Kohlberg's paper serves in many ways to exemplify interrelationships between cognitive and motivational theory within psychology. His topic cuts across many others found in this book, including political, sexual, and delinquent behavior. One could argue that, all things considered, the basic task (and problem) for socialization (including education) is the moralization of the individual. The processes and conditions of moral development therefore become grave matters of significance for psychological and educational study.

RECOMMENDED READINGS

Aronfreed, Justin. *Conduct and Conscience*. New York: Academic Press, 1968.

Golddiamond, Israel. Moral behavior: a functional analysis. *Psychology Today*, 1968, 2, 31–34, 70.

Hunt, Maurice P.   Some views on situational morality. *Phi Delta Kappan*, 1969, **50**, 452–456.

Junnell, Joseph. S.   Can our schools teach moral commitment? *Phi Delta Kappan*, 1969, **50**, 446–451.

Kohlberg, Lawrence.   Moral education in the schools: a developmental view. *The School Review*, 1966, **74**, 1–29.

Sears, Robert, Rau, Lucy, and Alpert, Richard.   *Identification and Child Rearing*. Palo Alto, Calif.: Stanford University Press, 1965.

2.3   Moral Development and the Education of Adolescents

Lawrence Kohlberg, HARVARD UNIVERSITY

Anyone who listens to adolescents knows that they are preoccupied, in one way or another, with formulating ideals for bringing order and value to their lives. It is reasonble to claim that moral concerns lie at the core of these ideals and the study of the individual's moral development is what I have long concerned myself with. Since most of my own psychological studies of moral development have been with adolescents, I have tried to collect the findings from them as they pertain to the education of adolescents.

It is usually supposed that psychology contributes to moral education by telling us appropriate *methods* of moral teaching and learning. A Skinnerian will speak of proper schedules of reinforcement in moral learning, a Freudian will speak of the importance of the balance of parental love and firmness which will promote superego-identification, and so on. When Skinnerians and Freudians speak on the topic of moral education, then, they start by answering Yes to the question "Is virtue something that can be taught?" and go on to tell us how. In *Walden Two*, Skinner not only tells us that virtue comes by practice and reinforcement, but designs an ideal center which educates all its children to be virtuous in this way.

My own response to these questions was more modest. When confronted by a group of parents who asked me, "How can we make our children virtuous?" I had to answer like Socrates, "You must think I am very fortunate to know how virtue is acquired. The fact is that far from

Reprinted by permission of Holt, Rinehart and Winston, Inc. from the forthcoming book, *Adolescents and the American High School* by Richard F. Purnell. Copyright © 1970 by Holt, Rinehart and Winston, Inc.

knowing whether it can be taught, I have no idea what virtue really is." Like most psychologists, I knew that science could teach me nothing as to what virtue is. Science could speak about causal relations, about the relations of means to ends, but it could not speak about ends or values themselves. If I could not define virtue or the ends of moral education, could I really offer advice as to means by which virtue should be taught? Could it really be argued that the means for teaching obedience to authority are the same as the means for teaching freedom of moral opinion, that the means for teaching altruism are the same as the means for teaching competitive striving, that the making of a good storm trooper involves the same procedures as the making of a democratic leader? My response to all this was that either we must be totally silent about moral education or else speak of the nature of virtue.

THE BAG OF VIRTUES

American educational psychology is Aristotelian in that it divides the personality up into cognitive abilities, passions or motives, and traits of character. Moral character, then, consists of a bag of virtues and vices. One of the earliest major American studies of moral character, that of Hartshorne and May (1928–1930), was conducted in the late twenties. Their bag of virtues included honesty, service, and self-control. A more recent major study by Havighurst and Taba (1949) added responsibility, friendliness, and moral courage to the Hartshorne and May's bag. Aristotle's original bag included temperance, liberality, pride, good temper, truthfulness, and justice. The Boy Scout bag is well known, a Scout should be honest, loyal, reverent, clean, and brave.

Given a bag of virtues, it is evident how we build character. Children should be exhorted to practice these virtues, should be told that happiness, fortune, and good repute will follow in their wake, adults around them should be living examples of these virtues, and children should be given daily opportunities to practice them. Daily chores will build responsibility, the opportunity to give to the Red Cross will build service or altruism, and so on.

You will not be surprised if I tell you that this approach to moral education does not work. Hartshorne and May found that participation in character education classes of this sort, in the Boy Scouts, in Sunday school did not lead to any improving in moral character as measured by experimental tests of honesty, service, and self-control, and more recent research does not provide any more positive evidence as to the effects of character-building programs.

The objection of the psychologist to the bag of virtues is that there are no such things. Virtues and vices are labels by which people award praise or blame to others, but the ways people use praise and blame toward others are not the ways in which they think when making moral decisions themselves. You or I may not find a Hell's Angel truly honest, but he may. Hartshorne and May found this out to their dismay 40 years ago by their monumental experimental studies of children's cheating and stealing. In brief, they and others since have found:

(1) You cannot divide the world into honest and dishonest people. Almost everyone cheats some of the time, cheating is distributed in bell-curve fashion around a level of moderate cheating.

(2) If a person cheats in one situation, it does not mean he will or will not in another. There is very little correlation between situational cheating tests. In other words, it is not a character-trait of dishonesty that makes a child cheat in a given situation. If it were, you could predict he would cheat in a second situation if he did in the first.

(3) People's verbal moral values about honesty have nothing to do with how they act. People who cheat express as much or more moral disapproval of cheating as those who do not cheat. More recently than Hartshorne and May, psychologists have studied moral character using psychoanalytically inspired words such as "resistance to temptation," "conscience strength," "superego strength," and "moral internalization." However, they have essentially used Hartshorne and May's tests and have obtained similar results of situational specificity.

A STUDY OF MORALITY

But the question still beckons: How can one study morality? Current trends in the fields of ethics, linguistics, anthropology, and cognitive psychology have suggested a new approach which seems to avoid the morass of semantical confusions, value-bias, and cultural relativity in which the psychonalytic and virtue approaches to morality have foundered. New scholarship in all these fields is now focusing upon structures, forms, and relationships that seem to be common to all societies and all languages rather than upon the features that make particular languages or cultures different.

For 12 years, my colleagues and I studied the same group of 75 boys, following their development at 3-year intervals from early adolescence through young manhood (Kohlberg, 1958, 1963, 1968; Kohlberg and Kramer, 1969; Turiel, 1966). At the start of the study, the boys were aged 10 to 16. We have now followed them through to ages 22 to 28. In addition, I have investigated moral development in other cultures— Great Britain, Canada, Taiwan, Mexico, and Turkey.

Inspired by Jean Piaget's (1948) pioneering effort to apply a structural approach to moral development, I have gradually elaborated over the years of my study a typological scheme describing general stages of moral thought which can be defined independently of the specific content of particular moral decisions or actions. In our study of 75 American boys from early adolescence on, these youths were continually presented with hypothetical moral dilemmas, all deliberately philosophical, some of them found in medieval works of casuistry. It was on the basis of their reasoning about these dilemmas at a given age that we constructed the typology of definite and universal levels of development in moral thought.

The typology contains three distinct levels of moral thinking, and within each of these levels two related stages are distinguished. These levels and stages may be considered separate moral philosophies, distinct views of the social-moral world.

We can speak of the child as having his own morality or series of moralities. Adults seldom listen to children's moralizing. If a child throws back a few adult cliches and behaves himself, most parents—and many anthropologists and psychologists as well—think that the child has adopted or internalized the appropriate parental standards.

Actually, as soon as we talk with children about morality, we find that they have many ways of making judgments that are not "internalized" from the outside, and that do not come in any direct and obvious way from parents, teachers, or even peers.

MORAL STAGES

The *pre-conventional* level is the first of three levels of moral thinking, the second level is *conventional*, and the third is *post-conventional* or autonomous. Although the pre-conventional child is often "well behaved" and is responsive to cultural labels of good and bad, he interprets these labels in terms of their physical consequences (punishment, reward, exchange of favors) or in terms of the physical power of those who enunciate the rules and labels of good and bad.

This level is usually occupied by children aged 4 to 10, a fact well known to sensitive observers of children. The capacity of "properly behaved" children of this age to engage in cruel behavior when there are holes in the power structure is sometimes noted as tragic (*Lord of the Flies, High Wind in Jamaica*), sometimes as comic (Lucy in *Peanuts*).

The second or *conventional* level also can be described as conformist, but that is perhaps too smug a term. Maintaining the expectations and rules of the individual's family, group, or nation is perceived as valuable in its own right. There is a concern not only with *conforming* to the individual's social order but in *maintaining*, supporting, and justifying this order.

The *post-conventional* level is characterized by a major thrust toward autonomous moral principles that have validity and application apart from authority of the groups or persons who hold them and apart from the individual's identification with those persons or groups.

Within each of these three levels there are two discernable stages. Table 1 contains the dual moral stages of each level just described.

TABLE 1. Definition of Moral Stages

I. Pre-Conventional Level

At this level the child is responsive to cultural rules and labels of good and bad, right or wrong, but interprets these labels in terms of either the physical or the hedonistic consequences of action (punishment, reward, exchange of favors) or in terms of the physical power of those who enunciate the rules and labels. The level is divided into the following two stages:

Stage 1: The punishment and obedience orientation. The physical consequences of action determine its goodness or badness regardless of the human meaning or value of these consequences. Avoidance of punishment and unquestioning deference to power are valued in their own right, not in terms of respect for an underlying moral order supported by punishment and authority (the latter being Stage 4).

Stage 2: The instrumental relativist orientation. Right action consists of that which instrumentally satisfies one's own needs and occasionally the needs of others. Human relations are viewed in terms like those of the market place. Elements of fairness, of reciprocity, and equal sharing are present, but they are always interpreted in a physical pragmatic way. Reciprocity is a matter of "you scratch my back and I'll scratch yours," not of loyalty, gratitude, or justice.

II. Conventional Level

At this level, maintaining the expectations of the individual's family, group, or nation is perceived as valuable in its own right, regardless of immediate and obvious consequences. The attitude is not only one of *conformity* to personal expectations and social order, but of loyalty to it, of actively *maintaining*, supporting, and justifying the order and of identifying with the persons or group involved in it. At this level, there are the following two stages:

Stage 3: The interpersonal concordance or "good boy—nice girl" orientation. Good behavior is that which pleases or helps others and is approved by them. There is much conformity to stereotypical images of what is majority or "natural" behavior. Behavior is frequently judged by intention—"he means well" becomes important for the first time. One earns approval by being "nice."

Stage 4:   The "law and order" orientation. There is orientation toward authority, fixed rules, and the maintenance of the social order. Right behavior consists of doing one's duty, showing respect for authority and maintaining the given social order for its own sake.

III. Post-Conventional, Autonomous, or Principled Level

At this level, there is a clear effort to define moral values and principles which have validity and application apart from the authority of the groups or persons holding these principles and apart from the individual's own identification with these groups. This level again has two stages:

Stage 5:   The social-contract legalistic orientation. Generally has utilitarian overtones. Right action tends to be defined in terms of general individual rights and in terms of standards which have been critically examined and agreed upon by the whole society. There is a clear awareness of the relativism of personal values and opinions and a corresponding emphasis upon procedural rules for reaching consensus. Aside from what is constitutionally and democratically agreed upon, the right is a matter of personal "values" and "opinion." The result is an emphasis upon the "legal point of view," but with an emphasis upon the possibility of changing law in terms of rational considerations of social utility (rather than freezing it in terms of Stage-4 "law and order"). Outside the legal realm, free agreement, and contract is the binding element of obligation. This is the "official" morality of the American government and Constitution.

Stage 6:   The universal ethical principle orientation. Right is defined by the decision of conscience in accord with self-chosen *ethical principles* appealing to logical comprehensiveness, universality, and consistency. These principles are abstract and ethical (the Golden Rule, the categorical imperative), they are not concrete moral rules such as the Ten Commandments. At heart, these are universal principles of *justice* of the *reciprocity* and *equality* of the human *rights* and of respect for the dignity of human beings as *individual persons*.

To understand what these stages mean concretely, let us look at them with regard to 2 of 25 basic moral concepts or aspects used to form the dilemmas. One such aspect, for instance, is "Motive Given for Rule Obedience or Moral Action." In this instance, the six stages look like this:

(1)   Obey rules to avoid punishment.
(2)   Conform to obtain rewards, have favors returned, and so on.

(3) Conform to avoid disapproval, dislike by others.
(4) Conform to avoid censure by legitimate authorities and resultant guilt.
(5) Conform to maintain the respect of the impartial spectator judging in terms of community welfare.
(6) Conform to avoid self-condemnation.

In another of these 25 moral aspects, the value of human life, the six stages can be defined thus:

(1) The value of human life is confused with the value of physical objects and is based on the social status or physical attributes of the possessor.
(2) The value of human life is seen as instrumental to the satisfaction of the needs of its possessor or of other persons.
(3) The value of human life is based on the empathy and affection of family members and others toward its possessor.
(4) Life is conceived as sacred in terms of its place in a categorical moral or religious order of rights and duties.
(5) Life is valued both in terms of its relation to community welfare and in terms of life being a universal human right.
(6) Belief in sacredness of human life as representing a universal human value of respect for the individual.

I have called this scheme a typology. This is because approximately 50 percent of most people's thinking will be at a single stage, regardless of the moral dilemma involved. We call our types *stages* because they seem to represent an *invariant developmental sequence*. "True" stages come one at a time and always in the same order.

All movement is forward in sequence, and does not skip steps. Children may move through these stages at varying speeds, of course, and may be found half in and half out of a particular stage. An individual may stop at any given stage and at any age, but if he continues to move, he must move in accord with these steps. Moral reasoning of the conventional or Stage 3-4 kind never occurs before the pre-conventional Stage-1 and Stage-2 thought has taken place. No adult in Stage 4 has gone through Stage 6, but all Stage-6 adults have gone at least through 4.

Although the evidence is not complete, my study strongly suggests that moral change fits the stage pattern just described.

As a single example of our findings of stage-sequence, take the progress of two boys on the aspect "The Value of Human Life." The first boy, Tommy, is asked, "Is it better to save the life of one important person or a lot of unimportant people?" At age 10, he answers, "All the people that aren't important because one man just has one house, maybe a lot of furniture, but a whole bunch of people have an awful lot of furniture and some of these poor people might have a lot of money and it doesn't look it."

Clearly Tommy is Stage 1: He *confuses* the value of a human being with the value of the property he possesses. Three years later (age 13) Tommy's conceptions of life's values are most clearly elicited by the question, "Should the doctor 'mercy kill' a fatally ill woman requesting death because of her pain?" He answers, "Maybe it would be good to put her out of her pain, she'd be better off that way. But the husband wouldn't want it, it's not like an animal. If a pet dies you can get along without it—it isn't something you really need. Well, you can get a new wife, but it's not really the same."

Here his answer is Stage 2: The value of the woman's life is partly contingent on its hedonistic value to the wife herself but even more contingent on its *instrumental* value to her husband, who cannot replace her as easily as he can a pet.

Three years later still (age 16) Tommy's conception of life's value is elicited by the same question, to which he replies: "It might be best for her, but her husband—it's a human life—not like an animal; it just doesn't have the same relationship that a human being does to a family. You can become attached to a dog, but nothing like a human you know."

Now Tommy has moved from a Stage-2 instrumental view of the woman's value to a Stage-3 view based on the husband's distinctively human *empathy* and love for someone in his family. Equally clearly, it lacks any basis for a universal human value of the woman's life, which would hold if she had no husband or if her husband did not love her. Tommy, then, has moved step by step through three stages during the age 10–16. Tommy, although bright (IQ 120), is a slow developer in moral judgment. Let us take another boy, Richard, to show us sequential movement through the remaining three steps.

At age 13, Richard said about the mercy-killing, "If she requests it, it's really up to her. She is in such terrible pain, just the same as people are always putting animals out of their pain," and in general showed a mixture of Stage-2 and Stage-3 responses concerning the value of life. At 16, he said, "I don't know. In one way, it's murder, it's not a right or privilege of man to decide who shall live and who should die. God put life into everybody on earth and you're taking away something from that person that came directly from God, and you're destroying something that is very sacred, it's in a way part of God and it's almost destroying a part of God when you kill a person. There's something of God in everyone."

Here Richard clearly displays a Stage-4 concept of life as sacred in terms of its place in a categorical moral or religious order. The value of human life is universal, it is true for all humans. It is still, however, dependent on something else, upon respect for God and God's authority; it is not an autonomous human value. Presumably if God told Richard to murder, as God commanded Abraham to murder Isaac, he would do so.

At age 20, Richard said to the same question: "There are more and more people in the medical profession who think it is a hardship on everyone, the person, the family, when you know they are going to die. When a person is kept alive by an artificial lung or kidney it's more like being a vegetable than being a human. If it's her own choice, I think there are certain rights and privileges that go along with being a human being. I am a human being and I have certain desires for life and I think everybody else does too. You have a world of which you are the center, and everybody else does too and in that sense we're all equal."

Richard's response is clearly Stage 5, in that the value of life is defined in terms of equal and universal human rights in a context of relativity ("You have a world of which you are the center and in that sense we're all equal"), and of concern for utility or welfare consequences.

At 24, Richard says: "A human life takes precedence over any other moral or legal value, whoever it is. A human life has inherent value whether or not it is valued by a particular individual. The worth of the individual human being is central where the principles of justice and love are normative for all human relationships."

This young man is at Stage 6 in seeing the value of human life as absolute in representing a universal and equal respect for the human as an individual. He has moved step by step through a sequence culminating in a definition of human life as centrally valuable rather than derived from or dependent on social or divine authority.

In a genuine and culturally universal sense, these steps lead toward an increased *morality* of value judgment, where morality is considered as a form of judging, as it has been in a philosophic tradition running from the analyses of Kant to those of the modern analytic or "ordinary language" philosphers. The person at Stage 6 has disentangled his judgments of—or language about—human life from status and property values (Stage 1), from its uses to others (Stage 2), from interpersonal affection (Stage 3), and so on; he has a means of moral judgment that is universal and impersonal. The Stage-6 person's answers use moral words like "duty" or "morally right," and he uses them in a way implying universality, ideals, impersonality: He thinks and speaks in phrases like "regardless of who it was," or ". . . I would do it in spite of punishment."

CULTURAL UNIVERSALITY

When I first decided to explore moral development in other cultures, I was told by anthropologist friends that I would have to throw away my culture-bound moral concepts and stories and start from scratch learning a whole new set of values for each new culture. My first try consisted of a brace of villages, one Atayal (Malaysian aboriginal) and the other Taiwanese.

My guide was a young Chinese ethnographer who had written an account of the moral and religious patterns of the Atayal and Taiwanese villages. Taiwanese boys in the 10–13 age group were asked about a story involving theft of food. A man's wife is starving to death but the store owner will not give the man any food unless he can pay, which he cannot. Should he break in and steal some food? Why? Many of the boys said, "He should steal the food for his wife because if she dies he'll have to pay for her funeral and that costs a lot."

My guide was amused by these responses, but I was relieved: they were of course "classic" Stage-2 responses. In the Atayal village, funerals were not such a big thing, so the Stage-2 boys would say, "He should steal the food because he needs his wife to cook for him."

This means that we have to consult our anthropologists to know what content a Stage-2 child will include in his instrumental exchange calculations, or what a Stage-4 adult will identify as the proper social order. But one certainly does not have to start from scratch. What made my guide laugh was the difference in form between the children's Stage-2 thought and his own, a difference definable independently of particular cultures.

Figures 1 and 2 indicate the cultural universality of the sequence of stages which we have found. Figure 1 presents the age trends for middle-class urban boys in the United States, Taiwan, and Mexico. At age 10 in each country, the order of use of each stage is the same as the order of its difficulty or maturity.

In the United States, by age 16 the order is the reverse, from the highest to the lowest, except that Stage 6 is still little-used. At age 13, the good-boy, middle-stage (Stage 3), is not used.

The results in Mexico and Taiwan are the same, except that development is a little slower. The most conspicuous feature is that at the age of 16, Stage-5 thinking is much more salient in the United States than in Mexico or Taiwan. Nevertheless, it *is* present in the other countries, so we know that this is not purely an American democratic construct.

Figure 2 shows strikingly similar results from two isolated villages, one in Yucatan, and one in Turkey. Although conventional moral

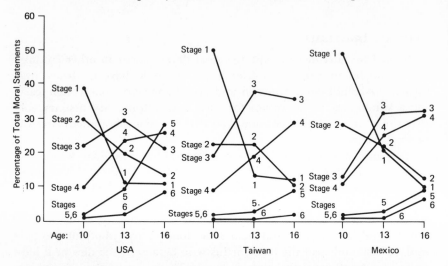

FIGURE 1. Middle-Class Urban Boys in the U.S., Taiwan, and Mexico. At Age 10, the Stages Are Used According to Difficulty. At Age 13, Stage 3 is Most Used by All Three Groups. At Age 16, U.S. Boys Have Reversed the Order of Age 10 Stages (With the Exception of 6). In Taiwan and Mexico, Conventional (3-4) Stages Prevail at Age 16, with Stage 5 Also Little Used.

thought increases steadily from ages 10 to 16 it still has not achieved a clear ascendency over pre-conventional thought.

Trends for lower-class urban groups are intermediate in the rate of development between those for the middle-class and for the village boys. In the three divergent cultures that I studied, middle-class children were found to be more advanced in moral judgment than matched lower-class children. This was not due to the fact that the middle-class children heavily ignored some one type of thought which could be seen as corresponding to the prevailing middle-class pattern. Instead, middle-class and working-class children move through the same sequences, but the middle-class children move faster and farther.

This sequence is not dependent upon a particular region, or any region at all in the usual sense. I found no important difference in the development of moral thinking among Catholics, Protestants, Jews, Buddhists, Moslems, and atheists. Religious values seem to go through the same stages as all other values.

In summary, the nature of our sequence is not significantly affected by widely varying social, cultural, or religious conditions. The only thing that is affected is the *rate* at which individuals progress through this sequence.

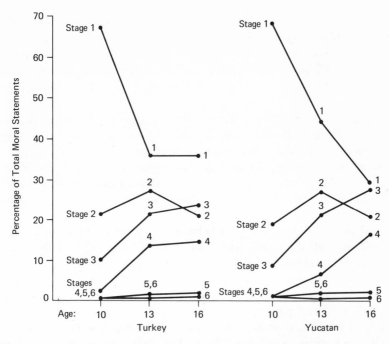

FIGURE 2. Two Isolated Villages, One in Turkey, the Other in Yucatan, Show Similar Patterns in Moral Thinking. There Is No Reversal of Order, and Pre-Conventional (1–2) Thought Does Not Gain a Clear Ascendancy Over Conventional Stages at Age 16.

IMPLICATIONS OF UNIVERSAL STAGES

Why should there be such a universal invariant sequence of development? In answering this question, we need first to analyze these developing social concepts in terms of their internal logical structure. At each stage, the same basic moral concept or aspect is defined, but at each higher stage this definition is more differentiated, more integrated, and more general or universal. When one's concept of human life moves from Stage 1 to Stage 2 the value of life becomes more differentiated from the value of property, more integrated (the value of life enters an organizational hierarchy where it is "higher" than property so that one steals property in order to save life), and more universalized (the life of any sentient being is valuable regardless of status or property). The same advance is true at each stage in the hierarchy. Each step of development, then, is a better cognitive organization than the one before it, one which takes account of everything present in the previous stage, but making new distinctions and organizing them into a more comprehensive or more equilibriated structure. The fact that this is the case has been demonstrated by a series of studies indicating that children and adolescents comprehend all stages up to their own, but not more than one stage beyond their own (Rest, 1969). And importantly, *they prefer this next stage*.

We have conducted experimental moral discussion classes (Blatt & Kohlberg, 1969) which show that the child at an earlier stage of development tends to move forward when confronted by the views of a child one stage further along. In an argument between a Stage-3 and Stage-4 child, the child in the third stage tends to move toward or into Stage 4, while the Stage-4 child understands but does not accept the arguments of the Stage-3 child.

Moral thought, then, seems to behave like all other kinds of thought. Progress through the moral levels and stages is characterized by increasing differentiation and increasing integration, and hence is the same kind of progress that scientific theory represents. Like acceptable scientific theory—or like *any* theory or structure of knowledge—moral thought may be considered partially to generate its own data as it goes along, or at least to expand so as to contain in a balanced, self-consistent way a wider and wider experiential field. The raw data in the case of our ethical philosophies may be considered as conflicts between roles, or values, or as the social order in which men live.

The social worlds of all men seem to contain the same basic structures. All the societies we have studied have the same basic institutions—family, economy, law, and government. In addition, however, all societies are alike because they *are* societies—systems of defined complementary roles. In order to *play* a social role in the family, school, or society, the child must implicitly take the role of others toward himself and toward others in the group. These role-taking tendencies form the basis of all social institutions. They represent various patternings of shared or complementary expectations.

In the pre-conventional and conventional levels (Stages 1–4), moral content or value is largely accidental or culture-bound. Anything from "honesty" to "courage in battle" can be the central value. But in the higher post-conventional levels, Socrates, Lincoln, Thoreau, and Martin Luther King tend to speak without confusion of tongues, as it were. This is because the ideal principles of any social structure are basically alike, if only because there simply are not that many principles that are articulate, comprehensive, and integrated enough to be satisfying to the human intellect. And most of these principles have gone by the name of justice.

THE CONCEPT OF JUSTICE

Now let me point out that justice is not a character trait in the usual sense. You cannot make up behavior tests of justice, as Hartshorne and May did for honesty, service, and self-control. One cannot conceive of a little set of behavior tests that would indicate that Martin Luther King or Socrates were high on the trait of justice. The reason for this is that justice is not a concrete rule of action, as that which lies behind virtues such as honesty. To be honest means don't cheat, don't steal, don't lie. Justice is not a rule or a set of rules, it is a moral principle. By a moral principle we mean a mode of choosing which is universal, a rule of choosing which we want all people to adopt always in all situations. We know it is all right to be dishonest and steal to save a life because it is just, because a man's right to life comes before another man's right to property. We know it is sometimes right to kill, because it is sometimes just. The Germans who tried to kill Hitler were doing right because respect for the equal values of lives demands that we kill someone who is murdering others in order to save their lives. There are exceptions to rules, then, but no exceptions to principles. A moral obligation is an obligation to respect the right or claim of another person. A moral principle is a principle for resolving competing claims, you versus me, you versus a third person. There is only one principled basis for resolving claims: justice or equality. Treat every man's claim impartially regardless of the man. A moral principle is not only a rule of action but a reason for action. As a reason for action, justice is called respect for persons.

As another example of our Stage 6, *orientation to universal moral principles,* let me cite Martin Luther King's letter from a Birmingham jail.

There is a type of constructive non-violent tension which is necessary for growth. Just as Socrates felt it was necessary to create a tension in the mind so that individuals could rise from the bondage of half-truths, so must we see the need for non-violent gadflies to create the kind of tension in society that will help men rise from the dark depths of prejudice and racism.

One may well ask, "How can you advocate breaking some laws and obeying others?" The answer lies in the fact that there are two types of laws, just and unjust. One has not only a legal but a moral responsibility to obey just laws. One has a moral responsibility to disobey unjust laws. An unjust law is a human law that is not rooted in eternal law and natural law. Any law that uplifts human personality is just, any law that degrades human personality is unjust. An unjust law is a code that a numerical or power majority group compels a minority group to obey but does not make binding on itself. This is difference made legal.

I do not advocate evading or defying the law as would the rabid segregationist. That would lead to anarchy. One who breaks an unjust law must do so openly, lovingly, and with a willingness to accept the penalty. An individual who breaks a law that conscience tells him is unjust, and willingly accepts the penalty of imprisonment in order to arouse the conscience of the community over its injustice, is in reality expressing the highest respect for the law.

King makes it clear that moral disobedience of the law must spring from the same root as moral obedience to law, out of respect for justice. We respect the law because it is based on rights, both in the sense that the law is designed to protect the rights of all and because the law is made by the principle of equal political rights. If civil disobedience is to be Stage 6, it must recognize the contractual respect for law of Stage 5, even to accepting imprisonment. That is why Stage 5 is a way of thinking about the laws which are imposed upon all, while a morality of justice which claims to judge the law can never be anything but a free personal ideal. It must accept being put in jail by its enemies not of putting its enemies in jail.

Both logic and empirical study suggests there is no shortcut to autonomous morality, no Stage 6 without a previous Stage 5.

MORAL JUDGMENT AND MORAL ACTION

Our claim is that knowledge of the moral good is one. We now will try to show that virtue in action is knowledge of the good. We have already said that knowledge of the good in terms of a bag of virtues that comes from opinion or conventional belief is not virtue. An individual may believe that cheating is very bad but that does not predict that he will resist cheating in real life. Espousal of unprejudiced attitudes toward Negroes does not predict actual action to assure civil rights in an atmosphere where others have some prejudice. However, true knowledge, knowledge of principles of justice does predict virtuous action. With regard to cheating, the essential elements of justice are understood by both our Stage-5 and Stage-6 subjects. In cheating, the critical issue is recognition of the element of contract and agreement implicit in the situation, and the recognition that while it does not seem so bad if one person cheats, what holds for all must hold for one. In a recent study, 100 sixth-grade children were given experimental cheating tests and our moral judgment interview. The majority of the children were below the principled level in moral judgment, they were at our first four moral stages. Seventy-five percent of these children cheated. In contrast, only 20 percent of the principled subjects, that is, Stage 5 or 6, cheated. In another study conducted at the college level, only 11 percent of the principled subjects cheated, in contrast to 42 percent of the students at lower levels of moral judgment.

In the case of cheating, justice and the expectations of conventional authority both dictate the same behavior. What happens when they are opposed?

An experimental study by Stanley Milgram (1963) involved such an opposition. Undergraduate subjects were ordered by an experimenter to administer increasingly more severe electric shock punishment to a stooge victim in the guise of a learning experiment. In this case, the principles of justice involved in the Stage-5 social contract orientation do not clearly prescribe a decision. The victim had voluntarily agreed to participate in the experiment and the subject himself had contractually committed himself to perform the experiment. Only Stage-6 thinking clearly defined the situation as one in which the experimenter did not have the moral right to ask them to inflict pain on another person. Accordingly, 75 percent of the Stage-6 subjects quit or refused to shock the victim as compared to only 13 percent of all the subjects at lower stages.

A study of Berkeley students carries the issue into political civil disobedience. Berkeley students were faced with the decision to sit in the Administration building in the name of political freedom of communication. Haan, Smith, and Block (1968) administered moral judgment interviews to over 200 of these students. Again the situation was similar to the Milgram situation. A Stage-5 social contract interpretation of justice, which was held by the University administration, could take the position that a student who came to Berkeley came with foreknowledge of the rules and could go elsewhere if he did not like them. About 50 percent of the Stage-5 subjects sat in. For Stage-6 students, the issue was clear-cut and 80 percent of them sat in. For students at the conventional levels, Stages 3 and 4, the issue was also clear-cut and only 10 percent of them sat in. These results will sound very heartwarming to those of us who have engaged in protest activities. Protesting is a sure sign of being at the most mature moral level. However, there was another group who was almost as disposed to sit in as the Stage-6 students. These were our Stage-2 instrumental relativists, of whom about 60 percent sat in. From our longitudinal studies, we know that most Stage-2 college students are in a state of confusion. In high school most were at the conventional level, and in college they kick conventional morality searching for their thing, for self-chosen values, but cannot tell an autonomous morality of justice from one of egoistic relativism, exchange, and revenge. Our longitudinal studies indicate that all of our middle-class Stage-2 college students grow out of it to become principled adults.

I make the point to indicate that protest activities, like other acts, are neither virtuous nor vicious; it is only the knowledge of the good which lies behind them that gives them virtue. As an example, I would take it that a Stage-6 sense of justice would have been rather unlikely to find the Dow Chemical sit-in virtuous. The rules being disobeyed by the protesters were not unjust rules, and the sit-in was depriving individuals of rights, not trying to protect individual rights. Principled civil disobedience is not illegitimate propaganda for worthy political causes, it is the just questioning of injustice.

Having, I hope, persuaded you of one view of virtue, let us briefly consider how it may be taught. In a sense, this view implies that knowledge of the good is always within but needs to be drawn out. In a series of experimental studies (Rest, Turiel, & Kohlberg, 1969; Rest, 1969), we have found that children and adolescents prefer the highest level of thought they can comprehend. Children comprehend all lower stages than their own, and often comprehend the stage one higher than their own and occasionally two stages higher, although they cannot actively express these higher stages of thought. If they comprehend the stage one higher than their own, they tend to prefer it to their own. This fact is basic to moral leadership in our society. Although the majority of adults in American society are at a conventional level, Stages 3 and 4, leadership in our society has usually been expressed at the level of Stages 5 and 6, as our example of Martin Luther King suggests.

Returning to the teaching of virtue as a drawing out, the child's preference for the next level of thought shows that it is greeted as already familiar, that it is felt to be a more adequate expression of that already within, of that latent in the child's own thought. If the child were responding to fine words and external prestige he would not pick the next stage continuous with his own, but something else.

Let us now suggest a different example of the sense in which moral teaching must be a drawing out of that already within. At the age of 4 my son joined the pacifist and vegetarian movement and refused to eat meat, because as he said, "it's bad to kill animals." Despite lengthy Hawk argumentation by his parents about the difference between justified and unjustified killing, he remained a vegetarian for 6 months. Like most doves, however, his principles recognized occasions of just or legitimate killing. One night I read to him a book of Eskimo life involving a seal-killing expedition. He got angry during the story and said, "You know there is one kind of meat I would eat, Eskimo meat. It's bad to kill animals so it's all right to eat them."

For reasons I will not detail, this eye for an eye, tooth for a tooth concept of justice is Stage 1. You will recognize, however, that it is a very genuine, although 4-year-old, sense of justice, and that it contains within it the Stage-6 sense of justice in shadowy form. The problem is to draw the child's perceptions of justice from the shadows of the cave step by step toward the light of justice as an ideal form. This last example indicates a truth not indicated by our experimental example, the truth that the child initially turned from the dark images of the cave toward the light still convinced that his dark images best represent the truth. The child is initially quite confident of his moral knowledge, of the rationality and efficacy of his moral principles. The notion that the child feels ignorant and is eager to absorb the wisdom of adult authority in the moral domain is one which any teacher or parent will know is nonsense. Let me give another example. Following a developmental time-table, my son moved to an expedient Stage-2 orientation when he was 6. He told me at that time, "You know the reason people don't steal is because they're afraid of the police. If there were no police around everyone would steal." Of course I told him that I and most people did not steal because we thought it wrong, because we would not want other people to take things from us, and so on. My son's reply was, "I just don't see it, it's sort of crazy not to steal if there are no police."

The story indicates that, like most ordinary fathers, I have no great skill in teaching true virtue. My son, of course, has always been virtuous in the conventional sense. Even when he saw no rational reason for being honest, he received E's on his report card on the bag of virtues on obedience, responsibility, and respect for property. Unlike what we usually think, it is quite easy to teach conventionally virtuous behavior but very difficult to teach true knowledge of the good.

The first step in teaching virtue, then, is the Socratic step of creating dissatisfaction in the student about his present knowledge of the good. This we do experimentally by exposing the student to moral conflict situations for which his principles have no ready solution. Second, we expose him to disagreement and argument about these situations with his peers. Our view holds that if we inspire cognitive conflict in the student and point the way to the next step up the divided line, he will tend to see things previously invisible to him.

In practice, then, our experimental efforts at moral education have involved getting students at one level, say Stage 2, to argue with those at the next level, stay Stage 3. The teacher would support and clarify the Stage-3 arguments. Then he would pit the Stage-3 students against the Stage-4 students on a new dilemma. Initial results with this method with a junior high group indicated that 50 percent of the students moved up one stage and 10 percent moved up two stages. In comparison, only 10 percent of a control group moved up one stage in the 4-month period involved (Blatt & Kohlberg, 1969).

Obviously the small procedures I have described are only a way station to genuine moral education. As my earlier comments suggested, a more complete approach means full student participation in a school in which justice is a living matter.

REFERENCES

Blatt, M., and Kohlberg, L. The effects of a classroom discussion program upon the moral levels of preadolescents. *Merrill Palmer Quarterly*, 1970, in press.

Haan, N., Smith, M. B., and Block, J. Political, family, and personality correlates of adolescent moral judgment. *Journal of Personality and Social Psychology*, 1968, **10**, 183–201.

Hartshorne, H., and May, M. A. *Studies in the Nature of Character*: Vol. 1: *Studies in Deceit*. Vol. 2: *Studies in Self-Control*. Vol. 3: *Studies in the Organization of Character*. New York: Macmillan, 1928–1930.

Havighurst, R. J., and Taba, H. *Adolescent Character and Personality*. New York: John Wiley, 1949.

Kohlberg, L. The development of modes of moral thinking and choice in the years ten to sixteen. Unpublished doctoral dissertation, University of Chicago, 1958.

Kohlberg, L. The development of children's orientations toward moral order: 1. Sequence in the development of moral thought. *Vita Humana*, 1963, **6**, 11–33.

Kohlberg, L. Stage and sequence: the cognitive developmental approach to socialization. In D. Goslin (Ed.) *Handbook of Socialization Theory*. Chicago: Rand McNally, 1969.

Kohlberg, L., and Kramer, R. Continuity and discontinuity in moral development from childhood to adulthood. *Human Development*, 1970, in press.

2.4 *Orientation*

A review of the growing literature concerned with creativity reflects a thorny chain of issues and problems. Although creativity has been contemplated and subjected to armchair study for centuries by the best scholars, one might argue that greater success has been achieved in obscuring than in clarifying the nature of creativity and its development. Gradually, more scientific approaches have been taken to this task of clarification. Currently a number of tentative generalizations are emerging about what we think we know about creativity. Despite this inroad, there clearly remains a lack of resolution of questions basic to a reasonable examination of the creativity phenomenon. Such questions, which range from those of definition and measurement to those concerning the antecedents of creative behavior, have become central to discussions of creativity and educational practice.

Although there appears to be an increasing commitment among educators to the idea of achieving creative outcomes among children and adolescents in the schools, there is a patent lack of specificity regarding these desired outcomes and techniques appropriate to their attainment. Few would deny that education, as an instrument of behavior change, is irrelevant to creative growth. However, can education possibly service creative growth in the absence of data which establish clear antecedent (instructional)-consequent (behavioral) relationships relevant to this aim? In short, educators must know what it is they are trying to accomplish, what it is they wish students to be able to do, before we can discuss how to "teach for" creativity in any legitimate fashion. Immediately the ugly head of the criterion problem is reared, the beast that gives rise to myriad related problems and issues. Most intimately fused with the criterion problem is its shadow, the measurement issue.

In the following paper, Stuart Golann provides a well-conducted tour of theory and research issues pertinent to creativity. The four emphases with respect to the study of creativity identified by Golann have continued since the original publication of this article. Certainly the issues he identifies continue to confront psychologists, particularly those concerned with the developmental characteristics of creativity during childhood and adolescence. Readers will note that Golann believes the exploration of personality characteristics to hold the greatest promise for those who wish a deeper understanding of creativity. Possibly other avenues of study will be equally fruitful. Although the identification of personality characteristics associated with creativity is important, the identification of conditions under which such characteristics develop is perhaps even more so, especially for educational purposes.

RECOMMENDED READINGS

Albert, Robert S.   Genius: present day status of the concept and its implications for the study of creativity and giftedness. *American Psychologist*, 1969, 24, 743–753.

Barron, Frank.   *Creativity and Personal Freedom*. Princeton, N.J.: Van Nostrand, 1968.

Gowan, John C., Demos, George D., and Torrance, E. Paul. *Creativity: Its Educational Implications*. New York, John Wiley, 1967.

Kagan, Jerome (Ed.) *Creativity and Learning.* Boston: Beacon Press, 1967.

Torrance, E. Paul. Fostering creative thinking during the high school years. *The High School Journal,* 1962, **45,** 281–288.

2.4   The Psychological Study of Creativity

Stuart E. Golann, AMERICAN PSYCHOLOGICAL ASSOCIATION

The purpose of the present paper is to review recent theory and research pertaining to the psychological study of creativity so as to highlight the issues and emphases reflected in the literature. Three issues are apparent: (*a*) What is creativity?—questions of definition and criteria, (*b*) How does creativity occur?—questions of the process viewed temporally, and, (*c*) Under what conditions is creativity manifest?—questions of necessary personal and environmental conditions. A striking feature of the literature on creativity is the diversity of interests, motives, and approaches characteristic of the many investigators. Creativity has been viewed as a normally distributed trait, an aptitude trait, an intrapsychic process, and as a style of life. It has been described as that which is seen in all children, but few adults. It has been described as that which leads to innovation in science, performance in fine arts, or new thoughts. Creativity has been described as related to, or equatable with, intelligence, productivity, positive mental health, and originality. It has been described as being caused by self-actualization and by sublimation and restitution of destructive impulses. Clearly there is a need for organization and integration within the psychological study of creativity. What are the many investigators studying? How are they studying it? Four contemporary emphases are apparent: products, process, measurement, and personality. The organization herein will follow this same order. The scope of the paper precludes an exhaustive presentation of all theoretical statements and research reports. The reader is referred to an annotated bibliographical volume prepared by Stein and Heinze (1960). French and Italian bibliographies (Bédard, 1959; 1960) are also available.

EMPHASIS ON PRODUCTS

The use of products as criteria of creativity is most frequently encountered in investigations in technological or industrial settings. In such studies creativity is assumed to be a unitary or multifaceted trait which is distributed in the population in a manner comparable to other intellec-

Reprinted from *Psychological Bulletin,* 1963, **60,** 548–565, by permission of the author and the American Psychological Association.

tive or personality traits (see Gamble, 1959, p. 292). Several authors believe that creativity can best be studied through products.

In the "Committee Report on Criteria of Creativity" (Gamble, 1959), it was stated that the products of creative behavior should be the first object of study. After the products are judged "creative" the term can be applied to the behavior which produced them, and also the individuals who performed the behavior can be classed as possessing to some degree the trait of creativity.

Several possible product criteria of creativity were proposed by McPherson (1956) who reviewed the problem of determining "inventive level" of patents. Ghiselin (1958) stated that the approach outlined by McPherson would not provide the true criteria of creativity and distinguished two levels of creativity. A higher level of creativity introduces some new element of meaning or some new order of significance while a lower level gives further development to an established body of meaning by initiating some advance in its use.

While the utility of studying creativity through products remains an issue, Harmon (1958), Taylor (1958), and C. Taylor (1959) have studied relationships between criterion variables and determinants of judges' creativity ratings. Harmon reported correlations of .61 and .76 between judged creativity and number of publications. D. Taylor reported a correlation of .69 between ratings of creativity and ratings of productivity given by supervisors of research personnel. In later reports, Taylor (1960; 1961) argued that distinctions among problem solving, decision making, and creative thinking can best be made in terms of the product. A large number of measures were refined by C. Taylor to yield 56 scores on each of a group of research scientists. Included in the refined measures were supervisor, peer, examiner, and self-evaluations; counts of reports and publications; official records; and membership in professional societies. Factor analysis yielded 27 factors. The findings that among the many correlations four out of any five variables were independent of a given criterion was cited as evidence for the "almost overwhelming complexity of the criterion problem."

EMPHASIS ON PROCESS

Creative Process and Illumination

An alternative to the study of creativity through products is to study the process of creativity. Wallas (1926) described the stages of forming a new thought as follows: preparation, incubation, illumination, and verification. While the four stages could be distinguished from one another, Wallas noted that they do not occur in an uninterrupted problem and solution sequence. Controversy has appeared concerning the distinctness of the stages and the relative importance of conscious or other modes of mental activity.

Dashiell (1931) noted the four stages of the creative process and related inspiration to insight in learning. Recall is dependent on the absence of interfering associations set up by excessive concentration on the recalling. Similarly, Woodworth (1954) stated that incubation implies a theory he prefers not to accept. Illumination, he believed is the result of laying aside a problem, giving the mind a chance to rest and at the same time to get rid of false sets and directions. Relating the recall of a forgotten name to creative insight, Woodworth stated that the sudden recall of a forgotten name after previous futile attempts suggests that an essential factor in illumination is the absence of interferences which block progress during the preliminary stage.

In addition to considering explanations of unconscious processes and the weakening of erroneous sets, Crutchfield (1961) suggested that incubation may permit, perhaps unaware to the individual, new and better cues from the environment and from ideation to develop while one engages in other activities. An experiment cited suggested that the subject's performance on a former task may facilitate insight on a later task even though they report no awareness of the relevant cue present in the preceding task. Instead of the study of distinct stages, Crutchfield recommended a functional analysis which would seek lawful accounts of the manner in which each step of the creative thinking process was functionally determined by prior steps and in turn governed succeeding steps.

Ghiselin (1956) described insight as the crucial action of the mind in creation. He too preferred to consider the creative process as consisting of fewer discrete steps, and stated that no sort of calculation from known grounds will suffice for creative production. Required for creativity is a fresh formulation, rather than copying with variations or elaborations. Although he believed that concepts of unconscious thoughts are imprecise, he did admit the importance of diversion which is conceptualized as being related to what he terms preconfigurative consciousness.

The illumination controversy could be enlarged upon and conceptually updated. However, the guidelines seem clear in regard to the creative process. Crutchfield's paper is helpful in that he attempted to translate the somewhat literary descriptions of the creative process into better conceptualized psychological variables.

Creative Process: Systematized, Goal Directed, or Plastic

For Harmon (1956) the creative process is any process by which something new is produced: an idea or object, a new form or arrangement of old elements. The essential requirement is that the new creation must contribute to the solution of a problem. The creative process is goal directed. Harris (1959) saw the creative process as consisting of six steps: (a) realizing the need, (b) gathering information, (c) thinking through, (d) imaging solutions, (e) verifying, and (f) putting the ideas to work. He stated that the difference between the electrified or illuminated minds of some geniuses and the processes in ordinary people is the speed with which they proceed from Step (a) to Step (d) (see also Arnold, 1959).

Taking a different view, I. Taylor (1959) stated that the rules of logic and scientific method are a psychological straight jacket for creative thought. He proposed five levels of creativity which he identified by the analysis of over 100 definitions of creativity.

Expressive creativity is most fundamental, according to Taylor, involving independent expression where skills, originality, and the quality of the product are unimportant. Spontaneity and freedom are apparent from which later creative talents develop. Individuals proceed from the expressive to the productive level of creativity when skills are developed to produce finished works. The product is creative in that a new level of accomplishment is reached by the person though the product may not be stylistically discernible from the work of others. Inventive creativity is operative when ingenuity is displayed. This level involves flexibility in perceiving new and unusual relationships between previously separate parts. It does not contribute to new ideas but to new uses of old parts. Innovative creativity requires strong abstract conceptualizing skill and is seen when basic foundation principles are sufficiently understood so as to allow improvement through modification. The highest form of creativity is "emergentive creativity," which involves the conception of an entirely new principle at a most fundamental and abstract level. The core of the creative process in Taylor's view is the ability to mold experiences into new and different organizations, the ability to perceive the environment plastically, and to communicate the resulting unique experiences to others.

Stein (1956) stated that creativity is a process of hypothesis formulation, hypothesis testing, and the communication of results which are the resultant of social transaction. Individuals affect and are affected by the environment in which they live. The early childhood family-environment transaction facilitates or inhibits creativity. An empirical definition of manifest creativity is suggested by Stein (1956):

Creativity is that process which results in a novel work that is accepted as tenable or useful or satisfying by a group at some point in time. (p. 172) .

Potential creativity is suggested when an individual does not satisfy the requirements of the stated definition, but nevertheless performs on psychological tests like individuals who do manifest creativity. In an earlier paper Stein (1953) elaborated upon his definition of creativity.

EMPHASIS ON MEASUREMENT

Factor Analytic Approach

Since the publication of Chassell's (1916) paper numerous investigators have attempted to devise or adapt tests that would measure creative abilities. Although the types of tests have not changed very much over the past 55 years, the methods of analysis have become more complex. For example, Guilford attempted to define the entire structure of intellect by factor analytic methods. In one of the more recent revisions of his system, he presented a "unified theory of intellect" making use of a cubical model of intellectual abilities in which each dimension represents a mode of variation among the factors (Guilford, 1959a). The lack of psychological knowledge in the area of creativity may be attributable, according to Guilford (1959b) to the inappropriateness of the SR model for the study of higher processes.

Instead, Guilford (1959b) recommended a trait approach for the study of creativity and stated that the most defensible way of discovering dependable trait concepts is factor analysis. He attempted to place his research on creativity within the larger context of the structure of intellect. Noting some 47 known factors of intellect, Guilford suggested that they can be put into a three-way classification according to: the kind of material or content of thought, the varieties of activities or operations performed, and the varieties of resultant products. In this system each primary intellectual ability represents the interaction of a kind of operation applied to a kind of material, yielding a kind of product. Most needed, according to Guilford, was a more thorough understanding of the nature and components of intellect. Accordingly, most of the data reported concern the isolation of a primary factor believed to be of importance for creativity.

The factorial aptitude traits that Guilford currently believes to be related to creativity are described as: ability to see problems, fluency of thinking (the factors of word fluency and ideational fluency), flexibility of thinking (the factors of spontaneous flexibility and adaptive flexibility), originality, redefinition, and elaboration. The types of cognitive abilities Guilford believes to be of importance for creativity are reflected in the measuring devices he has designed or adapted. Very briefly described, his tests require individuals to state defects or deficiencies in common implements or institutions; to produce words containing a specified letter or combination of letters; to produce in limited time as many synonyms as they can for a stimulus word; to produce phrases or sentences; to name objects with certain properties (for example, objects that are hard, white, and edible); or to give various uses for a common object. Guilford's (1959b) practice in scoring fluency factors is to emphasize sheer quantity— "quality need not be considered so long as responses are appropriate (p. 146)." Other tests employed ask examinees which of a given list of objects could best be adapted to make another object; or to construct a more complex object from one or two simple lines.

Guilford (1959b) presented three ways to measure the trait of originality: counting the number of responses that are judged to be clever, utilizing items calling for remote associations, and weighting the subject's responses in proportion to their infrequency of occurrence in a population of subjects. The first two procedures require a quality criterion.

Much of the research efforts of Guilford and associates has been devoted to the definition of factor traits by isolating patterns of concomitant variation (see Guilford, 1957; Guilford, Kettner, & Christensen, 1954, 1956; Kettner, Guilford, & Christensen, 1959). The studies reviewed herein cluster into two groups: (a) those studies demonstrating a relationship between measures of the factors and criterion variables and (b) those studies suggesting no relationship between measures of the factors and judged creativity.

Correlations of .25 between grades in an astronomy course and performance on a test of expressional fluency, .37 between scores on a test of ideational fluency and a criterion of engineer performance based on pay increases, and .31 between a measure of adaptive flexibility and the pay increase criterion were reported by Guilford (1956). Adaptive flexibility was reported to have consistently shown a relationship to performance in mathematics (average $r = .33$). Three Guilford originality tests (Unusual Uses, Consequences, and Plot Titles) were reported by Barron (1956) to correlate in the range of .30–.36 with 10 judges' ratings of originality. Significant multiple correlations were reported by Chorness (1956) between a composite factor score from the Guilford battery and United States Air Force student-instructor characteristics judged to be demonstrative of creative expression. The best single predictor was a test of controlled associations. Statistically removing the effects of intelligence demonstrated that the creativity tests could be employed as predictors of instructor performance since the factor composite predicted the student instructor grades for the phase of the program studied better than an intelligence index which had previously been relied on.

No significant differences between groups rated as creative or not creative on the factors of redefinition, closure, ideational fluency, associational fluency, spontaneous flexibility, sensitivity to problems, and originality were found by Drevdahl (1956). Similarly, Gerry, DeVeau, and Chorness (1957) reported no significant differences on the Guilford battery between awarded and non-awarded employees when the groups had been equated for intelligence, job performance, and education.

Surveying several years of research on creative, effective people, Mac-Kinnon (1961) stated that in all samples studied, the Guilford tests, scored for quantity or quality, did not correlate well with the degree of creativity as judged by experts in the subjects' own fields. Substantiating this, correlations reported by Gough (1961) between criterion ratings of creativity and several of the Guilford tests were: Unusual Uses (quantity $-.05$, quality .27); Consequences (quantity $-.27$, quality $-.12$); Matchsticks (.04); Gestalt Transformations (.27).

Relationship between Measured Creativity and Measured Intelligence

Using an IQ measure (Stanford-Binet, Wechsler Scale for Children, or Henmon-Nelson) and five creativity measures (Word Association, Uses for Things, Hidden Shapes, Fables, and Make-Up Problems), Getzels and Jackson (1959) selected two experimental groups. One group was composed of children who placed in the top 20 percent on the creativity measures when compared with same-sexed age peers, but below the top 20 percent in measured IQ. The second group consisted of subjects who placed in the top 20 percent in IQ, but below the top 20 percent on the creativity measures. Despite the similarity in mean IQ between the high creative group (IQ $= 127$) and total population (IQ $= 132$), and despite the 23-point difference in mean IQ between the two experimental groups in favor of the high intelligence group (IQ $= 150$), the achievement scores of the two experimental groups on standard subject-matter tests were equally superior to the achievement scores of the remainder of the school population. These data are discussed more fully in a recent volume (Getzels & Jackson, 1962).

The main criticisms of the Getzels-Jackson report have centered around the use of a single atypical school. Torrance studied creative thinking in the early school years (see Torrance, 1958; 1959a; 1959b; 1959c; 1959d; 1959e; 1960a; 1960b; 1960c; 1960d; Torrance, Baker, & Bowers, 1959; Torrance & Radig, 1959) and brought together eight partial replications of the Getzels-Jackson study. Two batteries of creativity tests were used; both consisted of modifications of Guilford-type tests with the exception of the Ask and Guess Test developed by Torrance (Torrance & Radig, 1959). The procedure followed by Torrance (1960c) is similar to Getzels and Jackson in that he selected groups who placed in the upper 20 percent on either the creativity or IQ measures, but not in the upper 20 percent on the remaining measure.

In six of Torrance's eight groups, there was no significant difference on measured achievement between the high creative and high intelligence groups. In two of the elementary schools (the small town school and the parochial school) there was a significant difference in measured achievement in favor of the high intelligence group. The question is then raised: Under what conditions do "highly creative" pupils achieve as well as "highly intelligent" ones? Additional data reported by Torrance suggest a tendency for the highly creative groups to be better on reading and language skills than on work-study or arithmetic skills.

Meer and Stein (1955) reported a significant relationship between research chemists scores on the Wechsler-Bellevue, Miller Analogies, and supervisors ratings of creativity. When education was controlled, they concluded that with opportunity held constant, IQ beyond the ninety-fifth percentile is not significant for creative work. Similarly, summarizing several studies, Barron (1961) suggested that a small correlation (about .40) exists between the total ranges of creativity and intelligence. However, beyond an IQ of about 120, measured intelligence is unimportant for creativity. He pointed instead to the importance of motivational and stylistic variables.

Criterion Group Empirical Approach

The Welsh Figure Preference Test (WFPT; Welsh, 1949; 1959a; 1959b) is a different type of psychometric instrument used in the study of creativity. In short, it is a nonlingual test composed of 400 India ink drawings, to each of which the examinee must respond "like" or "don't like." Of primary interest in the present context is an empirical scale derived by contrasting the likes and dislikes of 37 artists and art students with the likes and dislikes of 150 people in general (Barron & Welsh, 1952). This scale has since been revised by Welsh to eliminate any response set and in its present form the Revised Art (RA) scale consists of 30 drawings that artists like more frequently than people do in general, and 30 items that artists dislike more often than people do in general.

Rosen (1955) attempted to use the earlier form of the Art scale (BW) as a predictor of originality and level of ability among artists. He reported a significant difference between artists and art students as contrasted with nonartists, but no evidence that Art scale score increased as a function of level of training of the artist. One art product of each of the students was rated on a 5-point scale of originality by each of the art faculty. The correlation between the Art scale score and the average of the ratings was .40. The correlation between the Art scale score and the grade-point average of the students was .34.

Rank-order correlations of .40 and .35 between scores on the RA scale and creative writing instructor's ratings of originality and creativity of their students were reported by Welsh (1959a). Gough (1961) reported that the BW scale showed the highest single correlation (.41) with criterion judgments of research workers' creativity. Among the many measures which did not correlate well with the criterion judgments were three ability measures, the Allport-Vernon value scales, 56 of the 57 Strong Vocational Inventory scales, Barron's Originality scale, Barron's Preference for Complexity scale, the originality coefficient from Gough's Differential Reaction Schedule, and the six Guilford measures already noted.

Data obtained by MacKinnon (1961) indicated that a group of highly creative architects placed in the same range as artists on the BW scale, while a less creative group obtained lower scores, and a third group not distinguished for its creativity scored lowest.

EMPHASIS ON PERSONALITY

Personality is another major emphasis within the psychological study of creativity. It can be subdivided into: (a) the study of motivation of creative behavior and (b) the study of personality characteristics or life styles of creative individuals. Regarding motivation, two divergent viewpoints are apparent. One describes creative behavior as an emergent property which matures as the individual attempts to realize his fullest potentials in his interaction with his environment, while the second treats creativity as a byproduct of repressed or unacceptable impulses.

Among the concepts related to the first viewpoint are Allport's (1937) functional autonomy, Goldstein's (1939), Roger's (1954; 1956), and Yacorzynski's (1954) self-actualization; as well as May's (1959) and Schachtel's (1959) motives for creativity. Individuals are described as being creative because it is satisfying to them since they have a need to relate to the world around them so they may experience their selves in action.

Antithetical to these views are the concepts of psychoanalytic authors who have discussed creativity. Freud (1910; 1924; 1948) originally postulated that all cultural achievements are caused by the diversion of libidinal energy. This displacement, producing higher cultural achievements, he called sublimation (Freud, 1930). Several authors have described creativity as motivated by efforts to defend against unacceptable impulses (see Bergler, 1947; Bychowski, 1951) or as motivated by unconscious restitution for destructive urges (see Fairbairn, 1938; Lee, 1947; 1948; 1950; Rickman, 1957; Sharpe, 1930; 1950). Other reductionistic treatments of creativity can be found in the writings of Abraham (1949), Adler (1927), Bellack (1958), Bischler (1937), Brill (1931), Ehrenzweig (1949), Grotjahn (1957), Kohut (1957), Kris (1952), Levey (1940), Rank (1916), and Sachs (1951). Criticisms of sublimation theory were offered by Bergler (1945), Deri (1939), and Levey (1939).

It is difficult to compare these viewpoints experimentally for several reasons. Creativity has not been defined by either group and it does not seem that they are describing the same types of behaviors. The reductionistic authors most often discuss painting and writing in their attempts to explain creativity. The self-actualizing group seem to describe a much more global style of interacting with one's environment which could lead to products that would be judged as creative. Moreover, such concepts as sublimation and self-actualization are not easily definable or measurable. There are a few experimental studies which have yielded data of varying degrees of consistency or inconsistency with the two views of motivation for creative behavior.

Studies of Motivation for Creativity

Münsterberg and Mussen (1953) attempted to study several hypotheses derived from psychoanalytic formulations of the creative personality. They interpreted the data as supporting the following hypotheses: (a) more artists than non-artists have intense guilt feelings, (b) more artists are introverted and have a rich inner life, (c) more artists than non-artists are unable or unwilling to comply with their parents. No support was reported for the following hypotheses: (a) non-artists are more likely to show overt aggressive tendencies, (b) appreciation of the product supplies basic narcissistic gratification for the artist, (c) the artist interprets appreciation as evidence that others share his guilt. Evidence was reported supporting the single hypothesis which was not derived from psychoanalytic formulations—that more artists than non-artists show a need for creative self-expression.

Myden (1959) defined a highly creative group by choosing 20 subjects from "the top rank" of diverse fields of the arts. Content and formal analysis of the Rorschach suggested that the creative group did utilize primary process significantly more than the noncreative group. Myden stated that in the creative individual the primary process appeared to be integrated with the secondary process and did not seem to arise from, or increase, anxiety. Regression appeared to be a part of the thinking of creative individuals, rather than symptomatic of loss of ego control. No quantitative difference in anxiety was apparent between the two groups. The creative group was reported to employ significantly less repression than did the noncreative group. Myden believed that this may account for the finding that they show a greater amount of psycho-sexual ambivalence.

One large difference between the two groups, which is not considered in the psychoanalytic literature, was noted to be a significantly stronger sense of psychological role-in-life characteristic of the creative group. Myden (1959) described them as "inner-directed and not easily swayed by outside reactions and opinions." (p. 156).

Golann (1961; 1962) proposed a hypothetical construct—the creativity motive—through which he attempted to express the view that creative products are only one segment of creative behavior which becomes mani-fest when individuals actively interact with their environment so as to experience their fullest perceptual, cognitive, and expressive potentials. He argued that high creativity motive subjects should prefer stimuli and situations which allow for idiosyncratic ways of dealing with them. In an attempt to demonstrate this, and in an attempt toward explanation of positive correlations between the Art scales of the WFPT and judged creativity in painting, writing, and research, it was shown that the 30 RA scale items liked by artists were significantly more ambiguous than the RA items artists did not like. A second study revealed that individuals who scored high on the RA scale, subjects who preferred the ambiguous, evocative figures, indicated preference on a questionnaire for activities and situations which allowed more self-expression and utilization of creative capacity, in contrast to low RA subjects who preferred more routine, structured, and assigned activities.

Personality attributes of creative individuals have been treated through experimental study and theoretical descriptive reports. Maslow's (1959) description of self-actualizing creativeness and Roger's (1954) discussion of conditions within the individual that are closely associated with a potentially creative act are highly similar. Both authors placed a great deal of importance on openness to experience rather than premature conceptualization, and on an internal locus of evaluation rather than over concern with the opinions of others. The theme of individuals' desire to fully achieve their potentials through their interaction with the environment is prominent in these writings. Similar or related observations have been made by Fromm (1959), Murphy (1947; 1958), and Mooney (1953a; 1953b).

Studies of Personality Attributes of Creative Individuals

The experimental study of personality attributes of creative individuals tends to contrast criterion groups on either self-descriptions, others' descriptions, test performance, life history material, or work habits. The criterion groups have been selected on the basis of either ratings of creativity, performance on Guilford tests, scores on BW or RA of the WFPT, or nomination of individuals of outstanding creativity by a panel of experts in their field.

The relationship between self-description and degree of creativity has been studied by several investigators. Barron (1952) reported that subjects at the lower extreme on the BW scale described themselves as contented, gentle, conservative, unaffected, patient, and peaceable. In contrast, the high BW subjects characterized themselves as gloomy, loud, unstable, bitter, cool, dissatisfied, pessimistic, emotional, irritable, and pleasure seeking. Similar results were reported by Barron (1958) in a later study. Relating self-descriptions to a productivity criterion, VanZelst and Kerr (1954) reported that productive scientists described themselves as more original, imaginative, curious, enthusiastic, and impulsive, and as less contented and conventional. Stein (1956) reported that creative subjects regard themselves as assertive and authoritative, while less creative regard themselves as acquiescent and submissive. Self-descriptions for highly creative and less creative female mathematicians have been reported by Helson (1961) and by MacKinnon (1961) for groups of architects varying in creativeness. MacKinnon reported that the highly creative stress their inventiveness, independence, individuality, enthusiasm, determination, and industry while the less creative stress virtue, good character, rationality, and concern for others. He suggested that the highly creative are able to speak frankly, in a more unusual way about themselves because they are more self-accepting than their less creative colleagues (see also Barron, 1961).

A dimension similar to that apparent in the self-descriptions is reflected in the test performance of subjects varying in creativity. The values of subjects at the extremes on the BW scale were inferred by Barron (1952) from fine arts preferences. He reported that low BW subjects approved of good breeding, formality, religion, and authority and rejected the daring, esoteric, or sensual. In contrast, high BW subjects approved of the modern, experimental, primitive, and sensual while they disliked the aristocratic, traditional, and emotionally controlled.

Barron (1953) equated performance on the BW scale with a bipolar factor of preference for perceiving and dealing with complexity as opposed to preference for simplicity. Positive relationships reported for preference of complexity included: personal tempo, verbal fluency, impulsiveness, expansiveness, originality, sensuality, sentience, esthetic interest, and femininity in men. Negative relationships of preference for complexity included: rigidity, constriction, repressive impulse control, political-economic conservatism, subservience to authority, ethnocentrism, and social conformity. This dimension is discussed more fully in a later report (Barron, 1961).

Studying the relationship between aptitude and nonaptitude factors, Guilford (1957) stated that the intercorrelations were generally low. Subjects who scored higher on ideational fluency were more impulsive, self-confident, ascendent, more appreciative of originality and somewhat less inclined towards neuroticism. Subjects higher on originality were more interested in esthetic expression, reflective and divergent thinking, more tolerant of ambiguity, and felt less need for orderliness.

Independence as a personality attribute was stressed in several theoretical discussions of creativity. Barron (1953b) reported that subjects who did not yield to the incorrect group consensus in the Asch line judgment situation scored significantly higher on the BW scale than a group of yielders. Barron (1961) also noted that subjects who regularly perform in a creative or original manner on Guilford tests are independent in judgment when put under pressure to conform to a group opinion in conflict with their own.

The suggestion that the real difference between high and low creative individuals might be a function of the lows' defensiveness which inhibits generalization and communication of hypotheses was offered by Stein and Meer (1954). They administered the Rorschach to subjects at exposures ranging from .01 second to full. Their scoring system gave the highest score to a well-integrated response given to a difficult card at the shortest exposure. A biserial correlation of .88 between total weighted score and criterion creativity ratings was reported.

The work style of similarly employed individuals varying in creativity has also been the object of study. Roe (1949) reported that biologists selected for eminence in research were very unaggressive, had little interest in interpersonal relations, were unwilling to go beyond the data presented, and preferred concrete reality to the imaginary. Other data on Rorschach and Thematic Apperception Test performances of groups of eminent scientists are discussed in this and other reports (see Roe, 1946; 1949; 1951; 1952). Bloom (1956) administered projective techniques to outstanding scientists and reported personality and temperamental characteristics similar to those described by Roe. The willingness to work hard seems to be the most general characteristic of the samples studied.

Two research styles were reported by Gough (1961) to correlate with criterion ratings of creativity: the man who is dedicated to research and sees himself as a driving researcher with exceptional mathematical skills; the man with wide interests, analytic in thinking, who prefers research which lends itself to elegant, formal solutions. In a previous paper, Gough (1958) had described eight types of researchers and how these were conceptualized.

Another source of data bearing on creativity and personality is life history material. Roe (1953) reported that social scientists' interaction with their parents involved overprotection while physical and biological scientists developed early a way of life not requiring personal interaction.

A negative relationship between rated creativity and socioeconomic as well as educational status of the parents has been reported by Stein (1956). Creative subjects were more likely to feel that their parents were inconsistent in attitudes toward them. Less creative subjects were more likely to engage in group activities in childhood while the more creative preferred solitary activities. Similar trends were reported in extensive biographical studies by Cattell (1959). MacKinnon (1961) reported relationships between life history material and rated creativity which require and warrant further investigation.

Crutchfield (1961) attempted to describe personality attributes which tend to characterize creative individuals in general. He reported that in cognitive spheres they are more flexible and fluent; their perceptions and cognitions are unique. In approach to problems they are intuitive, empathic, perceptually open, and prefer complexity. In emotional-motivational spheres they demonstrate freedom from excessive impulse control, achieve via independence rather than conformity, are individualistic, and have strong, sustained, intrinsic motivation in their field of work.

Studies with Children

Few studies have been reported on creativity in children despite the great interest in the creativeness of childhood. Mattil (1953) attempted to study the relationship between the creative products of children and their adjustment. The data led Mattil to conclude that elements of adjustment and mental abilities are directly related to creative products.

Limited data on creativity in children are included in a monograph by Adkins and her associates (Adkins, Cobb, Miller, Sanford, Stewart, Aub, Burke, Nathanson, Stuart, & Towne, 1943). Teacher ratings of creativity in school children are reported to correlate positively with independent measures of the following variables: .81 with need for sentience (pleasures); .65 with intraception (imaginative, subjective, human outlook); .65 with the need to produce, organize, or build things; .63 with the need for understanding; .60 with the need to explain, judge, or interpret; .50 with the need to restrive after failure and to overcome weakness; .50 with the enjoying of thought and emotion for its own sake or preoccupation with inner activities. Negative correlations reported for the same teacher ratings include: −.79 with sameness (adherence to places, people, and modes of conduct; rigidity of habits); −.57 with the need of acquisition; and −.54 with the need to reject others.

Reid, King, and Wickwire (1959) reported that creative subjects exhibited superior performance on almost all cognitive variables, indicating that cognitive abilities (as measured by general intelligence, aptitude, and achievement instruments) are related to peer nominations of creativity. While these results can be interpreted as generally consistent with studies on adult populations, the findings that the creative group was significantly higher on *cyclothymia*, while the noncreatives were higher on *schizo-*

thymia, contradicts replicated results with adults who have been described as withdrawn or individualistic and have themselves said they preferred individual pursuits as children.

A recent study by Torrance (1959d), in which he attempted to explore some of the relationships between talkativeness and creative thinking, may help resolve the apparent contradiction. He reported that in the first grade, those children perceived as not speaking out their ideas tend to be more frequently seen as having good ideas, more frequently chosen as friends, higher on a measure of spontaneous flexibility, more intelligent, and higher on a nonverbal measure of creativity. This pattern gradually begins to shift, and by the fourth grade, the highly talkative individuals are more frequently perceived as having good ideas and receive more friendship choices. Thus, highly talkative children tend to earn higher scores on the verbal test of creativity, but not on the nonverbal measure. Torrance's results suggested that a sociometric criterion will select children with well-developed and exercised verbal abilities who are not necessarily more creative than many of their peers. A wide range of issues concerning the development of creativity in children is discussed in a paper by Lowenfeld (1959).

CRITICAL OVERVIEW

What is creativity? Creativity has been viewed as a normally distributed trait; as such its investigation has proceeded in an attempt to find product criteria from which the presence or absence of the trait in an individual could be inferred. Creativity has been viewed as the outcome of a complex of aptitude traits; as such its investigation has proceeded in an attempt to demonstrate the presence of such traits through factor analysis and to develop measuring instruments. Creativity has been viewed as a process culminating in a new thought or insight; as such its investigation has proceeded by introspective reporting, or investigator observation of the temporal sequence. Creativity has been described as a style of life, the personality in action; as such its investigation has been concerned with personality descriptions and assessment of people believed to be creative and investigation of motives for creativity.

All of the possible emphases within the study of creativity require no justification other than noting that each is capable of making important contributions. It would seem, however, that data reported by Taylor, Smith, and Ghiselin (1959), which indicated a very low degree of association among the many possible product criteria, argue against the likelihood of a product approach providing a comprehensive understanding of creativity. Crutchfield's (1961) discussion of the creative process should be helpful to those attempting experimental studies. His explanation of illumination will require careful study in the light of recent reports (see Spielberger, 1962) which suggest that the examiner's awareness of the subject's awareness may be a function of the extent of the postexperimental interview. Difficulty may arise when investigators, working within one area of emphases, with one explicit or implied definition and set of criteria, lose sight of the inherent limitations of their choices. The point can perhaps be illustrated by a reconsideration of the relationship between creativity and intelligence.

The studies by Getzels and Jackson (1959) and Torrance (1959e) indicated that measured intellectual ability and measured creative ability are by no means synonymous. Torrance presented additional data which indicated that in his sample, using only the Wechsler Intelligence Scale for Children, to determine giftedness would have excluded 70 percent of the children placing in the upper 20 percent on the creativity measures. The same ratios obtain using other measures of intelligence. Meer and Stein (1955), Barron (1961), and MacKinnon (1961) agree essentially that while there is a correlation over the entire ranges of intelligence and creativity, the magnitude of the correlation varies greatly at different levels of intelligence. Meer and Stein cite the ninety-fifth percentile, Barron an IQ of 120, as the approximate point above which intelligence is unimportant for creativity. The point that needs to be stressed is that these data are in a sense arbitrary: intelligence is not performance on a test; creativity is more than test performance or being judged as creative. What is needed for the understanding of the relationship between creativity and intelligence is not only data at the correlational level, but conceptual reorganization as well. Just as the choice of a series of Guilford tests or judgment procedures implies one definition of creativity, the choice of an intelligence test implies one of many possible definitions of intelligence. I. Taylor (1959), for example, believes intelligence to be an invention of Western culture, which stresses how fast relatively unimportant problems can be solved without making errors. He feels that another culture might choose to measure intelligence in a way more congruent with a high level of creativity.

For these reasons Guilford has attempted to employ a wide variety of criterion measures, grouped by factor analysis, and study relationships among the factors.

One could, however, select criterion measures on the basis of theoretical constructs and still pay careful attention to the predictive efficacy of the criterion and compare its predictive ability with other possible selection criterion. This author agrees with Guilford that what is needed is better understanding of the nature of intellect but does not agree that factor analysis presents the best way of defining one's constructs. The factor analytic approach does not solve the problem of how well the measuring instrument is sensitive to variations in the construct its user believes it to measure. It does not seem that factor analysis will, itself, enrich basic understanding of creative phenomena. Required are not only data at a correlational level, but a developmental understanding as well, and also an understanding of different situations where different correlations are obtained between the same criteria.

If the choice is made to select subjects on conceptual rather than factor analytic bases it would seem that the investigator should attempt in some manner to isolate the contribution of a single criterion choice. The point to be made can perhaps best be seen in the work reported by Barron and MacKinnon. Their studies utilized a compound criterion in the selection of subjects: creative, effective individuals. The criteria of creativity in all cases were judgments clearly the most carefully collected, reliable of all those reported, but judgments nonetheless. The reports by Harmon (1958) and D. Taylor (1958) indicated that judges' ratings of creativity seem heavily determined by the productivity of the individual. Note that the self-descriptions of productive scientists reported by Van-Zelst and Kerr (1954) are very similar to the self-descriptions of creative individuals reported by Gough, Harmon, and MacKinnon. While it is crucial that creative, productive people be studied as such, it must be kept in mind that the portion of the reported findings attributable to creativity cannot be separated from that portion attributable to that which makes for productivity, and that which leads to being seen by judges as creative. It is possible, and perhaps we are now ready to utilize personality and stylistic modes as criterion variables. In such an approach our criterion variables might be tolerance for or seeking of ambiguity, openness to experience, childlike traits, self-actualization or expression, internal frames of evaluation, or independence of judgment, to name but a few theoretically based descriptive concepts which appear again and again in the literature and deserve further investigation. The important questions would then become: how do these cognitive, stylistic, or motivational modes of interacting with one's environment develop? What are the environmental, interpersonal, and intrapersonal conditions that tend to facilitate or discourage them? How in turn are these factors related at different age levels to behavior which is judged to be creative, effective, and productive? In no sense would this approach solve the problem of using judgments. The argument is not that this approach corrects or circumvents most of the problems inherent in other approaches. However, it is my belief that the use of theoretically derived personality factors as criterion variables has, because of its own inherent difficulties, been neglected, yet holds most promise of providing a functional developmental understanding of creativity.

SUMMARY

In this review of the psychological study of creativity there are 4 emphases: products, process, measurement, and personality. Three main issues concern questions of: definition and criteria, the process viewed temporally, and necessary personal and environmental conditions. The relationship between creativity and intelligence is discussed to illustrate the need for conceptual reorganization as well as correlational data. We should now be able to utilize personality and stylistic modes as criterion variables and to study how these factors are related at different age levels to behavior that is judged to be creative. This approach holds promise for providing a functional, developmental understanding of creativity.

REFERENCES

Abraham, K. The influence of oral erotism on character formation. In *Selected Papers of Karl Abraham*. (Trans. by D. Bryan and A. Strachey). London: Hogarth Press, 1949, 393–406.

Adkins, Margaret M., Cobb, Elizabeth A., Miller, R. B., Sanford, R. W., Stewart, Ann H., Aub, J. C., Burke, Bertha, Nathanson, I. T., Stuart, H. C., and Towne, Lois. Physique, personality, and scholarship. *Monographs of the Society for Research in Child Development*, 1943, 8(1, Ser. No. 34).

Adler, A. *The Practice and Theory of Individual Psychology*. New York: Harcourt, Brace, 1927.

Allport, G. W. The functional autonomy of motives. *American Journal of Psychology*, 1937, **50**, 141–156.

Arnold, J. F. Creativity in engineering. In P. Smith (Ed.) *Creativity*. New York: Hastings House, 1959, 33–46.

Barron, F. Personality style and perceptual choice. *Journal of Personality*, 1952, **20**, 385–401.

Barron, F. Complexity-simplicity as a personality dimension. *Journal of Abnormal and Social Psychology*, 1953, **48**, 162–172. (a)

Barron, F. Some personality correlates of independence of judgment. *Journal of Personality*, 1953, **21**, 287–297. (b)

Barron, F. The disposition towards originality. In C. Taylor (Ed.) *The 1955 University of Utah Research Conference on the Identification of Creative Scientific Talent*. Salt Lake City: University of Utah Press, 1956, 156–170.

Barron, F. The needs for order and for disorder as motives in creative activity. In C. Taylor (Ed.) *The 1957 University of Utah Research Conference on the Identification of Creative Scientific Talent*. Salt Lake City: University of Utah Press, 1958, 119–128.

Barron, F.   Creative vision and expression in writing and painting. In *Conference on the Creative Person*. Berkeley: University of California, Institute of Personality Assessment and Research, 1961, Chap. 2.

Barron, F., and Welsh, G. S.   Artistic perception as a possible factor in personality style: Its measurement by a figure preference test. *Journal of Psychology*, 1952, **33**, 199–203.

Bédard, R. J.   *Creativity in the Arts, Literature, Science, and Engineering: A Bibliography of French Contributions*. (Creativity Research Exchange Bulletin No. 10) Princeton, N.J.: Educational Testing Service, 1959.

Bédard, R. J.   *Creativity in the Arts, Literature, Science, and Engineering: A Bibliography of Italian Contributions*. (Creativity Research Exchange Bulletin No. 9) Princeton, N.J.: Educational Testing Service, 1960.

Bellack, L.   Creativity: Some random notes to a systematic consideration. *Journal of Projective Techniques*, 1958, **22**, 363–380.

Bergler, E.   On a five-layer structure in sublimation. *Psychoanalytical Quarterly*, 1945, **14**, 76–97.

Bergler, E.   Psychoanalysis of writers and of literary productivity. In G. Roheim (Ed.) *Psychoanalysis and the Social Sciences*. Vol. 1. New York: International Universities Press, 1947, 247–296.

Bischler, W.   Intelligence and higher mental functions. *Psychoanalytical Quarterly*, 1937, **6**, 277–307.

Bloom, B. S.   Report on creativity research at the University of Chicago. In C. Taylor (Ed.) *The 1955 University of Utah Research Conference on the Identification of Creative Scientific Talent*. Salt Lake City: University of Utah Press, 1956, 182–194.

Brill, A. A.   Poetry as an oral outlet. *Psychoanalytical Review*, 1931, **18**, 357–378.

Bychowski, G.   Metapsychology of artistic creation. *Psychoanalytical Quarterly*, 1951, **20**, 592–602.

Cattell, R. B.   The personality and motivation of the researcher from measurements of contemporaries and from bibliography. In C. Taylor (Ed.) *The 1959 University of Utah Research Conference on the Identification of Creative Scientific Talent*. Salt Lake City: University of Utah Press, 1959, 77–93.

Chassell, L. M.   Tests for originality. *Journal of Educational Psychology*, 1916, **7**, 317–329.

Chorness, M. H.   An interim report on creativity research. In C. Taylor (Ed.) *The 1955 University of Utah Research Conference on the Identification of Creative Scientific Talent*. Salt Lake City: University of Utah Press, 1956, 132–153.

Crutchfield, R.   The creative process. In *Conference on the Creative Person*. Berkeley: University of California, Institute of Personality Assessment and Research, 1961, Chap. 6.

Dashiell, J. F.   *Fundamentals of General Psychology*. New York: Houghton Mifflin, 1931.

Deri, F.   On sublimation. *Psychoanalytical Quarterly*, 1939, **8**, 325–334.

Drevdahl, J. E.   Factors of importance for creativity. *Journal of Clinical Psychology*, 1956, **12**, 21–26.

Ehrenzweig, A.   The origin of the scientific and heroic urge. *International Journal of Psychoanalysis*, 1949, **30**, 108–123.

Fairbairn, W. R. D.   Prolegomena to a psychology of art. *British Journal of Psychology*, 1938, **28**, 288–303.

Freud, S.   *Three Contributions to the Theory of Sex.* New York: Nervous & Mental Disease Publishing Company, 1910.

Freud, S.   "Civilized" sexual morality and modern nervousness. (Orig. publ. 1908) In *Collected Papers*, Vol. 2. (Trans. by J. Riviere). London: Hogarth Press, 1924, 76–99.

Freud, S.   *Civilization and Its Discontents.* (Trans. by J. Riviere). New York: Cope & Smith, 1930.

Freud, S.   The relation of the poet to day-dreaming. (Orig. publ. 1908) In *Collected Papers*, Vol. 4. (Trans. by J. Riviere). London: Hogarth Press, 1948, 173–183.

Fromm, E.   The creative attitude. In H. Anderson (Ed.) *Creativity and Its Cultivation.* New York: Harper, 1959, 44–54.

Gamble, A. O.   Suggestions for future research. In C. Taylor (Ed.) *The 1959 University of Utah Research Conference on the Identification of Creative Scientific Talent.* Salt Lake City: University of Utah Press, 1959, 292–297.

Gerry, R., DeVeau, L., and Chorness, M.   *A Review of Some Recent Research in the Field of Creativity and the Examination of an Experimental Creativity Workshop.* (Proj. No. 56–24) Lackland Air Force Base, Texas: Training Analysis and Development Division, 1957.

Getzels, J. W., and Jackson, P. W.   The highly intelligent and the highly creative adolescent: A summary of some research findings. In C. Taylor (Ed.) *The 1959 University of Utah Research Conference on the Identification of Creative Scientific Talent.* Salt Lake City: University of Utah Press, 1959, 46–57.

Getzels, J. W., and Jackson, P. W.   *Creativity and Intelligence: Explorations with Gifted Children.* New York: John Wiley, 1962.

Ghiselin, B.   The creative process and its relation to the identification of creative talent. In C. Taylor (Ed.) *The 1959 University of Utah Research Conference on the Identification of Creative Scientific Talent.* Salt Lake City: University of Utah Press, 1956, 195–203.

Ghiselin, B.   Ultimate criteria for two levels of creativity. In C. Taylor (Ed.) *The 1957 University of Utah Research Conference on the Identification of Creative Scientific Talent.* Salt Lake City: University of Utah Press, 1958, 141–155.

Golann, S. E.   The creativity motive. Unpublished doctoral dissertation, University of North Carolina, 1961.

Golann, S. E.   The creativity motive. *Journal of Personality*, 1962, **30**, 588–600.

Goldstein, K.   *The Organism.* New York: American Book, 1939.

Gough, H. G.   Stylistic variations in the self-views and work attitudes of a sample of professional research scientists. Paper read at Western Psychological Association, Monterey, California, April 1958.

Gough, H. G. Techniques for identifying the creative research scientist. In *Conference on the Creative Person*. Berkeley: University of California, Institute of Personality Assessment and Research, 1961, Chap. 3.

Grotjahn, M. *Beyond Laughter*. New York: McGraw-Hill, 1957.

Guilford, J. P. The relation of intellectual factors to creative thinking in science. In C. Taylor (Ed.) *The 1955 University of Utah Research Conference on the Identification of Creative Scientific Talent*. Salt Lake City: University of Utah Press, 1956, 69–95.

Guilford, J. P. Creative abilities in the arts. *Psychological Review*, 1957, **64**, 110–118.

Guilford, J. P. Intellectual resources and their values as seen by scientists. In C. Taylor (Ed.) *The 1959 University of Utah Research Conference on the Identification of Creative Scientific Talent*. Salt Lake City: University of Utah Press, 1959, 128–149. (a)

Guilford, J. P. Traits of creativity. In H. Anderson (Ed.) *Creativity and Its Cultivation*. New York: Harper, 1959, 142–161. (b)

Guilford, J. P., Kettner, N. W., and Christensen, P. R. A factor-analytic study across the domains of reasoning, creativity, and evaluation: I. Hypotheses and description of tests. *University of Southern California Psychology Laboratory Reports*, 1954, No. 11.

Guilford, J. P., Kettner, N. W., and Christensen, P. R. A factor-analytic study across the domains of reasoning, creativity, and evaluation: II. Administration of tests and analysis of results. *University of Southern California Psychology Laboratory Reports*, 1956, No. 16.

Hadamard, J. *An Essay on the Psychology of Invention in the Mathematical Field*. Princeton, N.J.: Princeton University Press, 1945.

Harmon, L. R. Social and technological determiners of creativity. In C. Taylor (Ed.) *The 1955 University of Utah Research Conference on the Identification of Creative Scientific Talent*. Salt Lake City: University of Utah Press, 1956, 42–52.

Harmon, L. R. The development of a criterion of scientific competence. In C. Taylor (Ed.) *The 1957 University of Utah Conference on the Identification of Creative Scientific Talent*. Salt Lake City: University of Utah Press, 1958, 82–97.

Harris, R. A. Creativity in marketing. In P. Smith (Ed.) *Creativity*. New York: Hastings House, 1959, 143–166.

Helson, Ravenna. Creativity, sex, and mathematics. In *Conference on the Creative Person*. Berkeley: University of California, Institute of Personality Assessment and Research, 1961, Chap. 4.

Kettner, N. W., Guilford, J. P., and Christensen, P. R. A factor-analytic study across the domains of reasoning, creativity, and evaluation. *Psychological Monographs*, 1959, **73**(9, Whole No. 479).

Kohut, H. Observations on the psychological functions of music. *Journal of American Psychoanalysis Association*, 1957, **5**, 389–407.

Kris, E. *Psychoanalytic Explorations in Art.* New York: International Universities Press, 1952.

Lee, H. B. On the esthetic states of mind. *Psychiatry,* 1947, **10,** 281–306.

Lee, H. B. Spirituality and beauty in artistic experience. *Psychoanalytical Quarterly,* 1948, **17,** 507–523.

Lee, H. B. The values of order and vitality in art. In G. Roheim (Ed.) *Psychoanalysis and the Social Sciences,* Vol. 2. New York: International Universities Press, 1950, 231–274.

Levey, H. B. A critique of the theory of sublimation. *Psychiatry,* 1939, **2,** 239–270.

Levey, H. B. A theory concerning free creation in the inventive arts. *Psychiatry,* 1940, **3,** 229–293.

Lowenfeld, V. *Educational Implications of Creativity Research in the Arts.* (Creativity Research Exchange Bulletin No. 8). Princeton, N.J.: Educational Testing Service, 1959.

MacKinnon, D. W. The study of creativity and creativity in architects. In *Conference on the Creative Person.* Berkeley: University of California, Institute of Personality Assessment and Research, 1961, Chaps. 1 and 5.

McPherson, J. H. A proposal for establishing ultimate criteria for measuring creative output. In C. Taylor (Ed.) *The 1955 University of Utah Research Conference on the Identification of Creative Scientific Talent.* Salt Lake City: University of Utah Press, 1956, 62–68.

Maslow, A. H. Creativity in self-actualizing people. In H. Anderson (Ed.) *Creativity and Its Cultivation.* New York: Harper, 1959, 83–95.

Mattil, E. L. A study to determine the relationship between the creative products of children, aged 11–14, and their adjustments. Unpublished doctoral dissertation, Pennsylvania State University, 1953.

May, R. The nature of creativity. In H. Anderson (Ed.) *Creativity and Its Cultivation.* New York: Harper, 1959, 55–68.

Meer, B., and Stein, M. I. Measures of intelligence and creativity. *Journal of Psychology,* 1955, **39,** 117–126.

Mooney, R. L. *Classification of Items in "A Preliminary Listing of Indices of Creative Behavior."* Columbus: Ohio State University, Bureau of Educational Research, 1953. (a)

Mooney, R. L. *A Preliminary Listing of Indices of Creative Behavior.* Columbus: Ohio State University, Bureau of Educational Research, 1953. (b)

Münsterberg, Elizabeth, and Mussen, P. H. The personality structures of art students. *Journal of Personality,* 1953, **21,** 457–466.

Murphy, G. *Personality: A Biosocial Approach to Origins and Structure.* New York: Harper, 1947.

Murphy, G. *Human Potentialities.* New York: Basic Books, 1958.

Myden, W. Interpretation and evaluation of certain personality characteristics involved in creative production. *Perception and Motor Skills,* 1959, **9,** 139–158.

Rank, O., and Sachs, H. *The Significance of Psychoanalysis for the Mental*

Sciences. Washington, D. C.: Nervous & Mental Disease Publishing Company, 1916.

Reid, J. B., King, F. J., and Wickwire, Pat. Cognitive and other personality characteristics of creative children. *Psychological Reports,* 1959, 5, 729–737.

Rickman, J. On the nature of ugliness and the creative impulse. (Orig. publ. 1940) In W. Clifford and M. Scott (Eds.) *Selected Contributions to Psychoanalysis.* London: Hogarth Press, 1957, 68–89.

Roe, Anne. Artists and their work. *Journal of Personality,* 1946, 15, 1–40.

Roe, Anne. Psychological examinations of eminent biologists. *Journal of Consulting Psychology,* 1949, 13, 225–246.

Roe, Anne. A psychological study of eminent biologists. *Psychological Monographs,* 1951, 65(14, Whole No. 331).

Roe, Anne. *The Making of a Scientist.* New York: Dodd-Mead, 1952.

Roe, Anne. A psychological study of eminent psychologists and anthropologists and a comparison with biological and physical scientists. *Psychological Monographs,* 1953, 67(2, Whole No. 352).

Rogers, C. R. Toward a theory of creativity. *Etcetera,* 1954, 11, 249–260.

Rogers, C. R. What it means to become a person. In C. Moustakas (Ed.) *The Self.* New York: Harper, 1956, 195–211.

Rosen, J. C. The Barron-Welsh art scale as a predictor of originality and level of ability among artists. *Journal of Applied Psychology,* 1955, 39, 366–367.

Sachs, H. *The Creative Unconscious* (2d ed.) Cambridge, Mass.: Science-Art Publishers, 1951.

Schachtel, E. G. *Metamorphosis.* New York: Basic Books, 1959.

Sharpe, Ella F. Certain aspects of sublimation and delusion. *International Journal of Psychoanalysis,* 1930, 11, 12–23.

Sharpe, Ella F. Similar and divergent unconscious determinants underlying the sublimations of pure art and pure science. In M. Brierly (Ed.) *Collected Papers on Psychoanalysis.* London: Hogarth Press, 1950, 137–154.

Spielberger, C. D. The role of awareness in verbal conditioning. *Journal of Personality,* 1962, 30, 73–101.

Stein, M. I. Creativity and culture. *Journal of Psychology,* 1953, 36, 311–322.

Stein, M. I. A transactional approach to creativity. In C. Taylor (Ed.) *The 1955 University of Utah Research Conference on the Identification of Creative Scientific Talent.* Salt Lake City: University of Utah Press, 1956, 171–181.

Stein, M. I., and Heinze, Shirley. *Creativity and the Individual.* Glencoe, Ill.: Free Press, 1960.

Stein, M. I., and Meer, B. Perceptual organization in a study of creativity. *Journal of Psychology,* 1954, 37, 39–43.

Taylor, C. (Ed.) *The 1959 University of Utah Research Conference on the Identification of Creative Scientific Talent.* Salt Lake City: University of Utah Press, 1959.

Taylor, C. W., Smith, W. R., and Ghiselin, B. Analysis of multiple criteria of creativity and productivity of scientists. In C. Taylor (Ed.) *The 1959 University of Utah Research Conference on the Identification of Creative Scientific Talent*. Salt Lake City: University of Utah Press, 1959, 5–28.

Taylor, D. W. Variables related to creativity and productivity among men in two research laboratories. In C. Taylor (Ed.) *The 1957 University of Utah Research Conference on the Identification of Creative Scientific Talent*. Salt Lake City: University of Utah Press, 1958, 20–54.

Taylor, D. W. Thinking and creativity. *Annual New York Academy of Sciences,* 1960, **91**, 108–127.

Taylor, D. W. Environment and creativity. In *Conference on the Creative Person*. Berkeley: University of California, Institute of Personality Assessment and Research, 1961, Chap. 8.

Taylor, I. A. The nature of the creative process. In P. Smith (Ed.) *Creativity*. New York: Hastings House, 1959, 51–82.

Torrance, E. P. *Sex-role Identification and Creative Thinking*. Minneapolis: University of Minnesota, Bureau of Educational Research, 1958.

Torrance, E. P. *Explorations in Creative Thinking in the Early School Years: II. An Experiment in Training and Motivation*. Minneapolis: University of Minnesota, Bureau of Educational Research, 1959. (a)

Torrance, E. P. *Explorations in Creative Thinking in the Early School Years: V. An Experimental Study of Peer Sanctions against Highly Creative Children*. Minneapolis: University of Minnesota, Bureau of Educational Research, 1959. (b)

Torrance, E. P. *Explorations in Creative Thinking in the Early School Years: VI. Highly Intelligent and Highly Creative Children in a Laboratory School*. Minneapolis: University of Minnesota, Bureau of Educational Research, 1959. (c)

Torrance, E. P. *Explorations in Creative Thinking in the Early School Years: VII. Talkativeness and Creative Thinking*. Minneapolis: University of Minnesota, Bureau of Educational Research, 1959. (d)

Torrance, E. P. Explorations in creative thinking in the early school years: A progress report. In C. Taylor (Ed.) *The 1959 University of Utah Research Conference on the Identification of Creative Scientific Talent*. Salt Lake City: University of Utah Press, 1959, 58–71. (e)

Torrance, E. P. *Changing Reactions of Girls in Grades Four Through Six to Tasks Requiring Creative Scientific Thinking*. Minneapolis: University of Minnesota, Bureau of Educational Research, 1960. (a)

Torrance, E. P. *A Collection of Ideas for Developing the Creative Thinking Abilities Through the Language Arts*. Minneapolis: University of Minnesota, Bureau of Educational Research, 1960. (b)

Torrance, E. P. *Educational Achievement of the Highly Intelligent and the Highly Creative: Eight Partial Replications of the Getzels-Jackson Study*. Minneapolis: University of Minnesota, Bureau of Educational Research, 1960. (c)

Torrance, E. P.   *Social Stress in Homogeneous and Heterogeneous Groups.* Minneapolis: University of Minnesota, Bureau of Educational Research, 1960. (d)

Torrance, E. P., Baker, F. B., and Bowers, J. E.   *Explorations in Creative Thinking in the Early School Years: IV. Manipulation of Objects and Inventiveness.* Minneapolis: University of Minnesota, Bureau of Educational Research, 1959.

Torrance, E. P., and Radig, H. J.   *The Ask and Guess Test: Scoring Manual and Rationale.* Minneapolis: University of Minnesota, Bureau of Educational Research, 1959.

VanZelst, R. H., and Kerr, W. A.   Personality self-assessment of scientific and technical personnel. *Journal of Applied Psychology*, 1954, **38**, 145–147.

Wallas, G.   *The Art of Thought.* New York: Harcourt, Brace, 1926.

Welsh, G. S.   A projective figure-preference test for diagnosis of psychopathology: I. A preliminary investigation. Unpublished doctoral dissertation, University of Minnesota, 1949.

Welsh, G. S.   *Preliminary Manual: Welsh Figure Preference Test.* (Res. ed.) Palo Alto, Calif.: Consulting Psychologists Press, 1959. (a)

Welsh, G. S.   *Welsh Figure Preference Test.* (Res. ed.) Palo Alto, Calif.: Consulting Psychologists Press, 1959. (b)

Woodworth, R. S., and Schlosberg, H.   *Experimental Psychology.* (2d ed.) New York: Holt, Rinehart and Winston, 1954.

Yacorzynski, G. K.   The nature of man. In F. L. K. Hsu (Ed.) *Aspects of Culture and Personality.* New York: Abelard-Schuman, 1954, 173–186.

2.5   Orientation

In most discussions of adolescent problems found in the literature on adolescence, vocational choice ranks among the most critical. Noteworthy examples include the developmental functions of future orientation and vocational preparation revealed in Douvan and Adelson's (1966) large scale research, the concern and confusion over career planning among large percentages of adolescents disclosed by Remmers and Radler (1957), and Tennyson's (1968) recent review of career development theory and research. Therefore, a most relevant contribution to this volume is Samuel Osipow's succinct overview of conceptual approaches to the study of vocational (career) development. Osipow steps beyond a traditional descriptive review, however, to take the position that cognitive factors in development are necessary considerations if a more adequate understanding of vocational choice behavior is to be achieved.

Central to Osipow's cognitive orientation is a psychological construct known as *cognitive style*. This construct refers to the characteristic way in which an individual perceives, decodes, and encodes environmental stimuli. (An example of research based on cognitive style is provided in Part III of this volume.) If Osipow's cognitive style hypothesis weathers the empirical test successfully, a number of implications for vocational guidance should emerge. Osipow concludes his present discussion by charting several of these implications.

Although the study of vocational development could easily be justified on intrinsic grounds, there exist many important practical questions in this area of psychology. Some of the most important of these questions cluster within education. For example, can realistic vocational planning and choice be facilitated through educational programs which provide occupational information to adolescents? Can vocational guidance programs provide a foundation for positive vocational "adjustment" and reduce the incidence of job dissatisfaction among workers? Is it possible to derive more valid systems of testing which allow for the accurate prediction of vocational success? Data from the Osipow selection and references listed below will be helpful to students interested in these and other issues related to vocational development and guidance.

RECOMMENDED READINGS

Crites, J. O., and Semler, I. J. Adjustment, educational achievement, and vocational maturity as dimensions of development in adolescence. *Journal of Counseling Psychology*, 1967, 14, 489–496.

Douvan, Elizabeth, and Adelson, Joseph. *The Adolescent Experience.* New York: John Wiley, 1966.

Hollender, John W. Development of a realistic vocational choice. *Journal of Counseling Psychology*, 1968, 15, 23–30.

Krumboltz, J. D., and Schroeder, W. W. Promoting career planning through reinforcement. *Personnel and Guidance Journal*, 1966, 44, 611–614.

Remmers, H. H., and Radler, D. H. *The American Teenager.* Indianapolis: Bobbs-Merrill, 1957.

Simons, J. B. Existential view of vocational development. *Personnel and Guidance Journal*, 1966, 44, 604–614.

Stump, W. L., Jordan, J. E., and Friesen, E. W. Cross-cultural considerations in understanding vocational development. *Journal of Counseling Psychology*, 1967, 14, 325–331.

Tennyson, W. Wesley. Career development. *American Educational Research Journal*, 1968, 38, 346–366.

2.5 Some Cognitive Aspects of Career Development

Samuel H. Osipow, THE OHIO STATE UNIVERSITY

Over the years a great deal of attention has been focused on the study of vocational maturation, the antecedents of good decision-making, and methods of vocational choice implementation through the adolescent period. This attention is understandable, since our educational system is closely tied to vocational choice and training. Many of the educational decisions made and skills acquired during adolescence have significant implications for later vocational choice, attainment, performance, and satisfaction.

A number of perplexing questions have plagued the study of vocational development and implementation. It is troublesome not to be able to identify the early antecedents of good decision-making; it is bothersome not to understand more about the inter-individual differences in information processing for decision-making; it is awkward not to have a handy way to account for the wide tolerance of individual differences exhibited by occupations. A clear need exists for an adequate means to explain the process of vocational development.

Many theoretical descriptions of career development have been put forward (Osipow, 1968). The earliest of these views of vocational development were essentially aimed at identifying the individual traits most closely associated with particular occupational preferences, membership, and success. This approach took the point of view that vocational choice is at heart an irreversible decision made at a specific point in time. Thus, an attempt was made to identify the abilities and personality traits that best suit an individual to the pursuit of a particular career in order to reach the objective of matching the individual and occupational traits as closely as possible. A giant matrix of traits could potentially be developed, individual traits could be compared to the matrix associated for an occupation by means of statistical methods, and clients could sort through the matrix to make their decision. This procedure is theoretically feasible within the limits of current tests, inventories, and statistical formulas, since job tasks do draw on abilities differentially. Thus, automobile mechanics are likely to require certain mechanical, spatial, and manual skills and aptitudes; these demands differ substantially from the traits required for success in a medical career.

An original paper prepared especially for this volume.

In the personality realm, however, although occupational differences exist, a considerable and annoying overlap of traits has been observed. Possibly, the overlap occurs because, to some extent, job roles shape personality as well as the reverse. A job role may determine the ideal personality type to enter a given occupation. Once entered, however, "personality" interacts with the occupation. For example, there is a stereotype that depicts accountants to be compulsive. One would expect compulsive people to be highly attracted to careers as accountants. If a relatively uncompulsive individual were attracted to accounting, however, and some undoubtedly are, it may be expected that he would become more compulsive as a result of the nature of the duties involved in being an accountant. The job duties involved in accounting reinforce compulsive, careful behaviors.

Since personality traits significantly moderate the effect of aptitudes on career progress (through their impact on motivation, for example), the accuracy of the aptitude-oriented trait factor model breaks down. As a result, it actually has a limited impact on vocational decision-making despite its wide use by counselors. As the result of disillusionment, possibly premature and over-zealous, with the trait factor model, a shift in conceptions about careers has occurred in recent years. It is now popular to see vocational choice as a developmental process. Holders of this point of view suggest that career development is systematic, periodic, and essentially irreversible and cumulative in nature (Ginsberg et al., 1951), with antecedents in early development (Roe, 1957) occurring in clearly demarked stages (Super, 1953). Attention is focused on the compromises that people are required to make between their vocational preferences and their vocational opportunities and possibilities. Super's et al., more recent work (1963) has further enriched the developmental approach by the introduction of the notion of self-concept implementation through emerging career development. This introduction was, at least partially, an attempt to deal with the complexities of personality involvement in career choice.

The simplistic t-f approach has elicited a second type of theoretical reaction; that is, an attempt to devise a more sophisticated trait-factor model. Holland's (1966) work represents such a response. Holland has proposed six occupational environments, each of which demands a different personality style for optimum vocational functioning. According to Holland, people select occupations that represent occupational environments consistent with their personality types. Since people are rarely "pure" types, Holland has devoted considerable attention to personality constellations and their career concomitants, thus avoiding one of the serious shortcomings of the model. Nonetheless, although many studies indicate a relation between personality type and career (Holland, 1966; Osipow, 1968), the relationships are of modest magnitude, and the basis for much career functioning is not clearly established.

PERSONALITY AND CAREER

The notion that personality and career choice are closely intertwined and predictably related is intuitively very attractive. Evidence of this attractiveness lies in the many studies of the relationship between personality and career that have been conducted (Osipow, 1968). Despite the apparent appropriateness of this line of inquiry, most of the research indicates only minimal relationships between personality and career. The lack of stable relationships between personality and vocation is bewildering. The absence of a clear relationship between personality and career is probably partly the result of the wide overlap of personality styles that are possible in implementing certain careers. It also results partly from the deficiencies in instrumentation in the measurement of personality, as well as from the interaction between personality and career mentioned earlier. No adequate theoretical structure exists to explain the particular relationship between personality development and functioning and career choice. Roe's (1957) approach tried to relate some aspects of early personal development to later career entrance, representing one attempt to bridge the personality-career gap, but it met with little empirical success.

It would appear that some important conceptual ingredient is missing that could help explain the wide variance of personality traits, styles, and types tolerated by occupations. It would be helpful if some element were postulated that satisfactorily explained how different types of people function effectively in similar occupational environments and how similar people can be comfortable in a wide range of career activities. How is it that an observer may, for example, find impulsive, outgoing people operating successfully in a wide range of vocations? How is it possible that salesmen can have a wide range of interpersonal styles and personality organizations and yet be able to function successfully, effectively, and with satisfaction?

A partial answer is that effective career performance makes demands on several aspects of human psychological functioning. Among those that come to mind readily are intellective-aptitude requirements. Work involves the adequate performance of a series of tasks. Aptitudes determine the ease with which individuals can develop the skills necessary to become proficient in the performance of these tasks. People differ in the possession of aptitudes, this difference affecting the economy of their acquisition of job-related skills. Since some people are willing and able to practice more than others, aptitudes do not predict performance perfectly. Within limits, however, occupations make significant demands on aptitudes as evidenced in data such as presented by Thorndike and Hagan (1959).

A second type of demand made by careers involves interpersonal behavior. It is likely that people differ in both the inherent behaviors they bring to interpersonal relations as well as in their response to training in interpersonal behaviors. Occupations differ in their tolerance of various interpersonal styles, yet, as has been observed, wide personality style variations within one career are possible. Very little is really known about the antecedents of personal styles and their vocational implications.

A third area of importance to the vocational psychologist lies in the impact of motivation, interests, values, and attitudes on career development. A number of questions can be raised in this regard. What are "interests"? Do they refer to intrinsic subjective gratifications growing out of engagement in circumscribed activities? Are they best conceived as patterns of expressed preferences? Or is it more helpful to think of them as some combination of the two? Implicitly, it is assumed that interests in general are intrinsically related to vocational interests. How valid is that assumption? Are interests merely attitudes in that they predispose individuals to respond to stimulus events in some effective manner?

Do interests serve as motivators to vocationally related activities? Intuitively, it would seem they should, yet much data, often unpublished (for example, Osipow, 1966) indicate that, other things being equal (such as abilities), interests inferred from inventories do not differentially predict vocationally oriented academic performance.

A fourth area of interest to the vocational psychologist has to do with individual perceptual-conceptual organization. Sometimes these events are called cognitive styles. A number of definitions of cognitive style have been proposed. In general, it is an elusive construct. Broverman (1960a; 1960b) has considered cognitive styles to be evident in the observed "relationships between abilities within individuals." Murray and Jackson (1964) see cognitive styles as "perceptual attitudes" leading to stable responses to various stimuli. Wallach (1962) seems to use the term to describe the cognitively based generality of responses across situations. Witkin (1965) has defined cognitive styles as "characteristic, self-consistent ways of functioning in their perceptual and intellectual activities." All of these definitions have similar components. They all attempt to use the term to describe the individual's consistency in responding to various stimuli across situations. All the definitions are more concerned with intra-individual characteristics than with inter-individual similarities or differences.

Some operational examples of cognitive styles include creativity (for example, Getzels & Jackson, 1960), automatizing (Broverman, 1964), conceptual versus perceptual motor-dominance (Broverman, 1964), analytic-descriptive, inferential-categorical, and relational (Kagan, Moss, & Sigel, 1963), field dependence and independence (Witkin et al., 1962), and equivalence-range (Sloane, Gorlow, & Jackson, 1963). To Getzels and Jackson, creativity refers to the individual's ability to solve old problems in a unique fashion. The "automatizer" of Broverman is the person who is able to relegate routine perceptual motor functions to the background of his attention and concentrate on higher level conceptual skills. The analytic-descriptive style of Kagan, Moss, and Sigel refers to the tendency of certain individuals to label items in terms of objective attributes they possess; the inferential-categorical person labels or arranges stimuli in terms of their relationship to one another and other elements in the category, while the relational person arranges stimuli in terms of their functional relationships to one another. The field-independent person of Witkin is characterized by a clear self-concept, articulate body-image, and autonomous impulse control. The notion of equivalence-range, as used by Sloane and his associates, refers to the "range of things a person will treat the same"; individuals vary in the degree to which they use broad versus narrow notions of similarity. Many other examples of cognitive styles could be provided, but the above illustrate the concept well.

To summarize: An intellective-abilities focus on career development allows prediction of different levels of vocational proficiency; an interest-attitude-motivational emphasis lends itself to the prediction of job persistence and satisfaction; the interpersonal and cognitive style data suggest individual differences in work organization and emphasis. Little attention has been paid to this last topic.

Cognitive style appears to have some unique features which lend it potential to serve especially well as a unifying construct to integrate observations about careers and personality. The concept can, to some extent, account for the differential functioning of personality types in one occupation while at the same time allow the psychologist to explain the satisfactory functioning of the same personality in many kinds of occupations.

A volume of literature has already accumulated which reveals something about the antecedents of some cognitive styles. The family environment seems to be important. It can be observed from Helson's work (1968) that performance on cognitive tasks related to creativity seems to be correlated among siblings. Creative women seem to encounter more sibling competition with their brothers than with their sisters. Getzels and Jackson (1961) also report familial differences in creative cognitive styles. When comparing the parental environment of high IQ versus high creative children, they found a number of significant differences. Fathers of high IQ's were more likely to be college graduates than fathers of high creatives; mothers of high IQ's were more likely to have a graduate degree than mothers of high creatives; mothers of high IQ's were more likely to be full-time housewives than mothers of high creatives; parents of high IQ's were more likely to be two or more years apart in age than parents of creative children; mothers of high IQ's were more likely to be concerned with finances than mothers of high creatives; the families of high IQ's subscribed to more magazines than families of high creatives; and, finally, mothers of high IQ's seemed to be more satisfied with their child-rearing procedures than mothers of high creatives.

With respect to familial antecedents of cognitive styles, the work of Anne Roe also seems relevant. Roe (1957) hypothesized that early family environment affects later interpersonal orientation which, in turn, affects later vocational functioning. In her studies of eminent scientists she observed a number of interesting differences in early family experiences according to professional discipline (1951a; 1951b; 1953). Unfortunately, most research with other groups using her concepts has failed to indicate systematic differences related to later vocational entrance. However, the notion that a set of cognitive styles result from various kinds of early childhood experiences and that these styles serve as an intervening variable can be postulated to account for variations in later vocational functioning.

Dauw (1966) found significant differences in the kinds of vocational preferences expressed by high versus low creative thinking boys and girls. The high creative thinkers were more likely to express preferences for work in service organizations, general-cultural, and artistic and entertainment kinds of careers (in Roe's catagories), while the low creative boys were more likely to select technological careers disproportionately. For girls, low creative thinkers over-chose organizational careers while high creative over-chose general-cultural and artistic and entertainment careers. Getzels and Jackson (1960), comparing the choices of high and low creative adolescents, found significant differences in both the quantity and quality of the occupational goals expressed by the two groups. Highly creative subjects expressed preferences for more unusual occupations as well as more occupations than low creative thinkers, and had exhibited less concern with the adult world's conventional standards of vocational success.

The work of Kagan, Moss, and Sigel (1963) suggests that children differ in the rate at which their cognitive development occurs and, further, that these differences have a impact on the child's suitability for certain

educational experiences at critical developmental periods of discontinuity. This cognitively based differential receptivity to stimuli could
very well have a cumulative impact on a youngster's progress through
school. It could affect the kind and proportion of success-failure experiences that occur; it could influence an adolescent's developing attitudes
toward different types of tests; it could alter his tendency to respond
constructively to various educational-vocationally related tasks. For example, a critical style may be useful in the study of literature but
troublesome in eighth grade science.

Even such attributes as risk-taking differences may easily be viewed as
a cognitive style, one that would have substantial implications for vocational selection and effectiveness. Broverman, Broverman, Vogel, and
Palmer (1964) found that physical attributes of strong versus weak male
automatizers differ. The strong automatizers had thick, heavy-set hirsute
builds, suggesting a high-level male endocrine function which spurred
adolescent growth, whereas the low automatizers were not as highly developed physically. It is interesting to speculate about the implications
that early physical maturation have for the kind of climate that a young
man experiences during his adolescence. The psychological climate resulting from physical differences should substantially affect self-image, and
consequently, task preferences, and the general sense of competency in
performing educationally and vocationally related tasks.

In another study Broverman (1960a) found that conceptually dominated subjects were less easily distracted while performing a concentration demanding conceptual task than perceptual motor dominant
subjects, that strong automatizers were less easily distracted than weak
automatizers on an automatic kind of conceptual task, and that strong
automatizers were less distracted than weak automatizers on an automatic perceptual motor task. Once again, these results have interesting
implications. The results suggest that cognitive styles influence the differential functioning and resulting differential environmental feedback
to youth about their educational development. In still a third study
Broverman (1960b) found that individuals with different cognitive styles
vary with respect to their abilities. Conceptually dominated subjects
were observed to perform above their own mean level of performance
on concentration demanding tasks and below their own mean level on
concentration demanding perceptual motor tasks. The reverse finding
was observed for strong automatizers.

A more molar kind of behavioral style variation associated with different kinds of performance in one occupation is suggested by findings
reported by Gough and Woodworth (1960). They examined systematic
differences in style among professional research scientists. Through the

use of factor analysis, it was possible to identify eight types which highly differentiated the scientists behaviorly even though they performed the same function nominally. Upon close scrutiny it appears that the scientists performed very different work functions under the same vocational label. The eight factor types could represent distinctive syndromes of several cognitive styles of significance in the work environment.

Osipow (1969) observed a number of cognitive similarities and differences in women's functioning across several occupational types. Nursing students, for example, were observed to be relatively receptive to stimuli, field-dependent, uncritical, and narrow in equivalence range. Of interest was the finding that the measures could differentiate the nurses from such similar professionals as dental hygienists, who appeared field-independent, relatively non-supporting, and masculine in their overall cognitive style. Also of interest in Osipow's data was the evidence of considerable variation in the cognitive style that could be observed within an educational field. This suggests the possibility that people entering an occupation who exhibit a very distinctive cognitive style from the modal style for that field will organize their work tasks and occupational objectives in a very distinctive fashion from one another.

IMPLICATIONS FOR CAREER DEVELOPMENT

A number of immediate possible implications come to mind with respect to cognitive styles and careers. First of all, the impact of different cognitive styles on the development of vocational preferences and aversions can be considered. It is possible, for example, that the individual whose cognitive style includes a small equivalence range is likely to find that certain kinds of tasks demanding a narrow and intense focus to be more to his liking, more intrinsically satisfying, than tasks that require the collation of broad bands of behavior. Similarly, certain other cognitive styles are likely to support activities that are relatively repetitive as opposed to others that may support activities which include frequent exposure to novel stimuli. The highly creative individual, for example, is likely to blossom under an environment which includes novelty, while the low creative individual is likely to be inhibited by such an environment and, in fact, may function most effectively where he is not frequently exposed to novel events. The interaction between specific cognitive styles and task preference and performance is an empirical question, open to study.

People with different cognitive styles are likely to process information differently (Munsinger & Kessen, 1966). It has been shown that there are systematic differences in preferences for stimulus variability which are associated both with maturation as well as with experience. The Kagan work, dealing with maturation and cognitive style, is also relevant to this respect. Presumably the analytic, reflective youngster is likely to find satisfaction and success in different and more complex tasks than the relational kind of youngster. Furthermore, the experiences these two types of people have are likely to result in cumulative effects on their sense of task success, consequently influencing their sense of self-esteem and self-concepts. This feedback is likely to have long-term and sequential impact on vocationally related decisions.

Of even more interest to counselors concerned with decision-making is the effect of different cognitive styles on the decision-making process itself. One is not hardpressed to imagine that cognitive styles may influence the degree to which individuals are willing to make decisions on limited data versus the degree to which they are able to make decisions at all in the presence of a degree of uncertainty. This is a realm of inquiry which offers considerable potential for investigation.

Still another area that potentially should interest vocational psychologists has to do with the differential management of job tasks associated with various cognitive styles. The individual's perceptual organization should affect the way he chooses to organize daily tasks, the emphasis he gives to certain tasks as opposed to others and the differential job satisfaction that he derives from his vocational activities. All of these aspects of work affect anticipations of potential success, task success, interest performance, and advancement.

SUMMARY

This paper has attempted to illustrate the problem of developing an appropriate conceptual role for the operation of personality in career development. The use of the concept of cognitive style was proposed as a means to integrate personality data into career functioning. Some examples of the way cognitive functioning can influence development in general and educational and vocational development in particular were suggested. The role of cognitive styles remains speculative, however, and is a fresh avenue for research efforts.

REFERENCES

Broverman, D. M.   Dimensions of cognitive style. *Journal of Personality*, 1960, **28**, 167–185. (a)

Broverman, D. M.   Cognitive styles and intra-individual variation in abilities. *Journal of Personality*, 1960, **28**, 240–255. (b)

Broverman, D. M. Generality and behavioral correlates of cognitive styles. *Journal of Consulting Psychology*, 1964, **28**, 487–500.

Broverman, D. M., Broverman, Inge K., Vogel, W., and Palmer, R. D. The automatization cognitive style and physical development. *Child Development*, 1964, **35**, 1343–1359.

Dauw, D. C. Career choices of high and low creative thinkers. *Vocational Guidance Quarterly*, 1966, **15**, 135–140.

Getzels, J. W., and Jackson, P. W. Occupational choice and cognitive functioning: career aspirations of highly intelligent and of highly creative adolescents. *Journal of Abnormal and Social Psychology*, 1960, **61**, 119–123.

Getzels, J. W., and Jackson, P. W. Family environment and cognitive style: a study of the sources of highly intelligent and of highly creative adolescents. *American Sociological Review*, 1961, **26**, 351–359.

Ginzberg, E., Ginsburg, S. W., Axelrad, S., and Herma, J. L. *Occupational Choice: An Approach to a General Theory*. New York: Columbia University Press, 1951.

Gough, H. G., and Woodworth, D. G. Stylistic variations among professional research scientists. *Journal of Psychology*, 1960, **49**, 87–98.

Helson, Ravenna. Effects of sibling characteristics and parental values on creative interest and achievement. *Journal of Personality*, 1968, **36**, 589–607.

Holland, J. L. *The Psychology of Vocational Choice*. Waltham, Mass.: Blaisdell, 1966.

Kagan, J., Moss, H. A., and Sigel, I. E. Psychological significance of styles of conceptualization. *Monographs of the Society for Research in Child Development*, 1963, **28**, 73–111.

Munsinger, H., and Kessen, W. Stimulus variability and cognitive change. *Psychological Review*, 1966, **73**, 164–178.

Murray, J. E., and Jackson, D. N. Impulsivity and color-form abstraction. *Journal of Consulting Psychology*, 1964, **28**, 518–522.

Osipow, S. H. The relationship between interests, aptitudes, and academic achievement. Unpublished data, 1966.

Osipow, S. H. *Theories of Career Development*. New York: Appleton-Century-Crofts, 1968.

Osipow, S. H. Cognitive styles and educational-vocational preferences and selection. *Journal of Counseling Psychology*, 1969, **16**, 534–546.

Roe, Anne. A psychological study of eminent biologists. *Psychological Monographs*, 1951, **65**, No. 14 (whole No. 331). (a)

Roe, Anne. A psychological study of eminent physical scientists. *Genetic Psychology Monographs*, 1951, **43**, 121–239. (b)

Roe, Anne. A psychological study of eminent psychologists and anthropologists and a comparison with biological and physical scientists. *Psychological Monographs*, 1953, **67**, No. 2 (whole No. 352).

Roe, Anne. Early determinants of vocational choice. *Journal of Counseling Psychology*, 1957, **4**, 212–217.

Sloane, H. N., Gorlow, L., and Jackson, D. N. Cognitive styles in equivalent range. *Perceptual Motor Skills*, 1963, **16**, 389–404.

Super, D. E.   A theory of vocational development. *American Psychologist*, 1953, 8, 185–190.

Super, D. E., Starishevsky, R., Matlin, N., and Jordaan, J. P.   *Career Development: Self-Concept Theory.* New York: College Entrance Examination Board Research Monograph No. 4, 1963.

Thorndike, R. L., and Hagen, Elizabeth.   *Ten Thousand Careers.* New York: John Wiley, 1959.

Wallach, M. A.   Commentary: active-analytical versus passive-global cognitive functioning. In S. Messick and J. Ross (Eds.) *Measurement in Personality and Cognition.* New York: John Wiley, 1962.

Witkin, H. A.   Psychological differentiation and forms of pathology. *Journal of Abnormal and Social Psychology*, 1965, **70**, 317–336.

Witkin, H. A., Dyk, Ruth B., Faterson, Hanna F., Goodenough, D. R., and Karp, S. A.   *Psychological Differentiation.* New York: John Wiley, 1962.

2.6 Orientation

Following the notorious "Berkeley Incident" of 1964, a mushrooming of papers concerned with student activism occurred in the psychological and sociological literature. As might be expected the quality of this literature varies widely. In the opinion of this writer, however, some of the most representative of high quality literature on student protest appeared in a collection edited by Sampson (1967). In this collection a wide range of emphases is found developed by contributing authors to analyze student activism. For example, the influence of societal ingredients such as the Civil Rights Movement and the Vietnam War is argued. So also are patterns of socialization marked by a "democratic and permissive authority structure" which purportedly groom life styles conducive to protest behavior. Incongruities between student needs and expectations and the growing depersonalization of the American educational system are mentioned. So are individual differences in activist behavior and the motives behind this behavior. It is here that Kenneth Keniston enters the picture with a polished account of contemporary student dissent.

At least two properties distinguish Keniston's discussion. One is his differentiation of the "genuine" political activist from the culturally alienated student. These two "ideal types" represent for Keniston opposite poles of the dissent continuum. A second distinctive property is Keniston's specification of factors which set the stage for protest, including the "protest-prone personality" and the nature of a given institutional climate. Throughout his commentary Keniston attempts to weed from his conceptual garden various stereotyped views and questionable assumptions concerning dissent. Also notable are his projections with reference to the future of student activism.

Recent developments suggest that student dissent is no longer unique to the college or university setting. High school authorities are increasingly faced with incidents of protest. As yet undetermined is whether these younger students are modeling themselves after their college counterparts, being strongly influenced by publicized dissent via the mass media, executing directives from outside sources, or reacting justifiably to unsatisfactory school conditions and policies. Perhaps it is some combination of these and other factors. Regardless, the issues of how, when, and under what circumstances school authorities should respond to protest are critical. Some maintain that activism, while dramatic, has actually involved only a small minority of the adolescent population. If so, do political apathy and social conformity to established norms still prevail among most adolescents? Is it not paradoxical that many of the same adults seemingly become distressed over both dissent and apathy?

RECOMMENDED READINGS

Brammer, Lawrence. The coming revolt of high school students. *Bulletin for the National Association of Secondary School Principals*, 1968, 52, 13–21.

Evans, Ellis D. Student activism and teaching effectiveness: survival of the fittest? *Journal of College Student Personnel*, 1969, 10, 102–108.

Sampson, Edward E. (Ed.) Stirrings out of apathy: student activism and the decade of protest. *Journal of Social Issues*, 1967, 23, 139 pp.

Tannenbaum, A. J. (Ed.) Alienated youth. *Journal of Social Issues*, 1969, 25, 167 pp.

2.6   The Sources of Student Dissent

Kenneth Keniston, YALE UNIVERSITY

The apparent upsurge of dissent among American college students is one of the more puzzling phenomena in recent American history. Less than a decade ago, commencement orators were decrying the "silence"

Reprinted from *The Journal of Social Issues*, 1967, 22, 108–137, by permission of the author and the Society for the Psychological Study of Social Issues.

of college students in the face of urgent national and international issues; but in the past two or three years, the same speakers have warned graduating classes across the country against the dangers of unreflective protest, irresponsible action and unselective dissent. Rarely in history has apparent apathy been replaced so rapidly by publicized activism, silence by strident dissent.

This "wave" of dissent among American college students has been much discussed. Especially in the mass media—popular magazines, newspapers and television—articles of interpretation, explanation, deprecation and occasionally applause have appeared in enormous numbers. More important, from the first beginnings of the student civil rights movement, social scientists have been regular participant-observers and investigators of student dissent. There now exists a considerable body of research that deals with the characteristics and settings of student dissent (see Lipset & Altbach, 1966; Block, Haan, & Smith, forthcoming; Katz, 1967; Peterson, 1967 for summaries of this research). To be sure, most of these studies are topical (centered around a particular protest or demonstration), and some of the more extensive studies are still in varying stages of incompletion. Yet enough evidence has already been gathered to permit tentative generalizations about the varieties, origins, and future of student dissent in the 1960s.

In the remarks to follow, I will attempt to gather together this evidence (along with my own research and informal observations) to provide tentative answers to three questions about student dissent today. First, what is the nature of student dissent in American colleges? Second, what are the sources of the recent "wave of protest" by college students? And third, what can we predict about the future of student dissent?

TWO VARIETIES OF DISSENT

Dissent is by no means the dominant mood of American college students. Every responsible study or survey shows apathy and privatism far more dominant than dissent (see, for example, *Newsweek*, 1965; Katz, 1965; Reed, 1966; Peterson, 1966; Block, Haan, & Smith, forthcoming). On most of our twenty-two hundred campuses, student protest, student alienation and student unrest are something that happens elsewhere, or that characterizes a mere handful of "kooks" on the local campus. However we define "dissent," overt dissent is relatively infrequent and tends to be concentrated largely at the more selective, "progressive," and "academic" colleges and universities in America. Thus, Peterson's study of student protests (1966) finds political demonstrations concentrated in the larger universities and institutions of higher academic calibre, and almost totally absent at teachers colleges, technical institutes and non-academic denominational colleges. And even at the colleges that gather together the greatest number of dissenters, the vast majority of students —generally well over 95 percent—remain interested onlookers or opponents rather than active dissenters. Thus, whatever we say about student dissenters is said about a very small minority of America's six million college students. At most colleges, dissent is not visible at all.

Partly because the vast majority of American students remain largely uncritical of the wider society, fundamentally conformist in behavior and outlook, and basically "adjusted" to the prevailing collegiate, national and international order, the small minority of dissenting students is highly visible to the mass media. As I will argue later, such students are often distinctively talented; they "use" the mass media effectively; and they generally succeed in their goal of making themselves and their causes highly visible. Equally important, student dissenters of all types arouse deep and ambivalent feelings in non-dissenting students and adults—envy, resentment, admiration, repulsion, nostalgia, and guilt. Such feelings contribute both to the selective over-attention dissenters receive and to the often distorted perceptions and interpretations of them and their activities. Thus, there has developed through the mass media and the imaginings of adults a more or less stereotyped—and generally incorrect—image of the student dissenter.

The Stereotyped Dissenter

The "stereotypical" dissenter as popularly portrayed is both a Bohemian and political activist. Bearded, be-Levi-ed, long-haired, dirty and unkempt, he is seen as profoundly disaffected from his society, often influenced by "radical" (Marxist, Communist, Maoist, or Castroite) ideas, an experimenter in sex and drugs, unconventional in his daily behavior. Frustrated and unhappy, often deeply maladjusted as a person, he is a "failure" (or as one U.S. Senator put it, a "reject"). Certain academic communities like Berkeley are said to act as "magnets" for dissenters, who selectively attend colleges with a reputation as protest centers. Furthermore, drop-outs or "non-students" who have failed in college cluster in large numbers around the fringes of such colleges, actively seeking pretexts for protest, refusing all compromise and impatient with ordinary democratic processes.

According to such popular analyses, the sources of dissent are to be found in the loss of certain traditional American virtues. The "breakdown" of American family life, high rates of divorce, the "softness" of American living, inadequate parents, and, above all, overindulgence and "spoiling" contribute to the prevalence of dissent. Brought up in undisciplined homes by parents unsure of their own values and standards, dissenters channel their frustration and anger against the older generation, against all authority, and against established institutions.

Similar themes are sometimes found in the interpretations of more scholarly commentators. "Generational conflict" is said to underly the motivation to dissent, and a profound "alienation" from American society is seen as a factor of major importance in producing protests. Then, too, such factors as the poor quality and impersonality of American college education, the large size and lack of close student-faculty contact in the "multiversity" are sometimes seen as the latent or precipitating factors in student protests, regardless of the manifest issues around which students are organized. And still other scholarly analysts, usually men now disillusioned by the radicalism of the 1930s, have expressed fear of the dogmatism, rigidity and "authoritarianism of the left" of today's student activists.

Activism and Alienation

These stereotyped views are, I believe, incorrect in a variety of ways. They confuse two distinct varieties of student dissent; equally important, they fuse dissent with maladjustment. There are, of course, as many forms of dissent as there are individual dissenters; and any effort to counter the popular stereotype of the dissenter by pointing to the existence of distinct "types" of dissenters runs the risk of oversimplifying at a lower level of abstraction. Nonetheless, it seems to me useful to suggest that student dissenters generally fall somewhere along a continuum that runs between two ideal types—first, the political activist or protester, and second, the withdrawn, culturally alienated student.

The activist   The defining characteristic of the "new" activist is his participation in a student demonstration or group activity that concerns itself with some matter of general political, social or ethical principle. Characteristically, the activist feels that some injustice has been done, and attempts to "take a stand," "demonstrate" or in some fashion express his convictions. The specific issues in question range from protest against a paternalistic college administration's actions to disagreement with American Vietnam policies, from indignation at the exploitation of the poor to anger at the firing of a devoted teacher, from opposition to the selective service laws which exempt him but not the poor to—most important—outrage at the deprivation of the civil rights of other Americans.

The initial concern of the protester is almost always immediate, ad hoc and local. To be sure, the student who protests about one issue is likely to feel inclined or obliged to demonstrate his convictions on other issues as well (Heist, 1966). But whatever the issue, the protester rarely demonstrates because his *own* interests are jeopardized, but rather because he perceives injustices being done to *others* less fortunate than himself. For example, one of the apparent paradoxes about protests against current draft policies is that the protesting students are selectively drawn from that subgroup *most* likely to receive student deferments for graduate work. The basis of protest is a general sense that the selective service rules and the war in Vietnam are unjust to others with whom the student is identified, but whose fate he does not share. If one runs down the list of "causes" taken up by student activists, in rare cases are demonstrations directed at improving the lot of the protesters themselves; identification with the oppressed is a more important motivating factor than an actual sense of immediate personal oppression.

The anti-ideological stance of today's activists has been noted by many commentators. This distrust of formal ideologies (and at times of articulate thought) makes it difficult to pinpoint the positive social and political values of student protesters. Clearly, many current American political institutions like de facto segregation are opposed; clearly, too, most students of the New Left reject careerism and familism as personal values. In this sense, we might think of the activist as (politically) "alienated." But this label seems to me more misleading than illuminating, for it overlooks the more basic *commitment* of most student activists to other ancient, traditional, and creedal American values like free speech, citizen's participation in decision-making, equal opportunity and justice. In so far as the activist rejects all or part of "the power structure," it is because current political realities fall so far short of the ideals he sees as central to the American creed. And in so far as he repudiates careerism and familism, it is because of his implicit allegiance to other human goals he sees, once again, as more crucial to American life. Thus, to emphasize the "alienation" of activists is to neglect their more basic allegiance to creedal American ideals.

One of these ideals is, of course, a belief in the desirability of political and social action. Sustained in good measure by the successes of the student civil rights movement, the protester is usually convinced that demonstrations are effective in mobilizing public opinion, bringing moral or political pressure to bear, demonstrating the existence of his opinions, or, at times, in "bringing the machine to a halt." In this sense, then, despite his criticisms of existing political practices and social institutions, he is a political optimist. Moreover, the protester must believe in at least minimal organization and group activity; otherwise, he would find it impossible to take part, as he does, in any organized demonstrations or activities. Despite their search for more truly "democratic" forms of organization and action (for example, participatory democracy), activists agree that group action is more effective than purely individual acts. To be sure, a belief in the value and efficacy of political action is not equivalent to endorsement of prevalent political institutions or forms of action. Thus, one characteristic of activists is their search for new forms of social action, protest and political organization (community organization, sit-ins, participatory democracy) that will be more effective and less oppressive than traditional political institutions.

The culturally alienated   In contrast to the politically optimistic, active, and socially concerned protester, the culturally alienated student is far too pessimistic and too firmly opposed to "the System" to wish to demonstrate his disapproval in any organized public way.[1] His demonstrations of dissent are private: through nonconformity of behavior, ideology and dress, through personal experimentation and above all through efforts to intensify his own subjective experience, he shows his distaste and disinterest in politics and society. The activist attempts to change the world around him, but the alienated student is convinced that meaningful change of the social and political world is impossible; instead, he considers "dropping out" the only real option.

Alienated students tend to be drawn from the same general social strata and colleges as protesters. But psychologically and ideologically, their backgrounds are often very different. Alienated students are more likely to be disturbed psychologically; and although they are often highly talented and artistically gifted, they are less committed to academic values and intellectual achievement than are protesters. The alienated student's real campus is the school of the absurd, and he has more affinity for pessimistic existentialist ontology than for traditional American activism. Furthermore, such students usually find it psychologically and ideologically impossible to take part in organized group activities for any length of time, particularly when they are expected to assume responsibilities for leadership. Thus, on the rare occasions when they become involved in demonstrations, they usually prefer peripheral roles, avoid responsibilities and are considered a nuisance by serious activists (Draper, 1965).

Whereas the protesting student is likely to accept the basic political and social values of his parents, the alienated student almost always rejects his parents' values. In particular, he is likely to see his father as

[1] The following paragraphs are based on the study of culturally alienated students described in *The Uncommitted* (1965). For a more extensive discussion of the overwhelmingly anti-political stance of these students, see Keniston (1966) and also Rigney & Smith (1961), Allen & Silverstein (1967), Watts & Wittaker (1967), and Wittaker & Watts (1967).

a man who has "sold out" to the pressures for success and status in American society; he is determined to avoid the fate that overtook his father. Toward their mothers, however, alienated students usually express a very special sympathy and identification. These mothers, far from encouraging their sons toward independence and achievement, generally seem to have been over-solicitous and limiting. The most common family environment of the alienated-student-to-be consists of a parental schism supplemented by a special mother-son alliance of mutual understanding and maternal control and depreciation of the father (Keniston, 1965a).

In many colleges, alienated students often constitute a kind of hidden underground, disorganized and shifting in membership, in which students can temporarily or permanently withdraw from the ordinary pressures of college life. The alienated are especially attracted to the hallucinogenic drugs like marijuana, mescaline, and LSD, precisely because these agents combine withdrawal from ordinary social life with the promise of greatly intensified subjectivity and perception. To the confirmed "acid head," what matters is intense, drug-assisted perception; the rest—including politics, social action and student demonstrations—is usually seen as "role-playing."[2]

The recent and much-publicized emergence of "hippie" subcultures in several major cities and increasingly on the campuses of many selective and progressive colleges illustrates the overwhelmingly apolitical stance of alienated youth. For although hippies oppose war and believe in interracial living, few have been willing or able to engage in anything beyond

[2] The presence among student dissenters of a group of "non-students"—that is, dropouts from college or graduate school who congregate or remain near some academic center—has been much noted. In fact, however, student protesters seem somewhat *less* likely to drop out of college than do nonparticipants in demonstrations (Heist, 1966), and there is no evidence that dropping out of college is in any way related to dissent from American society (Keniston & Helmreich, 1965). On the contrary, several studies suggest that the academically gifted and psychologically intact student who drops out of college voluntarily has few distinctive discontents about his college or about American society (Suczek & Alfort, 1966; Pervin et al., 1966; Wright, 1966). If he is dissatisfied at all, it is with himself, usually for failing to take advantage of the "rich educational opportunities" he sees in his college. The motivations of students dropping out of college are complex and varied, but such motivations more often seem related to personal questions of self-definition and parental identification or to a desire to escape relentless academic pressures, than to any explicit dissent from the Great Society. Thus, although a handful of students have chosen to drop out of college for a period in order to devote themselves to political and societal protest activities, there seems little reason in general to associate the dropout with the dissenter, whether he be a protester or an alienated student. The opposite is nearer the truth.

occasional peace marches or apolitical "human be-ins." Indeed, the hippies's emphasis on immediacy, "love" and "turning-on," together with his basic rejection of the traditional values of American life, inoculates him against involvement in long-range activist endeavors, like education or community organization, and even against the sustained effort needed to plan and execute demonstrations or marches. For the alienated hippie, American society is beyond redemption (or not worth trying to redeem); but the activist, no matter how intense his rejection of specific American policies and practices, retains a conviction that his society can and should be changed. Thus, despite occasional agreement in principle between the alienated and the activists, cooperation in practice has been rare, and usually ends with activists accusing the alienated of "irresponsibility," while the alienated are confirmed in their view of activists as moralistic, "up-tight," and "un-cool."

Obviously, no description of a type ever fits an individual perfectly. But by this rough typology, I mean to suggest that popular stereotypes which present a unified portrait of student dissent are gravely over-simplified. More specifically, they confuse the politically pessimistic and socially uncommitted alienated student with the politically hopeful and socially committed activist. To be sure, there are many students who fall between these two extremes, and some of them alternate between passionate search for intensified subjectivity and equally passionate efforts to remedy social and political injustices. And as I will later suggest, even within the student movement, one of the central tensions is between political activism and cultural alienation. Nonetheless, even to understand this tension we must first distinguish between the varieties of dissent apparent on American campuses.

Furthermore, the distinction between activist and alienated students as psychological types suggests the incompleteness of scholarly analyses that see social and historical factors as the only forces that "push" a student toward one or the other of these forms of dissent. To be sure, social and cultural factors are of immense importance in providing channels for the expression (or suppression) of dissent, and in determining *which* kinds of dissenters receive publicity, censure, support or ostracism in any historical period. But these factors cannot, in general, change a hippie into a committed activist, nor a SNCC field worker into a full-time "acid-head." Thus, the prototypical activist of 1966 is not the "same" student as the prototypical student bohemian of 1956, but is rather the politically aware but frustrated, academically oriented "privatist" of that era. Similarly, as I will argue below, the most compelling alternative to most activists is not the search for kicks or sentience but the quest for scholarly competence. And if culturally sanctioned opportunities for the expression of alienation were to disappear, most alienated students would turn to private psychopathology rather than to public activism.

Stated more generally, historical forces do not ordinarily transform radically the character, values and inclinations of an adult in later life. Rather, they thrust certain groups forward in some eras and discourage or suppress other groups. The recent alternation in styles of student dissent in America is therefore not to be explained so much by the malleability of individual character as by the power of society to bring activists into the limelight, providing them with the intellectual and moral instruments for action. Only a minority of potential dissenters fall close enough to the midpoint between alienation and activism so that they can constitute a "swing vote" acutely responsive to social and cultural pressures and styles. The rest, the majority, are characterologically committed to one or another style of dissent.

THE SOURCES OF ACTIVISM

What I have termed "alienated" students are by no means a new phenomenon in American life, or for that matter in industrialized societies. Bohemians, "beatniks" and artistically inclined undergraduates who rejected middle-class values have long been a part of the American student scene, especially at more selective colleges; they constituted the most visible form of dissent during the relative political "silence" of American students in the 1950s. What is distinctive about student dissent in recent years is the unexpected emergence of a vocal minority of politically and socially active students.[3] Much is now known about the characteristics of such students, and the circumstances under which protests are likely to be mounted. At the same time, many areas of ignorance remain. In the account to follow, I will attempt to formulate a series of general hypotheses concerning the sources of student activism.[4]

[3] Student activism, albeit of a rather different nature, was also found in the nineteen thirties. For a discussion and contrast of student protest today and after the Depression, see Lipset (1966a).

[4] Throughout the following, I will use the terms "protester" and "activist" interchangeably, although I am aware that some activists are not involved in protests. Furthermore, the category of "activist" is an embracing one, comprising at least three sub-classes. First, those who might be termed *reformers*, that is, students involved in community organization work, the Peace Corps, tutoring programs, Vista, etc., but not generally affiliated with any of the "New Left" organizations. Second, the group of *activists proper*, most of whom are or have been affiliated with organizations like the Free Speech Movement at Berkeley, Students for a Democratic Society, the Student Non-violent Coordinating Com-

It is abundantly clear that no single factor will suffice to explain the increase of politically motivated activities and protests on American campuses. Even if we define an activist narrowly, as a student who (a) acts together with others in a group, (b) is concerned with some ethical, social, ideological or political issue, and (c) holds liberal or "radical" views, the sources of student activism and protest are complex and inter-related. At least four kinds of factors seem involved in any given protest. First, the individuals involved must be suitably predisposed by their personal backgrounds, values and motivations. Second, the likelihood of protest is far greater in certain kinds of educational and social settings. Third, socially directed protests require a special cultural climate, that is, certain distinctive values and views about the effectiveness and meaning of demonstrations, and about the wider society. And finally, some historical situations are especially conducive to protests.

THE PROTEST-PRONE PERSONALITY

A large and still-growing number of studies, conducted under different auspices, at different times and about different students, presents a remarkably consistent picture of the protest-prone individual (Aiken, Demerath, & Marwell, 1966; Flacks, 1967; Gastwirth, 1965; Heist, 1965, 1966; Lyonns, 1965; Somers, 1965; Watts & Whittaker, 1966; Westby & Braungart, 1966; Katz, 1967; and Paulus, 1967). For one, student protesters are generally outstanding students; the higher the student's grade average, the more outstanding his academic achievements, the more likely it is that he will become involved in any given political demonstration. Similarly, student activists come from families with liberal political values; a disproportionate number report that their parents hold views essentially similar to their own, and accept or support their activities. Thus, among the parents of protesters we find large numbers of liberal Democrats, plus an unusually large scattering of pacifists, socialists, and so on. A disproportionate number of protesters come from Jewish families; and if the parents of activists are religious, they tend to be concentrated in the more liberal denominations—Reform Judaism, Unitarianism, the Society of Friends, etc. Such parents are reported to

---

mittee or the Congress on Racial Equality or the Vietnam Summer Project. Finally, there is a much publicized handful of students who might be considered *extremists*, who belong to doctrinaire Marxist and Trotskyite organizations like the now-defunct May Second Movement. No empirical study with which I am acquainted has investigated the differences between students in these three subgroups. Most studies have concentrated on the "activist proper," and my remarks will be based on a reading of their data.

have high ethical and political standards, regardless of their actual religious convictions.

As might be expected of a group of politically liberal and academically talented students, a disproportionate number are drawn from professional and intellectual families of upper middle-class status. For example, compared with active student conservatives, members of protest groups tend to have higher parental incomes, more parental education, and less anxiety about social status (Westby & Braungart, 1966). Another study finds that high levels of education distinguish the activist's family even in the grandparental generation (Flacks, 1967). In brief, activists are not drawn from disadvantaged, status-anxious, underprivileged or uneducated groups; on the contrary, they are selectively recruited from among those young Americans who have had the most socially fortunate upbringings.

Basic Value Commitments of Activists

The basic value commitments of the activist tend to be academic and non-vocational. Such students are rarely found among engineers, future teachers at teachers colleges, or students of business administration (see Trent & Craise, 1967). Their overall educational goals are those of a liberal education for its own sake, rather than specifically technical, vocational or professional preparation. Rejecting careerist and familist goals, activists espouse humanitarian, expressive and self-actualizing values. Perhaps because of these values, they delay career choice longer than their classmates (Flacks, 1967). Nor are such students distinctively dogmatic, rigid or authoritarian. Quite the contrary, the substance and style of their beliefs and activities tends to be open, flexible and highly liberal. Their fields of academic specialization are non-vocational—the social sciences and the humanities. Once in college, they not only do well academically, but tend to persist in their academic commitments, dropping out *less* frequently than most of their classmates. As might be expected, a disproportionate number receive a B.A. within four years and continue on to graduate school, preparing themselves for academic careers.

Survey data also suggest that the activist is not distinctively dissatisfied with his college education. As will be noted below, activists generally attend colleges which provide the best, rather than the worst, undergraduate education available today. Objectively then, activists probably have less to complain about in their undergraduate educations than most other students. And subjectively as well, surveys show most activists, like most other American undergraduates, to be relatively well satisfied with their undergraduate educations (Somers, 1965; Kornhauser, 1967).

Thus, dissatisfaction with educational failings of the "impersonal multi-versity," however important as a rallying cry, does not appear to be a distinctive cause of activism.

In contrast to their relative satisfaction with the quality of their educations, however, activists *are* distinctively dissatisfied with what might be termed the "civil-libertarian" defects of their college administrations. While no doubt a great many American undergraduates distrust "University Hall," this distrust is especially pronounced amongst student protesters (Kornhauser, 1967; Paulus, 1967). Furthermore, activists tend to be more responsive than other students to deprivations of civil rights on campus as well as off campus, particularly when political pressures seem to motivate on campus policies they consider unjust. The same responsiveness increasingly extends to issues of "student power": that is, student participation and decisions affecting campus life. Thus, bans on controversial speakers, censureship of student publications, and limitations on off-campus political or social action are likely to insense the activist, as is arbitrary "administration without the consent of the administered." But it is primarily perceived injustice or the denial of student rights by the Administration—rather than poor educational quality, neglect by the faculty, or the impersonality of the multiversity—that agitates the activist.

Most studies of activists have concentrated on variables that are relatively easy to measure: social class, academic achievements, explicit values, and satisfaction with college. But these factors alone will not explain activism; more students possess the demographic and attitudinal characteristics of the protest-prone personality than are actually involved in protests and social action programs. Situational, institutional, cultural and historical factors (discussed below) obviously contribute to "catalysing" a protest-prone personality into an actual activist. But it also seems that, within the broad demographic group so far defined, more specific psychodynamic factors contribute to activism.

Activists . . . Not in Rebellion

In speculating about such factors, we leave the ground of established fact and enter the terrain of speculation, for only a few studies have explored the personality dynamics and family constellation of the activist, and most of these studies are impressionistic and clinical (for example, Coles, 1967; Ehle, 1965; Draper, 1965; Fishman & Solomon n.d., 1964; Gastwirth, 1965; Newfield, 1966; Schneider, 1966; Solomon & Fishman, 1963, 1964; Zinn, 1965). But certain facts are clear. As noted, activists are *not*, on the whole, repudiating or rebelling against explicit parental values and ideologies. On the contrary, there is some evidence that such students are living out their parents' values in practice; and one study suggests that activists may be somewhat *closer* to their parents' values than non-activists (Flacks, 1967). Thus, any simple concept of "generational conflict" or "rebellion against parental authority" is clearly oversimplified as applied to the motivations of most protesters.

Activists . . . Living Out Parental Values

It does seem probable, however, that many activists are concerned with *living out expressed but unimplemented parental values*. Solomon and Fishman (1963), studying civil rights activists and peace marchers, argue that many demonstrators are "acting out" in their demonstrations the values which their parents explicitly believed, but did not have the courage or opportunity to practice or fight for. Similarly, when protesters criticize their fathers, it is usually over their fathers' failure to practice what they have preached to their children throughout their lives. Thus, in the personal background of the protester there is occasionally a suggestion that his father is less-than-"sincere" (and even at times "hypocritical") in his professions of political liberalism. In particular, both careerism and familism in parents are the objects of activist criticisms, the more so because these implicit goals often conflict with explicit parental values. And it may be that protesters receive both covert and overt support from their parents because the latter are secretly proud of their children's eagerness to implement the ideals they as parents have only given lip-service to. But whatever the ambivalences that bind parents with their activist children, it would be wrong to over-emphasize them; what is most impressive is the solidarity of older and younger generations.

ACTIVISTS . . . FAMILY STRUCTURE

While no empirical study has tested this hypothesis, it seems probable that in many activist-producing families, the mother will have a dominant psychological influence on her son's development. I have already noted that the protester's cause is rarely himself, but rather alleviating the oppression of others. As a group, activists seem to possess an unusual *capacity for nurturant identification*—that is, for empathy and sympathy with the underdog, the oppressed and the needy. Such a capacity can have many origins, but its most likely source in upper-middle class professional families is identification with an active mother whose own work embodies nurturant concern for others. Flacks' finding that the mothers of activists are likely to be employed, often in professional or service roles like teaching and social work, is consistent with this hypothesis. In general in American society, middle-class women have greater social and financial freedom to work in jobs that are idealistically "fulfilling" as opposed to merely lucrative or prestigious. As a rule, then, in middle-class families, it is the mother who actively embodies in her life and work the humanitarian, social and political ideals that the father may share in principle but does not or cannot implement in his career.

Given what we know about the general characteristics of the families of protest-prone students, it also seems probable that the dominant ethos of their families is unusually egalitarian, permissive, "democratic," and highly individuated. More specifically, we might expect that these will be families where children talk back to their parents at the dinner table, where free dialogue and discussion of feelings is encouraged, and where "rational" solutions are sought to everyday family problems and conflicts. We would also expect that such families would place a high premium on self-expression and intellectual independence, encouraging their children to make up their own minds and to stand firm against group pressures. Once again, the mother seems the most likely carrier and epitome of these values, given her relative freedom from professional and financial pressures.

The contrast between such protest-prompting families and alienating families should be underlined. In both, the son's deepest emotional ties are often to his mother. But in the alienating family, the mother-son relationship is characterized by maternal control and intrusiveness, whereas in the protest-prompting family, the mother is a highly individuating force in her son's life, pushing him to independence and autonomy. Furthermore, the alienated student is determined to avoid the fate that befell his father, whereas the protesting student wants merely to live out the values that his father has not always worked hard enough to practice. Finally, the egalitarian, permissive, democratic and individuating environment of the entire family of the protester contrasts with the overcontrolling, over-solicitous attitude of the mother in the alienating family, where the father is usually excluded from major emotional life within the family.

These hypotheses about the family background and psychodynamics of the protester are speculative, and future research may prove their invalidity. But regardless of whether *these* particular speculations are correct, it seems clear that in addition to the general social, demographic and attitudinal factors mentioned in most research, more specific familial and psychodynamic influences contribute to protest-proneness.

THE PROTEST-PROMOTING INSTITUTION

However we define his characteristics, one activist alone cannot make a protest; the characteristics of the college or university he attends have much to do with whether his protest-proneness will ever be mobilized into actual activism. Politically, socially and ideologically motivated demonstrations and activities are most likely to occur at certain types of colleges; they are almost unknown at a majority of campuses. The effects of institutional characteristics on protests have been studied by Cowan (1966) and Peterson (1966), and by Sampson (1967) and Brown (1967).

In order for an organized protest or related activities to occur, there must obviously be sufficient *numbers* of protest-prone students to form a group, these students must have an opportunity for *interaction* with each other, and there must be *leaders* to initiate and mount the protest. Thus, we might expect—and we indeed find—that protest is associated with institutional size, and particularly with the congregation of large numbers of protest-prone students in close proximity to each other. More important than sheer size alone, however, is the "image" of the institution: certain institutions selectively recruit students with protest-prone characteristics. Specifically, a reputation for academic excellence and freedom, coupled with highly selective admissions policies, will tend to congregate large numbers of potentially protesting students on one campus. Thus, certain institutions do act as "magnets" for potential activists, but not so much because of their reputations for political radicalism as because they are noted for their academic excellence. Among such institutions are some of the most selective and "progressive" private liberal arts colleges, major state universities (like Michigan, California at Berkeley, and Wisconsin) which have long traditions of vivid undergraduate teaching and high admissions standards (Lipset & Altbach, 1966) and many of the more prestigious private universities.

Once protest-prone students are on campus, they must have an opportunity to interact, to support one another, to develop common outlooks and shared policies—in short, to form an *activist subculture* with sufficient mass and potency to generate a demonstration or action program. Establishing "honors colleges" for talented and academically motivated students is one particularly effective way of creating a "critical mass" of protest-prone students. Similarly, inadequate on-campus housing indirectly results in the development of off-campus protest-prone subcultures (for example, co-op houses) in residences where student activists can develop a high degree of ideological solidarity and organizational cohesion.

But even the presence of a critical mass of protest-prone undergraduates in an activist subculture is not enough to make a protest without leaders and issues. And in general, the most effective protest leaders have not been undergraduates, but teaching assistants. The presence of large numbers of exploited, underpaid, disgruntled and frustrated teacher assistants (or other equivalent graduate students and younger faculty members) is almost essential for organized and persistent protest. For one, advanced students tend to be more liberal politically and more sensitive to political issues than are most undergraduates—partly because education seems to have a liberalizing effect, and partly because students who persist into graduate school tend to be more liberal to start than those who drop out or go elsewhere. Furthermore, the frustrations of graduate students, especially at very large public universities, make them particularly sensitive to general problems of injustice, exploitation and oppression. Teaching assistants, graduate students and young faculty members also tend to be in daily and prolonged contact with students, are close enough to them in age to sense their mood, and are therefore in an excellent position to lead and organize student protests. Particularly at institutions which command little institutional allegiance from large numbers of highly capable graduate students (Lipset & Altbach, 1966) will such students be found among the leaders of the protest movement.

The Issues of Protest

Finally, issues are a necessity. In many cases, these issues are provided by historical developments on the national or international scene, a point to which I will return. But in some instances, as at Berkeley, "on-campus" issues are the focus of protest. And in other cases, off-campus and on-campus issues are fused, as in the recent protests at institutional cooperation with draft board policies considered unjust by demonstrating students. In providing such on-campus issues, the attitude of the university administration is central. Skillful handling of student complaints, the maintenance of open channels of communication between student leaders and faculty members, and administrative willingness to resist public and political pressures in order to protect the rights of students—all minimize the likelihood of organized protest. Conversely, a university administration that shows itself unduly sensitive to political, legislative or public pressures, that treats students arrogantly, ineptly, condescendingly, hypocritically or above all dishonestly, is asking for a demonstration.

Thus one reason for the relative absence of on-campus student protests and demonstrations on the campuses of private, non-denominational "academic" colleges and universities (which recruit many protest-prone students) probably lies in the liberal policies of the administrations. As Cowan (1966) notes, liberal students generally attend non-restrictive and "libertarian" colleges. Given an administration and faculty that supports or tolerates activism and student rights, student activists must generally find their issues off-campus. The same students, confronting an administration unduly sensitive to political pressures from a conservative board of regents or State legislature, might engage in active on-campus protests. There is also some evidence that clever administrative manipulation of student complaints, even in the absence of genuine concern with student rights, can serve to dissipate the potentialities of protest (Keene, 1966).

Among the institutional factors often cited as motivating student protest is the largeness, impersonality, atomization, "multiversitification" etc., of the university. I have already noted that student protesters do not seem distinctively dissatisfied with their educations. Furthermore, the outstanding academic achievements and intellectual motivations of activists concentrate them, within any college, in the courses and programs that provide the most "personal" attention: honors programs, individual instruction, advanced seminars, and so on. Thus, they probably receive relatively *more* individual attention and a *higher* calibre of instruction than do non-protesters. Furthermore, protests generally tend to occur at the best, rather than the worst colleges, judged from the point of view of the quality of undergraduate instruction. Thus, despite the popularity of student slogans dealing with the impersonality and irrelevance of the multiversity, the absolute level of educational opportunities seems, if anything, positively related to the occurrence of protest: the better the institution, the more likely demonstrations are.

Nor can today's student activism be attributed in any direct way to mounting academic pressures. To be sure, activism is most manifest at those selective colleges where the "pressure to perform" (Keniston, 1965b) is greatest, where standards are highest, and where anxieties about being admitted to a "good" graduate or professional school are most pronounced. But, contrary to the argument of Lipset and Altbach (1966), the impact of academic pressure on activism seems negative rather than positive. Protest-prone students, with their superior academic attainments and strong intellectual commitments, seem especially vulnerable to a kind of academic professionalism that, because of the enormous demands it makes upon the student's energies, serves to cancel or preclude activism. Student demonstrations rarely take place during exam periods, and protests concerned with educational quality almost invariably seek an improvement of quality, rather than a lessening of pressure. Thus, though the pressure to perform doubtless affects *all* American students, it probably acts as a deterrent rather than a stimulus to student activism.

Deprivation of Expectations

What probably does matter, however, is the *relative* deprivation of student expectations (see Brown, 1967). A college that recruits large numbers of academically motivated and capable students into a less-than-first-rate education program, one that oversells entering freshmen on the virtues of the college, or one that reneges on implicit or explicit promises about the quality and freedom of education may well produce an "academic backlash" that will take the form of student protests over the quality of education. Even more important is the gap between expectations and actualities regarding freedom of student expression. Stern (1967) has demonstrated that most entering freshmen have extremely high hopes regarding the freedom of speech and action they will be able to exercise during college: most learn the real facts quickly, and graduate thoroughly disabused of their illusions. But since activists, as I have argued above, are particularly responsive to these issues, they are apt to tolerate disillusion less lightly, and to take up arms to concretize their dashed hopes. Compared to the frustration engendered by disillusionment regarding educational quality, the relative deprivation of civil libertarian hopes seems a more potent source of protests. And with regard to both issues, it must be recalled that protests have been *fewest* at institutions of low educational quality and little freedom for student expression. Thus, it is not the absolute level either of educational quality or of student freedom that matters, but the gap between student hopes and institutional facts.

THE PROTEST-PROMPTING CULTURAL CLIMATE

Even if a critical mass of interacting protest-prone students forms in an institution that provides leadership and issues, student protests are by no means inevitable, as the quiescence of American students during the 1950s suggests. For protests to occur, other more broadly cultural factors, attitudes and values must be present. Protest activities must be seen as meaningful acts, either in an instrumental or an expressive sense; and activists must be convinced that the consequences of activism and protest will not be overwhelmingly damaging to them. During the 1950s, one much-discussed factor that may have militated against student activism was the conviction that the consequences of protest (blacklisting, F.B.I. investigations, problems in obtaining security clearance, difficulties in getting jobs) were both harmful to the individual and yet extremely likely. Even more important was the sense on the part of many politically conscious students that participation in left-wing causes would merely show their naiveté, gullibility and political innocence without furthering any worthy cause. The prevailing climate was such that protest was rarely seen as an act of any meaning or usefulness.

Academic Support . . .

Today, in contrast, student protesters are not only criticized and excoriated by a large segment of the general public, but—more crucial —are actively defended, encouraged, lionized, praised, publicized, photographed, interviewed and studied by a portion of the academic community. Since the primary reference group of most activists is not the general public, but rather that liberal segment of the academic world most sympathetic to protest, academic support has a disproportionate impact on protest-prone students' perception of their own activities. In addition, the active participation of admired faculty members in protests, teach-ins and peace marches, acts as a further incentive to students (Kelman, 1966). Thus, in a minority of American colleges, subcultures have arisen where protest is felt to be both an important existential act—a dignified way of "standing up to be counted"—and an effective way of "bringing the machine to a halt," sometimes by disruptive acts (sit-ins, strikes, and so on), more often by calling public attention to injustice.

Universalism . . .

An equally important, if less tangible "cultural" factor is the broad climate of social criticism in American society. As Parsons (1951; 1960), White (1961), and others have noted, one of the enduring themes of American society is the pressure toward "universalism," that is, an increasing extension of principles like equality, equal opportunity, and fair protection of the law to all groups within the society (and in recent years, to all groups in the world). As affluence has increased in American society, impatience at the slow "progress" of non-affluent minority groups has also increased, not only among students, but among other segments of the population. Even before the advent of the student civil rights movement, support for racial segregation was diminishing. Similarly, the current student concern for the "forgotten fifth" was not so much initiated by student activists as it was taken up by them. In this regard, student activists are both caught up in and in the vanguard of a new wave of extension of universalism in American society. Although the demands of student activists usually go far beyond the national consensus, they nonetheless reflect (at the same time that they have helped advance) one of the continuing trends in American social change.

A contrasting but equally enduring theme in American social criticism is a more fundamental revulsion against the premises of industrial— and now technological—society. Universalistic-liberal criticism blames our society because it has not yet extended its principles, privileges and benefits to all: the complaint is injustice and the goal is to complete our unfinished business. But alienated-romantic criticism questions the validity and importance of these same principles, privileges and benefits— the complaint is materialism and the goal is spiritual, aesthetic or expressive fulfillment. The tradition of revulsion against conformist, anti-aesthetic, materialistic, ugly, middle-class America runs through American writing from Melville through the "lost generation" to the "beat generation" and has been expressed concretely in the bohemian subcultures that have flourished in a few large American cities since the turn of the century. But today, the power of the romantic-alienated position has increased: one response to prosperity has been a more search-ing examination of the technological assumptions upon which prosperity has been based. Especially for the children of the upper middle-class, affluence is simply taken for granted, and the drive "to get ahead in the world" no longer makes sense for students who start out ahead. The meanings of life must be sought elsewhere, in art, sentience, philosophy, love, service to others, intensified experience, adventure—in short, in the broadly aesthetic or expressive realm.

Deviant Views . . .

Since neither the universalistic nor the romantic critique of modern society is new, these critiques affect the current student generation not only directly but indirectly, in that they have influenced the way many of today's college students were raised. Thus, a few of today's activists are children of the "radicals of the 1930s" (Lipset & Altbach, 1966); and Flacks' comments on the growing number of intellectual, professional upper middle-class families who have adopted "deviant" views of tradi-tional American life and embodied these views in the practices by which they brought up their children. Thus, some of today's activists are the children of bohemians, college professors, and so on. But in general, the explanation from parental "deviance" does not seem fully convincing. To be sure, the backgrounds of activists are "atypical" in a statistical sense, and thus might be termed empirically "deviant." It may indeed turn out that the parents of activists are distinguished by their emphasis on humanitarianism, intellectualism and romanticism, and by their lack of stress on moralism (Flacks, 1967). But it is not obvious that such parental values can be termed "deviant" in any but a statistical sense. "Concern with the plight of others," "desire to realize intellectual ca-pacities," and "lack of concern about the importance of strictly control-ling personal impulses"—all these values might be thought of as more normative than deviant in upper middle-class suburban American society in 1966. Even "sensitivity to beauty and art" is becoming increasingly acceptable. Nor can the socio-economic facts of affluence, freedom from status anxiety, high educational levels, permissiveness with children, training for independence, and so on be considered normatively deviant in middle-class America. Thus, the sense in which activists are the de-viant offspring of subculturally deviant parents remains to be clarified.

Psychological Flexibility . . .

Another explanation seems equally plausible, at least as applied to some student activists—namely that their activism is closely related to the social and cultural conditions that promote high levels of psychological flexibility, complexity and integration. As Bay (1967) has argued, social scientists may be too reluctant to entertain the possibility that some political and social outlooks or activities are symptomatic of psychological "health," while others indicate "disturbance." In fact, many of the personal characteristics of activists—empathy, superior intellectual attainments, capacity for group involvement, strong humanitarian values, emphasis on self-realization, etc.—are consistent with the hypothesis that, as a group, they are unusually "healthy" psychologically. (See also Heist, 1966 and Trent & Craise, 1967.) Similarly, the personal antecedents of activist—economic security, committed parents, humanitarian, liberal and permissive home environments, good education, and so on—are those that would seem to promote unusually high levels of psychological functioning. If this be correct, then former SDS president Tom Hayden's words (1966) may be a valid commentary on the cultural setting of activism:

Most of the active student radicals today come from middle to upper middle-class professional homes. They were born with status and affluence as facts of life, not goals to be striven for. In their upbringing, their parents stressed the right of children to question and make judgments, producing perhaps the first generation of young people both affluent and independent of mind.

In agreeing with Bay (1967) that activists may be more psychologically "healthy" as a group than non-activists, I am aware of the many difficulties entailed by this hypothesis. First, complexity, flexibility, integration, high levels of functioning, and so on, are by no means easy to define, and the criteria for "positive mental health" remain vague and elusive. (See Jahoda, 1958.) Second, there are obviously many individuals with these same "healthy" characteristics who are not activists; and within the group of activists, there are many individuals with definite psychopathologies. In any social movement, a variety of individuals of highly diverse talents and motivations are bound to be involved, and global descriptions are certain to be oversimplified. Third, the explanation from "psychological health" and the explanation from "parental deviance" are not necessarily opposed. On the contrary, these two arguments become identical if we assume that the preconditions for high levels of psychological functioning are both statistically and normatively deviant in modern American society. This assumption seems quite plausible.

Whatever the most plausible explanation of the socio-cultural sources of activism, the importance of prevailing attitudes toward student protest and of the climate of social criticism in America seems clear. In the past five years a conviction has arisen, at least among a minority of American college students, that protest and social action are effective and honorable. Furthermore, changes in American society, especially in middle-class child rearing practices, mean that American students are increasingly responsive to both the universalistic and romantic critique of our society. Both strands of social criticism have been picked up by student activists in a rhetoric of protest that combines a major theme of impatience at the slow fulfillment of the creedal ideals of American society with a more muted minor theme of aesthetic revulsion at technological society itself. By and large, activists respond most affirmatively to the first theme and alienated students to the second; but even within the student protest movement, these two themes coexist in uneasy tension.

THE PROTEST-PRODUCING HISTORICAL SITUATION

To separate what I have called the "cultural climate" from the "historical situation" is largely arbitrary. But by this latter term I hope to point to the special sensitivity of today's student activists to historical events and trends that do not immediately impinge upon their own lives. In other nations, and in the past, student protest movements seem to have been more closely related to immediate student frustrations than they are in America today. The "transformationist" (utopian, Marxist, universalistic or democratic) aspirations of activist youth in rapidly developing nations often seem closely related to their personal frustrations under oppressive regimes or at "feudal" practices in their societies; the "restorationist" (romantic, alienated) youth movements that have appeared in later stages of industrialization seem closely connected to a personal sense of the loss of a feudal, maternal, and "organic" past. (See Lifton, 1960; 1963; 1964.) Furthermore, both universalistic and romantic youth movements in other nations have traditionally been highly ideological, committed either to concepts of universal democracy and economic justice or to particularistic values of brotherhood, loyalty, feeling and nation.

Anti-ideological . . .

Today's activists, in contrast, are rarely concerned with improving their own conditions and are highly motivated by identification with the oppressions of others. The anti-ideological bias of today's student activists has been underlined by virtually every commentator. Furthermore, as Flacks notes, the historical conditions that have produced protest elsewhere are largely absent in modern America; and the student "movement" in this country differs in important ways from student movements elsewhere. In many respects, then, today's American activists have no historical precedent, and only time will tell to what extent the appearance of organized student dissent in the 1960s is a product of locally

American conditions, of the psycho-social effects of a technological affluence that will soon characterize other advanced nations, or of widespread
changes in identity and style produced by psycho-historical factors that
affect youth of all nations (thermonuclear warfare, increased culture contact, rapid communications, and so on).

Sensitivity to World Events

But whatever the historical roots of protest, today's student protester
seems uniquely sensitive to historical trends and events. In interviewing
student activists I have been impressed with how often they mention
some world-historical event as the catalyst for their activism—in some
cases, witnessing via television of the Little Rock demonstrations over
school integration, in another case, watching rioting Zengakuren students
in Japan protesting the arrival of President Eisenhower, in other cases,
particularly among Negro students, a strong identification with the rising
black nationalism of recently independent African nations.

Several factors help explain this sensitivity to world events. For one,
modern means of communication make the historical world more psychologically "available" to youth. Students today are exposed to world
events and world trends with a speed and intensity that has no historical
precedent. Revolutions, trends, fashions and fads are now world wide;
it takes but two or three years for fashions to spread from Carnaby
Street to New York, New Delhi, Tokyo, Warsaw, Lagos, and Lima. In
particular, students who have been brought up in a tradition that makes
them unusually empathic, humanitarian and universalistic in values may
react more intensely to exposure via television to student demonstrations
in Japan than to social pressures from their fellow seniors in Centerville
High. Finally, this broadening of empathy is, I believe, part of a general modern trend toward the *internationalization of identity*. Hastened
by modern communications and consolidated by the world-wide threat
of nuclear warfare, this trend involves, in vanguard groups in many
nations, a loosening of parochial and national allegiances in favor of
a more inclusive sense of affinity with one's peers (and non-peers) from
all nations. In this respect, American student activists are both participants and leaders in the reorganization of psycho-social identity and
ideology that is gradually emerging from the unique historical conditions of the twentieth century (Lifton, 1965).

A small but growing number of American students, then, exhibit a
peculiar responsiveness to world-historical events—a responsiveness based
partly on their own broad identification with others like them throughout the world, and partly on the availability of information about world
events via the mass media. The impact of historical events, be they the

world-wide revolution for human dignity and esteem, the rising aspirations of the developing nations, or the war in Vietnam, is greatly magnified upon such students; their primary identification is not their unreflective national identity, but their sense of affinity for Vietnamese peasants, Negro sharecroppers, demonstrating Zengakuren activists, exploited migrant workers, and the oppressed everywhere. One of the consequences of security, affluence and education is a growing sense of personal involvement with those who are insecure, non-affluent and uneducated.

THE FUTURE OF STUDENT ACTIVISM

I have argued that no single factor can explain or help us predict the future of the student protest movement in America; active expressions of dissent have become more prevalent because of an *interaction* of individual, institutional, cultural and historical factors. Affluence and education have changed the environment within which middle-class children are raised, in turn producing a minority of students with special sensitivity to the oppressed and the dissenting everywhere. At the same time, technological innovations like television have made available to these students abundant imagery of oppression and dissent in America and in other nations. And each of these factors exerts a potentiating influence on the others.

Given some understanding of the interaction of these factors, general questions about the probable future of student activism in America can now be broken down into four more specific questions: Are we likely to produce (a) more protest-prone personalities? (b) more institutional settings in which protests are likely? (c) a cultural climate that sanctions and encourages activism? and (d) a historical situation that facilitates activism? To three of the questions (a, b, and d), I think the answer is a qualified yes; I would therefore expect that in the future, if the cultural climate remains the same, student activism and protest would continue to be visible features on the American social landscape.

Consider first the factors that promote protest-prone personalities. In the coming generation there will be more and more students who come from the upper middle-class, highly educated, politically liberal professional backgrounds from which protesters are selectively recruited (Michael, 1965). Furthermore, we can expect that a significant and perhaps growing proportion of these families will have the universalistic, humanitarian, equalitarian and individualistic values found in the families of protesters. Finally, the expressive, permissive, democratic and autonomy-promoting atmosphere of these families seems to be the emerging trend of middle-class America: older patterns of "entrepreneurial-authoritarian" control are slowly giving way to more "bureau-cratic-democratic" techniques of socialization (Miller & Swanson, 1958). Such secular changes in the American family would produce a growing proportion of students with protest-prone personalities.

Institutional factors, I have argued, are of primary importance in so far as they bring together a critical mass of suitably protest-predisposed students in an atmosphere where they can interact, create their own subculture, develop leadership and find issues. The growing size of major American universities, their increasing academic and intellectual selectivity, and the emphasis on "quality" education (honors programs, individual instruction, greater student freedom)—all seem to promote the continuing development of activist subcultures in a minority of American institutions. The increasing use of graduate student teaching assistants in major universities points to the growing availability of large numbers of potential "leaders" for student protests. Admittedly, a sudden increase in the administrative wisdom in college Deans and Presidents could reduce the number of available "on-campus" issues; but such a growth in wisdom does not seem imminent.

CULTURAL CLIMATE MAY CHANGE

In sharp contrast, a maintenance of the cultural climate required for continuation of activism during the coming years seems far more problematical. Much depends on the future course of the war in Vietnam. Continuing escalation of the war in Southeast Asia will convince many student activists that their efforts are doomed to ineffectuality. For as of mid-1967, anti-war activism has become the primary common cause of student protesters. The increasing militancy and exclusivity of the Negro student civil rights movement, its emphasis on "Black Power" and on grass-roots community organization work (to be done by Negroes) is rapidly pushing white activists out of civil rights work, thus depriving them of the issue upon which the current mood of student activism was built. This fact, coupled with the downgrading of the war on poverty, the decline of public enthusiasm for civil rights, and the increasing scarcity of public and private financing for work with the underprivileged sectors of American society, has already begun to turn activists away from domestic issues toward an increasingly single-minded focus on the war in Vietnam. Yet at the same time, increasing numbers of activists overtly or covertly despair of the efficacy of student attempts to mobilize public opinion against the war, much less to influence directly American foreign policies. Continuing escalation in Southeast Asia has also begun to create a more repressive atmosphere toward student (and other) protesters of the war, exemplified by the question, "Dissent or Treason"? Already the movement of activists back to full-time academic work is apparent.

Thus, the war in Vietnam, coupled by the "rejection" of white middle-class students by the vestigial black Civil Rights Movement is producing a crisis among activists, manifest by a "search for issues" and intense disagreement over strategy and tactics. At the same time, the diminution of support for student activism tends to exert a "radicalizing" effect upon those who remain committed activists—partly because frustration itself tends to radicalize the frustrated, and partly because many of the less dedicated and committed activists have dropped away from the movement. At the same time, most activists find it difficult to turn from civil rights or peace work toward "organizing the middle-class" along lines suggested by alienated-romantic criticisms of technological society. On the whole, activists remain more responsive to universalistic issues like peace and civil rights than to primarily expressive or aesthetic criticisms of American society. Furthermore, the practical and organizational problems of "organizing the middle-class" are overwhelming. Were the student movement to be forced to turn away from universalistic issues like civil rights and peace to a romantic critique of the "quality of middle-class life," my argument here implies that its following and efficacy would diminish considerably. Were this to happen, observations based on student activism of a more "universalistic" variety would have to be modified to take account of a more radical and yet more alienated membership. Thus, escalation or even continuation of the war in Vietnam, particularly over a long period, will reduce the likelihood of student activism.

Yet there are other, hopefully more permanent, trends in American culture that argue for a continuation of protests. The further extension of affluence in America will probably mean growing impatience over our society's failure to include the "forgotten fifth" in its prosperity: as the excluded and underprivileged become fewer in number, pressures to include them in American society will grow. Similarly, as more young Americans are brought up in affluent homes and subcultures, many will undoubtedly turn to question the value of monetary, familistic and careerist goals, looking instead toward expressive, romantic, experiential, humanitarian and self-actualizing pursuits to give their lives meaning. Thus, in the next decades, barring a major world conflagration, criticisms of American society will probably continue and intensify on two grounds: first, that it has excluded a significant minority from its prosperity, and second, that affluence alone is empty without humanitarian, aesthetic or expressive fulfillment. Both of these trends would strengthen the climate conducive to continuing activism.

WORLD WIDE PROTEST-PROMOTING PRESSURES . . .

Finally, protest-promoting pressures from the rest of the world will doubtless increase in the coming years. The esteem revolution in developing nations, the rise of aspirations in the impoverished two-thirds of the world, and the spread of universalistic principles to other nations— all of these trends portend a growing international unrest, especially in the developing nations. If young Americans continue to be unusually responsive to the unfulfilled aspirations of those abroad, international trends will touch a minority of them deeply, inspiring them to overseas activities like the Peace Corps, to efforts to "internationalize" American foreign policies, and to an acute sensitivity to the frustrated aspirations of other Americans. Similarly, continuation of current American policies of supporting anti-communist but often repressive regimes in developing nations (particularly regimes anathema to student activists abroad) will tend to agitate American students as well. Thus, pressures from the probable world situation will support the continuance of student protests in American society.

In the next decades, then, I believe we can forsee the continuation, with short-range ebbs and falls, of activism in American society. Only if activists were to become convinced that protests were ineffectual or social action impossible is this trend likely to be fundamentally reversed. None of this will mean that protesters will become a majority among American students; but we can anticipate a slowly growing minority of the most talented, empathic, and intellectually independent of our students who will take up arms against injustice both here and abroad.

SUMMARY

Throughout this discussion, I have emphasized the contrast between two types of students, two types of family backgrounds, and two sets of values that inspire dissent from the Great Society. On the one hand, I have discussed students I have termed alienated, whose values are apolitical, romantic, and aesthetic. These students are most responsive to "romantic" themes of social criticism; that is, they reject our society because of its dehumanizing effects, its lack of aesthetic quality and its failure to provide "spiritual" fulfillment to its members. And they are relatively impervious to appeals to social, economic or political justice. On the other hand, I have discussed activists, who are politically involved, humanitarian and universalistic in values. These students object to our society not because they oppose its basic principles, but because it fails to implement these principles fully at home and abroad.

In the future, the tension between the romantic-alienated and the universalistic-activist styles of dissent will probably increase. I would anticipate a growing polarization between those students and student groups who turn to highly personal and experiential pursuits like drugs, sex, art and intimacy, and those students who redouble their efforts to change American society. In the past five years, activists have been in the ascendant, and the alienated have been little involved in organized political protests. But a variety of possible events could reverse this ascendency. A sense of ineffectuality, especially if coupled with repression of organized dissent, would obviously dishearten many activists. More important, the inability of the student protest movement to define its own long-range objectives, coupled with its intransigent hostility to ideology and efficient organization, means that *ad hoc* protests are too rarely linked to explicit intellectual, political and social goals that alone can sustain prolonged efforts to change society. Without some shared sustaining vision of the society and world they are working to promote, and frustrated by the enormous obstacles that beset any social reformer, student activists would be likely to return to the library.

How and whether this tension between alienation and activism is resolved seems to me of the greatest importance. If a growing number of activists, frustrated by political ineffectuality or a mounting war in Southeast Asia, withdraw from active social concern into a narrowly academic quest for professional competence, then a considerable reservoir of the most talented young Americans will have been lost to our society and the world. The field of dissent would be left to the alienated, whose intense quest for *personal* salvation, meaning, creativity and revelation dulls their perception of the public world and inhibits attempts to better the lot of others. If, in contrast, tomorrow's potential activists can feel that their demonstrations and actions are effective in molding public opinion and, more important, in effecting needed social change, then the possibilities for constructive change in post-industrial American society are virtually without limit.

REFERENCES

Aiken, M., Demerath, N. J., and Marwell, G. Conscience and confrontation: some preliminary findings on summer civil rights volunteers. University of Wisconsin, 1966. (mimeo)

Allen, M., and Silverstein H. Progress report: creative arts—alienated youth project. New York: March, 1967.

Bay, Christian. Political and apolitical students: facts in search of theory. *Journal of Social Issues*, 1967, **23**, 76–91.

Bernreuter, Robert G. The college student: he is thinking, talking, acting. *Penn State Alumni News*, July, 1966.

Block, J., Haan, N., and Smith, M. B. Activism and apathy in contemporary adolescents. In J. F. Adams (Ed.) *Contributions to the Understanding of Adolescence*. Brown, New York: Allyn and Bacon, 1968, 198–231.

Brown, Donald R. Student stress and the institutional environment. *Journal of Social Issues*, 1967, **23**, 92–107.

Coles, Robert. Serpents and doves: non-violent youth in the South. In Erik Erikson (Ed.) *The Challenge of Youth*. New York: Basic Books, 1963.

Coles, Robert. *Children of Crisis*. Boston: Little, Brown, 1967.

Cowan, John Lewis. Academic freedom, protest and university environments. Paper read at APA, New York, 1966.

Draper, Hal. *Berkeley, the New Student Revolt*. New York: Grove, 1965.

Ehle, John. *The Free Men*. New York: Harper and Row, 1965.

Erikson, Erik H. (Ed.) *The Challenge of Youth*. New York: Basic Books, 1963.

Fishman, Jacob R., and Solomon, Frederic. Psychological observations on the student sit-in movement. *Proceedings of the Third World Congress of Psychiatry*. Toronto: University of Toronto/Mcgill, n.d.

Fishman, Jacob R., and Solomon, Frederic. Youth and social action. *Journal of Social Issues*, 1964, **20**, (4), 1–28.

Flacks, Richard E. The liberated generation: an exploration of the roots of student protest. *Journal of Social Issues*, 1967, **23**, 52–75.

Gastwirth, D. Why students protest. Unpublished paper, Yale University, 1965.

Hayden, T. Quoted in *Comparative Education Review*, 1966, **10**, 187.

Heist, Paul. Intellect and commitment: the faces of discontent. *Order and Freedom on the Campus*. Western Interstate Commission for Higher Education and the Center for the Study of Higher Education, 1965.

Heist, Paul. The dynamics of student discontent and protest. Paper read at APA, New York, 1966.

Jahoda, Marie. *Current Concepts of Positive Mental Health*. New York: Basic Books, 1958.

Katz, J. The learning environment: social expectations and influences. Paper presented at American Council of Education, Washington, D.C., 1965.

Katz, J. The student activists: rights, needs and powers of undergraduates. Stanford: Institute for the Study of Human Problems, 1967.

Keene, S. How one big university laid unrest to rest. *The American Student*, 1966, **1**, 18–21.

Kelman, H. D. Notes on faculty activism. *Letter to Michigan Alumni*, 1966.

Keniston, Kenneth. American students and the 'political revival.' *The American Scholar*, 1962, **32**, 40–64.

Keniston, Kenneth. *The Uncommitted.* New York: Harcourt, Brace and World, 1965. (a)

Keniston, Kenneth. The pressure to perform. *The Intercollegian.* September, 1965. (b)

Keniston, Kenneth. The faces in the lecture room. In R. S. Morison (Ed.) *The American University.* Boston: Houghton-Mifflin, 1966. (a)

Keniston, Kenneth. The psychology of alienated students. Paper read at APA, New York, 1966. (b)

Keniston, Kenneth, and Helmreich, R. An exploratory study of discontent and potential drop-outs at Yale. Yale University, 1965. (mimeo)

Kornhauser, W. Alienation and participation in the mass university. Paper read at American Ortho-Psychiatric Association, Washington, D.C., 1967.

Lifton, Robert Jay. Japanese youth: the search for the new and the pure. *The American Scholar,* 1960, **30,** 332–344.

Lifton, Robert Jay. Youth and history: individual change in post-war Japan. In E. Erikson (Ed.) *The Challenge of Youth.* New York: Harper and Row, 1963.

Lifton, Robert Jay. Individual patterns in historical change. *Comparative Studies in Society and History.* 1964, **6,** 369–383.

Lifton, Robert Jay. Protean man. Yale University, 1965. (mimeo)

Lipset, Seymour M. Student opposition in the United States. *Government and Opposition,* 1966, **1,** 351–374. (a)

Lipset, Seymour M. University students and politics in underdeveloped countries. *Comparative Education Review,* 1966, **10,** 132–162. (b)

Lipset, Seymour M., and Altbach, P. G. Student politics and higher education in the United States. *Comparative Education Review,* 1966, **10,** 320–349.

Lipset, Seymour M., and Wolin, S. S. (Eds.) *The Berkeley Student Revolt.* Garden City, N.Y.: Doubleday, 1965.

Lyonns, G. The police car demonstration: a survey of participants. In S. Lipset and S. Wolin (Eds.) *The Berkeley Student Revolt.* Garden City, N.Y.: Doubleday, 1965.

Michael, Donald Nelson. *The Next Generation. The Prospects Ahead for the Youth of Today and Tomorrow.* New York: Vintage, 1965.

Miller, Michael, and Gilmore, Susan (Eds.) *Revolution at Berkeley.* New York: Dell, 1965.

Miller, Daniel R., and Swanson, Guy E. *The Changing American Parent.* New York: John Wiley, 1958.

Newfield, Jack. *A Prophetic Minority.* New York: New American Library, 1966.

Newsweek. Campus, 1965. March 22, 1965.

Parsons, Talcott. *The Social System.* Glencoe, Ill.: Free Press, 1951.

Parsons, Talcott. *Structure and Process in Modern Societies.* Glencoe, Ill.: Free Press, 1960.

Paulus, G. *A Multivariate Analysis Study of Student Activist Leaders, Student Government Leaders and Non-Activists.* Cited in Richard E. Peterson, *The Student Left in American Higher Education.* Draft for Puerto Rico Conference on Students and Politics, 1967.

Pervin, Lawrence A., Reik, L. E., and Dalrymple, W. (Eds.) *The College Drop-out and the Utilization of Talent.* Princeton: Princeton University, 1966.

Peterson, Richard E. *The Scope of Organized Student Protest in 1964-65.* Princeton, N.J.: Educational Testing Service, 1966.

Peterson, Richard E. The student Left in American higher education. Draft for Puerto Rico Conference on Students and Politics, 1967.

Reed, M. Student non-politics, or how to make irrelevancy a virtue. *The American Student*, 1966, 1, (3), 7-10.

Rigney, Francis J., and Smith, L. D. *The Real Bohemia.* New York: Basic Books, 1961.

Schneider, Patricia. A study of members of SDS and YD at Harvard. Unpublished B.A. thesis, Wellesley College, 1966.

Solomon, Frederic, and Fishman, Jacob R. Perspectives on the student sit-in movement. *American Journal of Ortho-Psychiatry*, 1963, 33, 873-874.

Solomon, Frederic, and Fishman, Jacob R. Youth and peace: a psycho-social study of student peace demonstrators in Washington, D.C. *The Journal of Social Issues*, 1964, 20, (4), 54-63.

Somers, R. H. The mainsprings of the rebellion: a survey of Berkeley students in November, 1964. In S. Lipset and S. Wolin (Eds.), *The Berkeley Student Revolt.* Garden City, N.Y.: Doubleday, 1965.

Stern, G. Myth and reality in the American college. *AAUP Bulletin*, Winter, 1966, 408-414.

Suczek, Robert Francis, and Alfert, E. Personality characteristic of college dropouts. University of California, 1966. (mimeo)

Trent, James W., and Craise, Judith L. Commitment and conformity in the American college. *Journal of Social Issues*, 1967, 23, 34-51.

Trow, Martin. Some lessons from Berkeley. Paper presented to American Council of Education, Washington, D.C., 1965.

Watts, William Arther, and Whittaker, D. Some socio-psychological differences between highly committed members of the Free Speech Movement and the student population at Berkeley. *Applied Behavioral Science*, 1966, 2, 41-62.

Watts, William Arther, and Whittaker, D. Socio-psychological characteristics of intellectually oriented, alienated youth: a study of the Berkeley non-student. University of California, Berkeley, 1967. (mimeo)

Westby, D., and Braungart, R. Class and politics in the family backgrounds of student political activists. *American Social Review*, 1966, 31, 690-692.

White, Winston. *Beyond Conformity.* Glencoe, Ill.: Free Press, 1961.

Whittaker, D., and Watts, W. A. Personality and value attitudes of intellectually disposed, alienated youth. Paper presented at APA, New York, 1966.

Wright, E. O. Student leaves of absence from Harvard College: A personality and social system approach. Unpublished paper, Harvard University, 1966.

Zinn, Howard. *SNCC, The New Abolitionists.* Boston: Beacon, 1965.

2.7 Orientation

The following paper by sociologist Ronald Akers provides a survey of the epidemiology, theory, and social problems surrounding the use of drugs and alcohol by adolescents and young adults. Current statistical data are provided to the reader after which major theoretical concepts pertinent to the alcohol and drug use phenomena are discussed. These concepts include reference group norm qualities, imitation learning, and the "rebellion" hypothesis. Possibly relevant to the latter are the purported reinforcing properties of drug and alcohol use whereby the "nirvana" induced by these substances provides an escape from the frustrations and insecurities of role confusion (recall the identity crisis hypothesis introduced in Part I). Akers takes the notion of reinforcement further, however, to outline a *differential association-reinforcement* view of drug-taking and drinking behavior. This view attempts to account for the process by which one learns these behaviors within an environment whose characteristics are conducive to such learning.

Akers offers in conclusion a commentary on the social problems that adolescent drinking and drug use represent. These social problems, contends Akers, are magnified (if not generated by) ineffective social policies with regard to drugs and alcohol. Few would argue that traditional moral and legal sanctions concerning these problems have served our society effectively. Although clear pathways to the solution of such problems remain to be marked, Akers offers some preliminary ideas that may be constructive toward this end. Unquestionably the burden for developing realistic pathways is one to be shared jointly by the helping professions, including education, the mass media, and our legal institutions. Ultimately, the structure of values upon which our views of these problems are based (including its internal consistency) must also be carefully examined and clarified in meaningful ways.

RECOMMENDED READINGS

Alexander, C. Norman, Jr. Consensus and mutual attraction in natural cliques: a study of adolescent drinkers. *American Journal of Sociology*, 1964, **69**, 395–403.

Carey, James T. *The College Drug Scene*. Englewood Cliffs, N.J.: Prentice-Hall, 1968.

Louria, Donald B. *The Drug Scene.* New York: McGraw-Hill, 1968.

Maddox, George L., and McCall, Bevode C. *Drinking among Teenagers.*
New Brunswick, N.J.: Rutgers Center of Alcohol Studies, 1964.

Reister, A. E., and Zucher, R. A. Adolescent social structure and drinking behavior. *Personnel and Guidance Journal,* 1968, **47,** 304–312.

2.7   Teenage Drinking and Drug Use

Ronald L. Akers, UNIVERSITY OF WASHINGTON

INTRODUCTION

Whether some set of circumstances or the behavior of some members of
society constitute social problems depends upon from whose perspective
they are viewed. For somewhat different reasons, drinking alcohol and
taking drugs are among the kinds of behavior of adolescents that the
adult community and authorities define as deviant. Young people may
not define doing things proscribed by adult authority as major social
problems. However, in American society, adolescence is a relatively powerless social status, and it is the adult's view that prevails. Drinking by
teenagers is deviant only because such behavior is reserved for adults in
our society; drug use is deviant because it is prohibited for the young and
old alike.

This difference notwithstanding, both adolescent drug use and drinking
continue to occupy top positions in the list of adult concerns about their
children, and many of the same questions continue to be asked about
both problems. How much is there? Who is doing it? Why do they do
it? Are those who drink alcohol or use drugs more likely to commit other
delinquent acts? What changes have taken place through the years? Is
the situation getting worse or better? What can be done about the problem? The purpose here is to examine empirical evidence on and theoretical explanations of teenage drinking and drug use in an attempt to furnish
some answers to these questions. The first section summarizes some data
on the epidemiology, extent, trends, and variations in these two types of
adolescent behavior. The second section presents some theories of teenage
drinking and drug use. The last section points to some questions deserving
further research and offers some comments and suggestions on public
policy relating to use of alcohol and drugs by adolescents.

Original paper prepared especially for this volume.

EPIDEMIOLOGY OF TEENAGE DRINKING AND DRUG USE

Drug Use

The various substances that are included in the drug problem fall into five major categories. The two major types are: the *opiates*, including principally heroin and morphine and opiate-like synthetics such as demerol and dolophine, and *hallucinogens*, including primarily marihuana and LSD. Others are: *depressants*, such as barbiturates, *stimulants*, such as the amphetamines and cocaine; and *deliriants*, such as airplane glue and aerosal sprays. Of these, the opiates invariably and the depressants sometimes produce physiological addiction. The others may be used habitually, but they do not produce physiological dependence. The epidemological information presented here related basically to the opiates and hallucinogens.

Adolescent drug use in this country was very small until after World War II. In the nineteenth century, opiate users and addicts were most likely to be rural, white, middle-class females, and the average age at first addiction was between 35 and 40 (Brown, 1966; Marshall, 1966). In the twentieth century, thanks largely to a changed enforcement policy which made the major source of drug supply through illegal channels, opiate use began to be concentrated among urban, lower-class, non-white, and delinquent or criminal males (Lindesmith, 1967, pp. 130–132; Lindesmith & Gagnon, 1964, pp. 163–167). The average age of first use and addiction remained well above adolescence, however, throughout the 1930s (Winick, 1965, pp. 7–9). Until this time marihuana use was virtually unknown in this country; it was confined to lower-class Mexican-Americans in the Southwest. In the 1930s marihuana use began to spread among young adult men, mainly lower-class Negroes and jazz musicians, and then began to trickle down to younger groups. Starting after World War II and continuing into the early 1950s, marihuana and heroin spread through the ghettoes and slums of northern large cities. During this time, official statistics and hospital admissions reflected a dramatic drop in the ages of users and addicts. Adolescence became a common age at which drug use began. But the youthful drug users of both heroin and marihuana were almost exclusively lower-class slum dwellers, although even in these areas the majority of the teenagers did not smoke marihuana and probably no more than 10 percent used heroin. Moreover, the trend toward increased drug use among adolescents began to taper off in the mid-fifties; in the late 1950s, the average age of drug users began to rise again (Winick, 1965, pp. 7–9; Ausubel, 1958, pp. 63, 93–94; Kobrin & Finestone, 1968; Bates, 1966, p. 66; Blum, 1967, p. 48; Lindesmith, 1967, pp. 237–239).

The increased number of adolescent opiate users was never enough to bring the average age of addicts down to the teenage years; it was enough to ensure that the typical opiate addict became and remains today a young adult. Opiate use has been and remains concentrated in the large urban centers of population (Ball & Cottrell, 1965, p. 473; Ball & Bates, 1966, p. 59; O'Donnell & Ball, 1966, p. 9). Further, it is concentrated in the slums, in the poorest, most deprived, most crowded, and unstable neighborhoods, and among members of minority ethnic groups and others at the bottom of the socio-economic scale (Blum, 1967, pp. 49–50; Chein, 1965, pp. 109–112; Chein, 1966, pp. 123–125; Chein et al., 1964, pp. 45–74; Winick, 1965, pp. 10–16; Kobrin & Finestone, 1968, pp. 114–115).

Marihuana use developed differently. Although it continues to be done in the same slum environment with heroin, marihuana smoking has become increasingly an activity of young, middle-class and upper-class whites. Starting in the early 1960s marihuana became the chief drug, along with LSD, in the psychedelic drug movement. The "classic" hippie groups were comprised mainly of young adults, but they were recruited from the college-aged and college-oriented children of the affluent. Subsequently, marihuana use appears to have spread among these well-to-do older adolescents and young adults, and then to have moved from college to high school to junior high school. In addition to marihuana and LSD, a variety of other drugs and combinations are used; speed and other amphetamines (stimulants), barbiturates (depressants), and a range of hallucinogenic drugs.

That drug use has increased among adolescents in recent years is evident; but just what proportions it has reached is virtually unknown. Arrests of persons under 21 for possession of marihuana have gone up at a rate far in excess of adult drug arrests, and most of the increase is accounted for by arrests of whites (Carey, 1968, pp. 44–46). Estimates in 1965 placed the number of college students who had experimented with marihuana at 10 to 11 percent (Blum, 1967, p. 24; Young & Hixson, 1966, p. 76). In a study of five California campuses, it was found that 21 percent of the students in 1967 and 57 percent in 1968 had smoked marihuana at least once; 4 percent in 1967 and 14 percent in 1968 reported themselves as regular smokers (Newsweek, 1969). Informal surveys on various college campuses during 1967 and 1968 found from about 6 percent to 30 percent of the undergraduates smoked marihuana at least once and 1 percent to 15 percent had tried LSD. A 1967 Gallup Poll among a representative sample of college students found only 6 percent reporting one or more marihuana experiences (Louria, 1968, pp. 8–12). This does not constitute very full knowledge of drug use among college-age people, but even less is known about drug use among high school-aged youth; the estimates of the percentage of high school and junior high school students who have smoked marihuana or taken LSD range all the way from 5 percent to 90 percent, depending upon whether one asks school officials or the students. A survey taken in Long Island, New York schools found 8 percent of the students had used marihuana and 2 percent had used LSD. A study in San Francisco high schools reported 20 percent of the students had smoked marihuana one or more times (Louria, 1968, p. 10). In another study of marihuana use among high school seniors in three California schools only about 10 percent (16 percent of the boys and 4 percent of the girls) reported having ever smoked marihuana (Mauss, 1969).

Drinking

The research evidence on teenage drinking is much clearer and leaves little doubt that most people in this country will have had alcoholic beverages by the time they are adults. It is also evident that the vast majority of the drinkers, both as adolescents and as adults, are moderate, social drinkers. Neither adult nor underage drinking is a matter of random individual variation; both vary in socially patterned ways by age, sex, religion, region, community, and social class.

Until the first part of this century, drinking was a pastime of a minority of the population; the overwhelming majority of drinkers were men who typically consumed relatively large quantities of hard liquor and did most of their drinking in public saloons. In the last 60 years, however, the quantity taken at any one sitting and the per capita consumption of absolute alcohol have decreased; beer has taken the place of spirit alcohol as the most popular beverage alcohol. A larger portion of the drinkers are women. More of the drinking is now done in private homes. A greater proportion of the population drink, but the typical pattern is now social drinking in moderation. Only about 6 percent of the drinkers are alcoholics (McCarthy, 1964). Studies of adults have consistently found that about 75 percent of the men and 60 percent of the women drink alcohol to some extent. About 20 percent of the males and 5 percent of the females are frequent or heavy drinkers. The highest proportions in all categories of drinkers, from light to heavy, occur in the early 20's to late 30's age range (Riley & Marden, 1959; Mulford, 1964; Cahalan *et al.*, 1967).

The place of underage drinking in this picture was not known until the 1940s. Questionnaire survey studies done at that time found that a little over 40 percent of the adolescent boys and less than 30 percent of the girls were drinking at least sometimes (McCarthy, 1959). Although there are regional variations (ranging from around 25 percent in the South to 90 percent in the Northeast), studies since then have consistently found that the majority of high school students have had alcohol to drink at least once, and an average of about half of the boys and about one-fourth of the girls have established at least an occasional pattern of drinking (Baur & McCluggage, 1958; Maddox & McCall, 1964; Maddox, 1964; MacKay et al., 1967; Slater, 1952; McCarthy, 1959; Windham et al., 1967).

These studies agree that as one passes through the teenage years, the probability that he will drink continues to increase. The majority of the boys and a sizeable minority of the girls will have had drinking experience by the time of high school graduation; by late adolescence, the proportion of drinkers equals or exceeds the overall adult rate (Straus & Bacon, 1962). The proportion of teenage users increases with community size. Those from Protestant families are less likely to be drinkers than those from Catholic or Jewish families. The findings on the relationship between social class and teenage drinking are not entirely consistent, but probably the most accurate picture is that the lowest rates of use are found in the middle-level status groups and the higher rates in the upper and lower strata (Baur & McCluggage, 1958; Maddox, 1964; Maddox & McCall, 1964).

Drugs, Drinking, and Delinquency

Besides drinking of alcohol being one traditional reason why juveniles are taken into custody, the evidence is fairly clear that there is a connection between drinking and other delinquent behavior. Comparisons of high school students and institutionalized delinquents have invariably shown that a higher proportion of the officially adjudicated delinquents are drinkers; moreover, although the percentages are relatively small in either case, institutionalized adolescents are more likely to be heavy and problem drinkers. The delinquent youths start drinking at an early age, their parents are more likely to be drinkers, and they are more likely to have friends who drink (Nelson, 1968; MacKay, Phillips, & Bryce, 1967; MacKay, 1963; Blacker et al., 1965). These findings are confirmed when abstainers, drinkers, and problem drinkers are compared on unofficial, self-reported delinquency involvement; the highest percentage of those scoring high in delinquency involvement is among "problem" drinkers and the lowest percentage is among those who do not drink (Globetti & Windham, 1967, pp. 150–155).

The relationship between drug use and the commission of other delinquent and illegal acts by adolescents has not been subject to the same systematic attention as that between drinking and delinquency. Research has shown that opiate addiction in adults is related to commission of income-producing crime (but not violent crimes), and presumably this would hold for juveniles (O'Donnell, 1966). One study done in Chicago in the early 1950s supports this contention, finding most adolescent drug users to engage in other forms of delinquency, although the delinquent acts both preceded and followed drug use (Kobrin & Finestone, 1968). There are no substantiated relationships between use of other drugs and commission of delinquent acts.

Summary of Epidemiology of Drinking and Drug Use

Opiate use among young people is still disproportionately a phenomenon of the urban slums and ghettoes where it is part of a drug-oriented subculture. The rate of opiate use among the whole adolescent population is relatively small and appears to have leveled off and remained relatively stable for the past 15 years. On the other hand, alcohol is the most frequently used intoxicating substance among teenagers; although its use is subject to systematic variations, it is known to some extent throughout all regions, communities, social classes, and ethnic groups. Hallucinogenic and other non-opiate drugs occupy an intermediate position between opiates and alcohol. They are used in the same slum subculture as opiates, but are certainly not confined to this setting. In fact, the increased prevalence of their use has come about as a result of the upsurge among affluent, middle and upper status youth. Marihuana use has not yet reached the proportions of drinking; its increase is largely confined to affluent, college-oriented teenagers in the metropolitan areas of the north and the east and west coasts and is virtually unknown in some areas. But if present trends continue, marihuana will come to compete with alcohol as the favorite intoxicant of teenagers.

The positive relationship between drinking and delinquency has been fairly well-established; property offenses are related to opiate addiction, but the relationship between use of other drugs and delinquency is unknown at this time.

SOCIOLOGICAL THEORIES OF ALCOHOL AND DRUG BEHAVIOR AMONG ADOLESCENTS

General Sociological Orientation

The general sociological view of drinking and drug behavior is that they are responses to socio-cultural and group influences. Both conforming and deviant use of alcohol and drugs are social phenomena, products of the general culture, and the more specific groups and social situations with which individuals are confronted. There are systematic variations in cultural traditions and systems of social control with regard to drugs and alcohol from one society to another and over time. The extent and nature of drug use and addiction, drinking and alcoholism in different societies around the world and through history reflect variations in customs and laws. Within the same society one will be subject to differential group and cultural influence depending upon his social status-roles and group memberships as defined by his location in the age, sex, socio-economic, religious, occupational, ethnic, and other systems in society. Thus, the differences in the functions served by alcohol, the way it is used and integrated into eating, ceremonial, social, and other contexts, and the rates of alcoholism reflect different cultural traditions. The community in which one lives, his location within that community, his family, class, religion, and other membership and reference groups all expose him to certain cultural and subcultural orientations toward drugs and alcohol. What he does with and thinks about these substances then will be affected by these orientations. (The best introductory overview of this general sociological perspective on *alcohol* is in Pittman (1967), Clinard (1968, pp. 388–444), Pittman and Snyder (1962), and Straus (1966). As applied to *drugs* in a general way see Ausubel (1958, pp. 57–67).)

Norm Qualities

One factor in the impact that the socio-cultural milieu has on alcohol and drug related behavior is the *quality or type* of norms to which one is exposed by his reference groups (groups with which he identified whether or not he is a member). Early studies of religious norms and drinking practices found that those who identified with religions that strongly prohibited drinking were less likely to start drinking, but those who did begin were more likely to become problem drinkers than were those identified with religions that permitted moderate imbibing (Mizruchi & Perruci, 1962; Skolnick, 1958).

Building upon these studies, Larsen and Abu-Laban identified three types of drinking norms: *proscriptive*, abstinence norms that prohibit any drinking; *prescriptive*, norms that permit drinking, but that provide definite guidelines and limits on acceptable drinking; and *nonscriptive*, vague, incomplete, permissive norms that neither prohibit nor provide adequate guidelines for proper drinking. They found that regardless of the reference group (parents, family, friends, religion, and co-workers) the highest percentage of drinkers was found among those who had been exposed to prescriptive norms, and the highest percentage of heavy drinkers were found among those who had been exposed to vague, nonscriptive drinking standards (Larsen & Abu-Laban, 1968).

These studies have been on adult drinking patterns, and their implication for teenage drinking or drug use has not been made clear. It would seem, however, that the norm-quality explanation would predict that teenagers whose reference groups carry proscriptive or nonscriptive norms concerning alcohol or drugs are not apt to use either, but if they do the probability is higher than for those from prescriptive milieux that they will become heavy drinkers or habitual drug users. Unfortunately, no one has yet examined this proposition in the context of drug use. There is research relevant to norm-qualities and teenage drinking, but the findings have not been entirely consistent (see Preston, 1969; Globetti, 1967; Alexander, 1967).

Teenage Drinking and Drug Use: Adolescent Rebellion or Imitation

Perhaps the most common explanation of teenage drinking or drug use is that they are forms of "adolescent rebellion" and alienation from adult patterns; this view is countered by that which sees them as the result of adolescent "imitation" of adult patterns. Sometimes both explanations are presented together. For instance, Straus notes that some young people drink to symbolize a negative break with family and religion, but that most teenage drinking is simply the outcome of positive identification with family, peers, and other groups supportive of drinking. Adolescents tend both to press for adult status and to reject restrictions against their drinking (Straus, 1966, pp. 253–255). As long as the argument is presented in this way, that some teenage behavior is rebellion and some is imitation, the two explanations are not necessarily contradictory. However, insofar as claims are made that *most* teenage drinking and drug taking results from one and not the other, the two theories can be seen as competing explanations.

The "rebellion" theory is that adolescents resent adult authority which proscribes drugs and alcohol for them. They get alienated from and rebel against the conventional system represented by their parents, the law, religion, and the school system. Alcohol and drugs then are turned to as ways of expressing that rebellion; in so doing they are supported by peer group pressures and norms which are contrary to the expectations of the adult system. Thus, using drugs or alcohol are right by peer group standards because they are wrong by adult standards.

The "imitations" argument is that alcohol and/or drugs are an integral part of our society and their use by teenagers is just one way of attempting to behave as adults do and become incorporated into society. Thus, they do not reject so much as they emulate or imitate adult patterns. It is an exercise in anticipatory socialization into adult status and runs counter to adult expectations only in that it is done at an inappropriate or premature age.

The rebellion versus imitation views with regard to drinking are obviously related to the studies on norm qualities. The finding that those whose drinking is positively sanctioned by prescriptive norms are more likely to drink, and in some cases to drink more frequently, suggests that drinking in this context is the natural outcome of socialization into adult normative drinking patterns. On the other hand, the finding that proscriptive injunctions are related to heavy drinking suggests that faced with total abstinence norms, some will rebel, break the traces of prohibition, and become alienated from the groups that are the sources of these norms.

Thus, Globetti (1967) and Alexander (1967), both of whom conducted studies of teenage drinking in abstinence settings, support the adolescent rebellion theory. Alexander maintains that drinking "may represent an expression of hostility toward the normative authority of the total society," or against an individual who has authority (1967, p. 543).

Globetti's study did not reveal any relationship between parent-child relations and drinking, but it did show that:

. . . drinkers may be characterized as higher in deviance than non-drinkers as indicated by their participation in mild forms of deviant behavior, by their pessimism and by their rejection of middle-class values. In addition, they appear to be estranged from such important socialization groups as the family, the school, the church, and the community. The users identified in this study, so the data suggest, seem to be teenagers with problems. Their drinking appears to be an expression of rebellion or hostility toward the normative authority of the community. (Globetti, 1967, p. 132).

This notion of rebellious youth engaging in anti-authority activities supported by a peer-group culture has also been applied to teenage drug taking. Ausubel, for instance, labels adolescent drug use "reactive addiction" and places it in the same category as truancy, use of alcohol and tobacco, and reckless driving in that:

. . . it is expressive of a general anti-adult orientation characterized by defiance of traditional norms and conventions and flouting of adult-imposed taboos and authority.

Like other forms of adolescent rebellion, reactive addiction is generated and propagated through peer groups. (Ausubel, 1958, p. 51).

Louria, likewise, pictures drug taking by young people as a reaction against what they perceive to be an inept, self-serving system; the estrangement takes the forms of both open rebellion and alienation and is characteristic of the hippies, ghetto minorities, and affluent youth alike (Louria, 1968, pp. 24–27). On the basis of research in the Berkeley, college-related drug scene, Carey argues that the first step into drug use is a strong sense of disillusionment and alienation from conventional society which is seen as basically hypocritical (Carey, 1968, pp. 48–49).

The distinctive dress and grooming styles that many young people display today, the problems of inter-generational conflict, the discontinuities wrought by rapid social change in the cultural atmosphere in which parents were reared and that in which they attempt to rear their own children, the flouting of adult rules, and many other matters of differences between generations would seem to underscore the rebellion of youth against the adult system in general and parents in particular. This impression has become particularly salient with the insertion into the rhetoric of youthful protesters of phrases indicating the corruption, hypocrisy, and inequities of the "establishment" manned by adults. Using proscribed substances may be one way of showing they want no part of it. At the same time, it is clear that the majority of adolescents are not in open revolt against either their parents or adult authority, and some theorists have argued that the youngster's indulgence or abstinence may simply reflect the interplay of various positive influences, with authority rejection playing little or no part.

For instance, Maddox and McCall, while not denying that peer group settings are the occasions for much drinking, label as a myth the notion that the "youth culture" of peers places irresistible pressure on the abstaining youth to drink. Furthermore, even peer-group drinking is more an emulation rather than rejection of adult patterns (Maddox & McCall, 1964, pp. 3–8; see also McKay, 1965, pp. 3–4). Their major contention, supported by their research findings, is that, in general, teenage drinking is expressive of identification with an anticipatory socialization into adult behavior (Maddox & McCall, 1965, pp. 77–98).

. . . Drinking may be used as a test of loyalty to peer groups precisely because it is discouraged by adults. The contrary evidence, however, is compelling. The probability of alcohol use increases with age, i.e., as assumption of adult roles is approached. There is a demonstrated relationship between the drinking behavior of parents and their offspring . . . a majority of adolescents in our society would in all probability come to use beverage alcohol eventually even if there were no peer group experience at all since young people tend to perceive some drinking as an integral part of normal adult behavior. The emphasis of this evidence overwhelmingly favors adolescent indentification with adulthood, rather than hostility to adult goals or authority. (Maddox & McCall, 1964, p. 7).

The idea that drug use like alcohol use by teenagers may also be more in the nature of modeling behavior after, rather than rejecting, conventional society is presented succinctly by Simon and Gagnon:

These new patterns of marihuana use . . . must be seen in terms of their continuity with general trends in contemporary American culture. One of these trends . . . is the fact that we have become as a nation, a population of pill-takers. Both the actual miracle and the myth of modern medicine have made the use of drugs highly legitimate, as something to be taken casually and not only during moments of acute and certified distress. Our children, in being casual about drugs . . . far from being in revolt against an older generation, may in fact be acknowledging how influential a model that generation was. (Simon & Gagnon, 1968, p. 60).

Or as Louria says, "If young persons see their parents egregiously misusing and overusing drugs is it any wonder that they should become part of the youthful drug cult?" (Louria, 1968, p. 17).

As Maddox and McCall point out, the evidence with regard to drinking beverage alcohol is that the bulk of teenage drinking is very much a matter of copying adult models. Peer groups are also important influences, but they function to undergird and support parental models.

In general, the variations in frequency, amount, and type of teenage drinking patterns by sex, religion, region, and community reflect fairly faithfully the pattern variations of the adult community. More specifically, the most accurate predictor of what the teenager does with and thinks about alcohol, is the attitudes and behavior of his parents. The abstainer is most likely to come from an abstaining home; the moderate drinker from a home in which the parents drink moderately; and the heavy drinker from homes in which heavy drinking has been the pattern (Maddox, 1964). Moreover, a sizeable portion of the drinking teenagers report that their first drinking experience and some current drinking occurs at home with parental approval. Maddox and McCall found that among those who have tasted alcohol, more than half the boys and two-thirds of the girls report that the occasion for this tasting included parents or other adult relatives. Next to parents, adolescent peer group influences are most important. But they appear not to function as counter-normative groups forcing the abstainer to drink; they do provide the occasions and setting for unsupervised drinking without parental approval. Peer group settings for drinking are more important for boys than for girls; the girls who drink at all tend more frequently than boys to drink at home and less frequently than boys to drink in clandestine, peer-only groups. The salience of drinking as a mark of "coming of age," symbolization of and rite of passage into adult status, and the general association of drinking with adult status is evidenced by the frequency with which adolescents attribute drinking by their peers to be for reasons of trying to act "smart" or "grown-up." (Maddox & McCall, 1964; Maddox, 1963; Ullman, 1962; Slater, 1952).

Unfortunately, the studies of drug use by adolescents have not investigated the impact of parental and adult influence in the same way that studies of drinking have. Some general and tentative observations can be made, however, concerning the extent to which teenage drug use is rebellion against or reflects positive adult influence in the way in which teenage drinking does.

There can be little question that we live in both a "cocktail" and a "pill-taking" culture; it is possible then that teenage drug use as well as teenage drinking is due to the positive identification of adolescents with the model provided by society. However, there are some essential differences at this point in history in the way in which American society is alcohol-oriented and the way in which it is drug-oriented. These differences would argue that the imitation of adult model explanation seems at this time to fit drinking better than it does drug use.

Alcohol is widely available to and used openly by adults. It is openly advertised, sold, and regularly stocked in many homes. Drinking for social, pleasurable, and recreational purposes is integrally incorporated as a nondeviant part of our culture. With adults, only its misuse or abuse is uniformly condemned. Its moderate use is denied only to minors, and even then, only the law is uniform on this point; many adults do not vigorously object to adolescent's drinking although they may consider it premature. Since it is associated primarily with adult role behavior, drinking alcohol serves well to symbolize the aspiration and attainment of adulthood. One does not reject a pattern by copying it. Only in completely abstinent family-religion settings does drinking serve well as an expression of adolescent rebellion.

On the other hand, the drugs that the teenagers are using are not legal nor socially approved even for adults. In fact, adults of the generation who are parents of teenagers typically know less about drugs, are more convinced of their undesirability, and are less likely to use drugs than their children. They are supported in the general negative connotations attached to drugs and those who use them by established religion, schools, and law enforcement. In a sense, most teenagers find themselves in the same sort of abstinent milieu with respect to drugs that some find themselves in with respect to alcohol.

It is true that youngsters see adults taking drugs. But the example of drug use among adults must be qualified by the fact that it is nearly always done, at least justified, within a medical context, either under medical supervision or self-medication. Adults do not normally use drugs solely for non-medical purposes; mood-changing drugs are used, but their use purely for sociability, recreation, or pleasure is not accepted nor regularly practiced. Non-medicinal use of drugs is not incorporated as a non-deviant practice in our society; their medicinal use is acceptable for adult and child alike. For these reasons, drugs would seem to serve poorly as symbols of adult status, but serve well as symbolic of "our thing" and rebellion against the adult establishment among adolescents.

It may be, however, that teenage drug taking is learned from adult models in different ways. The alienating shortcomings of the system which are often cited were not perceived by some sort of magic by the youth; rather they have long been cataloged and broadcast by adults. Today's youth were not born with greater knowledge and insight into the true nature of drugs than their parents: rather they have had the benefit of years of serious research and study by medical and social scientists, who have pointed up the misrepresentations, hoaxes, and outright lies about drugs propogated for so many years by law enforcement and the mass media. Moreover, the psychedelic drug movement is not now and never has been confined to college and high school youth. Middle-class adults also are and have been involved; in fact, have been leaders in the movement. The praises of LSD, marihuana, mescaline, and other drugs were first sung by adults, ably abetted by the same mass media that earlier had propagandized against drugs, long before adolescents took up the cry. Some of these adults have been middle-aged, but by and large, they have been adults of a generation somewhat younger than the parents of teenagers. They have nonetheless proven able mentors and models for the young to emulate. (For two excellent discussions of the influence of adults on young people in this sense see Simon and Gagnon (1968) and Louria (1968, pp. 38–45).)

There is already some evidence that marihuana use among high school students is in part a function of anticipatory socialization into college life style (Mauss, 1969). It would seem that in the future, adult users will more and more simply be those who continue the social use of drugs such as marihuana learned in high school and college today in much the same way that persons have learned to use alcohol. The major differences in social acceptability of marihuana and alcohol in society as a whole today can be expected gradually to lessen and disappear as the current adolescents and young adults come to be the definers of morality. Thus, marihuana (and perhaps other drugs) may come to find a place in society analogous to alcohol—social-pleasurable use acceptable for adults and legally denied to minors who will nonetheless engage in drug practices learned primarily from parents and peers.

DIFFERENTIAL ASSOCIATION-REINFORCEMENT

The author previously has collaborated on the formulation of a general social learning theory of deviant behavior to which the label "differential association-reinforcement" has been given (Burgess & Akers, 1966). It has been used to analyze opiate use, addiction, and relapse, and use of hallucinogenic drugs (Akers et al., 1968; Akers, 1969). Space precludes a full explication of this theory as applied to the combined problem of teenage drinking and drug use. Therefore, what follows should be seen as a suggestive outline, rather than a fully documented and tightly reasoned analysis.

The basic contention is that use or non-use of alcohol and drugs is a normally learned (conditioned) response which is shaped by the patterns of (primarily social) reinforcements and involves exposure to normative definitions favorable or unfavorable to use through association with both users and non-users. All of the theories discussed above are consistent with this approach for each implicitly or explicitly assumes that social learning is the basic process in teenagers coming to drink or use drugs. The quality of norms, reference groups, and the rules and authority of the adult community against which an anti-adult teenage culture may be opposed or which teenage behavior imitates, all constitute various conditions and contingencies comprising the environment in which drug and drinking behavior is learned. The differential association-reinforcement theory attempts to indicate the learning process that one undergoes in this environment in becoming a user.

This explanation of pre- and non-addictive drug use has been summarized as follows:

. . . before one will first try a drug he must: (1) find the drug available or learn how to obtain it, and (2) learn and apply either positive or neutralizing definitions to its use. He will not continue beyond the first experimental experiences unless he (3) learns to take the drug properly for optimal effect, (4) either finds the effects intrinsically rewarding or learns to define the effects as desirable, and/or (5) obtains other social rewards contingent upon taking the drug . . . such that rewards for use are frequent and great enough to offset the negative consequences of use and the rewards for alternative behavior. (Akers, 1969, p. 79).

It is contended here that such a process, although the substance of what is learned is different, is also operative in non-pathological drinking. Addictive drug behavior is "escape-avoidance" behavior which develops with opiate (and sometimes barbiturates) when one learns that he must take the drug to alleviate or avoid withdrawal distress. Addictive drinking would seem to be the same kind of escape behavior.

Availability and acquisition of ability to take drugs or drink alcohol are fairly obvious steps. For most adolescents availability of alcohol presents no real problems; it abounds in our society. Certain kinds of drugs, marihuana and mild hallucinogens, are becoming more readily available, although through illegal channels. Drinking or taking pills require no special ability; one need only swallow. But smoking marihuana properly and the effective use of the hypodermic and related apparatus do require some ability. The other steps in the process require fuller comment.

Even if drugs or alcohol are available, one is not likely to avail himself
of them if he does not see drinking or drug use as a permissible, desirable,
or positively rewarding experience that he would want to undergo or if
he does not see it as relatively safe, not as bad as some say, worth the
risk, or justifiable on some ground. Teenagers raised in a prescriptive
drinking environment learn from parents, peers, and other groups that
social drinking is an acceptable, positive experience for adults and that
within limits it is permissible for minors. Or they may learn essentially
neutral definitions of alcohol; it is something that one may try or not
as he pleases. The situation is similar for those whose initial introduction
to drugs is through a drug-oriented subculture of one kind or another;
they may learn positive definitions of drugs as cool or exciting. By the
time they reach adolescence, then, these people have few moral or personal obstacles to overcome in taking the first drink, pill, or fix.

For most, though, the first thing that is learned about drugs is that
they are dangerous and that their non-medical use is morally abhorrent.
Even in a prescriptive environment, one is also apt to first encounter
negative definitions of underage drinking; it is all right for adults, but
kids should leave it alone. In proscriptive religious, family, and community settings, he learns that drinking alcohol is bad for everybody.
Before one who learns these views will try drugs or alcohol he must
neutralize or replace them with definitions favorable to use; that is, drinking (or using drugs) is bad only if you get a habit and I can control it;
they lied about it; lots of people do it and it doesn't hurt them; and
so on. The teenager may learn these counter definitions through association or identification with groups other than those in which he received
his initial socialization. These may be adults or they may be groups of
peers and friends who provide him with rationales for rejecting his
earlier learning.

Through the application of such positive, permissive, or rationalizing
definitions one gets to the point of experimenting with drugs or alcohol.
Whether he will continue to use them depends upon the consequences
of his drinking or drug experiences. If the drug or alcohol effects one
experiences and/or the reactions of others who are present or know about
his taking them are rewarding, he will continue; if they are unpleasant
or unrewarding, he will not.

For the majority of adolescents the actual or expected sanctions from
parents, friends, and law enforcement in reaction to their drug taking
are most likely to be negative; for many this is also the most likely
reaction to their drinking. They are not, therefore, apt to try or to continue using drugs or alcohol. For the others, using one or the other of
these substances is a way of gaining acceptance, approval, recognition,
and other social rewards. In neither case is the non-user aggressively en-

ticed or forced to become a user, but the positive social sanctions of peer groups of friends are very important social reinforcers for both drinking and taking of drugs. In addition to this peer group support, the adolescent reared in a prescriptive or permissive drinking environment may receive various overt and subtle signs of approval (or lack of disapproval) from adults for his drinking. It is through such social reinforcement that one learns to find the use itself rewarding. The initial effects of alcohol or drugs may be intrinsically enjoyable, but for the most part enjoyment of either is a socially acquired taste. Typically one has received prior socialization into what he is supposed to experience; thus, if he has learned to expect what he takes to taste good or produce enjoyable effects, any intrinsic pleasure is likely to be heightened or he will interpret the effects, whatever they are, as pleasurable. For many, however, initial effects are anything but pleasant; the beverage or the smoke may taste or smell bad; he may get sick; the intoxication or high may be frightening. Some will keep up use, nonetheless, sustained entirely by the social rewards contingent upon continuation. But most of those who continue will become conditioned to enjoy the effects and the pleasurable reactions to taking drugs or alcohol will be combined with social reinforcement to sustain further use. As long as these rewards are forthcoming to a greater extent than they would be for alternative behavior and are not offset by current or expected aversive consequences, use will continue.

Concluding Remarks: Teenage Drinking and Drug Use as Sociological and Social Problems

It should be noted here that further research needs to be done to determine to what extent the foregoing analysis is capable of accurately accounting for adolescent behavior of this kind. In general, more research needs to be done on drugs of the type that has been conducted on teenage drinking among representative samples of the adolescent population. Research on both drinking and drugs should pay more attention to securing out-of-school samples. It is also important that further analysis and research attempt to study the two problems together. Despite the fact that similar questions are asked about and similar explanations are given for the two, they are most often considered separately. (One instance in which the two are at least discussed within the same article is Pollack (1966).) For this reason, there are some significant questions concerning the relationship between the use of drugs and the use of alcohol by adolescents for which good answers are unavailable and to which future research should be directed. What are the differences and similarities in the way drugs and alcohol are viewed by the same sample of persons of this age group? How similar or different are the social and physical settings and occasions in which alcohol and drugs are used? Is the current prevalence of drug use the same as, greater than, or less than alcohol use among adolescents? Does more drug use mean less, more, or no change in the teenage consumption of alcohol? Does the introduction of drugs in a significant way in recent years mean that the teenage population can be divided into identifiable social types with regard to their use or non-use of alcohol and drugs—the "straights" or "squares" who use neither; the "mixers" who use both; the "boozers" or drinkers who use only alcohol; and the "druggies" or "heads" who use only drugs? What are the relative numbers in each of these categories? To what extent are the motivations and learning patterns similar for consumption of alcohol and drugs?

To this point, we have been mainly concerned with this kind of adolescent behavior as a sociological problem—something to be described, explained, and researched. In conclusion, some comments will be offered on teenage drinking and drug use as social problems—something about which there is social concern and for which legal and social policies have evolved.

In constructing a social policy to deal with the problem of teenage drinking in this country a strongly proscriptive stance seems to have been the one most often represented. Every state has laws against under-age drinking, most stating absolute prohibitions against the use, purchase, or possession of alcoholic beverages by anyone under the arbitrary age of 21. Most states also have some sort of official, in-school or out-of-school, programs on teenage drinking. Many of these still carry strongly moralistic messages that condemn drinking in unqualified terms and carry exaggerated warnings of the personal and legal problems which it can entail. But the notion of drinking as an unmitigated evil has clearly lost out in this country. Only a minority continue to view it with unqualified disapproval. Most see teenage drinking as only mildly deviant, wrong only because it is done prematurely. Under some circumstances, especially for older adolescents, even this premature use is all right. The outcome of this normative conflict has been a history of ineffective educational programs and widespread violation of the law by both juveniles and adults. There would seem to be some consensus on the undesirability of excessive drinking, whether by adolescents or adults. It would seem advisable then to be less concerned with keeping adolescents totally abstinent and more with promoting a prescriptive atmosphere of responsible drinking.

The goals should not be to reduce drinking of any kind, but to increase the proportion that is responsible and moderate drinking—which is not likely to lead to abuse, accidents, delinquencies and other problems. This seems to be the direction in which expert opinion in the field of alcohol education is headed . . .

A slight modification in the nature or form of drinking habits is possible— a reduction in the number of drinkers probably is not. (Akers, 1968, pp. 8–9).

One way in which to do this is to lower what is now an unrealistically high minimum age for drinking which forces many adolescents to drink furtively in clandestine settings that are not especially conducive to learning responsible drinking. Another is educational programs that provide accurate and realistic information on the consequences of drinking.

Drinking probably never has been viewed by the majority of adults with the same horror as have drugs. Non-medical use of drugs continues to be viewed with moral repugnance, even for adults. Consequently, the legal prohibitions against drug use have consistently been more punitive than those against drinking. Illegal purchase of alcohol by teenagers, while clearly prohibited, is at most a delinquent charge, but illegal possession of drugs is a crime even for adults; it can be charged as a felony, carrying not just delinquent but criminal penalties. The reaction to the drug problem, to an even greater extent than the alcohol problem, has been an increasingly punitive law enforcement response. This was the case when drug use was confined to a relatively small group in the urban lower class. Now the increased use of a variety of drugs among affluent teenagers is being recognized with headline dismay, and again the reaction has been mainly a cry for more law enforcement. Although some are thereby deterred from taking drugs, the past history of such a response shows that it also results in the creation of a lucrative black market (Lindesmith, 1967; Schur, 1965).

Realistic laws are needed for drugs, just as for alcohol. Although they present special problems, reform in the laws and public policy relating to opiates and other strong drugs is needed (President's Commission, 1967). But such reform would seem to be especially relevant with regard to marihuana. It was predicted above that the differences in the societal situations of marihuana and alcohol will gradually diminish. My personal opinion is that this would be desirable and should alleviate some of the problems currently revolving around marihuana; I would recommend that marihuana be regulated in much the same manner as alcohol (including a legal age limit lower than 21).

There is just as much or more need for accurate information and education about drugs as about alcohol. The history of publicly disseminated information and education about drugs has been replete with wildly exaggerated claims and horror stories about the degenerating and crime producing effects of drug use. The vast majority of adults, lawmakers, and law-enforcers still believe that marihuana is extremely more dangerous than alcohol. Younger people have learned that much of what they have heard from adults about marihuana is not true and tend to believe that marihuana is not dangerous. (See the 1969 Gallup Poll results in Gunther (1969, p. 29).) The tendency then is to discount all adult-initiated information about drugs and thus increase the probability of trying more harmful drugs. Realistic, substantiated knowledge about the real problems that use of alcohol or drugs engender can be effective in curtailing the abuse of both. However, the more exaggerated, unreal, and hypocritical definitions of drugs and alcohol, the more likely they are to be neutralized and discounted by youth. Such a "scare" approach to the problem, far from effectively reducing drug and alcohol abuse among adolescents would seem to serve only to widen whatever credibility gap already exists between generations.

This critique of current policy does not deny that in addition to being troublesome for the community, many young people experience real personal problems with drugs and alcohol; some who partake do so to excess and others suffer ill effects in any case. The argument is simply that those with such problems are probably better helped by some alternative policy, such as community-based agencies and programs which dispense realistic information and aid. An excessively punitive policy may not help, and simply result in presenting both society and adolescents with problems above and beyond whatever difficulties are engendered by the effects of the drugs and alcohol.

REFERENCES

Akers, Ronald L. Teenage drinking: a survey of action programs and research. *Journal of Alcohol Education*, 1968, **13**, 1–10.

Akers, Ronald L. Deviant drug use. Unpublished manuscript, University of Washington, 1969.

Akers, Ronald L., Burgess, Robert L., and Johnson, Weldon T. Opiate use, addiction, and relapse. *Social Problems*, 1968, **15**, 459–469.

Alexander, C. Norman, Jr. Alcohol and adolescent rebellion. *Social Forces*, 1966, **46**, 542–550.

Ausubel, D. P. *Drug Addition: Physiological, Psychological, and Sociological Aspects*. New York: Random House, 1958.

Ball, John C., and Bates, William M. Migration and residential mobility of narcotic drug addicts. *Social Problems*, 1966, **14**, 56–69.

Ball, John C., and Cottrell, Emily S. Admissions of narcotic drug addicts to public health service hospitals, 1935–63. *Public Health Reports*, 1965, **80**, 471–475.

Bates, William M. Narcotics, Negroes, and the South. *Social Forces*, 1966, 45, 61–67.

Baur, E. Jackson, and McCluggage, Marston. Drinking patterns of Kansas high school students. *Social Problems*, 1958, 5, 347–356.

Blacker, Edward *et al.* Drinking behavior of delinquent boys. *Quarterly Journal of Studies on Alcohol*, 1965, 26, 223–237.

Blum, Richard. Mind-altering drugs and dangerous behavior. In President's Commission, Task Force Report: *Narcotics and Drug Abuse*. Washington, D.C.: U.S. Government Printing Office, 1967, 21–66.

Brown, Lucius P. Enforcement of the Tennessee anti-narcotics law. In John O'Donnell and John C. Ball (Eds.) *Narcotic Addiction*. New York: Harper and Row, 1966, 34–45.

Burgess, Robert L., and Akers, Ronald L. A differential association-reinforcement theory of criminal behavior. *Social Problems*, 1966, 14, 128–147.

Cahalan, Don, Cisin, Ira H., and Crossley, Helen M. *American Drinking Practices*. Washington, D.C.: Social Research Report #3, George Washington University, 1967.

Carey, James T. *The College Drug Scene*. Englewood Cliffs, N.J.: Prentice-Hall, 1968.

Chein, Isidor. The use of narcotics as a personal and social problem. In Daniel Wilner and Gene Kassebaum (Eds.) *Narcotics*. New York: McGraw-Hill, 1965, 103–117.

Chein, Isidor. Narcotics use among juveniles. In John A. O'Donnell and John C. Ball (Eds.) *Narcotic Addiction*. New York: Harper and Row, 1966, 123–141.

Chein, Isidor *et al*. *The Road to H: Narcotics, Delinquency, and Social Policy*. New York: Basic Books, 1964.

Clinard, Marshall B. *Sociology of Deviant Behavior*, 3d ed. New York: Holt, Rinehart and Winston, 1968.

Globetti, Gerald. Teenage drinking in an abstinence setting. *Kansas Journal of Sociology*, 1967, 3, 124–134.

Globetti, Gerald, and Windham, Gerald O. The social adjustment of high school students and the use of beverage alcohol. *Sociology and Social Research*, 1967, 51, 148–157.

Gunther, Max. Will the U.S. ever legalize pot? *True*, 1969, 28ff.

Kobrin, Solomon, and Finestone, Harold. Drug addiction among young persons in Chicago. In James F. Short, Jr. (Ed.) *Gang Delinquency and Delinquent Subcultures*. New York: Harper and Row, 1968, 110–130.

Larsen, Donald E., and Abu-Laban, Baha. Norm qualities and deviant drinking behavior. *Social Problems*, 1968, 15, 441–449.

Lindesmith, Alfred R. *The Addict and the Law*. New York: Vintage Books, 1967.

Lindesmith, Alfred R., and Gagnon, John. Anomie and drug addiction. In Marshall B. Clinard (Ed.) *Anomie and Deviant Behavior*. New York: Free Press, 1964, 158–188.

Louria, Donald B. *The Drug Scene*. New York: McGraw-Hill, 1968.

McCarthy, Raymond G. High school drinking studies. In Raymond G. McCarthy (Ed.) *Drinking and Intoxication*. New Haven: College and University Press, 1959, 205–211.

McCarthy, Raymond G. Consumption rates and trends from 1850 to 1962 in the U.S. and other countries: alcoholism rates. In Raymond G. McCarthy (Ed.) *Alcohol Education for Classroom and Community*. New York: McGraw-Hill, 1964, 132–142.

MacKay, James R. Problem drinking among juvenile delinquents. *Crime and Delinquency*, 1963, **9**, 29–38.

MacKay, James R. Alcohol, alcoholism, and youth. *New Hampshire Bulletin on Alcoholism*, 1965, **14**, 1–6.

MacKay, James R., Phillips, Derek L., and Bryce, Forbes O. Drinking behavior among teenagers: a comparison of institutionalized and non-institutionalized youth in New Hampshire. *Journal of Alcohol Education*, 1967, **13**, 20–22.

MacKay, James R. *et al.* Teenage drinking in New Hampshire. *New Hampshire Bulletin on Alcoholism*, 1967, **3**, 1–11.

Maddox, George L. Teenage drinking in the United States. In David Pittman and Charles R. Snyder (Eds.) *Society, Culture and Drinking Patterns*. New York: John Wiley, 1962, 23–245.

Maddox, George L. Adolescence and alcohol. In Raymond G. McCarthy (Ed.) *Alcohol Education for Classroom and Community*. New York: McGraw-Hill, 1964, 32–47.

Maddox, George L. High school student drinking behavior: Incidental information from two national surveys. *Quarterly Journal of Studies on Alcohol*, 1964, **25**, 339–347.

Maddox, George L., and McCall, Bevode C. *Drinking among Teenagers*. New Brunswick: Rutgers Center of Alcohol Studies, 1964.

Marshall, O. The opium habit in Michigan. In John O'Donnell and John C. Ball (Eds.) *Narcotic Addiction*. New York: Harper and Row, 1966, 45–54.

Mauss, Armand L. Anticipatory socialization toward college as a factor in adolescent marijuana use. *Social Problems*, 1969, **16**, 357–364.

Mizruchi, Ephraim H., and Perruci, Robert. Norm qualities and differential effects of deviant behavior. *American Sociological Review*, 1962, **27**, 391–399.

Mulford, Harold A. Drinking and deviant drinking, U.S.A., 1963. *Quarterly Journal of Studies on Alcohol*, 1964, **25**, 634–650.

Nelson, Dale O. A comparison of drinking and understanding of alcohol and alcoholism between students in selected high schools of Utah and in the Utah State Industrial School. *Journal of Alcohol Education*, 1968, **13**, 17–25.

Newsweek. The drug generation: growing younger. *Newsweek*, 1969, April 21, 107–108.

O'Donnell, John A. Narcotic addiction and crime. *Social Problems*, 1966, **13**, 374–385.

O'Donnell, John A., and Ball, John C. (Eds.) *Narcotic Addiction*. New York: Harper and Row, 1966.

Pittman, David J. International overview: social and cultural factors in drinking patterns, pathological and nonpathological. In David J. Pittman (Ed.) *Alcoholism*. New York: Harper and Row, 1967, 3–20.

Pittman, David J., and Snyder, Charles R. (Eds.) *Society, Culture, and Drinking Patterns*. New York: John Wiley, 1962.

Pollack, Jack H. Teenage drinking and drug addiction. *NEA Journal*, 1966, **55**, 8–12.

President's Commission on Law Enforcement and Administration of Justice Task Force Report: *Narcotics and Drug Abuse*. Washington, D.C.: United States Government Printing Office, 1967.

Preston, James. On norm qualities and deviant drinking behavior. *Social Problems*, 1969, **16**, 534–537.

Riley, John W., and Marden, Charles F. The social pattern of alcoholic drinking. In Raymond G. McCarthy (Ed.) *Drinking and Intoxication*. New Haven: College and University Press, 1959, 182–189.

Schur, Edwin M. *Crimes without Victims*. Englewood Cliffs, N.J.: Prentice-Hall, 1965.

Simon, William, and Gagnon, John H. Children of the drug age. *Saturday Review*, 1968, September 21, 60–63, 75–78.

Skolnick, Jerome. Religious affiliation and drinking behavior. *Quarterly Journal of Studies on Alcohol*, 1958, **19**, 452–470.

Slater, A. D. A study of use of alcoholic beverages among high school students in Utah. *Quarterly Journal of Studies on Alcohol*, 1952, **13**, 78–86.

Straus, Robert. Alcohol. In Robert Merton and Robert Nisbet (Eds.) *Contemporary Social Problems*, 2d ed. New York: Harcourt, Brace, and World, 1966, 236–280.

Straus, Robert, and Bacon, Seldon. The problem of drinking in college. In David J. Pittman and Charles R. Snyder (Eds.) *Society, Culture, and Drinking Patterns*. New York: John Wiley, 1962, 246–258.

Ullman, Albert D. First drinking experience as related to age and sex. In David J. Pittman and Charles R. Snyder (Eds.) *Society, Culture, and Drinking Patterns*. New York: John Wiley, 1962, 259–266.

Windham, Gerald, Preston, James D., and Armstrong, Harold B. The high school student in Mississippi and beverage alcohol. *Journal of Alcohol Education*, 1967, **13**, 1–12.

Winick, Charles. Epidemiology of narcotics use. In Daniel Wilner and Gene Kassebaum (Eds.) *Narcotics*. New York: McGraw-Hill, 1965, 3–18.

Young, Warren, and Hixson, Joseph. *LSD on Campus*. New York: Dell Publishing Co., 1966.

2.8 Orientation

Few school-related behavior patterns are more disturbing to parents and teachers than underachievement. In lay terms underachievement is generally indicated by the failure of a child or adolescent to "work up to his potential." This conceptualization poses several difficulties for research psychologists who wish to explore the underachievement syndrome and is but one of several issues examined in the following paper by Merville Shaw. Also included in this examination are a survey of alternate definitions for underachievement, criteria useful for an evaluation of underachievement research, and a review of selected "discrepancy model" studies of underachievement. Shaw's foremost objective is to meet various criticisms of the underachievement construct, many of which represent a challenge to its basic validity. That Shaw has a vested interest in this challenge is marked by his long-term personal involvement in underachievement research activity.

As Shaw points out, the literature on underachievement is at best enigmatic. This literature does reflect, however, classes of research endeavor similar to those applicable to other psychological constructs. For example, one major class of studies has involved research into the origins (causes) and onset of underachievement. Another has been concerned with cataloging the personal attributes of underachievers, including attitudes and motivational characteristics. Still another has been concerned with the amelioration of underachievement. Included in the latter are studies of the salutary effects on achievement deficits of counseling tactics, innovative teaching methods, and systematic reinforcement strategies. Such studies are based on the general assumption that underachievement is a fact and not an artifact of measurement techniques as some authorities have charged.

An incidental, yet significant feature of the underachievement literature is that most studies have dealt with the "gifted" underachiever, possibly because the discrepancy between high measured scholastic aptitude and low academic achievement is more readily apparent among such subjects. The fact that gifted or highly intelligent underachievers have, as subjects for study, dominated the underachievement research perhaps is also a function of a fundamental assumption underlying this research. This assumption, based in our aggregate of cultural values, is that everyone should work up to "capacity" in order to make his maximum contribution to society and, in turn, reap the maximum personal benefits which hopefully follow. A second major assumption implicit in the underachievement research is that persons who consistently fail to achieve according to their ability level are likely to be plagued with frustration; prone to self-depreciation; and faced with general unhappiness. Thus the view is maintained that underachievement is a possible hazard to mental health.

Other entries in this volume pertinent to underachievement include those of Meacham (Part II), Husted and Cervantes (Part III), and Staats and Butterfield (Part III). For a more thorough study of this phenomenon the reader is referred to the recommended readings below. Shaw's bibliography is also useful for this purpose.

RECOMMENDED READINGS

Baymur, Feriha B., and Patterson, C. B.   A comparison of three methods of assisting underachieving high school students. *Journal of Counseling Psychology*, 1960, **7**, 83–90.

Finney, Ben C., and Van Dalsem, Elizabeth.   Group counseling for gifted underachieving high school students. *Journal of Counseling Psychology*, 1969, **16**, 87–94.

Klein, Joel P., Quarter, Jack J., and Laxer, Robert M.   Behavioral counseling of underachievers. *American Educational Research Journal*, 1969, **6**, 415–424.

Kolb, David A.   Achievement motivation training for underachieving high school boys. *Journal of Personality and Social Psychology*, 1965, **2**, 783–792.

Jackson, R. M.   In support of the concept of underachievement. *Personnel and Guidance Journal*, 1968, **47**, 56–62.

Thorndike, Robert.   *The Concepts of Over- and Underachievement.* New York: Columbia University Teachers College Press, 1963.

2.8   Underachievement: Useful Construct or Misleading Illusion

Merville C. Shaw, CHICO STATE COLLEGE, CALIFORNIA

Within the last 10 years there has been a tremendous upsurge in the amount of research done on the topic of academic underachievement. This research has had little focus and even large volumes reporting on the various studies on underachievement (Kornrich, 1965) fail to synthesize existing research into any useful theoretical pattern. Partially as a

Reprinted from *Psychology in the Schools*, 1968, **5**, 41–46, by permission of the author and Psychology Press, Inc.

result of failure to organize research results on underachievement in any logical way and partly as a result of seemingly contradictory findings, the concept of underachievement has been called into question on several bases. Current negative criticisms of this research include the following:

(1) Studies on underachievement have resulted in inconsistent findings; therefore the existence of any consistent pattern of characteristics in association with this phenomenon is improbable.

(2) Underachievement is not a "real" phenomenon. It is, rather, due to errors of measurement.

(3) The results of studies of underachievement are not generalizable. What holds true for one group of underachievers may not be true of another.

(4) The present concepts of underachievement have been studied enough. It is time for a new conceptualization of the problem.

(5) Underachievement is not really a problem since underachievers are (allegedly) more independent, less conforming and more creative. We should not be concerned about this kind of behavior.

These criticisms represent a wide variety of very different kinds of dissatisfaction with the current status of research in underachievement. If any one of these criticisms is valid, it would have great implications both with respect to the value of previous research and also for the future of research on this particular topic. The purpose of this article is to examine the validity of these criticisms by summarizing a series of interrelated research studies, all of which utilized a similar definition of academic underachievement.

DEFINITIONS OF UNDERACHIEVEMENT

In addition to lack of focus, studies on underachievement have been characterized by the utilization of a wide variety of different kinds of definitions. Five different definitions of underachievement are most common in the research literature.

(1) A discrepancy model which utilizes the difference between attainment as reflected by grades and expected attainment as reflected in a measure of scholastic aptitude or intelligence.

(2) A discrepancy model which utilizes the difference between attainment as reflected by achievement test scores and expected attainment as reflected in a measure of scholastic aptitude or intelligence.

(3) A regression model which utilizes the interrelationship between achievement tests and tests of intelligence or scholastic aptitude.

(4) A regression model which utilizes the relationship between academic grades and objective measures of intelligence or scholastic aptitude.

(5) A concept which utilizes only grades or an objective measure of achievement as an index of "underachievement."

Type five is obviously not a measure of underachievement since it does not employ the relationship between predicted and actual achievement in any way. It is included here only because studies utilizing this kind of definition are found in the literature and are sometimes labeled as studies of underachievement. Regression models utilize a total population and attempt to predict achievement for that population. Discrepancy models permit the utilization of any particular segment of the population with respect to either ability or achievement and also permit the selection of highly divergent groups so that differences existing between such groups will be accentuated.

With respect to both the discrepancy and regression models, it is important to remember that the utilization of teacher grades as the criterion of achievement will result in the selection of *different* populations than will utilization of achievement test scores. This phenomenon was pointed out as early as 1961a (Shaw) and has been confirmed by Pippert (1963) and Farquhar (1964). Comparison of studies utilizing different criteria of achievement has undoubtedly contributed to the belief that research in this area has resulted in inconsistent results.

SOME NECESSARY CRITERIA FOR COMPARABILITY

The five questions raised about underachievement can be answered only through examination of studies which utilize all of the following criteria:

(1) Identical types of achievement criteria
(2) Identical (or nearly identical) ability criteria
(3) Similar distributions with respect to ability
(4) Identical (or nearly identical) measures of the trait(s) under study
(5) Identical statistical models

Attempts to compare studies which do not meet these demands simply do not make sense. We should expect neither similar conclusions nor logical relationships when attempts are made to compare studies which are in no way comparable. In the section which follows, a series of studies which meet these demands will be presented. Only conclusions will be presented here. The interested reader may refer to the actual studies for finer detail.

All of the following studies utilize a discrepancy model with teacher grades utilized as the criterion of actual achievement. It should be pointed out that the studies were done on a limited segment of the population with respect to ability. Generally speaking, they include only those in the upper 25 percent of their respective population. Thus, if a college freshman population is under discussion, the top 25 percent of that group with respect to measured ability was utilized in the study. If a twelfth-grade population is under consideration, only the top 25 percent of that particular population is utilized. In some of these studies the population was limited to those who were one standard deviation or more above the mean in ability, but the generalization still holds that only the upper segment of the population with respect to ability has been utilized.

THE STUDIES

In 1957, Shaw and Brown reported on an exploratory study they had carried out on underachievement at the college freshman level. The main finding of this study which is of interest for present purposes, was that underachievers attained significantly higher scores on the Social Scale of the Bell Preference Inventory (1947).[1] This indicated that underachievers responded to their social environment in a significantly more hostile way than did achievers.

In order to substantiate this finding and to determine whether or not it was generalizable at another academic level, Shaw and Grubb (1958) carried out a study specifically designed to determine whether or not high school underachievers would also respond in more hostile fashion than their achieving counterparts. In order to do this, a sample of tenth-grade high school students was administered the Hostility Scale from the Bell Preference Inventory (1947), the F and P Scales from the Guilford-Zimmerman Temperament Survey (1949), the Hostility Scale developed by Cook and Medley from the MMPI (1954) and the F Scale (Adorno, 1950). In this study male and female groups were treated separately, in contrast to the approach utilized in the previous study. Results indicated that male underachievers responded in a significantly more hostile way on the first three of these hostility scales and barely failed to attain a significant difference on the fourth.

In a subsequent study (Shaw & Black, 1960) it was decided to utilize the Rosenzweig Picture Frustration Study (Rosenzweig, Fleming, & Clark, 1947) in order to assess the qualitative dimensions of the hostility of

[1] Since that time this scale has been incorporated into the 1964 revision of the Bell Adjustment Inventory.

underachievers. In order to accomplish this, a sample of eleventh- and twelfth-grade students was drawn and, as a preliminary to the basic study, the hostility scale developed by Cook and Medley was administered to a sample of male achievers and underachievers. Again the underachieving males got significantly higher scores on this hostility scale. The other findings of this study, although interesting, are not germane to the present issue and will not be discussed here.

Following completion of the third hostility underachievement study, a new research approach was taken. Since hostility is generally assumed to reflect personal inadequacy, measures designed to reflect self-concept should also reveal differences between achievers and underachievers. Such a study was carried out and reported by Shaw, Edson, and Bell (1960) utilizing the Sarbin Adjective Check List (Sarbin & Rosenberg, 1955) with eleventh- and twelfth-grade students. Response differences between achievers and underachievers were compared. It was concluded that male underachievers were significantly more negative in their self-concepts than were male achievers. A similar difference was not found between female achievers and underachievers.

In order to cross validate this finding and to utilize a somewhat more objective technique, a different sample of eleventh- and twelfth-grade achievers and underachievers was selected and was administered the Bills Index of Adjustment and Values (1958). This is a self-concept measure which provides not only information on self-concept but on self-acceptance, ideal self and several other self scales. The most important finding of this study, for present purposes, was that male underachievers were found to have more negative self-concepts than male achievers. While certain differences were found between the two female groups, they did not relate specifically to self-concept (Shaw & Alves, 1963).

In a much more complex and comprehensive study of academic under-achievement (Shaw, 1961b), self-concept differences between achievers and underachievers was again a subject of study. Experimental subjects were from the fourth, seventh, and tenth grade. A 90 item Q Sort was the basic instrument utilized and 30 items on this Q Sort related to self-concept. Data were subjected to item analysis. Only a summary of findings can be presented here. The following statements are taken from the final report.

One of the most consistent differences relates to the more generally negative attitudes toward self seen among the underachievers. Accompanying this is a restriction in the range of attitudes that underachievers hold toward themselves which might be interpreted to mean that achieving children see themselves in a clearer and more specific fashion than do underachieving children. (p. 285).

While both achieving and underachieving groups show feelings of inadequacy, there is a marked difference between them. The achievers feel inadequate in specific areas, but the underachievers tend to feel inadequate in a general kind of way. (p. 286).

IMPLICATIONS OF THE STUDIES

Additional studies by the present author as well as by other research workers could be delineated to further verify the findings which have been cited, but that would be superfluous. The results summarized here have definite implications for all five of the criticisms of research on underachievement. These studies demonstrate a consistency of outcome seldom found in descriptive studies of psychological variables. This consistency obtains with respect to two characteristics (hostility and self-concept) with different samples and at different ages.

Where such consistency exists, it is difficult to support the notion that such results were obtained in the presence of persistent errors of measurement. Both underachievement, as defined by these studies, and the characteristics measured by the studies would seem to be very consistent. If one wants to argue that hostility was not really the variable measured by the hostility scales, this in no way refutes the essential similarities which exist among the results of the three studies of this variable.

Another comment heard with respect to measurement problems inherent in such research relates to the utilization of teacher grades as the achievement criterion. The argument most frequently used is that any given child might get one grade in Teacher A's class but that for exactly the same kind of performance might receive a very different grade in the class of Teacher B. This idea must, of course, be accepted as true. The point that most critics miss, however, is that student grades over a reasonably long period of time are remarkably stable, and it is not inappropriate to assume that we are dealing with a criterion that is at least as stable as any of the more commonly used psychometric measures. While any student may vary from his own norm in a given subject or even in a given year, the stability of grades from year to year in a group of achievers or underachievers is quite satisfactory. Students identified as underachievers in the last two years of high school have been shown to exhibit the same behavior in the earliest school years (Shaw & McCuen, 1960).

The above results would indicate that there is a certain generalizability with respect to findings on underachievement, although this is a statement cautiously made. There may be variables which are generally characteristic of underachievers in *any* situation as well as those which are specific to certain conditions, such as age, socio-economic level, ability level, and others. Among the populations of rather restricted ability and, to a lesser degree, age, which were studied in the present research, findings were similar, suggesting their possible generalizability to similar populations.

The criticism with respect to the need for reformulation of the concept of underachievement is a difficult one to answer because it is generally so vague. The general implication of such criticisms is that a new conceptualization should employ a more complex statistical model. Why? There is no inherent virtue in complexity, and if the regression approach is deemed "better," then this must be labeled a value judgment, not a verifiable fact. The fact that this approach permits study of a total population in contrast to certain limits which exist in this regard when the discrepancy model is utilized, in no way makes the regression approach superior. The researcher may deliberately elect to utilize a discrepancy model in order to *maximize* differences. This decision, too, is a value judgment on the part of the person conducting the research, not one dictated by what is methodologically correct.

Apart from the statistical problem of defining underachievement, there probably is a need to re-think the *meaning* of the term. Studies such as Pippert's (1963) as well as one by Brophy (1962) clearly suggest that the child who is capable but who receives poor grades is not generally an "underachiever" as far as objective measures of academic achievement are concerned. When these findings are coupled with results like those quoted in this report, it seems clear that these pupils manifest behavior characteristics which cause negative social judgments to be made about them. Thus, teacher grades for these individuals reflect not what the underachievers *know*, but rather the personal impact that they have on their teachers. This should not be construed as a criticism of teachers. If, for example, a child fails to turn in required work, either because of a basic hostility or a fear of failure resulting from negative self-concept, the teacher may be left without any basis on which to judge. This kind of example could be multiplied many times.

Underachievement viewed in this light appears to reflect *ineffective social behavior* which results in generally negative social judgments by others. These negative social judgments include poor grades. Thus, the underachiever does not actually fail to learn, but he fails to demonstrate that he did learn.

The final criticism relative to the importance of studying the concept of underachievement is hardly a research question. The question must be translated to include the idea of "important to whom?" To the research worker? To school personnel who may utilize the results of such research? To the underachiever himself? If *only* the two variables of hostility and self-concept are considered, it would appear important to both the school and the underachiever himself to focus attention on the problem. Hostile behavior is, presumably, disruptive to the learning environment of the school, while a negative self-concept is hardly a comfortable condition for the underachiever to live with. Understanding the phenomenon would appear to be desirable if intelligent attempts to change or prevent it are to be made.

The five criticisms of research on underachievement which have been made do not hold up in the light of the studies presented. It is necessary to conclude that the concept of underachievement discussed here is continuing to provide stable, meaningful data, and to abandon it simply in order to utilize a more complex model would appear to be ill advised. What is needed is not a new definition, but rather a synthesis of all available research utilizing similar definitions so that reasonable theories relative to underachieving behavior can be built on empirical data.

REFERENCES

Adorno, T. W., Frenkel-Brunswik, Else, Levinson, D. J., and Sanford, R. N. *The Authoritarian Personality.* New York: Harper, 1950.

Bell, H. M. *Personal Preference Inventory.* Palo Alto: Pacific Books, 1947.

Bills, R. E. *Manual for the Index of Adjustment and Values.* Auburn, Alabama: Polytechnical Institute, 1958.

Brophy, D. A. Interrelationships between achievement test scores, grades and IQ. Unpublished master's thesis, Chico State College, Chico, California, 1962.

Cook, W., and Medley, D. M. Proposed hostility and pharisaic virtue scales for the MMPI. *Journal of Applied Psychology,* 1954, **38,** 414–418.

Farquhar, W. A classification and comparison of techniques used in selecting under and overachievers. *Personnel and Guidance Journal,* 1964, **42,** 874–884.

Guilford, J. P., and Zimmerman, W. S. *Guilford-Zimmerman Temperament Survey.* Beverly Hills: Sheridan Supply Co., 1949.

Kornrich, M. *Underachievement.* Springfield, Ill.: Charles C. Thomas, 1965.

Pippert, R. A comparison of two methods for classifying underachievers with respect to selected criteria. *Personnel and Guidance Journal,* 1963, **41,** 788–791.

Rosenzweig, P. F., Fleming, Edith, and Clark, Helen. *Revised Scoring Manual for the Rosenzweig Picture Frustration Study.* Provincetown, Mass.: Journal Press, 1947.

Sarbin, T. R., and Rosenberg, B. G. Contributions to role taking theory: IV, a method for obtaining a quantitative estimate of self. *Journal of Social Psychology,* 1955, 42, 71–81.

Shaw, M. C. Definition and identification of academic underachievers. In L. M. Miller (Ed.) *Guidance for the Underachiever with Superior Ability.* U. S. Dept. Health, Education and Welfare, Bulletin No. 25, 1961. (a)

Shaw, M. C. The interrelationship of selected personality factors in high ability underachieving school children. Final report, Project 58-M-1, California State Department Public Health, August 1961. (b)

Shaw, M. C., and Alves, G. J. The self-concept of bright academic underachievers: continued. *Personnel and Guidance Journal*, 1963, 42, 401–403.

Shaw, M. C., and Black, M. D. The reaction to frustration of bright high school underachievers. *California Journal of Educational Research*, 1960, 11, 120–124.

Shaw, M. C., and Brown, D. J. Scholastic underachievement of bright college students. *Personnel and Guidance Journal*, 1957, 36, 195–199.

Shaw, M. C., Edson, K. C., and Bell, H. M. Self-concepts of bright underachieving high school students as revealed by an adjective check list. *Personnel and Guidance Journal*, 1960, 39, 193–196.

Shaw, M. C., and Grubb, J. Hostility and able high school underachievers. *Journal of Counseling Psychology*, 1958, 5, 263–266.

Shaw, M. C., and McCuen, J. T. The onset of academic underachievement in bright children. *Journal of Educational Psychology*, 1960, 51, 103–108.

2.9 *Orientation*

The potential power of psychological counseling as a vehicle for behavioral change has long been recognized. Although at times this recognition seems to be based more upon faith than upon observed fact, the extent of counseling services provided in the public schools has increased enormously in the past several decades. Frequently, these services are directed to assist youth "in trouble" or "in conflict." That is, students with personal, academic, vocational, and social problems may be referred (or occasionally refer themselves) to a school counselor. Among the techniques applied to these problems include psychological testing, interviewing, and the provision of information by counseling specialists. Numerous issues with reference to counseling philosophy and technique exist, however. The following paper by Merle Meacham builds upon current social and educational contexts, including the ferment taking place within many of the nation's secondary schools, to examine some of these issues, and the ambiguous role of the school counselor.

One of Meacham's principal concerns is for two distinct alternatives in counseling strategy, one based upon humanistic psychology, the other upon behaviorism. Readers are cautioned against establishing a false dichotomy between these two orientations, because their implications are not a matter of black and white. Meacham's objective, however, is to clarify some fundamental differences between these orientations. These include (1) the degree of precision reflected in counseling objectives, (2) the extent to which counseling may be systematized, (3) the degree to which the manipulations attempted by a counselor are disguised, and (4) the requirement of research evidence to validate counseling procedures.

The issue of research evidence and continual self-evaluation in counseling is critical. If one applies basic standards of scientific inquiry to research traditionally executed in the areas of "guidance and counseling," one finds few examples of high quality. Moreover, the evidence that counseling in the schools makes a real difference in student behavior has not been very convincing. Admittedly, research on the effects of counseling poses knotty problems. But, increasingly the question of whether counseling (as it is practiced in most schools) is valid for its expressed purposes is being asked. Fortunately, reviewers such and Peters and Wattenberg (1966) report recent signs of improvement in counseling research procedures.

Meacham's views expressed toward the end of his paper are reminiscent of Friedenberg's (1959) critique of psychological services within the schools. Friedenberg contends that, too often, counseling represents an attempt to induce conformity and reduce, rather than dramatize individual differences or personal uniqueness. According to this view, such attempts interfere directly with self-definition. Moreover, Friedenberg contends that counselors and school administrators too frequently violate the confidentiality of counseling relationships by releasing information obtained therein to agencies outside the school. The possibility of such violation, states Friedenberg, may create fear among adolescents which motivates them to avoid counseling even if they may desire it. These problems aside, the reader is encouraged to consider means for the improved effectiveness of counseling and feasible alternatives to counseling as a medium for personal guidance.

RECOMMENDED READINGS

Ehrle, Raymond. An alternative to "words" in the behavior modification of disadvantaged youth. *Vocational Guidance Quarterly*, 1968, **17**, 41–46.

MacLennan, Beryce W., and Felsenfeld, Naomi. *Group Counseling and Psychotherapy with Adolescents*. New York: Columbia University Press, 1968.

Peters, Mildred, and Wattenberg, William W. Adolescence: behavior disorders and guidance. *Review of Educational Research*, 1966, **36**, 474–484.

Rhodes, William C. Utilization of mental health professionals in the school. *Review of Educational Research*, 1968, **38**, 497–511.

Rogers, Carl, and Skinner, B. F. Some issues concerning the control of human behavior: a symposium. *Science*, 1900, **124**, 1057–1066.

Schneiders, Alexander A. (Ed.) *Counseling The Adolescent*. San Francisco: Chandler, 1967.

2.9   Counseling Strategies with the Adolescent

Merle L. Meacham, UNIVERSITY OF WASHINGTON

There seems to be considerable dispute at this time as to just what will be the role of the secondary school counselor in the immediate future. This is partly a function of the accelerating changes in the urban society (population concentration, minority problems, and challenges to traditional values) and partly a function of rapid changes in student and faculty attitudes toward education and the role of the school in general. There is no doubt that many of these attitudes are in conflict especially as we see students seeking more autonomy and more participation in the educational process and teachers seeking the same by challenging administrators and school boards. In all of this, the counselor, often in a poorly defined position at best, may find himself caught up in such a vortex of feelings and attitudes that he will have to define his position and function clearly or have it defined for him.

It does seem clear that the traditional role of "advisor" regarding educational and vocational goals, the one who helped the student fit into the proper niche in a fairly stable society, is no longer viable. For this implies a rather acquiescent student body and something stable to aim toward. It is not clear just what the best alternative is, although there are emerging points of view vying for acceptance as the "model" for contemporary counseling. Polarized, these seem to be a humanistic-therapeutic point of view as opposed to a behavioristic point of view. Neither of these would deny the value of educational and vocational planning but would place these in a much broader context of counseling. These points of view also reflect the division within the parent body of psychological thinking and show the impact that psychology is

An original paper prepared especially for this volume.

having on counseling. One is tempted to say that "guidance" as a construct is dead and that counseling psychology, albeit divided, is the new way. This is not quite true but there are strong forces within the profession working in this direction.

In this section, then, we will examine the contemporary student, the counselor, and the rationale for the two major points of view in counseling. We will even attempt some tentative prognostication, knowing full well the risks involved in so fluid a situation, but tempted to give some impetus to a self-fulfilling prophecy.

TODAY'S STUDENTS

Much has been and is being written about today's students and their characteristics. So much so that any meaningful analysis of the data must await a more comprehensive review than this. However, there are some trends that stand out and that are meaningful for the counselor. Our young people are becoming a more disturbing problem to the majority of adults. Disturbing in the sense that they are attacking some of the fundamental beliefs of the society as well as continuing some of the "usual" adolescent behavior. Perhaps it is this attack that the "older" generation finds most upsetting for here is a challenge to the traditional middle-class values and an assertion that a large segment of our society has "copped out" and has only a hypocritical attitude toward those values they espouse. Perhaps the most disturbing aspect of all is that the attack has gone beyond exchanges of rhetoric and the students are revolting! Symptomatically, if not typically, the students in a nearby junior high school walked out when they disagreed with the teacher. We daily read of riots, confrontations, and disturbances (a convenient euphemism for the former) on our high school and college campuses. Why?

Flacks (1967) has some interesting answers. His research has involved both the students and their families. He finds that there is a close relationship between student activism or non-activism and the values of their parents. If the parents have espoused the more traditional career-oriented values, the result is a self-concept in terms of occupational status. And the youngster becomes much more molded into the traditional middle-class pattern of achievement and dominance orienation. As Flacks puts it (p. 20): "Thus, experience must be organized in terms of career patterns which demand a strong future-oriented psychology—present experience is shaped to career requirements. And finally, in this conception, one's full potential for occupational achievement can be realized only to the extent that the emotional life is regulated and rationalized." The result is the status-oriented, other directed, emotionally controlled, consumer of goods and services who reflects moderation in his political activity and a willingness to do whatever the system requires as long as it leads to the status goals.

On the other hand, according to Flacks, there are families where the dominant values are humanistic. These center around two groups of values, one involving "free expression of emotions and feelings . . . as essential to the development and integrity of the individual." The other involving "ethical humanism" with a genuine concern for the welfare of other human beings and thus "politically aware and active parents who tend to share their views with their children."

For Flacks, then, the student activist, the one who is challenging the establishment, comes from a humanistic background and as such his behavior is a logical outgrowth of his training rather than a revolt against the society as such. "Result, not revolt" he puts it and, if this is true, it has far-reaching implications for schools and counseling. For, although the "movement" is relatively small it seems to be growing. And in growing it is coming more often in conflict with the dominant society. This is already leading to talk of severely repressive measures particularly where some overt action is taken. Flacks' conclusions are worth quoting at length:

Our parent-student research indicates strongly that the movement has a dynamic of its own, which is shaping student attitudes and their commitments. Our data show that the recent protest groups are made up, in part, of a central core of activists who come from humanistic subcultures and have a long history of active protest, and, in part, of a larger group of newly recruited students. Fascinatingly or alarmingly, depending on one's viewpoint, recent recruits more closely resemble the general student population. They come from widely diverse backgrounds, even from conservative and conventional parents. Protest appeals to an increasingly broader spectrum of students. The movement is spreading to the dominant culture.

As increasing numbers of adolescents reflect the new values, many counselors are faced with a dilemma, especially if they have a strong personal commitment to the more traditional modes. They may not be able to accept their clients or really get involved in a helping relationship with young people they do not respect. Of course, since the youth are quick to discern such attitudes, the counselor would probably have few seeking his services anyway. If he is seen as representing the "establishment" he will be of no help to those that are of greatest concern to the establishment. If he becomes an advocate for the students, he may alienate himself from many of his peers. Of course, if he is an anti-establishment counselor he will have similar problems with the more conventional students! However, this need not be the case. This writer feels that a counselor who is committed to the welfare and personal growth of his client can help a wide variety of young people even though his values may differ to some extent. But there must be this commitment whether he is existentially oriented or behavioristically oriented. He cannot have as his hidden agenda, as Thompson (1969) seems to have found, that the ideal client is a person "like me" and that the goals of counseling are to make the client more and more "like me." In this event schools should hire a wide variety of "counselor types" as models for the students and the student and counselor would select each other on the basis of compatability.

Kelly (1969) presents another very interesting point of view when he suggests that adolescents can be viewed as members of a suppressed minority group. This adds new dimensions to Flacks' position and gives us something more of a structure in which to fit our ideas about counseling. Let us examine this position closely.

Kelly lists six characteristics of minority groups which he feels applies to adolescents:

(1) The minority individual differs in significant ways from the larger society.
(2) The minority individuals share some common experiences.
(3) The activities of the minority group are curtailed or suppressed.
(4) The larger society stereotypes the individual in a minority group.
(5) The minority group and the majority group both use the same referent for the good life.
(6) Minority groups use a variety of methods to reduce the consequences of minority status.

Then he shows that each of these characteristics applies to the adolescent subculture: They are a unique group biologically and sociologically. Perhaps most of all, though, they are unique since they are viewed as such by the larger society. They have a role to play that to a significant extent is expected, and much of their behavior meets the expectations.

They do share a multiplicity of common experiences since they are placed together physically and have common physical and psychological characteristics. The dominant culture assigns privileges and imposes restrictions in a fairly uniform manner.

Many of their activities are suppressed to an almost incredible degree. One has only to look at the furor over dress and hair styles to see some of the absurd aspects of this control. However, there is more subtle control over ideas and values, precisely in those areas where the young people are beginning to challenge the older. Kelly suggests also that the adolescent is often exploited in that much is demanded of him but little credit goes to him.

They are stereotyped. The image for the group is mostly determined by the minority that gets the most publicity or notoriety. Any stereotyping contributes to lack of communication and with the adolescent this contributes to what is called "the generation gap." Stereotyping makes individual communication almost impossible. The adult tends to respond to the youth as a member of a class rather than as an individual. Young people rightly resent this for it is no different than any other bigotry or prejudice.

Although at first adolescent aspiration may not seem like those of the larger society, a closer look makes Kelly's point convincing. He argues that adolescent idealism is a re-affirmation of the value that Americans have traditionally placed on human beings. Thus, the contemporary adolescent is affirming what our society is supposed to be all about and in the process of this affirmation is exposing the hypocrisy of his elders. They seem to be saying, "We *really* believe that all people are equal and should be treated as equals. We do not accept these ideas as convenient myths to be trotted forth on patriotic occasions but ignored the rest of the time." When this point of view is combined with the youthful NOW, it becomes an explosive set of issues. The adolescent, in current counseling terminology, is confronting us with our inconsistencies. Another aspect of the generation gap is our unwillingness to accept this confrontation, for full acceptance would mean that we must change our ways or our ideals.

Finally, the adolescent does use various means to reduce the consequences of his minority status. Kelly classifies these as non-rebellious and rebellious. In the former the adolescent seems to conform or may conform to the societal demands. However, many of the young people this writer has talked with do this in a manner which they describe as "playing the system." They become alienated from any deep involvement in the society while they are getting all they can from it. They tend to argue that once they gain status within the larger society they will work for change toward more idealistic goals. Although this may, for many, be a rationalization, one is stuck with the possibility of an adolescent fifth column! The rebellious youth are less subtle and mount a frontal attack. In doing this they establish status positions for themselves with their peers and sympathetic adults. This in turn provides for recognition beyond the adolescent status. So by direct confrontation they do two things: change or try to change those conditions which they feel are unjust and achieve status for themselves in the larger community.

The counselor, then, is faced with an increasingly militant youth who may challenge some of his most cherished values. He lives in an era of "people revolutions" and insistence that the old ways must go and something better must take their place. Coupled with this, the students he works with have many of the characteristics of a suppressed minority group and this is the day of the attempt to end minority subjugation. With these pressures from the youth pushing him in one direction he is also met by peer pressures to maintain the status quo and even to join in repressive measures against the very youngsters he would like to help. We said earlier that the counselor must define his role or have it defined for him. What should this be? An advocate for youngsters who are attacking the established authority? A therapist? A person who represents the majority viewpoint and who attempts to guide youth to the "right" path? Let us take a look now at how counselors might function and some of the professional forces at work shaping his role.

Gelatt (1969) using the term "guidance" to cover all student personnel services for students, makes a plea for a comprehensive program that is relevant to today's student. He says (p. 150):

One important guidance objective is to identify and respond to current major issues which have psychological, social, and educational implications for children. For example, the current personal and social problems facing youth in regard to drug usage, student unrest and protest, and race relations require a vigorous guidance approach. The present problems of education in regard to the relevancy of the curriculum, the appropriateness of evaluation methods, and the need for "effective" learning also demand critical inquiry by guidance researchers. Guidance programs should include active efforts to influence the values, the policies, and the practices of schools based on the knowledge and understanding of student behaviors. Such a change will require guidance workers to become specialists in learning processes, leaders in introducing innovations, and activists in providing in-service training for personnel. It will require the courage to change and actively ask for change.

In such a setting the counselor would be deeply involved with making his position relevant to student needs. However, the involvement would be directly related to the outcomes of research and thus closely allied to a more scientific approach to understanding adolescent behavior and helping the schools to change programs in line with research findings. The counselor becomes at least a consumer of research and hopefully a contributor.

Brammer (1968) is even more explicit as he sees the general role of the counselor firmly based on the science of psychology. In fact, he would have the counselor change from being a "guidance specialist" to a counseling psychologist. The emphasis would be on behavioral change and the techniques would involve those counseling strategies that have scientific backing. However, it should be remembered that these authors feel that change could be therapeutic in nature (that is, helping the person to a healthier adjustment) or strictly behavioral (the student spends more time studying, and so on). More of this seeming dichotomy later.

But what does psychology have to offer the counselor? Is there a set of techniques that the counselor can use to help change the client's behavior or feelings in some desirable sort of way? This is a difficult question at best, but it is one that is at the heart of much of the controversy in counseling. For, if counseling is to be or already is a technology based on a scientific discipline, then Gelatt is right in insisting that what is done be based on scientific research. And Brammer is also right in asserting that the science is psychology and counseling does and will derive its respectability from the behavioral sciences. But if the science of psychology is split into opposing camps, what should the counselor do? Join one camp or the other or take from both?

The contemporary humanistic movement in counseling psychology is based to a large extent on the ideas developed by Carl Rogers. Although these appear in many places, a good summary is in Patterson (1966, pp. 403–439). The interested student should, of course, read the original sources and a good place to start would be Rogers (1951).

As the name would imply, the humanistic psychologists are committed to a basic respect for the individual and his right and ability for self-direction. They see each person striving for self-awareness, self-understanding, and self-actualization; that is, achieving all those things for which he has a potential. Basic to man's personality is a striving toward growth and a healthy adjustment. Given the proper environment and particularly the proper social environment he will mature to become a well-adjusted human being. This will be evidenced by his self-direction, congruency (being openly what he truly is; honest to himself and others), and warmth and respect for others. Thus if a youngster is having difficulties, is aggressive or hostile, he is reacting to the frustrations of the situation and, given the opportunity, he can overcome these feelings and continue to develop. As Patterson states it (1966, p. 405): "When the individual is provided with reasonable conditions for growth, he will develop his potential constructively, as a seed grows and becomes its potential."

Counseling, then, is that situation which provides an opportunity for the client to explore himself, gain self-understanding, and return to being a self-actualizing person. The counselor essentially provides the climate or situation in which the client can continue to grow. He does this by being absolutely accepting of the client as a person and absolutely honest in his reaction to the client. Thus in the course of counseling, the client has an opportunity for immediate "feedback" of another person or, in group counseling, persons reactions to him. Contrary to some interpretations of this approach, the counselor does not condone everything the client says or does even though he continues to accept the client as a person. He differentiates between accepting the person and accepting what he does. For the counselor is always responding to and aware of the basic human qualities of his client even though his behavior may temporarily be quite anti-social. His faith is that given a chance any person will regain his humanity.

This very sketchy overview of the humanistic position in counseling has not really done justice to the wealth of material available for the interested student. Much of this is based on research of a phenomeno-logical nature, such as measurement of self-concept and changes in self-concept as a consequence of some counseling intervention. But the point is that the research as well as the counseling is oriented toward the private world of the client, both toward himself and the world as he sees it. The psychologist only sees this through the eyes of the client as there can be no direct observation of another's mind. It is a therapeutically oriented point of view since the goal is to help the person become psychologically healthy.

In the midst of the contemporary problems faced by adolescents this kind of counselor would and does find himself very much in sympathy with the youth. Primarily, because today's youth are reacting more and more against the hypocrisy of a society which espouses certain values but does not live up to them. In humanistic terminology there is a lack of congruence between what the older members of the society say and what they do. Since congruence between self and behavior is a sign of health and the lack of it a sign of sickness, we are, from this point of view, living in a sick society. Therefore, not only should we help the youth as counselors but also we have a duty to help change the society which is sick and producing illness in others. This is a powerful argument whether the reader wishes to accept "sickness and health" or not. For it is another protest against the necessity for "compromise" with values that has plagued developing youth for centuries. Why should values like the worth of humans and the equality of all men be denied or adulterated as a part of growing up? "Why indeed?" asks the humanistic counselor.

What then is the quarrel with the behaviorists? There are two that are fundamental. The first is quite simply that the behaviorists argue that humanism is not scientific and should not pretend to be so. Private experience is not open to scientific investigation except through self-report. Science must be public so that the phenomena are at least potentially observable by others. Since this is not the case with the humanists they should forget about being scientific or making any claims along this line. The second is that the behaviorists do not accept the health-illness model for human behavior. They point out that so-called statements about health and illness are really disguised philosophical statements about how people ought or ought not to behave. What is good or bad. Thus each counseling intervention involves some ethical or moral consideration and it should be clearly labeled as such and not disguised under "health or illness." Before we consider some counter arguments, let us look at counseling as the behaviorist would practice it.

Krumboltz (1966) argues that the only scientific approach to the counseling process is through a behavioristic psychology. However, this does not deny the human questions involved, indeed it makes them more explicit. For he would have it that "The goals of counseling should be stated as those specific behavior changes (a) desired by each client, (b) compatible with the counselor's values, and (c) externally observable." Bring it all out in the open is the argument for both the goals and the "ought" associated with those goals. Then both the client and counselor can decide if there is anything that violates their moral and ethical principles. He feels that the traditional goals of counseling such as "self-actualization" are so vague as to have little or no meaning. How does either the client or counselor know when he is self-actualizing? Krumboltz says, "The use of behavioral goals would result in (a) a clearer anticipation of what counseling could accomplish, (b) a better integration of counseling psychology with the mainstream of psychological theory and research, (c) a facilitation of the search for new and more effective techniques for helping clients, and (d) the use of different criteria for assessing the outcomes of counseling with different clients." Counseling would become a much more understandable and open process from this point of view. Both the client and the counselor would know when specific goals had been reached and the goals would be individualized for each person. The argument here is that this is a truly human-oriented approach since each client is treated as unique and there is no pre-conception of what he should or should not be. There is no assumption about any built-in ethical nature of man although there is the implication of the worth of human beings.

Thoresen (1969) argues that not only has the traditional therapeutic counseling offered little or no evidence of its effectiveness but it has so obscured the complex relationship in "outrageous wordology" as to almost defy meaning. He feels that if counseling is to become a viable enterprise, it must proceed in such a manner as to make clear its goals and evaluate its processes. He argues that counseling is an applied behavioral science and as such is not limited to one technique or one view of man but to what works for any individual. He feels there should be much more flexibility in approach as long as the counselor is specific in his goals and willing to evaluate outcomes. The following summarizes his and the behavioristic point of view:

Counseling is not a predetermined, prescribed, and stylized activity. Clients are not fitted to one method and judged either ready or not ready for counseling. Rather counseling follows from the problems of clients; procedures and techniques are determined by the problems of the client. . . . And as a scientist the counselor pursues techniques *tentatively*, gathering data through careful observation and making evaluations as he proceeds. . . . No procedure is off-limits because of any doctrinal allegiance to a particular point of view. Any procedure is a viable contender so long as it is evaluated using direct observations and experience and is gauged against actual changes in client behaviors. (p. 845).

Therefore, the behaviorist would not be opposed to what the humanist does so long as he can demonstrate that what he does makes a difference in the client's behavior and the sort of difference that the client asked for. But what if the goal is an affective one, for example, a change in feeling or "outlook on life"? The behaviorist would argue that these can often be broken down into more specific goals and if there are "true" changes the client should do something different as a consequence of the experience. This is allied to what Campbell and Dunnette (1968) have labeled esthetic experiences. If a client, as a consequence of individual or group counseling, makes such statements as "This is the greatest experience of my life," or "I now have a completely new and wonderful outlook on life," the authors have no complaint as long as these are not substituted for behavioral change. These are private and esthetic experiences much like one gets from a good play, movie, or symphony. Although affective or esthetic experience may be an end in itself for the counselor and client, it should be substituted for behavioral change if change is the goal. One can talk about these experiences but from a behavioral point of view they are interesting but not terribly important if the client does nothing toward achieving his behavioral goal. Talking about experience is quite different from doing something.

The behavioral counselor might function in the school very much like the humanistic counselor. The primary differences would be a more explicit statement or attempt to state the client's goals and a more comprehensive evaluative process as these goals are sought. He could be equally the advocate for the student if he agreed with the student goals and would use, with the consent of the student, any counseling techniques that seemed suited to the problem the student had.

Rousseve (1969) feels that there is not as great discrepancy between a humanistic approach and a behavioristic approach as some may claim. Essentially he feels that both positions have something to say about man and, although there may be controversy over the ultimate nature of man (that is, free or not free), this does not eliminate the contributions of relevance which both positions may have for counselors. Rousseve seems to be arguing for a "humanistic behaviorism" (Meacham & Wiesen, 1969) when he says: "On with the task, then, of improving our understanding, prediction, and control of human behavior, so long as we acknowledge and accept the concomitant responsibility to attend to human values in the process." This writer would agree. If counseling is to be an applied behavioral science, it cannot ignore the findings of the behaviorist. If it is to be worthwhile, it cannot ignore the values of the humanists. There is a caution that applies to both camps but perhaps more to the humanists at least as currently practiced. There seems to be a tendency to polarize these points of view and in the process the client is caught in the middle. Thus the militant behaviorist or the equally militant humanist tends to take his own position as the "good" one. Consequently, either type of counselor subtly or not so subtly reinforces the adolescent for behavior just like his. This is certainly contrary to the expressed ideals of both groups. And they might well take as their fundamental dictum Emerson's advice: "Stop trying to make that man like you. One is enough."

REFERENCES

Brammer, L. M. The counselor is a psychologist. *Personnel and Guidance Journal*, 1968, **47**, 4–9.

Carson, M. R. *A Descriptive Study of Functions: Elementary School Counselors, Psychologists, Social Workers.* Thesis, University of Washington, 1969.

Campbell, J. B., and Dunnette, M. D. Effectiveness of T-group experiences in managerial training and development. *Psychological Bulletin*, 1968, **70**, 73–104.

Flacks, R. Student activists: result not revolt. *Psychology Today*, 1967, **1**, 18.

Kelly, H. Adolescents: a suppressed minority group. *Personnel and Guidance Journal*, 1969, **47**, 634–640.

Krumboltz, J. D. Behavioral goals for counseling. *Journal of Counseling Psychology*, 1966, **13**, 153–159.

Meacham, M. L., and Wiesen, A. E. *Changing Classroom Behavior: A Manual for Precision Teaching.* Scranton, Pa.: International Textbook, 1969.

Patterson, C. H. *Theories of Counseling and Psychotherapy.* New York: Harper and Row, 1966, 403–439.

Rogers, C. R. *Client Centered Therapy.* Boston: Houghton-Mifflin, 1951.

Thompson, C. L. The secondary school counselor's ideal client. *Journal of Counseling Psychology*, 1969, **16**, 69–74.

Thoresen, C. E. The counselor as an applied behavioral scientist. *Personnel and Guidance Journal*, 1969, **47**, 841–848.

part three
A Sampling of Research on Adolescents

3.1 Orientation

Our brief excursion through exemplary selections from the research literature on adolescence begins with a longitudinal study of behavior. The longitudinal approach to psychological study is one most preferred by researchers concerned with developmental stability and change over time. Thus, it requires the observation of the same individuals over extended time intervals whereby periodic behavior assessments are made. Resultant data are frequently interpreted to reflect the influence of age (and cumulative experience) on the progressive differentiation of behavioral patterns, such as motor style, or the quality of selected responses, such as problem solving skills. The following selection illustrates specifically the longitudinal study of *cognitive style,* a construct first introduced by Barbara Hauck in Part I and dealt with intently by Samuel Osipow in Part II. Current interest in this construct further illustrates a remarkable acceleration of research into the psychology of cognition during the past decade.

311

Herman Witkin, from whose theorizing the following study was inspired, is a primary contributor to the cognitive style research. His work in this area has been based upon the broader concept of *psychological differentiation*. Basically, this concept involves specialization and complexity of integration in a system. Progressive differentiation is thought by Witkin to be manifest in an increasing articulation of experience, that is, an increasing analysis and structuring of personal experience by the individual. Witkin operates from the hypothesis that psychological differentiation increases with age and that at any age level individuals will differ in the extent of their differentiation. Degree of differentiation is defined by such primary indicator areas as articulation of the self (including sense of identity and body image), behavioral controls and defenses, and the perceptual components of intellectual functioning. The cognitive style component of psychological differentiation is depicted by the continuum *field independence—dependence*. This continuum, defined below by Witkin *et al.*, symbolizes variations in learning style and is related to such diverse phenomena as socialization practices, creativity, reading behavior, assertiveness, pain reactivity, impulsivity, and persistence. Consistent sex differences have also appeared with regularity.

As is typical of new vistas in psychological research, the literature on cognitive style is somewhat disordered. For one thing different researchers tend to utilize different terms to describe similar, if not identical phenomena. For another, cognitive style research has invaded the cognitive-affective development relationship, the complexities of which will require time and intensive study to clarify. Sufficient research momentum has been achieved, however, to pursue these problems optimistically.

A final word is in order. The reader inexperienced in the study of psychological reports could possibly be overwhelmed by the statistical and graphic data included in this selection and those that follow shortly. However, such data provide the raw stuff from which interpretations are made. Presented in published form, these data can also be checked independently by interested parties for accuracy and relevancy. Their purpose therefore is not to complicate or confuse a research report but to provide the report with its life blood.

RECOMMENDED READINGS

Barclay, A., and Cusumano, D. R. Father absence, cross-sex identity, and field-dependent behavior in male adolescents. *Child Development,* 1967, **38,** 243–250.

Kagan, Jerome, Moss, Howard, and Sigel, Irving. Psychological significance of styles of conceptualization. *Monographs of the Society of Research in Child Development,* 1963, **28,** Series No. 86, 73–124.

Sheerer, Constance (Ed.) *Cognition: Theory, Research, Promise.* New York: Harper and Row, 1964.

Witkin, Herman A. Psychological differentiation and forms of pathology. *Journal of Abnormal Psychology,* 1965, **70,** 317–336.

3.1 Stability of Cognitive Style from Childhood to Young Adulthood

Herman Witkin, STATE UNIVERSITY OF NEW YORK
DOWNSTATE MEDICAL CENTER†
Donald Goodenough, STATE UNIVERSITY OF NEW YORK
DOWNSTATE MEDICAL CENTER
*Stephen Karp,** STATE UNIVERSITY OF NEW YORK
DOWNSTATE MEDICAL CENTER

For a number of years now we have been concerned in our studies with individual consistencies in behavior (Witkin, Dyk, Faterson, Goodenough, & Karp, 1962; Witkin, Lewis, Hertzman, Machover, Meissner, & Wapner, 1954). Starting with observations of individual differences in perception, a variety of other psychological areas was examined for individual differences congruent with those first identified in perception. As the evidence on individual consistencies grew, our concept of them was inevitably modified. With the accumulated evidence now available psychological differentiation has come to serve for us as a construct to conceptualize the particular communality we have observed in a person's

Reprinted from *Journal of Personality and Social Psychology,* 1967, **7,** 291–300, by permission of the authors and the American Psychological Association.

† Psychology Laboratory, Department of Psychiatry.
* Dr. Karp is now at Sinai Hospital, Baltimore, Maryland.

functioning in different psychological areas; and we conceive of the individual differences we have found in clusters of interrelated characteristics as differences in extent of psychological differentiation.

Extent of differentiation is reflected in the area of perception in degree of field dependence or independence. In a field-dependent mode of perceiving, perception is dominated by the overall organization of the field; there is relative inability to perceive parts of a field as discrete. This global quality is indicative of limited differentiation. Conversely, a field-independent style of perceiving, in which parts of a field are experienced as discrete from organized background, rather than fused with it, is a relatively differentiated way of functioning. Persons whose field-dependent perception suggests limited differentiation in their experience of the world about them also show limited differentiation in their experience of their bodies. For example, their drawings of the human figure are likely to lack articulation. Further, just as they rely on the surrounding visual field in their perception of a stimulus object within it, so do they tend to use the social context in which they find themselves for definition of attributes of the self. We have called this a lack of developed sense of separate identity and take it as indicative of a limitedly differentiated self. Finally, persons who perceive in field-dependent fashion are also likely to use such global defenses as repression and denial, suggestive of limited differentiation, whereas field-independent perceivers tend to use specialized defenses, as intellectualization and isolation, suggestive of developed differentiation. Thus, viewed from the standpoint of level of differentiation, people show consistency in their psychological functioning across such diverse areas as perception, body concept, sense of separate identity, and nature of defenses.

The differentiation concept carries a number of implications for problems of development. In this paper we examine two of these implications. One is that during the course of normal development differentiation may be expected to increase with age. The other is that level of differentiation will be relatively stable during development so that the child who at an early age is less differentiated than his peers will tend to occupy a similar position on the differentiation continuum as a young adult as well.

The grounds on which an increase in differentiation with age may be expected are self-evident; and there is already some evidence, now extended in the study to be reported, supporting this expectation. The main ground for predicting relative stability in level of differentiation during development is that formal or structural features of an individual's psychological makeup are likely to show considerable stability over time as compared to content features; differentiation is of course a structural property of a psychological system. Escalona and Heider (1959) have come to a similar conclusion about stability of structural characteristics in their empirical studies of continuity in development. They write:

Our best predictive successes have occurred in regard to the formal aspects of behavior. With few exceptions we have been better able to forecast *how* a child goes about moving, thinking, speaking, playing, than *what* he is likely to do, think, speak or play. (p. 73).

Data from several studies with adults have already shown marked stability for several measures of differentiation. In one kind of study attempts were made to alter field dependence experimentally. The methods used have included drugs, such as sodium amytal, dexedrine, chlorpromazine, imiprimine and alcohol (Franks, 1956; Karp, Witkin, & Goodenough, 1965; Pollack, Kahn, Karp, & Fink, 1960); stress (Kraidman, 1959); training (Witkin, 1948); and electroconvulsive shock (Pollack *et al.*, 1960). The results of the study in which shock was used are particularly striking. Psychiatric patients were tested on the rod-and-frame test prior to shock and again 4 weeks afterwards. Though on retest they suffered retrograde amnesia for the first test, and so experienced retesting as an entirely new situation, there was no significant change in their rod-and-frame test scores, and the test-retest correlation was very high (.88, $p < .01$). In a more naturalistic study, which examined the effect of important changes in life experiences, Bauman (1951), working with young adults, found no evidence of change in extent of field dependence over a 3-year period attributable to marriage, psychotherapy, or psychological trauma (as divorce). Bauman also examined the stability of measures of field dependence and of figure-drawing ratings (reflecting extent of differentiation of body concept). In most cases the test-retest correlations over the 3-year period were no lower than test-retest correlations obtained for very short intervals of time, indicating quite striking stability for these measures.

In the studies with adults just reviewed, stability over time was *absolute* in the sense that not only were correlations from test to retest very high, but mean scores were not significantly different. During the growth years, on the other hand, we would expect to find only *relative* stability. Though test-retest correlations for measures of differentiation are again likely to be high, the existence of a general developmental trend toward greater differentiation would make for a change in mean scores. The question of stability during the growth years may be put in this form: How well can we predict a person's adult level of psychological differentiation from the level of differentiation he shows as a child?

In the studies reported here the expectations of increasing differentiation with age and of relative stability have been checked through cross-sectional and longitudinal studies, covering the period from 8 to 24 years of age. Extensive testing has been done in order to examine extent of differentiation in a variety of areas of psychological functioning. This report is limited to the results of perceptual testing, in other words, results on cognitive style. Findings on assessments of differentiation in other areas will be given in later reports.

Of the variety of indicators of psychological differentiation that may be employed in the study of change and stability during development, measures of field dependence are of particular value and have in fact been used most extensively. These measures are not only easily obtained and objective, but the tests from which they are derived can be given in the same form to subjects differing widely in age. The very same tests of field dependence have been used all the way from 8-year-old children to geriatric groups with sufficient variability in performance at each age to permit effective study of individual differences throughout the age range.

For investigations of developmental trends there are obvious methodological advantages in having comparable data from both cross-sectional and longitudinal studies; the data obtained by one method help us deal with problems inherent in the other. In cross-sectional studies there is the inevitable question of comparability of different age samples. This difficulty does not exist in longitudinal studies, of course, where the same sample is used throughout. Accordingly, developmental trends identified in cross-sectional studies may be checked against trends found in longitudinal studies. Longitudinal studies, on the other hand, have their own methodological problems. Chief among these is the confounding effect of repeated measurement on the same individuals, especially when the subject may learn something on one test occasion that may be useful to him on subsequent testing. Cross-sectional studies are free of this difficulty, so that to establish the scope of practice effects, longitudinal data may profitably be checked against cross-sectional data.

SUBJECTS AND TESTS

In the cross-sectional study, the age groups included 8-, 10-, 11-, 12-, 13-, 15-, and 17-year-olds and, in addition, a group of college students (mean age of men, 21.2 years; mean age of women, 19.6 years). Each group consisted of approximately 25 boys and 25 girls, except the 10-year and college groups where the Ns were larger. In the longitudinal study there were two groups: a 10–24-year group and an 8–13-year group. The 10–24-year group consisted of 30 boys and 30 girls when the study began. The girls were seen again at ages 14 and 17, and the boys were seen at both these ages and in addition at age 24.[1] At age 17, 25 of the original group of 30 girls were seen for final testing. At age 24, all but 2 of the original group of 30 boys were seen for final testing. (At age 14, 27 boys and 26 girls were tested and at age 17, 28 boys were tested.) In the 8–13-year longitudinal study there were 26 boys and 27 girls at the outset. Both groups were retested at age 13, at which time 26 boys and 22 girls were seen. The exact number of subjects in each cross-sectional group on each test occasion is given in Table 1.[2]

Every subject in all the groups received the three main tests of perceptual field dependence: the rod-and-frame test, the tilting-room-tilting-chair test, and the embedded-figures test. The subjects in the longitudinal study received in addition a number of other tests not considered in this report. These were the Rorschach, the TAT, the figure-drawing test, a miniature-toys-play test (at ages 10 and 14) and the WAIS (at age 17 only); there were also interviews with the children and their mothers. The three perceptual tests used in these studies have been described in detail elsewhere (see Witkin *et al.*, 1962).

In the rod-and-frame test (RFT), the subject is seated in a completely darkened room and adjusts a tilted luminous rod, centered within a tilted luminous frame, to a position he perceives as upright, while the frame remains at its initial position of the tilt. The test consists of three series of eight trials each: In Series 1, body and frame are tilted to opposite sides; in Series 2, body and frame are tilted to the same side; and in Series 3, the body is erect and the frame is tilted. Twenty-eight-degree tilts of the body, frame, and rod are used. The subject's score for each series is the mean degrees absolute deviation of the rod from the true upright.

The tilting-room-tilting-chair test has two parts, the room-adjustment test (RAT) and the body-adjustment test (BAT). In each, the subject sits in a chair, which is initially tilted, within a small room, which is also initially tilted. In the eight trials of the room-adjustment test, the room is tilted 56 degrees and the chair 22 degrees, and the subject's task is to adjust the room to the upright while his chair remains tilted. In the six

[1] Some of the children were also tested at age 12. Because the sample was very incomplete at that age, with particular attrition at the field-dependent end of the distribution, the results are not included. The fact that some children had this additional testing does not seem to be a problem. As will be seen, the body-erect condition of the rod-and-frame test, the only test of field dependence for which results are considered in the longitudinal study, shows no practice effect.

[2] The 8-year longitudinal groups and the 8-year cross-sectional groups are the same. The 10-year cross-sectional groups include the 10-year longitudinal groups, but have additional cases as well.

TABLE 1. MEAN RFT, BAT, AND EFT SCORES FOR ALL GROUPS

Age	RFTa												BAT				EFT			
	8-13 longitudinal groupsb				10-24 longitudinal groups				Cross-sectional groups				Cross-sectional groups				Cross-sectional groups			
	M		F		M		F		M		F		M		F		M		F	
	M	N	M	N	M	N	M	N	M	N	M	N	M	N	M	N	M	N	M	N
8	17.1	26	20.7	21					17.1	26	21.5	27	17.1	26	15.4	27				
10					14.9	27	16.6	24	14.8	54	17.7	54	13.9	54	14.2	54	187.0	54	156.0	54
11									9.2	21	15.4	24	13.8	21	11.3	24	90.7	21	116.3	24
12									11.2	25	14.1	25	11.3	25	13.0	25	99.1	25	102.0	25
13	10.1	26	13.8	21	9.4	27	13.7	24	7.4	30	10.0	29	10.0	30	8.5	29	57.8	25	78.2	25
14																				
15									5.2	25	7.3	25	7.7	25	8.6	25	34.0	25	47.4	25
17					7.9	27	12.6	24	4.5	23	8.6	25	6.0	23	9.4	25	31.2	23	48.1	23
19															10.2	52				
21									7.2	51	12.5	51	8.4	52				39.8	51	57.7	51
24					8.1	27														

a RFT and BAT scores are given in mean degrees deviation from upright per trial. EFT scores are given in mean number of seconds to solution per trial. High scores on each test indicate relatively field-dependent performance.

b Only subjects tested at all ages are included in the longitudinal data.

318

trials of the body-adjustment test, the initial settings of the room and chair are 35 degrees and 22 degrees, respectively; here the subject's task is to make himself straight while the room remains tilted. The subject's score for each of the two tests is again the mean degrees absolute deviation of the item to be adjusted (room or chair) from the true upright when he perceives it as straight.

Finally, in the embedded-figures test (EFT) the subject must locate a previously seen simple geometric figure within a complex figure designed to embed it. The test is composed of 24 pairs of simple and complex figures, and the subject's score for the test is the mean amount of time required to locate each of the simple figures.

As our work developed, and new data accumulated (including data from the present study), it became evident, first, that not all the subtests of this battery of tests provide equally good measures of field dependence, and, second, that some of the tests show practice effects and are therefore not suitable for longitudinal studies which require repeated testing.

Evidence now available from a variety of sources (summarized in Witkin *et al.*, 1962) indicates that the RAT and the two RFT series conducted with body tilted (Series 1 and 2) yield less adequate measures of field dependence. In the RAT, the results of factor analytic studies make it clear that performance is not primarily determined by the field-dependence factor, although the nature of the confounding effect is not yet clear (Goodenough & Karp, 1961; Linton, 1952). In the body-tilted condition of the RFT, performance is partially determined by a tendency to perceive the apparent upright as displaced in the direction opposite to body tilt. This is the E-effect of Müller (1916), which in some subjects is very marked. The presence of individual differences in the E-effect confounds the interpretation of test scores. For these reasons results for the RAT and for RFT Series 1 and 2 are not considered in this paper.

Concerning learning effects, in the EFT knowledge of results is clearly available to the subject during the course of testing; there is accordingly every reason to expect improvement in performance with practice. A clear learning effect has in fact been demonstrated by Witkin *et al.* (1954) and by Goldstein and Chance (1965). In the present study a comparison between longitudinal and cross-sectional data for subjects of the same age also reveals a learning effect. Subjects in the longitudinal groups who had prior exposure to the EFT tend to do much better than subjects in cross-sectional groups of the same age who were receiving the EFT for the first time. This practice effect limits the usefulness of the EFT for longitudinal studies of development. In the BAT cues as to the location of the upright (and therefore some knowledge of results) may be obtained by the subject as his body is rotated through the objective upright, particularly on trials in which body and field are initially tilted to opposite sides. There is therefore reason to expect a practice effect on this test. Results of past studies have in fact indicated a practice effect (Witkin *et al.*, 1954). In the present study there was some tendency for longitudinal groups to do better than cross-sectional groups of the same age on the BAT. Although the differences between the two kinds of groups were not as clear-cut for the BAT as for the EFT, the value of the BAT in longitudinal studies is questionable. In the RFT, in contrast to the EFT and BAT, no knowledge of results is available to the subject and evidence from a variety of past studies indicates no learning effect (Witkin, 1948; Witkin *et al.*, 1954). The results of the present study are consistent with the past findings. No learning effect is evident when data from longitudinal and cross-sectional groups of the same age are compared (Table 1).

In view of these findings, for the longitudinal groups data for RFT trials conducted with body erect (Series 3) only will be considered.[3]

RESULTS

The results bear upon three main issues: developmental changes in performance on perceptual tests reflecting extent of differentiation; relative stability of perceptual performance within the context of developmental change; and individual consistency in perceptual functioning at different ages.

Change in Level of Differentiation
from Childhood to Young Adulthood

The data on change in field dependence with age are summarized in Table 1 and Figures 1 through 5. Analyses of variance which bear on the significance of these changes are summarized in Tables 2, 3, and 4.

In general, a trend toward increasing field independence during development is clearly evident in both the longitudinal and cross-sectional groups. The age effect is significant in both kinds of data (Tables 2 and 3).

Moreover, every single subject in the longitudinal groups went from relatively field-dependent to relatively field-independent performance without significant reversal.

For the most extensively studied longitudinal subjects (males of the 10–24-year group) mean scores on the RFT decline in a regular fashion

---

[3] "RFT" will hereafter refer to RFT Series 3.

TABLE 2. Unweighted Means Analysis of Variance[a]
for RFT, BAT, and EFT for Cross-Sectional Groups

Effect	RFT		BAT		EFT[b]	
	F	df	F	df	F	df
Sex	41.17**	1,499	<1	1,500	13.47**	1,439
Age	30.16**	7,499	15.36**	7,500	44.99**	6,439
Linear trend	154.65**	1,499	91.17**	1,500	230.61**	1,439
Quadratic trend	34.09**	1,499	9.76**	1,500	26.08**	1,439
Higher-order trends	4.48**	5,499	1.32	5,500	3.32**	4,439
Sex × Age	<1	7,499	1.68	7,500	<1	6,439

[a] See Winer (1962, pp. 222–224).
[b] EFT was not given to the 8-year-olds.
** $p < .01$.

TABLE 3. Analysis of Variance for RFT for Two Longitudinal Groups

Effect	10–17 grp.[a]		8–13 grp.	
	F	df	F	df
Sex	4.01	1,49	4.33*	1,45
Age	33.93**	2,98	65.67**	1,45
Sex × Age	2.43	2,98	<1	1,45

[a] In the longitudinal study, started at age 10, boys were followed until age 24 and girls to age 17. To permit a test of sex differences, the data for the 10–17-year period only were considered in this analysis.
* $p < .05$.
** $p < .01$.

from 10 to 17 years of age and show little change from 17 to 24 years (Table 1 and Figure 4). An analysis of age trends for this group shows significant linear and quadratic components (Table 4). In effect, these significant trend components indicate that there is an overall tendency for children to become less field dependent during development, but the rate of change slows down with increasing age.

The apparent leveling off of the trend toward increasing field independence may indicate that for the average child development of this function is completed by age 17. On the other hand, the leveling off may be an artifact of the RFT test procedure. Specifically, the mean RFT score for the male subjects of the 10–24-year longitudinal group at age 17 is approximately 8 degrees per trial, a value which approaches the minimum possible score of 0 degrees. This may be a limiting factor which in itself produces an apparent leveling off in average scores.

To evaluate this possibility a comparison was made of the seven boys in the 10–24-year group who in their RFT performance at age 10 were most field dependent and the seven who were most field independent. Plots of mean scores at each age for these two groups of subjects are shown in Figure 5. It is evident that the field-dependent group shows at least as much leveling off as the field-independent group, even though the mean scores for the field-dependent group at the older ages are much farther away from the minimum possible score. These subgroup

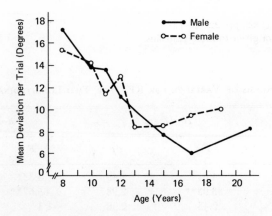

FIGURE 1. Developmental Curves for Body-Adjustment Test Based on Cross-Sectional Data

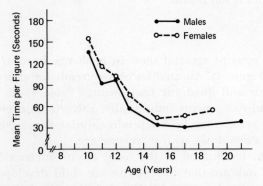

FIGURE 2. Developmental Curves for Embedded-Figures Test Based on Cross-Sectional Data

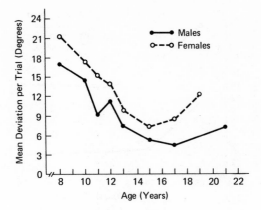

FIGURE 3. Developmental Curves for Rod-and-Frame Test Based on Cross-Sectional Data

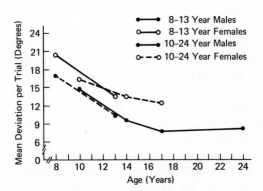

FIGURE 4. Developmental Curves for Rod-and-Frame Test Based on Longitudinal Data

TABLE 4. Trend Analysis for RFT for 10–24-Year Longitudinal Males

Effect	F	df
Age	37.09**	3,78
Linear trend	83.52**	1,78
Quadratic trend	26.87**	1,78
Higher order	<1	1,78

** $p < .01$.

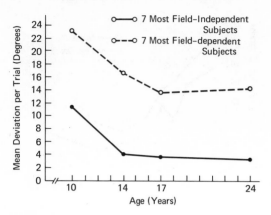

FIGURE 5. Developmental Curves for Rod-and-Frame Test for Seven Most Field-Dependent Males and Seven Most Field-Independent Males, at Age 10 in 10–24-Year Longitudinal Group

curves suggest that the leveling off is not entirely a test artifact, but more likely reflects completion of the development process by age 17.

The data for the remaining longitudinal groups and for the cross-sectional groups show similar developmental trends to those just described for the 10–24 male longitudinal group. In the cross-sectional data (Table 1; Figures 1, 2, and 3), although not in the longitudinal data (Table 1, Figure 4), there appears to be a tendency toward a return to more field-dependent performance after age 17, particularly among females. As we will see later, there is reason to believe that this reversal in trend at 17 years in the cross-sectional data is a sampling artifact.

Significant sex differences are found for the RFT and EFT, although not for the BAT, in the cross-sectional data (Table 2). In the data from the longitudinal study the sex difference for the RFT is significant for the 8–13-year group but does not reach significance for the 10–24-year group, although it is in the expected direction (Table 3). The overall tendency for males to be more field independent than females is consistent with the results of many other studies. (See Witkin *et al.* (1962) for a review of this evidence.)

Relative Stability of Level of Differentiation
during Development

Evidence on this issue comes from the data on RFT performance of the longitudinal groups, summarized in Table 5. For the 10–24-year groups of males and females test-retest correlations are all significant at better than the .01 level, and range in magnitude from .62 to .92. Even over the longest interval of time for which data are available (from age 10 to 24 for males) the correlation is quite high (.66). For the 8–13-year groups the test-retest correlations are also significant and fairly high.

TABLE 5. COEFFICIENTS OF STABILITY FOR RFT FOR TWO LONGITUDINAL GROUPS

Age		13		14		17		24	
	Sex	r	N	r	N	r	N	r	N
8	M	.76**a	26						
	F	.48*	21						
10	M			.71**	27	.72**	27	.66**	27
	F			.81**	24	.62**	24	–	–
14	M					.92**	27	.84**	27
	F					.76**	24	–	–
17	M							.90**	27
	F							–	–

ᵃ One-tailed test used.
* $p < .05$.
** $p < .01$.

These findings mean that despite a marked general increase in differentiation in perceptual functioning with age, each individual tends to maintain his relative position among his peers in the distribution of measures of differentiation from age to age. This relative stability is illustrated in the curves for the RFT in Figure 5. In these curves the field-dependent and field-independent groups clearly maintain their positions on the score continuum relative to each other, in the context of a marked decrease in scores for both groups. The evidence thus suggests a high degree of continuity during an individual's development in relative level of differentiation.

Consistency in Perceptual Functioning

The intercorrelations among measures from the various tests of field dependence in the cross-sectional groups at different ages are presented in Table 6. In general, the correlations tend to be in the expected direction (42 of 44 correlations) and significant (33 of 44 correlations). The correlations show no obvious age trend. Individual self-consistency in performance across tests of field dependence is thus evident at all ages examined.

TABLE 6. Intercorrelations among RFT, BAT, and EFT Scores for Cross-Sectional Groups

Test	Age	BAT				EFT[a]			
		M	N	F	N	M	N	F	N
RFT 3	8	.45*b	26	.17	27	–	–	–	–
	10	.42**	54	.40	54	.60**	54	.55**	54
	11	.27	21	.52**	24	.36	21	.60**	24
	12	.26	25	.54**	25	.56**	25	.49**	25
	13	.55**	30	.51**	29	.48**	25	.64**	25
	15	.32	25	.31	25	.56**	25	−.15	25
	17	.29	23	.42*	25	.52**	23	.40*	25
	College	.41**	46	.45**	45	.76**	46	.26*	45
BAT	10					.35**	54	.44**	54
	11					.39*	21	.66**	24
	12					.50**	25	.39*	25
	13					.41**	25	.40*	25
	15					.62**	25	−.18	25
	17					.26	23	.27	25
	College					.54**	46	.58**	45

[a] EFT was not given to 8-year-olds.
[b] Correlations are Pearson r's. A 1-tailed test of significance has been used.
* $p < .01$.
** $p < .05$.

Discussion

The developmental curves derived from both the cross-sectional and longitudinal data show a progressive decrease in field dependence up to age 17. In the period from 17 to young adulthood, however, the longitudinal data show no further change, whereas the cross-sectional data show a clear increase in field dependence. At a time before the longitudinal study had been completed, when we had the cross-sectional data alone, we considered that the rise in the cross-sectional curves after age 17 might signify the beginning of a "return to field dependence." We considered as an alternative possibility that the rise might be the result of a sampling artifact. We looked to the data from the longitudinal study for a choice between these two possibilities. The longitudinal data fail to show a rise and so support the sampling-artifact hypothesis. The manner in which we drew our samples for the cross-sectional study at different ages makes it likely that there was in fact a selection bias in a field-dependent direction in the young-adult sample responsible for the rise. Through age 17, the cross-sectional subjects were drawn from an elementary school and a high school near our laboratory. The young-adult group was drawn from a nearby college. Although a great majority of graduates of primary and secondary schools in this neighborhood do go on to college, some of them go to out-of-town colleges rather than the local college from which our young-adult sample was drawn. Fliegel (1955) has shown that young people who leave home at a relatively early age tend to be more field independent than those who do not, as might be expected from the observation that field-independent persons have a more developed sense of separate identity. The existence in the young-adult college group, as compared to the younger age groups, of a selection bias in the direction of relative field dependence thus seems a reasonable possibility, and would account for the observed rise in the cross-sectional curves after age 17.

Still another possible interpretation of the post-17-year difference between the cross-sectional and longitudinal data is that there is in fact a real tendency for field dependence to increase after age 17, but that this effect is obliterated in the longitudinal data by a counteracting practice effect. This interpretation may clearly be ruled out in view of the absence of a practice effect in the RFT, on which the longitudinal curves are based.

We would conclude from the evidence now on hand that the development of psychological differentiation tends to approach a plateau in young adulthood. This leveling off is clearly evident, as we have seen, when extent of differentiation is assessed in the area of perceptual functioning. It is equally evident in development of differentiation in other psychological areas. Faterson and Witkin, in an unpublished study, have used the figure drawings of the subjects from the longitudinal study to examine differentiation of body concept with age. The body concept of a person may be regarded as differentiated when he experiences it as articulated, that is, when he has a definite sense of parts of the body as discrete yet interrelated and formed into a definite structure. The drawings made by the male subjects of the 10–24-year longitudinal group at all ages were pooled and scored on a 9-point modification of the 5-point sophistication-of-body-concept scale devised in our earlier studies to assess articulation of body concept (Witkin et al., 1962). Placed in Category 1 were highly articulated drawings, that is, drawings showing realistic proportioning, representation of appendages and details in appropriate relation to body outline, and sex differentiation. Drawings placed in Category 9, at the opposite end of the rating scale, showed a low form level (as ovals, rectangles, sticks stuck onto each other), little or no representation of body parts, and an absence of sex identity or role. The developmental curve obtained when mean figure-drawing ratings were plotted against age was identical with the corresponding curve for RFT. Not only was there an increase in differentiation up to age 17, but there was also a leveling off of the curve after that age.

There is clear evidence from studies by Schwartz and Karp (1967), using RFT, BAT, and EFT, and by Comali (1965), using RFT and EFT, that a real "return to field dependence," probably signifying de-differentiation, does in fact occur, but much later in life. In both studies geriatric groups were found to be extremely field dependent. It seems clear that at some point between 24 years and old age the process of dedifferentiation begins. Results for the intermediate-age-groups studies by Schwartz and Karp and by Comali suggest that this point may be somewhere in the late 30's, on the average, after which the rate of de-differentiation may accelerate. This conclusion can only be tentative since the number of cases in the intermediate age groups studied was fairly small. Within the general trend toward dedifferentiation at later ages, we may reasonably expect the rate of dedifferentiation to show marked individual differences. Consistent with this expectation Karp, in an unpublished study, found that geriatric subjects who were still actively engaged in regular employment were more field independent than those no longer employed.

The youngest age group in this study was 8 years old. Data on tests of field dependence for younger age groups are, however, available from other studies. Goodenough and Eagle (1963), using a modification of the EFT more appropriate for young children, found a progressive decrease in field dependence in the 5–8-year period. Eagle and Goodenough, in an unpublished study, found the same trend in this age period with children's modifications of the RFT and BAT. Karp and Konstadt (1963) obtained a similar result for the same age period with a slightly different children's modification of the EFT. These observations suggest that 5-year-olds are more field dependent than 8-year-olds. From these earlier findings, taken together with those of the present study, comes the suggestion that the trend toward reduced field dependence is progressive from 5 to 17 years. Caution must however be exercised in simply extending the developmental curves of the present study downward to the 5-year level since the tests used in the 5–8-year period are not identical in format with those used in the present study in the 8–24-year period.[4]

[4] The studies by Goodenough and Eagle and by Karp and Konstadt as well as a study by Crudden (1941) suggest that there are no significant sex differences in field dependence in the 5–8-year period. In the geriatric group studied by Schwartz and Karp there were also no sex differences. Thus, the sex differences, found so consistently in older children and adults, appear to be absent in very young children and in the very old.

Level of differentiation, as assessed in perceptual functioning, shows high relative stability during the growth years, even over a time span as long as 14 years. This conclusion about stability is strongly supported by the evidence on articulation of body concept. For example, for the 10–24-year longitudinal male group, test-retest correlations for figure-drawing sophistication-of-body-concept scores, considered to reflect extent of differentiation in the area of body concept, range from .70 to .92 for the various age comparisons. The correlations between 10-year scores and 24-year scores, involving a 14-year interval, is .81.

In evaluating the high relative stability in level of differentiation we have found, it must be considered that a contributing factor may have been the stability in life circumstances of the particular longitudinal groups we studied. Stability of any psychological characteristic over time —and particularly in the growth years—is likely to depend on stability of the life situation during the period considered. Unstable life situations or important changes in life circumstances may well reduce continuity in relative level of differentiation from one stage of growth to another. The subjects in our longitudinal groups grew up in stable family and overall environmental settings. We do not have the data to say whether or not the high level of stability found in this study would be evident among children from less stable environments. This is an issue for further research.

The 14-year span from age 10 to age 24 covered by our most extended longitudinal study is of course a time of great personal change. This period covers the turbulent events of adolescence, the breaking of close family ties, psychosexual maturation, occupational commitment, and sometimes marriage and the assumption of family responsibility. The psychological impact of all this upon the developing person is of course very great and inevitably contributes to important changes in personal functioning. There is no doubt that many significant psychological changes did take place in our subjects over the 14-year period we studied them. Even with these changes we still find continuity in relative level of differentiation over time.

SUMMARY

Development of differentiation, as reflected in cognitive style, was followed longitudinally in 2 groups, 1 from 8 to 13 years, the other from 10 to 24 years. A battery of tests of field dependence was used to evaluate extent of differentiation in perceptual functioning. Comparable cross-sectional data were obtained from groups in the same age range. A progressive increase in extent of field independence is evident up to age 17, with no further change from 17 to 24. Within this general developmental trend, children show marked relative stability in extent of field dependence, even over 14 years. At each age, individual consistency in performance across tests of field dependence is found. Data from other psychological areas confirm the picture of development of differentiation derived from the perceptual data.

REFERENCES

Bauman, G. The stability of the individual's mode of perception and of perception-personality relationships. Unpublished doctoral dissertation, New York University, 1951.

Comali, P. E. Life span developmental studies in perception: theoretical and methodological issues. Paper presented at 18th annual meeting of the Gerontological Society, Los Angeles, November 13, 1965.

Crudden, C. H. Form abstraction by children. *Journal of Genetic Psychology*, 1941, **58**, 113–129.

Escalona, S., and Heider, G. M. *Prediction and Outcome*. New York: Basic Books, 1959.

Fliegel, Z. O. Stability and change in perceptual performance of a late adolescent group in relation to personality variables. Unpublished doctoral dissertation, New School for Social Research, 1955.

Franks, C. M. Différences déterminées par le personalité dans la perception visuelle de la verticalité. *Revue de Psychologie Appliquée*, 1956, **6**, 235–246.

Goldstein, A. G., and Chance, J. E. Effects of practice on sex-related differences in performance on embedded figures. *Psychonomic Science*, 1965, **3**, 361–362.

Goodenough, D. R., and Eagle, C. J. A modification of the embedded-figures test for use with young children. *Journal of Genetic Psychology*, 1963, **103**, 67–74.

Goodenough, D. R., and Karp, S. A. Field dependence and intellectual functioning. *Journal of Abnormal and Social Psychology*, 1961, **63**, 241–246.

Karp, S. A., and Konstadt, N. Manual for the children's embedded-figures test. Cognitive tests. Brooklyn: Authors, 1963. (P. O. Box 4, Vanderveer Station, 11210)

Karp, S. A., Witkin, H. A., and Goodenough, D. R. Alcoholism and psychological differentiation: the effect of alcohol on field dependence. *Journal of Abnormal Psychology*, 1965, **70**, 4, 262–265.

Kraidman, E. Developmental analysis of conceptual and perceptual functioning under stress and non-stress conditions. Unpublished doctoral dissertation, Clark University, 1959.

Linton, H. B. Relations between mode of perception and tendency to conform. Unpublished doctoral dissertation, Yale University, 1952.

Müller, G. E. Uber das Aubertsche Phanoman. *Zeitschrift für Psychologie*, 1916, **49**, 109–244.

Pollack, M., Kahn, R. L., Karp, E., and Fink, M. Individual differences in the perception of the upright in hospitalized psychiatric patients. Paper presented at the meeting of the Eastern Psychological Association, New York, 1960.

Schwartz, D. W., and Karp, S. A. Field dependence in a geriatric population. *Perceptual and Motor Skills*, 1967, 24, 495–504.

Winer, B. J. *Statistical Principles in Experimental Design*. New York: McGraw-Hill, 1962.

Witkin, H. A. The effect of training and of structural aids on performance in three tests of space orientation. Technical Report No. 80, 1948, Division of Research, Civil Aeronautic Authority, Washington, D. C.

Witkin, H. A., Dyk, R. B., Faterson, H. F., Goodenough, D. R., and Karp, S. A. *Psychological Differentiation*. New York: John Wiley, 1962.

Witkin, H. A., Lewis, H. B., Hertzman, M., Machover, K., Meissner, P., and Wapner, S. *Personality through Perception*. New York: Harper and Row, 1954.

3.2 Orientation

By way of David Elkind's discussion of adolescent egocentrism (Part I) the reader was introduced to the developmental psychology of Jean Piaget. It will be recalled that, according to Piaget, the developing person typically becomes capable of formal, logic thought during late pre-adolescence or early adolescence. The research reported below by Lee Yudin is an attempt to query Piaget's views on this developmental phenomenon. Of particular interest to Yudin is the extent to which the emergence of propositional logic is a function of intelligence, as measured by a conventional mental test. In other words, are there factors in addition to chronological age which influence the rate at which an individual develops increasingly complex thinking operations? Further, are there periods during which such development occurs more rapidly than in others? Yudin's concern with these questions is augmented by his interest in factors that affect the inductive concept learning efficiency of adolescents (concepts of number, form, and color).

Yudin's methodology is illustrative of many psychological studies of learning behavior, including the use of inductive concept learning materials. It is also illustrative of a major strategy for the study age-related behavioral change, namely, the *cross-sectional approach*. A cross-sectional approach to developmental study involves the simultaneous comparison of group subjects under coextensive research conditions where the critical difference between groups is chronological age. Thus Yudin has utilized identical criteria to compare 12-, 14-, and 16-year-olds otherwise similar in social class and other major variables. As the reader may have noted, the cross-sectional method stands in direct contrast to the longitudinal approach utilized by Witkin and his colleagues in the preceding study. While the cross-sectional method has obvious advantages, such as time savings, its principal weakness is that a researcher cannot be assured that his comparison groups represent samples from the same general population.

RECOMMENDED READINGS

Bruner, J. S. The course of cognitive growth. *American Psychologist,* 1964, **19,** 1–15.
Freyberg, P. S. Concept development in Piagetian terms in relation to school attainment. *Journal of Educational Psychology,* 1966, **57,** 164–168.
Jacobsen, L. S. *et al.* Relationship of intelligence and mediating processes to concept learning. *Journal of Educational Psychology,* 1969, **60,** 109–112.
Yudin, Lee, and Kates, Solis L. Concept attainment and adolescent development. *Journal of Educational Psychology,* 1963, **54,** 177–182.

3.2 Formal Thought in Adolescence as a Function of Intelligence

Lee William Yudin, IRVING SCHWARTZ INSTITUTE FOR CHILDREN AND YOUTH, PHILADELPHIA, PENNSYLVANIA

The purpose of this research was to investigate the development of concept attainment among adolescent males of low, middle, and high intelligence and to compare and contrast the attainment of concepts of color, number, and form, respectively. According to Inhelder and Piaget (1958), adolescence represents the stage when the concrete operations of childhood, with their emphasis on elementary logical groupings, gradually give way to the development of logical operations, and when the ability to reason by hypothesis becomes permanent. Yudin (1962; 1964) and Yudin and Kates (1963) have shown that 14- and 16-year-old males of

Reprinted from *Child Development,* 1966, **37,** 697–708, by permission of the author and the Society for Research in Child Development.

average intelligence are in fact superior in concept-attainment efficiency and strategies to 12-year-old males of similar IQ. In addition, they found no significant differences between the former two groups. What has not been made clear is whether adolescents of dissimilar intelligence will show this same pattern of development from age 12 to age 14 to age 16, or whether the attainment of formal thought and propositional logic will vary as a function of intellectual level.

Heidbreder (1946; 1947) has demonstrated that there is a rather definite and unchanging order with which concepts are attained. Her Ss repeatedly attained concepts more easily in going from the more to the less thinglike, in going from concepts of objects to concepts of form to concepts of color and, last, to concepts of number. Kates and Yudin (1964) and Yudin (1962; 1964) have shown that concepts of number are significantly more difficult to attain than concepts of color or form, while the latter two are of equal difficulty. The present study will explore this relation between the process of attainment and the nature of the concept type in a counterbalanced design which eliminates the confounding influence of practice and previous experience in the attainment of concepts.

This present research utilizes a reception paradigm defined as a set of conditions where Ss are presented with a series of instances which vary in accordance with a given schedule of information. Under this procedure, an individual has freedom, not in the instances he encounters, but only in the hypotheses he chooses to test in determining the relevant attributes from the nonrelevant, that is, in determining the criteria for acceptance. In a reception paradigm the instances presented to Ss can be either positive or negative, and they can either confirm a previous hypothesis or infirm it. These four contingencies are independent and mutually exclusive, and they exhaust the possibilities for testing particular hypotheses. The manner in which an individual attempts to deal with the information that is presented to him offers valuable clues for determining his level of cognitive development. Those individuals who maintain or alter a previous hypothesis on the basis of the information conveyed by the present instance and all previous instances can be said to be following an "ideal" strategy. In this manner a person will arrive at the correct concept on the basis of a minimum number of events encountered.

When the maintaining or changing of a hypothesis is compatible with the information conveyed by the present instance only, an individual is said to be following a "compatible" strategy and failing to assimilate fully the information presented. When a hypothesis is maintained in the face of an infirming instance or changed in the face of a confirming instance, an individual is following an "incompatible" strategy. In addition to defining the strategy or approach utilized by an individual in concept attainment, one can also note his efficiency. We would thus be interested in the presence or absence of perceptual errors (the offering of a hypothesis that is incompatible with the information presented by the present instance) as well as the amount of information required for attainment.

The following hypotheses are tested in this study.

(1) Intelligence is significantly related to concept-attainment performance. The greater the intelligence of S, the fewer instances that will be required for the attainment of concepts, the greater will be the percentage of strategies followed of an ideal nature, the smaller the percentages of strategies followed of a compatible and incompatible nature, and the fewer the perceptual errors.

(2) Among Ss of average intelligence, the performance of 12-year-olds is less efficient when compared with 14- and 16-year-olds. These 12-year-olds will require more instances for concept attainment, will follow more strategies defined as compatible and incompatible and fewer defined as ideal, and will make more perceptual errors. In addition, 14- and 16-year-olds of average intelligence will not differ in concept-attainment performance as measured.

(3) The development of formal thought among Ss of low intelligence is different from that of Ss of average intelligence. The attainment of logical operations is delayed among low-intelligence Ss and does not appear as a primary approach until the age period 14–16. Hence, no differences in performance from age 12 to age 14 are manifest. However, these same 14-year-olds as compared with these 16-year-olds (of low intelligence) will require a greater number of instances for attainment, will follow greater percentages of compatible and incompatible strategies and fewer percentages of ideal strategies in attaining the concepts, and will make a greater number of perceptual errors.

(4) Among Ss of high intelligence, age is negatively related to concept attainment in that younger Ss will require more instances for attainment, will follow more compatible and incompatible strategies and fewer ideal strategies, and will make more perceptual errors.

(5) Concepts of number are more difficult to attain than either concepts of color or concepts of form, and hence Ss require a greater number of instances, follow more compatible and incompatible strategies, make more perceptual errors, and follow fewer ideal strategies. In addition, performance in the attainment of concepts of color and form does not differ as measured.

METHOD

Subjects

There were 36 boys at each of the age levels, 12, 14, and 16. All *Ss* were within 6 months of their birthday and were enrolled in the same public school system in a small Massachusetts community of approximately 20,000 people. All 16-year-olds were tested in the town's one high school, while the younger children were tested in different buildings of the same elementary school. There were no major social-class differences among the different school locations (almost the entire community could be designated as lower-middle class), and all *Ss* tested were white. Within each age group, *Ss* were divided into three subgroups of 12 *Ss* each on the basis of their intelligence test scores on the Otis Beta and their average school achievement level as measured by the California Achievement Test. The low-intelligence subgroup ranged in IQ from 80 to 95 with a mean of 88.94. The *Ss* in the middle-intelligence subgroup had IQ's which ranged from 96 to 110 with a mean of 102.80, while the high-intelligence subgroup had IQ's which ranged from 115 to 130 with a mean of 121.26. All the *Ss* in the low-intelligence subgroup were achieving one or two grade levels below the average for their age group. The *Ss* who were achieving at their appropriate grade level were chosen for the middle-intelligence subgroup, while *Ss* who were achieving one or two grade levels above the mean for their age group were chosen for the high-intelligence subgroup.

Test Materials

A series of conceptual problems were presented to *Ss* by means of 2 × 2-inch color slides. Each slide contained either one or two instances. Each instance was composed of a figure characterized by four attributes: form, number, color, and number of borders surrounding the form(s). Each attribute was varied in three ways: Forms in each instance were one, two, or three circles (O), crosses (+), or squares (□). These forms were shown in red(R), green(G), or black(B), surrounded by one (1b), two (2b), or three (3b) black borders. For example, one instance consisted of one red circle with three borders (1RO3b); another was two green squares with one border (2G□1b); and still another was three black crosses with two borders (3B+2b). The instances presented to the *Ss* were composed of various combinations of these attribute values. In all problems the correct concept was defined by a single attribute, such as the color, red; the type of form, circles; the number, two; the number of borders, three borders.

Procedure

The 12 *Ss* within each of the three IQ subgroups at each age level were further subdivided into six different units of two *Ss* each and presented with the two instruction problems and the six experimental problems in a different order. These same six sequences were administered to each IQ subgroup within each age level.

All *Ss* received one instruction problem which was defined by one border and a second instruction problem defined by either red, three, or crosses. For three of the sequences, the border problem was the first instruction problem, and for three it was the second. These instruction problems and their particular order were randomly assigned to the six sequences with the one restriction that the second instruction problem deal with a different attribute from the first experimental problem. Of the six experimental problems, two were of color (green and black), two of number (one and two), and two of form (square and circles). The order in which these problems were presented was randomly chosen but with the following three restrictions: (*a*) that the two problems of number, color, or form not appear in the same half of the test series (the first three problems constituted the first half and the next three the second half); (*b*) that the two problems of number, color, and form not follow each other in the test series; and (*c*) that each attribute appear equally often in each position in the test series.

The concept problems were presented by means of a series of color slides, each of which was an exemplar of the correct concept. The first slide shown for each problem (the focus instance) was a single instance. Each succeeding slide contained this focus instance and an additional instance which differed in only one attribute value from the focus slide. For example, for the instruction problem "crosses," the focus slide was $2G + 2b$. The second slide showed this same $2G + 2b$ but with an additional instance $2R + 2b$ beneath it, thus indicating that color was not the correct concept (all instances have to show the *same* correct attribute and these two instances were of *different* color). A third slide showed the same focus instance and also $2G + 3b$). This slide eliminated borders as the relevant attribute. The fourth slide again showed the focus instance and also $1G + 2b$, thus eliminating the number of forms as the relevant attribute. Since neither the color of the forms, the number of borders, nor the number of forms was the relevant attribute, the type of forms, in this case "crosses," was the correct concept. After the focus slide, each succeeding cycle of three slides contained sufficient information to enable *Ss* to eliminate the nondefining attributes and to arrive at the correct concept. Ten slides were provided for each concept problem with *Ss* in groups of approximately six writing down their best guess about the correct concept. After recording their guess on an answer sheet, Ss were required to cover their hypotheses or guesses with a form provided by E. This form also provided Ss with a list of the abbreviations to be used in recording their guesses.

All Ss attained the two instruction problems with the assistance of E. To provide uniformity, all instructions and information concerning the nature of the test situation were transmitted by means of a tape recorder. To insure that Ss had received sufficient information and training to understand the procedure involved in the attainment of concepts, the following criteria were used as the basis for including each S. For the two instruction problems, (a) a guess had to be indicated after each instance was presented, (b) S had to offer the correct guess at that point where sufficient information had been provided to attain the concept, and (c) there had to be adequate comprehension of the nature of the single-attribute guess.

The dependent variables were the following: (a) Number of instances required for attainment. The S was considered to have attained the concept after he indicated the correct concept with no subsequent incorrect hypotheses. (b) Percentage of ideal strategies. This was calculated by dividing the number of ideal strategies followed by S until attainment of the concept by the total number of instances required for attainment. (c) Percentage of compatible strategies. This was calculated by dividing the number of compatible strategies followed by S until attainment of the concept by the total number of instances required for attainment. (d) Percentage of incompatible strategies. This was calculated by dividing the number of incompatible strategies followed by S by the total number of instances required for attainment. (e) Number of perceptual errors. This dependent variable indicated the number of times S offered a hypothesis which was not compatible with the information conveyed by the presenting instance.

All Ss solved the same six problems (but some, of course, in a different order). Each problem was introduced as a new and different problem to Ss, who were advised that *any one* of the four attributes might be the correct concept regardless of the attribute value that might have been correct for the previous problem.

RESULTS

Intelligence (First Hypothesis)

The Duncan Range test (Edwards, 1960, pp. 136–140) indicated that all dependent variables significantly differentiated the concept-attainment performance of Ss as a function of intelligence, with the exception of the dependent variable perceptual error (Table 1). Thus, these Ss of higher intelligence required significantly fewer instances to attain the concepts, followed greater percentages of strategies of the ideal type, and smaller percentages of strategies of the compatible and incompatible type. In addition, *Ss* in the low- and middle-intelligence subgroups made significantly more perceptual errors than those in the high-intelligence subgroup. The difference between the low- and middle-intelligence subgroups on this dependent variable was in the expected direction but failed to reach statistical significance.

TABLE 1. SUMMARY OF THE RESULTS OF DUNCAN RANGE TESTS BY INTELLIGENCE AND CONCEPT TYPE

	Number of Instances	Number of Perceptual Errors	Percentage of Ideal Strategies	Percentage of Compatible Strategies	Percentage of Incompatible Strategies
	$M_1:M_2$ [a]	$M_1:M_2$	$M_1:M_2$	$M_1:M_2$	$M_1:M_2$
Intelligence:					
Low vs. middle	7.57:5.48	.746:.477	43.15:65.92	37.03:25.26	19.86:8.92
Significance	<.05	N.S.	<.05	<.05	<.05
Low vs. high	7.57:4.55	.736:.130	43.15:78.56	37.05:17.90	19.86:3.67
Significance	<.05	<.05	<.05	<.05	<.05
Middle vs. high	5.48:4.55	.477:.130	65.92:78.56	25.26:17.90	8.92:3.67
Significance	<.05	<.05	<.05	<.05	<.05
Concept type:					
Color vs.					
number	4.90:7.70	.338:.634	72.46:45.36	17.84:42.51	9.43:12.22
Significance	<.05	<.05	<.05	<.05	N.S.
Color vs. form	4.90:4.96	.338:.370	72.46:69.81	17.84:19.83	9.43:10.80
Significance	N.S.	N.S.	N.S.	N.S.	N.S.
Number vs.					
form	7.76:4.96	.634:.370	45.36:69.81	51.24:19.83	12.22:10.80
Significance	<.05	<.05	<.05	<.05	N.S.

[a] M_1 = first mean; M_2 = second mean.

Age and the Middle-Intelligence Subgroup (Second Hypothesis)

The second hypothesis was fully confirmed. The 12-year-olds of average intelligence were significantly less efficient in concept attainment than either the 14- or 16-year-olds (Table 2). These former *Ss* required a significantly greater number of instances to attain the concepts, followed significantly fewer percentages of ideal strategies, followed higher percentages of compatible and incompatible strategies, and made a significantly greater number of perceptual errors. As further hypothesized, there were no significant differences on any of the dependent variables between the 14- and 16-year-old Ss.

TABLE 2. SUMMARY OF THE RESULTS OF DUNCAN RANGE TESTS
BY AGE AND INTELLIGENCE

	Number of Instances	Number of Perceptual Errors	Percentage of Ideal Strategies	Percentage of Compatible Strategies	Percentage of Incompatible Strategies
	$M_1:M_2$ [a]	$M_1:M_2$	$M_1:M_2$	$M_1:M_2$	$M_1:M_2$
Low intelligence:					
12 vs. 14	8.11:8.00	1.403:5.84	35.83:37.84	39.88:44.61	25.51:17.42
Significance	N.S.	<.05	N.S.	N.S.	N.S.
12 vs. 16	8.11:6:60	1.403:.222	35.83:55.77	39.85:26.63	25.51:16.64
Significance	<.05	<.05	<.05	<.05	N.S.
14 vs. 16	8.00:6.60	.584:.222	37.84:55.77	44.61:26.63	17.42:16.64
Significance	<.05	N.S.	<.05	<.05	N.S.
Middle intelligence:					
12 vs. 14	6.71:4.81	.931:.250	49.72:71.64	33.88:22.86	16.81:5.45
Significance	<.05	<.05	<.05	<.05	<.05
12 vs. 16	6.71:4.93	.931:.250	49.72:76.40	33.88:19.03	16.81:4.50
Significance	<.05	<.05	<.05	<.05	<.05
14 vs. 16	4.81:4.93	.250:.250	71.64:76.40	22.86:19.03	5.45:4.50
Significance	N.S.	N.S.	N.S.	N.S.	N.S.
High intelligence:					
12 vs. 14	5.31:4.31	.181:.125	67.99:77.64	27.16:16.88	4.59:5.46
Significance	N.S.	N.S.	N.S.	<.05	N.S.
12 vs. 16	5.31:3.89	.181:.083	67.99:90.05	27.16:9.67	4.59:.96
Significance	<.05	N.S.	<.05	<.05	N.S.
14 vs. 16	4.31:3.89	.125:.083	77.64:90.05	16.88:9.67	5.46:.96
Significance	N.S.	N.S.	N.S.	N.S.	N.S.

[a] M_1 = first mean; M_2 = second mean.

Age and the Low-Intelligence Subgroup (Third Hypothesis)

Duncan Range Tests indicated, as hypothesized, no significant differences in concept-attainment performance between the 12- and 14-year-old low-intelligence Ss for the number of instances or the percentages of ideal, compatible, or incompatible strategies (Table 2). Contrary to that which was expected, the 14-year-olds made significantly fewer perceptual errors than the 12-year-olds (Table 2). Unlike the adolescents of average intelligence who show no significant gains in efficiency from age 14 to 16, low-intelligence adolescents make significant gains during this period and make greater use of formal thought, employing efficient hypothesis testing in their problem solving. The 16-year-olds of low intelligence, as hypothesized, required significantly fewer instances for concept attainment, followed significantly greater percentages of ideal strategies, and significantly fewer percentages of compatible strategies (Table 2). It should be noted that their performance at age 16 was below that of the adolescents of average intelligence at the same age. The differences between these Ss for the dependent-variables percentage of incompatible strategies and number of perceptual errors was in the expected direction but failed to reach statistical significance (Table 2).

Age and the High-Intelligence Subgroup (Fourth Hypothesis)

The fourth hypothesis was, for the most part, not supported (Table 2). The only significant developmental findings were for the dependent-variable percentage of compatible strategies, with the high-intelligence 14-year-olds following significantly fewer of these strategies than the 12-year-olds of high intelligence. However, all differences between the 12-year-olds and the 14-year-olds and between the 14-year-olds and the 16-year-olds were in the expected direction except for the dependent-variable percentage of incompatible strategies. That the performance of these Ss did in fact improve is indicated by the findings that the 16-year-olds of high intelligence required significantly fewer instances for attainment, followed a significantly greater percentage of ideal strategies, and a significantly lower percentage of compatible strategies than the 12-year-olds (Table 2).

Concept Type (Fifth Hypothesis)

The fifth hypothesis was almost fully confirmed. In attaining concepts of number as compared with concepts of color or form, Ss required a significantly greater number of instances, followed significantly lower percentages of the ideal strategy, significantly greater percentages of compatible strategies, and made a significantly greater number of perceptual errors (Table 2). Further, Ss followed more incompatible strategies in attaining the number concepts as compared with the color and form concepts, but the differences were not significant. As hypothesized, there were no significant differences for any of the dependent variables in attaining concepts of color or form (Table 2).

The first guess that is offered for each problem represents a condition where the law of probability should operate. With the sequence of problems randomized from S to S and their being told that any one of the concept types could be the relevant attribute for a given problem, it might be expected that each of the four attributes would be offered as the first hypothesis with equal frequency. When we compare by χ^2 the frequency with which the four concept types were offered initially according to the ordinal position in the series, the following results are obtained. All six ordinal positions in the series are found to contain frequencies of the four concept types significantly different from that which would be expected on the basis of chance. All χ^2s are significant at or beyond the .05 level (Table 3). Further, in all but the first ordinal position (the first concept problem presented to Ss), the concept of number is found to be offered significantly less frequently than would be expected, while concepts other than number are offered significantly more frequently. For the first ordinal position, the difference between guesses of the concept number and guesses other than number was not significantly different. It should be added that, as experience increases, number appears to be offered as the initial guess less frequently than concepts other than number.

TABLE 3. A χ^2 COMPARISON OF THE FIRST HYPOTHESIS OFFERED BY Ss ACCORDING TO THE ORDINAL POSITION IN THE SERIES (OPS)

OPS	Number	Form	Color	Border	χ^2	p
1	18	38	25	27	7.67	< .02
2	17	25	34	32	6.59	< .05
3	16	35	23	34	9.26	< .01
4	14	15	36	43	24.07	< .001
5	13	35	23	37	13.93	< .001
6	13	25	33	37	12.44	< .001

DISCUSSION

Adolescent Development and Intelligence

Inhelder and Piaget's (1958) conception of adolescent development involves a reorganization of thought patterns (characterized by the presence of logical operations) beginning at about 12 years of age and reaching an equilibrium at about 14–16 years of age. That these older Ss of average intelligence are more efficient in problem solving than the younger ones is evident, but what is also highlighted is that the former individuals utilize strategies that are different from those followed by the younger Ss. A 14- or 16-year-old of average intelligence is more likely than a 12-year-old of similar intelligence to assimilate incoming information in an orderly and efficient manner. He is more capable of dealing with that information which is directly perceptible (thus making significantly fewer perceptual errors) and also of deciding when to maintain or to change a previously formulated hypothesis, being able to adequately consider both present and past information (thus following significantly greater percentages of ideal strategies and significantly lower percentages of compatible and incompatible strategies).

We have indicated above that individuals less favorably endowed intellectually (IQ range 70–89) manifest a retardation in their development and thus do not begin to fully utilize formal operations until 14–16 years of age. Whether this development will reach a point of equilibrium (from 16 to 18 years of age) comparable to that seen by the average-intelligence *Ss* from age 14 to 16, or whether these low-intelligence *Ss* will increase their performance still further and become more efficient, is a matter for further study.

The *Ss* of superior intelligence show an efficient use of logical operations even at age 12, indicating that development of these types of mental operations has begun for them earlier than for the low- or middle-intelligence subgroups. In addition, changes in performance from age 12 to age 14 to age 16 are more nearly linear, with a considerable (but not significant) increase with increasing age. It is exactly this quality of the mind, the ability to continue to profit from experience and to manifest continual growth, which characterizes the development of an individual of superior intelligence.

In a study of concept attainment by college students (mean age of 18), Kates and Yudin (1964) found their *Ss* capable of attaining concepts at a level above that reached by almost all of the *Ss* in the present research. This would indicate that further gains are made by the intellectually gifted from age 16 to age 18 on this type of concept task.

The most important implications of these findings are not that younger adolescents are less efficient in concept attainment than older adolescents or that low-intelligence adolescents are less efficient than brighter adolescents but, rather, that an interaction of both age and intelligence contributes toward cognitive development. The attainment of logical operations as an integral aspect of functioning is not uniform or rigid for all adolescents. All are capable of functioning in this most efficient manner, but not to the same extent. Thus, while previously we might have conceived of development as following an unchanging pattern with adolescence representing the focal point for the switch to hypothesis formation and testing, we now can understand more clearly that individuals of differing abilities not only achieve at different levels but that they follow significantly different patterns of development in their obtaining similar, more efficient approaches to problem solving. Development, whether accelerated or retarded, brings with it a shift in emphasis from concreteness to abstractness and a new way of dealing with facts and relations, but experience alone is not sufficient to bring about this shift.

Concept Type

As Heidbreder (1946; 1947) and others (Kates & Yudin, 1964; Yudin, 1962; 1964) have indicated, the attainment of concepts takes place in a hierarchy. The present results indicate that number concepts are more difficult to attain and that they impose increasing cognitive demands upon *Ss*. As a result, strategies utilized in the attainment of these concepts become significantly less efficient, and the ability of *Ss* to perceive adequately the environment and to utilize effectively the information provided decreases. It should be noted that to attain the number concept it is necessary to go beyond the directly perceptible in order to group the forms that are presented by the instances and to assign a symbol to them. For the color or form concepts, the grouping operation described above need not be carried out. Furthermore, the properties of "thingness" have to be discarded; the constancy, the shape-boundedness, and the dynamic properties of the forms all may interfere with the salience of the grouping operation.

The present findings also indicate that the number concepts were offered as the initial hypothesis for the various concept problems with the smallest frequency of all the concept types. It thus appears that number concepts are not only more difficult to attain but that a "perception" of number as a defining attribute is not readily aroused. Bruner (1957) points out that it is the ready perceiver who is able to proceed with a minimum of stimulus inputs and is thus able to use cognitive readiness not only for perceiving what *is* before him but what is *likely* to be before him. Bruner has further indicated that "the likelihood that a sensory input will be categorized in terms of a given category is not only a matter of fit between sensory input and category specification, it depends also on the accessibility, that is, given a sensory input with equally good fit to two nonoverlapping categories, the more accessible of the two categories would 'capture' the input" (p. 132). In the present research, the first guess for each problem provides a sensory input with equally good fit to four nonoverlapping categories, and results indicate that number is the least accessible. It is not surprising, therefore, that to attain a concept of number, *Ss* require significantly more stimulus input than they do for the other concepts. Their reduced efficiency is accompanied by the adoption of more primitive strategies (from a genetic standpoint), and all *Ss* tend to operate at a more concrete level.

SUMMARY

Adolescent males of 12, 14, and 16 were subdivided on the basis of their intelligence and presented with 2 instruction problems and 6 experimental problems. Results indicated that the development of formal thought in adolescence is an interaction of age and intelligence with significant gains being made by adolescents of average intelligence from 12 to 14 and by low-intelligence adolescents from 14 to 16. Ss of superior intelligence show an almost linear development. Further, concepts of number are significantly more difficult to attain than either concepts of color or form, but no significant differences are noted between the latter 2.

REFERENCES

Bruner, J. On perceptual readiness. *Psychological Review*, 1957, **64**, 123–152.
Edwards, A. *Experimental Design in Psychological Research*. New York: Holt, Rinehart and Winston, 1960.
Heidbreder, Edna. The attainment of concepts: II. The problem. *Journal of Genetic Psychology*, 1946, **35**, 190–223b.
Heidbreder, Edna. The attainment of concepts: III. The process. *Journal of Psychology*, 1947, **24**, 93–138.
Inhelder, Barbel, and Piaget, J. *The Growth of Logical Thinking*. London: Routledge, 1958.
Kates, S. L., and Yudin, L. W. Concept attainment and memory. *Journal of Educational Psychology*, 1964, **55**, 103–109.
Yudin, L. W. A developmental study of concept attainment. Unpublished Master's thesis, University of Massachusetts, 1962.
Yudin, L. W. Concept attainment and intelligence: a developmental study. Unpublished doctoral dissertation, University of Massachusetts, 1964.
Yudin, L. W., and Kates, S. L. Concept attainment and adolescent development. *Journal of Educational Psychology*, 1963, **55**, 1–9.

3.3 *Orientation*

In Stuart Golann's review of creativity (Part II) it was concluded that a functional understanding of this phenomenon may be enhanced by the study of personality factors. This approach to the study of creativity has resulted in several tentative contentions. One of these suggests that a unique aggregate of personality characteristics defines the creative adult, regardless of occupational speciality. A second is more presumptive, namely, that certain personality characteristics which may develop early in life predispose one toward creative productivity. Both of these contentions have provided the authors of the following research with a springboard from which to explore further the personality–creativity relationship. Involved are comparisons of more and less creative adolescents and adults for the purpose of determining whether basic traits or characteristics differentiate levels of creativity within both age groups. Taken as a whole, this study is anchored in a concern for the psychometric identification and prediction of creative potential. Perhaps the reader will be tempted to consider practical alternatives to the psychometric method for such purposes.

The principal psychometric tool employed in the present study, the California Psychological Inventory, is among the most respected of its type. All such measures, however, require for their validity the assumption that a respondent's test behavior corresponds to his behavior in natural (non-test) settings. Even if this assumption is met, an issue created by the present study involves whether personality data are sufficient by themselves for the prediction of creative performance. The reader is alerted to the researchers' discussion of this issue as well as the extent to which their general findings reinforce previous related research. Also notable is this study's finding concerning the apparent variation with age in personality characteristics facilitative to creativity. Finally, this study goes a long way to counter certain myths about the nature of creative people and their behavior. Especially significant for the adolescent sample is the emphasis upon "disciplined effectiveness" disclosed by the test data.

As in the Witkin et al. (1967) study presented earlier, a certain complexity in statistical reporting procedures marks the present research report. This complexity may be traced primarily to the authors' use of a technique, known as factor analysis. Briefly, this technique enables a researcher to extract from correlational matrices common, or relatively independent factors which describe clusters of closely related measurements. In this way vast amounts of test or observational data may be reduced to their lowest common denominators. Ultimately, this simplifies the task of codifying research data in broad, descriptive terms.

RECOMMENDED READINGS

MacKinnon, Donald W. Assessing creative persons. *Journal of Creative Behavior*, 1967, 1, 291–304.

Schaefer, Charles E., and Anastasi, Anne. A biographical inventory for identifying creativity in adolescent boys. *Journal of Applied Psychology*, 1968, **52**, 42–48.

Stein, Morris I. Creativity. In Edgar F. Borgatta and William W. Lambert (Eds.) *Handbook of Personality Theory and Research*. Chicago: Rand McNally, 1968, 900–942.

Williams, Frank E. Intellectual creativity and the teacher. *Journal of Creative Behavior*, 1967, **1**, 173–180.

3.3　Personality Characteristics which Differentiate Creative Male Adolescents and Adults*

Morris B. Parloff, NATIONAL INSTITUTE OF MENTAL HEALTH
Lois-ellin Datta, NATIONAL INSTITUTE OF MENTAL HEALTH
Marianne Kleman, BERKELEY FAMILY RESEARCH CENTER
Joseph H. Handlon, CASE WESTERN RESERVE UNIVERSITY

Creative performance is generally viewed as a consequence of a complex interaction among such variables as cognitive capacities, specific personality characteristics, and intercurrent environmental influences. Increasingly, the belief has grown among those who are particularly concerned with the role of personality that creative performance is stimulated, facilitated, and maintained by the presence of a rather limited and specifiable set of personality characteristics and patterns shared by all creative men. If there were in fact a strong and stable association between creativity and personality traits from childhood to adulthood then we could more confidently identify potentially creative individuals and could more effectively foster their development in order that their creative capacities might be given the fullest expression.

Independent surveys of the literature concerning relationships between personality and creativity have been performed by Stein (1962) and Barron (1965). They report that the more creative individual is differentiated from his less creative peer in that he is more assertive, forceful, and aggressive; less inhibited and less conventional; more bohemian, more radical, and more resistant to pressures toward conformity in thinking; lower in authoritarian values; more highly motivated and self-

Reprinted from the *Journal of Personality*, 1968, **36**, 528–552, by permission of the authors and the Duke University Press.

* We wish to express our gratitude to Barry Wolfe, Ann Drake, Jean Carter, and Claude Southerly for their assistance in gathering and processing these data. We are indebted to Drs. Karen Pettigrew and Samuel Greenhouse for their advice and aid in performing the statistical analyses.

disciplined; higher in impulse control; more persistent; higher in energy output; more constructively critical and less contented; more versatile and widely informed; broader in range of interests; and more open to feelings and emotions. He is also more introverted, reserved, and detached from interpersonal relationships (but not lacking in sensitivity or insight); higher in ego strength and stability (despite the fact that his performance on usual measures of adjustment may appear to be somewhat deviant); and he shows a stronger preference for aesthetic values, abstract thinking, and for comprehensiveness and elegance in explanations.

Despite this apparent consensus among investigators, these findings must be interpreted cautiously. The original studies are frequently not comparable due to marked differences in the definitions of criterion groups, in the selection of control groups, and in the choice of personality measures. Interpretation is further complicated in that the creative adult was studied only after he had achieved professional prominence. Such individuals may reasonably be expected to enjoy a reality-based sense of high self-esteem, a greater sense of autonomy, and to be less inhibited, more assertive, more resistant to conformity in thinking than their less honored colleagues. It is not clear, therefore, whether some or all of the personality characteristics which have been reported as differentiating the more from the less creative adults are in fact predisposing to or are the consequence of earlier creative performance.

The fact that personality characteristics have been found to differentiate between more and less creative groups *within* a specified vocation (Roe, 1949, 1952; Stein, 1957; Gough, 1961; Helson, 1961; MacKinnon, 1962a, 1962b; and Barron, 1963) has frequently been cited as evidence that "creative men," whatever their fields, share a unique set of personality features. However, studies which cut *across* two or more vocational fields (Roe, 1953; Cattell & Drevdahl, 1955; and Chambers, 1964) have thus far failed to present compelling evidence to support such a generalization.

Even less clear is the evidence for the common assumption that personality characteristics associated with creative performance among adults would also characterize the creative or potentially creative adolescents and children (Rivlin, 1959; Cashdan & Welsh, 1966).

The present investigation is addressed to two issues: (1) to test further the claim that creative adults, independent of field, share a common set of differentiating personality characteristics, and (2) to test whether such personality characteristics may be interpreted as conducive to or consequent to creative performance.

The first question was tested by a reanalysis of personality data obtained by investigators at the Institute for Personality Assessment and

Research (IPAR) at the University of California, Berkeley. In their studies of creative adults—architects, mathematicians, research scientists, and professional writers—the IPAR researchers had given careful attention to the selection of the criterion and control groups, and had administered appropriate and consistent batteries of personality measures.[1]

Although researchers at IPAR had individually studied groups of more and less creative adults, they had not done an overall analysis of levels of creativity, vocational affiliation, and the interaction of these two variables.

The second question could not be tested directly. No data were available concerning the personalities of these adults prior to their public recognition. An indirect test was undertaken by administering the same personality instrument employed in the study of the adult sample to a highly selected adolescent sample. The adolescents included two groups of male high school seniors who differed on judged creativity but were comparable on such variables as intelligence, science aptitude, level of school achievement (grades), and socio-economic status. Both high school groups had received a comparably high degree of recognition for their academic achievements.

Support for the hypothesis that a unique set of personality characteristics may be predisposing to creative performance would be clearest if both the more creative adolescent and adult groups were differentiated from their respective less creative groups in the same direction on the same set of personality dimensions. Support would also be inferred if the more creative groups in both age samples were mutually differentiated from their respective controls on an overlapping subset of personality dimensions. Such findings would suggest that personality characteristics may be conducive to creativity but that the facilitating personality features may vary from age period to age period. Similarly, if the adolescent groups were found to be differentiated from each other but the more creative and less creative groups of adults were not differentiated on any personality characteristics, support for the hypothesis would be equivocal but not precluded. Creative adults may have shown predisposing personality characteristics as adolescents comparable to those found among creative adolescents, but such personality differentiations were modified with age.

Lack of support for the hypothesis would be clearest if neither the

[1] We wish to express our deep appreciation to Dr. Donald MacKinnon, director of IPAR, and to the other members of his staff who generously furnished these data and invaluable assistance to the present writers. Special acknowledgement is made of the unstinting cooperation of Drs. Wallace B. Hall, Harrison Gough, Frank Barron, Richard Crutchfield, and Ravenna Helson.

adult nor the adolescent more and less creative groups were differentiated on any personality characteristics. Lack of support would also be inferred if only the adult and not the adolescent more creative groups were differentiated from their controls on personality dimensions.

METHOD

Adolescent Sample

The adolescent sample selected was drawn from more than 5,000 successful male entrants to the 22nd and 24th Annual Science Talent Search (STS). The stated aim of the STS competition is "to select from the nation's high school seniors those giving promise of being the creative scientists of tomorrow (Davis, 1963, p. 3)." From these applicants only those who scored above the 80th percentile on a nationally administered science aptitude examination[2] were invited to participate in our study. Of the 1,030 eligible, a total of 938 subjects (91 percent) accepted our invitation and completed the personality measures. By a criterion described below, 266 were classified as "more creative" and the remaining 672 as "less creative." No reliable differences were found in the rate of participation of these two groups.

A summary of the number of subjects classified by creativity level and vocation is presented in Table 1. Eight vocational groupings were identified in the adolescent sample. The less creative sample was found to be underrepresented in the area of mathematics and somewhat overrepresented in chemistry and engineering. In view of this, data analyses were performed to correct for effects of vocational imbalance in both the more and less creative groups.

In comparing the more and less creative groups no reliable differences were found between group means on the following variables: age (17.7), Science Aptitude Test[3] (50.03), Scholastic Aptitude Test-Verbal (681.5), high school grade-point average (3.7), socio-economic status (2.19),[4] and birth order (62.5 percent were first born or only children). Group differences were found on geographical and religious background variables. Forty-four percent of the more creative group

[2] The Science Aptitude Test was devised and is annually revised by Harold Edgerton, director of Performance Research, Inc., Washington, D.C.

[3] The raw scores for the sample drawn from the 22nd and 24th Annual Science Talent Search were separately transformed into standard scores and these scores were then pooled. The distribution of scores was limited to those representing the 80th percentile and above for the national samples tested in 1963 and 1965.

[4] The Hollingshead-Redlich Two Factor Index, which is based on paternal education and occupation, was used. Level 1 indicates the highest SES level.

TABLE 1. VOCATIONAL INTEREST DISTRIBUTION IN THE MORE AND LESS CREATIVE ADOLESCENT GROUPS USED IN CPI ANALYSES

Vocational choice	More creative		Less creative		Totals	
	N	Pct.	N	Pct.	N	Pct.
Mathematics	59	22.18	97	14.43	156	16.63
Physics	65	24.44	188	27.98	253	26.97
Biology and medicine	31	11.65	76	11.31	107	11.41
Chemistry	22	8.27	87	12.94	109	11.62
Engineering	18	6.77	79	11.76	97	10.34
Biochemistry	24	9.02	49	7.29	73	7.78
Other science	27	10.15	59	8.78	86	9.17
Nonscience	20	7.52	37	5.51	57	6.08
Totals	266	100.00	672	100.00	938	100.00

came from the Northeastern states, against only 38 percent of the less creative group; 51 percent of the more creative group lived in metropolitan areas having populations of more than 500,000 in contrast to 41 percent of the less creative group; and 46 percent of the more creative group reported Jewish parentage, as opposed to 32 percent of the less creative group.

It was assumed that the geographical background differences are unlikely to account for systematic personality differences between the two groups. Since religious differences may be associated with personality variables, we analyzed relationships between personality and creativity for students of Jewish and non-Jewish backgrounds. The observed relationships between creativity and personality were consistent for both religious background groups. Findings are therefore reported here without reference to religion. A detailed analysis of the association between religious background and creativity of 536 subjects of this sample has been discussed by Datta (1967).

In view of the comparability of the more and less creative groups on a number of aptitude and demographic variables, if personality differences were found, they could reasonably be expected to covary with creativity.

Judging Procedure: Adolescent Sample

Each entrant had submitted to a panel of judges a report of a research project which he had selected and independently conducted. Each project was independently rated by pairs of judges trained by Science Service, Inc. Judges represented different areas of specialization, such as mathematics, physics, chemistry, biology, etc. Projects were rated on a creativity scale ranging from A (high) to E (low). If the ratings of the pair of judges differed by more than one letter grade, the judges met to reconcile the discrepancies. On the basis of these ratings we classed subjects receiving grades of A and B in the "more creative" sample,[5] and all those receiving lower grades were placed in the "less creative" group.

The specific guidelines and instructions given to the raters by the administrators of the STS were quite broad. In the judging process two major criteria were used for evaluating the creativity of a project report: novelty and effectiveness. A novel project demonstrated ideas, concepts, and hypotheses which were judged to be original in a given area of study. (This definition was sometimes modified to represent originality from the viewpoint of the individual producing the area, rather than from the vantage point of the field.) Effectiveness was assessed according to the judges' standards of usefulness, tenability, plausibility, elegance, and so on, at a given point in time. Neither novelty nor effectiveness alone was sufficient to warrant the product's classification as creative. In employing this definition the judges were consistent with common practice, for the creative adult is usually identified by the value placed by his peers on a product (idea, theory, object, and so on) which he had conceived, formulated, "tested," and communicated.

Although many of the projects were judged to be of high creative caliber, the majority indicated potential rather than actual creativity. The ratings also reflected a subtle weighting of the facilities, equipment, and caliber of the teachers available to high school seniors. It is thus appropriate to identify the sample as Potentially Creative Scientists (PCS). The more creative adolescent group used in this investigation overlaps with but is more stringently selected than the group identified as "winners" in the Science Talent Search.[6]

[5] In 10 percent of the cases rated it was found that one judge had classed a project as "B" while the second judge had graded it "C." Such projects were assigned the grade of "B—" and were included in the more creative group. This practice resulted in limiting the level of absolute agreement between pairs of judges to 90 percent in the final assignment of cases to the more and less creative groups.

[6] The STS required that the subjects pass the Science Aptitude Test above the 40th percentile; the surviving subjects were then screened on a form designed to measure the quality and degree of previous achievement in science. The projects of those surviving the second hurdle were read and evaluated. (A random sample of all rejected projects was also read.) Subjects in our sample were limited to males who had passed the Science Aptitude Test above the 80th percentile. The projects of all such subjects were read and evaluated.

Adult Sample

The total adult sample consists of 200 subjects, of whom 101 were classified as "more creative" and 99 as "less creative." The sample included mathematicians, research scientists, writers, and architects. A detailed description of this sample is presented in Table 2.

TABLE 2. VOCATIONAL DISTRIBUTION AND MEAN AGE OF MORE AND LESS CREATIVE ADULT GROUPS

Vocation	More creative			Less creative			Totals		
	N	Pct.	Mean age	N	Pct.	Mean age	N	Pct.	Mean age
Mathematicians	27	26.7	38.7	29	29.3	37.9	56	28.0	38.3
Architects	40	39.6	50.9	41	41.4	50.2	81	40.5	50.5
Research scientists	15	14.9	34.1	15	15.2	36.8	30	15.0	35.5
Writers	19	18.8	48.5	14	14.1	56.7	33	16.5	52.0
Totals	101	100.0	44.7	99	100.0	45.5	200	100.0	45.1

Mathematicians   This sample was initially studied by Crutchfield (unpublished). A group of experts nominated 27 mathematicians as being outstandingly creative. A control group of 29 mathematicians judged to be of lesser creativity were selected on the basis of comparability of education and age.

Research scientists   This sample consisted initially of 45 industrial research workers, primarily physicists, mathematicians, and electronic engineers who had been studied by Gough (1957). Each subject was rated by two supervisors and by at least four of his fellow scientists. The present study was limited to the upper 15, who were classed as "more creative," and the lower 15, who comprised the "less creative" group.

Writers   Barron furnished material based on a sample of male writers: poets, novelists, and essayists who had been nominated by a panel of judges drawn from the English and drama departments of the University of California (Barron, 1965). Judges were asked to nominate writers of a conspicuously high degree of originality and creativeness. The control was composed of less creative but successful and productive writers who had clearly "made their mark." The 33 writers included 19 in the "more creative" and 14 in the "less creative" groups.

Architects   MacKinnon investigated the personality characteristics of three groups of architects representing different levels of assessed creativity (1962a, 1962b). The most creative sample (*N* = 40) was originally selected on the basis of nominations by judges who had been asked to name the 40 most creative architects in the United States. MacKinnon's original study included two control groups (Architects II and Architects III) selected from the *Directory of Architects, 1955*, who were comparable to the creative sample with respect to age and geographical location of practice. Since the subjects in Architects II had worked for one of the creative architects originally nominated, which might have reduced the variability of personality characteristics, this group was omitted from the present study. Control group III, consisting of 41 subjects, was included.

The average age of the 200 adult subjects is 45.1 years, ranging from 35.5 for the research scientists to 52.0 for the writers. The mean age of the 101 adults in the more creative sample, 44.7 years, did not differ significantly from that of the 99 less creative adults, 45.5.

Personality Measurement

Of the broad array of tests which had been administered to these samples only the California Psychological Inventory (CPI) (Gough, 1957) had been used in both the adult and adolescent studies. The CPI contains 18 scales measuring significant traits of personality that are involved in social interaction and in constructive achievement. This personality test has been used widely with school, college, and industrial populations, and has been used successfully in differentiating personality characteristics of more and less creative adults (MacKinnon, 1961).

Procedure and Design

Since the 18 scales of the CPI tend to show appreciable intercorrelation it was necessary to determine the independent dimensions represented. Although Gough has grouped these scales into four classes: (1) Poise, Ascendancy, and Self-assurance; (2) Socialization, Maturity, and Responsibility; (3) Achievement Potential and Intellectual Efficiency; and (4) Intellectual and Interest Modes, his groupings are not readily replicated (Crites, Bechtoldt, Goodstein, & Heilbrun, 1961; Leton & Walter, 1961; Mitchell & Pierce-Jones, 1960; Shure & Rogers, 1963). We therefore performed separate factor analyses for each of the present samples.

Separate correlation matrices were computed for the 18 CPI scale scores for the adolescent sample and for the adult sample. The two correlation matrices were subjected to a principal-components analysis

(Hotelling, 1933). All components with Eigenvalues greater than 1.00 were orthogonally rotated by the Varimax method (Kaiser, 1958). Each subject's score on the identified factors was determined.

Two-way analyses of variance, unweighted means solution (Winer, 1962) were performed separately for the adult and adolescent samples.[7] Two by eight analyses of variance were performed for the adolescents, representing two levels of creativity and eight vocational preference groups. The adult personality data were analyzed in two by four analyses of variance representing two levels of creativity and four vocational groupings.

To determine the strength and predictive utility of the association found between personality factors and creativity, discriminate function analyses were also computed for each sample.

RESULTS

Analyses of the CPI intercorrelation matrices for adolescent and adult samples yielded, for each sample, four factors with Eigenvalues greater than 1.00. Rotated solutions were computed by the Varimax procedure with the results shown in Table 3.

Coefficients of Congruence (Harman, 1960) were computed to determine whether similar factors had been found for the two matrices. The results indicate a high degree of similarity between the structure of the CPI for both the adolescent and adult groups since a good match is found for all factors. The Coefficients of Congruence between matching factors ranged from .96 to .86 with a mean of .91, while the coefficients for unmatched factors ranged from −.33 to .46 with a mean of .17. Since the factor analyses and rotations were completely independent, and since the samples were large and diverse, the results give strong evidence for a consistent organization of the CPI for both samples.

The four factors identified in the adolescent and adult samples in each instance accounted for a total of 69 percent of the variance (see Table 3). Analysis of the factor loadings on the CPI scales suggest the following descriptions and interpretations of the factors.

Factor I accounts for 28 percent and 23 percent of the total variance for the adolescent and adult samples respectively. The highest correlates of this component in each sample appear to be on the following scales:

[7] The original experimental design required four groups, representing the combinations of more and less creative and high and low scientific aptitude. A pilot study indicated that there were no low aptitude, high creative subjects in the STS group initially selected. Thus the final sample was limited to those who were high on the Science Aptitude Test.

TABLE 3. VARIMAX ROTATED FACTOR LOADINGS OF THE CALIFORNIA PSYCHOLOGICAL INVENTORY (CPI) FOR ADOLESCENT AND ADULT GROUPS

CPI scale	Group	Factor I	Factor II	Factor III	Factor IV
Do	Adolescent	.17	.79	−.14	.08
	Adult	.10	.80	−.18	.06
Cs	Adolescent	.29	.68	.31	−.02
	Adult	.18	.64	.35	.10
Sy	Adolescent	.21	.87	−.09	−.06
	Adult	−.15	.87	.09	.09
Sp	Adolescent	.03	.79	.27	−.23
	Adult	−.05	.77	.44	−.08
Sa	Adolescent	−.15	.86	−.07	−.02
	Adult	−.17	.83	.03	.04
Wb	Adolescent	.83	.20	.00	−.09
	Adult	.82	.16	.22	−.02
Re	Adolescent	.64	.07	−.11	.50
	Adult	.46	.10	.20	.60
So	Adolescent	.55	.00	−.37	.39
	Adult	.58	−.04	−.11	.39
Sc	Adolescent	.89	−.25	.04	.10
	Adult	.85	−.29	.15	.01

CPI scale	Group	Factor I	Factor II	Factor III	Factor IV
To	Adolescent	.78	.20	.27	.13
	Adult	.62	.29	.50	.08
Gi	Adolescent	.83	.06	.05	−.11
	Adult	.86	.05	−.06	−.10
Cm	Adolescent	.16	.21	−.55	.32
	Adult	.04	.29	−.33	.62
Ac	Adolescent	.75	.30	−.16	.21
	Adult	.72	.25	.11	.30
Ai	Adolescent	.50	.03	.64	.23
	Adult	.20	.05	.85	.11
Ie	Adolescent	.59	.44	.26	.07
	Adult	.41	.42	.54	.19
Py	Adolescent	.38	.20	.51	−.08
	Adult	.24	.03	.65	−.04
Fx	Adolescent	−.10	.06	.84	.10
	Adult	−.23	.06	.79	−.14
Fe	Adolescent	.10	−.18	.08	.84
	Adult	−.26	−.42	.27	.49
Percentage of total variance	Adolescent	28	21	12	8
	Adult	23	21	17	

355

Self-control, Good Impression, Well-being, Achievement via Conformance, Tolerance, and Socialization. The PCS sample also shows sizable loadings on scales measuring Responsibility and Intellectual Efficiency. The generality of this factor appears to be somewhat greater for the PCS sample than for the adult sample. Persons with high scores on these scales tend to be described as disciplined, painstaking, reliable; to be attentive to their impact on others; to have a comfortable sense of self-effectiveness and physical well-being; to be persistent, industrious, and capable of effective endeavor in structured settings; to be accepting of differing social beliefs and opinions; and to be efficient, persistent, productive, and reflective in the pursuit of intellectual goals.

This factor resembles the "adjustment by social conformity" factor identified by Mitchell and Pierce-Jones (1960) and the "Personal Integrity and Mental Health" factor obtained by Shure and Rogers (1963). The patterning of loadings in the present sample suggests that Factor I may best be described as *Disciplined Effectiveness*.

Factor II accounts for 21 percent of the total variance in both the adult and PCS samples. The scales which show the highest loadings on this component for both samples are Sociability, Self-acceptance, Dominance, Social Presence, and Capacity for Status. These are five of the six scales that Gough included as "Measures of Poise, Ascendancy, and Self-assurance." These scales describe an assertive, outgoing, self-confident, expressive, competitive style of relating to others. Such individuals are usually perceived as vigorous, ambitious, aggressive, and persuasive. This factor may be titled, *Assertive Self-Assurance*.

Factor III accounts for 12 percent of the total variance in the PCS sample and 17 percent of the total variance in the adult sample correlation matrix. The highest correlates of this component for both samples are Flexibility, Achievement via Independence, and Psychological Mindedness. High scorers on these scales tend to be characterized by individuality, spontaneity, self-reliance, intraception, lability, interpersonal perspicacity, and high motivation to work independently. Factor III may be entitled *Adaptive Autonomy*.

Factor IV accounts for 8 percent of the total variance in both the PCS and adult correlation matrices. For the PCS sample the only high loading occurs on the Feminity scale (.84) and the next highest loading is on Responsibility (.50); however, the latter scale has an even higher loading on Factor I (.64). The adult sample shows its highest factor loadings on Communality (.62), Responsibility (.60), and Femininity (.49). The Femininity scale loads almost as strongly on Factor II (−.42). It is to be noted that this factor tends also to be associated with the socialization scale for both samples (.39).

For the adolescents, Factor IV is perhaps best characterized by breadth of interest, sensitivity, and conscientiousness. For the adults, high scores on this factor appear to be associated with a tendency to hold and express conventional ideas, to be dependable, resourceful, sensitive, and efficient. Although this factor appears to be readily described by the general term Femininity for the PCS sample, for the adults this factor is more differentiated and suggests concern with others. Both the PCS and adult loadings have been tentatively subsumed under the term *Humanitarian Conscience*. A somewhat similar factor was described by Mitchell and Pierce-Jones (1960) with the term "Super-Ego Strength."

A summary of the mean factor scores of the more and less creative groups according to vocational preference classification is presented for adults and adolescents in Tables 4 and 5. Analyses of variance based on the CPI factor scores obtained with adult and adolescent groups are summarized in Table 6.

TABLE 4. FACTOR SCORE MEANS AND STANDARD DEVIATIONS[a] FOR MORE AND LESS CREATIVE ADULT GROUPS WITHIN VOCATIONS

	Factor I (Disciplined Effectiveness)				Factor II (Assertive Self-Assurance)			
	More creative		Less creative		More creative		Less creative	
Vocations	Mean	SD	Mean	SD	Mean	SD	Mean	SD
Architect	−3.12	6.00	4.30	4.76	.91	6.41	−.35	6.46
Writer	−4.99	7.64	−2.82	9.67	1.16	7.55	−1.09	8.90
Research scientist	2.35	4.24	1.99	6.10	4.52	6.05	3.03	5.90
Mathematician	−.99	6.72	1.52	6.45	−.95	5.39	−4.02	8.40
Totals	−1.69		1.25		1.41		−.61	

	Factor III (Adaptive Autonomy)				Factor IV (Humanitarian Conscience)			
	More creative		Less creative		More creative		Less creative	
Vocations	Mean	SD	Mean	SD	Mean	SD	Mean	SD
Architect	−1.27	5.13	−5.31	7.29	−1.23	6.16	−.09	6.98
Writer	1.43	5.40	−3.10	6.28	−.13	6.11	−2.21	7.94
Research scientist	4.00	5.88	2.43	6.21	−.25	4.46	−.78	5.92
Mathematician	4.55	5.81	2.24	6.65	2.33	9.05	1.34	7.24
Totals	2.18		−.94		.18		−.44	

[a] Factor scores multiplied by 100.

TABLE 5. FACTOR SCORE MEANS AND STANDARD DEVIATIONS[a] FOR MORE AND LESS CREATIVE ADOLESCENT GROUPS WITHIN VOCATIONS

| | Factor I (Disciplined Effectiveness) | | | | Factor II (Assertive Self-Assurance) | | | |
| | More creative | | Less creative | | More creative | | Less creative | |
Vocations	Mean	SD	Mean	SD	Mean	SD	Mean	SD
Mathematics	−.04	3.42	.36	2.98	−.21	3.32	−1.13	3.11
Physics	.61	3.07	.46	3.04	.21	3.00	0.43	3.12
Biology	−.31	3.25	−.61	2.88	1.50	3.67	1.47	3.23
Chemistry	.95	2.49	.12	3.25	.20	2.75	−.77	3.12
English	.59	3.31	−.41	3.57	.32	3.05	.17	3.17
Biochemistry	.34	3.02	−1.26	3.36	1.38	3.43	.62	2.84
Other science	.29	3.37	−.53	3.80	−1.37	3.17	−.38	3.72
Nonscience	−.06	3.14	−.91	3.43	2.61	3.29	.48	2.93
Totals	.30		−.35		.58		.00	

| | Factor III (Adaptive Autonomy) | | | | Factor IV (Humanitarian Conscience) | | | |
| | More creative | | Less creative | | More creative | | Less creative | |
Vocations	Mean	SD	Mean	SD	Mean	SD	Mean	SD
Mathematics	.92	3.25	.11	3.29	.31	3.60	.25	3.00
Physics	.27	2.70	.40	3.29	−.39	3.37	−.62	3.43
Biology	.25	3.21	−.59	2.92	−.34	2.98	.86	2.67
Chemistry	1.20	3.82	−.89	3.10	.42	2.54	.65	3.17
English	−1.18	3.20	−1.38	3.03	−.99	2.85	−.71	3.05
Biochemistry	−.32	2.97	−.15	3.63	1.12	3.25	.26	3.69
Other science	.52	3.42	−.15	2.83	−.22	3.13	−.10	3.40
Nonscience	2.44	1.78	.56	3.82	1.13	3.28	.06	2.79
Totals	.51		−.26		.13		.08	

[a] Multiplied by 100.

On Factor I (Disciplined Effectiveness) the main effect attributable to creativity was significant for both adults and adolescents ($p < .01$ and $p < .05$, respectively). An inspection of the means (see Tables 4 and 5) indicates that the more creative adolescents are higher on this factor than the less creative adolescents, whereas precisely the reverse discrimination is found between the more and less creative adult groups. While the adolescent groups show no main effect for vocation, the adult groups show significant effects for both vocation ($p < .01$) and the interaction

TABLE 6. ANALYSIS OF VARIANCE OF CPI FACTOR SCORES OBTAINED
WITH ADULT AND ADOLESCENT GROUPS

		Adults				Adolescents		
Factor	df	Mean square	F	p	df	Mean square	F	p
I. Disciplined Effectiveness								
Creativity	1	.036	8.69	<.01	1	.007	6.14	<.05
Vocation	3	.022	5.30	<.01	7	.002	1.61	n.s.
Interaction	3	.015	3.48	<.05	7	.001	.87	n.s.
Error								
(within cells)	192				922			
II. Assertive Self-Assurance								
Creativity	1	.017	3.68	<.10	1	.005	5.11	<.05
Vocation	3	.026	5.55	<.01	7	.007	7.19	<.001
Interaction	3	.001	.21	n.s.	7	.001	1.34	n.s.
Error								
(within cells)	192				922			
III. Adaptive Autonomy								
Creativity	1	.041	10.39	<.01	1	.009	9.04	<.01
Vocation	3	.062	15.68	<.001	7	.004	3.60	<.01
Interaction	3	.002	.50	n.s.	7	.001	1.39	n.s.
Error								
(within cells)	192				922			
IV. Humanitarian Conscience								
Creativity	1	.002	.32	n.s.	1	.000	.03	n.s.
Vocation	3	.009	1.82	n.s.	7	.003	2.46	<.05
Interaction	3	.002	.49	n.s.	7	.001	.87	n.s.
Error								
(within cells)	192				922			

($p < .05$). The interaction is due primarily to the fact that the mean factor score differences between the creative and control groups were larger for the architects, writers, and mathematicians than for the research scientists. Of major interest is the finding that the more creative adults are lower on Disciplined Effectiveness than their colleagues, while the more creative adolescents are higher on this factor than their less creative peers.

On Factor II (Assertive Self-Assurance) the findings for the adolescent and adult samples appear to be quite comparable: the main effect for creativity was significant at the .10 level for adults and the .05 level for adolescents. The main effect of vocation was significant for both samples

($p < .01$) but no significant interaction was found. In both samples the more creative groups tended to describe themselves as more self-assured than their less creative peers, independent of the fact that the absolute levels of self-assurance differ among vocations.

On Factor III (Adaptive Autonomy) the main effects of creativity and vocation were significant for both the adults and the adolescents ($p < .01$) and no interaction was found. The more creative groups showed significantly more autonomy than the less creative, independent of the fact that the levels of autonomy vary significantly among the different vocational groups represented.

Factor IV (Humanitarian Conscience) failed to differentiate the more and less creative groups within the adult or the adolescent sample. The adults showed no main effects attributable to vocation and no interaction. The adolescent sample revealed a vocational effect but no significant interaction.

In brief, the more creative adults and adolescents are similarly differentiated from their less creative colleagues by indicating greater tendencies toward Assertive Self-assurance and Adaptive Autonomy than do their controls; however, the adult and adolescent creative groups are distinguished from their respective less creative groups on the dimension of Disciplined Effectiveness in a diametrically contrasting fashion. Lower scores on this factor are associated with more creative performance among the adult groups, while higher scores are characteristic of the more creative adolescent group. That personality characteristics are differentially associated with vocational choice is evident, but specification of these differences is not germane to the purposes of this paper.

In order to determine the strength of the association between personality factors and creativity, as reflected in accuracy of identification of the more and less creative individuals within the adult and adolescent samples, discriminant function analyses were performed.

From the pool of subjects in each sample, an equal number of highs and lows were selected, (a) within a vocation and (b) across vocations, so that the "vocation specific" variance of the larger samples would not be overrepresented in the final prediction equation that was also to be applied to the smaller samples.[8] For the adult sample this yielded eight cells of 14 subjects each: 56 more creative and 56 less creative adults. For the adolescent sample there were 16 cells of 12 subjects each: 96 more creative and 96 less creative. A summary of the distribution of

[8] In order to fulfill the necessary assumption that the vocational and creativity subgroups represented random samples drawn from subsamples of equal means and variance, the raw factor scores were standardized within vocations to a mean of 50 and a standard deviation of 10.

correct and incorrect identifications of adults and adolescents on the basis of discriminant function analyses is reported in Table 7. Of the 112 adults, 65 percent were correctly identified by discriminant function analysis ($\chi^2 = 11.03$, $df = 1$, $p < .01$). When parallel procedures were

TABLE 7. IDENTIFICATION OF MORE AND LESS CREATIVE GROUPS WITHIN VOCATIONS BY APPLICATION OF SAMPLE-BASED DISCRIMINANT FUNCTION ANALYSIS[a]

Adults	More creative			Less creative			
Vocation	Correct	Incorrect	Pct. correct	Correct	Incorrect	Pct. correct	Totals correctly predicted (Pct.)
Writing	10	4	71	8	6	57	64
Mathematics	10	4	71	10	4	71	71
Research science	6	8	43	8	6	57	50
Architecture	10	4	71	11	3	79	75
Totals	36	20	64	37	19	66	65 ($\chi^2 = 9.15$, $df = 1$, $p < .01$)

Adolescents	More creative			Less creative			
Vocation	Correct	Incorrect	Pct. correct	Correct	Incorrect	Pct. correct	Totals correctly predicted (Pct.)
Mathematics	9	3	75	9	3	75	75
Physics	8	4	67	7	5	58	62.5
Biology	7	5	58	7	5	58	58
Chemistry	6	6	50	7	5	58	54
Engineering	6	6	50	8	4	67	58
Biochemistry	9	3	75	6	6	50	62.5
Other science	7	5	58	8	4	67	62.5
Other nonscience	9	3	75	7	5	58	67
Totals	61	35	64	59	37	61	63.5 ($\chi^2 = 11.03$, $df = 1$, $p < .01$)

[a] To balance effects of vocation and creativity, equal N's were randomly selected. Program restrictions on total N limited cell N's to 12 for the adolescents.

applied to the adolescent data, 63.5 percent of the 192 adolescents were correctly classified ($\chi^2 = 9.15$, $df = 1$, $p < .01$).

The prediction achieved within each creativity group appeared to be about equal. In the adult sample, 64 percent of the more creative individuals and 66 percent of the less creative individuals were correctly identified. The application of the sample-based discriminate function to each of the adult vocational subgroups indicated that prediction varied among the vocations. The more creative writers, mathematicians, and architects were correctly discriminated in 71 percent of the cases, while the research scientists were correctly identified in only 43 percent of the cases. The accuracy of identification of the less creative groups ranged from 79 percent for architects to 57 percent for writers and research scientists.

The discriminate function analyses permitted the correct identification of 64 percent of the more creative and 61 percent of the less creative adolescents. When the sample-based discriminate function was applied to each of the vocational groupings, it was found that the correct identification of individuals in the more creative groups ranged from a high of 75 percent for mathematicians, biochemists, and nonscientists to 50 percent for chemists and engineers. The correct identification of the less creative individuals ranged from 75 percent for mathematicians to 50 percent for biochemists.

In brief, although the personality factor mean differences between the more and less creative groups are statistically significant, the extent of the overlap in means permits misclassification in about one-third of the total cases.

In order to determine the utility of attempting to identify the potentially creative adolescent by using the combination of personality factor scores which best discriminates the adult more and less creative groups, the adult-based discriminate function formula was applied to the adolescent sample. On this basis the discrimination was reduced to about chance ($\chi^2 = 1.25$, $df = 1$, $p < .20$). It appears therefore that the identification of the more and less creative adolescent is better achieved by use of personality characteristics derived from the adolescent than by characteristics from the adult sample.

DISCUSSION

Although a nonchance association between personality and creativity has been demonstrated, the strength of association reflected in predictive efficiency is relatively modest. Given the fact that (1) CPI scale reliabilities, although high, are not perfect, (2) that the validity of judging of creativity must be assumed to be limited, and (3) that the fashioning of a creative product depends not only on personality predispositions but also on a variety of cognitive skills and conducive environmental circumstances, it would be overly optimistic indeed to expect that strong predictions of creativity could be made simply on the basis of a single specified set of personality characteristics. On this basis it may be gratifying to find that attention to personality characteristics alone enhances the identification of members of the more and less creative groups (adult or adolescent) to the degree demonstrated. On the other hand, the fact remains that the attempt to differentiate levels of creativity by use of a single set of personality characteristics would even under optimal conditions permit the misidentification of approximately one-third of the more and less creative individuals. It is likely that prediction and identification could be enhanced by further efforts to identify not simply the best central tendency representation but the variety and richness of various personality types associated with creative performance. Efforts to characterize the personality of "the creative man" must inevitably fail to describe a relatively sizable proportion of such individuals. It is appropriate here to consider the findings that were applicable to the majority of subjects. We note that despite the fact that personality characteristics are differentially associated with vocational choice, the more creative adults are distinguished from their less creative peers on a shared set of personality dimensions. These findings give support to the hypothesis that creative adults share a common set of differentiating personality characteristics. The hypothesis that these personality characteristics are predisposing to rather than the consequence of creative performance is also supported; however, the evidence suggests that facilitating personality characteristics may vary from one age period to another.

With the limitations that this investigation is based on but a single personality instrument (CPI) and seeks to identify and apply only group mean personality differences, the findings for the adult sample are remarkably consistent with the general picture of creative personality: relatively uninhibited and unconventional; appearing to have a greater need for independence, self-direction, and autonomy; and being more assertive, forceful, and seemingly self-assured.

With equal weight given to each cell mean, the absence of any true interaction between creativity and the various vocations represented gives the findings the weight of multiple replication. It is clear, however, that the mean differences between the more and less creative research scientist groups on the dimension of Disciplined Effectiveness are not consistent with the overall discrimination found between more and less creative adult groups (see Table 4). This inconsistency may be due to the fact that the more creative research scientists sample is the only group of adults that was not selected on the basis of demonstrated high levels of creativity. According to Gough, "the search was not for men of renown or outstanding creativity. To use an analogy from athletics, the sample was one of varsity players rather than of All-Americans (1961, p. III-6)." The degree to which creativity was represented in this sample may be relatively slight. There may also be a systematic selection factor in this group, based on the decision to enter and remain in an industrial research setting.

The adolescent more and less creative groups are also found to be reliably differentiated on the same three personality factors that differentiated the more and less creative adult groups. Again, despite the fact that personality differences were found among the various vocational interest groups, no significant interactions were found between creativity and vocation. In effect, the personality differences associated with the two levels of creativity are replicated in the various vocational groups. The stability of these findings gives added weight to the observation that the direction of the discrimination between more and less creative groups on Disciplined Effectiveness is reversed for the adult and adolescent samples. These findings suggests that the personality dimensions of Adaptive Autonomy and Assertive Self-assurance, which similarly discriminate the more and less creative groups of adults and adolescents, may indeed be predisposing to creative functioning; however, such characteristics as are described by low scores on the personality factor, Disciplined Effectiveness—unconventional behavior, lack of concern with maintaining the good opinion of others, and relative lack of inhibition —do not appear to be predisposing to adult creativity but may instead be a consequence of recognition or maturity. The data do not preclude the possibility that the creative adults achieve their most creative works and conceptions at a relatively young age, when their personality style was in fact more similar to that of the adolescent in this study than that of the adult. The reduction of concern with Disciplined Effectiveness may be associated not with an increase in creativity but with a decrease. That is a possible but not probable inference.

Creative performance among the adolescents appears to be facilitated rather than inhibited by a measure of social skills and self-control. This finding is consistent with the view that the adolescent, unlike the adult, is faced with the practical necessity of coping with the world in which his success is, in fact, dependent upon his ability to maintain a reasonable degree of cooperation with those who control the resources he needs to achieve his goals. Society is understandably more tolerant of the demands, eccentricities, and flouting of convention of adults who have demonstrated their creativity than it is of similar behavior from the brash, unrecognized adolescent. The adolescent who is unwilling to make appropriate allowances for this reality may perforce have to devote much of his effort to struggle and rebellion, with a resultant loss of energy which might otherwise have been available for creative productivity. An additional consideration is the possibility that the performance of the potentially creative adolescent may be facilitated rather than hindered by a self-discipline that permits him to learn principles, heuristics, and basic information, which he may then proceed to reintegrate and reorganize in a constructively creative fashion. It is important to recognize that although the more creative adolescent is sensitive to the feelings of others and aware of environmental constraints, he does not let such considerations limit his pursuit of an important goal; instead he may use such knowledge to work more effectively in achieving his ends.

The projected longitudinal study of the adolescent sample will provide an opportunity to test whether the more creative adolescents will in time relax their concerns with social acceptability while their seemingly less conforming and less creative colleagues will tend to become more staid, circumspect, and conforming. To develop and then to "outgrow" a capacity to adapt to the requirements of society is a far different maturation process from that in which such discipline was never developed or was excessively delayed.

Although it is recognized that the current cultural pressures on adolescents may differ from those which operated on contemporary adults during their adolescence, it is difficult to attribute the discrepancy observed on Disciplined Effectiveness to such cultural changes. The current emphasis on nonconformity, self-actualization, and self-expression is hardly consistent with the direction of discrimination in the adolescent sample.

A further implication of these findings is that in contrast to popular belief, the creative adolescent is able to combine (1) the exercise of self-discipline, (2) a reasonable circumspection in his dealings with others, and (3) a capacity to exercise autonomy and independence of thought and to make novel and effective integrations of ideas. Since it may be assumed that these personality dimensions have been affected by experience, it is apparent that independence of thought is not stifled by life experiences which led the individual to behave in a rather socially adept manner. It must be recognized that the degree of conformance is not high in terms of the general population norms for the CPI, but high only in relation to general adolescent norms (Gough, 1957).

Generalizations based on the adolescent groups must be restricted to those who have decided upon a career in science, have made this decision at a relatively early age, have demonstrated great competence and are willing to participate in a nationwide competition. That these findings may possibly apply to nonscience groups is suggested by the fact that groups of more and less creative adolescents who do not plan to make science their careers showed personality differentiations consistent with the science sample.

While students of creativity have emphasized the "creative act," it cannot be assumed that the personality characteristics which have been discussed here are limited primarily to the act per se. The creative man is one who has not only proposed a novel integration of ideas; he has rigorously tested the hypothesized relationship and has also vigorously communicated his findings. Each of these processes may reflect different personality characteristics. The formulation of new ideas may be associated with personality traits consistent with associative fluency, "regression in the service of the ego," and nonlogical thinking; hypothesis testing may be linked with persistence, logical thinking, self-control, and discipline; communication may be facilitated by such traits as dominance, aggressiveness, and assertiveness. Since the adolescent and adult samples reported here were limited to those who successfully met rigorous criteria of performance, those potentially creative individuals who did not complete all three steps of the process were not included in the sample.

These findings suggest that a particular personality dimension may be conducive to creative performance at one age level and may be less relevant or even inimical to creative performance at a later age.

One implication is that those who hope to identify the potentially creative young scientist on the basis of differentiated personality patterns will find it more appropriate to seek age-relevant differences than to adopt a single model based on characteristics which generally differentiate the more creative adults from the less creative adults.

The finding that Adaptive Autonomy and Assertive Self-assurance are predisposing to creativity in both the adolescent and adult samples is consonant with current cultural values placed on personality characteristics. The finding that Disciplined Effectiveness is associated with creative performance in the adolescent does appear to be overlooked in the popular belief regarding personality characteristics conducive to creativity.

We believe that these findings may be integrated in the following way: The creative individual recognizes and identifies new relationships among phenomena, and, by virtue of his respect for his own capacity, is willing to attempt new integrations. Such functioning is consistent with the factors of Adaptive Autonomy and Assertive Self-assurance. A creative product, however, must also be effective. A bizarre idea may be novel but not effective. To produce an effective idea the creative individual must have a thorough grasp of his field. This requires a high degree of competence, discipline, and motivation. These attributes may be reflected in the factor of Disciplined Effectiveness.

SUMMARY

More creative adult groups can be differentiated from less creative adult groups independent of their field on a shared set of personality characteristics.

Personality characteristics described by such factors as Adaptive Autonomy and Assertive Self-assurance appear to predispose to creative performance. An emphasis on Disciplined Effectiveness may be conducive to creative performance in the adolescent.

In contrast to popular belief, the creative adolescent has managed to learn to exercise self-discipline and to be reasonably circumspect in his dealings with others without detriment to his capacity to develop a high degree of independence in his thinking and his capacity to make novel and effective integrations of his ideas. A de-emphasis of this personality factor, as found in the more creative adult groups, may, however, be consequent to recognition. Whether the de-emphasis of Disciplined Effectiveness acts to further enhance the adult's continued creativity is presumed but not tested in this study.

The personality characteristics which differentiate between such adult groups thus cannot be applied without modification for the purpose of identifying the potentially creative adolescent.

REFERENCES

Barron, F. *Creativity and Psychological Health.* Princeton, N.J.: Van Nostrand, 1963.

Barron, F. The psychology of creativity. In F. Barron *et al.* (Eds.) *New Directions in Psychology.* Vol. 2. New York: Holt, Rinehart and Winston, 1965, 1–134.

Cashdan, S., and Welsh, G. Personality correlates of creative potential in talented high school students. *Journal of Personality,* 1966, **34,** 445–455.

Cattell, R. B., and Drevdahl, J. E. A comparison of the personality profile (16 PF) of eminent researchers with that of eminent teachers, administrators and of the general population. *British Journal of Psychology,* 1955, **46,** 248–261.

Chambers, J. A. Relating personality and biographical factors to scientific creativity. *Psychological Monographs,* 1964, **78,** No. 7.

Crites, J. O., Bechtoldt, H. P., Goodstein, L. D., and Heilbrun, A. G., Jr. A factor analysis of the California Psychological Inventory. *Journal of Applied Psychology*, 1961, 45, 408–414.

Datta, Lois-ellin. Religious background and early scientific creativity. *Sociological Review*, 1967, 32, 626–635.

Davis, W. *National Science Youth*. Washington, D. C.: Science Service, Inc., 1963.

Gough, H. G. *California Psychological Inventory Manual*. Palo Alto: Consulting Psychologists Press, 1957.

Gough, H. G. Techniques for identifying the creative research scientist. In *Proceedings*, Conference on "The Creative Person," Oct. 13–17, 1961, Lake Tahoe, Calif. Berkeley: University of California, University Extension, pp. III–1 to III–25.

Harman, H. H. *Modern Factor Analysis*. Chicago: University of Chicago Press, 1960.

Helson, Ravenna M. Creativity, sex, and mathematics. In *Proceedings,* Conference on "The Creative Person," Oct. 13–17, 1961, Lake Tahoe, Calif. Berkeley: University of California, University Extension, pp. IV–1 to IV–12.

Hotelling, H. Analysis of a complex of statistical variables into principal components. *Journal of Educational Psychology*, 1933, 24, 417–441, 498–520.

Kaiser, H. F. The varimax criterion for analytic rotation in factor analysis. *Psychometrika*, 1958, 23, 187–200.

Leton, D. A., and Walter, S. A. *A Factor Analysis of the California Psychological Inventory and Minnesota Counseling Inventory*. Santa Monica: System Development Corp., 1961. SP–204.

MacKinnon, D. W. The nature and nurture of creative talent. *American Psychologist*, 1962, 17, 484–495. (a). Reprinted in Ann Anastasi (Ed.) *Individual Differences*. New York: John Wiley, 1965, 282–295.

MacKinnon, D. W. The personality correlates of creativity: a study of American architects. In G. S. Nielsen (Ed.) *Proceedings of the XIV International Congress of Applied Psychology*, Copenhagen, 1961. Vol. 2. Copenhagen: Munksgaard, 1962, 11–39. (b)

Mitchell, J. V., and Pierce-Jones, J. A factor analysis of Gough's California Psychological Inventory. *Journal of Consulting Psychology*, 1960, 24, 453–456.

Rivlin, L. Creativity and the self-attitudes and sociability of high school students. *Journal of Educational Psychology*, 1959, 50, 147–152.

Roe, Anne. Psychological examinations of eminent biologists. *Journal of Consulting Psychology*, 1949, 13, 225–246.

Roe, Anne. Analysis of group Rorschachs of psychologists and anthropologists. *Journal of Projective Techniques*, 1952, 16, 212–224.

Roe, Anne. *The Making of a Scientist*. New York: Dodd, Mead, 1953.

Shure, G. H., and Rogers, M. S. Personality factor stability for three ability levels. *Journal of Psychology*, 1963, 55, 445–456.

Stein, M. I. Creativity and the scientist. In *The National Physical Laboratories, the Direction of Research Establishments*. Part 3. London: Her Majesty's Stationery Office, 1957, pp. 1–19.

Stein, M. I. Survey of the psychological literature in the area of creativity with the view toward needed research. Coop Research Project E-3. New York University, Research Center for Human Relations, 1962.
Winer, B. J. *Statistical Principles in Experimental Design.* New York: McGraw-Hill, 1962, pp. 241–244.

3.4 *Orientation*

The theme of individual differences basic to the preceding study of creativity is echoed by our next example of descriptive research. We now converge, however, upon the topic of moral judgment and associated variables. Previous discussions of political development (Sullivan), moral development (Kohlberg), and student dissent (Keniston) should provide the reader with a comprehensive frame of reference for the interpretation of this research.

A cornerstone of the following research is data yielded by the measurement of moral judgment. From this cornerstone the researchers have erected an elaborate latticework of inter-relationships involving students' protest behavior, self-concepts, and perceptions of parents. This latticework has also contributed to generalizations about three groups of moral types: the principled, the conventionally moral, and the pre-moral instrumental relativistic.

For a unique test of the relationship between measured moral judgment and public behavior, the present researchers have drawn upon events of the Berkeley Free Speech Movement. Consequently, their results reflect upon the validity of the Kohlberg Moral Judgment Scale selected for use in this study. Their data also indicate that similar (or identical) surface behavior (for example, "sitting-in") can represent diverse channels of moral reasoning. This finding fortifies the psychologist's need for systematic, objective means to measure motivational patterns.

Several studies related to the present research have recently appeared. For example, another Berkeley-based investigation has shown that student activists and non-conformists from a non-student subculture both express a high degree of *anomie* (a condition consisting of personal disorientation, anxiety, and feelings of isolation). These two groups differed, however, in that non-students were estranged from their parents, although student activists were not (Watts, Lynch, & Whittaker, 1969). A further exploration of difference between activists and non-activists reports the former to be higher in measured intelligence (Kerpelman, 1969). In addition, important personality differences *within* the student activist group were observed. As compared to "middle-" or "right-oriented" activists, "left-oriented" activists were significantly less concerned with social acceptance. Kerpelman has thus indicated the necessity to maintain a separation between activism and ideology in political behavior research.

Aside from the excellent discussion of findings by Haan, Smith, and Block, the reader is encouraged to note the data on student-parent conflict presented below. A concern for "generation-conflict" reappears in the Rivera and Short study of gang delinquency reproduced later in this section.

RECOMMENDED READINGS

Kohlberg, Lawrence.   Moral education in the schools: a developmental view. *The School Review*, 1966, **74**, 1–29.

Kerpelman, Larry C.   Student political activism and ideology: comparative characteristics of activists and nonactivists. *Journal of Counseling Psychology*, 1969, **16**, 8–13.

Ruma, Eleanor H., and Mosher, Donald L.   Relationship between moral judgment and guilt in delinquent boys. *Journal of Abnormal and Social Psychology*, 1967, **72**, 122–127.

Watts, William A., Lynch, Steve, and Whittaker, David.   Alienation and activism in today's college-age youth. *Journal of Counseling Psychology*, 1969, **16**, 1–7.

3.4   Moral Reasoning of Young Adults: Political-Social Behavior, Family Background, and Personality Correlates

Norma Haan, INSTITUTE OF HUMAN DEVELOPMENT,
  UNIVERSITY OF CALIFORNIA, AT BERKELEY
M. Brewster Smith,* INSTITUTE OF HUMAN DEVELOPMENT,
  UNIVERSITY OF CALIFORNIA, AT BERKELEY
Jeanne Block, INSTITUTE OF HUMAN DEVELOPMENT,
  UNIVERSITY OF CALIFORNIA, AT BERKELEY

Activist youth maintain that there are moral necessities for their social-political protest; this assertion bears upon a current, major research issue concerned with the relationship of moral judgment to behavior. If such

Reprinted from *Journal of Personality and Social Psychology*, 1968, **10**, 183–201, by permission of the authors and the American Psychological Association.

* Now at the University of Chicago.

a connection between moral reasoning and protesting behavior were found, and the activists were actually morally distinctive, a second issue concerned with the nature and context of the socialization experiences associated with morality and its related behavior would be of immediate interest.

The morality of young children has been studied more thoroughly than later morality, but a clearer understanding of the latter is crucial since it is the more critical issue for society. Various theoretical positions diverge in their assumptions about the kind of antecedent experiences that lead to a capability for principled judgments and behavior. In Kohlberg's (1964) developmental perspective the role of socializing agents and institutions is primarily that of providing role-taking opportunities since the young individual is viewed as developing morality in his own terms. On the other hand, various social learning points of view, for example, Aronfreed (1968), Bandura and McDonald (1963), generally ascribe moral attainment to selective reinforcement experiences and modeling behavior by the young and thereby suggest roles for socializing agents in children's development that are better characterized as countervening.

Conformity to the value content of some current social ideal, for example, the Protestant Ethic, or even "activism," is frequently taken as evidence of high morality. The value content of such orientations are clearly subject to considerable historical and cultural specificity, and the present generation's conceptualization of the "good man" is probably different from past ones. Moral philosophy draws attention, however, to the "calculus" (Baier, 1958) of moral reasoning, its processual properties, such as objectivity, generality, inclusiveness, universalizability, and impersonalness. The form of reasoning may likely have greater predictability and wider application than time-and-group-bound content; simple knowledge of socially approved ideals is known to be only a weak predictor of moral behavior. The present study focuses primarily on process criteria as indexed by the Kohlberg Moral Judgment Scale, but it also brings the Kohlberg typology of moral reasoning into relation with contemporary features of value content as indexed by descriptions of the ideal self.

This investigation identifies moral types based on the reasoning of college youth and Peace Corps volunteers in response to moral dilemmas of the Kohlberg Moral Judgment Scale and analyzes the differences between the types in political-social behavior, family background, perceptions of mother and father, and self-and ideal description. Other analyses from the larger study, of which this is part, have been reported by Block, Haan, and Smith (1968) and Smith, Haan, and Block (1969).

METHOD

Subjects

The original pool of 957 subjects who responded to the Kohlberg
Moral Judgment Scale included University of California and San Francisco State College students and Peace Corps volunteers in training. The
sexes were about equally divided; freshman and graduate students were
excluded and Peace Corps volunteers were somewhat older. Most student
subjects were contacted by letters sent to the membership of various
organizations and to students randomly drawn from the registration files
on the two campuses. Materials were subsequently sent to willing persons
and returned by them through the mail. Berkeley campus groups included arrestees in the Free Speech Movement (FSM), Young Democrats,
Young Republicans, California Conservatives for Political Action; San
Francisco State College groups were the student-body-sponsored Community Involvement Program, Tutorial Group, and Experimental College.
Some Peace Corps volunteers were tested in group meetings; others completed the tasks individually. The sample is not representative, since the
subjects were volunteers and the participation rate was uneven from
one contact group to another (cf. Smith *et al.*, 1969, for a discussion of
response rates). This analysis is concerned only with 54 percent of the
responding sample who could be assigned to one or another of five
"pure" moral types according to their responses to the Moral Judgment
Scale. (Table 2, to be discussed later, shows the source of the present
sample according to groups contacted.)

Kohlberg Moral Judgment Scale

Kohlberg has identified three general levels of moral judgment with
two types in each stage according to an age-developmental scheme which
was demonstrated both longitudinally (Kohlberg, 1964; Kramer, 1968)
and with cross-sectional age groups (Kohlberg, 1968; Turiel, 1969). The
general levels and the specific stages are described in Table 1 and the
alpha abbreviations identifying the various types are shown.

Five of the 10 Kohlberg stories were chosen for use in this study (a
sixth story concerned with the FSM sit-in of 1964 was included for Berkeley students, but is not considered in this paper).[1] The stories pose

[1] The five Kohlberg stories, the Biographical Information form, the Q-sort
item listing for describing self and ideal, and the supporting information for
Tables 7–10 have been deposited with the National Auxiliary Publications
Service. Order NAPS Document 0075 from ASSIS National Auxiliary Publica-
tions Service, c/o CCM Information Sciences, Inc., 22 West 34th St., New York,
New York 10001; remitting $1.00 for microfiche or $3.00 for photocopies.

TABLE 1. CLASSIFICATION OF MORAL JUDGMENT INTO LEVELS
AND STAGES OF DEVELOPMENT

Levels	Basis of moral judgment	Stages of development
I	Pre-moral Moral value resides in external, quasi-physical happenings, in bad acts, or in quasi-physical needs rather than in persons and standards.	Stage 1: Obedience and punishment orientation. Egocentric deference to superior power or prestige, or a trouble-avoiding set. Objective responsibility. Stage 2: Instrumental Relativists (IR) Naively egoistic orientation. Right action is that instrumentally satisfying the self's needs and occasionally others'. Awareness of relativism of value to each actor's needs and perspective. Naive egalitarianism and orientation to exchange and reciprocity.
II	Conventional Moral value resides in performing good or right roles, in maintaining the conventional order and the expectancies of others.	Stage 3: Personal Concordance (PC) Good-boy orientation. Orientation to approval and to pleasing and helping others. Conformity to stereotypical images of majority or natural role behavior, and judgment by intentions. Stage 4: Law and Order (LO) Authority and social-order maintaining orientation. Orientation to "doing duty" and to showing respect for authority and maintaining the given social order for its own sake. Regard for earned expectations of others.
III	Principled Moral value resides in conformity by the self to shared or shareable standards, rights or duties.	Stage 5: Social Contract (SC) Contractual legalistic orientation. Recognition of an arbitrary element or starting point in rules or expectations for the sake of agreement. Duty defined in terms of contract, general avoidance of violations of the will or rights of others, and majority will and welfare. Stage 6: Individual Principles (IP) Conscience or principle orientation. Orientation not only to actually ordained social rules but to principles of choice involving appeal to logical universality and consistency. Orientation to conscience as a directing agent and to mutual respect and trust.

NOTE. Adapted from Kohlberg (1967).

TABLE 2. DISTRIBUTION OF MORAL TYPES

Contact group	Pre-moral		Conventional				Principled				% Original sample	
	IR		PC		LO		SC		IP			
	M	F	M	F	M	F	M	F	M	F	M	F
UC random	4	2	16	25	33	22	11	2	2	1	64%	56%
FSM arrestees	6	1	4	3	3	5	11	8	6	6	46	45
Other UC	0	0	2	4	14	14	5	4	0	0	45	61
SF random	1	1	13	45	28	30	6	10	3	3	50	61
SF activist	2	0	7	8	3	6	4	6	3	1	53	58
Peace Corps	3	3	15	20	28	22	17	5	3	0	65	72
Total	16	7	57	105	109	99	54	35	17	11	51	56

NOTE. Moral types are designated by the following abbreviations: Instrumental Relativists (IR), Personal Concordance (PC), Law-Order (LO), Social Contract (SC), and Individual Principles (IP). Total $N = 510$.

classical moral dilemmas and are followed by questions which elicit the subject's resolution of the quandary, but more importantly ask for his supporting reasons. One situation concerns a husband who steals a drug for his wife because she is dying of cancer; the husband is unable to afford the drug, and all other means of his securing it are closed. Subsequent questions are concerned with the rightness or wrongness of his decision, the drug owner's rights, a husband's duties, one's obligations to nonrelatives, and the appropriate punishment for the husband. Sample answers for various stages and dilemmas can be found in Kohlberg (1964, p. 401).

Scoring   Three judges were trained by Kohlberg in a 4-day session. Scoring was based on sentence responses and relied upon a detailed manual worked out by Kohlberg. Each story was scored for approximately 200 subjects before the judges moved to the next in the series. A major overall type score, and a minor when needed, was assigned for each story. All stories were scored independently by two judges, and they did not know the sample membership or sex of the subjects.

Assignation of moral type   Subjects were mechanically assigned to their final "pure" type in accordance with a rule which required that the assigned type score must have twice the summed weight of any other for all five stories and two judges; major scores were weighted "2," or "3" if no minor was given, and minors, "1." This is a stringent criterion since there are 20 opportunities for a particular type score to appear.

As a result the types are quite homogeneous; for example, Stage 2 men have the following mean scores across the six stages: .8, 18.5, 3.9, 2.9, 6.1, 1.5. The subjects who met this qualification and their membership in the groups contacted are shown in Table 2. Only one subject representing Stage 1 was found, and he is not included in this report.

Reliability   Reliability of scoring was calculated in two main ways. A first estimate of reliability was based upon the percentage of agreement between the two judges in their individual modal designations. (Note this procedure, based upon individual judges, is different from the assignment of the final consensus type just described.) The agreement between the two judges' modal type designations was 85 percent, with agreement defined as either complete (both major and minor), major code only, or reversals of major and minor designations.

In the second instance, a subject's weighted score for each story was summed for each judge. The reliability estimate which resulted from correlating the first judge's total scores with the second was .82 for all 957 subjects.

The Kohlberg instrument is usually administered in an interview and the paper-and-pencil version probably caused some subjects to abbreviate their responses to these troublesome dilemmas. This may have lowered reliability and led to an inflated proportion of mixed types. The low incidence of Instrumental Relativism and Individual Principles in this large sample is an interesting indication of the restrictions in extreme types with a bright, college-age population and corroborates Kohlberg's observation that modal morality is conventional. Despite their small numbers, these two extreme types are included in all analyses because of their relevance to the outer limits of morality. The results for these groups particularly need to be tested with other samples.

Other Measurements

The subjects filled out a five-page Biographical Questionnaire which asked for checks, ratings, and rankings. Questions concerned college status, political-social activity and commitments, demographic information and parents, agreement with parents about issues commonly in dispute between generations, and the degree of influence attributed to different agents with respect to the person the subject now is, his political-social views, and his ethics and morality. (See footnote 1.)

A 63-adjective *Q* sort, adapted from one previously constructed by Jeanne Block, was sorted twice by the subjects to describe both their perceived and ideal selves. Adjectives were chosen to represent qualities which are deemed positive from various points of view. (See footnote 1.)

Another *Q* sort, the 91-item Child-Rearing Practices Report, developed by Block (1965), was used by the participants to give their description of the mother's child-rearing practices, and an identical set with an altered stem, the father's child-rearing practices. All Q sorts were done with a forced rectangular distribution of seven steps, so that group comparisons reflect an accumulation of differences in degrees of variable saliency within the individuals who make up contrast groups.

RESULTS

The results of this study are best presented as a series of integrated summaries for each moral level. Tables 3 through 11 provide the supporting information. Some descriptive information for the various types is reported as percentages, but a probability level of $\leq.05$ is adopted as the cutting point for reporting other results with χ^2 or F ratio being the test of significance. The authors recognize the strict inapplicability of probability statistics to these data. A few findings at the .10 level are presented when they are of special interest, and in this case the probability level is noted. The summaries start with the principled Social Contract (SC) and Individual Principles (IP) groups which are first considered as one. Differences between them are subsequently discussed. After the results for the typologies are presented several summary analyses specifically concerned with moral judgment and behavior and family milieu are reported.

Principled Morality Groups

Biographical information   The principled groups are more likely to have interrupted their college careers, live in apartments and houses on their own, are politically more radical, were strongly in support of the Free Speech Movement (FSM), more frequently indicate that they are agnostics, atheists, or areligious, were frequently raised in Jewish or areligious homes, tend to have politically liberal parents with mothers being comparatively better educated. (The fathers' education and occupational levels did not approach significance for any of the groups.) Even though the parents of these young people are liberals, their sons, and even more, their daughters, indicate that they are absolutely more discrepant and left wing than their parents. They moderately disagree with their parents in regard to political-social issues. Sons report that their fathers have influenced them less, personally and politically, while their close friends have been more influential. The principled women report strong influences from close friends in all domains, political influence from organized groups, and altogether less parental influence.

The political-social activity of the principled groups is the highest. They not only have affiliated with more organizations and movements but have also been much involved in them. Greater numbers have engaged in a large variety of activities with a heavy emphasis upon political protest. Social service activity does not significantly distinguish between groups, but the details in Table 7 show that principled youth have not devoted themselves solely to jarring the establishment.

Adjective Q sorts   *Idealistic* is the only self-characteristic common to both the male SC and IP groups (common refers to characteristics that are either highest or lowest for *both* the SC and IP groups). The principled men's distinctive conceptualization of the ideal, good man emphasizes both their commitment to taking the roles of others by the high value they place on *perceptive, empathic,* and *altruistic* and their rejection of *stubborn* and to self-expressiveness implied by *creative.* Their censure of contemporary society is evidenced by their idealization of *rebellious* and their rejection of *conventional.* The principled women described themselves dysphorically as *guilty, doubting, restless, impulsive,* and with the clearly moral word, *altruistic.* They do not see themselves as *foresightful, ambitious,* or *stubborn.* Both groups feel they are less *feminine* than any of the others ($p < .10$). The shared ideal conceptualization of the women is being *rebellious* and *free,* but not *ambitious, practical, responsible,* or *sociable.*

Perceptions of parental practices   The principled males reported that their mothers teased and made fun of them and that the relationship was the most conflicted. Fathers were seen as most willing to let their sons take chances and try new things. The mothers of the principled women are seen as most disappointed in their daughters, likely to let them know about maternal sacrifices, and least likely to comfort them when they are upset. They were least likely to take away privileges for punishment or to give extra ones for good behavior. Fathers did not take away privileges when their daughters were bad and least approved of competitive games, according to their daughters.

SC and IP differences   Scheffé tests were calculated for all significant F ratios but none significantly separated the SC and IP groups (except for SC males' self-description of being more practical). The Scheffé is a very conservative test of group contrasts, but there are a number of other nonsignificant differences which do form coherent patterns. IPs more than SCs have interrupted their college careers, live on their own, are more radical, and more pro-FSM. The men are more frequently agnostic. The IP women are more areligious, their mothers are more radical, but even so, their political discrepancy with parents

TABLE 3. Present Status of Subjects Assigned to Moral Types

Response category	Men						Women					
	IR	PC	LO	SC	IP	χ²	IR	PC	LO	SC	IP	χ²
Interruption of college career												
Yes	56%	27%	27%	29%	44%	7.23	40%	26%	20%	35%	**64%**	11.66*
Living arrangements												
On own	**75%**	34%	30%	42%	56%	16.12**	40%	36%	27%	62%	**100%**	31.55***
Political position						*F* ratio						*F* ratio
Radical-Conservative (8-pt. scale)	6.54	5.02	4.33	6.31	**6.81**	29.00***	5.00	4.95	4.44	6.31	**6.70**	11.30***
Pro FSM (5-pt. scale)	**4.29**	3.24	2.79	3.92	4.25	8.94***	**4.00**	3.26	3.01	3.62	**4.00**	2.59*
Present religious beliefs												
Protestant-Catholic	*0%*	53%	59%	17%	18%		60%	54%	**67%**	21%	*18%*	
Jewish	12%	*0%*	6%	12%	*0%*		*0%*	4%	3%	12%	*0%*	
Agnostic, etc.	**82%**	43%	27%	46%	70%		40%	32%	23%	**52%**	36%	
None	6%	4%	8%	25%	12%		*0%*	10%	7%	15%	**46%**	
Present church attendance (1 = never; 4 = weekly)												
	1.62	2.48	**2.59**	1.94	1.65	7.07***	2.20	2.49	**2.81**	1.88	*1.54*	7.55***

NOTE. Boldface X̄'s are highest; italics are lowest.   *p < .05.   **p < .01.   ***p < .001.

378

TABLE 4. FAMILY BACKGROUND

Response category	Men						Women					
	IR	PC	LO	SC	IP	F ratio	IR	PC	LO	SC	IP	F ratio
Mother and father												
Mother educated (5-pt. scale)	**2.38**	1.73	*1.62*	2.06	1.94	3.46*	3.00	*1.74*	1.98	2.09	1.91	2.73*
Mother radical-conservative (8-pt. scale)	4.56	3.94	*3.75*	4.51	**4.87**	3.58**	5.00	3.73	*3.65*	4.33	4.36	2.79*
Father radical-conservative	4.19	4.02	*3.69*	4.46	**4.50**	2.67*	3.60	3.69	*3.40*	**4.34**	4.00	2.41*
Family differences in radical-conservative												
Ss-Father	**2.69**	1.07	*.62*	1.86	2.27	10.19***	1.40	1.20	*.97*	1.97	**2.56**	3.51**
Ss-Mother	**2.38**	1.23	*.55*	1.89	1.86	8.83***	*.00*	1.12	.87	1.97	**2.30**	4.93***
Religious tradition of family												
Protestant-Catholic	*44%*	73%	**81%**	58%	56%		**80%**	78%	**80%**	*59%*	73%	
Jewish	**38%**	9%	*8%*	25%	25%		*0%*	7%	5%	**24%**	9%	
None	12%	11%	*5%*	8%	**19%**		**20%**	10%	9%	*6%*	9%	
All Others	6%	7%	6%	**9%**	*0%*		*0%*	5%	6%	**11%**	9%	

NOTE. Boldface X̄'s are highest; italics are lowest. * p ≤ .05. ** p ≤ .01. *** p ≤ .001.

379

TABLE 5. Agreements with Parents about Generational Gap Issues

	Men						Women					
Issue category	IR	PC	LO	SC	IP	F ratio	IR	PC	LO	SC	IP	F ratio
Agreement with father												
Religion	*2.33*	3.20	**3.21**	2.55	2.80	3.53**						
Friends	*2.67*	3.62	**3.81**	3.35	3.64	4.45**						
Politics	*2.56*	3.29	3.41	3.04	2.73	2.75*	3.40	3.13	**3.62**	2.72	*2.20*	5.56***
Demonstrations	2.31	2.86	**2.89**	*2.15*	2.62	3.14*						
S's occupational choice	*2.81*	3.90	3.73	3.34	4.00	3.13*	3.40	3.76	**4.08**	3.59	*2.60*	3.82**
Agreement with mother												
Friends	3.27	3.46	**3.93**	*3.26*	3.81	4.16**	4.00	3.06	**3.60**	2.85	*2.54*	5.00***
Politics	3.38	3.88	4.01	*3.36*	**4.27**	3.63**						
S's occupational choice												
Religion							*2.40*	3.27	**3.56**	2.82	2.91	3.12*

NOTE. Boldface $\overline{X}$'s are highest; italics are lowest.
 * $p \leq .05$.
 ** $p \leq .01$.
 *** $p \leq .001$.

380

TABLE 6. INFLUENCES FROM OTHER PERSONS: POLITICAL-SOCIAL;
ETHICS-MORALITY; AND "THE PERSON YOU NOW ARE"

Influencing agent	IR	PC	LO	SC	IP	F ratio
	S's political-social position					
Men						
Father	5.31	6.68	6.40	5.40	*5.19*	2.69*
	Persons they now are					
Father	6.33	6.83	7.19	5.90	*5.69*	3.07*
Close friends	6.67	6.11	*5.65*	6.50	6.94	2.97*
Older relatives	2.50	3.16	*2.40*	2.55	4.21	2.59*
	S's political-social position					
Women						
Mother	8.00	6.17	6.54	*4.84*	4.46	5.04***
Father	5.00	6.24	6.38	4.74	*3.36*	5.92***
Close friends	*6.00*	6.39	6.04	7.38	7.91	4.05**
Organized groups	3.80	*3.33*	4.13	5.16	6.30	4.78**
Older relatives	2.80	2.24	2.53	*1.33*	1.40	3.71**
Opposite sex	6.20	5.20	*4.41*	6.19	6.00	3.20*
	Persons they now are					
Mother	7.20	7.53	8.10	*6.76*	7.18	3.66**
Close friends	*5.20*	6.24	5.83	6.67	**7.82**	3.86**
Opposite sex	6.60	5.43	*4.50*	5.88	4.90	2.46*
Clergy	*1.00*	2.21	2.66	1.69	1.64	2.70*
	S's ethics-morality					
Mother	6.80	7.46	**7.78**	*6.39*	6.64	2.79*
Father	4.80	6.54	6.39	5.37	*4.64*	3.06*
Close friends	6.80	6.54	*5.63*	7.16	**7.36**	6.15***
Opposite sex	7.20	5.82	*4.64*	6.61	6.50	4.81**
Clergy	2.00	3.48	**4.33**	2.40	*1.50*	4.99**
Older relatives	2.00	2.33	**2.84**	1.61	*1.00*	2.92*

NOTE. Boldface $\overline{X}$'s are highest; italics are lowest. Scores are from a 10-step rank ordering with 10 representing highest influence.
* $p \le .05$.
** $p \le .01$.
*** $p \le .001$.

TABLE 7. PRESENT POLITICAL-SOCIAL BEHAVIOR

Category	Men						Women					
	IR	PC	LO	SC	IP	F ratio	IR	PC	LO	SC	IP	F ratio
Organizational participation												
Number	1.91	1.80	1.79	2.78	2.38	4.74**	3.00	1.50	2.14	2.38	2.67	4.18**
X̄ participation (5-pt. scale)	1.50	.71	.94	1.25	1.41	2.37*	.80	.84	1.11	1.71	1.64	3.38**
Summary activities												
Political (3-pt. scale)	.88	.38	.58	1.08	1.06	4.67**	.40	.22	.47	1.00	1.18	9.02***
Social service (6-pt. scale)	.38	.29	.25	.36	.35	.38	.20	.73	.65	.82	.54	.66
Protest (5-pt. scale)	1.81	.46	.30	1.62	2.47	21.50***	.20	.36	.39	1.62	2.00	15.82***
Total (14-pt. scale)	5.94	1.89	1.64	4.86	6.24	16.16***	1.40	1.63	2.21	5.09	7.27	14.78***

382

Kind of activity

Kind of activity	19%	12%	21%	31%	25%	20%	9%	16%	21%	45%
Precinct work	0	5	3	2	0	0	16	12	15	0
Hospital volunteer	31	7	19	25	19	0	13	11	26	27
Solicit funds	56	12	9	44	75	20	8	13	44	55
Picket	62	16	17	52	75	14	11	13	35	36
Teach-in	25	5	5	27	31	0	7	4	26	27
Sit-in	6	2	3	2	0	0	0	1	0	0
Civil Rights South	25	14	18	35	38	0	4	10	35	18
Petition work	0	3	4	8	6	40	14	13	3	0
Physical handicap										
Meetings	62	46	41	60	69	20	33	48	56	63
Distributing literature	44	11	20	42	50	20	10	21	44	55
Demonstrate	56	14	8	48	75	0	11	10	47	55
Peace march	56	12	5	40	62	20	11	10	44	64
Social agency	12	3	6	8	6	0	24	16	15	18
Tutor	25	9	11	15	25	0	3	7	32	27
School resource	0	7	2	4	0	20	7	5	18	9
Other	6	2	6	6	6				3	9

NOTE. Boldface $\overline{X}$'s are highest; italics are lowest. Summary Activities are the number of checks subjects made indicating their activities such as precinct work, and so on.

* $p < .05$.
** $p < .01$.
*** $p < .001$.

383

TABLE 8. MEANS OF SELF-DESCRIPTIONS (7-Step Scale)

Adjective	Males					Adjective	Females				
	IR	PC	LO	SC	IP		IR	PC	LO	SC	IP
.001 level											
Conventional	1.79	3.06	3.44	2.30	*1.60*	Ambitious	3.60	4.20	**4.30**	*2.84*	3.10
.01 level											
Ambitious	*3.29*	**5.09**	4.84	4.12	4.20	Guilty	3.20	3.13	*2.45*	3.53	**4.10**
Curious	5.64	5.28	*4.84*	5.64	**5.93**	Foresightful	3.60	3.85	**4.59**	3.38	*3.00*
Rebellious	4.50	2.98	2.71	3.58	3.93	Rebellious	4.20	2.78	*2.28*	3.28	**4.10**
Individualistic	**6.21**	*4.39*	5.00	5.34	5.60						
.05 level											
Idealistic	4.93	*4.20*	4.21	5.16	**5.27**	Fair	4.40	5.05	5.07	**5.25**	*3.70*
Creative	**5.79**	4.81	*4.24*	4.76	5.07	Aloof	**5.00**	2.35	*2.21*	2.25	2.30
Practical	2.86	3.52	**3.90**	3.16	*2.60*	Impulsive	*3.40*	4.02	3.52	4.25	**5.20**
Foresightful	3.64	3.80	**4.30**	*3.36*	3.93	Doubting	3.60	3.80	*3.16*	**4.50**	4.30
Orderly	*2.36*	3.89	4.14	3.52	2.80	Restless	3.20	3.14	*3.07*	4.16	**4.50**
Reserved	**4.00**	2.83	3.86	3.24	*2.40*	Stubborn	**6.60**	4.09	4.22	3.38	*3.30*
Sympathetic	4.93	4.20	**4.96**	4.72	5.40	Altruistic	*2.60*	3.25	3.66	4.25	3.90
Responsive	*3.64*	4.43	3.85	3.92	4.93						

NOTE. Boldface $\overline{X}$'s are highest; italics are lowest.

TABLE 9. MEANS OF IDEAL DESCRIPTIONS (7-STEP SCALE)

Adjective	Men					Adjective	Women				
	IR	PC	LO	SC	IP		IR	PC	LO	SC	IP
						.001 level					
Ambitious	2.93	5.11	5.07	3.38	3.50	Foresightful	4.40	4.35	4.96	4.36	3.10
Competitive	2.93	3.85	4.33	2.96	2.75	Rebellious	2.20	2.16	2.11	2.94	4.20
Doubting	3.14	1.80	1.63	2.10	2.19						
Practical	2.93	4.04	4.43	3.73	2.44						
Foresightful	3.43	4.67	5.07	4.31	4.00						
Orderly	2.79	3.98	4.25	3.35	2.62						
Rebellious	3.00	2.54	2.31	3.12	3.75						
						.01 level					
Playful	5.07	3.54	3.63	3.52	3.81	Ambitious	4.40	4.48	4.27	3.39	3.40
Idealistic	4.57	3.85	3.94	4.56	5.31	Competitive	2.20	3.08	3.34	2.39	2.30
Creative	6.36	5.94	5.72	6.40	6.38	Free	3.00	4.69	4.61	5.58	5.70
Free	5.46	4.76	4.24	5.42	4.81	Sensitive	6.20	4.45	4.54	5.58	6.20
Sensitive	5.07	4.56	4.37	4.87	6.12						
Responsive	5.36	5.20	4.50	5.04	5.31						

385

TABLE 9. MEANS OF IDEAL DESCRIPTIONS (7-STEP SCALE) *(continued)*

Men

Adjective	IR	PC	LO	SC	IP
Conventional	2.07	2.26	**2.30**	1.98	*1.38*
Loving	6.07	5.57	*5.16*	5.25	**6.12**
Artistic	**5.29**	4.32	*4.25*	4.88	5.06
Needs approval	*1.50*	1.76	**2.01**	1.69	1.44
Self-controlled	4.64	4.78	5.11	**5.12**	*4.06*
Aloof	**2.79**	1.74	1.84	1.83	*1.81*
Impulsive	**3.29**	2.82	*2.31*	2.94	2.81
Sociable	4.07	**4.82**	4.61	4.15	*3.44*
Perceptive	6.21	6.06	*5.95*	6.36	**6.69**
Responsible	*5.23*	5.76	**6.00**	5.33	5.31
Self-confident	5.57	5.78	**6.11**	*5.38*	5.62
Stubborn	**2.36**	1.91	1.74	1.54	*1.50*
Empathic	5.57	5.15	*4.94*	5.62	**6.00**
Uncompromising	**2.71**	1.85	2.03	*1.62*	2.19
Altruistic	*3.50*	4.04	3.98	4.27	**5.44**

.05 level

Women

Adjective	IR	PC	LO	SC	IP
Idealistic	**5.20**	3.81	4.27	3.77	5.10
Practical	**4.80**	3.71	3.89	3.23	*2.60*
Orderly	3.40	4.38	**4.55**	4.00	*3.30*
Sociable	4.60	**4.99**	4.55	4.03	*3.90*
Logical	*4.20*	4.94	**5.40**	4.90	4.50
Responsible	5.60	5.62	**6.11**	5.45	*5.20*
Self-denying	*2.20*	2.98	**3.36**	2.64	2.70
Stubborn	**3.60**	1.91	2.11	2.23	*1.70*
Individualistic	5.60	5.46	*4.99*	4.97	**6.10**

NOTE. Boldface $\overline{X}$'s are highest; italics are lowest. See footnote 1.

386

TABLE 10. MEANS OF MOTHER AND FATHER DESCRIPTIONS FOR THE MEN (7-STEP SCALE)

Q item	Mother					Q item	Father				
	IR	PC	LO	SC	IP		IR	PC	LO	SC	IP
.01 level											
Expected a lot from me	**5.79**	4.51	*4.48*	5.58	5.00	Liked time for self	5.29	4.80	*4.29*	4.61	**6.06**
.05 level											
Encouraged me to do my best	5.79	6.20	**6.42**	6.23	*5.65*	Often angry with me	**5.00**	3.22	3.45	4.04	4.50
Gave me extra privileges when I was good	*3.21*	4.36	3.53	3.71	3.47	Expressed affection by hugging, kissing	2.86	2.20	*2.08*	3.02	**2.12**
Felt too much affection weakens	2.29	2.89	3.18	2.23	2.59	Believed I always told truth	*3.21*	4.76	4.63	4.39	**3.56**
Sometimes made fun of me	1.93	2.06	*1.89*	**2.77**	2.47	Let me take chances and try new things	5.00	5.48	5.03	5.68	**6.25**
Good deal of conflict between us	3.21	2.54	2.59	3.52	**3.59**	Too wrapped up in children	1.57	2.20	2.37	**2.39**	*1.38*
Liked time for self	4.71	3.56	3.59	4.31	4.41	Felt too much affection harmed child	*2.93*	4.00	3.74	3.11	**4.19**
Always knew where I was and what I was doing	*3.14*	4.47	**4.94**	4.81	4.47	Good deal of conflict between us	**4.79**	*3.02*	3.38	4.04	4.12
						Wanted me to make good impression	**6.57**	*5.26*	5.71	5.80	5.75

NOTE. Boldface $\overline{X}$'s are highest; italics are lowest. See footnote 1.

387

TABLE 11. MEANS OF MOTHER AND FATHER DESCRIPTIONS FOR THE WOMEN

Q item	Mother					Q item	Father				
	IR	PC	LO	SC	IP		IR	PC	LO	SC	IP
.01 level											
Felt I was a disappointment	*1.80*	2.13	*1.98*	2.85	**3.90**	Felt I was a disappointment	3.60	2.48	*2.19*	2.81	**3.70**
.05 level											
Gave comfort when scared	6.80	5.39	5.84	5.21	*4.50*	Gave me family duties to perform	3.60	3.88	4.64	4.00	*3.30*
Punished me by taking away privileges	4.60	4.32	4.44	3.50	*3.10*	Had firm, well established rules for me	*3.00*	3.76	4.58	3.72	3.70
Gave me extra privileges when good	3.40	3.68	**3.88**	*3.00*	3.20	Punished me by taking away privileges	4.20	4.09	4.45	*3.22*	4.10
Let me know how much she sacrificed	*1.40*	3.69	2.99	3.74	4.10	Believed competitive games good	5.80	4.71	4.79	*4.03*	4.60
Found being with children interesting	6.00	*4.24*	4.71	4.44	5.20	Did not want me to be different from others	*3.20*	4.42	3.81	3.62	3.50

NOTE. Boldface $\overline{X}$'s are highest; italics are lowest. See footnote 1.

388

is greater. More SC women are from Jewish backgrounds. IPs generally agree with their parents less (the IP men, however, are in greatest agreement with both parents about occupational choice), and report less influence from parents and more from friends. The IPs have been the more politically-socially active.

Other differences where one group occupied an extreme position while the other had a middle rank show that the IP men see themselves as especially open to experience (*curious, sympathetic, responsive*, and not *reserved*) and less tradition oriented (not *conventional* and *practical*). The SCs described themselves as the most *foresightful*. The IP's ideal conceptualizations include a sense of interpersonal involvement: *idealistic, sensitive*, and *loving*, while devaluing *competitive, self-controlled, orderly, practical, aloof*, and *sociable*. The SCs only saliently value *self-controlled* while they reject *self-confident, uncompromising*, and *playful*.

Only a single self-difference separated the women: the SCs are highest for *fair*, whereas the IPs see themselves as the lowest. The IPs, like their male counterparts, uniquely combine their dissent from society with an idealization of interpersonal reactivity: they value *rebellious* and *individualistic* but also *sensitive* and *empathic* ($p < .10$), and place the least weight on *foresightful, orderly*, and *stubborn*. The more pragmatic SCs value *idealistic* least.

The parents of the SC men appear to place more emphasis on affection. The mothers of SC men were placed lowest in feeling that affection weakens a child. Their fathers openly express affection by kissing and hugging and are seen as too wrapped up in their children. On the other hand, the families of the IP boys seem to emphasize individuation, are less pressuring and rather factual with each other; the mothers were lowest in encouraging their sons to always do their best. The fathers seem like self-individuated men with clear standards for their sons. They most wanted time for themselves, felt too much affection would harm children, and were least wrapped up in their sons. (Note that the IP fathers were seen to be much more likely than any other group to let their sons take chances and try new things.)

The mothers of the SC and IP women are not differentiable; however, differences between fathers parallel the results for the males. The IP women were not given responsibilities by their fathers and feel they have disappointed their fathers.

Summarization for principled groups   The principled groups seem to have developed an autonomous sense of themselves. Their descriptions of the good man are a leitmotif of interpersonal responsiveness and self-expressiveness. Their dissonant political stands appear relatively ego-syntonic and tension free since they have the smallest discrepancy between self and ideal on rebelliousness which is placed approximately at the absolute $\overline{X}$ on both Q sorts. They seem to have been permitted, and perhaps were encouraged by their parents, to be importantly affected by their own life experiences in their own time and place. The result seems to be that these young people, having interacted with a different and highly fluid social context, are not in high political-social agreement with their elders nor do they give them credit for what they are today. It is more likely that they feel self-made.

These parents of principled youth are not seen by their offspring as permissive; instead they are viewed as actively involved and even conflict producing. They insist on their own rights as people at the same time that they respect the needs of their children. The mothers of the IP women emphasized their sacrifices, clearly an officially disapproved way for a "good mother" to act. The fathers of the men felt free to insist on time for themselves. The familial relationships are not seen as being importantly defined by formal powers of parents to give and take away. SC families are characterized as more concrete, loving, reactive, and conflicted, whereas IP families are seen as less expressive but clearer and more factual about the individuation and the responsibilities of its members.

The women's dysphoric self-descriptions, particularly the IPs, suggest that the development of autonomous morality—perhaps even autonomous ego functioning—may be a more arduous task for girls than boys and one that is not accomplished with comfort by this age group. There is a particular flavor of self-honesty and self-condemnation, consistent with Kohlberg's formulation of IPs, reflected in their report of guilt and lack of fairness.

In summary, principled young people are characterized by a firm sense of autonomy in their life patterns and ideological positions. They appear candid about themselves and their families and espouse both new values and their new politics. They are concerned with their interpersonal obligations while they reject traditional values implicit in the Protestant Ethic.

Conventionally Moral Groups

Biographical information   The Personal Concordance (PC) and Law-Order (LO) groups of both sexes share many characteristics indicating that they conduct their lives in expected ways: they least often interrupt their college careers, predominantly live in institutional, adult-approved arrangements, are politically more conservative (the means are in the moderate to conservative range), have small political difference with their most conservative parents, and were least in support of FSM (their absolute means are still in the range of approving). Their religious upbringing was often Protestant or Catholic, and they more often retain the religious beliefs of their childhood and still attend church. Their mothers are the least educated of all groups.

Family harmony and strong parental influence are reported: the men are in the highest agreement with their fathers in regard to most issues sampled and with their mothers in regard to friends. Moreover, they attribute considerable influence to their fathers, both politically and personally, and the least to close friends. Fathers and daughters agree politically and are in harmony with regard to the subjects' vocational choice. Mothers and daughters agree on both politics and religion. These women attribute considerable political, personal, and ethical influence to their mothers and political and ethical influence to their fathers. The clergy and older relatives have also influenced them while close friends and boyfriends have not.

The conventional groups have affiliated with few political-social organizations and were relatively inactive. Only small proportions engaged in political-social activities of any sort, except for attending meetings.

Adjective Q sorts   The self-descriptions for the male groups reflect traditional virtues: they see themselves as comparatively *conventional, ambitious, sociable, practical,* and *orderly,* and not as *curious, individualistic,* or *rebellious.* The women describe themselves as *ambitious* and *foresightful* and not as *guilty, restless,* or *rebellious.*

The shared conceptualizations of the good person by both sexes include values that emphasize efficient control of the self and social skillfulness, rather than the self-expressiveness and interpersonal responsiveness valued by the principled groups. The men value *ambitious, competitive, practical, foresightful, orderly, conventional,* and with other people they would be *responsible, self-confident, sociable,* and *needing approval.* They devalue *doubting, rebellious, idealistic;* self-expressiveness as reflected in *creative, free,* and *artistic;* and interpersonal responsiveness as reflected in *sensitive, perceptive,* and *empathic.* Although the women's conceptualizations of the ideal person have less commonality, the pattern is still like the men's. They value *orderly, logical, responsible,* and, paradoxically, both *competitive* and *self-denying. Rebellious* and *sensitive* are placed low.

Perceptions of parental practices   Father-son relations are reported as the least conflictual and angry, and fathers were seen as always believing that their sons told the truth and placed least emphasis on making a good impression. The mother-son relationships also were described as less conflicted; mothers expected the least from their sons, wanted the least time for themselves, but felt most that too much affection would weaken a child.

The women's descriptions of their parents have fewer shared characteristics. Nevertheless the commonalities reflect the use of parental power: their mothers gave extra privileges when they were good; fathers had firm, well-established rules, their daughters did not disappoint them, and they did not want their daughters to be different.

PC and LO differences   A systematic difference between the PC and the LO groups can be discerned by examination of the means in Tables 3 to 11 which shows that the LOs are more exaggerated in their traditionalism than the PCs. The LOs and their parents are the more conservative; there is both greater agreement with and influence from their parents. Their parents are less consciously ambivalent. The self- and ideal descriptions of the LOs more strongly emphasize the aggressive self-sufficiency and the interpersonal exteriorizing implied in the Protestant Ethic.

Scheffé tests between groups were calculated for the significant F ratios: the PC men are politically less conservative ($p \leq .10$) than the LOs, describe themselves as less reserved ($p \leq .10$), are more valuing of responsivity ($p \leq .05$), and their mothers were more likely to give extra privileges for good behavior ($p \leq .05$). Other differences where the LOs were in an extreme position and the PCs in the middle show that the LOs see themselves as most foresightful and put the least value on loving, responsive and impulsive. Their mothers least often teased them, most often knew where they were and what they were doing, and encouraged them always to do their best. Their fathers were seen as not expressing affection openly and wanting the least time for themselves while feeling reluctant to see their sons grow up, whereas the PC fathers were the least reluctant ($p \leq .10$).

Scheffé tests showed that the PC women, significantly more than the LOs, attribute close friends ($p \leq .05$) and boyfriends ($p \leq .10$) with having influence on their morals and ethics, see themselves as less foresightful ($p \leq .10$), and also value this characteristic less ($p \leq .05$). Of all groups, the LOs see themselves as least aloof and doubting and place the lowest value on individualism. LO fathers gave their daughters family responsibilities and took away privileges when they were bad. The PC women most value sociability and ambitiousness.

Summarization for the conventionally moral groups   The context for the moral reasoning of these young people is clear: they have harmonious, non-skeptical relations with traditional institutions—school, church, and politics—and with personal authorities—father, mother, and clergy. In this way they are probably well-insulated from conflicting values, and thus the impact of current political pressures and dilemmas upon them is attenuated. In this way, and consistent with the theory's expectations, the moral choices of the LOs can be guided by the rules of existing authorities and institutions while the PCs can consider the immediate wishes and good intentions of authorities in their attempt to maintain smooth role relationships, sociability, and to avoid guilt.

In summary, these young people describe their parents as relating to them in a manner consistent with the strategies generally recommended by social learning theory for the development of morality—clear rules, punishments, and rewards. There is ample evidence that they have modeled themselves after their parents and have accepted the traditional values of American society. It is clear that the child-rearing practices and the nature of the parent-child relationship described by the conventionalists make for a high degree of familial harmony, personal confidence, and political inactivity—even within the sphere of their own conventional ideology.

Pre-moral Instrumental Relativists

Biographical information   The Instrumental Relativists (IRs) of both sexes were more likely to have interrupted their college careers. The men more infrequently live on their own, generally consider themselves political liberals or radicals, are now most nontheistic, do not attend church, but are disproportionately from Jewish backgrounds. Both men and women most strongly supported FSM, although the women are only moderate liberals. Mothers of both are the best educated and are politically liberal; their fathers are more conservative. Discrepancies with the parents in political attitudes are the greatest for the men while women are in complete harmony with the political beliefs of their mothers. The men least agree with their fathers in regard to generational gap issues but acknowledge moderate paternal personal and political influence; they disagree with their mothers about the personal concerns of friends and occupational choice. The women, more than other groups, agree with their mothers about politics and attribute strong political influence to them, but religion is a cause of discord. They attribute opposite sex peers with stronger political, personal, and ethical influence than any other group.

IR men have belonged to only a moderate number of organizations, but their participation has been the most intense; their activity has involved both protest and politics. Conversely, the women have joined the most organizations but have been the most inactive.

Adjective Q sorts   Both men and women describe themselves as the most *rebellious,* but their rebellion is not ego-syntonic as reflected by their greatest discrepancy between self- and ideal item placements. The men's self-reports generally reflect a lack of involvement with others and an emphasis on personal freedom. The men see themselves as *reserved* and *nonresponsive,* but also *creative* and *individualistic;* they idealize the traits of *aloof, stubborn,* and *uncompromising* but also would like to be *responsive, playful, free,* and *artistic.* They reject most traditional virtues and place a lower value than any group on *altruism.* The women also reject interpersonal obligations but seem more intent on securing their own ends than on being personally expressive. They describe themselves as *stubborn* and *aloof* and report that they are neither *altruistic* nor *impulsive.* They place a low value on *self-denying, free,* and *empathic* ($p \leq .10$) and idealize a contradictory pattern of *practical* and *stubborn* coupled with *idealistic* and *sensitive.* They describe themselves as the most *feminine* ($p \leq .10$), consistent with their heterosexual commitment as reflected in the influence accorded their boyfriends.

The relations of the IR men with their fathers involve greater conflict and anger than any other group. In addition, the IRs most felt that their fathers expected them to make a good impression, doubted their reliability, discouraged trying new things if failure might result, and were the least concerned that too much affection was harmful. In terms of these emphases, it is of some interest that 5 of these 16 fathers were salesmen. Their well-educated mothers seem to have a detached, laissez-faire, indulging attitude; they were the lowest in teasing them, least often gave extra privileges when the sons were good, least often knew where they were, and most liked time for themselves. They, too, were not concerned that excess affection would weaken their sons. They held the highest aspirations for them, but with ambivalence suggested by the fact that they were not particularly encouraging.

The IR women described their mothers in unrelieved, positive terms: they comforted their daughters when they were afraid, found it interesting to be with them, were not disappointed by them, did not remind them of maternal sacrifice, and did not take away privileges as punishment. Fathers were seen as uninvolved and permissive: they did not establish firm rules or family duties, did not think scolding or criticism helped ($p \leq .10$), least cared if their daughters were different, but believed competitive games were good. Five or these seven fathers were engineers.

Summarization for the IRs   Male IRs are politically radical, active, and protesting; the women are political moderates and inactive, even though they are "joiners" and strongly supported FSM. In spite of these behavioral differences, there is commonality in their intrapsychic descriptions. Both see themselves as rebellious but wish they were less so. Both disclose in their self- and ideal descriptions (by the use of such words as aloof, reserved, stubborn, uncompromising, and most importantly, altruistic and self-denying) that they do not endorse the necessity or the interpersonal obligation to take the roles of others and are, instead, more concerned with personal fulfillment—the women by a stubborn practicality and the men for personal flair and expressiveness. These findings are consistent with the Kohlberg conceptualization of Stage 2 which emphasizes self-enhancement and rejects reciprocal obligations and satisfactions.

The IR families did not seem to encourage their children to evolve a sense of responsibility and autonomy. The IR men seem to have been alternately pressured, neglected, and indulged; the women's relationships with their mothers seem somewhat immature and suggest that these women are still quite dependent on their mothers. Taken altogether, there seems to be evidence to suggest that the IRs may have been indulged as children for purposes of maternal convenience in the case of the men and for enhancing the child's dependency in the case of the women. The problem with indulgence is that it can never be unambivalent, since the competition of rights between children and parents is inevitable, giving rise to the recrimination expressed by IR men. Because indulgence is often motivated by parental convenience and self-interest, there is unpredictability and a lack of clarification of rights and responsibilities, an unlikely context for moral development.

Since these educated and advantaged young people presumably have had opportunity for cognitive development, if not moral development, their premorality may be due more to affective disruption with social units and institutions than to experiential retardation. It is possible that the IR's present level of moral reasoning might be only temporarily regressive, due to personal crises, since Kramer (1968) did find such phenomena characterizing a small sample within a longitudinal study.

A Comparison of the IR and IP Groups

The reader will have noted that the male IR and IP groups have a number of similarities. Both groups, more than any of the others, report frequent interruption of their college careers, independent living arrangements, political liberalism-radicalism, pro-FSM positions, political involvement, and a lack of religious comment. Their self- and ideal descriptions both express the mode of present-day "liberated" youth. There are other considerations, however, which indicate that the distinction between the two types is valid and that their seemingly similar protesting and politicized behavior arises from different sources.

First, there is sufficient commonality between the intrapsychic descriptions of male and female IRs to suggest that the classification has meaning. Second, the behavior of the IR and IP women is in contrast; the former are inactive, merely joiners of organizations and politically moderate, whereas the IPs are active, protesting, and radical. Third, the fact that both IP men and women are active dissenters in this sample suggests a connection between this behavior and level of moral reasoning. However, the similarity of the male IR and IP groups needs to be examined.

There are pivotal differences. The following synopsis of the differences between IR and IP males follows the rule of citing only those contrasts where these two groups are at the opposite extremes of a dimension defined by all five groups. The rated occupational focus of the IPs is highest ($p \leq .10$), and their fathers agree with them about their choice. IRs and IPs belong to radical organizations in about equal numbers, but the IPs have the highest membership in liberal organizations; the IRs have none ($p \leq .05$). There are twice as many social science majors in the IP group (56 percent) as in the IR group (25 percent), but twice as many humanities majors in the IR (25 percent) as in the IP (12 percent).

The IRs describe themselves as most stubborn ($p \leq .10$) and *reserved*; the IPs see themselves as most *responsive* and *perceptive* ($p \leq .10$). The IRs idealize *aloof* and *stubborn* ($p \leq .10$) and *reserved;* the IPs *self-denying*. The correlations between the self and ideal Q sorts is highest for the IPs, .59, and lowest for the IRs, .43. The IPs see themselves as more *uncompromising* than they ideally would like to be, but the IRs have little wish for change in this respect ($p \leq .05$). The IR fathers were lowest in letting their sons take chances and try new things, lowest in trusting them to behave when they were not around ($p \leq .10$), and lowest in thinking that too much affection harms a child. The mothers of the two groups could not be distinguished by the criterion being used.

Altogether, this pattern of results indicates a distinct difference between the male IRs and IPs and suggests that ego effectiveness is a cleaving dimension. IR and IP women not only behave differently but are different intrapsychically. IR men and women behave differently but share some pivotal self- and ideal characteristics that are consistent with the theory's conceptualization of this type.

The two groups differ in their relationship to society and to authority. The IPs are independent and critical, but also involved, giving and responsive to others. The IRs are angry, also critical, but disjointed, uncommitted to others, and potentially narcissistic. It should not be surprising to find moral heterogeneity among protestees. Protest which opts for change and accommodation in the social order should draw support from individuals who question the justice of the status quo and are committed to improving it, as well as from those who want to win an issue simply because it is theirs.

Conflict and Disagreement with Parents

In the moral types' relations with their parents the role of conflict and disagreement seems central. Since moral decisions are imminently conflictual, the way that families and institutions view, structure, and resolve conflict should have important connections with the development of morality in the young. Figure 1 shows the position of the moral types on separate indexes of mother and father conflict generated by converting three measures of conflict to standard scores and compositing. The dimensions included: (a) subjects' discrepancy with each parent in political commitment, (b) mean disagreement between subject and parents on the generational gap issues, and (c) placement of the Q-sort item referring to degree of conflict with the parent. For the men, there is a curvilinear relationship between conflict and moral reasoning: intense family conflict, particularly with the father, being associated with premorality, least conflict with conventional morality, and moderate conflict with principled morality. For women, conflict with mother is positively related to increasing morality, whereas conflict with father is less important but is still positively related. The relationship with the same-sex parent is the more determinative. A difference between parents in level of conflict is most evident in the IR families.

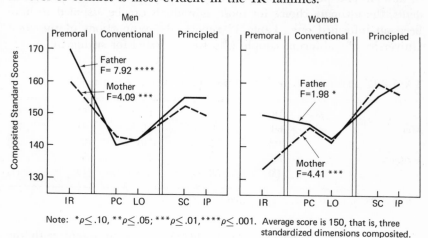

Note: $^*p \leq .10$, $^{**}p \leq .05$; $^{***}p \leq .01$, $^{****}p \leq .001$. Average score is 150, that is, three standardized dimensions composited.

FIGURE 1. Index of Parental Conflict and Disagreement for Various Moral Types

The findings for men are generally consistent with Kohlberg's (1966) suggestions that moral development is promoted by the cognitive reorganizations that occur when the moral conflicts of naturalistic social interactions are openly examined and negotiated. Langer (1969) has posited a similar vehicle for cognitive development—cognitive disequilibrium. Both the degree of conflict and its quality—affective rather than cognitive—may have retarded or disrupted the moral development in the IR men. This finding is consistent with well-accepted observations that intense or chronic affective states are stressful and disruptive of ego processes. In the female sample, conflict is positively related to moral maturity. Undoubtedly there would be an upper limit but it was not reached in this sample. The social milieu and expectations for women encourage dependency, which is one form of irresponsibility. Consequently, the development of autonomous, principled morality may be a more difficult task for girls because it involves conflict with the culturally defined feminine role. The principled women's dysphoria and their admission of disappointing their parents may be a manifestation of their moral growing pains.

The FSM Situation

The FSM sit-in provides us with an opportunity to view the public behavior of the University of California students in response to the same, well-publicized incident (cf. Lipset & Wolins, 1965, for a good chronology of the event and statement of the issues). Since this conflict took months to develop and public debate took place daily before thousands of students, the ultimate choice for most individuals can be assumed to have been an informed one. Table 12 reports the proportions of the total University of California sample who were arrested for sitting in.

TABLE 12. PERCENTAGES OF PURE MORAL TYPES ARRESTED IN THE FSM SIT-IN

	IR	PC	LO	SC	IP
Men	60	18	6	41	75
	(10)	(22)	(50)	(27)	(8)
Women	33	9	12	57	86
	(3)	(32)	(41)	(14)	(7)

NOTE. UC students only. *N*'s in parentheses.

These findings, based on a public behavior, are consistent with the subjects' reported activities and substantiate the general relationships of moral reasoning to behavior. The variety of moral reasons that can lead to the same behavior, civil disobedience in this instance, is shown by the fact that some conventionally moral people were also arrested. Most of these students supported their choice of sitting-in (which they reported in the special story concerned with the FSM situation) by reasoning which referred to their supposition that the University of California administrators had failed in their role of authorities—as good authorities for Stage 3, and as actual violators of proper legal understandings for Stage 4. Principled arrestees were more concerned with the basic issues of civil liberties and rights and the relationship of students as citizens within a university community. The IRs' reasons were more often concerned with their individual rights in a conflict of power. They frequently included the indubitable fact that the sit-in had worked to bring social-political reforms on the campus.

DISCUSSION

That there are comparatively few women in the extreme IR and IP groups, that the source samples were not representative, and that the Moral Judgment Scale is better administered in an interview have already been noted as limitations of this study. The reliance upon the subjects' descriptions of themselves and their view of their parents means that these results are to be regarded as descriptions of the subjects' present views—including defensive, wishful, or hostile distortions—of their history and current relationships.

Perceptions of parents are undoubtedly subject to developmental changes, and these subjects have described them during a period when separation from the family usually occurs. To the extent that the present results depend upon the character of concurrent relations and upon levels of moral reasoning that may still be evolving, the findings must be understood in a special light. Young people who have already become principled regard themselves as separated from their parents; those who are still conventionally moral, or who will remain conventionally moral, see themselves as stably attached to their parents; pre-moral men view their familial relationships as chaotically conflicted and indulging, and pre-moral women see theirs as mother-centered. Little is known about whether adult experiences affect moral development. Kramer (1968) did find continued growth in the late adolescent and young adult years, characterized by a decrease in lower stages rather than an increase in higher stages. This finding suggests that the pre-moral subjects might be the ones most likely to change.

Within these limitations and qualifications the results also show strong associations between political protest, social action, and principled reasoning—qualified by the finding that pre-moral men also protest—and that young people of conventional moral reasoning are inactive. Note that these findings do not suggest that protest in itself is moral. That judgment would have to depend upon the nature of the individual's reasoning and the specific aspects of the situation.

This finding and those concerned with parental relations raise a number of questions: What conceptualizations account for the association between the form of moral reasoning and related political-social behavior, since there is no political content in the Kohlberg stories? How can the family and social context of these young people be understood to support these outcomes? Can the Kohlberg conceptualization of moral reasoning account for the shift away from parental values that the principled protestors report?

Subsequent discussion of the above questions necessarily interweaves two concepts: the relation of moral thinking to the existing order of things and the individual's capability of taking another's or society's point of view when he is engaged in moral thought.

The frame of reference for the middle, conventional level of moral reasoning is that of maintaining society. Thus, the morally conventional individual—as he structures the interlocking pros and cons of a moral problem and considers its ramifications, consequences, and alternative solutions—views himself and his decisions as immanently within society. He will see and choose the good in those terms. Consequently, conventional moralizing does not often come to doubt the status quo, unless representatives of that order disappointingly and clearly prove themselves unworthy of their positions. In this way conventional morality circumscribes thinking and choosing the good, and it follows that such individuals are not likely to protest.

The IR must reject the status quo since it often does not comply with his egoistic view of his relationship to others and society and with his personally referenced definition of the good. His self-view does not permit him to see or take the roles of others including those in authority. This inability undoubtedly becomes an increasingly unworkable mode of choosing for people as they grow older.

Conventional, and particularly principled, morality is made possible by the capacity to take another's role which depends upon the ability to extend one's self and move from one's fixedness. The empathy of the PC moralist, although not equivalent to principled or IP role taking, is a precursor of it, as is the understanding respect the LO pays to representatives of society. When a principled person, particularly an IP, temporarily takes the position of another in a moral conflict situation— he may still end up rejecting the primary or legitimacy of the others' rights, such as the drug owner's in the story cited in this paper—considerable cognitive interplay and work is involved. Here thought has the properties of consistency, objectivity, universality, and impersonalness. The thought of the pre-moralist, however, does not show these characteristics; that is, he cannot objectively take another person's position, irrespective of who he is, and understand that ultimately the other has basic human needs that are roughly consistent with his own.

Political-social protest and premoral reasoning are probably not consistently linked across many samples, as the results for women suggest. Since the IR's concern about society is personally referenced, a generally politicized milieu is undoubtedly required for the IR to protest, and his ultimate criterion would often be whether it would work or not. Political protest itself is likely a fine expression of politicized IR's personal battles with a society which is seen as ungiving rather than immoral.

The principled individual is not automatically limited by the extant characteristics of a specified social order or arrangement. The SC, however, with his stronger sense of being contractually obligated, may not clearly or smoothly separate himself from the social order, even when he cognizes covenanted injustices. The IP's allegiance in a moral confrontation will be to universal and logically consistent, ideal principles of justice which necessarily include existing social agreements, but his principles will be primary if these two considerations should conflict. Kohlberg (1968) has observed that one cannot be at Stage 6 without first having been at Stage 5, that is, one cannot reject a social contract *on the basis of individual principles* without first understanding the essential contractual nature of social orders and human affairs. The IP takes the role of others in a most inclusive, abstract, and ideal sense. The "others" may frequently be all mankind and are not only those personally known or directly observed as with the PC, or occupants of formal positions as with the LO, or parties to contractual understandings as with the SC. The IP's sense of personal responsibility causes him to take roles in double sense, not only understanding the position of others, but also questioning what he would have others do to him if the tables were turned. This highly developed sense of interpersonal obligation was reflected in the IP's description of the person he would like to be— sensitive, empathic, and altruistic or self-denying. Principled thinking may or may not support the status quo, but since societies (and people) are only approximate representations of the good at any one time and place, the principled with his sense of obligation and his sense of himself as a chooser, and again the IP more than the SC, is the most likely to protest, as this study has shown.

Most studies that have related behavior to moral judgment have chosen behavior such as cheating, which is "bad" by everybody's agreement, and the required, criterion moral action is prohibitive (cf. Kohlberg, 1964; Maccoby, 1968 for reviews; also Krebs, 1967). The behavior studied here better represents "promotive" or "affiliative" morality as declaratory acts were analyzed. Only one other similar study has been reported. Kohlberg (1968) gave the Moral Judgment Scale to the students who were subjects in Milgram's pseudo-learning experiments. They were asked by the experimenter (an authority) to violate the universal dictate of not hurting others for insufficient reasons by shocking victims who did not learn rapidly. Since subjects needed to take emphatic and disobedient action to solve their dilemma, the situation is similar to ones that the student protestors often believe they are in. Kohlberg found that 75 percent of the subjects who used some Stage 6 thinking quit the experiment compared to only 13 percent of conventional or pure Stage 5 subjects. Milgram (1965) has commented that most people are without a language of disobedience when confronted with such situations. Kohlberg's study and the present one show, however, that Stage 6 individuals are the least likely to comply with requirements they regard as morally indefensible.

The relationships between the conventionally moral subjects, particularly the LOs, and their parents are consistent with moral replacement, a process Maccoby (1968) has labeled and used to describe the intergenerational process of value transmission as it is conceptualized by social learning theory. The conventionally moral report that their parents used child-rearing strategies which are consistent with social learning's recommendations for the development of morality—clear rules, punishments, and rewards—and there is ample evidence that they have modeled themselves after their parents. The present results suggest that these procedures do not release young people to be affected by their own experiences or to shift in response to social change as Maccoby had already deduced. The principled subjects, while not rejecting their parents with ambivalent anger as do the male pre-moralists, have adopted political-social and personal values that reflect contemporary leitmotif. Their responsiveness to social change, however, had a history of preparedness within politically liberal families who frankly experienced and examined conflict, and with parents who exercised their own rights as people, rather than the power and control that society automatically ascribes to them.

The families of the conventional moralists were probably not as conflict-free as their offspring describe, and were more likely reported to be conflictless because this was an important family value (an ideal parent sort would have provided certain information). When harmony is an ultimate value, individuals are prone to base their decisions on the approved solutions. Furthermore, conflictless experiences are probably inconsistent with both moral and cognitive growth. Both Turiel (1969) and Kohlberg (1968) have recently reported work which shows that moral development can be accelerated by moral arguments presented to children along with contradictory solutions and different levels of moral thought. The present authors have previously pointed out (Block et al., 1968), in accord with Inhelder and Piaget (1958), that adolescent cognitive development is characterized by the growth of capacities to entertain hypothetical ideas of what might be and to engage in reciprocity—there but for good fortune, go you or I. In this fluid, abstract, and person-oriented context moral disequilibriums undoubtedly occur and may result in change.

Undoubtedly new settings and new experiences, such as those encountered on a college campus, make for cognitive disequilibriums and the re-examination of moral commitments. Late adolescents who are open to experience are more likely to change than those who protect themselves from disharmonies. At the same time they may be the more vulnerable to temporary or permanent regressions, but then all growth is a chance. One does not know whether the stress and moral conflict of the FSM crisis and other Bay Area protests have affected the moral judgments of young people, but they may very well have. One does not know whether the net effect would be progressive or regressive, but it may be surmised that both occurred.

SUMMARY

College students and Peace Corps volunteers were assigned to a typology of moral reasoning according to their responses to the Kohlberg Moral Judgment Scale. Differences among 5 moral types in family-social background, self- and ideal descriptions, and descriptions of mother and father were analyzed. In general, Ss of principled moral reasoning, as contrasted with the conventionally moral, were more active in political-social matters, particularly in protest; their views on current issues were more discrepant from their parents who themselves were politically liberal; their self- and ideal conceptualizations emphasized interpersonal reactivity and obligation, self-expressiveness, and a willingness to live in opposition. Perceptions of parental relationships suggest that little conflict or separation occurred in the families of the conventionally moral with more in those of the principled.

REFERENCES

Aronfreed, J. *Conduct and Conscience: The Socialization of Internalized Control over Behavior.* New York: Academic Press, 1968.

Baier, K. *The Moral Point of View.* Ithaca: Cornell University Press, 1958.

Bandura, A., and McDonald, F. Influence of social reinforcement and the behavior of models in shaping children's moral judgments. *Journal of Abnormal and Social Psychology,* 1963, **67,** 274–281.

Block, J. The child-rearing practices report. Institute of Human Development, University of California, 1965. (Mimeo)

Block, J. H., Haan, N., and Smith, M. B. Activism and apathy in contemporary adolescents. In J. F. Adams (Ed.) *Understanding Adolescence: Current Developments in Adolescent Psychology.* Boston: Allyn & Bacon, 1968.

Inhelder, B., and Piaget, J. *The Growth of Logical Thinking.* New York: Basic Books, 1958.

Kohlberg, L. Development of moral character and moral ideology. In H. Hoffman and L. Hoffman (Eds.) *Review of Child Development Research.* Vol. 1. New York: Russell Sage Foundation, 1964.

Kohlberg, L. Moral and religious education and the public schools: A developmental view. In T. R. Sizer (Ed.) *Religion and Public Education.* New York: Houghton-Mifflin, 1967.

Kohlberg, L. Education for justice: a modern statement of the Platonic view. Ernest Burton Lecture on moral education, Harvard University, April 23, 1968.

Kramer, R. B. Changes in moral judgment response pattern during late adolescence and young adulthood: retrogression in a development sequence. Unpublished doctoral dissertation, University of Chicago, 1968.

Krebs, R. Some relations between moral judgment, attention, and resistance to temptation. Unpublished doctoral dissertation, University of Chicago, 1967.

Langer, J. Disequilibrium as a source of development. In P. Mussen, J. Langer, and M. L. Covington (Eds.) *Trends and Issues in Developmental Psychology.* New York: Holt, Rinehart and Winston, 1969.

Lipset, S. M., and Wilins, S. S. (Eds.) *The Berkeley Student Revolt: Facts and Interpretations.* Garden City, N. Y.: Doubleday, 1965.

Maccoby, E. Development of moral values and behavior. In J. Clausen (Ed.) *Socialization and Society.* New York: Little, Brown, 1968.

Milgram, S. Some conditions of obedience and disobedience to authority. *Human Relations,* 1965, **18,** 57–76.

Smith, M. B., Haan, N., and Block, J. Social-psychological aspects of student activism. In B. Rubenstein and M. Levitt (Ed.) *Rebels and the Campus Revolt.* New York: Prentice-Hall, 1969.

Turiel, E. Developmental processes in the child's moral thinking. In P. Mussen, J. Langer, and M. L. Covington (Eds.) *Trends and Issues in Developmental Psychology.* New York: Holt, Rinehart and Winston, 1969.

3.5 *Orientation*

It is virtually impossible to examine the psychological literature concerned with personality development and mental health without encountering a reference to the *self-concept*. Most generally, the self-concept is thought to represent an organized system of *expectancies* and *self-evaluative* tendencies. Such expectancies may be reflected by an individual's subjective estimates concerning what he can or cannot do; self-evaluative tendencies may be manifest by the feelings one has regarding the quality of his behavior. It is the extent to which one holds a favorable view of himself or tends to debase himself in which the authors of the following paper are interested. And their particular focus is the possible influence that racial segregation and integration policies may have upon the self-esteem of Negro youth.

Research on self-esteem and the self-concept is most typically grounded in *self-theory*. This point of view holds that behavior is to be understood primarily in terms of an individual's perception of himself and his environment and the meaning he attaches to his experience. Thus, according to self-theory, behavior is mediated by one's perceptions and self-reference tendencies regardless of how closely such perceptions correspond to reality and how appropriate self-references may be in an actual situation. Self-theory further suggests that behavior is motivated primarily in terms of the maintenance, enhancement, and actualization of self. The organization and generality of the self-concept are thought to increase successively with age.

Of the many problems faced by researchers oriented toward self-theory, the measurement of the self-concept has been a most critical one. The Tennessee Self-Concept Scale utilized by Williams and Byars exemplifies the psychometric approach to this problem. Data that have accumulated to date on the attributes of this instrument, including reliability and validity, are encouraging (Fitts & Crites, 1965). A theoretical issue has been raised, however, in connection with its use, an issue worthy of the reader's consideration. The Tennessee Scale presents 100 self-descriptive statements (for example, "I have a healthy body") to which an examinee must respond on a five-point scale ranging from "Completely True" to "Completely False." One, of course, must assume that an examinee will respond honestly to these statements. The more basic issue, however, is whether any self-concept measure can be genuinely phenomenological unless an examinee is permitted to use *his own words* to describe himself.

Problems of theory and measurement aside, the Williams and Byars study attends to a profoundly significant social (and psychological) issue and relates closely to the identity concept discussed in Part I. Among other things, the results of this study suggest that major psychological characteristics, such as one's self-concept, are not likely to be modified simply. Perhaps a broader implication of these findings is that integration *per se* may contribute little to the psychological strength of those whose racial or ethnic identity has served as a target for discriminatory practices in our society.

RECOMMENDED READINGS

Fitts, W. H., and Crites, J. O. Test reviews: Tennessee Self-Concept Scale. *Journal of Counseling Psychology*, 1965, **12**, 330–331.

Kvaraceus, William H. *et al. The Relationship of Education to Self-Concept in Negro Children and Youth.* New York: McGraw-Hill, 1965.

Rainwater, Lee. Crucible of identity: the Negro lower-class family. *Daedalus*, 1966, **95**, No. 1.

3.5   Negro Self-Esteem in a Transitional Society

Robert L. Williams, UNIVERSITY OF TENNESSEE
Harry Byars, WEST GEORGIA COLLEGE

Of the pernicious effects of racial segregation, perhaps none is more debilitating than the effect on the Negro's self-esteem. Research indicates that in a segregated social milieu, feelings of self-abasement originate early in life and have a pervasive and deep effect on the Negro personality. Clark and Clark (1947), by studying the reactions of Negro children to brown and white dolls, found that children as young as age three years show awareness of racial differences. At all ages studied (three to seven years) the majority of subjects preferred the white doll and attributed negative characteristics to the colored doll. Radke and Trager (1950) also found a greater tendency for Negro children to choose white dolls in play situations than for white children to choose brown dolls. In a similar vein, Pettigrew (1964) has proposed that Negro chil-

Reprinted from the *Personnel and Guidance Journal*, 1968, **47**, 120–125, by permission of the authors and the American Personnel and Guidance Association.

dren usually prefer white friends and often identify themselves as white. The injurious effect of segregation on the Negro personality is equally evident among older children and adults (Myers & Yochelson, 1948; Boykin, 1957; Grossack, 1957; Karon, 1958; McClain, 1967).

From a theoretical perspective, the debasing effect of segregation on Negro self-esteem is entirely explicable. Most self-concept theorists (Kelly & Rasey, 1952; Maslow, 1954; Combs & Snygg, 1959; Rogers, 1961) maintain that self-evaluation evolves basically from the evaluations of others. If society communicates to the Negro child that he is a second-rate, subservient individual, it is probable that he would come to view himself as an inferior person. There is no social institution that emphatically communicates to the Negro that he is an inferior individual more than segregation does.

The major purpose of the present study was to assess objectively the magnitude of self-esteem among Negro adolescents in what traditionally have been segregated Southern communities. The study was deemed advisable for two reasons: (a) many previous investigations have employed projective type instruments which permit considerable subjectivity of interpretation, (b) the sweeping changes in civil rights are most likely affecting Negro self-esteem. Although some research (Yarrow, Campbell, & Yarrow, 1958) suggests that short-term interracial contact has a facilitative effect on the Negro self-concept, other investigators (Pugh, 1943; Katz & Benjamin, 1960) have found that integration may initially create greater insecurity and self-hate. If a recent survey (Chesler, 1967) of the humiliating experiences of Negro children in desegregated Southern classrooms is at all valid, diminished self-esteem is not surprising.

However, despite these adverse experiences, many Negro leaders are ardently emphasizing the need for self-acceptance and racial pride. The focus of the present study is on Negro self-esteem in a transitional period when the Negro is being subjected to a multiplicity of new and often contradictory influences. Specifically, there were three major concerns in the investigation: (a) Negro-Caucasian self-concept disparities; (b) discrepancies between Negro self-images and normative self-concept scores; and (c) differences between the self-evaluations of Negroes in both integrated and segregated academic settings.

METHOD

Subjects

The sample consisted of 176 Caucasian students (88 males, 88 females) and 134 Negro students (67 males, 67 females) which were selected from a cross-section of rural and urban schools in Georgia. However, because of the inaccessibility of schools in heavily populated regions, the sample is more representative of students in rural and small urban Southern communities than those in larger metropolitan areas. The subjects were selected from both segregated and integrated academic settings and, within the participating schools, were chosen on a random basis. The Negro group was composed of 35 students attending integrated schools and 99 in segregated institutions. Most of the integrated schools had been desegregated within the last year, whereas the segregated schools were scheduled for desegregation the following year. To avoid contamination of results by the major physiological and emotional changes of early puberty, the experimenters selected students at the senior high level.

Instrument and Procedure

The Tennessee Self-Concept Scale (Fitts, 1965), a standardized Likert-type instrument, was used in assessing self-esteem. The norms for this scale were developed from a broad sample of 626 persons. The standardization sample included individuals from various parts of the country and ranged in age from 12 to 68. "There were approximately equal numbers of both sexes, both Negro and white subjects, representatives of all social, economic, and intellectual levels and educational levels from sixth grade through the Ph.D. degree" (Fitts, 1965, p. 13).

The Tennessee scale provides an assessment of Physical Self, Moral-Ethical Self, Personal Self, Family Self, Social Self, and Total Positive Self. Additional measures of the Tennessee scale used in the present study were Self-Criticism (obvious defensiveness), Total Conflict (confusion and contradiction in self-perception), Total Variability (inconsistency or lack of integration), True-False Ratio (response set or response bias), Defensive Positive Scale (subtle defensiveness), General Maladjustment (empirical index of adjustment-maladjustment), Psychosis Scale (empirical psychotic scale), Personality Disorder (basic personality defects), Neurosis Scale (empirical neurotic scale), and Personality Integration (empirical personal adjustment scale). The data were collected by both Negro and white examiners at the beginning of the academic year. The subjects were instructed that their responses would be used only for research purposes and would not be revealed to their teachers.

Results

The analysis of the data for the various dimensions of self-esteem produced pervasive differences between the Negro and Caucasian subjects but not between the Negroes attending integrated and segregated schools. The Negro students in integrated schools obtained slightly higher scores on most of the basic self-esteem dimensions than the Negroes in segregated settings but not to a significant degree.

In contrast, a series of 2×2 factorial design analyses, with race and sex as the independent variables, revealed that on 12 of 17 dimensions the combined Negro group scored below the Caucasian (see Table 1). The Self-Criticism scale provided the only relevant race $\times$ sex interaction. On each of the 17 scales the Negro mean was below the concomitant normative mean, in some instances as much as one or two standard deviations. The Negro subjects fared best on the assessment of Physical Self, with a mean score slightly above the Caucasian mean and slightly below the normative.

TABLE 1. Means, Standard Deviations, and Significance Levels for Self-Concept Scores

Scale	Normative Mean	Normative SD	Negro Mean	Caucasian Mean	Level of Significance
Physical Self	71.78	7.67	70.50	69.79	NS
Moral-Ethical Self	70.33	8.70	62.58	66.03	.005
Personal Self	64.55	7.41	59.85	62.32	.05
Family Self	70.83	8.43	65.32	66.97	NS
Social Self	68.14	7.86	63.46	65.40	.05
Total Positive	345.57	30.70	326.26	330.76	NS
Self-Criticism	35.54	6.70	33.40[a]	36.75[a]	.02
Defensive Positive	54.60	12.38	59.68	51.54	.005
Total Conflict	30.10	8.21	44.92	33.70	.005
Total Variability	48.53	12.42	53.92	53.89	NS
Distribution	120.44	24.19	120.66	113.53	.025
True/False Ratio	1.03	.29	1.61	1.09	.005
Personality Integration	10.42	3.88	6.08	8.58	.005
Personality Disorder[b]	76.39	11.72	64.74	68.50	.01
General Maladjustment[b]	98.80	9.15	88.87	91.67	.05
Neurosis[b]	84.31	11.10	79.78	79.81	NS
Psychosis[b]	46.10	6.49	54.84	48.24	.005

[a] Significant interaction, means computed only for males.
[b] Inverse Scale.

Of the five basic dimensions of self-evaluation, Moral-Ethical, Personal, and Social yielded significantly lower scores for the Negro subjects. The test manual describes the Moral-Ethical score as relating to perception of "moral worth, relationship to God, feelings of being a 'good' or 'bad' person, and satisfaction with one's religion or lack of it." The Personal Self score is reflective of "the individual's sense of personal worth, his feeling of adequacy as a person, and his evaluation of his personality apart from his body or his relationship to others"; and the Social Self measures an indication of "the person's sense of adequacy and worth in his social interactions with people in general (Fitts, 1965, p. 3)."

A basic consideration in the interpretation of self-description data is the willingness of the respondent to convey derogatory information about himself. The Tennessee scale includes two defensiveness measures: the Self-Criticism scale (SC) and the Defensive Positive scale (DP). The SC scale is composed of mildly discreditable statements that most people will admit to being true of themselves. The analysis of the SC data yielded a significant interaction effect, that is, Negro males were significantly lower than white males and Negro females, whereas the white and Negro females did not differ. This finding implies that the Negro male is more defensive about his reported self-esteem than the white male or Negro female.

The DP scale provides a more subtle assessment of defensiveness than the SC. In formulating the DP scale, Fitts identified 29 items which differentiated psychiatric patients with high self-esteem scores from the other groups. Fitts assumes that persons with established psychiatric disorders do have negative self-perceptions at some level of cognition even though the individuals may not be consciously aware of these negative perceptions. Scores on the DP scale indicate that the Negro participants exhibited significantly greater defensive distortion of their self-descriptions than the Caucasians.

Another cogent concern in evaluating the self-concept is the clarity, certainty, and consistency of the self-esteem judgments. Four scales—Total Conflict, Total Variability, Distribution (D), and True-False Ratio (T/F)—pertain to this issue. The Total Conflict score indicates "confusion, contradiction, and general conflict" within the basic self-concept areas (Fitts, 1965). On this scale the Negro mean was significantly above the Caucasian mean and almost two standard deviations above the corresponding normative mean. The Variability score is an assessment of inconsistency between the basic dimensions of esteem, for example, a high Personal Self in combination with a low Social Self. While the racial groups did not differ on the Total Variability scale, both were markedly above the normative mean. The Distribution score relates to certainty of self-perception. Individuals using the extremes, "completely false," or "completely true," of the Likert format would obtain high D scores.

Although the Negro subjects obtained significantly higher D scores than the whites, the results do not necessarily indicate a high level of certainty in self-delineation among Negroes. Actually, the Negro mean was commensurate with the normative mean. White defensiveness rather than Negro certainty would be a more appropriate interpretation of the D scores. High T/F scores denote that the individual is attempting to delineate his self-perception by focusing on what he *is*, and is relatively unable to eliminate what he is *not*. Low T/F scores indicate the converse orientation. On this dimension Negro participants obtained significantly higher ratios than the Caucasians; in fact, the Negro T/F ratio mean was approximately two standard deviations above the Caucasian and normative means.

The Personality Integration (PI), Personality Disorder (PD), General Maladjustment (GM), and Psychosis (Psy) scores, all empirical scales, indicated that Negro students are more similar in their test responses to individuals diagnosed as having adjustment problems than are the Caucasian adolescents. Although the groups did not differ on the Neurosis scale, both were substantially below the normative mean.

DISCUSSION

The results of this study portray the Southern Negro adolescent as generally negative in self-perception, quite defensive in his self-description, not having a clear, consistent picture of himself, and having extensive personality problems. The self-concept patterns for Negro students cannot be construed simply as an outgrowth of a geographic area, since Caucasian subjects from the same area obtained very different profiles. However, on certain dimensions the Caucasians and Negroes did not differ, whereas both were considerably below the normative means. The one scale on which the Negro subjects had the highest degree of self-confidence was the evaluation of physical prowess. Undoubtedly, the Negro's accomplishments in athletics at all levels of competition plus his proclivity for physical activities have enhanced the appraisal of physical self. However, on the remaining dimensions of self-evaluation, the Negro subjects obtained significantly lower scores than the Caucasian adolescents or scored almost a standard deviation below the normative mean.

The civil rights emphasis on racial pride and self-respect may partially account for the defensiveness manifested by the Negro subjects. It is socially expedient for the Negro to view himself as a capable, worthy human being. This refusal to admit derogatory self-perceptions is particularly pronounced among Negro males. Radke, Sutherland, and Rosenberg (1950) suggest that Negro females are more inclined to accept devaluation of their race than Negro males. Several researchers (Smuts,

1957; Gaier & Wambach, 1960; Ausubel & Ausubel, 1963) have affirmed that segregation has a more deleterious effect on the Negro male than female. Therefore, in the painful period of basic social reform the Negro male compared to the female may feel a deeper need to present himself in a positive light to society. The race of the examiner may also affect the defensiveness of Negro subjects. Grossack (1956) indicates that Negroes manifest greater racial pride if tested by a white examiner than by a Negro interviewer. To randomize the defensiveness which Negro subjects might exhibit toward examiners of particular racial identities, the experimenters randomly employed both Negro and white examiners in the collection of the data.

Self-concept theorists (Kelley & Rasey, 1952; Combs & Snygg, 1959) are in general agreement that the self-perceptions of a given individual accrue from the reactions of others toward that individual. Perhaps no cultural group within our society is experiencing more varied and contradictory social reactions than the Negro. The Negro has not entirely shed the shackles of segregation but is now faced with a multiplicity of new social currents which convey very different information concerning his identity and destiny. These new voices in a somewhat obstreperous fashion demand an audience, but to listen to one may exclude others. The myriad and contradictory social influences would undoubtedly produce ambiguity and confusion in self-identity.

The findings of the present study confirm this postulation. The Negro students obtained a mean almost two standard deviations above the normative mean on an assessment of conflict, contradiction, and confusion in self-image. The high T/F Ratios of the Negro participants imply that they have either a pronounced tendency to acquiesce or a clearer perception of what they are than what they are not. The ignominious abasement of past decades and the ostensible opportunities of the future have contributed to uncertainty in self-identity. The safest course may be to exclude no possibility in self-delineation, either positive or negative.

It seems reasonable to assume that the excruciating frustrations of the past plus the trauma of present social changes would have some effect on the general emotional adjustment of Negroes. The empirical scales indicated that the Negro subjects responded to the statements in a fashion similar to that of individuals who are judged to be poorly integrated, generally maladjusted, neurotic or psychotic, and having basic personality defects.

While the past decade has brought dramatic change in the social status of the Southern Negro, it has by no means totally remediated the ills of the past. The Negro students in recently integrated schools compared to those in segregated settings evidenced some trend toward improvement in self-esteem, however at present such improvement is minimal. Teachers and counselors in integrated schools should not assume that integration will magically ameliorate all the self-doubt and self-hate produced by years of racial discrimination. It may be extremely difficult to upgrade the academic achievement of the disadvantaged Negro child without first providing an atmosphere in which the child can more fully discover and respect himself. The problem is of such magnitude as to warrant a concerted attempt to train prospective teachers and counselors in the mechanics of self-theory and methodology of changing self-esteem.

SUMMARY

The focus of the study was on the self-esteem of Negro adolescents in Southern communities where desegregation of public facilities and schools is occurring. The major emphasis was Negro self-evaluation in a period of increasing social and academic integration. The Tennessee Self-Concept Scale, a standardized Likert-type instrument, was administered to 134 Negro and 176 Caucasian senior high school students. On 12 of 17 self-evaluation dimensions the Negro subjects obtained scores significantly below those of whites and on all 17 scales obtained mean scores below the corresponding normative means. Generally, the findings indicated that the Negro students were low in self-confidence, defensive in their self-descriptions, confused concerning their self-identity, and similar in their performance to neurotic and psychotic individuals. Negro students attending integrated schools did not differ significantly from those in segregated settings.

REFERENCES

Ausubel, D. P., and Ausubel, P. Ego development among segregated Negro children. In A. H. Passow (Ed.) *Education in Depressed Areas.* New York: Bureau of Publications, Teachers College, Columbia University, 1963, 109–141.

Boykin, L. L. The adjustment of 2,078 Negro students. *Journal of Negro Education,* 1957, 26, 75–79.

Chesler, M. A. *In Their Own Words: A Student Appraisal of What Happened after School Desegragation.* Atlanta: Southern Regional Council, 1967.

Clark, K. B., and Clark, M. P. Racial identification and preference in Negro children. In T. M. Newcomb and E. L. Hartley (Eds.) *Readings in Social Psychology.* New York: Holt, 1947, pp. 169–178.

Combs, A. W., and Snygg, D. *Individual Behavior: A Perceptual Approach to Behavior.* (Rev. ed.) New York: Harper and Brothers, 1959.

Fitts, W. H. *Tennessee Self-Concept Scale.* Nashville: Counselor Recordings and Tests, 1965.

Gaier, E. L., and Wambach, H. S. Self-evaluation of personality assets and liabilities of southern white and Negro students. *Journal of Social Psychology*, 1960, **51**, 135–143.

Grossack, M. M. Group belongingness among Negroes. *Journal of Social Psychology*, 1956, **43**, 167–180.

Grossack, M. M. Some personality characteristics of southern Negro students. *Journal of Social Psychology*, 1957, **46**, 125–131.

Karon, B. P. *The Negro Personality.* New York: Springer, 1958.

Katz, I., and Benjamin, L. Effects of white authoritarianism in biracial work groups. *Journal of Abnormal and Social Psychology*, 1960, **61**, 448–456.

Kelly, E. C., and Rasey, M. I. *Education and the Nature of Man.* New York: Harper and Brothers, 1952.

Maslow, A. H. *Motivation and Personality.* New York: Harper and Brothers, 1954.

McClain, E. W. Personality characteristics of Negro college students in the South—a recent appraisal. *Journal of Negro Education*, 1967 Summer Yearbook, **36**, 320–325.

Myers, H. J., and Yochelson, L. Color denial in the Negro: a preliminary report. *Psychiatry*, 1948, **11**, 39–46.

Pettigrew, T. F. *A Profile of the Negro American.* Princeton, N.J.: Van Nostrand, 1964.

Pugh, R. W. A comparative study of the adjustment of Negro students in mixed and separate high schools. *Journal of Negro Education*, 1943, **12**, 607–616.

Radke, M., Sutherland, J., and Rosenberg, P. Racial attitudes of children. *Sociometry*, 1950, **13**, 154–171.

Radke, M., and Trager, H. G. Children's perceptions of the social roles of Negroes and whites. *Journal of Psychology*, 1950, **29**, 2–33.

Rogers, C. R. *On Becoming a Person.* Boston: Houghton-Mifflin, 1961.

Smuts, R. W. The Negro community and the development of Negro potential. *Journal of Negro Education*, 1957, **26**, 456–465.

Yarrow, M. R., Campbell, J. D., and Yarrow, L. J. Acquisition of new norms: a study of racial desegregation. *Journal of Social Issues*, 1958, **14**, 8–28.

3.6 Orientation

In a technologically advancing society such as ours, unique problems are created by adolescents who elect to leave the school environment before completing their formal education. The relevance of such education for all adolescents is open for debate. There can be little argument, however, that the typical high school dropout fares less well in society than his "stay-in" counterpart. For one thing, the job-market is considerably more restricted for non-graduates of high school. What jobs are available generally do not provide impressive salaries or security. Leaving school may reduce developmentally important social opportunities for adolescents and the path toward delinquency seems to be more frequently traveled by high school dropouts.

Among the many concerns expressed by psychologists and sociologists for the dropout phenomenon, concern for its etiology is paramount. This concern is seemingly predicated on the assumption that one must understand fully the causes of a problem in order to deal adequately with that problem. The authors of the following piece of research address themselves precisely to causation in reference to the unsuccessful school behavior of adolescents. And, as the reader will see, these researchers have pinpointed the concept of *primary human relationships* as a critical variable in academic achievement.

It must be noted that the data upon which the primary relationships academic achievement association is founded do not constitute direct proof of this association. Rather, the researchers have combined these data with related empirical evidence and theory to articulate a plausible inference. This inferential strategy is necessitated by the design of their research which, incidentally, is representative of vast numbers of psychological studies. This strategy, sometimes referred to as the *causal-comparative design*, involves the selection of two or more groups of subjects, as equal as possible in all aspects save the variable(s) at issue in the research, and where said variable(s) represent something that has already happened to the subjects. Thus, Husted and Cervantes have studied two groups of adolescents, "equal" in age, IQ, and social class status, but different in that one group was composed of high school dropouts, the other of stay-ins. The next step in this method was to study intensively all subjects in the attempt to ferret out any background differences, psychological or otherwise, not initially apparent between the two groups. If successful, researchers frequently infer, although in *post hoc* fashion, that such differences somehow contribute to the criterial difference, which in the present case is school dropout behavior. One, of course, must exercise caution in assuming causation *post hoc*. Nevertheless, many problems of interest to behavioral scientists can be pursued only by using the causal-comparative method or variations thereof.

Finally, the reader is encouraged to examine carefully the dropout prediction table developed by Husted and Cervantes. Equipped with such data, educators may be helped to predict earlier and more efficiently those individuals who are imminent dropout candidates. It is likely that preventative measures applied prior to premature school leaving will be more effective than measures attempted once an individual has officially departed the school setting.

RECOMMENDED READINGS

Carlsmith, Lyn. Effect of early father absence on scholastic aptitude. *Harvard Educational Review*, 1964, 34, 3–21.

Cervantes, Lucius. *The Drop-Out: Causes and Cures.* Ann Arbor, Mich.: University of Michigan Press, 1965.

Combs, Janet, and Cooley, William W. Dropouts: in high school and after school. *American Educational Research Journal*, 1968, 5, 343–363.

Heckhausen, Heinz. *The Anatomy of Achievement Motivation.* New York: Academic Press, 1967.

Mannino, Fortune V. Family factors related to school persistence. *Journal of Educational Sociology*, 1962, 35, 193–202.

Schreiber, Daniel (Ed.) *Profile of the School Dropout.* New York: Random House, 1968.

Tannenbaum, Abraham J. The school dropout today. *IRCD Bulletin*, 1968, 4, No. 4.

3.6   The Psycho-Social Origins of Academic Achievement and the Maternal Role in Autonomy

Grace Platts Husted, ST. LOUIS UNIVERSITY
Lucius F. Cervantes, S.J., ST. LOUIS UNIVERSITY

National statistics indicate that during the present decade there are an accumulating 8,000,000 high school dropouts. The dropout group cuts across all ethnic, social class and geographic lines but the overwhelming percentage originates in the blue collar and lower-white collar socioeconomic classes. A majority of the dropouts fall within the average IQ range and have more than adequate talent to finish high school profitably. Many more have IQ's adequate for the completion of college, but are lost as "natural resources" to the nation by premature withdrawal from the secondary school process. In view of the contemporary society's

An original paper prepared especially for this volume.

educational expectation for modern youth and the dropout youth's inability to get a job in the computerized, specialized, technological society, the very state of being a dropout has all but become by definition the state of being a second-class citizen.

The greater the number of negative factors working to the disadvantage of the student, the greater the chance of his dropping out of school. More males than females drop out of high school, and the dropout rates among Negroes are twice that of whites.

The purpose of this article is to analyze data from a research project on the dropout in terms of a specific facet of the family background, namely the concept of primary relationships in the psycho-social origins of academic achievement.

THE HIGH SCHOOL DROPOUT STUDY

A research study was designed of "hard core" dropouts in six large urban centers. School authorities in Boston, St. Louis, New Orleans, Omaha, Denver, and Los Angeles assisted the research interviewers by providing 25 "matched" pairs of white youth, one of whom had dropped out of school, while the other member of the pair was completing the last semester of his high school education. The youth were matched on the variables of sex, age, IQ, and general socio-economic background. They originated in lower-class families (70 percent blue collar, 30 percent lower-white collar); the median income (1961) was slightly less than $5,000 per year. The 300 respondents with but fourteen exceptions were either 17 or 18 years of age.

The three instruments of research that were utilized in processing the teenage sample were a questionnaire, a taped interview of approximately forty minutes, and a Thematic Apperception Test.

The central research hypothesis that was basic to the selection and development of the research instruments used was that *academic achievement is positively related to the involvement of youth in primary relationships.*

A primary relationship (Broom & Selznick, 1963) is defined as the relation which is characterized by:

(1) depth and frequency of intercommunication,
(2) acceptance of the other as a person rather than as a role player,
(3) pleasure of association under a variety of circumstances (pp. 135–139).

One hypothesis that emerged from the research was that the *primary relationship with the mother* was the key variable in academic inadequacy of the child. It seems there is a twofold descent into inadequacy:

(1) absence or weak presence of the father, and
(2) maternal deficiency in developing the creative potentials of the child, including the achievement value and autonomy.

More important than any other environmental influence on the dropout was the influence of the mother. Children are inevitably unable to develop their full potential if they are brought up by mothers who are deficient in these responses:

(1) depth level intercommunication,
(2) acceptance of children as individuals in their own right,
(3) companions in pleasure.

Our evidence indicates that dropouts are characterized by the following variables:

DROPOUT PREDICTION TABLE
(Cervantes-Husted, 1965, pp. 198–199)

School

1. Two years behind in reading or arithmetic at seventh grade level. Majority of grades are below average.
2. Failure of one or more school years (1st, 2d, 8th, 9th grades most commonly failed; 85 percent of dropouts behind one year; 53 percent two or more years).
3. Irregular attendance and frequent tardiness. Ill-defined sickness given as a reason.
4. Performance consistently below potential.
5. No participation in extracurricular activies.
6. Frequent change of schools.
7. Behavior problems requiring disciplinary measures.
8. Feeling of "not belonging" (because of size, speech, personality development, nationality, social class, family disgrace, retardation in school, dress, lack of friends among schoolmates or staff, and so on).

Family

9. More children than parents can readily control (for example, only child for divorced and working mother; five or more for non-divorced and working mother of blue and lower white-collar class).
10. Parents inconsistent in affection and discipline.
11. Unhappy family situation (common acceptance, communication, and pleasurable experiences lacking; family solidarity minimal).

12. Father figure weak or absent.
13. Education of parents at eighth grade level.
14. Few family friends; among these few, many problem units (divorced, deserted, delinquents, dropouts).

Peers

15. Friends not approved by parents.
16. Friends not school-oriented.
17. Friends much older or much younger.

TAT (Psychological Orientation)

18. Resentful of all authority (home, school, police, job, church).
19. Deferred gratification pattern weak.
20. Weak self-image.

MATERNAL DEFICIENCY?

All of these negative psycho-social factors are debilitating to the total personality. But more important from the psychogenesis of the achievement orientation is the teasing hypothesis that the achievement value and autonomy emerge in the earliest years in the relationship between the mother and the child.

Throughout the study it was evident that the father had a more minor role in the life of the dropout from high school than in the life of the high school graduate. Two out of three dropouts were brought up in family systems in which the father had little or no authority (Mother Dominant or Laissez-Faire); while two out of three of the graduates were brought up in family systems in which the father was dominant or had equal influence with the mother (Father Dominant or Democratic).

TABLE 1. FAMILY AUTHORITY STRUCTURE

Father Dominant			Democratic		
	%	N		%	N
Dropouts	24.7	37	Dropouts	9.3	14
Graduates	38.0	57	Graduates	24.0	36
Laissez Faire			Mother Dominant		
	%	N		%	N
Dropouts	32.7	49	Dropouts	33.3	50
Graduates	4.7	7	Graduates	33.3	50

$N = 300$ (150 dropout and 150 graduate high school students).

The hypothesis that the father's authority is weaker in the case of the dropouts than it is in the case of the graduates is sustained ($D = .543$; X^2 (2 df) = 15.8; $p < .001$).

To the question, "Was it your father or your mother who was more insistent concerning your completing your education?" the pattern is again the same. The dropout's life history is marked to a significant degree by the absence of the father's influence.

In response to the question, "If you needed help and advice to make a big decision, to whom would you go for that advice?" it was found that 50 percent more graduates than dropouts would go to both the father and the mother, while the dropouts would more often seek their mother's help without consulting their fathers. A further question was, "At the point of leaving school, from whom did you seek help?" No dropout would seek help from a teacher in these critical questions, and those who did seek help from within the family circle sought this help two and a half times as frequently from the mother as from the father.

Consonant with our finding that the father-figure is minimal in the achievement value of the dropout is the finding of the non-existence of the authority of the teacher. Traditionally, the teacher is perceived as the parental-surrogate who instrumentalizes the middle-class values of the community, but in our study this was found to be completely a myth. There was not one dropout who at the time he was contemplating withdrawing from school considered asking counsel of a teacher. The teacher-student relationship was a secondary one.

There was a curious finding concerning the relative placement of the father's friends in the hierarchy of family friends. The youths were asked to list whether each friend of the family was primarily a friend of the father or of the mother or of both. The friends of the dropout's families were not only primarily the mother's, but those few friends and relatives of the father that were listed were ranked by the dropouts as being very low on their family's friend list. By central tendency the opposite was true of the graduates' families' friends: their fathers' friends were more frequently the best or second best friends and their mothers' friends more frequently lower on the list.

Seven out of ten of the family friends who were relatives were relatives of the mother in the case of the dropouts, while only six out of ten were such in the case of the graduates. Clearly the dynamic interrelationships of the dropout are matricentric.

THE MATERNAL ROLE IN THE PSYCHOGENESIS OF ACHIEVEMENT AND AUTONOMY

What does this mean in terms of academic achievement? The role of the "significant other" in influencing the child was ascertained by the question, "Which person do you judge to have been most influential in your life?" Both graduates and dropouts overwhelmingly chose the mother, and ignored the teacher and other possible choices.

This sample was predominantly a working-class sample. McClelland (1953) and Rosen (1956) suggest that middle-class parents place greater stress upon independence training than do lower-class parents. Also, Winterbottom (1958) examined the relationship between independence-mastery training and achievement motivation and found that achievement motivation is strongest among boys whose mothers expected relatively early indications of self-reliance and mastery from them. These expectations, involving standards of excellence, are more often found in the middle class than in the lower class. Achievement training stresses competition in situations involving standards of excellence, which insist that the child be able to perform certain tasks by himself. Independence training involves permitting the child to exercise freedom of action in decision-making, in order to develop autonomy. In these two dimensions, the direction and intensity of the response from the mother become paramount. Winterbottom (1958) found that mothers with children of high achievement gave somewhat more intense (positive) rewards than mothers with children of low achievement.

The positive direction and intensity of response from the mother is more than affection or discipline. It is perhaps the basic variable in the formulation of close attachments to the mother, which leads the child to accept the mother's values. The primary relationship between mother and child seems to be the central one in the achievement motivation of the child. It is formulated in the earliest years of interaction. Kagan (1969) says that "middle-class mothers spend a lot more time entertaining their babies, talking, smiling, playing face-to-face. Lower-class mothers talk from another room, or issue orders, and don't take time for reciprocal play with the child." (p. 15).

The relationship between mother and child is one of close attachment and influence, and the strategies of developing both achievement values and autonomy in the child stem from the response of the mother to the child in their mutual intercommunication. Expectancies on the part of the mother for the child develop from infancy and are incorporated into the child's self-concept. Erik Erikson (1967) says that "a sense of basic trust is the first component of mental health to develop in life, a sense of autonomous will the second, and a sense of initiative the third." (p. 188).

He further says that autonomy develops in the second and third years, after the sense of basic trust, and that initiative develops in the fourth or fifth years. "A baby may show something like 'autonomy' from the beginning, for example, in the particular way in which he tries to wriggle his head free when tightly held. However, under normal conditions, it is not until the second year that he begins to experience *the whole critical alternative between being an autonomous creature and being a dependent one*; and it is not until then that he is ready for a decisive encounter with his environment, an environment, which, in turn, feels called upon to convey to him its particular ideas and concepts of autonomy and coercion in ways decisively contributing to the character, the efficiency, and the health of his personality in his culture." (p. 189).

Gordon Allport (1961, p. 118) places the development of autonomy at the third year of life. He also suggests that the third year of life is the beginning of the desire for competition and achievement. "When the exploratory bent is frustrated, the child feels it a blow to his self-esteem. The ego is thwarted, resulting in humiliation and anger. The child becomes acutely aware of himself as a self. So conspicuous is this behavior that some psychologists say that the *need for autonomy* is the outstanding mark of self-hood in the third year of life."

The growth of self-awareness reaches a critical stage around the age of 2. One symptom is the burst of opposition to feeding, dressing, taking orders—to almost anything the parent desires. Levy (1953) has studied this type of "oppositional behavior" in nearly 1000 children brought to the clinic for medical examination and testing. The first signs of negativism (usually the cry "No, No") appear in half the cases by 18 months of age, but the negative mode may continue to the age of 4. Although he is negativistic, the child of 2 is not yet competitive. Allport (1961, p. 19) states that "only by the age of 3 can he be taught to 'get ahead' . . . . By the age of 6 or 7 in our culture we can safely say that self-esteem acquires a competitive flavor. In other cultures it is not so. Anthropologists tell us that while in most cultures individual competition is keen, in others, it is impossible to arouse rivalry within the group. The individual identifies his self-esteem with his esteem for the group."

Allport (1961) says that three aspects of self-awareness gradually evolve during the first three years of life: sense of bodily self, sense of continuing self-identity, and self-esteem and pride.

Contributing to the development are many influences: maturational (anatomical and physiological), recurrent bodily sensations, memory aided by verbal concepts, one's proper name as an anchorage point, frustrations during the process of exploring and manipulating the environment, a period of negativism where the child practices his emerging sense of self. At this stage the child begins to feel himself autonomous and separate from others. (p. 120).

Erikson (1959) points out that the chief feature of adolescence is the renewed search for identity. The 2-year-old has already gone through the preliminary stage. But later he has emerged with his family and peers and lost himself in group loyalties. Allport (1961) states: "Now in adolescence, the problem once more becomes acute." (p. 122). The adolescent's self-image is dependent on others. "He seeks popularity and is fearful of ostracism. His hair, his tastes in music, even his jalopy conform to the standards of the group. Seldom does the adolescent defy teenage mores. His self-image and sense of identity are not firm enough to stand the strain." (p. 125).

According to Allport (1961), the "well-known rebelliousness of the adolescent has an important relationship to his search for identity. *It is his final bid for autonomy.* Rejecting one's parents in whole or in part may be a necessary, if cruel stage in the process. It is the adolescent counterpart of the toddler's negativism. The search for identity is revealed in the way an adolescent tries on different masks. He first develops one line of chatter, then another, one style of hairdress and then another . . . . Since parents are usually scornful of these experiments, the youth tries them out with his peers, and chiefly with the opposite sex, and often over the telephone, to which he is greatly addicted." (p. 125).

The important point is that in adolescence, "long-range purposes and distant goals add a new dimension to the sense of self-hood" (Allport, 1961, p. 126). Both independence and achievement motivation are required for competence. In a sense, the achievement value is purposeful and goal-oriented; and independence training fosters strategy and tactics for attainment of the goal. According to Allport (1961, p. 126), this may be called *propriate striving.* "The cement holding a life together is its directness or intentionality. In order to be normal, an adolescent, and especially an adult, needs a defining objective, a line of promise. It is not necessary that the goals be rigidly focused, but only that a central theme of striving be present."

What is the mother's role in the development of autonomy and the sense of striving? The strength and intensity of the interaction between mother and child is continued into adolescence, whether the value system of the mother is academically orientated or not. The mother's value system is communicated to the child through the direction and intensity of her response to his successes and defeats from day to day, and mothers of high achievers communicate an expectation of both achievement and autonomy. Some children learn the achievement value, but are unable to instrumentalize it because they have not developed a sense of autonomy and are somewhat helpless in decision-making.

According to McClelland (1961, p. 345), "early mastery training promotes high achievement provided it does not reflect generalized restrictiveness, authoritarianism, or 'rejection' by the parents. The boy can be put on his own too early, as in the predominantly lower-class families, or too late, as in the predominantly middle-class families that expect achievement and independence quite late . . . . What is desirable is . . .

a stress on meeting certain achievement standards somewhere between the ages of 6 and 8 . . . neither too early for the boy's abilities nor too late for him to internalize those standards as his own."

SUMMARY

The central hypothesis of the research study is that academic achievement is positively related to the involvement of the youth in primary relationships.

The interpersonal matrix of the dropouts was found to be clearly one of weak primary relationships. The family with depth of intercommunication, acceptance of others as individuals, and companionship in pleasurable associations under a variety of circumstances is the family of graduates. Contrariwise, weak primary relationships with a minimum of host culture standards, a minimum of depth intercommunication, little acceptance of others as individuals, and little companionship in pleasure are characteristic of the matrix from which the dropout emerges.

Subsidiary to the prime conclusion are the following:

(1) The primary relationship with the mother was the key variable in academic inadequacy of the dropout.
(2) Our evidence supports the hypothesis that the primary relationship with the mother is the source of the achievement value and autonomy.
(3) The self-image is weak in the case of the dropout.

Supported by relevant literature are the findings that academic achievement orientations and autonomy are developed in the mother's selective responses to the child's movements and explorations. Achievement and autonomy are encouraged by the direction and intensity of the mother's response. Autonomy and the sense of competition are probably developed by the third year of life. The mother's role is critical in the development of achievement and autonomy.

SUGGESTIONS FOR PREVENTION OF DROPOUTS

Two suggestions are offered for the alleviation of the dropout phenomenon: First, the responses of lower-class mothers toward their children might be changed, by retraining the mothers. Second, following McClelland's research, the school system should pay particular attention to children between 6 and 8.

Both of these suggestions, retraining the mothers of lower-class infants, and centering on the achievement of the 6–8-year-old child, would require a major national commitment.

REFERENCES

Allport, Gordon W. *Pattern and Growth in Personality.* New York: Holt, Rinehart and Winston, 1961.

Broom, Leonard, and Selznick, Philip. *Sociology.* 3d ed. Evanston, Ill.: Row, Peterson and Company, 1963, Chap. V.

Bruner, Jerome S. *The Process of Education.* Cambridge: Harvard University Press, 1961.

Bruner, Jerome S. *Toward a Theory of Instruction.* Cambridge, Mass.: The Belknap Press of Harvard University, 1966.

Cervantes, Lucius F., and Husted, Grace Platts. *The Dropout.* Ann Arbor, Mich.: University of Michigan Press, 1965.

Erikson, Erik, in *Personality, in Nature, Society and Culture.* 2d ed. Clyde Kluckholn and Henry A. Murray with David M. Schneider (Eds.) New York: Alfred A. Knopf, 1967.

Erikson, Erik. Identity and the life cycle. *Psychological Issues,* 1959, 1, No. 1.

Kagan, Jerome, in Maya Pines, Why some 3 year olds get A's—and some get C's. *The New York Times Magazine,* July 6, 1969, pp. 4–17.

Levy, D. M. The early development of independent and oppositional behavior. In *Midcentury Psychiatry.* Springfield, Ill.: Charles C. Thomas, 1953, Chap. 5.

McClelland, D. C., Atkinson, J. W., Clark, R., and Lowell, E. *The Achievement Motive.* New York: Appleton-Century-Crofts, 1953.

McClelland, D. C. *The Achieving Society.* Princeton, N.J.: Van Nostrand, 1961.

Mead, Margaret. *Cooperation and Competition among Primitive Peoples.* New York: McGraw-Hill, 1937.

Piaget, Jean. *Judgment and Reasoning in the Child.* New York: The Humanities Press, 1952.

Piaget, Jean. *Logic and Psychology.* Manchester: Manchester University Press, 1956.

Rosen, B. C. The achievement syndrome: a psychocultural dimension of social stratification. *American Sociological Review,* 1956, **21**, 203–211.

Winterbottom, M. R. The relation of need for achievement in learning experiences in independence and mastery. In J. W. Atkinson, *Motives in Fantasy, Action, and Society.* Princeton, N.J.: Van Nostrand, 1958.

3.7 *Orientation*

That peer influences upon one's attitudes, values, and choice behavior increase during pre-adolescence and adolescence is a well-documented fact. Formal study of this increase has included, among other things, investigation into the development of conformity behavior. Since conformity behavior is one of the most popular topics for discussion by psychologists concerned with adolescence, the following example is included here. Although the topic alone makes John Darley's research purposeful, at least three additional features contribute to its attractiveness. One feature is Darley's theoretical rationale which, in concert with his methodology, leads to an attempted test of variables underlying conformity behavior. A recent critique of contemporary research on conformity states that many researchers have failed to distinguish carefully between descriptive and explanatory analyses of such behavior (Hollander & Willis, 1967). Darley seems to have set his sights upon explanatory concepts of conformity.

A second noteworthy item in the Darley paper is his use of genuine experimental procedures. The classic experimental model in psychology calls for at least two initially equal comparison groups. One group then receives an experimental treatment designed and executed by the researcher. The second group, referred to as the *control* group, receives no treatment. Subsequently, the two groups are compared on the basis of a selected criterion. This comparison allows one to examine what differences between these groups (if any) may be attributable to the experimental treatment. As the reader will see, Darley has expanded upon this model to include four groups. Three of these groups receive treatments, the fourth serves as a control. Darley's purpose is to establish a relationship between two antecedents—fear and social comparison—and consequent conformity behavior.

A third discernible feature of Darley's study is his exclusive use of females. Most of the research examples in this volume utilize males as subjects; by no means does this writer intend to be discriminatory! Darley's results, while applicable to females, may or may not be reproducible with males. The reader may wish to speculate on the generalizability and explanatory potential of these findings. Also worthy of consideration are the rather frightening implications of these findings for the control of behavior. A final question concerns the extent to which certain fears—fear of social rejection, for example—may motivate or contribute to peer group conformity in natural settings.

RECOMMENDED READINGS

Brittain, C. V. Age and sex of siblings and conformity toward parents versus peers in adolescence. *Child Development*, 1966, **37**, 709–714.

Endler, Norma S. Conformity as a function of different reinforcement schedules. *Journal of Personality and Social Psychology*, 1966, **4**, 175–180.

Hollander, Edwin P., and Willis, Richard H. Some current issues in the psychology of conformity and nonconformity. *Psychological Bulletin*, 1967, **68**, 62–76.

Nord, Walter R. Social exchange theory: an integrative approach to social conformity. *Psychological Bulletin*, 1969, **71**, 174–208.

Radloff, Roland. Affiliation and social comparison. In Edgar F. Borgatta and William W. Lambert (Eds.) *Handbook of Personality Theory and Research*. Chicago: Rand-McNally, 1968, 943–958.

Steiner, Ivan D., and Vannoy, Joseph S. Personality correlates of two types of conformity behavior. *Journal of Personality and Social Psychology*, 1966, **4**, 307–315.

3.7 Fear and Social Comparison as Determinants of Conformity Behavior

John M. Darley, PRINCETON UNIVERSITY

Several current observers of society (Fromm, 1941; Riesman, 1950) have suggested that the amount of conformity a person evidences in a particular situation is closely related to the amount of fear felt in that situation. Several psychological theories suggest why this might be so; why a momentary increase in a person's fear level might lead him to be more conforming, even when the conformity behavior does not reduce the specific threat. Considerable evidence has been accumulated to support the position that conformity, accepting the opinion or judgments of others in the absence of sufficient evidence to do so or in the face of evidence to the contrary, is a specific instance of dependency behavior (Berkowitz, 1957; Jakubezak & Walters, 1959).

A social learning theory suggests that an increase in a person's general anxiety state will increase the frequency of his learned responses to anxiety. Among these responses may be dependency behaviors. A series of studies by Walters gives empirical support to this expectation. Walters and Karal (1960) found that social isolation leads to increased susceptibility to social influence only if the experience of isolation is accompanied by anxiety. Walters and Ray (1960) conclude that anxiety increases the effectiveness of social reinforcers in the conditioning of young children. Walters, Marshall, and Shooter (1960) found that a high anx-

Reprinted from *Journal of Personality and Social Psychology*, 1966, **4**, 73–78, by permission of the author and the American Psychological Association.

iety group of subjects was more likely to conform to the judgments of the experimenter in the autokinetic situation. Staples and Walters (1961) found that first-born subjects threatened with electric shock for errors conformed more to the suggestions of the experimenter in the autokinetic situation than were either unthreatened subjects or later-born threatened subjects.

A further prediction about the fear-conformity situation may be developed from Schachter's (1959) explanation for the increased desire for affiliation caused by a fear-provoking threat. He found that subjects waiting to receive painful electric shocks wanted to wait together with other subjects who were also waiting for the electric shocks. Schachter concluded that the effect resulted from the subjects' desires to reduce their anxiety directly and to evaluate their emotional state produced in this novel situation by comparing it with the emotional state of others in the same boat. Further research has confirmed the finding that direct anxiety reduction and social comparison both take place when actual groups are formed (Wrightsman, 1960), and that social comparison was relatively more important than direct anxiety reduction in motivating the subject's choice of waiting partner (Darley & Aronson, 1967).

A fearful subject, then, who is in a group of other fearful subjects will feel more affiliative toward them. It is possible that the subject will also be more conforming to pressure from these other subjects, either because the shared threat makes the group a more cohesive one (for evidence that increased group cohesiveness leads to increased conformity, see Blake & Mouton, 1961), or because the subjects, each of whom desires to find out the emotional reactions of the other subjects, are generally more open to influence from these other subjects.

On the basis of these theories, two predictions were made in this study. First, that an increase in a person's fear level will cause him to be more conforming; second, that a threatened subject under conformity pressures from other subjects who share the threat will be more conforming to these subjects than to those who do not share the threat.

METHOD

To test whether an increase in a person's fear level does cause an increase in his conformity behaviors, it was necessary to create a situation in which a group of subjects could be made afraid by some external threat and to compare their comformity responses with those of a group of subjects who were not threatened, but were subjected to the same conformity pressures. To test the prediction made on the basis of Schachter's work, it was necessary that some of these frightened subjects believe they were under conformity pressures from one source while others believe they were under pressures from a difference source. To realize the situations experimentally, the following context was devised:

Subjects were told that they were to take part in an experiment concerning the contributions of certain inner-ear receptor centers to hearing acuity. They were further told that girls who had been assigned to the experimental group would later have these auditory receptor centers temporarily affected by the administration of a severe electric shock. Other girls, who had been assigned to the control group, would not get the electric shock. Then the subjects were told that before the electroshocks were given to the members of the experimental group, a "hearing acuity pretest" (which was actually an auditory version of the Asch conformity situation) would be given to all subjects. Following the actual administration of this test, the subjects were asked about their reactions to the previous part of the experiment, and then the true purpose of the experiment was explained and the subjects' reactions to it were discussed with them. Each subject was asked not to reveal the actual purpose of the experiment to others and paid for her time. No subject was given an electric shock.

To summarize, four groups of 12 subjects were run in this part of the experiment:

(1) A group of subjects who believed that they were to receive an electric shock and thus were highly fearful, and who believed that all the other girls in their testing session were also to get the shock and thus were also highly fearful (HH group).

(2) A group of subjects who believed that they were to receive an electric shock, and thus were highly fearful, and who believed that all the other girls in the experimental session were not to receive the electric shock and thus were not nervous (HL group).

(3) A group of subjects who believed that they were not going to receive an electric shock, and who believed that all the other girls in the experimental situation were to be given the electric shock (LH group).

(4) A group of subjects who believed that they were not going to receive an electric shock, and who believed that all the other girls in the experimental session were also not going to receive an electric shock (LL group).

Subjects

The subjects were 64 females between the ages of 17 and 21, obtained from a teacher's college in Cambridge, Massachusetts, who had volunteered to participate in "a psychology experiment." They were paid $1.50 per hour for doing so.

Experimental Procedures

A white-coated experimenter met each subject and showed her to a small room littered with electrical apparatus. The subject's attention was called to a form telling her whether she had been assigned to the experimental or the control condition, and also telling her the assignment of the other three girls whom she believed to be present in the testing session. The subject was told to put on headphones over which she would hear the instructions, and that the experiment would begin just as soon as all the subjects arrived. A minute or so later, a tape recording of a modification of the instructions developed by Schachter (1959) to induce fear by threat of electric shock was played to the subject.[1] It began with a justification for studies about hearing mechanisms, then mentioned that this study would involve modifying the hearing of the subjects by certain "physiological modification procedures," that would be given to experimental condition subjects but not to control condition subjects. These modification procedures would involve the administration of painful electric shocks described as follows:

Now, I do feel that I must be completely honest with you. These shocks, to produce the desired effect, must be quite intense, so that for the experimental group this part of the experiment will be painful. The shocks will hurt. Of course, no permanent damage will be done by the shocks and I'm sure you realize that what may be learned from this series of experiments has great potential value for the alleviation of suffering caused by hearing defects. Gains in science, like gains anywhere else, must be paid for.

Then the experimenter asked the subject to record her responses to the experiment, including the following question:

Given that you have been assigned to the ———— group, how nervous do you feel about taking part in your part of the experiment? (Circle the number that best describes your feelings.)

0	1	2	3	4	5	6	7
Completely calm		A little nervous		Quite nervous		Extremely nervous	

[1] A complete draft of the script of the tape recording played to the subjects, and the exact series of conformity trials, has been deposited with the American Documentation Institute. Order Document No. 8834 from ADI Auxiliary Publications Project, Photoduplication Service, Library of Congress, Washington, D. C. 20540. Remit in advance $1.25 for microfilm or $1.25 for photocopies and make checks payable to: Chief, Photoduplication Service, Library of Congress.

Next, a measure of the degree to which the subject wished to affiliate with the other members of the testing session was taken:

After the pre-test, but before we have given the electroshocks to the experimental group subjects, there is usually about a ten-minute wait while we recalibrate the apparatus used in the pre-test. During this time, we have arranged things so that you may either wait alone or together with the other three girls in this experimental session. Turn the page of the booklet now and check the choice that describes which of these alternatives you want to choose. One thing that I would ask of you: If you do choose to wait together with the other girls, please do not talk about the pre-test that you've just been in. You may talk about anything else, but please don't talk about the pre-test. Check now the alternative that you want to choose.

(+3) I very much prefer to wait with the other girls
(+2) I prefer to wait with the other girls
(+1) I slightly prefer to wait with the other girls
(0) I don't care
(−1) I slightly prefer to wait alone
(−2) I prefer to wait alone
(−3) I very much prefer to wait alone

After these forms were filled out, the experimenter collected them, and, after a pause suitable for tabulation, announced

Well, looking over your choices of whether you wanted to wait alone or wait together with the other girls, it seems that the thing that's consistent with most of your choices is to let you wait together as a group. So, after the pre-test and before the experimental group receives the electroshocks, you may all wait together. You may talk about anything else you want, but please do not talk about the experiment.

At this point in the conformity test, an auditory form of the Asch situation (Blake & Brehm, 1954) was given. It was the task of the subject to count the number of tape-recorded metronome clicks that she heard. The subject gave her answer after she heard the answer of the three other "subjects." In fact, these other subjects were confederates of the experimenter, and gave wrong but unanimous judgments on 12 of the 18 trials. The number of trials on which the subject gave the same wrong response as the confederates was the experimental measure of conformity. The responses of the confederates were delivered by a tape recorder so that every subject, regardless of condition, heard exactly the same conformity pressure.

RESULTS [2]

*Checks on the Manipulations: Differential Fear Caused
by Assignment to the Control of Experimental Group*

The fear manipulation succeeded in its purpose: The mean nervousness ratings for the four groups are given in Table 1; the difference in rated fearfulness between control and experimental condition subjects was highly significant. Clearly, the experimental group was relatively afraid, the control group was relatively calm.[3]

TABLE 1. SELF-RATINGS OF FEAR FOR THE FOUR EXPERIMENTAL GROUPS (0–7 SCALE)

	HH	HL	LH	LL
M	4.50	4.83	1.42	1.33
Mdn.	5.00	4.50	1.00	1.00
SD	2.15	2.94	.669	1.07

NOTE. $N = 12$ in each condition. HH + HL versus LH + LL $t = 7.617$, $df = 46$, $p < .001$, two-tailed.

Affiliation Scores

On the basis of the theory developed by Schachter, it was expected that the girls in the HH condition would wish to wait with the other girls before the electroshocks were given; the girls in the other three groups would have less strong affiliation desires. Again, the data indicate that the experimental manipulation had the desired effect; a fearful subject strongly wanted to wait together with the other subjects, provided that she also expected them to be afraid. Of the four groups, only

[2] The results of two subjects were dropped from the data analysis because final questioning indicated that they did not believe that there were any other girls present making the auditory judgments. Both had recently been in an experiment in which the presence of another subject had been simulated by tape recorder.

[3] Each subject also rated how anxiety provoking, in general, she thought her condition was, and how anxiety provoking she felt the other condition to be. There were no significant differences in the way in which any one of the four experimental groups rated either the "experimental" (shock) or the "control" (no-shock) condition. The mean rating for the general anxiety provokingness of the shock situation was 5.6; for the no-shock condition, 1.02.

the mean affiliation score of the HH group was significantly greater than zero, the "don't care" response ($t = 2.345$, $.02 < p < .05$). The mean affiliation score of none of the other three groups was significantly different from zero or from each other. The mean affiliation score of the HH group differed from the pooled mean affiliation scores of the other three groups ($t = 3.21$, $df = 46$, $p < .01$). The HH group wished to affiliate more than the HL group ($t = 3.45$, $df = 22$, $p < .01$).

TABLE 2. AFFILIATION RESPONSES OF THE SUBJECT (-3 TO $+3$ SCALE)

	HH	HL	LH	LL
M	2.00	0.33	0.66	0.58
Mdn.	2.00	0.00	1.00	0.50
SD	0.85	1.41	1.31	1.37

NOTE. $N = 12$ in each condition. HH versus other $t = 3.21$, $df = 46$, $p < .01$, two-tailed.

Conformity Scores of the Four Experimental Groups

It was predicted that the HH group would have the highest conformity scores, since the likelihood of a conformity response was thought to be increased both by a momentary increase in fear level and a desire to affiliate with those from whom the conformity pressures came. The girls in the HL group were expected to be more conforming than either of the low-fear groups. No differences in conformity scores were predicted between the two low-fear groups.

The mean and median conformity scores of each of the four groups are given in Table 3. They show a trend in the direction predicted by the hypothesis. Since the scores were distributed in a markedly non-normal fashion, non-parametric statistics were used in the analysis of the conformity scores.

TABLE 3. CONFORMITY RESPONSES OF THE FOUR EXPERIMENTAL GROUPS (FROM 0 TO 12 CONFORMITY RESPONSES WERE POSSIBLE)

	HH	HL	LH	LL
M	8.417	5.750	2.25	2.833
Mdn.	8.500	6.000	2.00	2.000
SD	2.940	2.100	2.77	3.440

NOTE. $N = 12$ in each condition.

To test for the significance of the obtained relationships between experimental group assignment and conformity scores, these steps were followed:

No difference in conformity scores between the two low-fear groups (LH and LL) was predicted. The Mann-Whitney test (Siegel, 1956) indicated no significant difference between the two low-fear groups, so the conformity scores of the members of these two groups were pooled to form a single, low-fear group for the next statistical tests.

The appropriate nonparametric significance test when an ordered prediction is made is Jonckheere's (1954) distribution-free K sample test against ordered alternatives. Applying that test to these data, it was found that they are in the predicted order; the limit-normal z, that is, the final Jonckheere statistic for samples of this size was 2.28 ($p < .01$).

The rank-order correlation coefficient between the conformity scores and the predicted ordering of the two high-fear groups and the pooled low-fear group for these data was $\tau = .67$, indicating quite a strong relationship between the direct and indirect effects of fear and the amount of conformity a person displays in the test situation.

This conclusion was supported by Mann-Whitney U tests between successive groups. The comparison of the HL group with the pooled LL and LH groups was significant at the .001 level ($Z = 3$). The comparison between the HH and the HL groups was significant, $p < .02$ ($U = 20$, $n_1 = 12$, $n_2 = 12$).

Birth Order

Ordinal position in the family was not found to be related to either the level of fear aroused by the high-fear instructions, the strength of the desire for affiliation, or the final conformity scores of the subjects.

A Possible Alternative Explanation

One possible explanation for the finding that fear leads to increased conformity is that the high-fear subjects were simply paying less attention to the stimuli, being more concerned with their feelings, or the ways in which they will face the future shock. Realizing their own preoccupation and the resulting inaccuracy of their counts, they had only the judgment of the other girls to rely on, and were more likely to conform to these judgments since they were justly less confident of their own. Fear, then, simply acts as a distraction.

If fear serves as a distraction for the fearful subjects, it would then be expected that the *accuracy* of their judgments should decrease even when there is no pressure on them to conform. To see whether this were true, two further groups of subjects were run, drawn from the same population of subjects as were the previous groups. One group of eight subjects was treated exactly like the two high-fear (HH and HL) conformity groups *except* that these subjects did not hear the tape-recorded judgments of the other girls and thus were not under pressure to conform to a group norm. These subjects heard exactly the same experimental instructions as the other groups, rated their own fear in the same way, and made their affiliative choices in the same way. They were given the same pretest instructions and heard the same tape recording of the clicks. An electrical switching device enabled the experimenter to block out the tape-recorded voices of the three confederates. Therefore, the delay between the clicks and the real subjects' report was exactly the same as for the conformity group subjects. (Four of these accuracy group subjects were treated as the HL group; four as the HH group, their fear and affiliation ratings were similar to these groups.)

For the eight subjects run in the high-fear accuracy condition, the mean error score was .89 and the median was 1 (on the 12 trials that were the conformity trials for the conformity groups). For the six low-fear subjects who made judgments about the stimulus tapes, the error score was 1.16 and the median was 1. The results show no difference in conformity rates for the two groups; thus, the accuracy-decrement explanation for the results is not supported by the available experimental evidence.

DISCUSSION

It seems possible to conclude that an increase in a subject's momentary level of fear leads to increased conformity. There seems to be both a direct relationship between fear and conformity, as evidenced by the generally higher conformity scores of the fearful subjects regardless of the source of the influence, and an indirect relationship between fear and conformity that is mediated by the increased desire for affiliation among the fearful subjects.

The fact that a fearful subject is more susceptible to conformity pressures, regardless of the source of the pressures, is evidence for the view that conformity is an instance of dependency behavior, and that dependency responses are increased by a momentary increase in a person's fear level. Several possible explanations suggest themselves for the affiliation-mediated fear-conformity relationships:

The explanation originally suggested is that the frightened subject desires and accepts social comparison information from other subjects who share her plight. Primarily, she seeks information from others that will enable her to evaluate her own emotional reactions to the novel and unexpected experimental situation. There is evidence (Wrightsman,

1960) that she is receptive to information about the emotional levels of others—that is, her rating of her own emotional level is pulled toward the emotional level of others. This willingness to accept the reaction of others may have generalized enough to make the subject willing to accept the opinions of others about stimulus events.

A second possibility is to interpret the variations in the source of conformity pressures for the high-fear subjects as a cohesiveness manipulation—the high-fear subject surrounded by other high-fear subjects feels herself to be in a highly cohesive group, the high-fear subject surrounded by low-fear subjects feels herself to be in a low-cohesive group. (Evidence for this is the significantly higher affiliation choice of the HH group over the HL group.) Increased cohesiveness has been shown in other experiments to lead to increased conformity behavior.

A third possible explanation is that the high-fear subjects surrounded by other high-fear subjects conform more because they are avoiding deviation in order to avoid *future* rejection from the group, either because they do not wish to be rejected from a highly cohesive group, or because rejection would preclude the possibility of future emotional social comparison.

The relationships between fear and conformity found in this experiment may give the beginnings of explanations for several sorts of observed behaviors of naturally created groups. Various authors have written about the "herd instinct" in man, usually drawing examples to support their claims from the extreme suggestibility and blind mob behavior of a panicked crowd. It is interesting to note that the circumstances that often are the cause for the formation of a panic mob are exactly those that produced the highest conformity rate in this experiment: a person made afraid by some external threat (perhaps by a fire in a theater or nightclub), and that person surrounded by other persons who are also threatened by the same circumstances. It is in situations such as these that the extreme suggestibility of panic mob occurs, in which the entire crowd initiates the senseless and maladaptive act of one of its panicked members.

SUMMARY

Sixty-four female *Ss* were run in an experiment testing the prediction that an increase in a person's fear level would produce increased conformity. The rate of conformity (in the Asch situation) of *Ss* threatened by future electric shock was compared with the conformity rate of unthreatened *Ss*. The results were: (a) High-fear *Ss* conformed more than

John M. Darley 437

low-fear *Ss*; and (*b*) high-fear *Ss* who believed that conformity pressures came from similarly threatened *Ss* conformed more than did high-fear *Ss* under pressure from unthreatened *Ss*. The correlation coefficient between effects of fear and conformity was .67 (*p* < .01). It was concluded that (*a*) an increase in fear causes increased conformity and (*b*) this increase is greatest if the conformity pressures come from people toward whom *S* feels affiliative.

REFERENCES

Berkowitz, L. Effects of perceived dependency relationships upon conformity to group expectations. *Journal of Abnormal and Social Psychology*, 1957, **55**, 350–354.

Blake, R. R., and Brehm, J. W. The use of tape recording to simulate a group atmosphere. *Journal of Abnormal and Social Psychology*, 1954, **49**, 311–313.

Blake, R. R., and Mouton, J. S. Conformity, resistance, and conversion. In I. A. Berg and B. M. Bass (Eds.) *Conformity and Deviation*. New York: Harper, 1961, 1–37.

Darley, J. M., and Aronson, E. Self evaluation vs. direct anxiety reduction as determinants of the fear-affiliation relationship. *Journal of Experimental Social Psychology*, 1967, **3**, 40–47.

Fromm, E. *Escape from Freedom*. New York: Farrar & Rinehart, 1941.

Jakubezak, L. F., and Walters, R. H. Suggestibility as dependency behavior. *Journal of Abnormal and Social Psychology*, 1959, **59**, 102–107.

Jonckheere, A. R. A distribution-free K sample test against ordered alternatives. *Biometrika*, 1954, **41**, 133–145.

Riesman, D. *The Lonely Crowd*. New Haven: Yale University Press, 1950.

Schachter, S. *The Psychology of Affiliation*. Stanford: Stanford University Press, 1959.

Siegel, S. *Nonparametric Statistics for the Behavioral Sciences*. New York: McGraw-Hill, 1956.

Staples, F. R., and Walters, R. H. Anxiety, birth order, and susceptibility to social influence. *Journal of Abnormal and Social Psychology*, 1961, **62**, 716–719.

Walters, R. H., and Karal, P. Social deprivation and verbal behavior. *Journal of Personality*, 1960, **28**, 89–107.

Walters, R. H., Marshall, W. S., and Shooter, J. R. Anxiety, isolation, and susceptibility to social influence. *Journal of Personality*, 1960, **28**, 518–529.

Walters, R. H., and Ray, E. Anxiety, social isolation, and reinforcer effectiveness. *Journal of Personality*, 1960, **28**, 358–367.

Wrightsman, L. S., Jr. Effects of waiting with others on changes in level of felt anxiety. *Journal of Abnormal and Social Psychology*, 1960, **61**, 216–222.

3.8 *Orientation*

In the opinion of this writer, no study of adolescence would be complete without a consideration of group behavior in a natural setting. For this purpose a research into the conditions of delinquent gang behavior by Ramon Rivera and James Short, Jr., has been selected. Like many such researches, the present study is concerned with a comparison of gang and non-gang adolescents. Comparative studies often disclose differences that contribute to our understanding of the motives behind gang behavior. The Rivera and Short research is unique, however, for at least two reasons. First, it is attendant specifically to the nature of adolescent-adult relationships in a subcultural milieu of gang delinquency. Secondly, it is addressed to the nature and extent of opportunity structures available to adolescents which affect their social (and economic) mobility.

The theoretical framework for the present study is the theory of *differential opportunity* explained below. The Rivera and Short data can also be interpreted as a commentary to some degree upon the *conflict-rebellion hypothesis* cited frequently in the adolescence literature. Roughly, this hypothesis refers to a nearly inevitable conflict between adults and adolescents as the latter seek their independence and social identity. Independence striving and sundry reactive mechanisms purportedly combine to motivate various forms of rebellion against established norms. Among the most intense or severe forms of rebellion is the acting-out, anti-social behavior of delinquent gangs. Rivera and Short have found, in contrast to this view, that their delinquent gang subjects did not necessarily profess antagonism toward adults.

Additional values of the Rivera and Short study are at least twofold. First, methodology suitable for ecological study is demonstrated. A second value is the implications of the study for the type and accessibility of adult models for adolescents. Suitable models seem desirable especially for adolescents whose deviancy poses a hazard to themselves as well as to society. This notion provides a direct path to Irwin Sarason's work with delinquent adolescents described in the following paper. Rivera and Short's broad human relations orientation is further reminiscent of Husted and Cervante's study of the antecedents to school dropout behavior.

RECOMMENDED READINGS

Dunphy, Dexter C. The social structure of urban adolescent peer groups. *Sociometry*, 1963, **26**, 230–246.

Empey, Lamar T. Delinquency theory and recent research. *Journal of Research in Crime and Delinquency*, 1967, 4, 28–42.

Kohrs, E. V. The disadvantaged and lower class adolescent. In James F. Adams (Ed.) *Understanding Adolescence*. Boston: Allyn and Bacon, 1968, 287–317.

Sherif, Muzafer, and Sherif, Carolyn W. *Problems of Youth*. Chicago: Aldine, 1965. (See Parts III and IV.)

3.8 Significant Adults, Caretakers, and Structures of Opportunity: An Exploratory Study

Ramon J. Rivera, CENTER FOR URBAN EDUCATION
James F. Short, Jr., WASHINGTON STATE UNIVERSITY

The primary purpose of the Chicago study of "Street Corner Groups and Patterns of Delinquency" was to generate information concerning gang delinquency.[1] The research was designed in such a way as to permit comparative study of observations and responses of Negro and white boys in each of the following categories: lower-class gang and non-gang, and middle-class non-gang. Boys in the gang categories were broadly representative of Chicago's "worst" during the period of study, particularly in the areas of conflict, excessive consumption of alcohol, illicit sexual behavior, and property crimes of great variety. The YMCA of Metropolitan Chicago, through their Program for Detached Workers, was in effective contact with the gangs, having been directed to them by various community agencies and by field investigations which sought to locate representatives of major (hypothesized) "delinquent subcultures."

Reprinted from the *Journal of Research in Crime and Delinquency*, 1967, 4, 76–79, by permission of the authors and the National Council on Crime and Delinquency.

[1] The most comprehensive discussion of the design of this study is found in James F. Short, Jr., and Fred L. Strodtbeck, *Group Process and Gang Delinquency*. Chicago: University of Chicago Press, 1965, 1–26.

Lower-class non-gang boys were contacted through social agencies in the gang areas, such as YMCA's, Boys' Clubs, and Settlement Houses. Their non-gang status was attested to by agency personnel and the detached workers. A measure of research control was thus obtained over "community factors" in selectivity for gang membership. Middle-class boys were chosen from HiY Clubs in two areas of the city which, by conventional ecological criteria, justified this classification. We were directed to these clubs by YMCA personnel who agreed that these boys provided the best "contrast" groups in the city, so far as their class orientation was concerned. The white middle-class boys, especially, had the reputation of being the "cream of the YMCA crop."

These samples of Chicago adolescents have become the subjects of a series of special inquiries deriving mainly from current theory and speculation in the area of adolescent behavior, and delinquent behavior in particular. This paper presents a continuation of that series and has as its special point of interest the relationships existing between these youngsters and the world of adults which surrounds them.

ADULTS AND ADOLESCENTS:
SOME THEORETICAL CONSIDERATIONS

In 1937 this passage appeared in an article by Edward Reuter:

An adolescent world—an area of human experience lying between childhood and adulthood and in a measure apart from each—appears to be a phenomenon of our time and a product of our cultural organization. . . . As any other culture complex, it is essentially a system of collective definitions that creates a world apart.[2]

These sentences appeared in 1962 in a book by Ernest Smith:

The exclusion of American youth from significant adult activities, combined with the widespread conflict between youth and adults, leads to the withdrawal of youth from institutions sponsored or controlled by adults.[3]

. . . the underlying conflict of the two cultures—youth versus adult—is fundamental and may develop into crises as both parental exasperation and youth resentment accumulate.[4]

There is an obvious continuity in these passages, and the point of view represented—the "youth culture" perspective—received strong support

---

[2] Edward Reuter, "The Sociology of Adolescence," *American Journal of Sociology*, November 1937, p. 421.

[3] Ernest Smith, *American Youth Culture*. New York: Free Press, 1962, 26.

[4] Smith, p. 19.

between 1937 and 1962 in the relevant works of Benedict, Davis, Parsons, and Coleman.[5] In fact, the "youth culture" perspective can be described as the accepted and traditional mode of theorizing about adult-adolescent relationships in modern America. It is not unfair to label these works as contributions to a theory of *divisiveness*. The integration of adolescents and adults is viewed as an attribute of some societies, present during earlier, certainly more idyllic days, but clearly absent from the contemporary scene. Adolescents, in this view, are more adolescent than they used to be. They most certainly do *not* seem to be persons becoming adults and interacting with adults in any meaningful way.

There have been occasional departures from this point of view. Nye, Withey, and Douvan, Douvan and Kaye, and Elkin and Westley have challenged implicitly or directly the existence of a pervasive and continuing tension between adolescents and adults.[6] Our research on this problem, while cognizant of the "youth culture" perspective and its critics, was even more directly shaped by an attempt to evaluate and operationalize a theory which stems from a different tradition entirely— Cloward and Ohlin's "theory of differential opportunity."[7]

Briefly, this theory argues that the genesis of specialized types of delinquent adaptation lies, to an important degree, in differential exposure

[5] See, for example, Ruth Benedict, "Continuities and Discontinuities in Cultural Conditioning," *Psychiatry*, May 1938, pp. 161–67; Kingsley Davis, "Adolescence and the Social Structure," *Annals of the American Academy of Political and Social Science*, November 1944, pp. 8–16; Kingsley Davis, "The Sociology of Parent-Youth Conflict," *American Sociological Review*, August 1940, pp. 523–35; Talcott Parsons, "Age and Sex in the Social Structure of the United States," *Personality in Nature, Society, and Culture*, Clyde Kluckhohn and H. A. Murray (Eds.) New York: Alfred A. Knopf, 1949, 269–81; James S. Coleman, *The Adolescent Society*. New York: Free Press, 1961.

[6] Ivan Nye, "Adolescent-Parent Adjustment: Socio-Economic Level as a Variable," *American Sociological Review*, June 1951, pp. 341–49; S. B. Withey and E. Douvan, *A Study of Adolescent Boys*. Ann Arbor: University of Michigan, Survey Research Center, 1955, mimeo; E. Douvan and E. Kaye, *Adolescent Girls*. Ann Arbor: University of Michigan, Survey Research Center, 1957, mimeo; Frederick Elkin and William Westley, "The Myth of Adolescent Culture," *American Sociological Review*, 1955, pp. 680–85; Frederick Elkin and William Westley, "The Protective Environment and Adolescent Socialization," *Social Forces*, March 1957, pp. 243–49. The implications of these works and others for the "theory of youth culture" are discussed in Ramon J. Rivera, *The Sociology of Adolescence: A Selective Review of the Literature*. Chicago: University of Chicago, National Opinion Research Center, 1963, 5–29.

[7] Richard A. Cloward and Lloyd E. Ohlin, *Delinquency and Opportunity: A Theory of Delinquent Gangs*. New York: Free Press, 1960.

to structures of opportunity. The theory is familiar to criminologists and has been summarized in other project papers.[8] Cloward and Ohlin's use of such terms as "opportunity structures," "legitimate and illegitimate means," "role models," "integration of age levels," and so on, clearly implies that somewhere within the institutional or informal social context of an adolescent's life there exist individuals who can offer or withhold keys to certain sectors of adult status. Presumably these individuals are often *adults*. An important question then is: Who are the older persons who function, for the adolescent, as mediators of values and opportunities?

Direct field observation and continuing interviews with the detached workers provided a valuable "window" through which we were able to observe the behavior of delinquent boys within the context of local community life. Very early in the project our attention was drawn to the relationships that existed between these adolescents and the adults who were part of their everyday world.[9] We began to explore the possibility of some type of community study (or series of studies) that would put us into direct contact with these adults.

A survey of the literature revealed that an undertaking of this type would be almost unique in the field of juvenile delinquency.[10] The literature also suggested that such a study might prove *impossible* because of the "underlying conflict" between adolescents and adults it so often refers to. We were faced with a curious dilemma. On one hand, we had evidence (the observer and detached worker reports) which argued that adolescents quite frequently interacted with community adults; on the other hand were arguments that meaningful contact of this type was virtually nonexistent. The problem struck us as intriguing

[8] See, for example, James F. Short, Jr., Ramon J. Rivera, and Ray A. Tennyson, "Perceived Opportunities, Gang Membership, and Delinquency," *American Sociological Review*, February 1965, pp. 56–57.

[9] For an analysis of the behavior of Negro gang boys which relies heavily on qualitative material describing adult-adolescent integration, see Short and Strodtbeck, footnote 1, pp. 102–116.

[10] The New York School of Social Work, in conjunction with Mobilization for Youth, Inc., interviewed a stratified random sample of the adult residents of Manhattan's Lower East Side. Several of the questionnaire items employed in the New York survey were adapted for use in the Chicago study, but, in sample design and in intent, the two studies seem to be quite different. For an early report on the New York findings, see Richard A. Cloward and James A. Jones, "Social Class: Educational Attitudes and Participation," *Education in Depressed Areas*, A. Harry Passow (Ed.) New York: Bureau of Publications, Teachers College, Columbia University, 1963, 190–216.

enough to warrant a modest investment of funds for research. This paper outlines the research strategy followed and presents a number of findings from the study which ensued.

SECURING NOMINATIONS

We hoped to be able to locate and to interview samples of adults who were in effective contact with the boys. Initially, we considered straight-forward community studies of selected areas, for example, contacting every nth dwelling unit in a given neighborhood and interviewing a sample of randomly selected local residents. This strategy was rejected, largely on the grounds that such a procedure could never guarantee that the adults contacted had any meaningful relationship with the boys. We were, of course, interested in the characteristics of community adults, but this interest was made selective by our conviction that primary attention should be directed to those older persons who figured significantly in the lives of the boys.

An alternate strategy was adopted, one that *placed the major burden of sample selection on the youngsters themselves.* Our solution was simply to encourage the *boys to provide us with the names of those adults with whom they regularly interacted.* (We assumed that the adolescents *would* know adults who could meet this criterion.) At the moment this decision was made, we were in the early stages of administering a personal interview to many of the youngsters involved in the program. The interview schedule was quickly adapted to include a sequence of items requesting from each boy the names, addresses, and occupations of *"the four adults with whom you have the most contact."* We were primarily concerned with the character of adolescent-adult relations within the broad context of community life and, in line with this emphasis, a respondent's immediate *family members were explicitly excluded from nomination.* As it turned out (cf. Table 2 below), other boys were quick to fill this gap by nominating a large number of adult relatives of their peers. At the close of interviewing, relevant data (names, addresses, and so on) had been secured from 458 boys.

Each boy had been asked for four names and the sheer volume of adults identified by this procedure, together with our limited financial resources, dictated a narrowing of research interests to a more manageable number of potential respondents. The basic design of the overall study suggested the appropriateness of selecting a sample of adults from each of the six categories which had guided the initial choice of adolescents in this study (NG, NLC, and so on). Since the gang and lower-class control youngsters were selected from the same areas of the city, we could easily match the gang samples with their appropriate LC controls and thus compare the characteristics and responses of adults nominated by gang and non-gang boys in the *same* neighborhood.

Accordingly, two lower-class communities (Negro and white) were selected on the basis of the delinquency involvement of the gang boys and the relative richness of supporting material from other sources of data collection.[11] Our limited selection of middle-class adolescents yielded two groups (Negro and white) and two communities which seemed fairly representative, given our previous experience with these categories of urban adolescents. Our attention was thus centered on four Chicago communities, the adolescents within them, and the adults who had captured their attention.

NOMINEES AND SAMPLES FOR THE SIX GROUPS

Table 1 indicates the name and size of each group of adolescents selected to generate respondents for the adult interviews. Each boy had been asked to nominate four adults and the third column of the table indicates, at least for non-gang boys, that this request was generally followed by the adolescents. We might pause to underline the significance of this point. *The boys seemed to have little difficulty in nominating adults beyond their family circles with whom they were in regular contact.* These data, if taken as rough indicators of age-grade integration, suggest that integration of this type *is* characteristic of the communities selected, although it is somewhat *less pronounced* among boys who are members of delinquent gangs.

TABLE 1. THE NOMINATION PROCESS

Status of Nominators (Adolescents)	N	Total Number of Adult Nominations	Mean Number of Nominations per Adolescent
NG—Rattlers	33	105	3.2
NLC—Market St. Y.	15	59	3.9
NMC—Omegas	12	44	3.7
WG—Pizza Grill	19	59	3.1
WLC—St. Paul Settlement	45	176	3.9
WMC—Admirals Hi-Y	34	136	4.0

11 The Negro gang (Rattlers) was highly involved in conflict activities. The delinquent behavior of boys in the white gang (Pizza Grill Boys) was less specialized. The WG (and WLC) area, however, showed evidence of being an "integrated community,"—that is, an area with stable relationships between carriers of conventional and criminal values.

The table also documents a second point which was seriously to modify our research strategy. A total of 158 adolescents offered a total of 579 adult nominations. Even allowing for *multiple* nominations—that is, the fact that more than one boy in a group may have nominated the same adult—the adolescents had generated six samples of adults that offered more potential respondents than we could afford to interview. However, the fact that a large number of multiple nominations had been received suggested a tactic for reducing the caseloads for our interviewers and, hopefully, for enhancing the relevance of the study.

The tactic was a simple one. Each sample of adults was stratified into two categories: those persons who had been nominated by more than one boy were placed in a special category; those adults nominated only once were grouped separately. We set out to interview *every* adult who was a multiple nominee, plus randomly selected adults nominated by only one boy in each of the six groups. At this point our samples had become frankly purposive, the selection procedure depending largely on the relative salience of a given adult for a given group of adolescents. Our departure from conventional sampling procedures, imposed mainly by requirements of economy, was made more palatable because of the probability that we would be interviewing those adults who were important to *a number* of boys within the original groups of adolescents.

Locating multiple nominees proved to be a relatively simple task. Since more than one boy had volunteered the name and address, we were provided with a built-in check on the accuracy of our identifying information. The check was a welcome corrective device, especially in the lower-class areas where youngsters were apt to be hazy about the precise addresses of the adults they had nominated. The problems we encountered in tracking down respondents in these communities are suggested by the following exchange that occurred as a Negro gang boy nominated a girl named "Dee Dee."

Interviewer: "Under what circumstances do you see Dee Dee?"
Respondent: "Mostly I see her in a restaurant on Market and Rockford. I dance with her."
Interviewer: Does Dee Dee have a job?"
Respondent: "She a prostitute."
Interviewer: "Where does she live?"
Respondent: "I don't know." (Probe) "Somewhere on Rockford. The 1200 block."

Dee Dee was nominated only once, but she was among those randomly selected for interviews in the NG adult sample. We never managed to locate her (she apparently had moved from the neighborhood). At the height of our search we had the active cooperation of the Rattlers (the gang from which her nomination came) and a number of Dee Dee's former colleagues, but all to no avail.

Instances of vagueness concerning names and addresses were relatively common and they seemed to be most prevalent among lower-class (G and LC) boys.

CHARACTERISTICS OF THE RESPONDENTS

Interviews were successfully completed with 146 adults. A high proportion of these persons (85 percent) either lived or worked in the communities where the boys themselves had been found. Another 11 percent had lived or worked there at one time, but at the moment of their interview they were located elsewhere in the city. The boys had not been asked to limit their choices to neighborhood adults, but, given an opportunity to define the scope of their adult contacts, most of the youngsters had restricted themselves to older persons in their immediate milieu.

Table 2 presents additional data describing the adult respondents. The mean number of (adolescents) nominations per (adult) respondent, ranging from 1.3 to 2.5, directly reflects our effort to enhance the representation of *multiple nominees*, that is, adults nominated by more than one boy. The median ages of the six categories of respondents ranges between 35 and 47 years. These figures do not demonstrate a consistent pattern by race, class, or gang status, but it is interesting to note that the adolescent nominators (who are roughly 16 to 17 years of age) did *not* concentrate their choices within a young adult age category (for example, 20 to 29 years). Typically, they selected persons who were more mature. At first glance this finding suggests a hopeful note for it implies that these youngsters may have been open to the influence of more *experienced* members of the civilian labor force. Presumably, these would be individuals well situated to advise adolescents on existing career opportunities and the contemporary realities of the world of work.

The fourth column of the table presents the percentage of females in each category of adults. The column has special relevance. Most discussions of the social organization of the American Negro community emphasize the prevalence of female dominance within the typical Negro household.[12] Here we shift our attention from the immediate family to the wider community and examine the relative dominance of females

[12] See E. Franklin Frazier, *The Negro Family in the United States*. Chicago: University of Chicago Press, 1939, and Charles E. King, "The Negro Maternal Family: A Product of an Economic and a Culture System," *Social Forces*, October 1945, pp. 100–104.

TABLE 2. SELECTED CHARACTERISTICS OF ADULTS INTERVIEWED, BY RACE, CLASS, AND GANG STATUS OF NOMINATORS

Status of Nomi- nators	Adequate Inter- views	Mean Number of Nomi- nations per Interview	Median Age of Adults Inter- viewed	Percent of Adults Who Are Female	Percent of Adults with Adolescents In Their Household	Percent of Adults Who Occupy "Caretaker" Roles
NG	23	2.2	45	47.8	40.9	9.1
NLC	20	2.5	45	45.0	52.6	60.0
NMC	20	1.3	39	50.0	60.0	20.0
WG	27	1.5	35	22.2	22.2	18.5
WLC	23	1.5	41	43.5	50.0	31.8
WMC	33	1.3	47	24.2	51.5	42.4

within the adult milieu of these adolescents. A glance at the column of figures tells us that females constitute a *minority* of the respondents for each group although, within this overall pattern, we note that females are more often found in the Negro samples than in the white.

The next column of the table presents the proportion of adult respondents with adolescent members in their own households. Perusal of the completed interviews indicates that this designation ordinarily identifies adults who come to the attention of the boys in the normal course of interaction between a youngster and his age mates. The boys come to know parents of friends, adult relatives of girls they date, boarders at friends' homes, and older persons (with teenagers of their own) whose interest in adolescents has led them to volunteer work with Boy Scout troops, and so on. These are adult-adolescent relationships, but they represent a particular *type* of relationship—one that is made available to youngsters through their peer relationships.

The preceding category of respondents suggests the appropriateness of examining the distribution of a related (and occasionally overlapping) type of adult nominee: adults who come to the attention of adolescents in a more *formal* or *more strictly institutional setting*. Borrowing from Gans,[13] we shall call them *caretakers*; in the context of this report, the term caretaker will be used to refer to any adult, who, in the course of his ordinary daily activities, comes into contact with adolescents *as a representative of some larger adult-dominated institution that is formally committed to guide or to change the behavior of youth*. The proportion

[13] Herbert Gans, *The Urban Villagers*. New York: Free Press, 1962, 142–45.

of caretakers in each sample of adolescents appears in the final column of Table 2. As we examine this column of figures, we note also the specific types of caretakers contacted (see Table 3) and the significance of their activities in the local community.

1. *Types of caretakers*   Table 3 lists the specific caretaker roles that were identified within each group of adult respondents. Initially we might observe that there were more than a few such persons; on an overall basis almost one-third (30 percent) of the 146 adults interviewed could be classified as occupants of caretaker roles. Their functions can be summarized as follows:

Caretaker Roles	Percent As a Proportion of All Caretakers	Percent As a Proportion of the Combined Samples
Detached worker and other YMCA and Youth Center Personnel	40	12
High school teachers and related personnel	27	8
Clergy and related personnel	20	6
Boy Scout personnel	7	2
Other	7	2
	101%	30%

The proportion of YMCA and other Youth Center personnel in these samples comes as no surprise. The study located its youngsters through agencies such as these so it is reasonable that, when the boys were asked to nominate "significant" adults, a number of them would refer us back to the staff of their local youth center. Perhaps it is noteworthy that there were not more such nominations. That is, given our method of locating youngsters, the fact that *only* 12 percent of *all* adult respondents were agency personnel may strike some as surprising. The proportion may be viewed as rather large, or rather small, depending on one's point of view.

Small clusters of caretaker roles can be identified with other major institutional settings. Thus we find additional groups of adult respondents whose relationships with children would seem to flow primarily from their positions as teachers (27 percent of all caretakers), religious figures (20 percent), and Scouting personnel (7 percent). The *significance* of

TABLE 3. "CARETAKER" ROLES OF COMMUNITY ADULTS NOMINATED BY ADOLESCENTS; BY STATUS OF NOMINATORS

Status of Nominators

NG	NLC	NMC	WG	WLC	WMC
Detached Worker (9)[a]	Girl's Secretary YMCA (7)	Physical Director, YMCA (2)	Detached Worker (5)	Program Director, St. Paul (9)	Executive Secretary, YMCA (5)
Minister (1)	Phys. Ed. Programmer, YMCA (6)	Physical Director, YMCA (1)	Asst. Director, Youth Club (1)	Teacher and Athletic Coach (3)	Teacher and Chairman, Phys. Ed. Department (3)
	Program Director, Youth Club (6)	Group Worker, YMCA (1)	Community Relations Aide, Chicago Public Housing (1)	Teacher (2)	Assistant Scoutmaster (2)
	Group Worker, Youth Club (3)	Teacher (1)	Counselor, Chicago Youth Advisors (1)[b]	Teacher (1)	School Counselor (2)
	Administrative Assistant YMCA (3)		Lawyer (1)[c]	Teacher (1)	Minister (2)
	Executive Secretary, YMCA (2)			Volunteer Group Worker, St. Paul (1)	Minister and Pastor of Youth (1)
	Game Room Instructor, Youth Club (2)			Minister (1)	Minister and Pastor of Youth (1)
	Porter, YMCA (1)				Minister (1)
	Secretary, Youth Club (1)				Priest (1)
	Teacher (1)				Scoutmaster (1)
	Teacher (1)				Teacher and High School Band Director (1)
	Teacher (1)				Sunday School Teacher and Member, Boy Scout Troop Committee (1)
					Teacher (1)
					Straight Life Group Worker (1)[d]

[a] Numbers in parentheses indicate the number of boys nominating this adult.
[b] This organization provides voluntary counseling services for adolescents on probation or parole.
[c] This adult has defended several of the WG boys in court.
[d] A religious organization aimed at guiding the moral development of adolescents.

449

adolescent exposure to these specialized adult roles, and the more basic question of their availability to young persons, is likely to vary from community to community and, *within* communities, from adolescent group to adolescent group. These questions are addressed below.

    2. Caretakers: Their availability and significance   At this point it is appropriate to ask: What does the *presence* of caretakers (and the *types* of caretakers who are present) tell us about the communities that were surveyed in Chicago? Let us begin with a NG-NLC neighborhood —the Market Street area.

    Market Street is overwhelmingly populated by Negroes and largely dilapidated. To the typical caretaker, it offered what amounted to a textbook example of a neighborhood gone to seed. Caretakers existed in large numbers. Did the boys notice them?

    The non-gang boys did. Sixty percent of the NLC adults interviewed were caretakers, a figure that is about 50 percent larger than the comparable proportion of NG adult respondents. The difference is considerable and readers are reminded that these nominations were offered by boys who lived in the *same* community. It is also useful to remember that the Detached Worker Program was specifically aimed at those young persons who were felt to be largely ignored by conventional caretaker agencies. The fact that nine NG boys (27 percent of the Rattlers) nominated their worker as a "significant" adult and that only *one* other caretaker appears in the NG adult sample suggests that the YMCA's motives were not entirely illusionary. It is also instructive to examine the *types* of caretakers interviewed from the NLC nominations, if only to underline their absence from the NG adult sample.

    Thus we note, within the group of NLC adult respondents, nine YMCA or Youth Center caretakers and three school teachers. Together these individuals collected 34 nominations from the boys, which amounts to 58 percent of all the nominations that the NLC offered to our interviewers. Our NLC comparison group, then, is heavily dominated by institutionalized roles, and their adult incumbents actually seem to have "captured" the loyalty of their "clients." *Given all of their adult contacts to choose from, the NLC boys tended to nominate their caretakers.* The contrast with NG boys is striking.

    We find a somewhat similar picture if we examine the number and the type of caretakers interviewed in our low status white categories. WLC adult respondents more often represent institutionalized roles, but in this case the margin over the WG group of adults is only 13 percent. More instructive are the specific caretaker roles which appear in each sample.

WG boys nominated caretakers who exist *to answer the special needs of boys who are in trouble*: a detached worker, a lawyer, and a probation officer, as well as a civic emissary (community relations aide) assigned to a neighborhood that needs "help." Other adolescents (WLC) in the same community nominated their teachers, a minister, and the officers of their local recreation centers. In this comparison it appears that the types of caretakers who become salient to groups of adolescent boys reflect the degree to which they are "in trouble."

The middle-class groups present quite different profiles. NMC adults are seldom caretakers, but they are often community adults *with teenage children of their own*. The group of WMC adult respondents is also weighted in this direction, but it includes a sizeable number of clergymen, teachers, and scouting personnel. The picture presented by the WMC adult sample is close to that offered by Elkin and Westley in their study of a Canadian suburb.[14] Control of the environment and protection of adolescents from disruptive events is a task shared *jointly* by parents and caretakers. For the NMC group it is the *parents* of group members (rather than caretakers) who predominate in this particular type of community context.

A final point should be made concerning the presence of caretakers. Relative to the educational and income characteristics of the entire civilian labor force, *professional caretakers tend to be persons of high socio-economic status*. The Duncan SES scale, for example, ranks teachers, group workers, and clergymen (along with lawyers, engineers, and real estate agents) at the "top of the heap"—that is, at the ninth or tenth decile in an SES ranking of all American occupations.[15] (See Table 4.)

The significance of this fact for low-status youngsters should not be overlooked. In urban slums, groups of adolescents which act to maximize contact with caretakers are likely also to maximize exposure to individuals *qualified to serve as role models for a middle-class way of life*. Table 5 contains relevant data.

Section A of the table presents the mean (Duncan SES) decile rank of all adult respondents who are caretakers. Not unexpectedly, the mean ranks are quite high, ranging between 8.7 and 10.0.[16] Other community

---

[14] Elkin and Westley, footnote 6.

[15] Duncan's scale is presented in Albert J. Reiss, Jr., *Occupations and Social Status*. New York: Free Press, 1962, 263–75. Table 4 is adapted from Duncan's list of occupations.

[16] It should be noted that not all caretakers will receive a rank of 9 or 10. One adult in the NLC group is a porter. Adults who worked as caretakers on a volunteer basis received an SES score on the basis of the way they made a living, and not on the basis of their caretaker activities. Finally, female care-

TABLE 4. Selected Occupations by Decile Rank and Socio-Economic Index

Occupation	Decile	Socio-economic index
Lawyer	10	93
Electrical Engineer	10	84
Accountant	10	78
Teacher	10	70
Recreation or Group Worker	10	67
Social Worker (except group)	9	64
Real Estate Agent	9	62
Clergyman	9	52
Sales Clerk	8	47
Electrician	8	44
Policeman	8	40
TV Repairman	7	36
Plumber	7	34
Bus Driver	6	24
Welder	6	25
Auto Mechanic	5	19
Bartender	5	19
Operative (manufacturing)	4	17
Waiter	4	16
Cook	4	15
Laborer (metal industry)	3	14
Farm Owner or Tenant	3	14
Taxi Driver	2	10
Janitor	2	9
Construction Laborer	2	7
Porter	1	4

adults tend to be much lower in status; on an overall basis, a margin of 3.6 deciles separates caretaker roles from other community adult respondents. This differential in adult status is especially characteristic of lower-class communities and it is most obvious in Negro communities.

Since the number and the proportion of caretakers vary across categories, their net contribution to the SES "mix" of a community varies as well. Part B of the table takes this factor into account, comparing the SES rank of all adult respondents to the status position of the families of the boys responsible for their nomination. Examining the bottom

takers, if they were married, were coded in terms of their husband's occupation, the assumption being that the husband's position determines the SES location of the family.

TABLE 5. MEAN DECILE RANKS: SOCIAL STATUS OF CARETAKERS AND OTHER ADULTS, BY STATUS OF ORIGIN OF ADOLESCENT NOMINATORS

A. Caretakers and Other Community Adult Respondents

Source of Mean Decile Ranks	Status of Nominators					
	NG	NLC	NMC	WG	WLC	WMC
Adult Respondents Who Are Caretakers	9.5(2)	9.3(12)	10.0(4)	9.4(5)	8.7(7)	9.6(14)
Other Community Adult Respondents	3.6(21)	2.6(8)	7.9(16)	5.4(22)	5.3(15)	9.2(19)
Observed Difference	+5.9	+6.7	+2.1	+4.0	+3.4	+0.4

B. All Community Adult Respondents and Adolescent Nominators

Source of Mean Decile Ranks	Status of Nominators					
	NG	NLC	NMC	WG	WLC	WMC
All Community Adult Respondents	4.1(23)	6.7(20)	8.3(20)	6.1(27)	6.4(22)	9.4(33)
Status of Origin of Nominators (Adolescents)	3.0(33)	3.7(15)	6.1(12)	3.9(19)	5.5(45)	9.2(34)
Observed Difference	+1.1	+3.0	+2.2	+2.2	+0.9	+0.2

453

row of the table ("Observed Difference") we find in every case that the boys have nominated adults who tend, on the average, to be superior to them in terms of social status. An important part of this status differential is due to the contribution made by caretakers to the mean position of all community adult respondents. *It would seem that the presence of caretakers or their relative absence may profoundly affect the SES characteristics of those adult roles available to youngsters in slum communities.*

Adolescent-Adult Contacts: General

During the course of their personal interview, each adult respondent was handed a list of all the boys in the group from which his nomination had been drawn. He was asked to indicate which names identified boys that were known personally and, for each identification made, the number of times each week that he saw the boy. These data appear in Table 6.

TABLE 6. ADOLESCENT-ADULT CONTACTS

		When presented with a roster of the names of the boys in the group responsible for nomination, the typical adult respondent:	
Status of Nominators (Adolescents)	*Number of Boys in Group*	*Was Able to Recognize the Names of . . .*	*And Said that He (She) Saw Each of These Boys, During an Average Week, about . . .*
NG	33	6 boys	5 times
NLC	15	11 boys	3 times
NMC	12	4 boys	3 times
WG	19	7 boys	2 times
WLC	45	4 boys	4 times
WMC	34	6 boys	3 times

The typical adult respondent was able to recognize about six names on the group rosters. Stated differently (and taking into account the different sizes of the adolescent groups involved), the average adult was able to identify about 24 percent of the boys in the group from which his nomination had come. Note that our "index of recognition" required each adult to know the first and last names of the boys involved.

The proportion of boys recognized on this basis (24 percent) strikes us as misleadingly low. Certainly, among gang boys of both races, this figure could have been raised by including nicknames as part of our "index of recognition." The addition of photographs of the boys would have enhanced the probability of identification among *all* groups. Unfortunately, neither of these methods was employed.

Table 6 also indicates that the average adult had from two to five contacts per week with each boy identified. There is no consistent pattern by race or class or gang affiliation, in the figures given. However, substantive differences *are* revealed if we ask *where* these contacts occurred and about the *types of conversations* that took place. These data appear in Tables 7 and 8.

TABLE 7. SELECTED RESPONSES OF COMMUNITY ADULTS TO THE QUESTION: "WHERE DO YOU GENERALLY SEE THESE BOYS?," BY RACE, CLASS, AND GANG STATUS OF NOMINATORS

Settings For Adult-Adolescent Contact	Status of Nominators					
	NG	NLC	NMC	WG	WLC	WMC
Around the Neighborhood	68.2	38.9	20.0	76.0	47.8	51.5
Centers for Organized Adolescent Activities	0.0	50.0	35.0	4.0	30.4	97.0
Home of Adult, or Home of Adolescent	22.7	11.1	85.0	28.0	56.5	48.5
At Work	9.0	22.0	10.0	32.0	17.4	9.1
100% =	22	18	20	25	23	33

N	141
NA	5
Total N (Adults)	146

Table 7 presents the answers that adults gave to the question "Where do you generally see these boys? (Where do you generally have most of your contact with them?)." Responses categorized as "around the neighborhood" include a range of answers. Usually the adult has said "on the street" or something similar (for example, "I see them on my way to the store," or "I only see them when I walk my dog"). We note that street-centered answers of this type are primarily characteristic of *adults nominated by gang boys*. Given what we already know of the characteristics of our adult respondents, the pattern of remaining answers is

TABLE 8. SELECTED RESPONSES OF ADULTS TO THE QUESTION:
"WHAT ARE SOME OF THE THINGS YOU'RE LIKELY TO TALK ABOUT WHEN
YOU SEE THEM?," BY RACE, CLASS, AND GANG STATUS OF NOMINATORS

Selected Responses	Status of Nominators					
	NG	*NLC*	*NMC*	*WG*	*WLC*	*WMC*
School	4.5	55.6	60.0	7.7	47.8	72.7
Work	36.4	22.2	20.0	42.3	30.4	12.1
Conventional Adolescent Interests (Cars, Sports, etc.)	18.0	55.6	60.0	49.9	87.0	63.7
Neighborhood Gossip, Casual Greetings, etc.	54.6	38.9	30.0	61.5	34.7	26.3
100% =	22	18	20	26	23	33

N	142
NA	4
Total N	146

largely predictable. Thus, NLC boys have been "captured" by caretakers. The adults they nominate tend to see the boys in caretaker-dominated centers for adolescent activities (for example, the YMCA). NMC boys nominated a large number of adults with teenagers of their own; these adults see the boys in the course of visits to the boys' homes or in their own. WLC adults (compared to their NLC counterparts) are less often agency-centered. They see the boys "around the neighborhood" or at home. WMC adults report an especially large number of agency contacts and secondary encounters in the neighborhood or during home visits. What types of conversation occur when the generations meet? An answer is suggested in Table 8.

After identifying his usual place of contact with the boys, each adult was asked "What are some of the things you're likely to talk about when you see them? (What's likely to come up in conversation?)" A glance at the first category of responses ("School") shows striking differences between adults nominated by gang boys and all other respondents. The general issue of one's *education* almost *never* comes up in a conversation between a gang boy and the "significant" adults we interviewed. This is the most decisive pattern in the table, but other differences are also important:

(1) There is a tendency for gang-nominated adults to report a somewhat *higher* proportion of discussions concerning the world of *work*,[17] but fewer conversations about conventional adolescent interests such as sports and cars.

(2) Gang boy-adult conversations involve chiefly neighborhood gossip and casual exchanges of greetings.

These points are worth underlining, if only because they are so obviously relevant to the general problem of structures of opportunity. In their conversations with adults, gang boys reveal themselves as relatively indifferent to more conventional adolescent interests, surely more indifferent to school, and much more likely to enter into conversations that, from a middle-class perspective, would seem to be without much content.

But are such conversations actually without content? They do seem to lack the *instructional* quality that appears to be an important component of exchanges between the generations in middle-class communities. Middle-class adults talk to adolescents about school. In so doing it seems likely that sentiments are conveyed such as "school is important" and "you must get all the education you can." As they talk, they *teach*. When the conversation does not dwell on education, it turns on topics that are specific to middle-class images of adolescent life—sports, cars, and so on. Discussions such as these would seem to stress a measure of *distance* between the age grades. That is, MC adults appear to be presenting themselves as persons who are tolerant and encouraging about adolescent interests, but they also present themselves as persons who are more expert and sophisticated than adolescents, and thus as persons who are strategically situated to offer them *advice*.

This is exactly the quality that seems to be lacking in adult conversations with gang boys. These persons exchange greetings; they gossip; occasionally they speak of the world of work. By and large they are *not* communicating in a fashion that would underline, for the youngster, any sense of dependence on the expertise of persons who are older. The generations appear to interact on a basis of *equality*, sharing concerns and exchanging information in a manner that seems to *deny* that there is any special significance in their positions as adults and adolescents. Consider the following selection of responses which gang-nominated

[17] It is interesting to note that adult-gang boy conversations involving work infrequently touch upon the problem of finding a job for the adolescent. In almost two-thirds (63 percent) of the work conversations described in the gang adult interviews, the boys and the adult respondents were simply comparing notes on the jobs that each held. This finding is consistent with our interpretation of other differences in the table.

adults gave to the question, "What are some of the things you're likely to talk about when you see them (the boys)?"

An NG adult (Case #150—Housewife): "Nothing but how do you do? How is your mother? Where are you going?"

A WG adult (Case #512—Unemployed Entertainer): "Nothing, we just bull-shit around. Nothing in particular."

An NG adult (Case #125—Laborer, Poultry Market): "This depends on what they are doing when I see them. Sometimes they're shooting craps in the alley. I say, what are you trying to do? Get some rest in California? That sort of stuff."[18]

A WG adult (Case #543—Laborer, Road Maintenance): "Who's in jail? What happened to this one? How's your brother? That's about it."

Exchanges such as these are hardly likely to convince adolescents that older persons may be capable of offering entree to a more desirable way of life. If they suggest anything at all to a person familiar with these environments, they are likely to remind him of conversations between adults.

Gang-nominated adults usually are not *pushing* anything. Note the contrast between the answers cited above and some typical responses of middle-class respondents to the same question:

A WMC adult (Case #314—Physician): "Electronics, radio, hi-fi; how to fix things—that sort of thing. I have a complete workshop—I teach the boys how to do these things."

An NMC adult (Case #334—Housewife): "We talk about so many things—sports, different players and the schools they went to. We discuss current events. Then we talk about school."

A WMC adult (Case #730—Salesman, Electrical Equipment): "Where are you going to school? Did you get a scholarship? What are you going to major in? Are you going to play baseball or football at school?"

ADOLESCENT-ADULT RELATIONS AS STRUCTURES OF OPPORTUNITY

The material in the preceding table appropriately introduces our final topic—intergenerational relations as structures of opportunity. Here we are concerned primarily with the extent to which community adults *intervene* in the lives of the younger generation to shape the life chances that they will encounter. We begin at a very basic level by asking whether "significant" adults are at all *concerned* about the eventual fate of young-sters. After some general questions about the boys in their neighborhood,

18 The term "get some rest in California" is a lower-class Negro slang expres-sion that refers to serving a sentence in the Cook County Jail. This facility is located on California Avenue in Chicago's South Side.

each adult respondent was asked: "Have you ever wondered about the kind of life these youngsters will lead when they grow up?" The proportion of adults answering "yes" appears in Table 9.

TABLE 9. PERCENT OF ADULTS RESPONDING "YES" TO THE QUESTION: "HAVE YOU EVER WONDERED ABOUT THE KIND OF LIFE THESE YOUNGSTERS WILL LEAD WHEN THEY GROW UP?," BY RACE, CLASS, AND GANG STATUS OF NOMINATORS

Status of Nominators					
NG	NLC	NMC	WG	WLC	WMC
65.2			55.6		
(23)			(27)		
	95.0			95.6	
	(20)			(23)	
		85.0			84.8
		(20)			(33)

			N	146	
			NA	0	
			Total N	146	

Taking these proportions as rough indicators of adult interest, we find that interest is *highest* among adults in touch with youngsters *who are not in gangs. Interest is almost universal among LC adults.* Note that the question was phrased in terms of the adult ever *wondering* about what would happen to the boys. The choice of this term was deliberate. We could have asked, for example, if they were *interested* or *concerned* or whether they ever *worried* about the subject at all. As it was finally phrased, the question was intended to cover all of these gradations (which might be seen as points along a continuum reflecting each adult's sense of *personal involvement* in the life chances of the youngsters he knew). This point is worth mentioning because the probability is high that LC adults tended to *wonder* because they were *worried*. LC adults (and NLC adults in particular) are often caretakers; LC adults tend to dislike the neighborhoods where they work and often live.[19] For persons

[19] Data relevant to this point were obtained. Middle-class adults are most likely to "like" the communities where the boys were found. NLC adults have the most negative attitudes concerning their neighborhood.

such as these, wondering about the fate of adolescents will often reflect a conviction that youngsters must be protected from the more threatening events that exist in their environment. On the other hand, it seems likely that middle-class adults *wonder* because they are *interested*. They are interested because it is "only natural" for MC adults to be interested in the life chances of adolescents, just as it is "only natural" for them when they meet, to talk of school and sports.[20] (See Table 8.)

Gang-nominated adults *wonder* less often. Perhaps they are less interested, or less concerned, or less worried. Perhaps they view the outcome of the lives of these boys as a foregone conclusion. In the absence of any follow-up items in the schedule to clarify these questions, any conclusion drawn is necessarily speculative. However, accepting the logic of the question they were asked, we are left to conclude that gang-nominated adults *less* often report a sense of *personal involvement in the life chances of the youngsters they know.*

As we have already suggested, there may be a number of dimensions to this sense of personal involvement. Still, the entire issue might not occur to some persons if it were not *forced* upon their attention by the adolescents themselves. A relevant question then becomes: How many of these respondents have ever been *approached* by boys concerned about their performance in conventional structures of opportunity? This question was asked, and the relevant data appear in Table 10.

Looking first at Section A of the table (school problems), we note a pattern of responses similar to that observed in Table 9. Nongang boys are *most* likely to approach community adults concerning their problems at school; gang boys are *least* likely to do so. The answers are especially striking because they bear almost no relation to the number and the severity of the problems that these boys experience in school. Gang boys, by a large margin, are most likely to experience difficulties in school,[21] yet they are least likely to bring these problems to the attention of the older persons they know.

[20] According to this line of reasoning, the small proportion of MC adults who do not wonder about the fate of adolescents (about 15 percent in both the NMC and WMC groups) do not wonder about the problem because the outcome is a foregone conclusion—the boys will do very well for themselves when they grow up.

[21] For a discussion of the school adjustments of the boys in the Chicago study, see Jonathan Freedman and Ramon Rivera, "Education, Social Class, and Patterns of Delinquency," paper read at the annual meeting of the American Sociological Association, 1962. Within each race, middle-class boys are most successful in school, followed by LC boys. Gang boys make the poorest adjustments to school.

TABLE 10. SCHOOL AND WORK

A. Problems at School

Percent of Adults Responding "Yes" to the Question:
"Has Any Boy on That List Ever Spoken to You about His Problems
at School?," by Race, Class, and Gang Status of Nominators

Status of Nominator					
NG	*NLC*	*NMC*	*WG*	*WLC*	*WMC*
39.1 (23)			40.0 (25)		
	85.0 (20)			78.3 (23)	
		50.0 (20)			59.4 (32)

N	143
NA	3
Total N	146

B. Finding a Job

Percent of Adults Responding "Yes" to the Question:
"Has Any Boy on That List Ever Spoken to You about How He Should Go
about Finding a Job?," by Race, Class, and Gang Status of Nominators

Status of Nominator					
NG	*NLC*	*NMC*	*WG*	*WLC*	*WMC*
47.8 (23)			53.8 (26)		
	75.0 (20)			73.9 (23)	
		50.0 (20)			33.3 (33)

N	145
NA	1
Total N	146

Section B of the table tells a similar story. More than any other group, the gang boys need jobs and need advice about finding them, yet it is mainly their LC peers who turn to adults for consultation. Above we noted that gang-nominated adults less often feel subjectively involved in the life chances of these boys. One reason for this fact may well be that gang boys *less often approach adults to discuss the problems they experience in conventional structures of opportunity.*

Table 11 presents further data relevant to this point. In constructing the interview schedule we attempted to develop a list of school problems that would give adequate coverage to difficulties encountered by boys of widely divergent social backgrounds. The list was constructed on the basis of data from pretest versions of our instrument, supplemented by information from interviews with the boys and observational material concerning their adjustment to school. The list of specific school problems that was eventually handed to the respondents contained 22 items. Each adult was asked to read the list and then to indicate the particular problems that had been mentioned in his conversations with the boys.

TABLE 11. PERCENT OF NG AND NLC COMMUNITY ADULTS WHO HAVE DISCUSSED SPECIFIC SCHOOL PROBLEMS WITH BOYS THEY KNOW

Question: "Have you ever spoken to a teenage boy who (cite specific problem) and advised him about what to do?" Problems Cited	Status of Nominators		
	NG	NLC	Observed Difference
Hadn't learned much from his earlier school work and was finding it difficult to catch up	17.4	70.0	+52.6
Was having difficulty getting along with his fellow students	4.3	55.0	+50.7
Was a slow learner and having a hard time making fair grades at school	30.4	80.0	+49.6
Felt that it cost too much money to continue with school	13.0	60.0	+47.0
Wanted to return to school, but felt that he was too old to go back	21.7	65.0	+43.3
Felt that he had to help out his parents financially and couldn't stay in school	21.7	65.0	+43.3
Wanted more spending money and felt he couldn't get it if he stayed in school	21.7	65.0	+43.3
Just didn't like the school he went to	17.4	60.0	+42.6
Couldn't decide what to take at school	8.7	50.0	+41.3

TABLE 11. *(continued)*

Was wondering about how to finance a college education	4.3	45.0	+40.7
Was wondering about the college he should apply to	4.3	45.0	+40.7
Felt that he wanted to enter the Armed Services instead of going to school	30.4	70.0	+39.6
Simply wasn't applying himself to his school work	26.1	65.0	+38.9
Felt that his teachers weren't doing a good job	21.7	60.0	+38.3
Tried hard, but just didn't seem to be lucky in school	21.7	60.0	+38.3
Just couldn't seem to get interested in his school work	39.1	75.0	+35.9
Felt that his teachers were asking him to do too much work	30.4	65.0	+34.6
Was trying to decide whether he should go to college	8.7	40.0	+31.3
Was having difficulty getting along with his teachers and felt they didn't like him	43.5	70.0	+26.5
Wanted to return to school, but didn't know how to go about getting back in	26.1	50.0	+23.9
Felt that he wanted to get married instead of going to school	21.7	40.0	+18.3
Was a truant and spent a lot of time away from school	43.5	55.0	+11.5
100% =	23	20	

N	43
NA	0
Total N (NG and NLC Adults)	43

We were confident that a large number of these items would evoke sizeable differences in the responses of gang and LC respondents; many of the items, in fact, were aimed directly at problems that we knew were much more severe among members of delinquent gangs. The data in Table 11, reporting the responses of NG and NLC adults, suggest that our whole approach to this problem, however commendable it may have seemed at the time, was dead wrong. *NLC adults are more likely to report conversations with the boys regardless of the type of problem involved.*

We know that gang boys get poorer grades in school, but NLC boys more often talk to adults about this problem. We know that financial problems are more likely to interrupt the schooling of gang boys, but NLC boys more often bring this issue to the attention of the older persons they know. To put it simply, *we were unable to locate any school problem at all that NG boys were more likely to discuss with adults. Yet NG boys, objectively, are much less successful in their adjustments to school.*

The decision *not* to turn to adults for assistance probably is related to a variety of factors, including the attitudes of the adults. Perhaps the boys sense that adults are less than concerned about their future. Another factor, suggested earlier, is that the generations tend to interact as *equals*; gang-nominated adults are not cast in the role of helpers for these youngsters and the boys are able to avoid the sense of dependence that such a relationship would involve. It is no surprise, therefore, to learn that gang boys are *less* likely to define local adults as effective individuals. This finding, based on interviews conducted with the boys, has been reported elsewhere.[22] Finally, we should note that gang-nominated adults less often view these boys as victims of a system of events and circumstances in which they (the adults) are a key link. If the boys do poorly in school it is *their own fault.* Gang-nominated adults, when they were asked to identify the cause of the school problems of gang boys, overwhelmingly laid the blame on the *personal characteristics* of the boys themselves. The youngsters were described as "stupid," "lazy," "indifferent," and so on. One WG respondent, when asked why the boys were apt to do poorly in school, phrased it this way (Case #539—Grocery Store Owner): "They just don't care about school. They're lazy bums. All they care about is running around and having fun."

This man's comment amounts to a self-fulfilling prophecy. The boys will do poorly in school and on the jobs they get. Why bother to help? So, of course, adults don't help; and the boys do poorly.

CONCLUSIONS

From the material presented above and from other project data, it is obvious that gang boys are enmeshed in an interlocking chain of circumstances which profoundly affect their chances for mobility. Its major elements can be outlined as follows:

(1) Members of delinquent gangs tend to be involved with older persons who possess few of the characteristics that might qualify an

[22] See Short, Rivera, and Tennyson, footnote 8, for the relevant data (especially Tables 1 and 2).

adult to improve an adolescent's performance in conventional structures of opportunity. The adults they know tend to be low in status. Few of them are committed to the goal of "helping adolescents" as part of a formal caretaker role.

(2) Compared to other respondents, the typical gang-nominated adult is simply less concerned with the whole problem of offering opportunities to youngsters. For gang communities, the generations do not interact in a fashion that makes this problem explicit. Adults are seldom reminded that they may have an important role to play in affecting the life chances of a younger generation.

(3) NG and WG adults, as disinterested and uninvolved witnesses to the failure of gang boys in conventional structures of opportunity, pin the blame for these failures on the boys. The youngsters, they feel, are incompetent.

(4) Perhaps the boys sense that this evaluation has been made. We do know that gang boys are less likely to describe their adult neighbors as effective individuals. Gang-nominated adults present a negative picture of the personal qualities of the boys they know; and the boys respond in kind.

(5) Finally, and inevitably, when problems arise for these youngsters, especially problems affecting their life-chances, *they are less often referred to older persons for solution*. Adults (the boys seem to be saying) do not *care*; and even if they do care, they are powerless to act.

This study, like that of Kobrin and his associates,[23] suggests modification of the Cloward and Ohlin theory of delinquent gangs and of other formulations concerning youth subcultures. The adolescent boys in this study were neither as isolated from adults nor as antagonistic toward them as some theorists would have us believe. Both Negro gang boys (the Rattlers are primarily a 'conflict' group) and white gang boys (who live in an area where criminal and conventional elements are 'integrated') have regular contacts with older persons in their communities. Perhaps the most important contribution of this study, however, is that it is a beginning attempt to *specify* the manner in which adult-adolescent relations operate to guide (or fail to guide) the passage of youngsters through conventional structures of opportunity. Within the *same* urban communities there are profound gang–non-gang differences in the *types*

[23] See Kobrin *et al.*, "Criteria of Status among Street Gangs," *Journal of Research in Crime and Delinquency*, 1967, **4**, 98–118.

of intergenerational contacts that occur. Non-gang boys are given guidelines and advice that are likely to enhance their life chances; gang-
nominated adults may live in the same community but they do little
to help boys they know to live, as adults, in a better world.

SUMMARY

During the Chicago study of "Street Corner Groups and Patterns of
Delinquency," adolescent boys (gang and non-gang lower-class, and middle-class) were asked to nominate adults with whom they were in regular
contact. Family members were excluded from nomination and the resulting rosters of adults, many of whom were local community residents,
were included in a program of personal interviews.

This article is a first report on these interviews and focuses on patterns
of adolescent-adult relations in the communities under study. Particular
attention is given to the fashion in which adults operate to shape the
social and economic opportunities that youngsters will encounter. There
are marked differences in this regard among the groups of adults studied.
Adults close to gang boys are less likely to express concern for the life
chances of boys they know and they are less likely to be sought out by
the boys for advice in handling problems that the boys have encountered
in school.

3.9 *Orientation*

Once behavior has been described and hypotheses about its acquisition or development are established, several questions may emerge.
For example, if a given behavior is maladaptive, should this behavior be changed? The answer to this question requires a value
judgment and hence raises a philosophical or moral-ethical issue.
Once a decision is made to attempt to modify maladaptive behavior in positive ways, however, the question that follows is clearly
psychological: Under what conditions or by what means can this
behavior be changed? Precisely such a question is the province of
the following report by Irwin Sarason.

Sarason describes below the evolvement of researches with delinquent adolescents ranging from the formulation of treatment
(modification) procedures to the construction of means to assess
behavioral changes attributable to such procedures. The conceptual

pulse of Sarason's project is supplied by observational learning and modeling. As such it shares broadly with the Rivera and Short selection, a theoretical view about learning and its conditions. The reader will recall Rivera and Short's previous dramatization, namely, the relative lack of opportunity for gang-oriented adolescents to model themselves after competent adults with whom personally significant communication channels have been established and who care about the lives of these adolescents. Sarason, however, logically extends his talents to consider the degree to which modeling opportunities (when provided) may assist toward the rehabilitation of delinquent adolescent males. The reader is particularly alerted to Sarason's modeling procedures, the relevance of which is not limited to the amelioration of delinquency. Involved is role playing based upon observational learning experiences. This role playing simulates real life situations, such as job-interviewing and the like. These simulations have been designed to highlight in meaningful ways certain values, such as personal initiative and responsibility, not apparent in the behavior of many delinquent adolescents.

In addition to the simulation procedures, Sarason's project is revealing in at least three ways. One of these concerns the learning outcomes associated with various combinations of experiences (for example, modeling with and without guided discussion and televised feedback). A second is the extent to which a subject's anxiety level seemingly modulates the impact of these learning experiences. A third area of significance is comprised of questions produced by Sarason's investigation which warrant further research.

RECOMMENDED READINGS

Empey, LaMar T., and Rabow, Jerome. The Provo experiment in delinquency rehabilitation. *American Sociological Review*, 1961, **26,** 679–696.

Hunt, David E., and Hardt, Robert C. Developmental stage, delinquency, and differential treatment. *Journal of Research in Crime and Delinquency*, 1965, **2,** 20–31.

Stralton, John R., and Terry,. Robert M. (Eds.) *Prevention of Delinquency: Problems and Programs.* New York: Macmillan, 1968.

Wattenberg, William W. (Ed.) *Social Deviancy among Youth.* 65th Yearbook of the National Society for the Study of Education (Part I). Chicago: University of Chicago Press, 1966.

3.9 An Observational Learning Approach to Juvenile Delinquency

Irwin G. Sarason, UNIVERSITY OF WASHINGTON

The need to cope in a positive fashion with the social problem of juvenile delinquency is being recognized increasingly. The delinquent is deficient in socially acceptable behavior and his reactions to school and work situations are maladaptive. Attempts at coping with this problem of the adolescent period have taken a variety of directions. Two components of these are efforts at (1) ferreting out the causes of delinquent, antisocial behavior and (2) changing the attitudes and personality attributes of the adolescents who display this behavior. At the same time, anomalously, we know both a great deal and very little about the causes and cures of delinquency. In a general sense, cultural deprivation and an inadequate home life are implicated in its occurrence. But at the level of the individual teenager it is often difficult to assign weights to these and other determinants. In some cases cultural deprivation may not be a specific cause of adolescent acting-out behavior. In many cases deprived youngsters overcome the handicapping limitations of their environments.

Clinical observations and sociological and psychological theories suggest that the behavioral deficiencies of many adolescents often result from lack of opportunity to observe models of socially adaptive and useful behavior. Certainly, much of juvenile delinquency need not be viewed in terms of a mental illness conception. Rather, it can be seen as a reflection of inadequate learning experiences. The delinquent is someone who has fallen out of the mainstream of his culture and who functions maladaptively. His deviant behavior may be viewed as part of a rebellion against societal norms and as a failure to have introjected socially useful roles and ways of responding. This failure comes about as a result of inadequate opportunities to observe, display, and subsequently, receive reinforcement for conventional behavior.

Building on these theoretical assumptions, an attempt has been made to devise a procedure different from the usual psychotherapeutic and counseling approaches. It provides juvenile delinquents with observa-

---

A paper prepared especially for this volume. The studies in this article were supported by a research and demonstration grant from the Social and Rehabilitation Service.

tional opportunities that might enhance their wherewithal in a variety of situations, especially those in which concepts of social motivation and self-control play important roles. This attempt took place within the context of a research investigation carried out under as well-controlled conditions as could be arranged within an institutional setting. As part of this project the behavior of adolescent delinquent boys continues to be evaluated as a function of special modeling and identification opportunities. The content of the observational opportunities is especially important to adolescents: vocational planning, motivations and interests, attitudes toward work and education, and the utility of socially appropriate behavior.

A major aim of the research has been to demonstrate that when juvenile delinquents are given opportunities to (1) observe socially adaptive behavior in healthy, accepting persons, and (2) replicate and practice this type of behavior, their repertories of pro-social responses will enlarge and strengthen. If the modeling process could be put to the positive advantage of the delinquent in a research and demonstration effort covering an admittedly relatively short time span, it would then be reasonable and promising to consider the development of more lengthy and complex identification opportunities, such as might be provided in special educational, social, and vocational centers. These centers might or might not be parts of existing institutions and be designed especially to maximize the possibility of the delinquents' and pre-delinquents' observations of healthy models. Another implication of the research described here concerns the training of non-professional personnel who often work with persons displaying behavior problems. It was our hope at the outset of the project that it might provide useful and practical leads for training these staff members to be therapeutic models for young offenders. This possibility in the case of adolescent delinquents would have important implications for society's efforts to help these youngsters overcome their social and emotional handicaps.

The project began in 1966 and is still in progress. Its locus is the Cascadia Juvenile Reception-Diagnostic Center in Tacoma, Washington. Cascadia receives a 100 percent sample of those committed to the Department of Institutions by the Juvenile Courts of the State of Washington. Its cottages, each with 20–25 juvenile offenders in residence, are staffed by personnel who work in shifts around the clock.

Initially we focused on answering several specific questions. What types of observational opportunities would be interesting and ego-involving for juvenile delinquents? How should models behave toward them in order to maximize the effects of observational opportunities? What sorts of control groups would be needed? What types of dependent variables should be measured in order to evaluate the effects of modeling opportunities? Early in our work it became clear that observational learning situations must be relatively uncomplicated and objective and must be clearly labeled and easily discriminable events. The following orientation was devised and given to the subjects at the beginning of their modeling "course":

"One important way that people learn how to do something is by observing someone else doing it. Frequently, just explaining something to someone isn't as effective as actually doing it first while the other person watches. For example, it is easier to learn to swim or even to put a puzzle together if you have a chance to watch someone else do it first. We think that small groups working together can learn a lot about appropriate ways of doing things by just playing and watching others play different roles. These roles will include common situations that many people experience, like how to apply for a job, or how to talk to a boss or teacher. Everyone in the group will both play roles for themselves and watch others play the same roles.

"We'll be playing a different role situation each day. We'll outline each scene as we go along.

"First, we'll describe the situation to you, then play out the roles involved. We want you to watch us, then take turns in pairs playing the same roles yourselves. We'll want you to stick closely to the roles the way we play them, but also you may add your own personal touch to your role."

The boys, whose average age was 17 years (range of 15½ to 18), seemed to accept the modeling situations as they were presented to them: opportunities to enhance their ability to cope with situations that for them represented problem areas. Each session is attended by two models (psychology graduate students) and four Cascadia boys and follows this sequence: (1) A model introduces and describes the scene for the day; (2) the models role play the scene while the boys observe; (3) one boy is called upon to summarize and explain the content and outcome of the situation; (4) the models briefly review the scene; (5) pairs of boys imitate and rehearse the roles and behaviors; (6) a short break is taken while soft drinks are served; (7) the remaining boys act out the scene; and (8) a final summary is made. On the basis of our first year's work the following points emerged: (1) The more specificity about how the group would proceed the better. (2) Great care must be taken to define for the boys why they are doing what they are doing and the relevance of what the models are doing for the boys. (3) It is desirable to maximize the involvement of the boys themselves concerning the application of the modeling situation to their own lives, and especially, to their future after being released. (4) Emphasis should be placed on the expression of affect and feeling. (5) It is necessary to permit the boys considerable freedom to use their own spontaneous styles and creativity when engaging in role playing.

The modeling scenes touch upon a variety of problem areas, including: (1) presenting oneself effectively to a potential employer; (2) dealing effectively with work situations and authority figures; (3) coping with peer pressures to engage in delinquent acts; (4) planning for the future; and (5) resisting temptations.

One of the modeling sessions deals with what we call a Job Interview Scene. These are the major points of emphasis in enactments of this scene: (1) The importance of presenting oneself well. The job-seeker must take initiative instead of waiting around passively for things to happen. Getting a job has a significant "selling yourself" aspect to it. (2) How to deal in job situations with the fact that one has a record. Again, the emphasis is on taking the initiative rather than displaying passivity and/or dishonesty. (3) It is understandable to feel anxious when being interviewed because getting a job is important. (4) Persistence is a trait employers like. In the case of the Job Interview Scene persistence is an important reason why the young man gets the job. In all of our scenes positive outcomes are related to skill in interpersonal relations rather than to luck.

Typical of the modeling meetings is the one concerned with how an adolescent approaches school problems. In the two scenes described below the models enact two scenes, one illustrating the ineffective behavior of a teenager with an academic problem, the other demonstrating a more effective approach. The four subjects observe these scenes, are stimulated by questions about them and then, following the leads provided by the models, take turns in pairs in role-playing adaptive behavior.

TACKLING SCHOOL PROBLEMS SCENE

Scene I

Introduction: Almost everyone has run into some difficulties with at least a few courses in school. Either the teacher doesn't seem to explain things clearly enough or the course just seems to be too hard or the subject isn't interesting and seems unimportant to our later lives or some other problem comes up and interferes with our getting much out of the course. While everyone has experienced these difficulties at one time or another, some people seem to be able to solve school problems better than others. Others just let these problems ride and continue to add up, until they are really behind in the course and have a bad attitude toward the course and toward school in general. It is hard for a person to remain interested in school and want to continue going to school when he is getting farther and farther behind and not trying to solve the various school problems as they arise.

One of the best ways of solving school problems is to tackle them as soon as they appear. This should be done by talking over course problems with the teacher. To ensure that a talk with the teacher is helpful, the following rules are worthwhile to keep in mind.

(1) Don't put off these discussions. Go in as soon as the problem arises. Don't wait until the end of the semester and then walk in just before grades are due and tell the teacher you don't understand anything from the first week on.

(2) Have a specific problem in mind. A teacher can only help you when you are able to talk clearly about the things that are giving you trouble.

(3) Don't just dump the whole problem in the teacher's lap and expect it to be solved. Follow through on the suggestions he makes to ensure that you really understand better what to do.

In the scene today you'll see the right way and the wrong way to talk out a school problem with a teacher. In both scenes a boy is having trouble with math and has come in to see his teacher about it. In the first scene Mr. _____ and I will just act out the wrong way. It is too bad, but probably many discussions with teachers turn out to be just as unsuccessful as this one.

Teacher:	"Come in, Bob. Did you want to see me?"
Bob:	"Yeah. I'm having an awful lot of trouble with your course and I thought I'd better come in and see you since we're going to have an exam in a couple of days."
Teacher:	"Well, I'll be glad to try and help. What's giving you trouble?
Bob:	(Laughing and shrugging his shoulders) "Well . . . math."
Teacher:	(Smiling) "Well, maybe you can pin it down better than that."
Bob:	"I don't know. I guess I haven't understood much from the second chapter on."
Teacher:	"Well, now Bob, we finished that chapter over 4 weeks ago. If you didn't understand something in Chapter 2, you should have come in then, when you started to have difficulties."

Bob: "Yeah, I guess so, but I thought maybe I'd catch on after a while. But now, I don't know. It seems to be getting worse all the time."

Teacher: "I don't know if I can be much help now. The material in Chapter 9 and in Chapter 10 that I assigned today is pretty much impossible to understand if you didn't get the concepts in the previous chapters. Are you reading the book as we go along in class? Are you up to where the rest of the class is?"

Bob: "Well, no, not really. I just sort of gave up after Chapter 4."

Teacher: "Are you having trouble understanding the book? Does it make sense to you when you read it?"

Bob: "No, I think it's pretty hairy . . . hard to understand. And I haven't understood much of what you've said in class lately, either."

Teacher: "Well, I think what we'd better do is to get you so you understand the basic concepts and then try to catch you up with the class. Now, we don't use this book, but it has the same material. Some people find it a little easier to understand. What you should do is try to read the first four chapters in it and try to understand that material and then come in and see me again and we'll talk over any problems you've had with it. Then maybe you can start again in the regular text and read Chapters 5 through 10. I think they'll make better sense to you then. And remember to work a couple of problems at the end of each section that you read. If anything gives you trouble, bring it along with you when you come in to see me."

Bob: "Boy, that's an awful lot of work. I don't know if I'm gonna have time to do that by Friday."

Teacher: "Yes, it's going to take extra effort on your part to catch up. But it's not too bad. You don't have to work all the problems and the new book will go fairly fast, I think. I'll let you skip the exam Friday. You can take a make-up when you get caught up."

Bob: "Well, I didn't expect when I came in here that I'd have *more* work to do. I kind of had some plans lined up for the next few weekends."

Teacher: "Now, Bob, if you're going to catch up and make a passing grade in my class you'll have to sacrifice something. After all, you've let this problem slip too long. You should have come in right away when you first started having trouble."

TACKLING SCHOOL PROBLEMS SCENE

Scene II

Scene:	The setting of this scene is the same as Scene I.
Teacher:	"Come in, Bob. Did you want to see me?"
Bob:	"Yeah, I'm having trouble with this section that you assigned yesterday and I thought I'd better come in and see you before I got all messed up."
Teacher:	"Well, I'm glad you did. Have you read the section?"
Bob:	"Yeah, I read it last night, but I didn't understand it too well. When I went to work these problems here at the end I couldn't get anywhere with them. Could you work through this example problem here? This is where I really got fouled up."
Teacher:	"Yes, of course. How have you been doing up to now?"
Bob:	"Okay. I thought everything was clear until I ran into this junk."
Teacher:	"I'm glad you came in early before you started to really get behind. This is an important section and the material in it is important for the things we'll be studying for the rest of the course. But this section must be much harder to understand than the rest. The author doesn't explain things as well as usual here. I've had about four people come in and ask me for help with this assignment."
Bob:	"Really? I thought I was the only one having trouble."
Teacher:	"Oh, no. As a matter of fact, it's a good thing that you are all coming in and asking me about it. I had planned to give a quiz on this section tomorrow to see if you are all keeping up with the work. But if some of you are having trouble understanding this section, there's no use testing you on it."
Bob:	"Geez, I couldn't pass a test on this stuff."
Teacher:	"Well, I planned instead to just spend tomorrow going over the section step by step, since it's giving so many people trouble."
Bob:	"Yeah, that'd probably be better."
Teacher:	"Also, if you want, you could read these three pages in this other book by Walters. He has a better explanation of what's going on than our textbook."
Bob:	"Yeah, okay. I can do that in study hall and get the book back to you right away."

Teacher: "That's fine. Now about this sample problem, let me explain it as I work it on the board."

Having built our modeling vehicle, we turned to some equally important questions. How might the effects of modeling opportunities be assessed? By means of what sorts of procedures can we judge how worthwhile modeling is as a behavior enhancing method? Since our research was carried out in an institutional setting, we asked: Does the delinquent boy who participates in modeling sessions behave differently on his cottage than does the boy not so involved? What sorts of control and comparison groups would be needed? In several studies we used as comparisons or controls groups of boys who engaged in role playing but who did not have the opportunity to observe models.

Cottage staff supplied two kinds of pre- and post-ratings. One was on a Behavior Rating Scale which all the staff filled out on each boy. The scale consisted of 25 items describing different types of behavior, for example, table manners, lying, self-control. Each item was checked on a 9-point scale, from high to low. The second rating, the Weekly Behavior Summary, included seven categories of behavior; for example, peer relationships, staff relationships, and work detail performance. Ratings were made for each boy after his initial 10 days on the cottage and again just prior to his discharge. Table 1 shows the post-minus pre-results for one of our studies in which experimental and control groups were compared. The scores summarized in it suggest that the experimental condition had a positive effect.

TABLE 1. BEHAVIOR RATING CHANGES, POST-MINUS PRE-RATING SCORES
(A PLUS (+) CHANGE MEANS IMPROVEMENT)

Group	N	Change Score
Experimental	16	+3.47
Control	16	− .59

In addition to using the staff's descriptions of the boys' behavior, we also assessed the boys themselves on a number of psychological dimensions. One of these was anxiety level. On the basis of previous research (Sarason, 1960; Sarason, 1968; Sarason, Pederson, & Nyman, 1968) we thought that anxious boys might be more responsive to a modeling approach than would boys whose levels of tension were relatively low. It seemed reasonable that an individual who is personally dissatisfied with his behavior and who is capable of expressing fear is more likely to desire personal change than one who is complacent and unconcerned. Much psychological research has made it amply clear that anxiety is a state that people desire to terminate and that in severe doses over long periods of time it may even become intolerable. One of the measures gathered on each boy was his level of test anxiety and how he reacts to situations in which he feels that he is being evaluated. Our findings indicate that boys who are characterized by high degrees of anxiety and neuroticism respond most favorably to observational opportunities. Table 2 provides data from one of our experiments that support this conclusion. The experimental group had the modeling experience; the control group did not. Table 2 is based on behavior ratings of the boys made by institutional personnel having day-to-day contact with them. Modeling opportunities may not significantly affect the behavior of certain types of low-anxious delinquents; for example, sociopaths. But those delinquents who feel anxiety about their maladaptive behavior do seem to be benefited significantly.

TABLE 2. NUMBERS OF HIGH AND LOW TEST-ANXIOUS SUBJECTS SHOWING EITHER CHANGE OR NO (OR NEGATIVE) CHANGE IN BEHAVIOR RATINGS

	Experimental Group		Control Group	
	Positive Change	No or Negative Change	Positive Change	No or Negative Change
High Test Anxiety	11	2	4	7
Low Test Anxiety	5	5	6	6

From Sarason, I. G., Verbal learning, modeling, and juvenile delinquency. *American Psychologist*, 1968, **23**, 254–266.

An experiment subsequent to the ones whose results are summarized in Tables 1 and 2 is the one that has been our most comprehensive effort at evaluating the contribution that modeling can make to the rehabilitation of delinquent boys. The experiment proper took over one year to complete. It involved better-defined conditions, larger N's and more reliable dependent measures than we had employed in our earlier studies. Some of its procedures were different from those of the earlier studies. Since counseling and psychotherapy are techniques frequently employed with delinquents, we decided to use, for comparison purposes, a procedure similar to "talking therapy." The procedure we developed consists of guided discussion group meetings. Subjects participating in guided group discussions have the same number of sessions as do modeling groups. In addition, the content of each session is similar. For example, while a modeling group acts out a job interview scene, a guided discussion group considers the problems posed by and possible solutions to the problems of handling job interviews. In guided discussion groups boys are encouraged to talk about common situations and problems, including those they will face after returning to society, controlling anger, and avoiding being pressured by friends into doing destructive things. These groups are told: "Sometimes we will talk about the situations you fellows have to cope with, as persons who have been in an institution. We use four rules in these groups: (1) one person talks at a time; (2) everyone contributes to the discussion; (3) what goes on here won't be taken outside the group—it will be confidential and not used by staff; and (4) no ranking—constructive criticism and comments are good, but ranking doesn't help anyone."

The following are the instructions for the guided discussion group analog to the modeling job interview scene:

"Having a job can be very important. It is a way to get money for things we need, but it is also a way to earn something for ourselves through our own efforts and it makes us feel more independent. Getting a job isn't easy. Today we want to talk about some of the things involved in getting jobs. Also, since you fellows have been in trouble with the law, you may have some extra problems getting jobs that other young fellows wouldn't have. We can talk about that, too. Let's start today by finding out what sorts of jobs you fellows have had (ask each person in the group to describe the kinds of jobs he has had in the past).

"A very important part of getting a job is, of course, the job interview. There are lots of ways to handle a job interview, so let's talk about that for a while."

One of the leaders then asks the boys what sorts of interviews they have had, what sorts of questions were asked of them during the interviews, and how they handled them. He asks others to comment on each boy's discussion. He raises questions about what kinds of things are important in an interview: How one should dress, what does it mean when an interviewer says, "We'll keep your application and call you." Should you apply for more than one job at a time? We devoted considerable time during the second year to creating the guided group discussion because we regard it, not just as a comparison group, but also as a potentially useful behavior modification approach in itself.

Besides employing the guided group discussions, the other new element in our major experiment was the introduction of closed-circuit television as a means of increasing the number of exposures subjects have to observational learning. Since our earlier work suggested that the modeling sessions contribute a desirable step forward for the boys, perhaps more observational trials were needed in order to strengthen their prosocial repertories. Therefore, we increased the number of modeling sessions, televised them, and played back excerpts from them to the boys. This gave the boys an opportunity, not only to observe others (models and peers) but also to observe themselves. Since the use of television is part of the experimental design, it was used with half of the modeling and half of the guided discussion groups. This permits assessment of its effectiveness across situations. Also included in the study was an untreated control group.

Although our major experiment has been completed, data are still being gathered. We are doing follow-ups on boys in the modeling, guided discussion, and control (no treatment) groups. When we finish this phase of the research we shall have a fairly clear idea of how the experiment affected the subjects' behavior as long as 1½ years after they left Cascadia. We already have available results concerning the relationship between the experimental procedures and the boys' behavior at Cascadia. Let us turn to them next.

Briefly, the findings are that of the five groups in the experiment (four combinations of modeling and discussion and TV–no-TV, plus a control group) the modeling no-TV shows the most improvement in (1) behavior as rated by Cascadia staff, and (2) pre-post assessment comparisons (for example, anxiety, self-concept, goals for the future). Using twelve dependent measures gathered at Cascadia (various behavior ratings and assessment measures) the modeling–no-TV group showed the greatest number of positive or favorable changes. On one cottage there was positive change on all twelve measures for the modeling–no-TV group. This demonstration of the efficacy of modeling is consistent with our earlier studies and our theoretical framework.

Unexpectedly, the modeling and group discussion formats, on the one hand, and the TV–no-TV variable, on the other, were found to interact. Televised feedback appeared to have opposite effects on the subjects receiving these treatments. Televised feedback was facilitative for the guided discussion but not the modeling groups. (This interaction is statistically independent of the main effects comparison for treatments.) Overviewing all of our measures it would appear that the most effective treatment is that involving observational learning without TV feedback, while the guided group discussion treatment with TV feedback is runner-up.

Major impetus for introducing the television variable into the research design was the desire to increase the impact of observational opportunities in the modeling condition. A review of our procedures together with reactions gleaned from subjects' spontaneous comments suggests one factor that may have caused the findings that we obtained. The televised feedback for the modeling experience (which is a highly novel one compared with the group discussions) accentuated for the subjects the disparity between their role playing ability and the more effective role playing of the models (both subjects and models were seen on the TV tapes). On the other hand, for guided group discussions, group leaders were on-camera fewer times and when they did appear on TV it was almost always as a benign, supportive, questioner rather than as someone with whom the subject might compare himself on a dimension analogous to that of adequacy of role playing. In the modeling situation the models provided the subjects with an easily recognized standard of excellence. This was not nearly so much the case in the discussion groups. The modeling subjects in the no-TV condition, of course, were exposed to standards of excellence but the general superiority of this condition obviously indicates that observing "live" standards is not *per se* detrimental. Clearly, further inquiry is required concerning the cognitive impacts of observation of "live" and televised behavior of self and others.

As is true in every scientific investigation, we have both answered and raised questions. The experiment just described confirmed earlier indications that observational learning might be a fruitful therapeutic approach to juvenile delinquency. The follow-up study still under way will shed light on the long-term rehabilitative benefits of this approach. Is modeling as valuable in the development of our subjects after their institutionalization as during it? The following is an excerpt from an interview with a boy who received the modeling–no-TV treatment. The interview took place 1½ years after the boy left Cascadia and suggests that he not only remembered the modeling experience, but used it as well when he returned to his community. This part of the interview began by the interviewer asking the boy, Harold, what he remembered of the Cascadia skits:

"Well, I remember the ones that we did, about half of them helped me and they helped me in how to get along in different situations, well, to think before I react and, like do a skit where you ah, meet a policeman, you know, just pretent like and ah, how to, you know, talk to him, and different things like that. The ones that, you know, didn't apply to me, really didn't help me that much but the majority of them helped me."

(*Interviewer:* "Which of the scenes do you remember, you mentioned the one about the policeman?")

"Well, like there were different ones, the one with the policeman, and I liked doing the ones like someone tries to talk you into stealing a car or something like that because you, you know, you figure out ways, ah, ways to avoid that type of person and then you ah, then you take his place and see how bad it really was to try and talk him into doing something like that."

(*Interviewer:* "What do you remember about the cop scene?")

"Well, well, that was ah, you know, like curfew, where you'd ah, be walking home from your girlfriend's house, and then, they, if you made, well, like some guys make a joke out of it, you know, and ah, but with me, I didn't make a joke out of it, I just ah, went, went on through it and ah, if you walk home and a policeman would stop you and ah, you'd say you just got back from your girlfriend's and the policeman would want to call your girlfriend's house and you didn't want him to because that would look kind of bad for you."

(*Interviewer:* "What kind of an idea was that trying to get across?")

"Well, you now, just to be honest, you know just, you know, tell him where you're going and everything instead of trying to, you know, detour around it."

(*Interviewer:* "Have you ever been put in this type of position since you got out on parole?")

"Yes, I have, like, you know, we had this trouble up here on Broad Street and then, ah, one night I got stopped by ah, six different police cars all in the same night because they put it on a different curfew and in the paper it said all teenagers were going to be stopped by the cops. I just, you know, told them I was heading home, you know, just didn't make them feel particularly that they were bothering me or anything or take me into jail with a bunch of questions or anything like that."

(*Interviewer:* "That was the other one you mentioned, something to do with the cops?")

"Well, that didn't really, well, I suppose it did help me because ah, I knew some kids that were, you know, stealing cars and they wanted me to go in on it, that's why one of them is in jail now for stealing cars, he just got arrested for it."

(*Interviewer:* "This is something that just happened?")

"They tried to get me to, you know, steal a car with them but I didn't want to. And then there was ah, just, you know, drinking beer and things like that and I just got out of the habit of doing really. Except that I might have one beer with a pizza or something but that's all."

Unforeseen when we planned our research was the interaction between the modeling and group discussion approaches, on the one hand, and the TV–no-TV condition, on the other. Whereas our ongoing follow-up study will answer the question of the long-term effects of our experimental treatments, new research efforts will be required to clarify the variables implicated in this video effect.

REFERENCES

Sarason, I. G. Empirical findings and theoretical problems in the use of anxiety scales. *Psychological Bulletin*, 1960, **57**, 403–415.

Sarason, I. G. Verbal learning, modeling, and juvenile delinquency. *American Psychologist*, 1968, **23**, 254–266.

Sarason, I. G., Pederson, A. M., and Nyman, B. Test anxiety and the observation of models. *Journal of Personality*, 1968, **36**, 493–511.

3.10 *Orientation*

Our brief sampling of research on adolescents concludes with a study of behavior modification based upon the concept of reinforcement. The reader will recall the introduction of this concept in Part I by Herbert Lefcourt. The present study is concerned with the powerful influence of positive reinforcement. Technically, positive reinforcement may be defined as any stimulus following a response that has the effect of maintaining or increasing the strength or rate of that response. Hence, psychologists armed with the concept of positive reinforcement focus upon the management of consequences which follow responding. In applied settings, such as the classroom, this approach requires that a situation for behaving be structured so as to maximize the probability that a desirable response (or approximation thereof) occurs so that it can immediately be reinforced. In this way, learning or behavior change takes place.

From an empirical point of view the consequences of behavior are defined as reinforcing only if they affect the frequency or strength of that behavior. The problem tackled by the researchers whose report appears below involved the management of positive reinforcements as a consequence of reading behavior. Their purpose was very specific: To increase significantly the frequency of correct reading responses performed by a disadvantaged adolescent with severe academic deficits. The accomplishment of this goal required the development of a reinforcement system that would "motivate" and provide meaningful feedback to this non-reader, thus facilitating the learning process.

Both the design and methodology set the Staats and Butterfield study apart from those that have previously appeared in this section. For example, only one subject is involved in the present research, whereas preceding studies have all employed groups of subjects from which generalizations were derived. The study of individual response rate and conditions which affect such rate is firmly associated with the descriptive behaviorism of B. F. Skinner and his followers. In applied form this approach at least includes the (1) assessment of response frequency prior to treatment, (2) systematic arrangement of reinforcement contingencies, and (3) continuous response measurement during treatment. The latter permits the observation of cumulative response frequency that may occur. This measurement strategy stands in contrast to summative approaches which are designed to examine terminal behavior only at the end of an experiment.

Still further points of interest in the Staats and Butterfield research may be identified. For one, the study represents an apparently successful attempt to apply laboratory-derived procedures to practical problems. It also suggests a complex interrelationship between school failure and deviant behavior; in this case desirable allied changes in school behavior seem to be associated with increased success in reading. A third point of interest is the remarkable acceleration in reading achievement accomplished by the subject over a comparatively short period. This acceleration attests to the potency of carefully arranged teaching conditions, including well-programmed materials and contingent reinforcement. Recent breakthroughs in the study of contingent reinforcement such as this represent an invaluable contribution to the psychologist's understanding of behavioral change. Such studies have also contributed greatly to the development of more effective techniques for behavior modification.

RECOMMENDED READINGS

Baer, Donald, Wolf, Montrose, and Risley, Todd. Some current dimensions of applied behavior analysis. *Journal of Applied Behavior Analysis*, 1968, 1, 91–97.

Bijou, Sidney W. An empirical concept of reinforcement and a functional analysis of child behavior. *Journal of Genetic Psychology*, 1964, 104, 215–223.

Haring, Norris G., and Hauck, Mary Ann. Improved learning conditions in the establishment of reading skills with disabled readers. *Exceptional Children*, 1969, **35**, 341–352.

Premack, David. Toward empirical behavior laws: I. Positive reinforcement. *Psychological Review*, 1959, **66**, 219–233.

Skinner, B. F. Contingencies of reinforcement in the design of a culture. *Behavioral Science*, 1966, **11**, 159–166.

Whelan, Richard, and Haring, Norris. Modification and maintenance of behavior through systematic application of consequences. *Exceptional Children*, 1966, **32**, 281–285.

3.10 Treatment of Nonreading in a Culturally Deprived Juvenile Delinquent: An Application of Reinforcement Principles

Arthur W. Staats, UNIVERSITY OF HAWAII
*William H. Butterfield,** UNIVERSITY OF MICHIGAN

Staats (1964c; Staats & Staats, 1963) has previously discussed behavior problems and their treatment in terms of learning principles. In doing so it was indicated that problem behaviors can arise in part (1) because behavior that is necessary for adjustment in our society is absent from the individual's repertoire, (2) because behaviors considered undesirable by the society are present in the individual's repertoire, or (3) because the individual's motivational (reinforcement) system was inappropriate in some respect.

Although a complete account is not relevant here, several points pertinent to the above conceptions will be made in introducing the present study. The notion that many behavior problems consist of deficits in behavior is important in the study of child development. Behaviorally speaking, a child is considered to be a problem when he does not acquire behaviors as other children do. It is conceivable that a deficit in behavior could arise because the child simply cannot acquire the behavior involved, even though the conditions of learning have been entirely adequate.

Reprinted from *Child Development*, 1965, **36**, 925–942, by permission of the author and the Society for Research in Child Development.

* Currently a pre-doctoral fellow at the University of Michigan in the area of social work and psychology.

It would be expected, however, that behavioral deficits would also arise in cases where the conditions of learning have been defective. Learning conditions can be defective in different ways. For example, the child may never have received training in the behavior he must later exhibit. Or the training may be poor, even though the "trainers," parents or teachers, and so on, have the best intentions.

In addition, however, a child may be exposed to learning conditions that are appropriate for most children but, due to the particular child's past history of learning, are not appropriate for him. It is especially in these cases that people are most likely to conclude erroneously that since other children learn in the same circumstances, the child's deficit must be because of some personal defect. For example, in cases where the training is long term, adequate reinforcement must be available to maintain the attentional and work behaviors necessary for learning. As Staats has indicated (1964c; Staats & Staats, 1963; Staats, Staats, Schutz, & Wolf, 1962), the reinforcers present in the traditional schoolroom are inadequate for many children. Their attentional behaviors are not maintained, and they do not learn. Thus, a deficit in an individual's behavioral repertoire may arise although he has been presented with the "same" training circumstances from which other children profit. Learning does not take place because the child's previous experience has not provided, in this example, the necessary reinforcer (motivational) system to maintain good "learning" behaviors. It would seem that in such a circumstance the assumption that the child has a personal defect would be unwarranted and ineffective.

However, after a few years of school attendance where the conditions of learning are not appropriate for the child, he will not have acquired the behavioral repertoires acquired by more fortunate members of the class—whose previous experiences have established an adequate motivational system. Then, lack of skilled behavior is likely to be treated aversively. That is, in the present case, the child with a reading deficit (or other evidence of underachievement) is likely to be gibed at and teased when he is still young and ignored, avoided, and looked down upon when he is older. Although the individuals doing this may not intend to be aversive, such actions constitute the presentation of aversive stimuli. Furthermore, this presentation of aversive stimuli by other "successful" children, and perhaps by a teacher, would be expected to result in further learning, but learning of an undesirable nature. These successful children, teachers, academic materials, and the total school situation can in this way become learned negative reinforcers, which may be translated (see Staats, 1964b) to say the child acquires negative attitudes toward school.

At this point, the child is likely to begin to "escape" the school situation in various ways (daydreaming, poor attendance, and so on) and to behave aversively in turn to the school and its inhabitants (vandalism, fighting, baiting teachers and students, and the like). Thus, a deficit in behavior, resulting from an inappropriate motivational system, can lead to the further development of inappropriate reinforcers and inappropriate behaviors.

The foregoing is by no means intended as a complete analysis of delinquency, dropouts, and the like. However, it does indicate some of the problems of learning that may occur in school. In addition, it does suggest that an analysis in terms of laboratory-established learning principles, when applied to problems such as in classroom learning of the above type, can yield new research and applied hypotheses. It was with this general strategy that the study of reading acquisition employing learning principles and reinforcement procedures were commenced (Staats, 1964a; Staats *et al.*, 1962; Staats, Finley, Minke, & Wolf, 1964a; Staats, Minke, Finley, Wolf, & Brooks, 1964b). The present study is a replication and an extension of these various findings to the development of a program for training nonreaders to read. The program, which adapts standard reading materials, is based upon the principle of the reinforcer system employed in the previous studies with the younger children, thus testing the principles of reinforcement in the context of remedial reading training, as well as the feasibility of using the type of reinforcement system with a new type of S. As such, the study has implication for the study of nonreading children of pre-adolescent, adolescent, and young adult ages. In the present case, S was also a culturally deprived delinquent child—and the study thus involves additional information and implications for the special problems associated with education in this population of children.

METHODS

Subject

The S was a 14-year-and-3-month-old boy of Mexican-American ancestry. He was the fifth child in a family of 11 children and the mother and father. The parental techniques for controlling their children's behavior consisted of physical and verbal abuse. Both parents described their own childhood conditions as primitive. The father was taken out of school after completing the fifth grade to help with his father's work. Each of S's four older brothers had been referred to the juvenile court for misbehavior. The parents appeared to be at loss as to how to provide effective control for family members.

The S had a history of various miscreant behaviors, having been referred to the juvenile department nine times for such things as running away, burglary, incorrigibility, and truancy. During the course of the study S was again referred on a complaint (with three other boys) of malicious mischief for shooting light bulbs and windows in a school building with a BB gun. He associated with a group of boys who had been in marked difficulty with the law. The S smoked, and on occasion he drank excessively.

The study commenced when S was residing with his family. However, after the complaint on malicious mischief S was sent to a juvenile detention home. During his stay there he was allowed to attend school in the daytime. The study was finally concluded when S was committed to an industrial school for juvenile-delinquent boys. This occurred because S baited the attendants at the detention home and caused disturbances which, although not serious, were very unpleasant and disruptive.

On the Wechsler Bellevue Form I, given when S was 13-10, he received Verbal and Performance IQ's of 77 and 106, respectively, for a Full Scale IQ of 90. The examiner concluded that S was probably within the normal range for this test. On the basis of this test and HTP Projective Drawings, S was characterized as having a poor attention span and poorly integrated thought processes and as lacking intellectual ambitiousness. He was also described as seeking satisfaction in fantasy and as having good conventional judgment.

The S had continually received failing grades in all subjects in school. He was described as having "been incorrigible since he came here in the second grade. He has no respect for teachers, steals and lies habitually and uses extremely foul language." The S had been promoted throughout his school career simply to move him on or to "get rid of him." He was disliked by the teachers and administrators in grade school because of his troublesome behavior and was described by the principal as mentally retarded even though one of the tests taken there indicated a score within the normal range. Another test taken there gave him an IQ of 75. During the study S was attending a local high school and taking classes for low-level students.

Reinforcer System

In previous studies (Staats, 1966, Staats et al., 1964a; 1964b), a reinforcer system was demonstrated that was capable of maintaining attention and work behaviors for long-term experimental studies. This system worked well with preschool children of ages 2 to 6 and with educable and trainable retardates of ages 8 to 11. The principle of the system was based upon token reinforcers. The tokens were presented contingent upon correct responses and could be exchanged for items the child could keep. In the previous studies toys of various values could be obtained when a sufficient number of tokens had been accrued in visible containers.

This system was adapted for use with the adolescents S of the present study. In the adaptation there were three types of token, distinguished by color. The tokens were of different value in terms of the items for which the tokens could be exchanged. A blue token was valued at $\frac{1}{10}$ of one cent. A white token was valued at $\frac{1}{5}$ of a cent. A red token was worth $\frac{1}{2}$ of a cent.

The child's acquisition of tokens was plotted so that visual evidence of the reinforcers was available. The tokens could be used to purchase a variety of items. These items, chosen by the subject, could range in value from pennies to whatever the subject wished to work for. Records were kept of the tokens earned by S and of the manner in which the tokens were used.

Reading Materials

The reading material used was taken from the Science Research Associates (SRA) reading-kit materials. The SRA kits consist of stories developed for and grouped into grade levels. Each story includes a series of questions which can be used to assess the reader's comprehension of the story. The reading training program was adapted from the SRA materials as follows:

Vocabulary words   A running list was made of the new words that appeared in the series of stories. The list finally included each different word that appeared in the stories that were presented. From this list, the new vocabulary for each story was selected, and each word was typed on a separate 3 × 5 card.

Oral reading materials   Each paragraph in the SRA stories was typed on a 5 × 8 card. Each story could thus be presented to S paragraph by paragraph.

Silent-reading and comprehensive-question materials   Each SRA story, with its comprehensive questions, was typed on an 8½ × 13 sheet of white paper.

Procedure

Vocabulary presentation   The procedure for each story in the series commenced with the presentation of the new words introduced in that story. The words were presented individually on the cards, and S was asked to pronounce them. A correct response to a word-stimulus card was reinforced with a midvalue token. After a correct response to a word, the card was dropped from the group of cards yet to be presented. The S was instructed to indicate words that he did not know the meaning of, and this information was provided in such cases.

When an incorrect response to a word stimulus occurred, or when S gave no response, E gave the correct response. The S then repeated the word while looking at the stimulus word. However, the word card involved was returned to the group of cards still to be presented. A card was not dropped from the group until it was read correctly without prompting. After an error on a word stimulus, only a low-value token was given on the next trial when the word was read correctly without prompting. The vocabulary-presentation phase of the training was continued until each word was read correctly without prompting.

Oral reading   Upon completion of the vocabulary materials, each paragraph was individually presented to S in the order in which the paragraph occurred in the story. When correct reading responses were made to each word in the paragraph, a high-value token was given upon completion of the paragraph. When a paragraph contained errors, S was corrected, and he repeated the word correctly while looking at the word. The paragraph was put aside, and when the other paragraphs had been completed, the paragraph containing errors was again presented. The paragraph was repeated until it was done correctly in its entirety—at which time a midvalue token was presented. When all paragraphs in a story had been completed correctly, the next phase of the training was begun.

Silent reading and comprehensive questions   Following the oral reading S was given the sheet containing the story and questions. He was instructed to read the story silently and to answer the questions beneath the story. He was also instructed that it was important to read to understand the story so that he could answer the questions.

Reinforcement was given on a variable interval schedule for attentive behavior during the silent-reading phase. That is, as long as S appropriately scanned the material he was given a low-value reinforcer an average of every 15 seconds. The exact time for reinforcement was determined by a table of random numbers varying from 1 to 30 seconds. Whenever he did anything else than peruse the material, no reinforcement was given. The next interval was then timed from the moment S returned to the silent reading, with the stipulation that no reinforcement be given sooner than 5 seconds after S returned to the reading. If the interval was less than 5 seconds, a token was not given until the next interval had also occurred. Timing was done by a continuously running stopwatch. The S was also given an extra midvalue token at the end of the silently read story on those occasions where he read without moving his lips.

Upon completion of the story, S wrote his answers to the questions typed below the story and gave his answers to E. For each correct answer, S received a high-value token. For an answer with a spelling error, S was reinforced with a midvalue token when he had corrected the answer. For incorrect answers S had to reread the appropriate paragraph, correct his answer, and he then received a midvalue token.

Vocabulary review   Some of the vocabulary words presented to S in the first phase of training were words he already could read. Many others, however, were words that the procedure was set up to teach. The oral-reading-phase performance indicated the level of S's retention of the words he had learned—and also provided further training trials on the words not already learned. A further assessment of S's retention of the words that he did not know in the vocabulary training was made after each 20 stories of the SRA materials had been read. This test of individually presented words, for each story, was started about 3 days after completion of the 20 stories and constituted fairly long-term retention.

This test was also used as a review for S, and further training on the words was given. This was first done by reinforcing S with a low-value token for every word he read correctly. However, S's attention was not well maintained by this reinforcement, and the procedure was changed to provide a midvalue token for correctly read words. When S could not read a word, or missed one, he was prompted and had to correctly repeat the name of the word while looking at the word. This word card was then put aside and presented later, at which time S was reinforced with a low-value token if he read it correctly. If not, the procedure was repeated until a correct unprompted trial occurred.

Achievement tests   Prior to the commencement of the training, S was tested to assess his reading performance, and during the period of experimental training he was given two additional reading-achievement tests. The first one given was the Developmental Reading Test. (At this time the S's vision and hearing were also tested and found to be normal.) After 45 training sessions another reading test was given S, this time the California Reading Test, Form BB, for grades 1, 2, 3, and L-4. Twenty-five sessions later, just before the termination of the study, S was given the California Reading Test, Form BB, for grades 4, 5, and 6. The S's performance on the three reading tests constituted one of the measures of his progress. The tests were given at the Arizona State University Reading Center.

Training sessions   The training sessions would ordinarily last for 1 hour or less, although a few sessions were as short as 30 minutes or as long as 2 hours. Not all of this time was spent in reading, however. A good deal of time was spent in arranging the materials, recording *S*'s performances, keeping count of the reinforcers, plotting the reinforcers accrued, and so on. The time spent actually reading was tabulated. During the 4½-month experimental period, 70 training sessions were conducted, with an average of about 35 minutes spent per session for a total of 40 hours of reading training.

RESULTS AND CONCLUSIONS

During the period of training *S* made many reading responses. Figure 1 shows the number of single-word reading responses *S* made as a function of the hours of time spent in training. An estimate of the number of single-word reading responses was obtained from tabulating each presentation of a word card, the number of words in the stories, and the reading-comprehension questions at the end of each story, as well as the words presented to *S* in the later single-word retention test. Actually, the number of words in the stories was an estimate obtained from the mean number of words in two out of each five stories. Thus, rather than giving the true absolute number of reading responses made, the figure gives an estimate. However, the most important aspect of the figure is to indicate

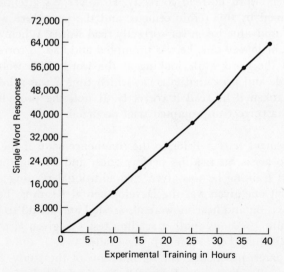

FIGURE 1. Number of Single-Word Reading Responses as a Function of the Time in Experimental Reading Training

the rate of this single-word reading-response measure as a function of time in experimental training. As can be seen, as the training progressed S covered the reading material at a slightly more rapid rate, as is shown by the slight positive acceleration in the curve. The importance of this result is to indicate that the child's behavior of attending to the task and making the appropriate reading responses did not diminish throughout the period of training. Thus, the reinforcement system employed was capable of maintaining the behavior for a long period of time. During this time the attentional and cooperative behaviors instigated resulted in many, many, learning trials—a *sine qua non* for the acquisition of achievement in any skill.

Before reading each story S was presented with individual cards for all the words included in that story which had not been presented in a previous story. When these words were presented, S would read a certain proportion correctly on first presentation, the other words being missed on the first presentation. The ones missed were considered to be new words for S, words that he had not previously learned. These words were separately tabulated. The cumulative number of these new words as a function of every 5 SRA stories read is shown by the top curve of Figure 2. (The data for the first 10 stories are not presented since they were not available for all three curves.) As this curve indicates, 761 new words were presented to S during the training.

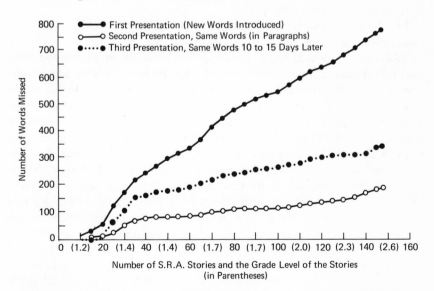

FIGURE 2. Number of Words Missed on First, Second, and Third Presentations for the 150 SRA Stories

Thus, S missed 761 words when they were first presented to him. However, he was given training trials on these words, and then he read them again in the oral reading of the paragraph. The number of these words that he missed in this oral-reading phase is plotted in the bottom curve of Figure 2, above. This curve indicates the number of errors made on the second reading test of the words that had been previously learned. Thus, only 176 words out of the 761 (about 23 percent) were missed in the oral-reading phase—showing retention for 585 words. The results indicate that the criterion of one correct unprompted reading trial in the original vocabulary-learning phase produced considerable learning when the words were read in context.

The middle curve in Figure 2 involves a measure of long-term retention of the words that had been learned. This measure was obtained by testing S on the words, presented singly, that had been learned in the preceding 20 stories. This test was given 10 to 15 days after the training occurred. The training thus included the previous single-word presentations of the words, as well as those same words read orally and silently. In addition, however, S had also learned a considerable number of other words by the time of this test. As the middle curve shows, when tested 10–15 days later, S read 430 of the 761 words correctly, or, conversely, 331 words (about 43 percent) were missed. Thus, the procedures produced retention when the words were later presented out of context after a considerable intervening period.

The results appearing in Figure 2 indicate that the child covered a considerable amount of reading material, that he learned to read a number of new words when presented individually or in context, and that he retained a good proportion of what he had learned. The results also indicate that the child improved during the training in his retention. That is, his rate of getting new words in the first-presentation phase continues at a high rate throughout the study. (This supports the results shown in Figure 1 indicating that the child's behavior did not weaken during the training.) However, his "rate" of missing the new words on the second and third presentations decreased, that is, he retained more of the words he had learned. Thus, tabulation indicated that for the first 35 stories only about 33 percent of the words learned were retained 10–15 days later, whereas S's subsequent retention increased to about 55 percent. It should be noted that this improvement occurred even though the difficulty of the words (as shown in Figure 2 by the numbers in parentheses) became progressively greater during the training, moving from the 1.2-grade level of difficulty to the 2.6-grade level.

These results receive support from the data presented in Figure 3. As already indicated, on the first presentation of the vocabulary of a story, some words were missed out of the total presented—and S was then presented with training on these words. Figure 3 shows the number of the words presented and missed in ratio to the total number presented, as this ratio is related to the number and difficulty of the stories presented. A smaller ratio indicates that S missed fewer of the total vocabulary words when they were presented for the first time. As can be seen in Figure 3, as the child read more stories in his training (even though they become more difficult), he missed fewer and fewer words that were presented to him. It should be stressed that he was thus improving in the extent to which he correctly responded to new words on *first* presentation. This improvement appeared to be correlated with other observations that indicated the S was also beginning to learn to sound out words as a function of the training. For example, he remarked when in the judge's office that he thought a sign said "information," because he could read the "in" and the "for" and the "mation." In addition, S reported a number of times that the training was helping him in school, that reading was getting easier for him in school, that he liked the reading training better as he went along, and so on. It would be expected (as will be supported by other data) that as the reading training improved his reading in school, the things he learned in school would also improve his performance in the reading training. It is this effect that may also be reflected in his increasing ability to read the new words presented to him.

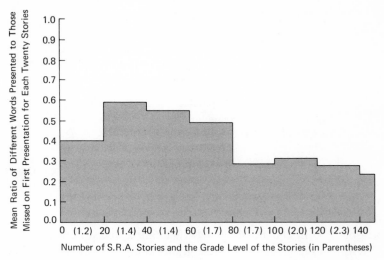

FIGURE 3. Ratio of Words Presented to Those Missed on First Presentation for the 150 SRA Stories

In addition to this direct evidence of the child's progress in reading training, and the foregoing indirect evidence that the reading training was having general effects upon the child's behavior, the study was formulated to obtain other sources of information concerning the child's progress. One means of doing this was to give the child reading-achievement tests before beginning the reading training as well as during the training. The results of these tests are shown in Figure 4. The first point on the curve is a measurement obtained by use of the Developmental Reading Test giving a total score of reading achievement showing that S was performing at the grade-2 level. After 45 reading-training sessions, S's performance on the California Reading Test showed a gain to the 3.8-grade level. By the end of the training, after 25 more training sessions, S had advanced to the 4.3-grade level on the California Reading Test.

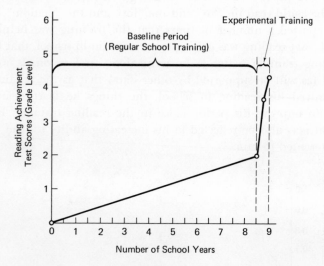

FIGURE 4. **Reading-Achievement Test Scores as a Function of 8½ Years of School Training and 4½ Months of Experimental Training**

Another indication of the general effect of the reading training came from the child's performance in school, both in school achievement and deportment. The period of reading training coincided with a school term. The boy received passing grades in all subjects: A C in physical education, a D in general shop, a D in English, and a D in mathematics. It should be emphasized that these grades represent the first courses that this child had ever passed, and thus his finest academic performance.

Furthermore, *S* began to behave better while in school. The boy had always been a behavior problem in school, and this continued into the period during which *S* received reading training. As Figure 5 shows, during the first month of the training *S* committed 10 misbehaviors that resulted in the receipt of demerits. The behaviors were as follows: disturbance in class (2 times), disobedience in class (5 times), loitering (2 times), and tardiness. In the second month he was given demerits for scuffling on the school grounds and also for creating a disturbance. In the third month he was given demerits for cutting a math class and for profanity in class. As the figure shows, however, no misbehaviors occurred in the fourth month or in the half month after this until the conclusion of the school term.

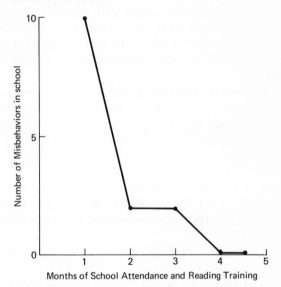

FIGURE 5. Number of Official Misbehaviors in School as a Function of Time in the Experimental Training

The *S* requested that the tokens be exchanged for items that he wanted in sessions 12, 17, 25, 31, 35, 43, 49, 55, and in the last session he was given the value of the remaining tokens in cash. Items included were a pair of "beatle" shoes, hair pomade, a phonograph record, an ice cream sundae, a ticket to a school function, money for his brother who was going to reform school, and so on. Further information regarding the reinforcement system is given in Figure 6. The vertical axis of the graph represents the ratio of the number of tokens obtained by *S* relative to the number of single-word reading responses which he emitted. Lesser ratios thus indicate more reading responses per reinforcer. This ratio was plotted as a function of the progress S made in the training program, as given by the number of SRA stories he had completed. As the training progressed S gradually made an increasingly greater number of reading responses per reinforcer. This effect was not accomplished by changing the rules by which the reinforcers were administered. The effect, which was planned in the training program, resulted from the fact that the SRA stories became longer as the grade level was raised. Since, for example, paragraph reading was reinforced by the paragraph, the longer the paragraph, the greater the number of reading responses that had to be emitted before reinforcement was obtained. At the end of training, thus, S was getting about half as much reinforcement per response as at the beginning of training. It should also be indicated that the stories were more difficult as the training progressed, so the effort involved in reading was increasing—although reinforcement for the reading was decreasing.

During the $4\frac{1}{2}$ months of training, which involved 40 hours of reading training and the emission of an estimated 64,307 single-word reading responses, S received \$20.31.

DISCUSSION

In this section the various aspects of the reading-training procedures will first be discussed. Then the implications of the results and analysis will be outlined both for further studies of remedial reading training as well as for a learning conception of certain aspects of cultural deprivation and delinquency.

The method of reading training used in the present study was derived from previous study (Staats, 1964a; 1966; Staats et al., 1962) with preschool children in which words were first presented singly, then in sentences, and finally in short stories. The present study indicated that SRA materials can be adapted for a similar type of presentation in conjunction with the type of reinforcer system previously developed (Staats et al., 1964a; 1964b). From the SRA materials it was possible to present single-word training trials and oral-reading training and to develop a silent-reading training procedure, all involving reinforcement.

When the training of reading, at least in part, is considered as operant discrimination learning, the learning task consists of having S emit the correct speech response while looking at the verbal stimulus—this process being followed by reinforcement. This basic procedure was elaborated in the present study to include two levels of reinforcement. An unprompted reading response on the first trial was reinforced more heavily than one that had been previously missed. This procedure appeared to produce learning that was retained very well when the child later read the words orally in a paragraph, with considerable retention also occurring when the child was tested on the individual words 10–15 days later.

It may seem incongrous at first to attempt to reinforce silent reading, since this behavior is not observable. However, it should be remembered that the subject actually has two types of behavior in the silent-reading act. He looks at the verbal stimuli—that is, attends—and he makes "reading" verbal responses to the verbal stimuli. While the reading responses cannot be monitored when they are covert, the attending behavior can be. Of course, there is a danger involved in reinforcing the behavior of just looking at something. Perhaps the child will do nothing else. If he is heavily reinforced for sitting and looking at a page, and the actual reading responses are effortful, he may not emit the reading responses. The present procedure was set up to eliminate this possibility by using a double contingency. The child was reinforced for simple attention, but the reinforcement was low in value. The opportunity for a greater amount of reinforcement came during the answering of the questions. Thus, although simple attention was reinforced lightly, attention and reading responses were reinforced much more heavily. In this way it was possible to use reinforcement in a procedure designed to maintain reading for "understanding," in addition to simple "word-naming." (These results could be generalized to other types of learning.) Furthermore, this procedure provided an opportunity to train the subject to read silently. Although he had a tendency to make vocal or lip responses while reading, it was possible to strengthen reading without these other responses through differentially reinforcing the correct silent reading.

Thus, it may be concluded that the reading program increased the child's reading vocabulary as shown by the various measures of retention used in the study, the tests of reading achievement, as well as the child's improved school performance and his verbal description of improved attitude toward and performance in reading in school. There were also suggestions that the child was acquiring a "unit-reading repertoire," that is, the general ability to sound out words through making the correct response to single letters and syllables. Thus, for example, the child made errors on fewer and fewer of the new words presented as the training progressed, even though the words were of greater difficulty. In addition, he retained a greater proportion of the words he learned as he went on. Further research of the present type must be conducted to test the possibilities for using a more phonic system of remedial reading training with the present type of subject.

A final point should be made concerning the training procedures used in the present study. The procedures are very specific and relatively simple. Thus, it was not necessary to have a person highly trained in education to administer the training. In the present case the trainer-experimenter was a probation officer. It might also be suggested that anyone with a high school education and the ability to read could have administered the training. This has implications for the practical application of the present methods, since one of the questions that arises in this context concerns the economy of the procedures. Although the procedures as described involved a one-trainer-to-one-student ratio, as many remedial teaching procedures do, in the present case the simplicity of the procedures suggests the possibility that savings may be effected because the trainer need not be so highly trained. Thus, the procedures could be widely applied or adapted by various professionals, for example, social workers, prison officials, remedial teachers, tutors, and so on. In an even more economical application, helpers of professionals could be used to actually administer the procedures; for example, selected delinquents (or prisoners) could administer the procedures to other delinquents. Thus, the procedures could be utilized in various situations, such as settlement houses, homes for juvenile delinquents, prison training programs, parts of adult education, and so on. All that is needed is a suitable system of reinforcers to back up the tokens.

It is relevant to add here that the type of token reinforcer system employed in the present study was developed by the first author in 1959 in the context of an exploratory study of remedial reading. This token-reinforcer system has since been applied widely by others in a number of behavior modification studies of various behavior problems—producing results which support the preceding conclusions. Furthermore, additional studies have been conducted in the present project to further substantiate the general efficacy of the token-reinforcer system and the reading procedures, with various types of subjects. Thus, the present training procedures have been employed successfully in a study involving 18 additional children (including 7 educable retardates as well as several emotionally disturbed children) of junior high school age. The instructional-technicians were 9 average high school students and 9 adult volunteers (Staats, Minke, Goodwin, & Landeen, 1967).

In a later study conducted with the assistance of Karl A. Minke and Priscilla Butts which is now being prepared for publication, 32 Negro ghetto children with behavior problems were given the treatment. The instructional-technicians were literate Negro high school children from ghetto schools and two formerly unemployed Negro adults who were employed on the project in full-time positions. The treatment was conducted for a semester and the results were again successful. Increases were shown in achievement tests, grades, attendance, and deportment, in comparison to a control group of 32 children. In addition, Staats (see 1968) has conducted a long-term project with young children in the study and treatment of cognitive deficits in such areas as first reading acquisition, number skill learning, and writing acquisition. The present methods and principles receive strong support as being generally applicable from these various studies.

In the same context, it may be worthwhile pointing out that the results indicated that the child advanced as many years in reading achievement, as measured by the tests, during the experimental training as he had in his previous school history. A comparison of the relative costs—in the present case, about 70 hours of time of a person not necessarily trained in teaching and $20.31 for the reinforcers versus 8½ years of trained teachers' time, albeit in a group situation—suggests that the procedure introduced in the present study may not be uneconomical, even without improvements in the method. And, as will be further described, the child's failure in school may in many cases be considered as a contributor to the child's delinquency—which also carries a high cost to society. The present results, in suggesting that the training procedures may also effect general improvements in behavior, including misbehaviors in school, thus have further implications concerning the economy of the procedures.

The present study, among other things, tests the feasibility of using the type of reinforcing system, previously applied successfully to younger children, to the study of learning in older children—in this case a 14-year-old juvenile delinquent. The reinforcer system worked very well with the present S, maintaining his attention and working behaviors in good strength for a long period of time. And there was every reason to expect that the study could have been continued for a much longer period, probably as long as it would have taken to train the child to read normally.

It should be noted that although the amount of reinforcement given decreases during the training, as shown in Figure 6, the reading behavior is maintained in good strength throughout the study, as shown in Figures 1 and 2; thus, less and less reinforcement is needed to maintain the behavior even though the material increases in difficulty. As already described, this occurred because a progressively greater number of reading responses was necessary per reinforcer. This is analogous to gradually raising the ratio of responses to the reinforcers as considered in terms of ratio schedules of reinforcement. Staats has suggested that this type of gradual increase must occur to produce good work behaviors in humans (Staats & Staats, 1963).

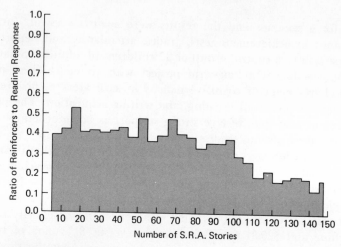

FIGURE 6. Ratio of the Number of Tokens Received Divided by the Number of Reading Responses Made as a Function of the Number of SRA Stories Read

This result in the present study is in part an answer to the question whether the use of extrinsic reinforcers in training will produce a child who is dependent upon these reinforcers. It is not possible to discuss this topic fully now. However, it may be said that the extrinsic reinforcement can be gradually decreased until, as was happening with the present child, reading becomes reinforcing itself, or other sources of reinforcement maintain the behavior.

A word should be said concerning the relevance of reinforcement variables in the treatment of nonlearning in culturally deprived children. Typically, as in the present case, such children do not, as a result of their home experiences, acquire "reinforcer systems" appropriate for maintaining learning in the traditional classroom. Rosen (1956) has shown that, in the present terminology, lower-class children do not have experiences that make school achievement and learning itself positively reinforcing. This deficit, among others that affect the reinforcer system, can be expected to lead to poor school learning and other behavioral deficits. In such cases, there are increased opportunities for other poor social attitudes and undesirable behaviors to develop, as suggested in the introduction and exemplified in the present case.

The present study suggests that these conditions can be reversed through the application of learning principles and reinforcement variables to the task of repairing the child's behavioral-achievement deficit. There were indications that this treatment resulted in improvement in the reinforcement value of (attitudes toward) school for this child and consequently in the decrease in incidence of misbehaviors in school. The results thus suggest that under appropriate conditions the deficit in behavior stemming from the child's inadequate reinforcing system may be, at least in part, repaired by a properly administered, effective reinforcement system, resulting in a decrease in undesirable behaviors.

A comment should be made about the possibility of a Hawthorne effect, that is, that the social reinforcement by the E and possible extra-experimental reinforcement contributed to the results in the present study. It would be expected that such reinforcers could contribute to the overall effect—and in the present case the expenditure for the material reinforcers was small. In general, it can be expected that individuals will vary in the extent to which social reinforcers will be effective. For example, in pre-school children social reinforcement is ineffective for long-term training (Staats, 1964c; Staats et al., 1962), and the same would be expected for many individuals with behavior problems. Ordinarily, it might be expected that the weaker other sources of reinforcement are for the individual, the stronger must be the reinforcer system of the treatment procedure.

In conclusion, the present study helps support and replicate the previous findings and extends the general procedures and principles to the study of an adolescent child who is culturally deprived and is also a juvenile delinquent. The various sources of data used suggest that the present procedures and principles are applicable to this population also. Based upon these suggestions, further studies will be conducted on culturally deprived children, delinquent and nondelinquent, as well as studies of other types of nonachieving or underachieving readers.

It should also be indicated that the present study indicates the possibility for developing procedures for the objective application and test of laboratory-derived learning principles within the context of an actual problem of behavior. As previously indicated (Staats, 1964a), verification of learning principles in the context of a problem of human behavior constitutes one way to further the generality of the principles themselves. It may thus be suggested that such studies have two types of implication: they have implications for people interested in dealing with the problems of human behavior, as well as for those interested in the extension and verification of the basic science.

SUMMARY

A 14-year-old, Mexican-American delinquent boy, who had a long history of school failure and misbehavior and second-grade reading achievement, was given 40 hours of reading training which extended over a 4½-month period. Science Research Associates reading materials were adapted for use in conjunction with a token system of reinforcement. During the training, S's attention and participation were maintained in good strength by the reinforcers, he made many reading responses and learned and retained 430 new words, his reading achievement increased to the 4.3-grade level, he passed all his courses for the first time, and his misbehaviors in school decreased to zero.

REFERENCES

Rosen, B. C. The achievement syndrome: a psychocultural dimension of social stratification. *American Sociological Review*, 1956, **21**, 203–211.

Staats, A. W. A case in and a strategy for the extension of learning principles to problems of human behavior. In A. W. Staats (Ed.) *Human Learning.* New York: Holt, Rinehart and Winston, 1964. (a)

Staats, A. W. Conditioned stimuli, conditioned reinforcers, and word meaning. In A. W. Staats (Ed.) *Human Learning.* New York: Holt, Rinehart and Winston, 1964. (b)

Staats, A. W. (Ed.) *Human Learning.* New York: Holt, Rinehart and Winston, 1964. (c)

Staats, A. W. An integrated-functional learning approach to complex human behavior. In B. Kleinmuntz (Ed.) *Problem Solving: Research, Method and Theory.* New York: John Wiley, 1966.

Staats, A. W., Finley, J. R., Minke, K. A., and Wolf, M. Reinforcement variables in the control of unit reading responses. *Journal of Experimental Analytical Behavior*, 1964, **7**, 139–149. (a)

Staats, A. W., Minke, K. A., Finley, J. R., Wolf, M., and Brooks, L. O. A reinforcer system and experimental procedure for the laboratory study of reading acquisition. *Child Development*, 1964, **35**, 209–231. (b)

Staats, A. W., and Staats, C. K. *Complex Human Behavior.* New York: Holt, Rinehart and Winston, 1963.

Staats, A. W., Staats, C. K., Schutz, R. E., and Wolf, M. The conditioning of textual responses utilizing "extrinsic" reinforcers. *Journal of Experimental Analytical Behavior*, 1962, **5**, 33–40.

In Retrospect

At least four major areas of adolescent adjustment, or areas in which achieved competence is desirable for personality growth during adolescence, have elsewhere been systematically derived: status, sociality, sexuality, and values and morality (McCandless, 1970). In the opinion of this editor, the range of material found in the present book clearly encompasses these goals of adolescence. Related in one way or another to the *status* goal (a goal that includes achievement-related skill development and respect for competence) are discussions of behavioral effectiveness (Heilbrun, Part I), cognitive development (Elkind, Part I), achievement difficulties (Shaw, Part II; Husted and Cervantes, Part III), and vocational development (Osipow, Part II). *Sociality*, which includes the cultivation of satisfactory peer relationships, is addressed from a variety of viewpoints. Among them are Hauck's treatment of sex differences in social development and behavior (Part I), Spindler's examination of school functions regarding social behavior (Part II), Darley's study of conformity (Part III), and Burlingame's analysis of the youth culture (Part I). Wagner (Part I) and Payne (Part II) attend specifically to the third area—*sexuality*. The fourth dimension—*morality and the*

503

development of values—is treated by Sullivan (Part I), Kohlberg (Part II), and Haan *et al.* (Part III), to name just a few.

In addition to an augmentation of the quadripartite framework conceived by McCandless (1970), this book has been oriented toward at least four major outcomes. One involves a recognition of and appreciation for the multi-disciplinary nature of adolescent study. As the literature suggests, a combination of such disciplines as psychology, sociology, and cultural anthropology for the purpose of adolescent study offers a greater wealth of insights than does any one discipline examined independently. For that matter, one might argue that a separation of the behavioral sciences for this purpose is artificial and could interfere with progress toward an understanding of adolescent behavior and development. Examples of selections in this volume that provide a multidisciplinary flavor of one sort or another include those supplied by Wagner, Evans and Potter, and Burlingame (Part I); Spindler, Payne, Keniston, and Akers (Part II); and Williams and Byars and Rivera and Short (Part III).

A second major outcome attempted by the editor of this book of readings involves insight into some significant processes or conditions of development and learning. These range from *identification* (Heilbrun, Part I) and *observational learning* (Sarason, Part III) to *reinforcement* (Lefcourt, Part I; Staats and Butterfield, Part III) and *cognitive conflict* (Kohlberg, Part II). Accepting their validity, these processes or conditions also carry implications for (1) behavioral change within a context of formal education (Spindler, Part II), (2) a better understanding of various social behavior patterns (Akers, Part II), (3) the treatment of socially deviant behavior (Sarason, Part III), and (4) techniques for the solution of specific learning problems (Staats and Butterfield, Part III).

A third underlying "theme" of this book has been the importance and desirability of *positive human relations* as a condition for effective development during adolescence. This theme has appeared in various guises, often implicitly, although it cannot be stressed too strongly. In this regard, consider again selections in Part I concerning identity (Evans and Potter) and identification (Heilbrun), Meacham's discussion of counseling strategies based upon respect for individuality, and at least three research papers in Part III (Williams and Byars; Husted and Cervantes; and Rivera and Short).

The fourth principal theme or objective of this book involves an appreciation of the value (and complexities) of research on adolescence. As indicated in the Preface to this volume, a great variety characterizes such research. Accordingly, the ten selections appearing in Part III herein represent an attempt collectively to illustrate (*a*) an increasing diversification of research interests among behavioral scientists, and (*b*) evidence for the qualitative improvement of research believed by this editor to have occurred in recent years. Although the description of behavior and development continues as a major avenue for research activity (for example, Witkin *et al.* and Parloff *et al.*, Part III), progress is being made toward clearer definitions of antecedent-consequent relationships and procedures for behavior modification. These latter two areas have profited greatly in recent times from more sophisticated applications and variations of the experimental method (for example, Darley, Sarason, and Staats and Butterfield, Part III). In short, although certain facets of the literature on adolescence need increased research attention (for example, more frequent and intensive study of adolescent females, parent-adolescent relationships, the effects of educational programs for adolescents, and the measurement of complex adolescent behavior), this writer finds much about which to be encouraged. Hopefully the reader who has completed a study of this book shares this outlook.

REFERENCE

McCandless, Boyd R. *Adolescence: Behavior and Development.* Hinsdale, Ill.: Dryden Press, 1970.

Author Index

Subject Index

517